Lecture Notes in Computer Science   8858

Commenced Publication in 1973
Founding and Former Series Editors:
Gerhard Goos, Juris Hartmanis, and Jan van ˇ

T0236536

Editorial Board

Jacques Garrigue (Ed.)

Programming Languages and Systems

12th Asian Symposium, APLAS 2014
Singapore, Singapore, November 17-19, 2014
Proceedings

 Springer

Volume Editor

Jacques Garrigue
Nagoya University, Graduate School of Mathematics
Chikusa-ku, Nagoya 464-8602, Japan
E-mail: garrigue@math.nagoya-u.ac.jp

ISSN 0302-9743　　　　　　　　e-ISSN 1611-3349
ISBN 978-3-319-12735-4　　　　 e-ISBN 978-3-319-12736-1
DOI 10.1007/978-3-319-12736-1
Springer Cham Heidelberg New York Dordrecht London

Library of Congress Control Number: 2014951872

LNCS Sublibrary: SL 2 – Programming and Software Engineering

Typesetting: Camera-ready by author, data conversion by Scientific Publishing Services, Chennai, India

Printed on acid-free paper

Springer is part of Springer Science+Business Media (www.springer.com)

Preface

This volume contains the proceedings of the 12th Asian Symposium on Programming Languages and Systems (APLAS 2014), held in Singapore, during November 17–19, 2014. APLAS aims at stimulating programming language research by providing a forum for the presentation of the latest results and the exchange of ideas in topics concerned with programming languages and systems. APLAS is based in Asia, but is an international forum that serves the worldwide programming language community. Past APLAS symposia were successfully held in Melbourne (2013), Kyoto (2012), Kenting (2011), Shanghai (2010), Seoul (2009), Bangalore (2008), Singapore (2007), Sydney (2006), Tsukuba (2005), Taipei (2004), and Beijing (2003) after three informal workshops.

The topics covered in the conference include, but are not limited to, semantics, logics, and foundational theory; design of languages, type systems and foundational calculi; domain-specific languages; compilers, interpreters, and abstract machines; program derivation, synthesis, and transformation; program analysis, verification, and model-checking; software security; concurrency and parallelism; and tools and environments for programming, verification, and implementation.

This year, 57 papers were submitted to APLAS. Each submission was reviewed by three or more Program Committee members. After thoroughly evaluating the relevance and quality of each paper, the committee chose to accept 24 papers for presentation at the conference.

This year's program also continued the APLAS tradition of invited talks by distinguished researchers:

- Zhenjiang Hu (NII) on "What Is the Essence of Bidirectional Programming?"
- Julien Verlaguet (Facebook) on "Incremental Adoption of Static-Typing"
- Dexter Kozen (Cornell University) on "NetKAT: A Formal System for the Verification of Networks"

This program would not have been possible without the unrelenting efforts of several people, whom we would like to thank. First, the Program Committee and additional reviewers for the hard work put in toward ensuring the high quality of the proceedings. Our thanks also go to the Asian Association for Foundation of Software (AAFS), founded by Asian researchers in cooperation with many researchers from Europe and the USA, for sponsoring and supporting APLAS. We would like to warmly thank the Steering Committee in general and Wei-Ngan Chin and Cristian Gherghina for their support in organizing the conference and the poster session. Finally, we are grateful to Andrei Voronkov whose EasyChair system eased the processes of submission, paper selection, and proceedings compilation.

September 2014   Jacques Garrigue

Organization

Program Committee

Xiaojuan Cai	Shanghai Jiao Tong University, China
James Chapman	IoC, Tallinn University of Technology, Estonia
Jacques Garrigue	Nagoya University, Japan
Cristian Gherghina	Singapore University of Technology and Design
Eric Goubault	CEA, France
Fei He	Tsinghua University, China
Gerwin Klein	NICTA and UNSW, Australia
Raghavan Komondoor	Indian Institute of Science, Bangalore, India
Paddy Krishnan	Oracle, Australia
Daan Leijen	Microsoft Research, USA
Yasuhiko Minamide	University of Tsukuba, Japan
Shin-Cheng Mu	Academia Sinica, Taiwan
Sungwoo Park	Pohang University of Science and Technology, South Korea
Julian Rathke	University of Southampton, UK
Sukyoung Ryu	KAIST, South Korea
Alexandra Silva	Radboud University Nijmegen, The Netherlands
Martin Sulzmann	Hochschule Karlsruhe, Germany
Munehiro Takimoto	Tokyo University of Science, Japan
Jan Vitek	Northeastern University, USA
Hongwei Xi	Boston University, USA

Additional Reviewers

Andronick, June
Athaiya, Snigdha
Basold, Henning
Boyland, John
Chuang, Tyng-Ruey
Clairambault, Pierre
Costea, Andreea
Cristescu, Ioana
Danish, Matthew
Fahrenberg, Uli
Fernandez, Matthew
Ferrara, Pietro

Geuvers, Herman
Hage, Jurriaan
He, Chaodong
Im, Hyeonseung
Jeannin, Jean-Baptiste
Jongmans, Sung-Shik T.Q.
K.R., Raghavendra
Krebbers, Robbert
Laird, James
Lewis, Corey
Liang, Hongjin
Liangze, Yin

Liu, Jiaxiang
Lopes, Antónia
Mackie, Ian
Mcbride, Conor
Mimram, Samuel
Miné, Antoine
Moy, Yannick
Murray, Toby
Oh, Hakjoo
Petri, Gustavo
Pouzet, Marc
Pérez, Jorge A.
Rama, Girish Maskeri
Ren, Zhiqiang
Robert, Thomas

Roux, Pierre
Sammartino, Matteo
Santosa, Andrew
Sato, Haruhiko
Schöpp, Ulrich
Sewell, Thomas
Sharma, Asankhaya
Sneyers, Jon
Ta, Quang Trung
Taghdiri, Mana
Tzevelekos, Nikos
Vazou, Niki
Voigtländer, Janis
Wang, Bow-Yaw

Invited Presentations

What Is the Essence
of Bidirectional Programming?

Zhenjiang Hu

National Institute of Informatics, Japan
hu@nii.ac.jp

Bidirectional transformations [8, 4, 13] provide a novel mechanism for synchronizing and maintaining the consistency of information between input and output. The idea of bidirectional transformations is originated from the *view updating* mechanism in the database community [1, 5, 9], and has been attracting a lot of attention from a wide range of communities, including programming languages, software engineering and databases, which has motivated the proposal of a vast number of bidirectional approaches aiming to solve the problems of different bidirectional applications.

A bidirectional transformation basically consists of a pair of transformations: the *forward* transformation *get s* is used to produce a target view v from a source s, while the *putback* transformation *put s v* is used to reflect modifications on the view v to the source s. These two transformations should be *well-behaved* in the sense that they satisfy the following round-tripping laws.

$$put\ s\ (get\ s) = s \qquad\qquad \text{GETPUT}$$
$$get\ (put\ s\ v) = v \qquad\qquad \text{PUTGET}$$

The GETPUT property requires that no change in the view shall be reflected as no change in the source, while the PUTGET property requires all changes in the view to be completely reflected to the source so that the changed view can be computed again by applying the forward transformation to the changed source.

Bidirectional programming is to develop well-behaved bidirectional transformations in order to solve various synchronization problems. A straightforward approach to bidirectional programming is to write two unidirectional transformations. Although this solution provides full control over both get and putback transformations and can be realized using standard programming languages, the programmer needs to show that the two transformations satisfy the well-behavedness laws, and a modification to one of the transformations requires an adaptation of the other transformation as well as a new well-behavedness proof.

It should be preferable to write just a single program that can denote both transformations, in order to ease and enable maintainable bidirectional programming. Then what should this single program be? Most existing bidirectional programming languages are to aid programmers in writing a forward transformation *get* and deriving a backward transformation *put* for free [8, 3, 2, 11, 12, 16, 20, 15, 19, 10]. However, the maintainability offered by such languages comes at the cost of expressiveness and (more importantly) predictability because the ambiguity of synchronization handled by the putback transformation is solved by default strategies over which programmers have little control.

One interesting but less known fact is that while *get* usually loses information when mapping from a source to a view, *put* must preserve information when putting back from the view to the source, according to the PUTGET property. Furthermore, it has been shown in [7, 6] that, for a putback transformation *put*, if there exists a forward transformation *get* then such *get* is uniquely determined by *put*. In other words, the essence of bidirectional programming is nothing but to write putback transformation.

In this talk, I will report our recent progress on putback-baesd bidirectional programming, explaining how to design user-friendly languages for supporting putback-based bidirectional programming [17, 18], showing how to systematically check whether the definition of a *put* is in a valid form that guarantees that the corresponding unique *get* exists [14], demonstrating how to apply putback-based bidirectional programming to solve practical problems [6, 21], and highlighting important issues and challenges for future work.

References

1. Bancilhon, F., Spyratos, N.: Update semantics of relational views. ACM Transactions on Database Systems 6(4), 557–575 (1981)
2. Bohannon, A., Foster, J.N., Pierce, B.C., Pilkiewicz, A., Schmitt, A.: Boomerang: resourceful lenses for string data. In: POPL 2008, pp. 407–419. ACM (2008)
3. Bohannon, A., Pierce, B.C., Vaughan, J.A.: Relational lenses: a language for updatable views. In: PODS 2006, pp. 338–347. ACM (2006)
4. Czarnecki, K., Foster, J.N., Hu, Z., Lämmel, R., Schürr, A., Terwilliger, J.F.: Bidirectional transformations: A cross-discipline perspective. In: Paige, R.F. (ed.) ICMT 2009. LNCS, vol. 5563, pp. 260–283. Springer, Heidelberg (2009)
5. Dayal, U., Bernstein, P.: On the correct translation of update operations on relational views. ACM Transactions on Database Systems 7, 381–416 (1982)
6. Fischer, S., Hu, Z., Pacheco, H.: "Putback" is the Essence of Bidirectional Programming, GRACE Technical Report 2012-08, National Institute of Informatics, 36 p. (2012)
7. Foster, J.: Bidirectional Programming Languages. Ph.D. thesis, University of Pennsylvania (December 2009)
8. Foster, J.N., Greenwald, M.B., Moore, J.T., Pierce, B.C., Schmitt, A.: Combinators for bidirectional tree transformations: A linguistic approach to the view-update problem. ACM Transactions on Programming Languages and Systems 29(3), 17 (2007)
9. Gottlob, G., Paolini, P., Zicari, R.: Properties and update semantics of consistent views. ACM Transactions on Database Systems 13(4), 486–524 (1988)
10. Hidaka, S., Hu, Z., Inaba, K., Kato, H., Matsuda, K., Nakano, K.: Bidirectionalizing graph transformations. In: ICFP 2010, pp. 205–216. ACM (2010)
11. Hofmann, M., Pierce, B.C., Wagner, D.: Symmetric lenses. In: POPL 2011, pp. 371–384. ACM (2011)
12. Hofmann, M., Pierce, B.C., Wagner, D.: Edit lenses. In: POPL 2012, pp. 495–508. ACM (2012)

13. Hu, Z., Schürr, A., Stevens, P., Terwilliger, J.F.: Dagstuhl Seminar on Bidirectional Transformations (BX). SIGMOD Record 40(1), 35–39 (2011)
14. Hu, Z., Pacheco, H., Fischer, S.: Validity checking of putback transformations in bidirectional programming. In: Jones, C., Pihlajasaari, P., Sun, J. (eds.) FM 2014. LNCS, vol. 8442, pp. 1–15. Springer, Heidelberg (2014)
15. Matsuda, K., Hu, Z., Nakano, K., Hamana, M., Takeichi, M.: Bidirectionalization transformation based on automatic derivation of view complement functions. In: ICFP 2007, pp. 47–58. ACM (2007)
16. Pacheco, H., Cunha, A., Hu, Z.: Delta lenses over inductive types. BX 2012. Electronic Communications of the EASST 49 (2012)
17. Pacheco, H., Hu, Z., Fischer, S.: Monadic combinators for "putback" style bidirectional programming. In: PEPM 2014, pp. 39–50. ACM (2014)
18. Pacheco, H., Zan, T., Hu, Z.: BiFluX: A bidirectional functional update language for XML. In: PPDP 2014. ACM (2014)
19. Voigtländer, J.: Bidirectionalization for free! (pearl). In: POPL 2009, pp. 165–176. ACM (2009)
20. Xiong, Y., Liu, D., Hu, Z., Zhao, H., Takeichi, M., Mei, H.: Towards automatic model synchronization from model transformations. In: ASE 2007, pp. 164–173. ACM (2007)
21. Zan, T., Pacheco, H., Hu, Z.: Writing bidirectional model transformations as intentional updates. In: ICSE 2014 (NIER Track), pp. 488–491. ACM (2014)

Incremental Adoption of Static-Typing

Julien Verlaguet

Facebook

Over the last year, Facebook migrated nearly its entire PHP codebase to Hack: a gradually typed language that interoperates seamlessly with PHP. At Facebook's scale, it would have been difficult to completely transition to Hack right away. To make this transition successful, the language and its type-system had to be designed with interoperability in mind. In this talk, we will review the design decisions that were made during the conception of the language. We will discuss the tradeoffs that had to be considered to find a balance between ease of use and safety.

Hack is an interesting case study of retrofitted static-typing into a dynamic language. Some parts are specific to PHP, but we are hopeful that the lessons learnt will be valuable to anyone interested in dynamic languages and type-systems in general.

NetKAT — A Formal System for the Verification of Networks

Dexter Kozen

Cornell University, Ithaca, NY 14853-7501, USA
kozen@cs.cornell.edu
http://www.cs.cornell.edu/~kozen

Abstract. This paper presents an survey of recent work in the development of NetKAT, a formal system for reasoning about packet switching networks, and its role in the emerging area of software-defined networking.

Keywords: Kleene algebra, Kleene algebra with tests, NetKAT, software defined networking, packet switching, OpenFlow, Frenetic.

Table of Contents

Invited Presentation

Regular Papers

NetKAT — A Formal System
for the Verification of Networks

Dexter Kozen

Cornell University, Ithaca, NY 14853-7501, USA
kozen@cs.cornell.edu
http://www.cs.cornell.edu/~kozen

Abstract. This paper presents a survey of recent work in the development of NetKAT, a formal system for reasoning about packet switching networks, and its role in the emerging area of software-defined networking.

Keywords: Kleene algebra, Kleene algebra with tests, NetKAT, software defined networking, packet switching, OpenFlow, Frenetic.

1 Introduction

NetKAT is a relatively new language and logic for reasoning about packet switching networks. The system was introduced quite recently by Anderson et al. [1] and further developed by Foster et al. [10]. The present paper provides an accessible self-contained introduction to the NetKAT language, some examples of things one can do with it, and a flavor of ongoing work. All the results described here have appeared previously [1, 10].

1.1 Software-Defined Networking

Traditional network architecture is fairly low-level, consisting of routers and switches that do little besides maintaining routing tables and forwarding packets. The components of the network are typically configured locally, making it difficult to implement end-to-end routing policies and optimizations that require a global perspective. This state of affairs is ill-suited to modern data centers and cloud-based applications that require a higher degree of coordination among network components to function effectively.

Software-defined networking (SDN) is a relatively new paradigm for network management. The main idea behind SDN is to permit centralized control of the network in the form of a controller that communicates with the individual network components. As the Open Networking Foundations's 2012 white paper "Software-Defined Networking: The New Norm for Networks" [11] describes it,

> In the SDN architecture, the control and data planes are decoupled, network intelligence and state are logically centralized, and the underlying network infrastructure is abstracted from the applications. As a

J. Garrigue (Ed.): APLAS 2014, LNCS 8858, pp. 1–18, 2014.

result, enterprises and carriers gain unprecedented programmability, automation, and network control, enabling them to build highly scalable, flexible networks that readily adapt to changing business needs.

One can think of a centralized controller or set of controllers that have global knowledge of the topology of the network over which they exercise control and can interact with individual network components via a standardized communication interface. The controller can receive traffic flow information and operational status from the components and can reconfigure them on the fly if necessary to balance load, reroute traffic to circumvent failures, or implement security policies.

1.2   NetKAT

NetKAT is a new domain-specific language and logic for specifying and verifying network packet-processing functions that fits well with the SDN paradigm. It is part of the Frenetic suite of network management tools [9, 12, 28, 29]. NetKAT is based on Kleene algebra with tests (KAT), a generic algebraic system for reasoning about partial correctness that has been studied since the 1990's [23]. KAT, in turn, is based on Kleene algebra (KA), the algebra of regular expressions [19]. NetKAT is essentially KAT with primitives for modifying and testing packet headers and encoding network topologies along with axioms for reasoning about those constructs.

One might at first be skeptical about the expressive power of regular expressions in this context, but in fact regular expressions are sufficient to encode network topology and express many common reachability and security queries, which can now be verified automatically. In §3 we give some examples of the types of queries one can express with NetKAT. This expressive power, coupled with NetKAT's formal mathematical semantics, complete deductive system, and decision procedure, make NetKAT a viable tool for SDN programming and verification.

2   NetKAT Basics

In this section we describe the syntax and semantics of NetKAT. This requires us to say a few words about Kleene algebra (KA) [19] and Kleene algebra with tests (KAT) [23] on which NetKAT is based.

2.1   Kleene Algebra (KA)

Kleene algebra is the algebra of regular expressions. Regular expressions are normally interpreted as regular sets of strings, but there are many other useful interpretations: binary relation models used in programming language semantics, the (min, +) algebra used in shortest path algorithms, models consisting of convex sets used in computational geometry. Perhaps surprisingly, a formal model of packet-switching networks can also be added to this list.

Abstractly, a *Kleene algebra* is any structure

$$(K, +, \cdot, ^*, 0, 1)$$

where K is a set, $+$ and $\cdot$ are binary operations on K, * is a unary operation on K, and 0 and 1 are constants, satisfying the following axioms:

$$
\begin{array}{ll}
p + (q + r) = (p + q) + r & p(qr) = (pq)r \\
p + q = q + p & 1 \cdot p = p \cdot 1 = p \\
p + 0 = p + p = p & p \cdot 0 = 0 \cdot p = 0 \\
p(q + r) = pq + pr & (p + q)r = pr + qr \\
1 + pp^* \leq p^* & q + px \leq x \Rightarrow p^*q \leq x \\
1 + p^*p \leq p^* & q + xp \leq x \Rightarrow qp^* \leq x
\end{array}
$$

where we define $p \leq q$ iff $p + q = q$. The axioms above not involving * are succinctly stated by saying that the structure is an idempotent semiring under $+, \cdot, 0$, and 1, the term *idempotent* referring to the axiom $p + p = p$. Due to this axiom, the ordering relation $\leq$ is a partial order. The axioms for * together say that p^*q is the $\leq$-least solution of $q + px \leq x$ and qp^* is the $\leq$-least solution of $q + xp \leq x$.

One of the nice things about KA is that all properties are expressed as equations and equational implications (Horn formulas), and reasoning is purely equational. No specialized syntax or rules are needed, only the axioms and rules of classical equational logic. This is also true of KAT and NetKAT.

2.2 Kleene Algebra with Tests (KAT)

To get KAT from KA, we add Boolean tests. Formally, a KAT is a two-sorted structure $(K, B, +, \cdot, ^*, ^-, 0, 1)$, where $B \subseteq K$ and

- $(K, +, \cdot, ^*, 0, 1)$ is a Kleene algebra
- $(B, +, \cdot, ^-, 0, 1)$ is a Boolean algebra
- $(B, +, \cdot, 0, 1)$ is a subalgebra of $(K, +, \cdot, 0, 1)$.

The elements of B are called *tests*. Note that the semiring operations $+, \cdot, 0, 1$ are heavily overloaded, but this does not create any conflict. On tests, $+$ and $\cdot$ behave as Boolean disjunction and conjunction, respectively, and 0 and 1 stand for falsity and truth, respectively. The overline $^-$ is the Boolean negation operator, sometimes written as a prefix operator $\neg$.

The axioms of Boolean algebra are

$$
\begin{array}{ll}
a + bc = (a + b)(a + c) & ab = ba \\
a + 1 = 1 & a + \bar{a} = 1 \\
a\bar{a} = 0 & aa = a
\end{array}
$$

in addition to the axioms of KA above. KAT can model standard imperative programming constructs

$$p\,;q = pq$$
$$\text{if } b \text{ then } p \text{ else } q = bp + \bar{b}q$$
$$\text{while } b \text{ do } p = (bp)^*\bar{b}$$

as well as Hoare partial correctness assertions $\{b\}\,p\,\{c\}$, which can be written in any one of three equivalent ways:

$$bp \leq pc \qquad\qquad bp = bpc \qquad\qquad bp\bar{c} = 0.$$

Hoare-style rules become universal Horn sentences in KAT. For example, the Hoare while-rule

$$\frac{\{bc\}\,p\,\{c\}}{\{c\}\text{ while } b \text{ do } p\,\{\bar{b}c\}}$$

becomes the universal Horn sentence

$$bcp \leq pc \;\Rightarrow\; c(bp)^*\bar{b} \leq (bp)^*\bar{b}\bar{b}c.$$

For purposes of program verification, KAT expressions are typically interpreted in binary relation models. Each expression is interpreted as a binary relation on the set of program states, the input/output relation of the program. The tests are interpreted as *subidentities*, subsets of the identity relation on states; a test acts as a guard that either passes the state through unaltered or fails with no output state.

2.3   NetKAT

NetKAT, in its simplest form, is a version of KAT in which the atomic actions and tests take a particular network-specific form, along with some additional axioms for reasoning about programs built using those primitives. The atomic actions are for modifying, duplicating, and forwarding packets, and the atomic tests are for filtering packets based on values of fields.

Formally, the atomic actions and tests are

- $x \leftarrow n$ (assignment)
- $x = n$ (test)
- dup (duplication)

We also use pass and drop for 1 and 0, respectively.

We will describe the formal semantics below, but intuitively, a NetKAT expression is a program that transforms input packets to output packets. The assignment $x \leftarrow n$ assigns the constant value n to the field x in the current packet. The test $x = n$ tests whether the current value of the field x of the current packet is n and drops the packet if not. For example, the expression

$$switch = 6\,;\,port = 8\,;\,dest \leftarrow 10.0.1.5\,;\,port \leftarrow 5$$

expresses the command: "For all packets incoming on port 8 of switch 6, set the destination IP address to 10.0.1.5 and send the packet out on port 5."

The NetKAT axioms consist of the following equations in addition to the KAT axioms:

$$
\begin{array}{rcll}
x \leftarrow n\,;\,y \leftarrow m & = & y \leftarrow m\,;\,x \leftarrow n & (x \neq y) \qquad (2.1) \\
x \leftarrow n\,;\,y = m & = & y = m\,;\,x \leftarrow n & (x \neq y) \qquad (2.2) \\
x = n\,;\,\mathsf{dup} & = & \mathsf{dup}\,;\,x = n & \qquad (2.3) \\
x \leftarrow n\,;\,x = n & = & x \leftarrow n & \qquad (2.4) \\
x = n\,;\,x \leftarrow n & = & x = n & \qquad (2.5) \\
x \leftarrow n\,;\,x \leftarrow m & = & x \leftarrow m & \qquad (2.6) \\
x = n\,;\,x = m & = & 0 \quad (n \neq m) & \qquad (2.7) \\
(\sum_n x = n) & = & 1 & \qquad (2.8)
\end{array}
$$

These equations have the following intuitive interpretations:

(2.1) Assignments to distinct fields may be done in either order.
(2.2) An assignment to a field does not affect the value of a different field.
(2.3) When a packet is duplicated, the field values are preserved.
(2.4) An assignment of a value to a field causes that field to have that value.
(2.5) An assignment to a field of a value that the field already has is redundant.
(2.6) With two assignments to the same field, the second assignment erases the effect of the first.
(2.7) A field may have no more than one value.
(2.8) A field must have at least one value.

2.4 Semantics

The standard model of NetKAT is a packet-forwarding model. Operationally, a NetKAT expression describes a process that maps an input packet to a set of output packets. However, in order to reason about packet trajectories, we need to keep track of changes to the packet as it moves through the network. Thus the standard semantics interprets an expression as a function that maps an input *packet history* to a set of output *packet histories*.

Formally, a *packet* π is a record with constant values n assigned to fields x. A *packet history* is a nonempty sequence of packets

$$\pi_1 :: \pi_2 :: \cdots :: \pi_k.$$

The *head packet* is π_1, which represents the current values of the fields. The remaining packets $\pi_2, \ldots, \pi_k$ describe the previous values from youngest to oldest.

Every NetKAT expression e denotes a function:

$$[\![e]\!] : H \to 2^H$$

where H is the set of all packet histories. The function $[\![e]\!]$ takes an input packet history $\sigma \in H$ and produces a set of output packet histories $[\![e]\!](\sigma) \subseteq H$.

The semantics of expressions is compositional and is defined inductively. For the primitive actions and tests,

$$[\![x \leftarrow n]\!](\pi :: \sigma) = \{\pi[n/x] :: \sigma\}$$

$$[\![x = n]\!](\pi :: \sigma) = \begin{cases} \{\pi :: \sigma\} & \text{if } \pi(x) = n \\ \varnothing & \text{if } \pi(x) \neq n \end{cases}$$

$$[\![\mathsf{dup}]\!](\pi :: \sigma) = \{\pi :: \pi :: \sigma\}$$

where $\pi[n/x]$ denotes the packet π with the field x rebound to the value n. Thus the assignment $x \leftarrow n$ rebinds the value of x to n in the head packet; the test $x = n$ simply drops the packet (logically, the entire history) if the test is not satisfied and passes it through unaltered if it is satisfied, thus behaving as a packet filter; and dup simply duplicates the head packet. The KAT operations are interpreted as follows:

$$[\![p + q]\!](\sigma) = [\![p]\!](\sigma) \cup [\![q]\!](\sigma)$$

$$[\![pq]\!](\sigma) = \bigcup_{\tau \in [\![p]\!](\sigma)} [\![q]\!](\tau)$$

$$[\![p^*]\!](\sigma) = \bigcup_n [\![p^n]\!](\sigma)$$

$$[\![1]\!](\sigma) = [\![\mathsf{pass}]\!](\sigma) = \{\sigma\}$$

$$[\![0]\!](\sigma) = [\![\mathsf{drop}]\!](\sigma) = \varnothing$$

$$[\![\neg b]\!](\sigma) = \begin{cases} \{\sigma\} & \text{if } [\![b]\!](\sigma) = \varnothing \\ \varnothing & \text{if } [\![b]\!](\sigma) = \{\sigma\} \end{cases}$$

To compose p and q sequentially, the action p is done first, producing a set of packet histories $[\![p]\!](\sigma)$, then q is performed on each of the resulting histories individually and the results accumulated. This is often called *Kleisli composition*.

The operation $+$ simply accumulates the actions of the two summands. Thus the expression $(port \leftarrow 8) + (port \leftarrow 9)$ describes the behavior of a switch that sends copies of the packet to ports 8 and 9. This is a departure from the usual Kleene interpretation of $+$ as nondeterministic choice—NetKAT treats $+$ as *conjunctive* in the sense that both operations are performed, rather than *disjunctive*, in which one of the two operations would be chosen nondeterministically. Nevertheless, the axioms of NetKAT are sound and complete over this interpretation [1].

3 Examples

In this section we show some useful things that can be done with NetKAT. These examples are all from $[1, 10]$, except some minor improvements have been made in some cases. We will show how various reachability and security properties can be represented as equations between NetKAT terms, thus can be checked automatically by NetKAT's bisimulation-based decision procedure $[10]$. Specifically, we show how to encode the following queries:

- Reachability: Can host A communicate with host B? Can every host communicate with every other host?
- Security: Does all untrusted traffic pass through the intrusion detection system located at C?
- Loop detection: Is it possible for a packet to be forwarded around a cycle in the network?

Several automated tools already exist for answering such questions $[16, 17, 27]$. Many of these encode the topology and policy as a logical structure, then translate the query into a Boolean formula and hand it to a SAT solver. In contrast, NetKAT expresses such properties as equations between NetKAT terms, which can then be decided by the NetKAT decision procedure.

3.1 Encoding Network Topology

The topology of the network can be specified by a directed graph with nodes representing hosts and switches and directed edges representing links. In NetKAT, the topology is expressed as a sum of expressions that encode the behavior of each link. To model a link, we use an expression

$$switch = A \, ; port = n \, ; switch \leftarrow B \, ; port \leftarrow m$$

where A and n are the switch name and output port number of the source of the link and B and m are the switch name and input port number of the target of the link. This expression filters out all packets not located at the source end of the link, then updates the switch and port fields to the location of the target of the link, thereby capturing the effect of sending the packet across the link.

3.2 Switch Policies

Each switch may modify and forward packets that it receives on its input ports. The policy for switch A is specified by a NetKAT term

$$switch = A \, ; p_A$$

where p_A specifies what to do with packets entering switch A. For example, if a packet with IP address a entering on port n should have its IP address modified to b and sent out on ports m and k, this behavior would be expressed by

$$port = n \, ; ip = a \, ; (port \leftarrow m + port \leftarrow k) \, ; ip \leftarrow b$$

and p_A is the sum of all such behaviors for A.

Let t be the sum of all link expressions and p the sum of all switch policies. The product pt describes one step of the network in which each switch processes its packets, then sends them along links to the next switch. Axioms (2.4) and (2.7) guarantee that cross terms in the product vanish, thus the expression correctly captures the linkage. The expression $(pt)^*$ describes the multistep behavior of the network in which the single-step behavior is iterated.

3.3   Reachability

To encode the question of whether it is possible for any packet to travel from an output port of switch A to an input port of switch B given the topology and the switch policies, we can ask whether the expression

$$switch = A \,; t(pt)^* \,; switch = B \qquad (3.1)$$

is equivalent to 0 (drop). Intuitively, the prefix $switch = A$ filters out histories whose head packet does not satisfy $switch = A$, and the postfix $switch = B$ filters out histories whose head packet does not satisfy $switch = B$.

However, more can be said. Using the axioms (2.1)–(2.8), it can be shown that (3.1) is equivalent to a sum of terms of the form

$$switch = A \,; x_1 = n_1 \,; \cdots \,; x_k = n_k \,; x_1 \leftarrow m_1 \,; \cdots \,; x_k \leftarrow m_k \,; switch = B$$

and each such nonzero term describes initial conditions under which a packet can travel from A to B. Note that only the initial and final values of the fields appear; the intermediate values vanish due to axioms (2.4), (2.6), and (2.7). We can retain the intermediate values using dup if we wish; an example of this is given below.

3.4   All-Pairs Reachability

We may wish to check whether every host in the network can physically communicate with every other host. To test this, we use the switch policies

$$switch = A \,; \sum_n port = n \,; \sum_m port \leftarrow m \qquad (3.2)$$

where the first sum is over all the active input ports n of node A and the second is over all the active output ports m of A. This expression simply tests whether the packet is currently located at an input port of A and if so forwards it out over all active output ports unaltered. This is a little different from the query of §3.3 in that the switch policies of §3.2, which can modify packets and thus affect traffic flow, are not taken into account, but only the physical network topology.

Let q be the sum of all policies (3.2) over all A. Then q performs this action for all A. Let t be the encoding of the topology as described in §3.1. Consider the equation

$$(qt)^* = \sum_A (switch = A \,; \sum_n port = n) \,; \sum_B (switch \leftarrow B \,; \sum_m port \leftarrow m)$$

where n ranges over all active input ports of A and m ranges over all active input ports of B. The expression qt represents a program that forwards all packets from the input port of any node along all outgoing links to an input port of a node that is reachable in one step. The left-hand expression $(qt)^*$ is the multistep version of this; it starts at an input port of any node A and forwards to all input ports of all nodes reachable from A. The right-hand expression represents a program that, given any packet located a some input port of some node, no matter where it is located, immediately forwards to all input ports of all possible nodes. The left-hand side is contained in the right, since intermediate nodes in a path are elided by axiom (2.6); and if there are A, n, B, m such that input port m of B is not reachable from input port n of A, then

$$switch = A \; ; port = n \; ; switch \leftarrow B \; ; port \leftarrow m$$

will be contained in the right-hand side but not the left.

3.5   Waypointing

A *waypoint* W between A to B is a location that all packets must traverse enroute from A to B. It may be important for security purposes to ensure that all traffic of a certain type traverse a waypoint; for example, we may wish to ensure that all traffic from an untrusted external source to a trusted internal destination traverse a firewall.

We can do this by modifying the switch policy to duplicate the head packet in the firewall component F. That is, the expression $switch = F \; ; p_F$ in the sum p is replaced by $switch = F \; ; \mathsf{dup} \; ; p_F$. This is a way to mark traffic through F. Now we ask whether

$$switch = A \; ; t(pt)^* \; ; switch = B$$
$$\leq switch = A \; ; t(pt)^* \; ; switch = F \; ; \mathsf{dup} \; ; p_F \; ; t(pt)^* \; ; switch = B$$

which holds if and only if all output packet histories contain a dup generated by traversing F (assuming $F \notin \{A, B\}$).

The solution to this problem presented in [1] inserted a dup in all switch policies; however, the complexity of the decision procedure of [10] is exponential in the number of occurrences of dup, so for performance reasons it is desirable to minimize this quantity. The solution given here has four occurrences.

3.6   Forwarding Loops

A network has a *forwarding loop* if some packet would endlessly traverse a cycle in the network. Forwarding loops are a frequent source of error and have caused outages in both local area networks and on the Internet [15]. They are usually handled by introducing a TTL (time-to-live) field, a runtime mechanism in which a counter is decremented at each hop and the packet is dropped when the counter hits 0.

We can use NetKAT to check for loops by checking whether there is a packet that visits the same state twice. This is done by checking

$$\alpha \, ; pt(pt)^* \, ; \alpha = 0$$

for each valuation α such that

$$in \, ; (pt)^* \, ; \alpha$$

does not vanish. Here α represents a valid assignment to all fields and in represents a set of initial conditions on packets. The set of α that need to be checked is typically sparse. This algorithm has been used to check for loops in networks with topologies containing thousands of switches and configurations with thousands of forwarding rules on each switch.

3.7   Other Applications

The papers [1, 10] present a few other important applications: traffic isolation, access control, and correctness of a compiler that maps a NetKAT expression to a set of individual flow tables that can be deployed on the switches. It is interesting that so much can be done with regular expressions.

4   Soundness and Completeness

Let $\vdash$ denote provability in ordinary equational logic, assuming the NetKAT axioms (the axioms of KAT plus (2.1)–(2.8)) as premises.

Theorem 1 ([1]). *The NetKAT axioms are sound and complete with respect to the packet-switching semantics of §2.4. That is, $\vdash p = q$ if and only if $[\![p]\!] = [\![q]\!]$.*

The completeness proof is quite interesting. It introduces a *language model* for NetKAT that is isomorphic to the packet-switching model of §2.4. The language model also plays a role in the decision procedure of [10]. The language model consists of the regular sets of *reduced strings* of the form

$$\alpha p_0 \, \mathsf{dup} \, p_1 \, \mathsf{dup} \, p_2 \cdots p_{n-1} \, \mathsf{dup} \, p_n, \quad n \geq 0, \qquad (4.1)$$

where α is a *complete test* $x_1 = n_1 \, ; \cdots \, ; x_k = n_k$, the p_i are *complete assignments* $x_1 \leftarrow n_1 \, ; \cdots \, ; x_k \leftarrow n_k$, and $x_1, \ldots, x_k$ are all of the fields occurring in the expressions of interest in some arbitrary but fixed order. Every string of atomic actions and tests is equivalent to a reduced string modulo the NetKAT axioms. The set of reduced strings is described by the expression $\mathsf{At} \cdot P \cdot (\mathsf{dup} \cdot P)^*$, where At is the set of complete tests and P the set of complete assignments. The complete tests are the atoms (minimal nonzero elements) of the Boolean algebra generated by the primitive tests. Complete tests and complete assignments are in one-to-one correspondence as determined by the sequence of values $n_1, \ldots, n_k$.

The standard interpretation over this model is the map G that assigns a regular set of reduced strings to each NetKAT expression:

$$G(x \leftarrow n) = \{\alpha p_\alpha[x \leftarrow n] \mid \alpha \in \mathsf{At}\}$$
$$G(x = n) = \{\alpha p_\alpha \mid \alpha \in \mathsf{At}, \ x = n \text{ appears in } \alpha\}$$
$$G(\mathsf{dup}) = \{\alpha p_\alpha \, \mathsf{dup} \, p_\alpha \mid \alpha \in \mathsf{At}\}$$
$$G(p + q) = G(p) \cup G(q)$$
$$G(pq) = \{xy \mid \exists \beta \ xp_\beta \in G(p), \ \beta y \in G(q)\}$$
$$G(p^*) = \bigcup_{n \geq 0} G(p^n)$$

where $p[x \leftarrow n]$ denotes the complete assignment p with the assignment to x replaced by $x \leftarrow n$, α_p is the complete test corresponding to the complete assignment p, and p_β is the complete assignment corresponding to the complete test β.

It follows that for $p \in P$ and $\alpha \in \mathsf{At}$,

$$G(p) = \{\alpha p \mid \alpha \in \mathsf{At}\} \qquad\qquad G(\alpha) = \{\alpha p_\alpha\}.$$

The NetKAT axioms (2.1)–(2.8) take a simpler form for reduced strings:

$$\alpha \, \mathsf{dup} = \mathsf{dup} \, \alpha \qquad p\alpha_p = p \qquad \alpha p_\alpha = \alpha$$

$$\alpha\alpha = \alpha \qquad \alpha\beta = 0, \ \alpha \neq \beta \qquad qp = p \qquad \sum_{\alpha \in \mathsf{At}} \alpha = 1.$$

5 NetKAT Coalgebra and a Decision Procedure

Coalgebra is a general framework for modeling and reasoning about state-based systems [3,4,31,33,35]. A central aspect of coalgebra is the characterization of equivalence in terms of *bisimulation*. The bisimulation-based decision procedure for NetKAT presented in [10] was inspired by similar decision procedures for KA and KAT [3,4,31]. However, to apply these techniques to NetKAT, it is necessary to develop the coalgebraic theory to provide the basis of the algorithm and establish correctness.

5.1 NetKAT Coalgebra

Formally, a NetKAT coalgebra consists of a set of states S along with *continuation* and *observation maps*

$$\delta_{\alpha\beta} : S \to S \qquad\qquad \varepsilon_{\alpha\beta} : S \to 2$$

for $\alpha, \beta \in \mathsf{At}$. A deterministic NetKAT automaton is a NetKAT coalgebra with a distinguished start state $s \in S$. The inputs to the automaton are the NetKAT reduced strings (4.1); that is, elements of the set $N = \mathsf{At} \cdot P \cdot (\mathsf{dup} \cdot P)^*$ consisting of strings of the form

$$\alpha p_0 \, \mathsf{dup} \, p_1 \, \mathsf{dup} \cdots \mathsf{dup} \, p_n$$

for some $n \geq 0$. Intuitively, $\delta_{\alpha\beta}$ attempts to consume αp_β dup from the front of the input string and move to a new state with a residual input string. This succeeds if and only if the reduced string is of the form αp_β dup x for some $x \in (P \cdot \mathsf{dup})^* \cdot P$, in which case the automaton moves to a new state as determined by $\delta_{\alpha\beta}$ with residual input string βx. The observation map $\varepsilon_{\alpha\beta}$ determines whether the reduced string αp_β should be accepted in the current state.

Formally, acceptance is determined by a coinductively defined predicate $\mathsf{Accept} : S \times N \to 2$:

$$\mathsf{Accept}(t, \alpha p_\beta \, \mathsf{dup} \, x) = \mathsf{Accept}(\delta_{\alpha\beta}(t), \beta x)$$
$$\mathsf{Accept}(t, \alpha p_\beta) = \varepsilon_{\alpha\beta}(t).$$

A reduced string $x \in N$ is *accepted* by the automaton if $\mathsf{Accept}(s, x)$, where s is the start state.

5.2   The Brzozowski Derivative

The Brzozowski derivative for NetKAT comes in two versions: semantic and syntactic. The semantic version is defined on subsets of N and gives a coalgebra $(2^N, \delta, \varepsilon)$ that is a final coalgebra for the NetKAT signature.

$$\delta_{\alpha\beta} : 2^N \to 2^N \qquad\qquad \varepsilon_{\alpha\beta} : 2^N \to 2$$

$$\delta_{\alpha\beta}(A) = \{\beta x \mid \alpha p_\beta \, \mathsf{dup} \, x \in A\} \qquad \varepsilon_{\alpha\beta}(A) = \begin{cases} 1 & \text{if } \alpha p_\beta \in A, \\ 0 & \text{if } \alpha p_\beta \notin A. \end{cases}$$

One can show that this is the final coalgebra for the NetKAT signature by showing that bisimilarity implies equality.

There is also a syntactic derivative

$$D_{\alpha\beta} : \mathsf{Exp} \to \mathsf{Exp} \qquad\qquad E_{\alpha\beta} : \mathsf{Exp} \to 2,$$

where Exp is the set of reduced NetKAT expressions. The syntactic derivative also gives a coalgebra (Exp, D, E). The maps D and E are defined inductively:

$$D_{\alpha\beta}(p) = 0 \qquad D_{\alpha\beta}(b) = 0 \qquad D_{\alpha\beta}(\mathsf{dup}) = \alpha \cdot \begin{cases} 1 & \text{if } \alpha = \beta, \\ 0 & \text{if } \alpha \neq \beta. \end{cases}$$

$$D_{\alpha\beta}(e_1 + e_2) = D_{\alpha\beta}(e_1) + D_{\alpha\beta}(e_2)$$
$$D_{\alpha\beta}(e_1 e_2) = D_{\alpha\beta}(e_1) \cdot e_2 + \sum_\gamma E_{\alpha\gamma}(e_1) \cdot D_{\gamma\beta}(e_2)$$
$$D_{\alpha\beta}(e^*) = D_{\alpha\beta}(e) \cdot e^* + \sum_\gamma E_{\alpha\gamma}(e) \cdot D_{\gamma\beta}(e^*)$$

$$E_{\alpha\beta}(p) = \begin{cases} 1 & \text{if } p = p_\beta, \\ 0 & \text{if } p \neq p_\beta \end{cases} \qquad E_{\alpha\beta}(b) = \begin{cases} 1 & \text{if } \alpha = \beta \leq b, \\ 0 & \text{otherwise} \end{cases}$$

$$E_{\alpha\beta}(\mathsf{dup}) = 0 \qquad E_{\alpha\beta}(e_1 + e_2) = E_{\alpha\beta}(e_1) + E_{\alpha\beta}(e_2)$$

$$E_{\alpha\beta}(e_1 e_2) = \sum_\gamma E_{\alpha\gamma}(e_1) \cdot E_{\gamma\beta}(e_2)$$

$$E_{\alpha\beta}(e^*) = \sum_\gamma E_{\alpha\gamma}(e) \cdot E_{\gamma\beta}(e^*) + \begin{cases} 1 & \text{if } \alpha = \beta, \\ 0 & \text{if } \alpha \neq \beta. \end{cases}$$

Note that the definitions for * are circular, but both are well defined if we take the least fixpoint of the resulting system of equations.

The standard language interpretation $G : \mathsf{Exp} \to 2^N$ is the unique coalgebra morphism to the final coalgebra.

5.3   Matrix Representation

By currying, one can view the signature of NetKAT coalgebra as

$$\delta : X \to X^{\mathsf{At} \times \mathsf{At}} \qquad\qquad \varepsilon : X \to 2^{\mathsf{At} \times \mathsf{At}}$$

and observe that $X^{\mathsf{At} \times \mathsf{At}}$ and $2^{\mathsf{At} \times \mathsf{At}}$ are isomorphic to the families of square matrices over X and 2, respectively, with rows and columns indexed by At. Moreover, as the reader may have noticed, many of the operations used to define the syntactic derivative $D_{\alpha\beta}, E_{\alpha\beta}$ closely resemble matrix operations. Indeed, we can view $\delta(t)$ as an $\mathsf{At} \times \mathsf{At}$ matrix over X and $\varepsilon(t)$ as an $\mathsf{At} \times \mathsf{At}$ matrix over 2. Moreover, if X is a KAT, then the family of $\mathsf{At} \times \mathsf{At}$ matrices over X again forms a KAT, denoted $\mathsf{Mat}(\mathsf{At}, X)$, under the standard matrix operations [7]. Thus we have

$$\delta : X \to \mathsf{Mat}(\mathsf{At}, X) \qquad\qquad \varepsilon : X \to \mathsf{Mat}(\mathsf{At}, 2).$$

With this observation, the syntactic coalgebra defined in §5.2 takes the following concise form:

$$D(p) = 0 \qquad D(b) = 0 \qquad D(\mathsf{dup}) = J \qquad D(e_1 + e_2) = D(e_1) + D(e_2)$$
$$D(e_1 e_2) = D(e_1) \cdot I(e_2) + E(e_1) \cdot D(e_2) \qquad D(e^*) = E(e^*) \cdot D(e) \cdot I(e^*),$$

where $I(e)$ is the diagonal matrix with e on the main diagonal and 0 elsewhere and J is the matrix with α on the main diagonal in position $\alpha\alpha$ and 0 elsewhere; and

$$E(\mathsf{dup}) = 0 \qquad\qquad E(e_1 + e_2) = E(e_1) + E(e_2)$$
$$E(e_1 e_2) = E(e_1) \cdot E(e_2) \qquad\qquad E(e^*) = E(e)^*.$$

In this form E becomes a KAT homomorphism from Exp to $\mathsf{Mat}(\mathsf{At}, 2)$.

Likewise, we can regard the set-theoretic coalgebra presented in §5.2 as having matrix type

$$\delta : 2^N \to \mathsf{Mat}(\mathsf{At}, 2^N) \qquad\qquad \varepsilon : 2^N \to \mathsf{Mat}(\mathsf{At}, 2).$$

Again, in this form, ε becomes a KAT homomorphism.

This matrix representation is exploited heavily in the implementation of the decision procedure of [10] described below in §6.

5.4   Kleene's Theorem for NetKAT

The correctness of the bisimulation algorithm hinges on the relationship between the coalgebras described in §5.1 and the packet-switching and language models described in §2.4 and §4, respectively. This result is the generalization to NetKAT of Kleene's theorem relating regular expressions and finite automata.

Theorem 2 ([10]). *A set of NetKAT reduced strings is the set accepted by some finite-state NetKAT automaton if and only if it is $G(e)$ for some NetKAT expression e.*

Given a NetKAT expression e, an equivalent finite NetKAT automaton can be constructed from the derivatives of e modulo associativity, commutativity, and idempotence (ACI), with e as the start state. The continuation and observation maps are the syntactic derivative introduced in §5.2. A careful analysis shows that the number of states is at most $|\mathsf{At}| \cdot 2^\ell$, where ℓ is the number of occurrences of dup in e.

6   Implementation

The paper [10] describes an implementation of the decision procedure for NetKAT term equivalence. It converts two NetKAT terms to automata using Brzozowski derivatives, then tests bisimilarity. The implementation comprises roughly 4500 lines of OCaml and includes a parser, pretty printer, and visualizer. The implementation has been integrated into the Frenetic SDN controller platform and has been tested on numerous benchmarks with good results.

The bisimilarity algorithm is fairly standard. Given two NetKAT terms, all derivatives are calculated, and the E matrices of corresponding pairs are checked for equality. The procedure fails immediately if they are not. This coinductive algorithm can be implemented in almost linear time in the combined size of the automata using the union-find data structure of Hopcroft and Karp [13] to represent the bisimilarity classes.

6.1   Optimizations

The implementation incorporates a number of important enhancements and optimizations to avoid combinatorial blowup. It uses a symbolic representation that exploits symmetry and sparseness to reduce the size of the state space. Intermediate values that do not contribute to the final outcome are aggressively pruned. To further improve performance, the implementation incorporates a number of other optimizations: hash-consing and memoization, sparse multiplication, base compaction, fast computaton of fixpoints. These enhancements are described in detail in [10].

Although the algorithm is still necessarily exponential in the worst case (the problem is PSPACE-complete), the tool tends to be fast in practice due to the constrained nature of real-world problems.

7   Related Work

Software-defined networking (SDN) has emerged in recent years as the dominant paradigm for network programming. A number of SDN programming languages and verification tools have appeared [2,5,8,9,12,16–18,26,28–30,34,36–39], and SDN is being actively deployed in industry [14,20,21].

NetKAT [1, 10] was developed as a part of the Frenetic project [9, 12, 28, 29]. Compared to other tools, NetKAT is unique in its focus on algebraic and coalgebraic structure of network programs. NetKAT largely inherits its syntax, semantics, and application methodology from these earlier efforts but adds a complete deductive system and PSPACE decision procedure.

The algebraic and coalgebraic theories of KA and KAT and related systems have been studied extensively [6, 22–25, 33, 35]. This work has uncovered strong relationships between the algebraic/logical view of systems and the combinatorial/automata-theoretic view. These ideas have figured prominently in the development of NetKAT.

The implementation uses many ideas and optimizations from the coalgebraic implementations of KA and KAT and other related systems [3, 4, 31] to provide enhanced performance, making automated decision feasible even in the face of PSPACE completeness.

8   Conclusion

This paper surveys recent work on NetKAT, a relatively new language and logic for specifying and verifying network packet-processing functions. NetKAT was introduced in [1] and further developed in [10]. We have attempted to make the presentation self-contained and accessible, but a more comprehensive treatment can be found in the original papers.

NetKAT consists of Kleene algebra with tests [23] with specialized primitives for expressing properties of networks, along with equational axioms for reasoning with those constructs. The standard semantics is a packet-switching model that interprets NetKAT expressions as functions from packet histories to sets of packet histories. There is also a language model that is isomorphic to the packet-switching model and a coalgebraic model that is related to the other two models via a version of Kleene's theorem. The NetKAT axioms are sound and complete over these interpretations. The coalgebraic model admits a bisimulation-based decision procedure that is efficient in many cases of practical interest, although the general problem is PSPACE-complete. There is a full implementation in OCaml that is efficient in practice and compares favorably with the state of the art. Several applications of interest have also been described.

Acknowledgments. Special thanks to my coauthors Carolyn Jane Anderson, Nate Foster, Arjun Guha, Jean-Baptiste Jeannin, Matthew Milano, Cole Schlesinger, Alexandra Silva, Laure Thompson, and David Walker for their kind permission to include results from [1, 10] in this survey. Thanks also to Konstantinos Mamouras, Andrew Myers, Mark Reitblatt, Ross Tate, and the rest of the Cornell PLDG group for many insightful discussions and helpful comments.

References

1. Anderson, C.J., Foster, N., Guha, A., Jeannin, J.-B., Kozen, D., Schlesinger, C., Walker, D.: NetKAT: Semantic foundations for networks. In: Proc. 41st ACM SIGPLAN-SIGACT Symp. Principles of Programming Languages (POPL 2014), San Diego, California, USA, pp. 113–126. ACM (January 2014)
2. Ball, T., Bjorner, N., Gember, A., Itzhaky, S., Karbyshev, A., Sagiv, M., Schapira, M., Valadarsky, A.: Vericon: Towards verifying controller programs in software-defined networks. In: PLDI (to appear, 2014)
3. Bonchi, F., Pous, D.: Checking NFA equivalence with bisimulations up to congruence. In: Proc. 40th ACM SIGPLAN-SIGACT Symp. Principles of Programming Languages, POPL 2013, pp. 457–468. ACM (2013)
4. Braibant, T., Pous, D.: Deciding Kleene algebras in Coq. Logical Methods in Computer Science 8(1:16), 1–42 (2012)
5. Canini, M., Venzano, D., Perešíni, P., Kostić, D., Rexford, J.: A NICE way to test OpenFlow applications. In: NSDI (2012)
6. Chen, H., Pucella, R.: A coalgebraic approach to Kleene algebra with tests. Electronic Notes in Theoretical Computer Science 82(1) (2003)
7. Cohen, E., Kozen, D., Smith, F.: The complexity of Kleene algebra with tests. Technical Report TR96-1598, Computer Science Department, Cornell University (July 1996)
8. Ferguson, A.D., Guha, A., Liang, C., Fonseca, R., Krishnamurthi, S.: Participatory networking: An API for application control of SDNs. In: SIGCOMM (2013)
9. Foster, N., Harrison, R., Freedman, M.J., Monsanto, C., Rexford, J., Story, A., Walker, D.: Frenetic: A network programming language. In: ICFP (September 2011)
10. Foster, N., Kozen, D., Milano, M., Silva, A., Thompson, L.: A coalgebraic decision procedure for NetKAT. Technical Report, Computing and Information Science, Cornell University (March 2014), http://hdl.handle.net/1813/36255, POPL 2015 (to appear)
11. Open Networking Foundation. Software-defined networking: The new norm for networks. White paper (2012), https://www.opennetworking.org/images/stories/downloads/sdn-resources/white-papers/wp-sdn-newnorm.pdf
12. Guha, A., Reitblatt, M., Foster, N.: Machine-verified network controllers. In: PLDI (June 2013)

13. Hopcroft, J.E., Karp, R.M.: A linear algorithm for testing equivalence of finite automata. Technical Report 71-114. University of California (1971)
14. Jain, S., Kumar, A., Mandal, S., Ong, J., Poutievski, L., Singh, A., Venkata, S., Wanderer, J., Zhou, J., Zhu, M., Zolla, J., Hölzle, U., Stuart, S., Vahdat, A.: B4: Experience with a globally-deployed software defined WAN. In: SIGCOMM (2013)
15. Katz-Bassett, E., Scott, C., Choffnes, D.R., Cunha, Í., Valancius, V., Feamster, N., Madhyastha, H.V., Anderson, T., Krishnamurthy, A.: Lifeguard: Practical repair of persistent route failures. In: SIGCOMM (2012)
16. Kazemian, P., Varghese, G., McKeown, N.: Header space analysis: Static checking for networks. In: NSDI (2012)
17. Khurshid, A., Zou, X., Zhou, W., Caesar, M., Godfrey, P.B.: VeriFlow: Verifying network-wide invariants in real time. In: NSDI (2013)
18. Kim, H., Feamster, N.: Improving network management with software defined networking. IEEE Communications Magazine 51(2), 114–119 (2013)
19. Kleene, S.C.: Representation of events in nerve nets and finite automata. In: Shannon, C.E., McCarthy, J. (eds.) Automata Studies, pp. 3–41. Princeton University Press, Princeton (1956)
20. Koponen, T., Amidon, K., Balland, P., Casado, M., Chanda, A., Fulton, B., Ganichev, I., Gross, J., Gude, N., Ingram, P., Jackson, E., Lambeth, A., Lenglet, R., Li, S.-H., Padmanabhan, A., Pettit, J., Pfaff, B., Ramanathan, R., Shenker, S., Shieh, A., Stribling, J., Thakkar, P., Wendlandt, D., Yip, A., Zhang, R.: Network virtualization in multi-tenant datacenters. In: NSDI (2014)
21. Koponen, T., Casado, M., Gude, N., Stribling, J., Poutievski, L., Zhu, M., Ramanathan, R., Iwata, Y., Inoue, H., Hama, T., Shenker, S.: Onix: A distributed control platform for large-scale production networks. In: OSDI (2010)
22. Kozen, D.: A completeness theorem for Kleene algebras and the algebra of regular events. Infor. and Comput. 110(2), 366–390 (1994)
23. Kozen, D.: Kleene algebra with tests. Transactions on Programming Languages and Systems 19(3), 427–443 (1997)
24. Kozen, D.: On the coalgebraic theory of Kleene algebra with tests. Technical Report. Computing and Information Science, Cornell University (March 2008), http://hdl.handle.net/1813/10173
25. Kozen, D., Smith, F.: Kleene algebra with tests: Completeness and decidability. In: van Dalen, D., Bezem, M. (eds.) CSL 1996. LNCS, vol. 1258, pp. 244–259. Springer, Heidelberg (1997)
26. Loo, B.T., Hellerstein, J.M., Stoica, I., Ramakrishnan, R.: Declarative routing: Extensible routing with declarative queries. In: SIGCOMM (2005)
27. Mai, H., Khurshid, A., Agarwal, R., Caesar, M., Godfrey, P.B., King, S.T.: Debugging the data plane with Anteater. In: SIGCOMM (2011)
28. Monsanto, C., Foster, N., Harrison, R., Walker, D.: A compiler and run-time system for network programming languages. In: POPL (January 2012)
29. Monsanto, C., Reich, J., Foster, N., Rexford, J., Walker, D.: Composing software-defined networks. In: NSDI (April 2013)
30. Nelson, T., Guha, A., Dougherty, D.J., Fisler, K., Krishnamurthi, S.: A balance of power: Expressive, analyzable controller programming. In: HotSDN (2013)
31. Pous, D.: Relational algebra and KAT in Coq (February 2013), http://perso.ens-lyon.fr/damien.pous/ra
32. Rutten, J.J.M.M.: Universal coalgebra: A theory of systems. Theoretical Computer Science 249, 3–80 (2000)

33. Rutten, J.J.M.M.: Automata and coinduction (an exercise in coalgebra). In: Sangiorgi, D., de Simone, R. (eds.) CONCUR 1998. LNCS, vol. 1466, pp. 194–218. Springer, Heidelberg (1998)
34. Scott, R.C., Wundsam, A., Zarifis, K., Shenker, S.: What, Where, and When: Software Fault Localization for SDN. Technical Report UCB/EECS-2012-178, EECS Department, University of California, Berkeley (2012)
35. Silva, A.: Kleene Coalgebra. PhD thesis, University of Nijmegen (2010)
36. Voellmy, A., Hudak, P.: Nettle: Functional reactive programming of OpenFlow networks. In: Rocha, R., Launchbury, J. (eds.) PADL 2011. LNCS, vol. 6539, pp. 235–249. Springer, Heidelberg (2011)
37. Voellmy, A., Wang, J., Yang, Y.R., Ford, B., Hudak, P.: Maple: Simplifying SDN programming using algorithmic policies. In: SIGCOMM (2013)
38. Xie, G.G., Zhan, J., Maltz, D.A., Zhang, H., Greenberg, A.G., Hjálmtýsson, G., Rexford, J.: On static reachability analysis of IP networks. In: INFOCOM (2005)
39. Zeng, H., Kazemian, P., Varghese, G., McKeown, N.: Automatic test packet generation. In: CoNEXT (2012)

Optimized Compilation of Multiset Rewriting with Comprehensions*

Edmund Soon Lee Lam and Iliano Cervesato

Carnegie Mellon University, Qatar Campus, Doha, Qatar
sllam@qatar.cmu.edu, iliano@cmu.edu

Abstract. We extend the rule-based, multiset rewriting language CHR with multiset comprehension patterns. Multiset comprehension provides the programmer with the ability to write multiset rewriting rules that can match a variable number of entities in the state. This enables implementing algorithms that coordinate large amounts of data or require aggregate operations in a declarative way, and results in code that is more concise and readable than with pure CHR. We call this extension CHR^{cp}. In this paper, we formalize the operational semantics of CHR^{cp} and define a low-level optimizing compilation scheme based on join ordering for the efficient execution of programs. We provide preliminary empirical results that demonstrate the scalability and effectiveness of this approach.

1 Introduction

CHR is a declarative logic constraint programming language based on pure forward-chaining and committed choice multiset rewriting. This provides the user with a highly expressive programming model to implement complex programs in a concise and declarative manner. Yet, programming in a pure forward-chaining model is not without its shortfalls. Expressive as it is, when faced with algorithms that operate over a dynamic number of constraints (e.g., finding the minimum value satisfying a property or finding *all* constraints in the store matching a particular pattern), a programmer is forced to decompose his/her code over several rules, as a CHR rule can only match a fixed number of constraints. Such an approach is tedious, error-prone and leads to repeated instances of boilerplate code, suggesting the opportunity for a higher form of abstraction. This paper develops an extension of CHR with *multiset comprehension patterns* [11,2]. These patterns allow the programmer to write multiset rewriting rules that can match dynamically-sized constraint sets in the store. They enable writing more readable, concise and declarative programs that coordinate large amounts of data or use aggregate operations. We call this extension CHR^{cp}.

In previous work [7], we presented an abstract semantics for CHR^{cp} and concretized it into an operational semantics. This paper defines a compilation scheme for CHR^{cp} rules that enables an optimized execution for this operational semantics. This compilation scheme, based on *join ordering* [4,6], determines an optimized sequence of operations to carry out the matching of constraints and guards. This ordering is optimized in that it utilizes the most effective supported indexing methodologies (e.g., hash map

---

* This paper was made possible by grant NPRP 09-667-1-100, *Effective Programming for Large Distributed Ensembles*, from the Qatar National Research Fund (a member of the Qatar Foundation). The statements made herein are solely the responsibility of the authors.

J. Garrigue (Ed.): APLAS 2014, LNCS 8858, pp. 19–38, 2014.

indexing, binary tree search) for each constraint pattern and schedules guard condition eagerly, thereby saving potentially large amounts of computation by pruning unsatisfiable branches as early as possible. The key challenge of this approach is to determine such an optimized ordering and to infer the set of lookup indices required to execute the given CHR^{cp} program with the best possible asymptotic time complexity. Our work augments the approach from [6] to handle comprehension patterns, and we provide a formal definition of this compilation scheme and an abstract machine that implements the resulting compiled CHR^{cp} programs.

Altogether, this paper makes the following contributions: We define a scheme that compiles CHR^{cp} rules into optimized join orderings. We formalize the corresponding CHR^{cp} abstract matching machine. We prove the soundness of this abstract machine with respect to the operational semantics. We provide preliminary empirical results to show that a practical implementation of CHR^{cp} is possible.

The rest of the paper is organized as follows: Section 2 introduces CHR^{cp} by examples and Section 3 gives its syntax. In Section 4, we describe an operational semantics for CHR^{cp} and define our compilation scheme in Section 5. Section 6 builds optimized join orderings of CHR^{cp} rules. Section 7 defines the abstract state machine and Section 8 establishes correctness results. In Section 9 we present preliminary empirical results. Section 10 situates CHR^{cp} in the literature and Section 11 outlines directions of future work.

2 A Motivating Example

In this section, we illustrate the benefits of comprehension patterns in multiset rewriting with an example. A comprehension pattern $\lceil p(\vec{t}) \mid g \rfloor_{\vec{x} \in t}$ represents a multiset of constraints that match the atomic constraint $p(\vec{t})$ and satisfy guard g under the bindings of variables $\vec{x}$ that range over the elements of the *comprehension domain* t.

Consider the problem of two agents wanting to swap data that they each possess on the basis of a pivot value P. We express an integer datum I belonging to agent X by the constraint $data(X, I)$. The state of this dynamic system is represented by a multiset of ground constraints, the constraint store. Given agents X and Y and a value P, we want all of X's data with value I less than or equal to P to be transferred to Y and all of Y's data J such that J is greater than or equal to P to be transferred to X. Notice that the value P satisfies the conditions both for I and J. The following CHR^{cp} rule implements this swap procedure:

$$selSwap @ \begin{array}{c} swap(X, Y, P) \\ \lceil data(X, I) \mid I \leq P \rfloor_{I \in Xs} \\ \lceil data(Y, J) \mid J \geq P \rfloor_{J \in Ys} \end{array} \Longleftrightarrow \begin{array}{c} \lceil data(Y, I) \rfloor_{I \in Xs} \\ \lceil data(X, J) \rfloor_{J \in Ys} \end{array}$$

The swap is triggered by the constraint $swap(X, Y, P)$ in the rule head on the left of $\Longleftrightarrow$. All of X's data I such that $I \leq P$ are identified by the comprehension pattern $\lceil data(X, I) \mid I \leq P \rfloor_{I \in Xs}$. Similarly, all Y's data J such that $J \geq P$ are identified by $\lceil data(Y, J) \mid J \geq P \rfloor_{J \in Ys}$. The instances of I and J matched by each comprehension pattern are accumulated in the comprehension domains Xs and Ys, respectively. Finally, these collected bindings are used in the rule body on the right of $\Longleftrightarrow$ to complete the rewriting by redistributing all of X's selected data to Y and vice versa. The CHR^{cp} semantics enforces the property that each comprehension pattern captures a *maximal multiset* of constraints in the store, thus guaranteeing that no data that is to be swapped is left behind.

Comprehension patterns allow the programmer to easily write rules that manipulate dynamic numbers of constraints. By contrast, consider how the above program would be written in pure *CHR* (without comprehension patterns). To do this, we are forced to explicitly implement the operation of collecting a multiset of *data* constraints over several rules. We also need to introduce an accumulator to store bindings for the matched facts as we retrieve them. A possible implementation of this nature is as follows:

$$
\begin{aligned}
init\ @\ swap(X, Y, P) &\Longleftrightarrow grab1(X, P, Y, []), grab2(Y, P, X, []) \\
gIter1\ @\ grab1(X, P, Y, Is), data(X, I) &\Longleftrightarrow I \leq P \mid grab1(X, P, Y, [I \mid Is]) \\
gEnd1\ @\ grab1(X, P, Y, Is) &\Longleftrightarrow unrollData(Y, Is) \\
gIter2\ @\ grab2(Y, P, X, Js), data(Y, J) &\Longleftrightarrow J \geq P \mid grab2(Y, P, X, [J \mid Js]) \\
gEnd2\ @\ grab2(Y, P, X, Js) &\Longleftrightarrow unrollData(X, Js) \\
unrollIter\ @\ unrollData(L, [D \mid Ds]) &\Longleftrightarrow unrollData(L, Ds), data(L, D) \\
unrollEnd\ @\ unrollData(L, []) &\Longleftrightarrow true
\end{aligned}
$$

In a *CHR* program with several subroutines of this nature, such boilerplate code gets repeated over and over, making the program verbose. Furthermore, the use of list accumulators and auxiliary constraints (e.g., *grab1*, *grab2*, *unrollData*) makes the code less readable and more prone to errors. Most importantly, the swap operation as written in CHR^{cp} is *atomic* while the above *CHR* code involves many rewrites, which could be interspersed by applications of other rules that operate on *data* constraints. Observe also that this pure *CHR* implementation assumes a priority semantics [3]: rule *gEnd1* is to be used only when rule *gIter1* is *not* applicable, and similarly for rules *gEnd2* and *gIter2*. Rule priority guarantees that all eligible *data* constraints participate in the swap. We may be tempted to implement the swap procedure as follows in standard *CHR*:

$$
\begin{aligned}
swap1\ @\ swap(X, Y, I), data(X, I) &\Longleftrightarrow I \leq P \mid swap(X, Y, I), data(Y, I) \\
swap2\ @\ swap(X, Y, J), data(Y, J) &\Longleftrightarrow J \geq P \mid swap(X, Y, J), data(X, J) \\
swap3\ @\ swap(X, Y, D) &\Longleftrightarrow true
\end{aligned}
$$

This, however, does not work in general. This is because the matching conditions of *swap1* and *swap2* are potentially overlapping: if we have $data(X, P)$ in the constraint store, applying *swap1* to it will produce $data(Y, P)$, which will inevitably be reversed by an application of *swap2*, thereby locking the execution in a non-terminating cycle. This code is however correct were the conditions on X's and Y's values to be complementary (e.g., $I < P$ and $J \geq P$). But it is still non-atomic and relies on prioritization as the last rule should be triggered only when neither of the first two is applicable. By contrast, multiset comprehensions in CHR^{cp} provides a high-level abstraction that relinquishes all these technical concerns from the programmer's hands.

3   Syntax and Notations

In this section, we define the abstract syntax of CHR^{cp} and highlight the notations used throughout this paper. We write $\bar{o}$ for a multiset of syntactic objects o, with $\varnothing$ indicating the empty multiset. We write $\langle \bar{o}_1, \bar{o}_2 \rangle$ for the union of multisets $\bar{o}_1$ and $\bar{o}_2$, omitting the brackets when no ambiguity arises. The extension of multiset $\bar{o}$ with syntactic object o is similarly denoted $\langle \bar{o}, o \rangle$. Multiset comprehension at the meta-level is denoted by

Variables: x Predicates: p Rule names: r Primitive terms: t_α Occurrence index: i

$$\begin{aligned}
\textit{Terms:}\quad & t ::= t_\alpha \mid \bar{t} \mid \{t \mid g\}_{\bar{x}\in t} \\
\textit{Guards:}\quad & g ::= t = t \mid t \dot{\in} t \mid t < t \mid t \le t \mid t > t \mid t \ge t \mid g \wedge g
\end{aligned}$$

Atomic Constraints:	$A ::= p(\vec{t})$	*Head Constraints:*	$H ::= C : i$
Comprehensions:	$M ::= \{A \mid g\}_{\bar{x}\in t}$	*Rules:*	$R ::= r @ \bar{H} \Longleftrightarrow g \mid \bar{B}$
Rule Constraints:	$C, B ::= A \mid M$	*Programs:*	$\mathcal{P} ::= \bar{R}$

Fig. 1. Abstract Syntax of CHR^{cp}

$\{o \mid \Phi(o)\}$, where o a meta object and $\Phi(o)$ is a logical statement on o. We write $\vec{o}$ for a comma-separated tuple of o's. A list of objects o is also denoted by $\vec{o}$ and given o, we write $[o \mid \vec{o}]$ for the list with head o and tail $\vec{o}$. The empty list is denoted by $[\,]$. We will explicitly disambiguate lists from tuples where necessary. Given a list $\vec{o}$, we write $\vec{o}[i]$ for the ith element of $\vec{o}$, with $\vec{o}[i] = \bot$ if i is not a valid index in $\vec{o}$. We write $o \in \vec{o}$ if $\vec{o}[i] \ne \bot$ for some i. The set of valid indices of the list $\vec{o}$ is denoted $range(\vec{o})$. The concatenation of list $\vec{o}_1$ with $\vec{o}_2$ is denoted $\vec{o}_1 ++ \vec{o}_2$. We abbreviate a singleton list containing o as $[o]$. Given a list $\vec{o}$, we write $\{\vec{o}\}$ to denote the multiset containing all (and only) the elements of $\vec{o}$. The set of the free variables in a syntactic object o is denoted $FV(o)$. We write $[\vec{t}/\vec{x}]o$ for the simultaneous replacement within object o of all occurrences of variable x_i in $\vec{x}$ with the corresponding term t_i in $\vec{t}$. When traversing a binding construct (e.g., a comprehension pattern), substitution implicitly α-renames variables to avoid capture. It will be convenient to assume that terms get normalized during substitution. The composition of substitutions θ and ϕ is denoted $\theta\phi$.

Figure 1 defines the abstract syntax of CHR^{cp}. An atomic constraint $p(\vec{t})$ is a predicate symbol p applied to a tuple $\vec{t}$ of terms. A comprehension pattern $\{A \mid g\}_{\bar{x}\in t}$ represents a multiset of constraints that match the atomic constraint A and satisfy guard g under the bindings of variables $\vec{x}$ that range over t. We call $\vec{x}$ the *binding variables* and t the *comprehension domain*. The variables $\vec{x}$ are locally bound with scope A and g. We implicitly α-rename binding variables to avoid capture. The development of CHR^{cp} is largely agnostic to the language of terms [7]. In this paper however, we assume for simplicity that t_α are arithmetic terms (e.g., 10, $x + 4$). We also include tuples and multisets of such terms. Term-level multiset comprehension $\{t \mid g\}_{x \in m}$ filters multiset m according to guard g and maps the result as specified by t.

A *CHR* head constraint $C : i$ is a constraint C paired with an occurrence index i. As in *CHR*, a CHR^{cp} rule $r @ \bar{H} \Longleftrightarrow g \mid \bar{B}$ specifies the rewriting of the *head constraints* $\bar{H}$ into the *body* $\bar{B}$ under the conditions that guards g are satisfied; r is the name of the rule.[1] If the guard g is always satisfied (i.e., *true*), we drop that rule component entirely. All free variables in a CHR^{cp} rule are implicitly universally quantified at the head of the rule. A *CHR* program is a set of *CHR* rules and we require that each head constraint has a unique occurrence index i. For simplicity, we assume that a rule body is grounded by the head constraints and that guards do not appear in the rule body.

---

[1] *CHR* rules traditionally have a fourth component, the propagation head, which we omit in the interest of space as it does not fundamentally impact the compilation process or our abstract machine. See [7] for a treatment of comprehension patterns in propagation heads.

Matching: $\bar{C} \triangleq_{\mathbf{lhs}} St$ $C \triangleq_{\mathbf{lhs}} St$

$$\frac{\bar{C} \triangleq_{\mathbf{lhs}} St \quad C \triangleq_{\mathbf{lhs}} St'}{\langle \bar{C}, C \rangle \triangleq_{\mathbf{lhs}} \langle St, St' \rangle} \,(1_{mset\text{-}1}) \qquad \frac{}{\varnothing \triangleq_{\mathbf{lhs}} \varnothing} \,(1_{mset\text{-}2}) \qquad \frac{}{A \triangleq_{\mathbf{lhs}} A} \,(1_{atom})$$

$$\frac{[\vec{t}/\vec{x}]A \triangleq_{\mathbf{lhs}} A' \quad \models [\vec{t}/\vec{x}]g \quad \langle A \mid g \rangle_{\vec{x} \in ts} \triangleq_{\mathbf{lhs}} St}{\langle A \mid g \rangle_{\vec{x} \in \langle ts, \vec{t} \rangle} \triangleq_{\mathbf{lhs}} \langle St, A' \rangle} \,(1_{comp\text{-}1}) \qquad \frac{}{\langle A \mid g \rangle_{\vec{x} \in \varnothing} \triangleq_{\mathbf{lhs}} \varnothing} \,(1_{comp\text{-}2})$$

Residual Non-matching: $\bar{C} \triangleq^{\neg}_{\mathbf{lhs}} St$ $C \triangleq^{\neg}_{\mathbf{lhs}} St$

$$\frac{\bar{C} \triangleq^{\neg}_{\mathbf{lhs}} St \quad C \triangleq^{\neg}_{\mathbf{lhs}} St}{\langle \bar{C}, C \rangle \triangleq^{\neg}_{\mathbf{lhs}} St} \,(1^{\neg}_{mset\text{-}1}) \qquad \frac{}{\varnothing \triangleq^{\neg}_{\mathbf{lhs}} St} \,(1^{\neg}_{mset\text{-}2})$$

$$\frac{}{A \triangleq^{\neg}_{\mathbf{lhs}} St} \,(1^{\neg}_{atom}) \qquad \frac{A \not\sqsubseteq_{\mathbf{lhs}} M \quad M \triangleq^{\neg}_{\mathbf{lhs}} St}{M \triangleq^{\neg}_{\mathbf{lhs}} \langle St, A \rangle} \,(1^{\neg}_{comp\text{-}1}) \qquad \frac{}{M \triangleq^{\neg}_{\mathbf{lhs}} \varnothing} \,(1^{\neg}_{comp\text{-}2})$$

Subsumption: $A \sqsubseteq_{\mathbf{lhs}} \langle A' \mid g \rangle_{\vec{x} \in ts}$ iff $A = \theta A'$ and $\models \theta g$ for some $\theta = [\vec{t}/\vec{x}]$

Fig. 2. Semantics of Matching in CHR^{cp}

4 Operational Semantics of CHR^{cp}

This section recalls the operational semantics of CHR^{cp} [7]. Without loss of generality, we assume that atomic constraints in a rule have the form $p(\vec{x})$, including in comprehension patterns. This simplified form pushes complex term expressions and computations into the guard component of the rule or the comprehension pattern. The satisfiability of a ground guard g is modeled by the judgment $\models g$; its negation is written $\not\models g$.

Similarly to [5], this operational semantics defines a goal-based execution of a CHR^{cp} program $\mathcal{P}$ that incrementally processes store constraints against rule instances in $\mathcal{P}$. By "incrementally", we mean that goal constraints are added to the store one by one, as we process each for potential match with the head constraints of rules in $\mathcal{P}$. We present the operational semantics in two sub-sections: Section 4.1 describes in isolation, the processing of a rule's left-hand side (*semantics of matching*) and right-hand-side execution. Section 4.2 presents the overall operational semantics. We assume that the constraint store contains only ground facts, a property that is maintained during execution. This entail that matching (as opposed to unification) suffices to guarantee the completeness of rule application.

4.1 Semantics of Matching and Rule Body Execution

The semantics of matching, specified in Figure 2, identifies applicable rules in a CHR^{cp} program by matching their head with the constraint store. The matching judgment $\bar{C} \triangleq_{\mathbf{lhs}} St$ holds when the constraints in the store fragment St match *completely* the multiset of constraint patterns $\bar{C}$. It will always be the case that $\bar{C}$ is ground (i.e., $FV(\bar{C}) = \emptyset$). Rules $(1_{mset\text{-}*})$ iterate rules (1_{atom}) and $(1_{comp\text{-}*})$ on St, thereby partitioning it into fragments matched by these rules. Rule (1_{atom}) matches an atomic constraint A to the singleton store A. Rules $(1_{comp\text{-}*})$ match a comprehension pattern

$\boxed{\text{Rule Body: } \bar{C} \gg_{\mathbf{rhs}} St \quad C \gg_{\mathbf{rhs}} St}$

$$\frac{\bar{C} \gg_{\mathbf{rhs}} St \quad C \gg_{\mathbf{rhs}} St'}{\lfloor \bar{C}, C \rfloor \gg_{\mathbf{rhs}} \lfloor St, St' \rfloor} \,(\mathbf{r}_{mset-1}) \qquad \frac{}{\varnothing \gg_{\mathbf{rhs}} \varnothing} \,(\mathbf{r}_{mset-2}) \qquad \frac{}{A \gg_{\mathbf{rhs}} A} \,(\mathbf{r}_{atom})$$

$$\frac{\models [\vec{t}/\vec{x}]g \quad [t/\vec{x}]A \gg_{\mathbf{rhs}} A' \quad \lfloor A \mid g \rfloor_{\vec{x} \in ts} \gg_{\mathbf{rhs}} A'}{\lfloor A \mid g \rfloor_{\vec{x} \in \lfloor ts, \vec{t} \rfloor} \gg_{\mathbf{rhs}} \lfloor St, A' \rfloor} \,(\mathbf{r}_{comp-1})$$

$$\frac{\not\models [\vec{t}/\vec{x}]g \quad \lfloor A \mid g \rfloor_{\vec{x} \in ts} \gg_{\mathbf{rhs}} St}{\lfloor A \mid g \rfloor_{\vec{x} \in \lfloor ts, \vec{t} \rfloor} \gg_{\mathbf{rhs}} St} \,(\mathbf{r}_{comp-2}) \qquad \frac{}{\lfloor A \mid g \rfloor_{\vec{x} \in \varnothing} \gg_{\mathbf{rhs}} \varnothing} \,(\mathbf{r}_{comp-3})$$

$\boxed{\text{Residual Non-unifiability: } \mathcal{P} \triangleq_{\mathbf{unf}}^{\neg} \bar{B} \quad g \rhd \bar{H} \triangleq_{\mathbf{unf}}^{\neg} \bar{B}}$

$$\frac{g \rhd \bar{H} \triangleq_{\mathbf{unf}}^{\neg} \bar{B} \quad \mathcal{P} \triangleq_{\mathbf{unf}}^{\neg} \bar{B}}{\mathcal{P}, (r @ \bar{H} \Longleftrightarrow g \mid \bar{C_b}) \triangleq_{\mathbf{unf}}^{\neg} \bar{B}} \,(\mathbf{u}_{prog-1}^{\neg}) \qquad \frac{}{\varnothing \triangleq_{\mathbf{unf}}^{\neg} \bar{B}} \,(\mathbf{u}_{prog-2}^{\neg})$$

$$\frac{g \rhd \bar{H} \triangleq_{\mathbf{unf}}^{\neg} \bar{B} \quad g \rhd C \triangleq_{\mathbf{unf}}^{\neg} \bar{B}}{g \rhd \lfloor \bar{H}, C : i \rfloor \triangleq_{\mathbf{unf}}^{\neg} \bar{B}} \,(\mathbf{u}_{mset-1}^{\neg}) \qquad \frac{}{g \rhd \varnothing \triangleq_{\mathbf{unf}}^{\neg} \bar{B}} \,(\mathbf{u}_{mset-2}^{\neg}) \qquad \frac{}{g \rhd A \triangleq_{\mathbf{unf}}^{\neg} \bar{B}} \,(\mathbf{u}_{atom}^{\neg})$$

$$\frac{g \rhd B \not\sqsubseteq_{\mathbf{unf}} M \quad g \rhd M \triangleq_{\mathbf{unf}}^{\neg} \bar{B}}{g \rhd M \triangleq_{\mathbf{unf}}^{\neg} \lfloor \bar{B}, B \rfloor} \,(\mathbf{u}_{comp-1}^{\neg}) \qquad \frac{}{g \rhd M \triangleq_{\mathbf{unf}}^{\neg} \varnothing} \,(\mathbf{u}_{comp-2}^{\neg})$$

$$g \rhd A \sqsubseteq_{\mathbf{unf}} \lfloor A' \mid g' \rfloor_{\vec{x} \in ts} \text{ iff } \theta A \equiv \theta A', \models \theta g', \models \theta g \text{ for some } \theta$$

$$g'' \rhd \lfloor A \mid g \rfloor_{\vec{x} \in ts} \sqsubseteq_{\mathbf{unf}} \lfloor A' \mid g' \rfloor_{\vec{x}' \in ts'} \text{ iff } \theta A \equiv \theta A', \models \theta g'', \models \theta g', \models \theta g \text{ for some } \theta$$

Fig. 3. Rule Body Application and Unifiability of Comprehension Patterns

$\lfloor A \mid g \rfloor_{\vec{x} \in ts}$. If the comprehension domain is empty ($x \in \varnothing$), the store must be empty rule (1_{comp-2}). Otherwise, rule (1_{comp-1}) binds $\vec{x}$ to an element $\vec{t}$ of the comprehension domain ts, matches the instance $[\vec{t}/\vec{x}]A$ of the pattern A with a constraint A' in the store if the corresponding guard instance $[\vec{t}/\vec{x}]g$ is satisfiable, and continues with the rest of the comprehension domain. To guarantee the maximality of comprehension patterns, we test a store for *residual matchings* using the residual non-matching judgment $\bar{C} \triangleq_{\mathbf{lhs}}^{\neg} St$ (Also shown in Figure 2). For each comprehension pattern $\lfloor A' \mid g \rfloor_{\vec{x} \in ts}$ in $\bar{C}$, this judgment checks that no constraints in St matches A' satisfying g.

Once a CHR^{cp} rule instance has been identified, we need to *unfold* the comprehension patterns in its body into a multiset of atomic constraints that will be added to the store. The judgment $\bar{C} \gg_{\mathbf{rhs}} St$ does this unfolding: given $\bar{C}$, this judgment holds if and only if St is the multiset of all (and only) constraints found in $\bar{C}$, after comprehension patterns in $\bar{C}$ have been unfolded. Figure 3 defines this judgment.

An important property of CHR is *monotonicity*: if a rule instance r transforms store Ls to Ls', then r transforms $\lfloor Ls, Ls'' \rfloor$ to $\lfloor Ls', Ls'' \rfloor$ for any Ls''. This property allows for incremental processing of constraints ([5]) that is sound w.r.t. the abstract semantics of CHR. Monotonicity does not hold in CHR^{cp}. We showed in [7] that to guarantee the sound incremental goal-based execution of a CHR^{cp} program $\mathcal{P}$, we must identify those rule body constraints are *monotone*, and only incrementally store monotone constraints, while non-monotone constraints are immediately stored. A monotone

$$\text{Goal Constraint} \quad G ::= \texttt{init } \bar{B} \mid \texttt{lazy } A \mid \texttt{eager } A\#n \mid \texttt{act } A\#n\, i$$

Goal Stack $\quad Gs ::= [\,] \mid [G \mid Gs]$ $\quad$ Store $\quad Ls ::= \varnothing \mid \langle Ls, A\#n \rangle$ $\quad$ State $\quad \sigma ::= \langle Gs\, ;\, Ls \rangle$

$dropIdx(C : i) ::= C \quad getIdx(C : i) ::= \{i\} \quad dropLabels(A\#n) ::= A \quad getLabels(A\#n) ::= \{n\}$

$newLabels(Ls, A) ::= A\#n$ $\quad$ such that $n \notin getLabels(Ls)$

$\mathcal{P}[i] \quad ::= $ if $R \in \mathcal{P}$ and $i \in getIdx(R)$ then R else $\bot$

Fig. 4. Execution States and Auxiliary Meta-operations

constraint in program $\mathcal{P}$ is a constraint A that can never be matched by a comprehension head constraint of any rule in $\mathcal{P}$. To test that a comprehension pattern M has no match in a store Ls (i.e., $M \triangleq_{\text{lhs}}^{\neg} Ls$), it suffices to test M against the subset of Ls containing just its non-monotone constraints (see [7] for proofs). We call this property of CHR^{cp} *conditional monotonicity*. Given a CHR^{cp} program $\mathcal{P}$, for each rule body constraint B in $\mathcal{P}$, if for every head constraint comprehension pattern $M : j$ and rule guard g in $\mathcal{P}$, B is not unifiable with M while satisfying g (denoted $g \triangleright M \sqsubseteq_{\text{unf}} B$), then we say that B is *monotone* w.r.t. program $\mathcal{P}$, denoted by $\mathcal{P} \triangleq_{\text{unf}}^{\neg} B$. These judgments are defined in the bottom half of Figure 3.

4.2   Operational Semantics

In this section, we define the overall operational semantics of CHR^{cp}. This semantics explicitly supports partial incremental processing of constraints that are monotone to a given CHR^{cp} program. Execution states, defined in Figure 4, are pairs $\sigma = \langle Gs\, ;\, Ls \rangle$ where Gs is the *goal stack* and Ls is the *labeled store*. Store labels n allow us to distinguish between copies of the same constraint in the store and to uniquely associate a goal constraint with a specific stored constraint. Each goal in a goal stack Gs represents a unit of execution and Gs itself is a list of goals to be executed. Goal labels `init`, `lazy`, `eager` and `act` identify the various types of goals.

Figure 4 defines several auxiliary operations that either retrieve or drop occurrence of indices and store labels: $dropIdx(H)$ and $getIdx(H)$ deal with indices, $dropLabels(\_)$ and $getLabels(\_)$ with labels. We inductively extend $getIdx(\_)$ to multisets of head constraints and CHR^{cp} rules, to return the set of all occurrence indices that appear in them. We similarly extend $dropLabels(\_)$ and $getLabels(\_)$ to be applicable with labeled stores. As a means of generating new labels, we also define the operation $newLabels(Ls, A)$ that returns $A\#n$ such that n does not occur in Ls. Given program $\mathcal{P}$ and occurrence index i, $\mathcal{P}[i]$ denotes the rule $R \in \mathcal{P}$ in which i occurs, or $\bot$ if i does not occur in any of $\mathcal{P}$'s rules. We implicitly extend the matching judgment ($\triangleq_{\text{lhs}}$) and residual non-matching judgment ($\triangleq_{\text{lhs}}^{\neg}$) to annotated entities.

The operational semantics of CHR^{cp} is defined by the judgment $\mathcal{P} \triangleright \sigma \mapsto_{\omega} \sigma'$, where $\mathcal{P}$ is a CHR^{cp} program and σ, σ' are execution states. It describes the goal-oriented execution of the CHR^{cp} program $\mathcal{P}$. Execution starts in an *initial* execution state σ of the form $\langle [\texttt{init } \bar{B}]\, ;\, \varnothing \rangle$ where $\bar{B}$ is the initial multiset of constraints. Figure 5 shows the transition rules for this judgment. Rule (*init*) applies when the leading goal has the form `init` $\bar{B}$. It partitions $\bar{B}$ into $\bar{B}_l$ and $\bar{B}_e$, both of which are unfolded into St_l and St_e respectively (via rule body application, Section 4.1). $\bar{B}_l$ contains the multiset of constraints which are monotone w.r.t. to $\mathcal{P}$ (i.e., $\mathcal{P} \triangleq_{\text{unf}}^{\neg} \bar{B}_l$). These constraints are *not* added to the store immediately, rather we incrementally process them

$(init)$	$\mathcal{P} \rhd \langle [\texttt{init } \lfloor \bar{B}_l, \bar{B}_e \rfloor \mid Gs] ; Ls \rangle \mapsto_\omega \langle lazy(St_l) ++ eager(Ls_e) ++ Gs ; \lfloor Ls, Ls_e \rfloor \rangle$ such that $\mathcal{P} \triangleq_{\mathbf{unf}}^{\neg} \bar{B}_l \quad \bar{B}_e \gg_{\mathbf{rhs}} St_e \quad \bar{B}_l \gg_{\mathbf{rhs}} St_l \quad Ls_e = newLabels(Ls, St_e)$ where $\; eager(\lfloor Ls, A\#n \rfloor) ::= [\texttt{eager } A\#n \mid eager(Ls)] \qquad eager(\varnothing) ::= []$ $\qquad\quad lazy(\lfloor St_m, A \rfloor) ::= [\texttt{lazy } A \mid lazy(St_m)] \qquad\quad lazy(\varnothing) ::= []$
$(lazy\text{-}act)$	$\mathcal{P} \rhd \langle [\texttt{lazy } A \mid Gs] ; Ls \rangle \mapsto_\omega \langle [\texttt{act } A\#n \; 1 \mid Gs] ; \lfloor Ls, A\#n \rfloor \rangle$ such that $\lfloor A\#n \rfloor = newLabels(Ls, \lfloor A \rfloor)$
$(eager\text{-}act)$	$\mathcal{P} \rhd \langle [\texttt{eager } A\#n \mid Gs] ; \lfloor Ls, A\#n \rfloor \rangle \mapsto_\omega \langle [\texttt{act } A\#n \; 1 \mid Gs] ; \lfloor Ls, A\#n \rfloor \rangle$
$(eager\text{-}drop)$	$\mathcal{P} \rhd \langle [\texttt{eager } A\#n \mid Gs] ; Ls \rangle \mapsto_\omega \langle Gs ; Ls \rangle \qquad\qquad \text{if } A\#n \notin Ls$
$(act\text{-}apply)$	$\mathcal{P} \rhd \langle [\texttt{act } A\#n \; i \mid Gs] ; \lfloor Ls, Ls_h, Ls_a, A\#n \rfloor \rangle \mapsto_\omega \langle [\texttt{init } \theta \bar{B} \mid Gs] ; Ls \rangle$ if $\mathcal{P}[i] = (r \; @ \; \lfloor \bar{H}_h, C : i \rfloor \Longleftrightarrow g \mid \bar{B})$, there exists some θ such that $\models \theta g \qquad \theta C \triangleq_{\mathbf{lhs}} \lfloor Ls_a, A\#n \rfloor \qquad \theta \bar{H}_h \triangleq_{\mathbf{lhs}} Ls_h \qquad \theta \bar{H}_h \triangleq_{\mathbf{lhs}}^{\neg} Ls \qquad \theta C \triangleq_{\mathbf{lhs}}^{\neg} Ls$
$(act\text{-}next)$	$\mathcal{P} \rhd \langle [\texttt{act } A\#n \; i \mid Gs] ; Ls \rangle \mapsto_\omega \langle [\texttt{act } A\#n \; (i+1) \mid Gs] ; Ls \rangle$ if $(act\text{-}apply)$ does not applies.
$(act\text{-}drop)$	$\mathcal{P} \rhd \langle [\texttt{act } A\#n \; i \mid Gs] ; Ls \rangle \mapsto_\omega \langle Gs ; Ls \rangle \qquad\qquad \text{if } \mathcal{P}[i] = \bot$

Fig. 5. Operational Semantics of CHR^{cp}

by only adding them into the goal as 'lazy' goals (lazily stored). Constraints $\bar{B}_e$ are not monotone w.r.t. to $\mathcal{P}$, hence they are immediately added to the store and added to the goals as 'eager' goals (eagerly stored). Rule $(lazy\text{-}act)$ handles goals of the form lazy A: we initiate active matching on A by adding it to the store and adding the new goal act $A\#n$ 1. Rules $(eager\text{-}act)$ and $(eager\text{-}drop)$ deal with goals of the form eager $A\#n$. The former adds the goal 'act $A\#n$ 1' if $A\#n$ is still present in the store; the later simply drops the leading goal otherwise. The last three rules deal with leading goals of the form act $A\#n$ i: rule $(act\text{-}apply)$ handles the case where the active constraint $A\#n$ matches the ith head constraint occurrence of $\mathcal{P}$. If this match satisfies the rule guard, matching partners exist in the store and the comprehension maximality condition is satisfied, we apply the corresponding rule instance. These matching conditions are defined by the semantics of matching of CHR^{cp} (Figure 2). Note that the rule body instance $\theta \bar{B}$ is added as the new goal init $\bar{B}$. This is because it potentially contains non-monotone constraints: we will employ rule $(init)$ to determine the storage policy of each constraint. Rule $(act\text{-}next)$ applies when the previous two rules do not, hence we cannot apply any instance of the rule with $A\#n$ matching the ith head constraint. Finally, rule $(act\text{-}drop)$ drops the leading goal if occurrence index i does not exist in $\mathcal{P}$. The correctness of this operational semantics w.r.t. a more abstract semantics for CHR^{cp} is proven in [7].

5 Compiling CHR^{cp} Rules

While Figures 2–5 provide a formal operational description of the overall multiset rewriting semantics of CHR^{cp}, they are high-level in that they keep multiset matching abstract. Specifically, the use of judgments $\triangleq_{\mathbf{lhs}}$ and $\triangleq_{\mathbf{lhs}}^{\neg}$ in rule $(act\text{-}apply)$ hides away crucial details of how a practical implementation is to conduct these expensive operations. In this section, we describe a scheme that compiles CHR^{cp} head constraints into a lower-level representation optimized for efficient execution, without using $\triangleq_{\mathbf{lhs}}$ or $\triangleq_{\mathbf{lhs}}^{\neg}$. This compilation focuses on CHR^{cp} head constraints (left-hand side), where the bulk of execution time (and thus most optimization opportunities) comes from.

$$p_1(E, Z) : 1$$
$$\{p_2(Y, C, D) \mid D \in Ws, C > D\}_{(C,D) \in Ds} : 2$$
$$p_3(X, Y, F, Z) : 3 \qquad\qquad\qquad E \le F$$
$$p_4(Z, Ws) : 4 \qquad\qquad \Longleftrightarrow \quad Ws \ne \varnothing \qquad \cdots$$
$$\{p_5(X, P) \mid P \in Ws\}_{P \in Ps} : 5 \qquad\qquad Ps \ne \varnothing$$

i. Active $p_1(E, Z) : 1$	*vi.* CompreDomain $5\ P\ Ps$
ii. LookupAtom $\langle true; \{Z\}\rangle\ p_4(Z, Ws) : 4$	*vii.* CheckGuard $Ps \ne \varnothing$
iii. CheckGuard $Ws \ne \varnothing$	*viii.* LookupAll $\langle D \in Ws; \{Y\}\rangle\ p_2(Y, C, D) : 2$
iv. LookupAtom $\langle E \le F; \{Z\}\rangle\ p_3(X, Y, F, Z) : 3$	*ix.* FilterGuard $4\ C \ge D$
v. LookupAll $\langle P \in Ws; \{X\}\rangle\ p_5(X, P) : 5$	*x.* CompreDomain $4\ (C, D)\ Ds$

Fig. 6. Optimized Join Ordering for $p_1(E, Z) : 1$

As described in Section 4, an active constraint act $A\#n\ i$ is matched against an occurrence of head constraint H_i in a rule r, and all other head constraints H_k in r are matched against distinct constraints in the store. We call H_i the *active head constraint* and the other H_k *partner head constraints* (or simply, *active pattern* and *partners* respectively). Computing complete matches for the multiset of constraint patterns is a combinatorial search problem. In general, any ordering of partners leads to the computation of intermediate data that may ultimately be discarded, resulting in redundant storage and processing time. Therefore, we want to determine an optimized ordering of partners that minimizes this intermediate data. Join ordering [4,6] leverages the dependencies among rule heads and rule guards to do precisely this. This allows pruning search branches early and utilizing lookup methods (e.g., indexing on hash maps, balanced trees) that provide the best possible asymptotic time complexity. Our work extends traditional approaches to *CHR* compilation [6] to handle comprehension head constraints and augments them with optimizations specific to them. In particular, our approach is an extension of *static* join-ordering techniques (e.g., [4]) that relies on a heuristic cost model to determine optimized orderings at compile-time.

5.1 Introducing CHR^{cp} Join Ordering

The top of Figure 6 shows an example rule with five head constraints. In this example, all predicates are different, hence each head constraint will always match distinct constraints from the store (in Section 5.3, we discuss the case where different rule heads match the same constraint). To better appreciate the benefits of join ordering, consider an example constraint store Ls of the form:

$$p_1(t_{E1}, t_{Z1}), \; \biguplus_{i=1}^{n_2} p_2(t_{Yi}, t_{Ci}, t_{Di}), \; \biguplus_{i=1}^{n_3} p_3(t_{Xi}, t_{Yi}, t_{Fi}, t_{Zi}), \; \biguplus_{i=1}^{n_4} p_4(t_{Zi}, t_{Wsk}), \; \biguplus_{i=1}^{n_5} p_5(t_{Xi}, t_{Pi})$$

where $\biguplus_{i=1}^{n} p(\vec{t_i})$ denotes a store fragment containing n ground constraints of the form $p(\vec{t_i})$. Hence n_2, n_3, n_4 and n_5 are the number of constraints in the store for the predicates p_2, p_3, p_4 and p_5, respectively. As we carry out this analysis, we optimistically assume that each of the n_2 instances of p_2 has a different term t_{Yi} in its first argument, and similarly for each argument position and predicate.

Consider a naive execution of the rule in Figure 6 in the textual order with active constraint act $p_1(t_{E1}, t_{Z1})\#n\ i$ for some n and i, so that $p_1(E, Z) : 1$ is the active pattern. This binds variables E and Z to terms t_{E1} and t_{Z1} respectively. Next, we identify all constraints $p_2(t_{Yi}, t_{Ci}, t_{Di})$ such that $C > D$, and for each bindings t_{Yi} for Y, we build the comprehension range Ds from the t_{Ci}'s and t_{Di}'s. Since this pattern shares no common variables with the active pattern and variable Ws is not ground, to build the above match we have no choice but examining all n_2 constraints for p_2 in the store. Furthermore, the guard $D \in Ws$ would have to be enforced at a later stage, after $p_4(Z, Ws)$ is matched, as a post comprehension filter. We next seek a match for $p_3(X, Y, F, Z) : 3$. Because it shares variables Y and Z with patterns 1 and 2, we can find matching candidates in constant time, if we have the appropriate indexing support $(p_3(\_, Y, \_, Z))$. The next two patterns $(p_4(Z, Ws) : 4$ and $\wr p_5(X, P) \mid P \mathbin{\dot{\in}} Ws\!\int_{P \in Ps} : 5)$ are matched in a similar manner and finally $Ps \neq \varnothing$ is checked at the very end. This naive execution has two main weaknesses: first, scheduling partner 2 first forces the lower bound of the cost of processing this rule to be $O(n_2)$, even if we find matches to partners 3 and 4 in constant time. Second, suppose we fail to find a match for partner 5 such that $Ps \neq \varnothing$, then the execution time spent computing Ds of partner 2, including the time to search for candidates for partners 3 and 4, was wasted.

Now consider the join ordering for the active pattern $p_1(E, Z) : 1$ shown in Figure 6. It is an optimized ordering of the partner constraints in this instance: Task (i) announces that $p_1(E, Z) : 1$ is the constraint pattern that the active constraint must match. Task (ii) dictates that we look up the constraint $p_4(Z, Ws)$. This join task maintains a set of possible constraints that match partner 4 and the search proceeds by exploring each constraint as a match to partner 4 until it finds a successful match or fails; the *indexing directive* $I = \langle true; \{Z\} \rangle$ mandates a hash multimap lookup for p_4 constraints with first argument value of Z (i.e., $p_4(Z, \_)$). This allows the retrieval of all matching candidate constraints from Ls in amortized constant time (as oppose to linear $O(n_4)$). Task (iii) checks the guard condition $Ws \neq \varnothing$: if no such $p_4(Z, Ws)$ exists, execution of this join ordering can terminate *immediately* at this point (a stark improvement from the naive execution). Task (iv) triggers the search for $p_3(X, Y, F, Z)$ with the indexing directive $\langle E \leq F; \{Z\} \rangle$. This directive specifies that candidates of partner 3 are retrieved by utilizing a two-tiered indexing structure: a hash table that maps p_3 constraints in their fourth argument (i.e., $p_3(\_, \_, \_, Z)$) to a binary balance tree that stores constraints in sorted order of the third argument (i.e., $p_3(\_, \_, F, \_)$, $E \leq F$). The rule guard $E \leq F$ can then be omitted from the join ordering, since its satisfiability is guaranteed by this indexing operation. Task (v) initiates a lookup for constraints matching $p_5(X, P) : 5$ which is a comprehension. It differs from Tasks (ii) and (iv) in that rather than branching for each candidate match to $p_5(X, P) : 5$, we collect the set of all candidates as matches for partner 5. The multiset of constraints matching this partner is efficiently retrieved by the indexing directive $\langle P \mathbin{\dot{\in}} Ws; \{X\} \rangle$. Task (vi) computes the comprehension domain Ps by projecting the multiset of instances of P from the candidates of partner 5. The guard $Ps \neq \varnothing$ is scheduled at Task (vii), pruning the current search immediately if Ps is empty. Tasks $(viii - x)$ represent the best execution option for partner 2, given that composite indexing ($D \mathbin{\dot{\in}} Ws$ and $C \leq D$) is not yet supported in our implementation: Task $(viii)$ retrieves candidates matching $p_2(Y, C, D) : 2$ via the indexing directive $\langle D \mathbin{\dot{\in}} Ws; \{Y\} \rangle$, which specifies that we retrieve candidates from a hash multimap that indexes p_2 constraints on the first and third argument (i.e., $p_2(Y, \_, D)$); values of D are enumerated from Ws. Task (ix) does a post-comprehension filter, removing candidates of partner 2 that do not satisfy $C \leq D$. Finally, task (x) computes the comprehension domain Ds. While we still conduct a post comprehension filtering (Task (ix)), this filters from a small set of candidates (i.e., $p_2(Y, \_, D)$ where $D \mathbin{\dot{\in}} Ws$) and hence is likely more efficient than linear enumeration and filtering on the store (i.e., $O(|Ws|)$ *vs* $O(n_2)$).

$i.$ Active $\boxed{p_2(Y, C, D) : 2}$ $iv.$ CheckGuard $Ws \neq \varnothing,$ $\boxed{D \dot{\in} Ws}$

$ii.$ $\boxed{\text{CheckGuard } C > D}$ $v.$ LookupAtom $\langle E \leq F; \{Z\}\rangle\, p_3(X, Y, F, Z) : 3$

$iii.$ LookupAtom $\langle true; \{Z\}\rangle\, p_4(Z, Ws) : 4$ $vi.$ Bootstrap $\{C, D\}$ 2

                                   ... (Similar to Tasks $v - x$ of Figure 6)

Fig. 7. Optimized Join Ordering for $\wr p_2(Y, C, D) \mid D \dot{\in} Ws, C > D \wr_{(C,D) \in Ds} : 2$

Such optimized join orderings are statically computed by our compiler and the constraint store is compiled to support the set of all indexing directives that appears in the join orderings. In general, our implementation always produces join orderings that schedule comprehension partners after all atom partners. This is because comprehension lookups (LookupAll) never fail and hence do not offer any opportunity for early pruning. However, orderings within each of the partner categories (atom or comprehension) are deliberate. For instance, $p_4(Z, Ws) : 4$ was scheduled before $p_3(X, Y, F, Z) : 3$ since it is more constrained: it has fewer free variables and $Ws \neq \varnothing$ restricts it. Comprehension partner 5 was scheduled before 2 because of guard $Ps \neq \varnothing$ and also that 2 is considered more expensive because of the post lookup filtering (Task (ix)). Cost heuristics are discussed in Section 6.

5.2 Bootstrapping for Active Comprehension Head Constraints

In the example in Figure 6, the active pattern is an atomic constraint. Our next example illustrates the case where the active pattern H_i is a comprehension. In this case, the active constraint $A\#n$ must be part of a match with the comprehension rule head $H_i = \wr A' \mid g \wr_{x \in xs} : i$. While the join ordering should allow early detection of failure to match A with A' or to satisfy comprehension guard g, it must also avoid scheduling comprehension rule head H_i before atomic partner constraints are identified. Our implementation uses *bootstrapping* to achieve this balance: Figure 7 illustrates this compilation for the comprehension head constraint $\wr p_2(Y, C, D) \mid D \dot{\in} Ws, C > D \wr_{(C,D) \in Ds} : 2$ from Figure 6 playing the role of the active pattern. The key components of bootstrapping are highlighted in boxes: Task (i) identifies $p_2(Y, C, D)$ as the active pattern, treating it as an atom. The match for atom partners proceeds as in the previous case (Section 5.1) with the difference that the comprehension guards of partner 2 ($D \dot{\in} Ws, C > D$) are included in the guard pool. This allows us to schedule them early ($C > D$ in Task (ii) and $D \dot{\in} Ws$ in Task (iv)) or even as part of an indexing directive to identify compatible partner atom constraints that support the current partial match. Once all atomic partners are matched, at Task (vi), Bootstrap $\{C, D\}$ 5, clears the bindings imposed by the active constraint, while the rest of the join ordering executes the actual matching of the comprehension head constraint similarly to Figure 6.

5.3 Uniqueness Enforcement

In general, a CHR^{cp} rule r may have overlapping head constraints, i.e., there may be a store constraint $A\#n$ that matches both H_j and H_k in r's head. Matching two head constraints to the same object in the store is not valid in CHR^{cp}. We guard against this by providing two uniqueness enforcing join tasks: If H_j and H_k are atomic head constraints, join task NeqHead j k (figure 9) checks that constraints $A\#m$ and $A\#p$

$r @ p(D_0) : 1, \; q(P) : 2, \; \{p(D_1) \mid D_1 > P\}_{D_1 \in Xs} : 3, \; \{p(D_2) \mid D_2 \leq P\}_{D_2 \in Ys} : 4 \iff \dots$

i. Active $p(D_0) : 1$ *vi.* LookupAll $\langle D_2 \leq P; \varnothing \rangle \, p(D_2) : 4$

ii. LookupAtom $\langle true; \emptyset \rangle \, q(P) : 2$ *vii.* FilterHead 4 1

iii. LookupAll $\langle D_1 > P; \varnothing \rangle \, p(D_1) : 3$ *viii.* $\boxed{\text{FilterHead 4 3}}$

iv. FilterHead 3 1   *ix.* CompreDomain 4 D_2 Ys

v. CompreDomain 3 D_1 Xs

Fig. 8. Uniqueness Checks: Optimized Join Ordering for $p(D_0) : 1$

matching H_j and H_k respectively are distinct (i.e., $m \neq p$). If either H_j or H_k (or both) is a comprehension, the join ordering must include a FilterHead join task.

Figure 8 illustrates filtering for active pattern $p(D_0) : 1$. Task *(iv)* FilterHead 3 1 states that we must filter constraint(s) matched by rule head 1 away from constraints matched by partner 3. For partner 4, we must filter from 1 and 3 (Tasks *(vii − viii)*). Notice that partner 2 does not participate in any such filtering, since its constraint has a different predicate symbol and filtering is obviously not required. However, it is less obvious that task *(viii)*, highlighted, is in fact not required as well: because of the comprehension guards $D_1 > P$ and $D_2 \leq P$, partners 3 and 4 always match distinct sets of p constraints. Our implementation uses a more precise check for non-unifiability of head constraints ($\sqsubseteq_{\mathbf{unf}}$) to determine when uniqueness enforcement is required.

6   Building Join Orderings

In this section, we formalize join orderings for CHR^{cp}, as illustrated in the previous section. We first construct a valid join ordering for a CHR^{cp} rule r given a chosen sequencing of partners of r and later discuss how this sequence of partners is chosen. Figure 9 defines the elements of join orderings, join tasks and indexing directives. A list of join tasks $\vec{J}$ forms a join ordering. A join context Σ is a set of variables. Atomic guards are as in Figure 1, however we omit equality guards and assume that equality constraints are enforced as non-linear variable patterns in the head constraints. For simplicity, we assume that conjunctions of guards $g_1 \wedge g_2$ are unrolled into a multiset of guards $\bar{g} = \{g_1, g_2\}$, with $\models \bar{g}$ expressing the satisfiability of each guard in $\bar{g}$. An indexing directive is a tuple $\langle g; \vec{x} \rangle$ such that g is an indexing guard and $\vec{x}$ are hash variables. The bottom part of Figure 9 defines how valid index directives are constructed. The relation $\Sigma; A \rhd t \mapsto x$ states that from the join context Σ, term t connects to atomic constraint A via variable x. Term t must be either a constant or a variable that appears in Σ and $x \in FV(A)$. The operation $idxDir(\Sigma, A, g)$ returns a valid index directive for a given constraint A, the join context Σ and the atomic guard g. This operation requires that Σ be the set of all variables that have appeared in a prefix of a join ordering. It is defined as follows: If g is an instance of an order relation and it acts as a connection between Σ and A (i.e., $\Sigma; A \rhd t_i \mapsto t_j$ where t_i and t_j are its arguments), then the operation returns g as part of the index directive, together with the set of variables that appear in both Σ and A. If g is a membership relation $t_1 \dot{\in} t_2$, the operation returns g only if $\Sigma; A \rhd t_2 \mapsto t_1$. Otherwise, g cannot be used as an index, hence the operation returns $true$. Finally, $allIdxDirs(\Sigma, A, \bar{g})$ defines the set of all such indexing derivable from $idxDir(\Sigma, A, g)$ where $g \in \bar{g}$.

Join Context Σ	$::=$	$\vec{x}$	Index Directive	I	$::=$	$\langle g; \vec{x} \rangle$
Join Task	J	$::=$	Active H	LookupAtom I H		LookupAll I H
			Bootstrap $\vec{x}$ i	CheckGuard $\bar{g}$		FilterGuard i $\bar{g}$
			NeqHead i i	FilterHead i i		CompreDomain i $\vec{x}$ x

$\Sigma; A \triangleright t \mapsto x$ iff t is a constant or t is a variable such that $t \in \Sigma$ and $x \in FV(A)$

$$idxDir(\Sigma, A, g) \quad ::= \quad \begin{cases} \langle g; \Sigma \cap FV(A) \rangle & \begin{cases} \text{if } g = t_1 \ op \ t_2 \text{ and } op \in \{\leq, <, \geq, >\} \\ \text{and } \Sigma; A \triangleright t_i \mapsto t_j \text{ for } \{i,j\} = \{1,2\} \end{cases} \\ \langle g; \Sigma \cap FV(A) \rangle & \text{if } g = t_1 \doteq t_2 \text{ and } \Sigma; A \triangleright t_2 \mapsto t_1 \\ \langle true; \Sigma \cap FV(A) \rangle & \text{otherwise} \end{cases}$$

$$allIdxDirs(\Sigma, A, \bar{g}) \quad ::= \quad \lfloor idxDir(\Sigma, A, g) \mid \text{for all } g \in \bar{g} \cup true \rfloor$$

Fig. 9. Join Tasks and Indexing Directives

An indexing directive $\langle g; \vec{x} \rangle$ for a constraint pattern $p(\vec{t})$ determines what type of indexing method can be exploited for the given constraint type. For example, $\langle true; \vec{x} \rangle$ where $\vec{x} \neq \emptyset$ states that we can store constraints $p(\vec{t})$ in a hash multimap that indexes the constraints on argument positions of $\vec{t}$ where variables $\vec{x}$ appear, supporting amortized $O(1)$ lookups. For $\langle x \doteq ts; \vec{x} \rangle$, we store $p(\vec{t})$ in the same manner, but during lookup we enumerate the values of x from ts, hence we get amortized $O(m)$ lookups, where m is size of ts. Directive $\langle x \ op \ y; \emptyset \rangle$ specifies binary tree storage and binary search lookups, while $\langle x \ op \ y; \vec{x} \rangle$ specifies a composite structure: a hash map with binary trees as contents. The default indexing directive is $\langle true; \emptyset \rangle$, that corresponds to a linear iteration lookup on $p(\vec{t})$. For full details, refer to [8].

Figure 10 defines the operation $compileRuleHead(H_i, \vec{H}_a, \vec{H}_m, \bar{g})$ which compiles an active pattern H_i, a particular sequencing of partners, and rule guards of a CHR^{cp} rule (i.e., $r @ \lfloor \vec{H}_a, \vec{H}_m, H_i \rfloor \Longleftrightarrow \bar{g} \mid \bar{B}$) into a *valid* join ordering for this sequence. A join-ordering $\vec{J}$ is valid w.r.t. to a CHR rule r if and only if it possesses certain well-formedness properties (See [8] for details of these properties) that allows for its sound execution of the abstract matching machine (Section 7). The topmost definition of *compileRuleHead* in Figure 10 defines the case for H_i being an atomic constraint, while the second definition handles the case for a comprehension. The auxiliary operation $buildJoin(\vec{H}, \Sigma, \bar{g}, \vec{H}_h)$ iteratively builds a list of join tasks from a list of head constraints $\vec{H}$, the join context Σ and a multiset of guards $\bar{g}$, the *guard pool*, with a list of head constraints $\vec{H}_h$, the *prefix head constraints*. The join context contains the variables that appear in the prefix head constraints, while the guard pool contains guards g that are available for either scheduling as tests or as indexing guards. The prefix head constraints contain the list of atomic constraint patterns observed thus far in the computation. If the head of $\vec{H}$ is atomic $A : j$, the join ordering is constructed as follows: the subset $\bar{g}_1$ of $\bar{g}$ that are grounded by Σ are scheduled at the front of the ordering (CheckGuard $\bar{g}_1$). This subset is computed by the operation $scheduleGrds(\Sigma, \bar{g})$ which returns the partition of $\bar{g}$ such that $\bar{g}_1$ contains guards grounded by Σ and $\bar{g}_2$ contains all other guards. This is followed by the lookup join task for atom $A : j$ (i.e., LookupAtom $\langle g_i; \vec{x} \rangle$ $A : j$) and uniqueness enforcement join tasks $neqHs(A : j, \vec{H}_h)$ which returns a join tasks NeqHead j k for each occurrence in $\vec{H}_h$ that has the same

$compileRuleHead(A : i, \vec{H}_a, \vec{H}_m, \bar{g})$ ::= $[\texttt{Active}\ A : i \mid J_a]\!+\!\!+\!J_m\!+\!\!+\!checkGrds(\bar{g}'')$
where $(J_a, \Sigma, \bar{g}') = buildJoin(\vec{H}_a, FV(A_i), \bar{g}, [])$ and $(J_m, \Sigma', \bar{g}'') = buildJoin(\vec{H}_m, \Sigma, \bar{g}', \vec{H}_a)$

$compileRuleHead(\langle A \mid \bar{g}_m \rangle_{\vec{x} \in xs} : i, \vec{H}_a, \vec{H}_m, \bar{g})$
   ::= $[\texttt{Active}\ A : i \mid J_a]\!+\!\!+\![\texttt{Bootstrap}\ FV(A) - FV(\vec{x}) \mid J_m]\!+\!\!+\!checkGrds(\bar{g}'')$
   where $(J_a, \Sigma, \bar{g}') = buildJoin(\vec{H}_a, FV(A_i), \bar{g} \cup \bar{g}_m, [])$
        $(J_m, \Sigma', \bar{g}'') = buildJoin(\langle A_i \mid \bar{g}_m \rangle_{\vec{x} \in xs} \mid \vec{H}_m], \Sigma - \vec{x}, \bar{g}', \vec{H}_a)$

$buildJoin([A : j \mid \vec{H}], \Sigma, \bar{g}, \vec{H}_h)$
   ::= $([\texttt{CheckGuard}\ \bar{g}_1, \texttt{LookupAtom}\ \langle g_i; \vec{x} \rangle\ A : j]\!+\!\!+\!neqHs(A : j, \vec{H}_h)\!+\!\!+\!\vec{J}, \Sigma, \bar{g}_r)$
   where $(\bar{g}_1, \bar{g}_2) = scheduleGrds(\Sigma, \bar{g})$ and $\langle g_i; \vec{x} \rangle \in allIdxDirs(\Sigma, A, \bar{g}_2)$
        $(\vec{J}, \Sigma', \bar{g}_r) = buildJoin(\vec{H}, \Sigma \cup FV(A), \bar{g}_2 - g_i, \vec{H}_h\!+\!\!+\![A : j])$

$buildJoin([\langle A \mid \bar{g}_m \rangle_{\vec{x} \in xs} : j \mid \vec{H}], \Sigma, \bar{g}, \vec{H}_h)$
   ::= $([\texttt{CheckGuard}\ \bar{g}_1, \texttt{LookupAll}\ \langle g_i; \vec{x}' \rangle\ A : j, \texttt{FilterGuard}\ (\bar{g}_m - \{g_i\})]$
        $+\!\!+\!filterHs(\langle A \mid \bar{g}_m \rangle_{\vec{x} \in xs} : j, \vec{H}_h)\!+\!\!+\![\texttt{CompreDomain}\ j\ \vec{x}\ xs \mid \vec{J}], \Sigma, \bar{g}_r)$
   where $(\bar{g}_1, \bar{g}_2) = scheduleGrds(\Sigma, \bar{g})$ and $\langle g_i; \vec{x}' \rangle \in allIdxDirs(\Sigma, A, \bar{g}_2 \cup \bar{g}_m)$
        $(\vec{J}, \Sigma', \bar{g}_r) = buildJoin(\vec{H}, \Sigma \cup FV(A), \bar{g}_2 - g_i, \vec{H}_h\!+\!\!+\![\langle A \mid \bar{g}_m \rangle_{\vec{x} \in xs} : j])$

$buildJoin([], \Sigma, \bar{g}, \vec{H}_h)$ ::= $([], \Sigma, \bar{g})$
$scheduleGrds(\Sigma, \bar{g})$ ::= $(\{g \mid g \in \bar{g}, FV(g) \subseteq \Sigma\}, \{g \mid g \in \bar{g}, FV(g) \not\subseteq \Sigma\})$
$neqHs(p(\_) : j, p'(\_) : k)$ ::=   if $p = p'$ then $[\texttt{NeqHead}\ j\ k]$ else $[]$
$filterHs(C : j, C' : k)$ ::=   if $true \rhd C' \sqsubseteq_{\textbf{unf}} C$ then $[\texttt{FilterHead}\ j\ k]$ else $[]$

Fig. 10. Building Join Ordering from CHR^{cp} Head Constraints

predicate symbol as A. The rest of the join ordering $\vec{J}$ is computed from the tail of $\vec{H}$. Note that the operation picks *one* indexing directive $\langle g_i; \vec{x} \rangle$ from the set of all available indexing directives ($allIdxDirs(\Sigma, A, \bar{g}_2)$). Hence from a given sequence of partners, *compileRuleHead* defines a family of join orderings for the same inputs, modulo indexing directives. If the head of $\vec{H}$ is a comprehension, the join ordering is constructed similarly, with the following differences: 1) a $\texttt{LookupAll}$ join tasks in created in the place of $\texttt{LookupAtom}$; 2) the comprehension guards $\bar{g}_m$ are included as possible indexing guards ($allIdxDirs(\Sigma, A, \bar{g}_2 \cup \bar{g}_m)$); 3) immediately after the lookup join task, we schedule the remaining of comprehension guards as filtering guards (i.e., $\texttt{FilterGuard}\ \bar{g}_m - g_i$); 4) $\texttt{FilterHead}$ uniqueness enforcement join tasks are deployed ($filterHs(C : j, C' : k)$) as described in Section 5.3; 5) We conclude the comprehension partner with $\texttt{CompreDomain}\ \vec{x}\ xs$.

We briefly highlight the heuristic scoring function we have implemented to determine an optimized join ordering for each rule occurrence H_i of a CHR^{cp} program (refer to [8] for more details). This heuristic augments [6] to handle comprehensions. While we do not claim that such heuristics always produce optimal join-orderings, in practice it produces join-orderings that perform generally better than arbitrary ordering (see Section 9). Given a join ordering, we calculate a numeric score for the cost of executing $\vec{J}$: a weighted sum value $(n - 1)w_1 + (n - 2)w_2 + ... + w_n$ for a join ordering with n partners, such that w_j is the join cost of the jth partner H_j. Since earlier partners have higher weight, this scoring rewards join orderings with the least expensive partners scheduled earlier. The join cost w_j for a partner constraint $C : j$ is a tuple (v_f, v_l) where v_f is the *degree of freedom* and v_l is the *indexing score*. The degree of freedom v_f counts the number of new variables introduced by C, while the indexing score v_l is the negative of the number of common variables between C and all other partners matched before it. In general, we want to minimize v_f since a higher value indicates larger numbers of candidates matching C, hence larger branching factor

$$\begin{array}{ll} \text{Matching Context } \Theta \ ::= \ \langle A\#n; \vec{J}; Ls \rangle & \begin{array}{l} \text{Backtrack Branch } Br \ ::= \ (pc, \theta, Pm) \\ \text{Candidate Match } U \ ::= \ (\theta, A\#n) \\ \text{Partial Match } Pm \ ::= \ Pm, i \mapsto \bar{U} \mid \emptyset \end{array} \\ \text{Matching State } \mathcal{M} \ ::= \ \langle J; pc; \vec{Br}; \theta; Pm \rangle & \end{array}$$

$match(A, A') \ ::= \ \text{if exists } \phi \text{ such that } \phi A = A' \text{ then } \phi \text{ else } \bot$

$lookupCands(Ls, A', \langle g; \vec{x}' \rangle) \ ::= \ \{ (\phi, A\#n) \mid \text{ for all } A\#n \in Ls \text{ s.t. } match(A, A') = \phi \text{ and } \phi \neq \bot \text{ and } \models g \}$

Fig. 11. *LHS* Matching States and Auxiliary Operations

for `LookupAtom` join tasks, and larger comprehension multisets for `LookupAll` join tasks. Our heuristics also accounts for indexing guards and early scheduled guards: a lookup join tasks for $C : j$ receives a bonus modifier to w_j if it utilizes an indexing directive $\langle g_\alpha; \_ \rangle$ where $g_\alpha \neq true$ and for each guard (`CheckGuard` g) scheduled immediately after it. This rewards join orderings that heavily utilizes indexing guards and schedules guards earlier. The filtering guards of comprehensions (`FilterGuard`) are treated as penalties instead, since they do not prune the search tree.

For each rule occurrence H_i and partner atomic constraints and comprehensions $\bar{H}_a$ and $\bar{H}_c$ and guards $\bar{g}$, we compute join orderings from all permutations of sequences of $\bar{H}_a$ and $\bar{H}_c$. For each such join ordering, we compute the weighted sum score and select an optimized ordering based on this heuristic. Since CHR^{cp} rules typically contain a small number of constraints, join ordering permutations can be practically computed.

7   Executing Join Orderings

In this section, we define the execution of join orderings by means of an abstract state machine. The CHR^{cp} *abstract matching machine* takes an active constraint $A\#n$, the constraint store Ls and a valid join ordering $\vec{J}$ for a CHR^{cp} rule r, and computes an instance of a head constraint match for r in Ls.

Figure 11 defines the elements of this abstract machine. The inputs of the machine are the *matching context* Θ, $A\#n$, a join ordering $\vec{J}$ and the constraint store Ls. A *matching state* $\mathcal{M}$ is a tuple consisting of the current join task J, a program counter pc, a list of backtracking branches $\vec{Br}$, the current substitution θ and the current partial match Pm. A partial match is a map from occurrence indices i to multisets of candidates U, which are tuples $(\theta, A\#n)$. We denote the empty map as $\varnothing$ and the extension of Pm with $i \mapsto U$ as $(Pm, i \mapsto U)$. We extend the list indexing notation $Pm[j]$ to retrieve the candidates that Pm maps j to. We define two auxiliary meta-operations: $match(A, A')$ returns a substitution ϕ such that $\phi A = A'$ if it exists and $\bot$ otherwise; $lookupCands(Ls, A', \langle g; \vec{x} \rangle)$ retrieves the multiset of candidates $A\#n$ in store Ls that match pattern A' and satisfy g for indexing directive $\langle g; \vec{x} \rangle$.

Given an execution context $\Theta = \langle A\#n; \vec{J}; Ls \rangle$, the state transition operation, denoted $\Theta \triangleright \mathcal{M} \longmapsto_{lhs} \mathcal{M}'$, defines a transition step of this abstract machine. Figure 12 defines its transition rules: rule (*active*) executes `Active` $A' : i$ by matching the active constraint $A\#n$ with A' ($\phi = match(A, \theta A')$). If this match is successful ($\phi \neq \bot$), the search proceeds. Rule (*lookup-atom*) executes `LookupAtom` $\langle g; \vec{x} \rangle$ $A' : j$ by retrieving ($lookupCands(Ls, \theta A, \langle \theta g; \vec{x} \rangle)$) constraints in Ls that match $A' : j$. If there is at least one such candidate $(\phi, A''\#m)$, the search proceeds with it as the match to partner j and all other candidates as possible backtracking branches (Br'). This is the only type of join task where the search branches. Rule (*check-guard*)

$(active)$	$\Theta \rhd \langle \texttt{Active}\ A' : i; pc; Br; \theta; Pm \rangle \rightarrowtail_{lhs} \langle \vec{J}[pc]; pc{+}1; Br; \theta\phi; Pm, i \mapsto (\phi, A\#n) \rangle$ if $\phi = match(A, \theta A')$ and $\phi \neq \bot$
$(lookup\text{-}atom)$	$\Theta \rhd \langle \texttt{LookupAtom}\ \langle g; \vec{x} \rangle\ A' : j; pc; Br; \theta; Pm \rangle$ $\rightarrowtail_{lhs} \langle \vec{J}[pc]; pc{+}1; Br'{+}{+}Br; \theta\phi; Pm, j \mapsto (\phi, A''\#m) \rangle$ if $\lfloor \bar{U}, (\phi, A''\#m) \int = lookupCands(Ls, \theta A', \langle \theta g; \vec{x} \rangle)$ $Br' = \int (pc, \theta\phi, Pm, j \mapsto (\phi, A''\#m))\ $	for all $(\phi, A''\#m) \in \bar{U} \int$
$(check\text{-}guard)$	$\Theta \rhd \langle \texttt{CheckGuard}\ \bar{g}; pc; Br; \theta; Pm \rangle \rightarrowtail_{lhs} \langle \vec{J}[pc]; pc{+}1; Br; \theta; Pm \rangle\quad$ if $\models \theta\bar{g}$
$(lookup\text{-}all)$	$\Theta \rhd \langle \texttt{LookupAll}\ \langle g; \vec{x} \rangle\ A' : j; pc; Br; \theta; Pm \rangle \rightarrowtail_{lhs} \langle \vec{J}[pc]; pc{+}1; Br; \theta; Pm, j \mapsto \bar{U} \rangle$ where $\bar{U} = lookupCands(Ls, \theta A', \langle \theta g; \vec{x} \rangle)$
$(filter\text{-}guard)$	$\Theta \rhd \langle \texttt{FilterGuard}\ j\ \bar{g}; pc; Br; \theta; Pm, j \mapsto \bar{U} \rangle \rightarrowtail_{lhs} \langle \vec{J}[pc]; pc{+}1; Br; \theta; Pm, j \mapsto \bar{U}' \rangle$ where $\bar{U}' = \int (\phi', C)\ $	for all $(\phi', C) \in \bar{U}$ s.t. $\models \theta\phi'\bar{g} \int$
$(neq\text{-}head)$	$\Theta \rhd \langle \texttt{NeqHead}\ j\ k; pc; Br; \theta; Pm \rangle \rightarrowtail_{lhs} \langle \vec{J}[pc]; pc{+}1; Br; \theta; Pm \rangle$ if $Pm[j] = (\_, A'\#m)$ and $Pm[k] = (\_, A'\#n)$ such that $m \neq n$
$(filter\text{-}head)$	$\Theta \rhd \langle \texttt{FilterHead}\ j\ k; pc; Br; \theta; Pm, j \mapsto \bar{U}, k \mapsto \bar{U}' \rangle$ $\rightarrowtail_{lhs} \langle \vec{J}[pc]; pc{+}1; Br; \theta; Pm, j \mapsto \bar{U}'', k \mapsto \bar{U}' \rangle$ where $\bar{U}'' = \int (\phi, A''\#m)\ $	for all $(\phi, A''\#m) \in \bar{U}$ s.t. $\neg\exists(\_, A''\#m) \in \bar{U}' \int$
$(compre\text{-}dom)$	$\Theta \rhd \langle \texttt{CompreDomain}\ j\ \vec{x}\ xs; pc; Br; \theta; Pm \rangle \rightarrowtail_{lhs} \langle \vec{J}[pc]; pc{+}1; Br; \theta\phi; Pm \rangle$ where $Pm[j]$ and $\phi = [\int \phi'\vec{x}\ $	for all $(\phi', \_) \in \bar{U} \int / xs]$
$(bootstrap)$	$\Theta \rhd \langle \texttt{Bootstrap}\ \vec{x}\ j; pc; Br; \theta[\_/\vec{x}]; Pm, j \mapsto \_ \rangle \rightarrowtail_{lhs} \langle \vec{J}[pc]; pc{+}1; Br; \theta; Pm \rangle$
$(backtrack)$	$\Theta \rhd \langle \_; pc; [(pc', \theta', Pm') \| Br]; \theta; Pm \rangle \rightarrowtail_{lhs} \langle \vec{J}[pc']; pc'{+}1; Br; \theta'; Pm' \rangle$ if neither $(lookup\text{-}atom)$, $(check\text{-}guard)$ nor $(neq\text{-}head)$ applies.
$(fail\text{-}match)$	$\Theta \rhd \langle \_; pc; \varnothing; \theta; Pm \rangle \rightarrowtail_{lhs} \bot$ if neither $(active)$, $(lookup\text{-}atom)$, $(check\text{-}guard)$, $(neq\text{-}head)$ nor $(backtrack)$ applies.

Fig. 12. Execution of CHR^{cp} Join Ordering

executes $\texttt{CheckGuard}\ \bar{g}$ by continuing the search only if all guards $\bar{g}$ are satisfiable under the current substitution ($\models \theta\bar{g}$). Rule $(lookup\text{-}all)$ defines the case for $\texttt{LookupAll}\ \langle g; \vec{x} \rangle\ A' : j$, during which candidates matching A' are retrieved ($\bar{U} = lookupCands(Ls, \theta A, \langle \theta g; \vec{x} \rangle)$). But rather than branching, the search proceeds by extending the partial match with all candidates (i.e., $j \mapsto \bar{U}$). Rule $(filter\text{-}guard)$ defines the case for $\texttt{FilterGuard}\ j\ \bar{g}$, in which the search proceeds by filtering from $Pm[j]$ candidates that do not satisfy the guard conditions $\bar{g}$. Rule $(neq\text{-}head)$ defines the case for $\texttt{NeqHead}\ j\ k$: if $Pm[j]$ and $Pm[k]$ maps to unique constraints, the search proceeds. Rule $(filter\text{-}head)$ executes $\texttt{FilterHead}\ j\ k$ by filtering from $Pm[j]$ any candidates that appear also in $Pm[k]$. Rule $(compre\text{-}dom)$ executes $\texttt{CompreDomain}\ j\ \vec{x}\ xs$ by extending the current substitution θ with $\phi = [ps/xs]$ where ps is the multiset of projections of $\vec{x}$ extracted from each candidate of $Pm[j]$. Rule $(bootstrap)$ executes $\texttt{Bootstrap}\ \vec{x}\ j$ by removing mappings of j from current partial matches and mappings of $\vec{x}$ from the current substitution. Rule $(backtrack)$ backtracks when rules $(lookup\text{-}atom)$, $(check\text{-}guard)$ and $(neq\text{-}head)$ are not applicable. Backtracking is achieved by accessing the head of the backtracking branches (pc', θ', Pm'), and restoring the execution state to that particular state: the current join task becomes $\vec{J}[pc']$, the program counter $pc' + 1$, the current substitution θ' and the partial matches Pm'. If there are no more backtracking options, rule $(fail\text{-}match)$ declares failure to find a match. Execution of this machine implicitly terminates when pc reaches an index outside the join ordering (i.e., $\vec{J}[pc] = \bot$).

8   Correctness of CHR^{cp} Abstract Matching Machine

In this section, we highlight the correctness results of the CHR^{cp} abstract matching machine. Specifically, we show that our abstract machine always terminates for a valid matching context $\langle A\#n; \vec{J}; Ls \rangle$. By valid, we mean that Ls is finite, that $A\#n \in Ls$, and that $\vec{J}$ is a join ordering constructed by *compileRuleHead*. We also show that it produces sound results w.r.t. the CHR^{cp} operational semantics. Finally, we show that it is complete for a class of CHR^{cp} rules that are not *selective* on comprehension patterns. We assume that matching ($match(A, A')$) and guard satisfiability tests ($\models g$) are decidable procedures. Proofs and details for these results can be found in [8].

We denote the exhaustive transition of the CHR^{cp} abstract matching machine as $\Theta \rhd \mathcal{M} \rightarrowtail^*_{lhs} \mathcal{M}'$. There, $\mathcal{M}'$ is a *terminal* state of the form $\langle \bot; \_; \_; \_; \_ \rangle$: $\bot$ since the program counter has gone past the last index of $\vec{J}$. An *initial* state has the form $\langle \vec{J}[0]; 1; \varnothing; \cdot; \varnothing \rangle$. For our CHR^{cp} abstract matching machine to be effective, we need some guarantees that if we run it on a valid join ordering $\vec{J}$ and a finite constraint store Ls, execution either terminates at some terminal state (i.e., $\langle \bot; \_; \_; \_; \_ \rangle$), or returns $\bot$.

Theorem 1 (Termination of the CHR^{cp} Abstract Matching Machine).   *For any valid $\Theta = \langle A\#n; \vec{J}; Ls \rangle$, we have $\Theta \rhd \langle \vec{J}[0]; 1; \varnothing; \cdot; \varnothing \rangle \rightarrowtail^*_{lhs} \mathcal{M}$ such that either $\mathcal{M} = \langle \bot; \_; \_; \theta; Pm \rangle$ or $\mathcal{M} = \bot$.*

The CHR^{cp} abstract matching machine is also sound w.r.t. the semantics of matching of CHR^{cp}: in the final state of a valid execution, θ and Pm corresponds to head constraint match as specified by the semantics of matching of CHR^{cp} (Figure 2). The operation $constr(Pm, i)$ returns the multiset of all constraints in partial match Pm mapped by i.

Theorem 2 (Soundness of the CHR^{cp} Abstract Matching Machine).   *For any CHR^{cp} head constraints $C : i$, $\vec{H}_a$, $\vec{H}_m$ and $\bar{g}$, such that $\vec{J} = compileRuleHead(C : i, \vec{H}_a, \vec{H}_m, \bar{g})$, given a constraint store Ls and an active constraint $A\#n$, if $\langle A\#n; \vec{J}; Ls \rangle \rhd \langle \vec{J}[0]; 1; \varnothing; \cdot; \varnothing \rangle \rightarrowtail^*_{lhs} \langle \_; \_; \_; \theta; Pm \rangle$, then for some Ls_{act}, Ls_{part}, Ls_{rest} such that $Ls = \lfloor Ls_{act}, Ls_{part}, Ls_{rest} \rfloor$ and $Ls_{act} = constr(Pm, i)$ and $Ls_{part} = constr(Pm, getIdx(\lfloor \vec{H}_a, \vec{H}_m \rfloor))$, we have 1) $\models \theta g$, 2) $C : i \triangleq_{lhs} Ls_{act}$, 3) $\theta \lfloor \vec{H}_a, \vec{H}_m \rfloor \triangleq_{lhs} Ls_{part}$, and 4) $\theta \lfloor \vec{H}_a, \vec{H}_m, C : i \rfloor \triangleq^\neg_{lhs} Ls_{rest}$.*

However, our CHR^{cp} abstract matching machine is not complete in general. Incompleteness stems from the fact that it *greedily* matches comprehension patterns: comprehensions that are scheduled early consume all matching constraints in the store Ls. Consider a rule r with guard g, a comprehension head constraint $M : i$ and another head constraint $C : j$ with i and j unifiable. If guards g is satisfiable only for some particular partitions of i and j, we call r a *comprehension selective* rule. Our abstract machine will not necessary be able to identify this partitioning: suppose that a join ordering executes j before i, then the join task `FilterHead` i j always forces all constraints that can match either with i or j to be in j. The abstract matching machine is complete for CHR^{cp} rules that are non-selective on comprehensions.

Theorem 3 (Completeness of the CHR^{cp} Abstract Matching Machine).   *Let r be any CHR^{cp} rule that is non-selective on comprehension rule heads. Let its head constraints be $C : i$, $\vec{H}_a$, $\vec{H}_m$ and $\bar{g}$ with $\vec{J} = compileRuleHead(C : i, \vec{H}_a, \vec{H}_m, \bar{g})$. If*

Program	Standard rules only			With comprehensions			Code reduction (lines)
Swap	5 preds	7 rules	21 lines	2 preds	1 rule	10 lines	110%
GHS	13 preds	13 rules	47 lines	8 preds	5 rules	35 lines	34%
HQSort	10 preds	15 rules	53 lines	7 preds	5 rules	38 lines	39%

Program	Input Size	Orig	$+OJO$	$+OJO$ $+Bt$	$+OJO$ $+Mono$	$+OJO$ $+Uniq$	All	Speedup
Swap	$(40, 100)$	241 *vs* 290	121 *vs* 104	*vs* 104	*vs* 103	*vs* 92	*vs* 91	33%
	$(200, 500)$	1813 *vs* 2451	714 *vs* 681	*vs* 670	*vs* 685	*vs* 621	*vs* 597	20%
	$(1000, 2500)$	8921 *vs* 10731	3272 *vs* 2810	*vs* 2651	*vs* 2789	*vs* 2554	*vs* 2502	31%
GHS	$(100, 200)$	814 *vs* 1124	452 *vs* 461	*vs* 443	*vs* 458	*vs* 437	*vs* 432	5%
	$(500, 1000)$	7725 *vs* 8122	3188 *vs* 3391	*vs* 3061	*vs* 3290	*vs* 3109	*vs* 3005	6%
	$(2500, 5000)$	54763 *vs* 71650	15528 *vs* 16202	*vs* 15433	*vs* 16097	*vs* 15835	*vs* 15214	2%
HQSort	$(8, 50)$	1275 *vs* 1332	1117 *vs* 1151	*vs* 1099	*vs* 1151	*vs* 1081	*vs* 1013	10%
	$(16, 100)$	5783 *vs* 6211	3054 *vs* 2980	*vs* 2877	*vs* 2916	*vs* 2702	*vs* 2661	15%
	$(32, 150)$	13579 *vs* 14228	9218 *vs* 8745	*vs* 8256	*vs* 8617	*vs* 8107	*vs* 8013	15%

Execution times (ms) for various optimizations on programs with increasing input size.

Fig. 13. Preliminary Experimental Results

$\langle A\#n; \vec{J}; Ls \rangle \,\triangleright\, \langle \vec{J}\,[0\,]; 1; \varnothing; \cdot; \varnothing \rangle \,\longmapsto^{*}_{lhs}\, \bot$ *for a constraint store Ls and an active constraint $A\#n$, then there exists no applicable rule instance of r from Ls.*

9   Prototype and Preliminary Empirical Results

In this section, we report preliminary experimental results of our CHR^{cp} implementation. We have implemented a prototype (available for download at https://github.com/sllam/chrcp) that utilizes a source-to-source compilation of CHR^{cp} programs: our compiler is written in Python and translates CHR^{cp} programs into a sequence of join orderings. Then, it generates C++ code that implements multiset rewriting as specified by the operational semantics of CHR^{cp}. To support unifiability analysis for constraint monotonicity (Section 4.1), we have deployed a conservative implementation of the relation test routine $\sqsubseteq_{unf}$, discussed in [9].

We have conducted preliminary experiments aimed at assessing the performance of standard CHR programs (without comprehension patterns), CHR^{cp} programs with comprehension patterns and also to investigate the effects of the optimizations described in this paper: OJO optimized join ordering (Section 6), Bt bootstrapping of active comprehension head constraints (Section 5.2), $Mono$ incremental storage for monotone constraints (Section 4.1) and $Uniq$ non-unifiability test for uniqueness enforcement (Section 5.3). When OJO is omitted, join ordering are of arbitrary matching ordering (e.g., textual order). When Bt is omitted, an active comprehension pattern aggressively collects all matching constraints and filters non-matches away in later stages of the join ordering execution. When $Mono$ is omitted, all goals are treated as eager goals, hence eagerly stored and forsaking any opportunity of incremental processing. Finally, when $Uniq$ is omitted, join ordering produced conservatively (exhaustively) include uniqueness enforcement tasks for each pairs of rule head constraints. Optimization OJO is not specific to comprehension patterns: we use it to investigate the performance gains for programs with comprehension patterns relative to standard CHR variants. All other optimizations are specific to comprehension patterns, and hence we do not anticipate any performance gains for standard CHR programs. We have analyzed performance on three CHR^{cp} programs of varying sizes (refer to [8] for codes): *swap* is the swapping data example (Section 2) with input size (s, d) where s is number of swaps and

d is number of data constraints. *GHS* is a simulation of the GHS distributed minimal spanning tree algorithm with input sizes (v, e) where v is number of vertices and e is number of edges. Finally, *HQSort* is a simulation of the hyper-quicksort algorithm with input sizes (n, i) where n is number of nodes and i number of integers in each node.

Figure 13 displays our experimental results. All experiments were conducted on an Intel $i7$ quad-core processor with 2.20 GHz CPUs and 4 Gb of memory. All execution times are averages from ten runs of the same experiments. The column *Orig* contains results for runs with all optimizations turned off, while *All* contains results with all optimizations. In between, we have results for runs with optimized join ordering and at least one optimization specific to comprehension patterns. For *Orig* and $+OJO$, we show two values, n *vs* m, where n is the execution time for the program implemented with standard rules and m for code using comprehension patterns. Relative gains demonstrated in *Orig* and $+OJO$ comes at no surprise: join ordering and indexing benefit both forms of programs. For the *Swap* example, optimization $+Uniq$ yields the largest gains, with $+Bt$ for *GHS*. $+Mono$ yields the least gains across the board and we believe that this is because, for programs in this benchmark, constraints exclusively appear as atomic constraint patterns or in comprehension patterns. The last column shows the speedup of the CHR^{cp} code with all optimizations turned on w.r.t. the standard CHR code with join ordering. Our experiments, although preliminary, show very promising results: comprehensions not only provide a common abstraction by reducing code size, but, maybe more surprisingly, we get significant performance gains over CHR.

10 Related Work

Compilation optimization for CHR has received a lot of attention. Efficient implementations are available in Prolog, HAL [6], Java [13] and even in hardware (via FPGA) [12]. Join-ordering in pure CHR are extensively studied in [4,6]. The multiset matching technique implemented in these systems are based on the LEAPS algorithm [1]. Our work implements a variant of this algorithm, augmented to handle matching of comprehension patterns. These systems utilize optimization techniques (e.g., join ordering, index selection) that resemble query optimization in databases. The main difference is that in the multiset rewriting context we are interested in finding *one* match, while relational queries return *all* matches. Two related extensions to CHR have been proposed: negated head constraints allows encoding of a class of comprehension patterns[14], while an extension that allows computation of limited form of aggregates is discussed in [11]. Like the present work, both extensions introduce non-monotonicity into the semantics. By contrast, we directly address the issue of incrementally processing of constraints in the presence of non-monotonicity introduced by comprehension patterns. The logic programming language LM (Linear Meld) [2] offers features like aggregates and comprehension patterns, that are very similar to our work here. By contrast, comprehension patterns discussed here are more generalized: aggregates in LM can be expressed in CHR^{cp} as term-level comprehension and reduce operations.

11   Conclusion and Future Works

In this paper, we introduced CHR^{cp}, an extension of CHR with multiset comprehension patterns. We highlighted an operational semantics for CHR^{cp}, followed by a lower-level compilation scheme into join orderings. We defined an abstract machine that executes these join orderings, and proved its soundness with respect to the operational semantics. We have implemented a prototype CHR^{cp} system and have demonstrated promising results in preliminary experimentation. In future work, we intend to further develop our prototype implementation of CHR^{cp} by investigating the possibility of adapting other orthogonal optimization techniques found in [6,13,12]. Next, we intend to expand on our empirical results, testing our prototype with a larger benchmark and also testing its performance against other programming frameworks. We also intend to extend CHR^{cp} with some result form prior work in [10].

References

1. Batory, D.: The LEAPS Algorithm. Technical report, University of Texas at Austin (1994)
2. Cruz, F., Rocha, R., Copen Goldstein, S., Pfenning, F.: A linear logic programming language for concurrent programming over graph structures. CoRR, abs/1405.3556 (2014)
3. De Koninck, L., Schrijvers, T., Demoen, B.: User-definable rule priorities for chr. In: PPDP 2007, pp. 25–36. ACM, New York (2007)
4. De Koninck, L., Sneyers, J.: Join ordering for constraint handling rules. In: CHR (2007)
5. Duck, G.J., Stuckey, P.J., García de la Banda, M., Holzbaur, C.: The Refined Operational Semantics of Constraint Handling Rules. In: Demoen, B., Lifschitz, V. (eds.) ICLP 2004. LNCS, vol. 3132, pp. 90–104. Springer, Heidelberg (2004)
6. Holzbaur, C., de la Banda, M.G., Stuckey, P.J., Duck, G.J.: Optimizing compilation of constraint handling rules in HAL. CoRR, cs.PL/0408025 (2004)
7. Lam, E.S.L., Cervesato, I.: Constraint Handling Rules with Multiset Comprehension Patterns. In: CHR 2014 (2014)
8. Lam, E.S.L., Cervesato, I.: Optimized Compilation of Multiset Rewriting with Comprehensions (Full-Version). Technical Report CMU-CS-14-119, Carnegie Mellon (June 2014)
9. Lam, E.S.L., Cervesato, I.: Reasoning about Set Comprehension. In: SMT 2014 (2014)
10. Lam, E.S.L., Cervesato, I.: Decentralized Execution of Constraint Handling Rules for Ensembles. In: PPDP 2013, Madrid, Spain, pp. 205–216 (2013)
11. Sneyers, J., Van Weert, P., Schrijvers, T., Demoen, B.: Aggregates in Constraint Handling Rules. In: Dahl, V., Niemelä, I. (eds.) ICLP 2007. LNCS, vol. 4670, pp. 446–448. Springer, Heidelberg (2007)
12. Triossi, A., Orlando, S., Raffaetà, A., Frühwirth, T.W.: Compiling CHR to parallel hardware. In: PPDP 2012, pp. 173–184 (2012)
13. Van Weert, P., Schrijvers, T., Demoen, B., Leuven, K.U.: JCHR: A user-friendly, flexible and efficient CHR system for Java. In: CHR 2005, pp. 47–62 (2005)
14. Weert, P.V., Sneyers, J., Schrijvers, T., Demoen, B.: Extending CHR with Negation as Absence. In: CHR 2006, pp. 125–140 (2006)

Logic Programming and Logarithmic Space

Clément Aubert[1], Marc Bagnol[1], Paolo Pistone[1], and Thomas Seiller[2,*]

[1] Aix Marseille Université, CNRS, Centrale Marseille, I2M UMR 7373
13453 Marseille, France
[2] I.H.É.S., Le Bois-Marie, 35, Route de Chartres, 91440 Bures-sur-Yvette, France

Abstract. We present an algebraic view on logic programming, related to proof theory and more specifically linear logic and geometry of interaction. Within this construction, a characterization of logspace (deterministic and non-deterministic) computation is given *via* a syntactic restriction, using an encoding of words that derives from proof theory.

We show that the acceptance of a word by an observation (the counterpart of a program in the encoding) can be decided within logarithmic space, by reducing this problem to the acyclicity of a graph. We show moreover that observations are as expressive as two-ways multihead finite automata, a kind of pointer machine that is a standard model of logarithmic space computation.

Keywords: Implicit Complexity, Unification, Logic Programming, Logarithmic Space, Proof Theory, Pointer Machines, Geometry of Interaction, Automata.

1 Introduction

Proof Theory and Implicit Computational Complexity. Very generally, the aim of implicit computational complexity (ICC) is to describe complexity classes with no explicit reference to cost bounds: through a type system or a weakened recursion scheme for instance. The last two decades have seen numerous works relating proof theory (more specifically linear logic [15]) and ICC, the basic idea being to look for restricted substructural logics [19] with an expressiveness that corresponds exactly to some complexity class.

This has been achieved by various syntactic restrictions, which entail a less complex[1] cut-elimination procedure: control over the modalities [31,10], type assignments [14] or stratification properties [5], to name a few.

Geometry of Interaction. In recent years, the cut-elimination procedure and its mathematical modeling has become a central topic in proof theory. The aim of the geometry of interaction research program [16] is to provide the tools for such a modeling [1,25,32].

---

* This work was partly supported by the ANR-10-BLAN-0213 Logoi and the ANR-11-BS02-0010 Récré.

[1] Any function provably total in second-order Peano Arithmetic [15] can be encoded in second-order linear logic.

As for complexity theory, these models allow for a more synthetic and abstract study of the resources needed to compute the normal form of a program, leading to some complexity characterization results [6,20,2].

Unification. Unification is one of the key-concepts of theoretical computer science: it is a classical subject of study for complexity theory and a tool with a wide range of applications, including logic programming and type inference algorithms.

Unification has also been used to build syntactic models of geometry of interaction [18,6,21] where first-order terms with variables allow for a manipulation of infinite sets through a finite language.

Logic Programming. After the work of Robinson [29] on the resolution procedure, logic programming has emerged as a new computation paradigm with concrete realizations such as the languages PROLOG and DATALOG.

On the theoretical side, constant efforts have been provided to clarify expressiveness and complexity issues [11]: most problems arising from logic programming are undecidable in their most general form and some restrictions must be introduced in order to make them tractable. For instance, the notion of *finitely ground program* [9] is related to our approach.

Pointer Machines. Multi-head finite automata provide an elegant characterization of logarithmic space computation, in terms of the (qualitative) type of memory used rather than the (quantitative) amount of tape consumed. Since they can scan but not modify the input, they are usually called "pointer machines", even if this nomenclature can be misleading [8].

This model was already at the heart of previous works relating geometry of interaction and complexity theory [20,3,2].

Contribution and Outline. We begin by exposing the idea of relating geometry of interaction and logic programming, already evoked [18] but never really developed, and by recalling the basic notions on unification theory needed for this article and some related complexity results.

We present in Sect. 2 the algebraic tools used later on to define the encoding of words and pointer machines. Section 2.2 and Sect. 2.3 introduce the syntactical restriction and associated tools that allow us to characterize logarithmic space computation. Note that, compared to earlier work [2], we consider a much wider class of programs while preserving bounded space evaluation: we switch from representation of permutations to a class defined by a syntactical restriction on height of variables, which contains permutations as a strict subset.

The encoding of words enabling our results, which comes from the classical (Church) encoding of lists in proof theory, is given in Sect. 3. It allows to define the counterpart of programs, and a notion of acceptance of a word by a program.

Finally, Sect. 4 makes use of the tools introduced earlier to state and prove our complexity results. While the expressiveness part is quite similar to earlier presentations [3,2], the proof that acceptance can be decided within logarithmic space has been made more modular by reducing this problem to the standard problem of cycle search in a graph.

1.1   Geometry of Interaction and Logic Programming

The geometry of interaction program (GoI), started in 1989 [17], aims at describing the dynamics of computation by developing a fully mathematical model of cut-elimination. The original motivations of GoI must be traced back, firstly, to the *Curry-Howard correspondence* between sequent calculus derivations and typed functional programs: it is on the basis of this correspondence that cut-elimination had been proposed by proof-theorists as a paradigm of computation; secondly, to the finer analysis of cut-elimination coming from linear logic [15] and the replacement of sequent calculus derivations with simpler geometrical structures (proof-nets), more akin to a purely mathematical description.

In the first formulation of GoI [16], derivations in second order intuitionistic logic LJ^2 (which can be considered, by *Curry-Howard*, as programs in System F) are interpreted as pairs (U, σ) of elements (called *wirings*) of a $\mathbb{C}^*$-algebra, U corresponding to the axioms of the derivation and σ to the cuts.

The main property of this interpretation is *nilpotency, i.e.* if there exists an integer n such that $(\sigma U)^n = 0$. The cut-elimination (equivalently, the normalization) procedure is then interpreted by the application of an *execution operator*

$$EX(U, \sigma) = \sum_k (\sigma U)^k$$

From the viewpoint of proof theory and computation, nilpotency corresponds to the *strong normalization property*: the termination of the normalization procedure with any strategy.

Several alternative formulations of geometry of interaction have been proposed since 1989 (see for instance [1,25,32]); in particular, wirings can be described as logic programs [18,6,21] made of particular clauses called *flows*, which will be defined in Sect. 2.1.

In this setting the resolution rule induces a notion of product of wirings (Theorem 8) and in turn a structure of semiring: the *unification semiring* $\mathcal{U}$, which can replace the $\mathbb{C}^*$-algebras of the first formulations of GoI[2].

The $EX(.)$ operator of wirings can be understood as a way to compute the fixed point semantics of logic programs. The nilpotency property of wirings means then that the fixed point given by $EX(.)$ is finite, which is close to the notion of *boundedness*[3] [11] of logic programs.

---

[2] By adding complex scalar coefficients, one can actually extend $\mathcal{U}$ into a $\mathbb{C}^*$-algebra [18].

[3] A program is *bounded* if there is an integer k such that the fixed point computation of the program is stable after k iterations, independently of the facts input.

In definitive, from the strong normalization property for intuitionistic second order logic (or any other system which enjoys a GoI interpretation), one obtains through the GoI interpretation a family of bounded (nilpotent) logic programs computing the recursive functions typable in System F.

This is quite striking in view of the fact that to decide whenever a program is *bounded* is – even with drastic constraints – an undecidable problem [22], and that in general boundedness is a property that is difficult to ensure.

1.2   Unification and Complexity

We recall in the following some notations and some of the numerous links between complexity and unification, and by extension logic programming.

Notations. We consider a set of first-order terms T, assuming an infinite number of variables $x, y, z, \ldots \in$ V, a binary function symbol • (written in *infix notation*), infinitely many constant symbols a, b, c, $\ldots$ including the (multipurpose) dummy symbol $\star$ and, for any $n \in \mathbb{N}^*$, at least one n-ary function symbol A_n.

Note that the binary function symbol • is not associative. However, we will write it by convention as *right associating* to lighten notations: $t \cdot u \cdot v := t \cdot (u \cdot v)$.

For any $t \in$ T, we write $\mathtt{Var}(t)$ the set of variables occurring in t (a term is *closed* when $\mathtt{Var}(t) = \varnothing$) and $\mathtt{h}(t)$ the *height* of t: the maximal distance from the root to any leaf in the tree structure of t.

The *height of a variable occurrence* in a term t is its distance from the root in the tree structure of the term. A *substitution* θ is a mapping from variables to terms such that $x\theta = x$ for all but finitely many $x \in$ V. A *renaming* is a substitution α mapping variables to variables and that is bijective. A term t' is a *renaming* of t if $t' = t\alpha$ for some renaming α.

Definition 1 (unification, matching and disjointness). *Two terms t, u are*

- unifiable *if there exists a substitution θ, called a* unifier *of t and u, such that $t\theta = u\theta$. A unifier θ such that any other unifier of t and u is an instance of θ is called a* most general unifier *(MGU) of t and u,*
- matchable *if t', u' are unifiable, where t', u' are renamings of t, u such that $\mathtt{Var}(t') \cap \mathtt{Var}(u') = \varnothing$,*
- disjoint *if they are not matchable.*

A fundamental result [29] of the theory of unification is that two unifiable terms indeed have a MGU and that it can be computed.

More specifically, the problem of deciding whether two terms are unifiable is PTIME-complete [12, Theorem 1], which implies that parallel algorithms for this problem do not improve much on serial ones. Finding classes of terms where the MGU research can be efficiently parallelized is a real challenge.

It has been proven that this problem remains PTIME-complete even if the arity of the function symbols or the height of the terms is bounded [27, Theorems 4.2.1 and 4.3.1], if both terms are linear or if they do not share variables [12,13]. More recently [7], an innovative constraint on variables helped to discover an upper bound of the unification classes that are proven to be in NC.

Regarding space complexity, the result stating that the *matching problem* is in DLOGSPACE [12] (recalled as Theorem 36) will be used in Sect. 4.2.

2   The Unification Semiring

This section presents the technical setting of this work, the *unification semiring*: an algebraic structure with a composition law based on unification, that can be seen as an algebraic presentation of a fragment of logic programming.

2.1   Flows and Wirings

Flows can be thought of as very specific Horn clauses: safe (the variables of the head must occur in the body) clauses with exactly one atom in the body.

As it is not relevant to this work, we make no technical difference between predicate symbols and function symbols, for it makes the presentation easier. Anyway, to retrieve the connection with logic programming, simply assume a class of function symbols called "predicate symbols" (written in boldface) that can only occur at the root of a term.

Definition 2 (flows). *A flow is a pair of terms $t \leftharpoonup u$ with $\mathtt{Var}(t) \subseteq \mathtt{Var}(u)$. Flows are considered up to renaming: for any renaming α, $t \leftharpoonup u = t\alpha \leftharpoonup u\alpha$.*

An example of flow that indeed is a clause of logic programming would be for instance $\mathbf{colored}(x) \leftharpoonup \mathbf{blue}(x)$ which states that if x is blue, then it is colored.

Facts, which are usually defined as ground (using only closed terms) clauses with an empty body, can still be represented as a special kind of flows.

Definition 3 (facts). *A fact is a flow of the form $t \leftharpoonup \star$.*

Remark 4. Note that this implies that t is closed.

Following on the example above, $\mathbf{blue}(c) \leftharpoonup \star$ would be the fact stating that the object c is blue.

The main interest of the restriction to flows is that it yields an algebraic structure: a semigroup with a partially defined product.

Definition 5 (product of flows). *Let $u \leftharpoonup v$ and $t \leftharpoonup w$ be two flows. Suppose we have representatives of the renaming classes such that $\mathtt{Var}(v) \cap \mathtt{Var}(w) = \varnothing$. The product of $u \leftharpoonup v$ and $t \leftharpoonup w$ is defined if v, t are unifiable with MGU θ as $(u \leftharpoonup v)(t \leftharpoonup w) := u\theta \leftharpoonup w\theta$.*

Remark 6. The condition on variables ensures that facts form a "left ideal" of the set of flows: if $\mathbf{u}$ is a fact and f a flow, then $f\mathbf{u}$ is a fact when it is defined.

Example 7. $(\mathbf{f}(x) \leftharpoonup x)(\mathbf{f}(x) \leftharpoonup \mathbf{g}(x)) = \mathbf{f}(\mathbf{f}(x)) \leftharpoonup \mathbf{g}(x)$
$(x \bullet \mathrm{d} \leftharpoonup (y \bullet y) \bullet x)((\mathrm{c} \bullet \mathrm{c}) \bullet x \leftharpoonup y \bullet x) = x \bullet \mathrm{d} \leftharpoonup y \bullet x$
$(\mathbf{f}(x \bullet \mathrm{c}) \leftharpoonup x \bullet \mathrm{d})(\mathrm{d} \bullet \mathrm{d} \leftharpoonup \star) = \mathbf{f}(\mathrm{d} \bullet \mathrm{c}) \leftharpoonup \star$
$(x \leftharpoonup \mathbf{g}(\mathbf{h}(x)))(\mathbf{g}(y) \leftharpoonup y) = x \leftharpoonup \mathbf{h}(x)$

The product of flows corresponds to the resolution rule in the following sense: given two flows $f = u \leftharpoonup v$ and $g = t \leftharpoonup w$ and a *MGU* θ of v and t, then the resolution rule applied to f and g would yield fg.

To finish with our logic programming example, the product of the flows **colored**$(x) \leftharpoonup$ **blue**(x) and **blue**$(c) \leftharpoonup \star$ would yield **colored**$(c) \leftharpoonup \star$.

Wirings then correspond to logic programs (sets of clauses) and the nilpotency condition can be seen as an algebraic variant of the notion of boundedness of these programs.

Definition 8 (wirings). Wirings *are finite sets of flows. The product of wirings is defined as* $FG := \{ fg \mid f \in F, g \in G, fg \text{ defined} \}$.

We write $\mathcal{U}$ *for the set of wirings and refer to it as the* unification semiring.

The set of wirings $\mathcal{U}$ has the structure of a semiring. We use an *additive notation* for sets of flows to stress this point:

- The symbol $+$ will be used in place of $\cup$.
- We write sets as the sum of their elements: $\{ f_1, \ldots, f_n \} := f_1 + \cdots + f_n$.
- We write 0 for the empty set.
- The unit is $I := x \leftharpoonup x$.

We will call *semiring* any subset $\mathcal{A}$ of $\mathcal{U}$ such that

- $0 \in \mathcal{A}$,
- if $F \in \mathcal{A}$ and $G \in \mathcal{A}$ then $FG \in \mathcal{A}$.
- if $F, G \in \mathcal{A}$, then $F + G \in \mathcal{A}$,

A subset satisfying only the first two conditions will be called a *semigroup*.

Definition 9 (nilpotency). *A wiring F is* nilpotent *if* $F^n = 0$ *for some* $n \in \mathbb{N}$. *We may use the notation* $\mathbf{Nil}(F)$ *to express the fact that F is nilpotent.*

As mentioned in Sect. 1.1, nilpotency is related with the notion of *boundedness* [11] of a logic program. Indeed, if we have a wiring F and a finite set of facts $\mathbf{U}$, let us consider the set of facts that can be obtained through F, $\{ \mathbf{u} \mid \mathbf{u} \in F^n \mathbf{U} \text{ for some } n \}$ which can also be written as $(I + F + F^2 + \cdots) \mathbf{U}$ or $EX(F)\mathbf{U}$ (where $EX(.)$ is the execution operator of Sect. 1.1). If F is nilpotent, one needs to compute the sum only up to a finite rank that does not depend on $\mathbf{U}$, which implies the boundedness property.

Among wirings, those that can produce at most one fact from any fact will be of interest when considering deterministic *vs.* non-deterministic computation.

Definition 10 (deterministic wirings). *A wiring F is* deterministic *if given any fact $\mathbf{u}$,* $\mathrm{card}(F\mathbf{u}) \leq 1$. *We will write* $\mathcal{U}_d$ *the set of deterministic wirings.*

It is clear from the definition that $\mathcal{U}_d$ forms a semigroup. The lemma below gives us a class of wirings that are deterministic and easy to recognize, due to its more syntactic definition.

Lemma 11. *Let $F = \sum_i u_i \leftharpoonup t_i$. If the t_i are pairwise disjoint (Theorem 1), then F is deterministic.*

Proof. Given a closed term t there is at most one of the t_i that matches t, therefore $F(t \leftharpoonup \star)$ is either a single fact or 0.   □

2.2 The Balanced Semiring

In this section, we study a constraint on variable height of flows which we call *balance*. This syntactic constraint can be compared with similar ones proposed in order to get logic programs that are *finitely ground* [9]: balanced wirings are a special case of *argument-restricted* programs in the sense of [26].

We will be able to decide the nilpotency of balanced wirings in a space-efficient way, thanks to the results of Sect. 2.3.

Definition 12 (balance). *A flow $f = t \leftharpoonup u$ is* balanced *if for any variable $x \in \mathsf{Var}(t) \cup \mathsf{Var}(u)$, all occurrences of x in either t or u have the same height (recall notations p. 42) which we write $\mathsf{h}_f(x)$, the height of x in f. A wiring F is* balanced *if it is a sum of balanced flows.*

We write $\mathcal{U}_b$ for the set of balanced wirings and refer to it as the balanced semiring.

In Theorem 7, only the second line shows the product of balanced flows.

The basic idea behind the notion of balance is that it forbids variations of height which may be used to store information "above" a variable. Typically, the flow $\mathsf{f}(x) \leftharpoonup x$ is not balanced.

Definition 13 (height). *The height $\mathsf{h}(f)$ of a flow $f = t \leftharpoonup u$ is $\max\{\mathsf{h}(t), \mathsf{h}(u)\}$. The height $\mathsf{h}(F)$ of a wiring F is the maximal height of flows in it.*

The following lemma summarizes the properties that are preserved by the product of balanced flows. It implies in particular that $\mathcal{U}_b$ is indeed a semiring.

Lemma 14. *When it is defined, the product fg of two balanced flows f and g is still balanced and its height is at most $\max\{\mathsf{h}(f), \mathsf{h}(g)\}$.*

Proof (sketch). By showing that the variable height condition and the global height are both preserved by the basic steps of the unification procedure.   □

2.3 The Computation Graph

The main tool for a space-efficient treatment of balanced wirings is an associated notion of graph. This section focuses on the algebraic aspects of this notion, proving various technical lemmas, and leaves the complexity issues to Sect. 4.2.

A separating space can be thought of as a finite subset of the Herbrand universe associated with a logic program, containing enough information to decide the problem at hand.

Definition 15 (separating space). *A separating space for a wiring F is a set of facts $\mathbf{S}$ such that*

- *For all $\mathbf{u} \in \mathbf{S}$, $F\mathbf{u} \subseteq \mathbf{S}$.*
- *$F^n\mathbf{u} = 0$ for all $\mathbf{u} \in \mathbf{S}$ implies $F^n = 0$.*

We can define such a space for balanced wirings with Theorem 14 in mind: balanced wirings behave well with respect to height of terms.

Definition 16 (computation space). *Given a balanced wiring F, we define its* computation space $\mathbf{Comp}(F)$ *as the set of facts of height at most $\mathbf{h}(F)$, built using only the symbols appearing in F and the constant symbol $\star$.*

Lemma 17 (separation). *If F is balanced, then $\mathbf{Comp}(F)$ is separating for F.*

Proof. By Theorem 14, $F(u \hookleftarrow \star)$ is of height at most $\max\{\mathbf{h}(F), \mathbf{h}(u)\} \leq \mathbf{h}(F)$ and it contains only symbols occurring in F and u, therefore if $\mathbf{u} \in \mathbf{Comp}(F)$ we have $F\mathbf{u} \subseteq \mathbf{Comp}(F)$.

By Theorem 14 again, F^n is still of height at most $\mathbf{h}(F)$. If $(F^n)\mathbf{u} = 0$ for all $\mathbf{u} \in \mathbf{Comp}(F)$, it means the flows of F^n do not match any closed term of height at most $\mathbf{h}(F)$ built with the symbols occurring in F (and eventually $\star$). This is only possible if F^n contains no flow, *ie.* $F^n = 0$. □

As F is a finite set, thus built with finitely many symbols, $\mathbf{Comp}(F)$ is also a finite set. We can be a little more precise and give a bound to its cardinality.

Proposition 18 (cardinality). *Let F be a balanced wiring, A the maximal arity of function symbols occurring in F and S the set of symbols occurring in F, then $\mathrm{card}(\mathbf{Comp}(F)) \leq (\mathrm{card}(S)+1)^{P_{\mathbf{h}(F)}(A)}$, where $P_k(X) = 1+X+\cdots+X^k$.*

Proof. The number of terms of height $\mathbf{h}(F)$ built over the set of symbols $S \cup \{\star\}$ of arity bounded by A is at most as large as the number of complete trees of degree A and height $\mathbf{h}(F)$ (that is, trees where nodes of height less than $\mathbf{h}(F)$ have exactly A childs), with nodes labeled by elements of $S \cup \{\star\}$. □

Then, we can encode in a directed graph[4] the action of the wiring on its computation space.

Definition 19 (computation graph). *If F is a balanced wiring, we define its* computation graph $\mathbf{G}(F)$ *as the directed graph:*

- *The vertices of $\mathbf{G}(F)$ are the elements of $\mathbf{Comp}(F)$.*
- *There is an edge from $\mathbf{u}$ to $\mathbf{v}$ in $\mathbf{G}(F)$ if $\mathbf{v} \in F\mathbf{u}$.*

We state finally that the computation graph of a wiring contains enough information on the latter to determine its nilpotency. This is a key ingredient in the proof of Theorem 35, as the research of paths and cycles in graphs are problems that are well-known [24] to be solvable within logarithmic space.

Lemma 20. *A balanced wiring F is nilpotent (Theorem 9) iff $\mathbf{G}(F)$ is acyclic.*

---

[4] Here by directed graph we mean a set of *vertices* V together with a set of *edges* $E \subseteq V \times V$. We say that there is an edge *from* $e \in V$ *to* $f \in V$ when $(e, f) \in E$.

Proof. Suppose there is a cycle of length n in $\mathbf{G}(F)$, and let $\mathbf{u}$ be the label of a vertex which is part of this cycle. By definition of $\mathbf{G}(F)$, $\mathbf{u} \in (F^n)^k \mathbf{u}$ for all k, which means that $(F^n)^k \neq 0$ for all k and therefore F cannot be nilpotent.

Conversely, suppose there is no cycle in $\mathbf{G}(F)$. As it is a finite graph, this entails a maximal length N of paths in $\mathbf{G}(F)$. By definition of $\mathbf{G}(F)$, this means that $F^{N+1}\mathbf{u} = 0$ for all $\mathbf{u} \in \mathbf{Comp}(F)$ and with Theorem 17 we get $F^{N+1} = 0$.

□

Moreover, the computation graph of a deterministic (Theorem 10) wiring has a specific shape, which in turn induces a deterministic procedure in this case.

Lemma 21. *If F is a balanced and deterministic wiring, $\mathbf{G}(F)$ has an out-degree (the maximal number of edges a vertex can be the source of) bounded by 1.*

Proof. It is a direct consequence of the definitions of $\mathbf{G}(F)$ and determinism.   □

2.4   Tensor Product and Other Semirings

Finally, we list a few other semirings that will be used in the next section, where we define the notions of representation of a word and observation.

The binary function symbol $\bullet$ can be used to define an operation that is similar to the algebraic notion of tensor product.

Definition 22 (tensor product). *Let $u \leftharpoonup v$ and $t \leftharpoonup w$ be two flows. Suppose we have chosen representatives of their renaming classes that have disjoint sets of variables. We define their* tensor product *as $(u \leftharpoonup v) \dot{\otimes} (t \leftharpoonup w) := u \bullet t \leftharpoonup v \bullet w$. The operation is extended to wirings by $(\sum_i f_i) \dot{\otimes} (\sum_j g_j) := \sum_{i,j} f_i \dot{\otimes} g_j$. Given two semirings $\mathcal{A}, \mathcal{B}$, we define $\mathcal{A} \dot{\otimes} \mathcal{B} := \{ \sum_i F_i \dot{\otimes} G_i \mid F_i \in \mathcal{A}, \ G_i \in \mathcal{B} \}$.*

The tensor product of two semirings is easily shown to be a semiring.

Example 23. $(\mathtt{f}(x) \bullet y \leftharpoonup y \bullet x) \dot{\otimes} (x \leftharpoonup \mathtt{g}(x)) = (\mathtt{f}(x) \bullet y) \bullet z \leftharpoonup (y \bullet x) \bullet \mathtt{g}(z)$

Notation. As the symbol $\bullet$, the $\dot{\otimes}$ operation is not associative. We carry on the convention for $\bullet$ and write it as *right associating*: $\mathcal{A} \dot{\otimes} \mathcal{B} \dot{\otimes} \mathcal{C} := \mathcal{A} \dot{\otimes} (\mathcal{B} \dot{\otimes} \mathcal{C})$.

Semirings can also naturally be associated to any set of closed terms or to the restriction to a certain set of symbols.

Definition 24. *Given a set of closed terms E, we define the following semiring $E^{\leftharpoonup} := \{ \sum_i t_i \leftharpoonup u_i \mid t_i, u_i \in E \}$. If S is a set of symbols and $\mathcal{A}$ a semiring, we write $\mathcal{A}^{\backslash \mathsf{S}}$ the semiring of wirings of $\mathcal{A}$, that do not use the symbols in S.*

This operation yields semirings because composition of flows made of closed terms involves no actual unification: it is just equality of terms and therefore one never steps out of $E^{\leftharpoonup}$.

Finally, the unit $I = x \leftharpoonup x$ of $\mathcal{U}$ yields a semiring.

Definition 25 (unit semiring). *The* unit semiring *is defined as $\mathcal{I} := \{0, I\}$.*

3   Words and Observations

We define in this section the global framework that will be used later on to obtain the characterization of logarithmic space computation. In order to discuss the contents of this section, let us first define two specific semirings.

Definition 26 (word and observation semirings). *We fix two (disjoint) infinite sets of constant symbols* P *and* S, *and a unary function symbol* M. *We denote by* M(P) *the set of terms* M(p) *with* p $\in$ P. *We define the following two semirings that are included in* $\mathcal{U}_b$:

- *The* word semiring *is the semiring* $\mathcal{W} := \mathcal{I} \dot{\otimes} \mathcal{I} \dot{\otimes} \mathtt{M(P)}^{\leftharpoonup}$.
- *The* observation semiring *is the semiring* $\mathcal{O} := \mathtt{S}^{\leftharpoonup} \dot{\otimes} \mathcal{U}_b^{\backslash \mathtt{P}}$.

Remark 27. The expression $\mathcal{I} \dot{\otimes} \mathcal{I} \dot{\otimes} \mathtt{M(P)}^{\leftharpoonup}$ may seem odd at first sight, as the intuition from algebra is that $\mathcal{I} \dot{\otimes} \mathcal{I} \simeq \mathcal{I}$. But remember that we are here in a *syntactical* context and therefore we need to be careful with things that can usually be treated "up to isomorphism", as it may cause some unifications to fail where they should not.

These two semirings will be used as parameters of a construction $\mathcal{M}_\Sigma(.)$ over an alphabet Σ (we suppose $\star \notin \Sigma$), that will define the representation of words and a notion of abstract machine, that we shall call observations.

Definition 28. *We fix the set of constant symbols* LR := $\{\mathtt{L}, \mathtt{R}\}$.
Given a set of constant symbols Σ *and a semiring* $\mathcal{A}$ *we define the semiring* $\mathcal{M}_\Sigma(\mathcal{A}) := (\Sigma \cup \{\star\})^{\leftharpoonup} \dot{\otimes} \mathtt{LR}^{\leftharpoonup} \dot{\otimes} \mathcal{A}$.

In the following of this section, we will show how to represent lists of elements of Σ by wirings in the semiring $\mathcal{M}_\Sigma(\mathcal{W})$. Then, we will explain how the semiring $\mathcal{M}_\Sigma(\mathcal{O})$ captures a notion of abstract machine. In the last section of the paper we will explain further how observations and words interact, and prove that this interaction captures logarithmic space computation.

3.1   Representation of Words

We now show how one can represent words by wirings in $\mathcal{M}_\Sigma(\mathcal{W})$. We recall this semiring is defined as $\left((\Sigma \cup \{\star\})^{\leftharpoonup} \dot{\otimes} \mathtt{LR}^{\leftharpoonup}\right) \dot{\otimes} \mathcal{I} \dot{\otimes} \mathcal{I} \dot{\otimes} \mathtt{M(P)}^{\leftharpoonup}$.

The part $(\Sigma \cup \{\star\})^{\leftharpoonup} \dot{\otimes} \mathtt{LR}^{\leftharpoonup}$ deals with, and is dependent on, the alphabet Σ considered; this is where the input and the observation will interact. The two instances of the unit semiring $\mathcal{I}$ correspond to the fact that the word cannot affect parts of the observation that correspond to internal configurations. The last part, namely the semiring $\mathtt{M(P)}^{\leftharpoonup}$, will contain the *position constants* of the representation of words.

Notation. We write $t \leftrightharpoons u$ for $t \leftharpoonup u + u \leftharpoonup t$.

Definition 29 (word representations). *Let* $W = c_1, \ldots, c_n$ *be a word over an alphabet* Σ *and* $p = p_0, p_1, \ldots, p_n$ *be pairwise distinct constant symbols.*

Writing $p_{n+1} = p_0$ *and* $c_0 = c_{n+1} = \star$, *we define the* representation *of* W *associated with* $p_0, p_1, \ldots, p_n$ *as the following wiring:*

$$\bar{W}_p = \sum_{i=0}^{n} c_i \bullet R \bullet x \bullet y \bullet M(p_i) \leftrightharpoons c_{i+1} \bullet L \bullet x \bullet y \bullet M(p_{i+1}) \tag{1}$$

We will write $\mathcal{R}(W)$ *the set of representations of a given word* W.

To better understand this representation, consider that each symbol in the alphabet Σ comes in two "flavors", *left* and *right*. Then, one can easily construct the "context" $\bar{W} = \sum_{i=0}^{n} c_i \bullet R \bullet x \bullet y \bullet M([\ ]_i) \leftrightharpoons c_{i+1} \bullet L \bullet x \bullet y \bullet M([\ ]_{i+1})$ from the list as the sums of the arrows in the following picture (where x and y are omitted):

Then, choosing a set $p = p_0, \ldots, p_n$ of position constants, intuitively representing physical memory addresses, the representation $\bar{W}_p$ of a word associated with p is obtained by filling, for all $i = 0, \ldots, n$, the hole $[\ ]_i$ by the constant p_i.

This abstract representation of words is not an arbitrary choice. It is inspired by the interpretation of lists in geometry of interaction.

Indeed, in System F, the type of binary lists corresponds to the formula $\forall X\ (X \Rightarrow X) \Rightarrow (X \Rightarrow X) \Rightarrow (X \Rightarrow X)$. Any lambda-term in normal form of this type can be written as $\lambda f_0 f_1 x. f_{c_1} f_{c_2} \cdots f_{c_k} x$, where $c_1 \cdots c_k$ is a word over $\{0, 1\}$. The GoI representation of such a lambda-term yields the abstract representation just defined[5]. Notice that the additional symbol $\star$ used to represent words corresponds to the variable x in the preceding lambda-term. Note also the fact that the representation of integer is *cyclic*, and that the symbol $\star$ serves as a reference for the starting/ending point of the word.

Let us finally stress that the words are represented as *deterministic* wirings. This implies that the restriction to deterministic observations will correspond to restricting ourselves to deterministic pointer machines. The framework, however, allows for a number of generalization and variants. For instance, one can define a representation of trees by adapting Theorem 29 in such a way that every vertex is related to its descendants; doing so would however yield non-deterministic wirings. In the same spirit, a notion of "one-way representations of words", defined by replacing the symbol $\leftrightharpoons$ by the symbol $\leftharpoonup$ in Eq. 1 of Theorem 29, could be used to characterize one-way multi-head automata.

3.2   Observations

We now define *observations*. We will then explain how these can be thought of as a kind of abstract machines. An observation is an element of the semiring

$$\mathcal{M}_\Sigma(\mathcal{O}) = (\Sigma \cup \{\star\})^{\leftharpoonup} \dot{\otimes} LR^{\leftharpoonup} \dot{\otimes} (S^{\leftharpoonup} \dot{\otimes} \mathcal{U}_b^{\backslash P})$$

---

[5] A thorough explanation can be found in previous work by Aubert and Seiller [3].

Once again, the part of the semiring $(\Sigma \cup \{\star\})^{\leftharpoonup} \dot{\otimes} \mathsf{LR}^{\leftharpoonup}$ is dependent on the alphabet Σ considered and represents the point of interaction between the words and the machine. The semiring $\mathsf{S}^{\leftharpoonup}$ intuitively corresponds to the *states* of the observation, while the part $\mathcal{U}_b^{\backslash \mathsf{P}}$ forbids the machine to act non-trivially on the *position constants* of the representation of words. The fact that the machine cannot perform any operation on the memory addresses – the position constants – of the word representation explains why observations are naturally thought of as a kind of *pointer machines*.

Definition 30 (observation). *An* observation *is any element O of $\mathcal{M}_\Sigma(\mathcal{O})$.*

We can define the language associated to an observation. The condition of acceptance will be represented as the nilpotency of the product $O\bar{W}_p$ where $\bar{W}_p \in \mathcal{R}(W)$ represents a word W and O is an observation.

Definition 31 (language of an observation). *Let O be an observation on the alphabet Σ. We define the* language accepted by O *as*

$$\mathcal{L}(O) := \left\{ W \in \Sigma^* \mid \forall p,\ \mathbf{Nil}(O\bar{W}_p) \right\}$$

One important point is that the semirings $\mathcal{M}_\Sigma(\mathcal{W})$ and $\mathcal{M}_\Sigma(\mathcal{O})$ are not completely disjoint, and therefore allow for non-trivial interaction of observations and words. However, they are sufficiently disjoint so that this computation does not depend on the choice of the representative of a given word.

Lemma 32. *Let W be a word, and $\bar{W}_p, \bar{W}_q \in \mathcal{R}(W)$. For every observation $O \in \mathcal{M}_\Sigma(\mathcal{O})$, $\mathbf{Nil}(O\bar{W}_p)$ if and only if $\mathbf{Nil}(O\bar{W}_q)$.*

Proof. As we pointed out, the observation cannot act on the position constants of the representations $\bar{W}_p$ and $\bar{W}_q$. This implies that for all integer k the wirings $(O\bar{W}_p)^k$ and $(O\bar{W}_q)^k$ are two instances of the same *context, i.e.* they are equal up to the interchange of the positions constants $\mathsf{p}_0, \dots, \mathsf{p}_n$ and $\mathsf{q}_0, \dots, \mathsf{q}_n$. This implies that $(O\bar{W}_p)^k = 0$ if and only if $(O\bar{W}_q)^k = 0$. □

Corollary 33. *Let O be an observation on the alphabet Σ. The set $\mathcal{L}(O)$ can be equivalently defined as the set*

$$\mathcal{L}(O) = \left\{ W \in \Sigma^* \mid \exists p,\ \mathbf{Nil}(O\bar{W}_p) \right\}$$

This result implies that the notion of acceptance has the intended sense and is finitely verifiable: whether a word W is accepted by an observation O can be checked without considering all representations of W.

This kind of situation where two semirings $\mathcal{W}$ and $\mathcal{O}$ are disjoint enough to obtain Theorem 33 can be formalized through the notion of *normative pair* considered in earlier works [20,3,2].

4   Logarithmic Space

This section starts by explaining the computation one can perform with the observations, and prove that it corresponds to logarithmic space computation by showing how pointer machines can be simulated. Then, we will prove how the language of an observation can be decided within logarithmic space.

This section uses the complexity classes DLogspace and coNLogspace , as well as notions of completeness of a problem and reduction between problems. We use in Sect. 4.2 the classical theorem of coNLogspace -completeness of the acyclicity problem in directed graphs, and in Sect. 4.1 a convenient model of computation, two-ways multi-head finite automata [23], a generalization of automata also called "pointer machine". Note that the non-deterministic part of our results concerns coNLogspace , or equivalently NLogspace by the famous Immerman-Szelepcsényi theorem.

4.1   Completeness: Observations as Pointer Machines

Let $h_0, x, y \in V$, p_0, p_1, A_0 constants and $\Sigma = \{0, 1\}$, the excerpt of a dialogue in Figure 1 between an observation $O = o_1 + o_2 + \cdots$ and the representation of a word $\bar{W}_p = w_1 + w_2 + \cdots$ should help the reader to grasp the mechanism.

$$\star \cdot \mathbf{R} \cdot \mathbf{init} \cdot A_0 \cdot M(h_0) \;\leftharpoondown\; \star \cdot \mathbf{L} \cdot \mathbf{init} \cdot A_0 \cdot M(h_0) \qquad (o_1)$$

$$1 \cdot \mathbf{L} \cdot x \cdot y \cdot M(p_1) \;\leftharpoondown\; \star \cdot \mathbf{R} \cdot x \cdot y \cdot M(p_0) \qquad (w_1)$$

$$1 \cdot \mathbf{L} \cdot b \cdot A_0 \cdot M(h_0) \;\leftharpoondown\; 1 \cdot \mathbf{L} \cdot \mathbf{init} \cdot A_0 \cdot M(h_0) \qquad (o_2)$$

$$\star \cdot \mathbf{R} \cdot x \cdot y \cdot M(p_0) \;\leftharpoondown\; 1 \cdot \mathbf{L} \cdot x \cdot y \cdot M(p_1) \qquad (w_2)$$

By unification,

$$1 \cdot \mathbf{L} \cdot \mathbf{init} \cdot A_0 \cdot M(p_1) \;\leftharpoondown\; \star \cdot \mathbf{L} \cdot \mathbf{init} \cdot A_0 \cdot M(p_0) \qquad (w_1 o_1)$$

$$1 \cdot \mathbf{L} \cdot b \cdot A_0 \cdot M(p_1) \;\leftharpoondown\; \star \cdot \mathbf{L} \cdot \mathbf{init} \cdot A_0 \cdot M(p_0) \qquad (o_2 w_1 o_1)$$

$$\star \cdot \mathbf{R} \cdot b \cdot A_0 \cdot M(p_0) \;\leftharpoondown\; \star \cdot \mathbf{L} \cdot \mathbf{init} \cdot A_0 \cdot M(p_0) \qquad (w_2 o_2 w_1 o_1)$$

This can be understood as the small following dialogue:

o_1: [*Is in state* **init**] "I read $\star$ from left to right, what do I read now?"
w_1: "Your position was p_0, you are now in position p_1 and read 1."
o_2: [*Change state to* **b**] "I do an about-turn, what do I read now?"
w_2: "You are now in position p_0 and read $\star$."

Fig. 1. The beginning of a dialogue between an observation and the representation of a word

We just depicted two transitions corresponding to an automata that reads the first bit of the word, and if this bit is a 1, goes back to the starting position, in state **b**. We remark that the answer of w_1 differs from the one of w_2: there is no need to clarify the position (the variable argument of M), since h_0 was already replaced by p_1. Such an information is needed only in the first step of the computation: after that, the updates of the position of the pointer take place on the word side. We remark that neither the state nor the constant A_0 is an object of dialogue.

Note also that this excerpt corresponds to a deterministic computation. In general, several elements of the observation could get unified with the current configuration, yielding non-deterministic transitions.

Multiple Pointers and Swapping. We now add some computational power to our observations by adding the possibility to handle several pointers. The observations will now use a k-ary function A_k that allows to "store" k additional positions in the variables $h_1, \ldots, h_k$. This part of the observation is not affected by the word, which means that only one head (the *main pointer*) can move. The observation can exchange the position of the main pointer and the position stored in A_k: we therefore refer to the arguments of A_k as *auxiliary pointers* that can become the main pointer at some point of the computation. This is of course strictly equivalent to having several heads with the ability to move.

Consider the following flow, that encodes the transition "if the observation reads 1•R in state **s**, it stores the position of the main pointer (the variable h_0) at the i-th position in A_k and start reading the input with a new pointer":

$$\star\text{•}R\text{•}s'\text{•}A_k(h_1, \ldots, h_0, \ldots, h_k)\text{•}M(h_i) \leftharpoondown 1\text{•}R\text{•}s\text{•}A_k(h_1, \ldots, h_i, \ldots, h_k)\text{•}M(h_0)$$

Suppose that later on, when reading 0•L in state **r**, we want to give back to that pointer the role of main pointer. That means to swap again the position of the variables h_0 and h_i, in order to store the position that was currently read and to restore the position that was "frozen" in A_k.

$$\_\text{•}L\text{•}r'\text{•}A_k(h_1, \ldots, h_i, \ldots, h_k)\text{•}M(h_0) \leftharpoondown 0\text{•}L\text{•}r\text{•}A_k(h_1, \ldots, h_0, \ldots, h_k)\text{•}M(h_i)$$

The occurrence of L in the head of the previous flow reflects that we want to read the input from left to right, but the "_" slot cannot be a free variable, for that would break the safety of our clauses, the fact that all the variable of the head (the left-member) appears in the body (the right-member). So this slot should be occupied by the last value read by the pointer represented by the variable h_0, an information that should be encoded in the state $\mathbf{r}$[6].

Acceptance and Rejection. Remember (Theorem 33) that the language of an observation is the set of words such that the wiring composed of the observation applied to a representation of the word is nilpotent. So one could add a flow with the body corresponding to the desired situation leading to acceptance, and the head being some constant ACCEPT that appears in the body of no other flow, thus ending computation when it is reached. But in fact, it is sufficient not to add any flow: doing nothing is accepting!

---

[6] That is, we should have states $\mathbf{r_\star}$, $\mathbf{r_0}$ and $\mathbf{r_1}$, and flows accordingly.

The real challenge is to reject a word: it means to loop. We cannot simply add the unit $(I := x \leftharpoondown x)$ to our observation, since that would make our observation loop *for any input*. So we have to be more clever than that, and to encode rejection as a re-initialization of the observation: we want the observation to put all the pointers on $\star$ and to go back to an **init** state. So, a rejection is in fact a "perform for ever the same computation".

Suppose the main pointer was reading from right to left, that we are in state **b** and that we want to re-initialize the computation. Then, for every $c \in \Sigma$, it is enough to add the transitions (go-back-c) and (re-init) to the observation,

$$c \cdot L \cdot b \cdot A(h_1, \dots, h_k) \cdot M(h_0) \leftharpoondown c \cdot R \cdot b \cdot A(h_1, \dots, h_k) \cdot M(h_0) \qquad \text{(go-back-c)}$$

$$\star \cdot R \cdot \textbf{init} \cdot A(h_0, \dots, h_0) \cdot M(h_0) \leftharpoondown \star \cdot R \cdot b \cdot A(h_1, \dots, h_k) \cdot M(h_0) \qquad \text{(re-init)}$$

Once the main pointer is back on $\star$, (re-init) re-initializes all the positions of the auxiliary pointers to the position of $\star$ and changes the state for **init**.

There is another justification for this design: as the observation and the representation of the word are sums, and as the computation is the application, any transition that can be applied will be applied, *i.e.* if the body of a flow of our observation and the head of a flow of the word can be unified, the computation will start in a possibly "wrong" initialization. That some of these incorrect runs accept for incorrect reason is no trouble, since only rejection is "meaningful" due to the nilpotency criterion. But, with this framework, an incorrect run will be re-initialized to the "right" initialization, and perform the correct computation: in that case, it will loop if and only if the input is rejected.

Two-Ways Multi-Heads Finite Automata and Completeness. The model we just developed has clearly the same expressivity as two-ways multi-head finite automata, a model of particular interest to us for it is well studied, tolerant to a lot of enhancements or restrictions[7] and gives an elegant characterization of DLOGSPACE and NLOGSPACE [23,28].

Then, by a plain and uniform encoding of two-ways multi-head finite automata, we get Theorem 34. That acceptance and rejection in the non-deterministic case are "reversed" (*i.e.* all path have to accept for the computation to accept) makes us characterize CONLOGSPACE instead of NLOGSPACE.

Note that encoding a *deterministic* automaton yields a wiring of the form of Theorem 11, which would be therefore a deterministic wiring.

Theorem 34. *If $L \in$ CONLOGSPACE, then there is an observation O such that $\mathcal{L}(O) = L$. If moreover $L \in$ DLOGSPACE, then O can be chosen deterministic.*

---

[7] In fact, most of the variations (the automata can be one-way, sweeping, rotating, oblivious, etc.) are studied in terms of number of states and additional heads needed to simulate a variation with another, but most of the time they keep characterizing the same complexity classes.

4.2 Soundness of Observations

We now use the results of Sect. 2.3 and Sect. 3.2 to design a procedure that decides whether a word belongs to the language of an observation within logarithmic space. This procedure will reduce this problem to the problem of testing the acyclicity of a graph, that is well-known to be tractable with logarithmic space resources.

First, we show how the computation graph of the product of the observation and the word representation can be constructed deterministically using only logarithmic space; then, we prove that testing the acyclicity of such a graph can be done within the same bounds. Here, depending on the shape of the graph (which is dependent in itself of determinism of the wiring, recall Theorem 21), the procedure will be deterministic or non-deterministic.

Finally, using the fact that logarithmic space algorithms can be composed [30, Fig. 8.10], Theorem 20 and Theorem 33, we will obtain the expected result:

Theorem 35. *If O is an observation, then $\mathcal{L}(O) \in$ CONLOGSPACE. If moreover O is deterministic, then $\mathcal{L}(O) \in$ DLOGSPACE.*   •

A Foreword on Word and Size. Given a word W over Σ, to build a representation $\bar{W}_p$ as in Theorem 29 is clearly in DLOGSPACE: it is a plain matter of encoding. By Theorem 32, it is sufficient to consider a single representation. So for the rest of this procedure, we consider given $\bar{W}_p \in \mathcal{R}(W)$ and write $F := O\bar{W}_p$. The size of Σ is a constant, and it is clear that the maximal arity and the height of the balanced wiring F remain fixed when W varies. The only point that fluctuates is the cardinality of the set of symbols that occurs in F, and it is linearly growing with the length of W, corresponding to the number of position constants. In the following, any mention to a logarithmic amount of space is to be completed by "relatively to the length of W".

Building the Computation Graph. We need two main ingredients to build the computation graph (Theorem 19) of F: to enumerate the computation space $\mathbf{Comp}(F)$ (recall Theorem 16), and to determine whether there is an edge between two vertices.

By Theorem 18, card($\mathbf{Comp}(F)$) is polynomial in the size of W. Hence, given a balanced wiring F, a logarithmic amount of memory is enough to enumerate the members of $\mathbf{Comp}(F)$, that is the vertices of $\mathbf{G}(F)$.

Now the second part of the construction of $\mathbf{G}(F)$ is to determine if there is an edge between two vertices. Remember that there is an edge from $\mathbf{u} = u \leftharpoonup \star$ to $\mathbf{v} = v \leftharpoonup \star$ in $\mathbf{G}(F)$ if $\mathbf{v} \in F\mathbf{u}$. So one has to scan the members of $F = O\bar{W}_p$: if there exists $(t_1 \leftharpoonup t_2)(t_1' \leftharpoonup t_2') \in F$ such that $(t_1 \leftharpoonup t_2)(t_1' \leftharpoonup t_2')(u \leftharpoonup \star) = v \leftharpoonup \star$, then there is an edge from $\mathbf{u}$ to $\mathbf{v}$. To list the members of F is in DLOGSPACE, but unification in general is a difficult problem (see Sect. 1.2). The special case of matching can be tested with a logarithmic amount of space:

Theorem 36 (matching is in DLOGSPACE [12, p. 49]). *Given two terms t and u such that either t or u is closed, deciding if they are matchable is in* DLOGSPACE.

Actually, this result relies on a subtle manipulation of the representation of the terms as *simple directed acyclic graphs* [4], where the variables are "shared". Translations between this representation of terms and the usual one can be performed in logarithmic space [12, p. 38].

Deciding if G(F) is Acyclic We know thanks to Theorem 20 that answering this question is equivalent to deciding if F is nilpotent. We may notice that $\mathbf{G}(F)$ is a directed, potentially unconnected graph of size card($\mathbf{Comp}(F)$).

It is well-know that testing for acyclicity of a directed graph is a CONLOG-SPACE [24, p. 83] problem. Moreover, if F is deterministic (which is the case when O is), then $\mathbf{G}(F)$ has out-degree bounded by 1 (Theorem 21) and one can test its acyclicity without being non-deterministic: it is enough to list the vertices of $\mathbf{Comp}(F)$, and for each of them to follow card($\mathbf{Comp}(F)$) edges and to test for equality with the vertex picked at the beginning. If a loop is found, the algorithm rejects, otherwise it accepts after testing the last vertex. Only the starting vertex and the current vertex need to be stored, which fits within logarithmic space, and there is no need to do any non-deterministic transitions.

5   Conclusion

We presented the unification semiring, a construction that can be used both as an algebraic model of logic programming and as a setting for a dynamic model of logic. Within this semiring, we were able to identify a class of wirings that have the exact expressive power of logarithmic space computation.

If we try to step back a little, we can notice that the main tool in the soundness proof (Sect. 4.2) is the computation graph, defined in Sect. 2.3. More precisely, the properties of this graph, notably its cardinality (that turns out to be polynomial in the size of the input), allow to define a decision procedure that needs only logarithmic space. The technique is modular, hence not limited to logarithmic space: identifying other conditions on wirings that ensure size bounds on the computation graph would be a first step towards the characterization of other space complexity classes.

Concerning completeness, the choice of encoding pointer machines (Sect. 4.1) rather than log-space bounded Turing machines was quite natural. Balanced wirings correspond to the idea of computing with pointers: manipulation of data without writing abilities, and thus with no capacity to store any information other than a fixed number of positions on the input.

By considering other classes of wirings or by modifying the encoding it might be possible to capture other notions of machines characterizing some complexity classes: we already mentioned at the end of Sect. 3.1 a modification of the representation of the word that would model one-way finite automata.

The relation with proof theory needs to be explored further: the approach of this paper seems indeed to suggest a sort of "Curry-Howard" correspondence for logic programming.

As Sect. 1.1 highlighted, there are many notions that might be transferable from one field to the other, thanks to a common setting provided by geometry of interaction and the unification semiring. Most notably, the notion of nilpotency (on the proof-theoretic side: strong normalization) corresponds to a variant of boundedness of logic programs, a property that is usually hard to ensure.

Another direction could be to look for a proof-system counterpart of this work: a corresponding "balanced" logic of logarithmic space.

Acknowledgments. The authors would like to thank the anonymous referees for helpful suggestions and comments.

References

1. Asperti, A., Danos, V., Laneve, C., Regnier, L.: Paths in the lambda-calculus. In: LICS, pp. 426–436. IEEE Computer Society (1994)
2. Aubert, C., Bagnol, M.: Unification and logarithmic space. In: Dowek, G. (ed.) RTA-TLCA 2014. LNCS, vol. 8560, pp. 77–92. Springer, Heidelberg (2014)
3. Aubert, C., Seiller, T.: Characterizing co-nl by a group action. Arxiv preprint abs/1209.3422 (2012)
4. Baader, F., Snyder, W.: Unification theory. In: Robinson, J.A., Voronkov, A. (eds.) Handbook of Automated Reasoning, pp. 445–532. Elsevier and MIT Press (2001)
5. Baillot, P., Mazza, D.: Linear logic by levels and bounded time complexity. Theoret. Comput. Sci. 411(2), 470–503 (2010)
6. Baillot, P., Pedicini, M.: Elementary complexity and geometry of interaction. Fund. Inform. 45(1-2), 1–31 (2001)
7. Bellia, M., Occhiuto, M.E.: N-axioms parallel unification. Fund. Inform. 55(2), 115–128 (2003)
8. Ben-Amram, A.M.: What is a "pointer machine"? Science of Computer Programming 26, 88–95 (1995)
9. Calimeri, F., Cozza, S., Ianni, G., Leone, N.: Computable functions in ASP: Theory and implementation. In: Garcia de la Banda, M., Pontelli, E. (eds.) ICLP 2008. LNCS, vol. 5366, pp. 407–424. Springer, Heidelberg (2008)
10. Dal Lago, U., Hofmann, M.: Bounded linear logic, revisited. Log. Meth. Comput. Sci. 6(4) (2010)
11. Dantsin, E., Eiter, T., Gottlob, G., Voronkov, A.: Complexity and expressive power of logic programming. ACM Comput. Surv. 33(3), 374–425 (2001)
12. Dwork, C., Kanellakis, P.C., Mitchell, J.C.: On the sequential nature of unification. J. Log. Program. 1(1), 35–50 (1984)
13. Dwork, C., Kanellakis, P.C., Stockmeyer, L.J.: Parallel algorithms for term matching. SIAM J. Comput. 17(4), 711–731 (1988)
14. Gaboardi, M., Marion, J.Y., Ronchi Della Rocca, S.: An implicit characterization of pspace. ACM Trans. Comput. Log. 13(2), 18:1–18:36 (2012)
15. Girard, J.Y.: Linear logic. Theoret. Comput. Sci. 50(1), 1–101 (1987)
16. Girard, J.Y.: Geometry of interaction 1: Interpretation of system F. Studies in Logic and the Foundations of Mathematics 127, 221–260 (1989)
17. Girard, J.Y.: Towards a geometry of interaction. In: Gray, J.W., Ščedrov, A. (eds.) Proceedings of the AMS-IMS-SIAM Joint Summer Research Conference held, June 14-20. Categories in Computer Science and Logic, vol. 92, pp. 69–108. AMS (1989)

18. Girard, J.Y.: Geometry of interaction III: Accommodating the additives. In: Girard, J.Y., Lafont, Y., Regnier, L. (eds.) Advances in Linear Logic. London Math. Soc. Lecture Note Ser., vol. 222, pp. 329–389. CUP (1995)

19. Girard, J.Y.: Light linear logic. In: Leivant, D. (ed.) LCC 1994. LNCS, vol. 960, pp. 145–176. Springer, Heidelberg (1995)

20. Girard, J.Y.: Normativity in logic. In: Dybjer, P., Lindstrm, S., Palmgren, E., Sundholm, G. (eds.) Epistemology versus Ontology. Logic, Epistemology, and the Unity of Science, vol. 27, pp. 243–263. Springer (2012)

21. Girard, J.Y.: Three lightings of logic. In: Ronchi Della Rocca, S. (ed.) CSL. LIPIcs, vol. 23, pp. 11–23. Schloss Dagstuhl - Leibniz-Zentrum für Informatik (2013)

22. Hillebrand, G.G., Kanellakis, P.C., Mairson, H.G., Vardi, M.Y.: Undecidable boundedness problems for datalog programs. J. Log. Program. 25(2), 163–190 (1995)

23. Holzer, M., Kutrib, M., Malcher, A.: Multi-head finite automata: Characterizations, concepts and open problems. In: Neary, T., Woods, D., Seda, A.K., Murphy, N. (eds.) CSP. EPTCS, vol. 1, pp. 93–107 (2008)

24. Jones, N.D.: Space-bounded reducibility among combinatorial problems. J. Comput. Syst. Sci. 11(1), 68–85 (1975)

25. Laurent, O.: A token machine for full geometry of interaction (extended abstract). In: Abramsky, S. (ed.) TLCA 2001. LNCS, vol. 2044, pp. 283–297. Springer, Heidelberg (2001)

26. Lierler, Y., Lifschitz, V.: One more decidable class of finitely ground programs. In: Hill, P.M., Warren, D.S. (eds.) ICLP 2009. LNCS, vol. 5649, pp. 489–493. Springer, Heidelberg (2009)

27. Ohkubo, M., Yasuura, H., Yajima, S.: On parallel computation time of unification for restricted terms. Tech. rep., Kyoto University (1987)

28. Pighizzini, G.: Two-way finite automata: Old and recent results. Fund. Inform. 126(2-3), 225–246 (2013)

29. Robinson, J.A.: A machine-oriented logic based on the resolution principle. J. ACM 12(1), 23–41 (1965)

30. Savage, J.E.: Models of computation - exploring the power of computing. Addison-Wesley (1998)

31. Schöpp, U.: Stratified bounded affine logic for logarithmic space. In: LICS, pp. 411–420. IEEE Computer Society (2007)

32. Seiller, T.: Interaction graphs: Multiplicatives. Ann. Pure Appl. Logic 163, 1808–1837 (2012)

Automatic Memory Management Based on Program Transformation Using Ownership

Tatsuya Sonobe, Kohei Suenaga, and Atsushi Igarashi

Kyoto University, Kyoto, Japan

Abstract. We present a type-based program transformation for an imperative programming language with manual memory-management primitives (e.g., `malloc` and `free` in C). Our algorithm, given a program with potential memory leaks, inserts memory-deallocating instructions to the program so that the resulting program does not contain memory leaks. We design the algorithm as type reconstruction for an extension of the ownership-based type system by Suenaga and Kobayashi.

Keywords: Memory leaks, Type system, Program transformation.

1 Introduction

Memory leaks are one of the most serious bugs in the programming languages with manual memory management (e.g., C language [11] and C++ [21]). It is hard to find via testing because it is the result of illegal *inaction* (i.e., not appropriately deallocating an allocated memory cell), not the result of illegal action that can be detected instantly.

Various approaches to this problem have been proposed [8, 9, 10, 14, 23]. We henceforth focus on *static verification*, in which a verifier analyzes source code at compile time to verify memory-leak freedom.

A difficulty in using static verification consists in pinpointing errors. A verifier warns possibility of a memory leak if the verification fails. In order to determine why the warning is issued, a programmer often needs to understand how the verifier works. However, this is in general difficult especially if the verifier is based on highly mathematical theory.

To address this problem, the current paper proposes *automated correction* of a program with memory leaks. If verification of a program fails, our algorithm inserts a call to the memory deallocation instruction **free** to the program; the resulting program is guaranteed to be memory-leak free. Figure 1 exemplifies the proposed transformation; our algorithm, given the program that contains a memory leak (Figure 1a), inserts a memory-deallocating instruction **free**(x) producing a memory-leak free program (Figure 1b).

Our algorithm is based on the type system proposed by Suenaga and Kobayashi [23]. Before describing our algorithm, we first review that system. Inspired by several type systems [2, 10, 24], they augment the pointer-type

J. Garrigue (Ed.): APLAS 2014, LNCS 8858, pp. 58–77, 2014.

(a)	(b)
let $x = $ **malloc**() **in**	let $x = $ **malloc**() **in**
let $y = $ **malloc**() **in**	let $y = $ **malloc**() **in**
$*x \leftarrow y;$	$*x \leftarrow y;$
free(y)	**free**(x);
	free(y)

Fig. 1. Example of transformation. (a) Input program that may causes a memory leak. (b) Result of transformation of (a).

constructor τ **ref** with a *fractional ownership*[1] (or, simply an *ownership*) f. A fractional ownership is a member of $\{x \in \mathbb{Q} \mid 0 \leq x \leq 1\}$ where $\mathbb{Q}$ is the set of rational numbers. A fractional ownership describes how each pointer should be and can be used. Hence, a reference type in the type system is of the form τ **ref**$_f$.

We explain how ownerships work in our type system; for more intuitive explanation, we refer one to Suenaga and Kobayashi [23] and Suenaga, Fukuda, and Igarashi [22].

First, we note that the type system is designed to be a flow-sensitive one so that different types can be assigned to different occurrences of a variable. The type system assigns the ownership 1 to a pointer, say x, at the program point where x is bound to a fresh memory cell; we write $*x$ for the memory cell pointed to by x. Then, suppose that a pointer x has a type **int ref**$_f$ at a certain program point[2]. Then, the usage of x at the program point should respect the following rules.

1. Rule on deallocation: The memory cell pointed to by x should be deallocated eventually if $f > 0$.
2. Rules on accesses:
   (a) Read on $*x$ is allowed only if $f > 0$ at the program point of the read.
   (b) Write on $*x$ is allowed only if $f = 1$ at the program point of the write.
   (c) **free**(x) is allowed only if $f = 1$; the ownership f is set to 0 at the program point just after the **free**(x).
3. Rule on ownership passing: If it is statically known that x is an alias of y at a program point (i.e., x is a *must-alias* of y at the program point), then ownerships can be transferred between x and y.

An important invariant of the rules above is that, for each memory cell, the sum of the ownerships of the pointers to the cell is exactly equal to 1. Therefore,

---

[1] Our use of the term ownership is different from that of the ownership types [3]. By ownership, we intend to denote information about obligation *and* permission in accessing a memory cell whereas ownership types are used to control permission to access an object.

[2] Although the formalization of their type system and the current paper does not contain the type of integers **int**, we use it here for explanation; extension of the frameworks with integers is straightforward.

Program	Type env. after each instruction
0 :	$/ * \emptyset * /$
1 : **let** $x =$ **malloc**() **in**	$/ * x : $**int ref**$_1 * /$
2 : **let** $y =$ **malloc**() **in**	$/ * x : $**int ref**$_1, y : $**int ref**$_1 * /$
3 : $*x \leftarrow y$;	$/ * x : $**int ref**$_1, y : $**int ref**$_1 * /$
4 : **free**(x);	$/ * x : $**int ref**$_0, y : $**int ref**$_1 * /$
5 : **free**(y)	$/ * x : $**int ref**$_0, y : $**int ref**$_0 * /$

Fig. 2. Example of typing

by forcing that no ownership is left at the end of a program, we can guarantee memory-leak freedom. Moreover, the rule 2c guarantees that the deallocated cell is not accessed since there is no pointer to the cell that has a positive ownership after the deallocation. Suenaga and Kobayashi [23] proved that a well-typed program does not lead to a memory leak.

Figure 2 shows an example of typing; the figure includes a program and the type of each variable at each program point. The types of x and y at Lines 1 and 2, respectively, show that the ownership 1 is assigned just after memory allocation. The ownership 1 of x at Line 3 allows the write on $*x$ (Rule 2b). The instructions **free**(x) and **free**(y) at Line 4 and 5, respectively, are allowed because of the ownership 1 of x and y (Rule 2c). There is no ownership left at Line 5; hence, Rule 1 is satisfied.

Suenaga and Kobayashi formalized the type system, proposed a constraint-based type inference algorithm. They also conducted an experiment using an implementation of the verification algorithm [23].

Their verifier, if verification fails, reports the failure with little supplemental information. Then, understanding the cause of verification failure requires the knowledge about the type system. To address this problem, the extension proposed in the current paper enables the verifier to *insert* memory-deallocating instructions. Even if a given program contains a memory leak, the verifier tries to transform it to a well-typed program by inserting calls to the instruction **free** to appropriate locations and, if it succeeds, returns the transformed programs.

Our main idea is to consider missing deallocations as *implicit type conversions*. Then, insertion of **free** is a procedure that makes the implicit conversions explicit. This procedure is essentially type reconstruction for a type system with subtyping.

To this end, we introduce a pseudo instruction called a *cast* $\langle \Gamma_1 \trianglelefteq \Gamma_2 \rangle$ to the framework where Γ_1 and Γ_2 are type environments. A cast $\langle \Gamma_1 \trianglelefteq \Gamma_2 \rangle$ is interpreted as a shorthand for instructions that coerce the type environment Γ_1 at a program point to Γ_2; the typing rule for cast instructions is designed so that a well-typed program admits such interpretation. The transformation algorithm, given a program, first inserts a cast template (e.g., a cast whose ownership parts are left unknown) to every program point, and then conducts type inference to the program. After fixing the unknown ownerships, the algorithm replaces each cast with its interpretation.

Consider the program in Figure 1a. Given this program, our algorithm inserts cast templates to every location[3].

let $x =$ **malloc**() in $\langle x\!:\!$**int ref**$_{\varphi_1} \trianglelefteq x\!:\!$**int ref**$_{\varphi_2}\rangle$;
let $y =$ **malloc**() in $\langle x\!:\!$**int ref**$_{\varphi_3}, y\!:\!$**int ref**$_{\varphi_4} \trianglelefteq x\!:\!$**int ref**$_{\varphi_5}, y\!:\!$**int ref**$_{\varphi_6}\rangle$;
$*x \leftarrow y$; $\langle x\!:\!$**int ref**$_{\varphi_7}, y\!:\!$**int ref**$_{\varphi_8} \trianglelefteq x\!:\!$**int ref**$_{\varphi_9}, y\!:\!$**int ref**$_{\varphi_{10}}\rangle$;
free(y); $\langle x\!:\!$**int ref**$_{\varphi_{11}}, y\!:\!$**int ref**$_{\varphi_{12}} \trianglelefteq x\!:\!$**int ref**$_{\varphi_{13}}, y\!:\!$**int ref**$_{\varphi_{14}}\rangle$;
$\langle x\!:\!$**int ref**$_{\varphi_{15}} \trianglelefteq x\!:\!$**int ref**$_{\varphi_{16}}\rangle$.

Here, φ_i are variables for ownerships.

Then, the algorithm conduct type inference to calculate an ownership assignment that makes the program above well-typed. One of the possible assignments produces the following.

let $x =$ **malloc**() in $\langle x\!:\!$**int ref**$_1 \trianglelefteq x\!:\!$**int ref**$_1\rangle$;
let $y =$ **malloc**() in $\langle x\!:\!$**int ref**$_1, y\!:\!$**int ref**$_1 \trianglelefteq x\!:\!$**int ref**$_1, y\!:\!$**int ref**$_1\rangle$;
$*x \leftarrow y$; $\langle x\!:\!$**int ref**$_1, y\!:\!$**int ref**$_1 \trianglelefteq x\!:\!$**int ref**$_0, y\!:\!$**int ref**$_1\rangle$;
free(y); $\underline{\langle x\!:\!$**int ref**$_0, y\!:\!$**int ref**$_1 \trianglelefteq x\!:\!$**int ref**$_0, y\!:\!$**int ref**$_0\rangle}$;
$\langle x\!:\!$**int ref**$_0 \trianglelefteq x\!:\!$**int ref**$_0\rangle$.

The underlined cast expresses that the ownership of x should be converted from 1 to 0 there for this program to be well-typed; that is, **free**(x) has to be inserted there. By replacing each cast with corresponding instructions (e.g., $\langle x\!:\!$**int ref**$_1, y\!:\!$**int ref**$_1 \trianglelefteq x\!:\!$**int ref**$_0, y\!:\!$**int ref**$_1\rangle$ with **free**(x)), the verifier obtains the program in Figure 1b.

Remark 1. One restriction of the current framework is that we can deal with only casts from the ownership 1 to 0, excluding a cast like $\langle x\!:\!$**int ref**$_{0.5} \trianglelefteq x\!:\!$**int ref**$_0\rangle$ which would be useful in disposing read-only pointers; dealing with such cast requires manual annotations called *assertions*.

The current paper proposes a theoretical framework in a simple setting that does not incorporate structures. Although we have a prototype of the implementation of the proposed algorithm, the conducted experiment is still limited. We have not measured performance yet. Extension of the framework and demonstrating its feasibility is deferred to future work.

This paper is structured as follows. We first review the framework by Suenaga and Kobayashi [23] in Section 2. We then present the transformation algorithm in Section 3. After reviewing related work in Section 4, we conclude in Section 5.

Notation. $\mathbb{Q}$ is the set of rational numbers. Given a (partial) function $f : X \rightarrow Y$, we write $f[x \mapsto y]$, where $x \in X$ and $y \in Y$, for the (partial) function defined as follows: $f[x \mapsto y](x') = y$ if $x = x'$ and $f[x \mapsto y](x') = f(x')$ otherwise. We write $\widetilde{x}$ for a finite sequence $x_1, \ldots, x_n$. We also write X^* for the set $\{x_1 \ldots x_n | x_i \in X\}$. The number $n \geq 0$ shall be clear from context or does not matter when we use the notations X^* and $\widetilde{x}$.

---

[3] For simplicity, the cast insertion here is slightly different from that in Section 3.

$$
\begin{array}{llll}
x, y, z, \ldots & \text{(variables)} & \in \mathbf{Vars} \\
F & \text{(fun. names)} & \in \mathbf{FunN} \\
v & \text{(values)} & ::= \mathbf{null} \mid x \\
s & \text{(statements)} & ::= \mathbf{skip} \mid s_1; s_2 \mid \mathbf{let}\ x = v\ \mathbf{in}\ s \mid F(x_1, \ldots, x_n) \\
& & \mid\ \mathbf{let}\ x = \mathbf{malloc}()\ \mathbf{in}\ s \mid \mathbf{free}(x) \mid \mathbf{let}\ x = *y\ \mathbf{in}\ s \\
& & \mid\ *x_1 \leftarrow y_2 \mid \mathbf{ifnull}\ x\ \mathbf{then}\ s_1\ \mathbf{else}\ s_2 \\
& & \mid\ \mathbf{assert}(x_1 = x_2) \mid \mathbf{assert}(x_1 = *x_2) \\
d & \text{(fun. def.)} & ::= (x_1, \ldots, x_n)s \\
D & \text{(fun. env.)} & ::= \{F_1 \mapsto d_1, \ldots, F_n \mapsto d_n\} \\
P & \text{(program)} & ::= \langle D, s \rangle
\end{array}
$$

Fig. 3. Syntax of the language

2   Suenaga–Kobayashi Type System

To make the current paper self-contained, we recapitulate the Suenaga–Kobayashi type system [23].

2.1   Language

Syntax. Figure 3 presents the syntax of the language. We fix countably infinite sets **Vars** of variables and **FunN** of function names. A value of the language is **null** or a variable representing a pointer. The meta-variable s ranges over statements. The intuition of each statement is as follows.

- **skip** does nothing.
- $s_1; s_2$ executes s_1 until it terminates and then executes s_2.
- **let** $x = v$ **in** s binds x to the value v and executes s.
- $F(x_1, \ldots, x_n)$ calls a function F with parameters $x_1, \ldots, x_n$; we assume that $x_1 \ldots x_n$ are different from each other.
- **let** $x = \mathbf{malloc}()$ **in** s allocates a memory cell, binds x to the pointer to the cell, and executes s.
- **free**(x) deallocates the cell pointed to by x.
- **let** $x = *y$ **in** s dereferences y, binds x to the result, and executes s.
- $*x_1 \leftarrow x_2$ writes x_2 to the cell pointed to by x_1.
- **ifnull** x **then** s_1 **else** s_2 executes s_1 if x is **null** and s_2 otherwise.
- **assert**$(x_1 = x_2)$ does nothing if x_1 is equal to x_2; it raises *assertion failure* otherwise. This statement and the statement **assert**$(x_1 = *x_2)$ are used as auxiliary information for the type system. More detail is in Section 2.2.
- **assert**$(x_1 = *x_2)$ does nothing if x_1 is equal to the value stored in the memory cell pointed to by x_2; it raises assertion failure otherwise.

A *function definition* (or, simply *definition*) d is of the form $(x_1, \ldots, x_n)s$ representing a function that takes arguments, binds $x_1, \ldots, x_n$ to the arguments, and executes s. We use the meta-variable D for *function environments*

$$\frac{\langle H, R, s_1 \rangle \to_D \langle H', R', s_1' \rangle}{\langle H, R, s_1; s_2 \rangle \to_D \langle H', R', s_1'; s_2 \rangle} \quad \text{(Sem-Seq1)}$$

$$\langle H, R, \textbf{skip}; s_2 \rangle \to_D \langle H, R, s_2 \rangle \quad \text{(Sem-Seq2)}$$

$$\frac{x' \text{ is fresh}}{\langle H, R, \textbf{let } x = v \textbf{ in } s \rangle \to_D \langle H, R[x' \mapsto v], [x'/x]s \rangle} \quad \text{(Sem-Let)}$$

$$\frac{D(F) = (x_1, \ldots, x_n)s}{\langle H, R, F(y_1, \ldots, y_n) \rangle \to_D \langle H, R, [y_1, \ldots, y_n/x_1, \ldots, x_n]s \rangle} \quad \text{(Sem-Call)}$$

$$\frac{y \text{ and } x' \text{ are fresh.} \qquad v \text{ is an arbitrary value.}}{\langle H, R, \textbf{let } x = \textbf{malloc}() \textbf{ in } s \rangle \to_D \langle H[x' \mapsto v], R[y \mapsto x'], [y/x]s \rangle} \quad \text{(Sem-Malloc)}$$

$$\frac{y \in \textbf{dom}(H)}{\langle H, R[x \mapsto y], \textbf{free}(x) \rangle \to_D \langle H \backslash y, R[x \mapsto y], \textbf{skip} \rangle} \quad \text{(Sem-Free)}$$

$$\langle H, R[x \mapsto \textbf{null}], \textbf{free}(x) \rangle \to_D \langle H, R[x \mapsto \textbf{null}], \textbf{skip} \rangle \quad \text{(Sem-FreeNull)}$$

$$\frac{x' \text{ is fresh}}{\langle H[z \mapsto v], R[y \mapsto z], \textbf{let } x = *y \textbf{ in } s \rangle \to_D \langle H[z \mapsto v], R[y \mapsto z, x' \mapsto v], [x'/x]s \rangle} \quad \text{(Sem-Deref)}$$

$$\langle H[R(x) \mapsto v'], R, *x \leftarrow y \rangle \to_D \langle H[R(x) \mapsto R(y)], R, \textbf{skip} \rangle \quad \text{(Sem-Assign)}$$

$$\frac{R(x) \neq \textbf{null}}{\langle H, R, \textbf{ifnull } x \textbf{ then } s_1 \textbf{ else } s_2 \rangle \to_D \langle H, R, s_1 \rangle} \quad \text{(Sem-IfNull1)}$$

$$\frac{R(x) \neq \textbf{null}}{\langle H, R, \textbf{ifnull } x \textbf{ then } s_1 \textbf{ else } s_2 \rangle \to_D \langle H, R, s_2 \rangle} \quad \text{(Sem-IfNull2)}$$

$$\frac{R(x) = R(y)}{\langle H, R, \textbf{assert}(x = y) \rangle \to_D \langle H, R, \textbf{skip} \rangle} \quad \text{(Sem-AssertEq)}$$

$$\frac{H(R(y)) = R(x)}{\langle H, R, \textbf{assert}(x = *y) \rangle \to_D \langle H, R, \textbf{skip} \rangle} \quad \text{(Sem-AssertDerefEq)}$$

Fig. 4. Semantics of the language

$\{F_1 \mapsto d_1, \ldots, F_n \mapsto d_n\}$. A function environment gives a mapping from function names to their definitions. Finally, a program of our language consists of a function environment D and a main statement s, written $\langle D, s \rangle$.

Occurrences of x are bound in s of **let** $x = v$ **in** s and of **let** $x = *y$ **in** s; $x_1, \ldots, x_n$ are bound in s of $(x_1, \ldots, x_n)s$; and $F_1, \ldots, F_n$ are bound in $d_1, \ldots, d_n$, and s in $\langle \{F_1 \mapsto d_1, \ldots, F_n \mapsto d_n\}, s \rangle$. We identify statements and programs that differ only in the name of bound variables. We assume that bound variables are renamed so that each of them is unique.

Semantics. A *heap*, ranged over by H, and a *register file*, ranged over by R, are partial functions from **Vars** to the set of values. A register file is used to record bindings of programs variables, whereas a heap to record those of heap locations; we abuse **Vars** for the domains of both. We assume that the domain of a heap and that of a register file are finite. We write **dom**(X) for the domain

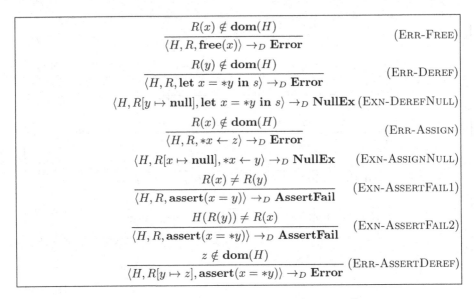

Fig. 5. Semantics of the language (continued)

of X where X is a heap or a register file. We also write $X \backslash S$, where $S \subseteq \mathbf{Vars}$, for the restriction of X on $\mathbf{dom}(X) \backslash S$. If S is a singleton $\{x\}$, we write $X \backslash x$ for $X \backslash \{x\}$.

Figures 4 and 5 define the operational semantics of the language. The semantics is given as D-parameterized rewriting relations $\langle H, R, s \rangle \to_D \langle H', R', s' \rangle$ and $\langle H, R, s \rangle \to_D E$; here, $\langle H, R, s \rangle$ is a *configuration* that models a state of computation and $E \in \{\mathbf{Error}, \mathbf{NullEx}, \mathbf{AssertFail}\}$ is an *exception*. We write $\to_D^*$ for the reflexive transitive closure of $\to_D$.

An exception E represents an exceptional state; **Error** represents an access to a memory cell that is already deallocated; **NullEx** represents an access to **null**[4]; **AssertFail** represents an assertion failure. One of the properties the type system summarized later guarantees is that **Error** is not reachable; **NullEx** and **AssertFail** are not seen as erroneous.

Definition 1. *A program* $\langle D, s \rangle$ *is* safe *if* $\langle \emptyset, \emptyset, s \rangle \to_D^* \mathbf{Error}$ *does not hold.*

A program is said to be memory-leak free if the program does not leave any memory cell allocated when it terminates. Notice that the property mentions only terminating programs. Dealing with non-terminating programs is beyond the scope of the current paper, though we are looking at this direction.

Definition 2. *A program* $\langle D, s \rangle$ *is* memory-leak free *if* $\langle \emptyset, \emptyset, s \rangle \to_D^* \langle H, R, \mathbf{skip} \rangle$ *implies* $H = \emptyset$.

2.2   Type System

Figure 6 defines the syntax of types.

---

[4] **free(null)** is not considered exceptional following the convention of the C language.

f (ownerships)	$\in \{x \in \mathbb{Q} \mid 0 \leq x \leq 1\}$
τ (types)	$\in \{0\}^* \to \mathbf{Own}$
Γ (type environments)	$::= \{x_1 \mapsto \tau_1, \ldots, x_n \mapsto \tau_n\}$
Θ (function type environments)	$::= \{F_1 \mapsto (\widetilde{\tau_1}) \to (\widetilde{\tau_1'}), \ldots, F_n \mapsto (\widetilde{\tau_n}) \to (\widetilde{\tau_n'})\}$

Fig. 6. Definition of types and type environments

- Ownerships, ranged over by f, are rational numbers in $[0, 1]$.
- Reference types, ranged over by τ, are maps from $\{0\}^*$ (the set of sequences of zeros) to ownerships. We use a meta-variable w that ranges over $\{0\}^*$; we write $|w|$ for the length of w and ϵ for the empty sequence. Intuition is as follows. Suppose that a variable x has a type τ at a program point such that $\tau(w) = f$. Then, the program has to follow the ownership f at the program point to access the memory cell $|w|$-hop away from x. A reference type $\tau_1 + \tau_2$ is defined by $(\tau_1 + \tau_2)(w) = \tau_1(w) + \tau_2(w)$. Due to a technical reason [23], we assume that a reference type τ satisfies the following rule: if $\tau(w) = 0$ then $\tau(0w) = 0$.
- Type environments, ranged over by Γ, are maps from variables to reference types. We assume that the domain of a type environment is a finite set. We write $x_1 : \tau_1, \ldots, x_n : \tau_n$ for $\{x_1 \mapsto \tau_1, \ldots, x_n \mapsto \tau_n\}$. If $x \notin \mathbf{dom}(\Gamma)$, we write $\Gamma, x : \tau$ for $\Gamma \cup \{x \mapsto \tau\}$.
- *Function type environments*, ranged over by Θ, are maps from function names to *function types* $(\widetilde{\tau}) \to (\widetilde{\tau'})$; the types $\widetilde{\tau}$ in a function type $(\widetilde{\tau}) \to (\widetilde{\tau'})$ are the types of the parameters at function invocation, whereas $\widetilde{\tau'}$ are those at the end of the function execution. We assume the length of $\widetilde{\tau}$ is the same as that of $\widetilde{\tau'}$.

We write $\mathbf{1}$ for the type τ such that $\tau(w) = 1$ for any w; $\mathbf{0}$ for one such that $\tau(w) = 0$. We also write $\tau \, \mathbf{ref}_f$ for the type τ' such that $\tau'(\epsilon) = f$ and $\tau'(0w) = \tau(w)$ for any w. The order $\tau_1 \leq \tau_2$ is defined pointwise by: $\tau_1(w) \leq_\mathbb{Q} \tau_2(w)$ for all w. We write $\mu\alpha.\tau$ for the least type τ such that $\alpha = \tau$ on this order $\leq$; for example, $\mu\alpha.\alpha \, \mathbf{ref}_1 = \mathbf{1}$ because $\alpha = \alpha \, \mathbf{ref}_1$ holds only if $\alpha = \mathbf{1}$.

Remark 2. We use $\{0\}^*$, not $\mathbb{N}$, for the domain of reference types so that our types can be smoothly extended to complex heap objects. For example, we can incorporate pointers to pairs by using $\{0, 1\}^*$ as the domain of the pointer types. Such extension has been already done by Suenaga and Kobayashi [23].

Remark 3. A reference type $\tau \, \mathbf{ref}_f$ describes the usage of a variable. For example, if x has the type $\mathbf{0} \, \mathbf{ref}_1$ at a program point, it means that the memory cell pointed to by $*x$ is accessible only via x and that the cell pointed to by $**x$ cannot be accessed via x. If $**x$ has not been deallocated, there should be other aliases that have ownership to access to the cell. See [23] for more detailed presentation.

$$\Gamma \vdash_\Theta \mathbf{skip} \Longrightarrow \Gamma \qquad \text{(T-SKIP)}$$

$$\frac{\Gamma_1 \vdash_\Theta s_1 \Longrightarrow \Gamma \qquad \Gamma \vdash_\Theta s_1 \Longrightarrow \Gamma_2}{\Gamma_1 \vdash_\Theta s_1; s_2 \Longrightarrow \Gamma_2} \qquad \text{(T-SEQ)}$$

$$\frac{\Gamma, x{:}\tau_1, y{:}\tau_2 \vdash_\Theta s \Longrightarrow \Gamma', x{:}\mathbf{0}}{\Gamma, y{:}\tau_1 + \tau_2 \vdash_\Theta \mathbf{let}\ x = y\ \mathbf{in}\ s \Longrightarrow \Gamma'} \qquad \text{(T-LET)}$$

$$\frac{\Gamma, x{:}\tau' \vdash_\Theta s \Longrightarrow \Gamma', x{:}\mathbf{0}}{\Gamma \vdash_\Theta \mathbf{let}\ x = \mathbf{null}\ \mathbf{in}\ s \Longrightarrow \Gamma'} \qquad \text{(T-LETNULL)}$$

$$\frac{\Theta(F) = (\tau_1, \ldots, \tau_n) \to (\tau'_1, \ldots, \tau'_n)}{\Gamma, x_1{:}\tau_1, \ldots, x_n{:}\tau_n \vdash_\Theta F(x_1, \ldots, x_n) \Longrightarrow \Gamma, x_1{:}\tau'_1, \ldots, x_n{:}\tau'_n} \qquad \text{(T-CALL)}$$

$$\frac{\Gamma, x{:}\mathbf{0}\ \mathbf{ref}_1 \vdash_\Theta s \Longrightarrow \Gamma', x{:}\mathbf{0}}{\Gamma \vdash_\Theta \mathbf{let}\ x = \mathbf{malloc}()\ \mathbf{in}\ s \Longrightarrow \Gamma'} \qquad \text{(T-MALLOC)}$$

$$\Gamma, x{:}\mathbf{0}\ \mathbf{ref}_1 \vdash_\Theta \mathbf{free}(x) \Longrightarrow \Gamma, x{:}\mathbf{0} \qquad \text{(T-FREE)}$$

$$\frac{\Gamma, x{:}\tau_1, y{:}\tau_2\ \mathbf{ref}_f \vdash_\Theta s \Longrightarrow \Gamma', x{:}\mathbf{0} \qquad f > 0}{\Gamma, y{:}(\tau_1 + \tau_2)\ \mathbf{ref}_f \vdash_\Theta \mathbf{let}\ x = {*}y\ \mathbf{in}\ s \Longrightarrow \Gamma'} \qquad \text{(T-DEREF)}$$

$$\Gamma, x{:}\mathbf{0}\ \mathbf{ref}_1, y{:}\tau_1 + \tau_2 \vdash_\Theta {*}x \leftarrow y \Longrightarrow \Gamma, x{:}\tau_1\ \mathbf{ref}_1, y{:}\tau_2 \qquad \text{(T-ASSIGN)}$$

$$\frac{\Gamma, x{:}\tau' \vdash_\Theta s_1 \Longrightarrow \Gamma' \qquad \Gamma, x{:}\tau\ \mathbf{ref}_f \vdash_\Theta s_2 \Longrightarrow \Gamma'}{\Gamma, x{:}\tau\ \mathbf{ref}_f \vdash_\Theta \mathbf{ifnull}\ x\ \mathbf{then}\ s_1\ \mathbf{else}\ s_2 \Longrightarrow \Gamma'} \qquad \text{(T-IFNULL)}$$

$$\frac{\tau_1 + \tau_2 = \tau'_1 + \tau'_2}{\Gamma, x{:}\tau_1, y{:}\tau_2 \vdash_\Theta \mathbf{assert}(x = y) \Longrightarrow \Gamma, x{:}\tau'_1, y{:}\tau'_2} \qquad \text{(T-ASSERT)}$$

$$\frac{\tau_1 + \tau_2 = \tau'_1 + \tau'_2 \qquad f > 0}{\Gamma, x{:}\tau_1, y{:}\tau_2\ \mathbf{ref}_f \vdash_\Theta \mathbf{assert}(x = {*}y) \Longrightarrow \Gamma, x{:}\tau'_1, y{:}\tau'_2\ \mathbf{ref}_f} \quad \text{(T-ASSERTDEREF)}$$

$$\frac{x_1{:}\tau_1, \ldots, x_n{:}\tau_n \vdash_\Theta s \Longrightarrow x_1{:}\tau'_1, \ldots, x_n{:}\tau'_n}{\vdash_\Theta (x_1, \ldots, x_n)s{:}(\tau_1, \ldots, \tau_n) \to (\tau'_1, \ldots, \tau'_n)} \qquad \text{(T-DEF)}$$

$$\frac{\vdash_\Theta D(F){:}\Theta(F)\ \text{for each}\ F \in \mathbf{dom}(D) \qquad \mathbf{dom}(D) = \mathbf{dom}(\Theta)}{\vdash D{:}\Theta} \qquad \text{(T-DEFS)}$$

$$\frac{\vdash D{:}\Theta \qquad \emptyset \vdash_\Theta s \Longrightarrow \emptyset}{\vdash \langle D, s \rangle} \qquad \text{(T-PROG)}$$

Fig. 7. Typing rules

The operation $\tau_1 + \tau_2$ is extended to type environments as follows:

$$(\Gamma_1 + \Gamma_2)(x) := \begin{cases} \Gamma_1(x) & \text{if } x \in \mathbf{dom}(\Gamma_1) \backslash \mathbf{dom}(\Gamma_2) \\ \Gamma_2(x) & \text{if } x \in \mathbf{dom}(\Gamma_2) \backslash \mathbf{dom}(\Gamma_1) \\ \Gamma_1(x) + \Gamma_2(x) & \text{otherwise.} \end{cases}$$

Figure 7 defines the type judgments of the type system. The main one is that for statements: $\Gamma_1 \vdash s \Longrightarrow \Gamma_2$. Here, Γ_1 describes the type of each variable at the program point just before s; Γ_2 describes that of just after s. We call Γ_1 the *pre type environment* of s and Γ_2 the *post type environment*.

It should be easy to see that the intuition of ownerships explained in Section 1 is encoded in the typing rules. We give remarks about further important features of the typing rules. For rule-by-rule explanation, readers are referred to [23].

- When an alias z to a variable w is created, the ownership on w transferred to z. For example, in T-LET, the ownership on y represented by $\tau_1 + \tau_2$ at the pre type environment of **let** $x = y$ **in** s is split and transferred to x. This feature is observed also in T-DEREF and T-ASSIGN.
- The ownership on a bound variable is forced to be **0** at the end of scope of the variable. For example, in T-LET, the type of x at the post type environment of s (i.e., the type environment at the end of the scope of x) is **0**. This is because x is made unreachable beyond this program point. Such a feature is observed also in T-LETNULL, T-MALLOC, and T-DEREF[5].
- If a program applies a destructive instruction to a variable of the type τ **ref**$_f$, then τ needs to be **0**. requires the type of x in the pre type environment to be **0 ref**$_1$. This is because $*x$ cannot be accessed beyond this program point. The same feature appears in T-ASSIGN where the type of x at the pre type environment is required to be **0 ref**$_1$.
- The instructions **assert**$(x = y)$ and **assert**$(x = *y)$ enable ownership transfer between variables. These instructions are provided as hints to a type checker. Such transfer is legitimate only if the assertions indeed hold. Although such annotation could be automatically generated using a must-alias analysis, the current implementation assumes that the annotations are inserted manually.

The following theorem is from Suenaga and Kobayashi [23].

Theorem 1 (Type soundness [23]). *If* $\vdash \langle D, s \rangle$, *then* $\langle D, s \rangle$ *is safe and memory-leak free.*

3   Program Transformation

As we mentioned in Section 1, the main idea of the algorithm is to see missing deallocations as type coercions and to discover such coercions. To this end, we introduce a pseudo-instruction $cast \langle \Gamma_1 \trianglelefteq \Gamma_2 \rangle$, which is interpreted as a sequence of instructions that coerce Γ_1 to Γ_2. The algorithm first inserts a *cast template* (i.e., a cast in which ownerships are left unknown) to every program point and then conducts constraint-based type inference to the resulting program. The algorithm decides which cast template should be replaced with deallocating statements based on the result of the type inference.

This section first introduces a cast. Then, we introduce the syntax of constraints, which is followed by the definition of the algorithm.

---

[5] Note that this does *not* necessary mean that the memory cell pointed to by x cannot escape; the ownership retained by x in s may be transferred to other variables before the scope of x ends.

$$\tau \trianglelefteq \tau \qquad \text{(S-Refl)}$$

$$\frac{\tau_1 \trianglelefteq \tau_2 \qquad \tau_2 \trianglelefteq \tau_3}{\tau_1 \trianglelefteq \tau_3} \quad \text{(S-Trans)}$$

$$\mathbf{0} \ \mathbf{ref}_1 \trianglelefteq \mathbf{0} \qquad \text{(S-Free)}$$

$$\mathbf{1} \trianglelefteq \mathbf{0} \qquad \text{(S-FreeList)}$$

$$\frac{f > 0 \qquad \tau_1 \trianglelefteq \tau_2}{\tau_1 \ \mathbf{ref}_f \trianglelefteq \tau_2 \ \mathbf{ref}_f} \quad \text{(S-Deref)}$$

$$\emptyset \trianglelefteq \emptyset \quad \text{(S-TEnvEmpty)}$$

$$\frac{\tau_1 \trianglelefteq \tau_2 \qquad \Gamma_1 \trianglelefteq \Gamma_2}{\Gamma_1, x{:}\tau_1 \trianglelefteq \Gamma_2, x{:}\tau_2} \qquad \text{(S-TEnv)}$$

Fig. 8. Definition of $\tau_1 \trianglelefteq \tau_2$ and $\Gamma_1 \trianglelefteq \Gamma_2$

$$\left[\!\!\left[\ \overline{\emptyset \trianglelefteq \emptyset} \ ^{\text{S-TEnvEmpty}}\right]\!\!\right] = \mathbf{skip}$$

$$\left[\!\!\left[\ \frac{\overset{\mathcal{D}_2}{\Gamma_1 \trianglelefteq \Gamma_2} \quad \overset{\mathcal{D}_1}{\tau_1 \trianglelefteq \tau_2}}{\Gamma_1, x{:}\tau_1 \trianglelefteq \Gamma_2, x{:}\tau_2} \ ^{\text{S-TEnv}}\right]\!\!\right] = \left[\!\!\left[\ \overset{\mathcal{D}_2}{\Gamma_1 \trianglelefteq \Gamma_2}\right]\!\!\right] ; \left[\!\!\left[\ \overset{\mathcal{D}_1}{\tau_1 \trianglelefteq \tau_2}\right]\!\!\right]_x$$

$$\left[\!\!\left[\ \overline{\tau \trianglelefteq \tau} \ ^{\text{S-Refl}}\right]\!\!\right]_x = \mathbf{skip}$$

$$\left[\!\!\left[\ \frac{\overset{\mathcal{D}_1}{\tau_1 \trianglelefteq \tau_3} \quad \overset{\mathcal{D}_2}{\tau_3 \trianglelefteq \tau_2}}{\tau_1 \trianglelefteq \tau_2} \ ^{\text{S-Trans}}\right]\!\!\right]_x = \left[\!\!\left[\ \overset{\mathcal{D}_1}{\tau_1 \trianglelefteq \tau_3}\right]\!\!\right]_x ; \left[\!\!\left[\ \overset{\mathcal{D}_2}{\tau_3 \trianglelefteq \tau_2}\right]\!\!\right]_x$$

$$\left[\!\!\left[\ \overline{\mathbf{0} \ \mathbf{ref}_1 \trianglelefteq \mathbf{0}} \ ^{\text{S-Free}}\right]\!\!\right]_x = \mathbf{free}(x)$$

$$\left[\!\!\left[\ \overline{\mathbf{1} \trianglelefteq \mathbf{0}} \ ^{\text{S-FreeList}}\right]\!\!\right]_x = \mathit{freelist}(x)$$

$$\left[\!\!\left[\ \frac{\overset{\mathcal{D}_1}{\tau_1 \trianglelefteq \tau_2} \quad f > 0}{\tau_1 \ \mathbf{ref}_f \trianglelefteq \tau_2 \ \mathbf{ref}_f} \ ^{\text{S-Deref}}\right]\!\!\right]_x = \mathbf{let}\ y = {*}x\ \mathbf{in}\ \left[\!\!\left[\ \overset{\mathcal{D}_1}{\tau_1 \trianglelefteq \tau_2}\right]\!\!\right]_y ; \mathbf{assert}(y = {*}x)$$

Fig. 9. Semantics of casts

3.1　Casts

We define a relation between types $\tau_1 \trianglelefteq \tau_2$ as the least reflexive transitive relation that satisfies the rules in Figure 8. This relation captures that the values of a type τ_1 can be coerced to those of a type τ_2 by certain sequence of statements[6]. The relation $\tau_1 \trianglelefteq \tau_2$ is extended to that between type environments $\Gamma_1 \trianglelefteq \Gamma_2$ in the pointwise manner.

We write $\langle \Gamma_1 \trianglelefteq \Gamma_2 \rangle$ for a statement that coerces Γ_1 to Γ_2; we call $\langle \Gamma_1 \trianglelefteq \Gamma_2 \rangle$ a *cast* from Γ_1 to Γ_2. The semantics of a cast $\langle \Gamma_1 \trianglelefteq \Gamma_2 \rangle$, defined in Figure 9, is given as a map from a derivation of $\Gamma_1 \trianglelefteq \Gamma_2$ to a statement. It is not defined if Γ_1 and Γ_2 do not match any cases in Figure 9. For example, we interpret a

---

[6] As the rule S-Free suggests, the current framework inserts $\mathbf{free}(x)$ only at a program point where x has the type $\mathbf{0}\ \mathbf{ref}_1$. Hence, if a pointer has an ownership less than 1, one first needs to insert assertions so that the pointer has type $\mathbf{0}\ \mathbf{ref}_1$. Relaxing this restriction is left as future work.

$$\varphi \quad \in \mathbf{OVar}$$
$$\tau, \sigma ::= (\mu\alpha.\alpha \; \mathbf{ref}_f) \; \mathbf{ref}_{f'}$$
$$q \quad \in \{x \in \mathbb{Q} \mid 0 \leq x \leq 1\}$$
$$f \quad ::= \varphi \mid q \mid f_1 + f_2$$
$$c \quad ::= \tau_1 \trianglelefteq \tau_2 \mid f_1 \leq f_2 \mid c_1 \implies c_2$$
$$C \quad :: \{c_1, \ldots, c_n\}$$

Syntax sugars:

$$(f_1 = f_2) := \{f_1 \leq f_2, f_2 \leq f_1\}$$
$$(\tau_1 = \tau_2) := \{\tau_1 \trianglelefteq \tau_2, \tau_2 \trianglelefteq \tau_1\}$$
$$\mathbf{empty}((\mu\alpha.\alpha \; \mathbf{ref}_f) \; \mathbf{ref}_{f_1}) := (f = 0) \cup (f_1 = 0)$$
$$\mathbf{wf}((\mu\alpha.\alpha \; \mathbf{ref}_f) \; \mathbf{ref}_{f'}) := (f' = 0 \implies f = 0)$$

Fig. 10. Syntax of constraints

derivation

$$\frac{}{x:0 \; \mathbf{ref}_1 \trianglelefteq x:0} \; \text{S-Free}$$

as **free**(x), whereas

$$\frac{}{x:0 \trianglelefteq x:0} \; \text{S-Refl}$$

as **skip**. We define $[\![s]\!]$ as a statement that is obtained by applying $[\![\cdot]\!]$ to each occurrence of a cast in s. $[\![(\widetilde{x})s]\!]$ and $[\![\langle D, s\rangle]\!]$ are defined in the same way.

The definition in Figure 9 uses as a function *freelist*. This function, given a pointer x to a list of cells, deallocates all the cells reachable from x. Concretely, *freelist* is defined as follows:

$$freelist(x) = \mathbf{ifnull} \; x \; \mathbf{then} \; \mathbf{skip} \; \mathbf{else} \; \mathbf{let} \; y = *x \; \mathbf{in} \; freelist(y); \mathbf{free}(x).$$

In the rest of the paper, we assume that D contains the definition above and that Θ contains *freelist*$:(1) \to (0)$.

With this relation, the typing rule for cast instructions is as follows:

$$\frac{\Gamma_1 \trianglelefteq \Gamma_2}{\Gamma_1 \vdash_\Theta \langle \Gamma_1 \trianglelefteq \Gamma_2 \rangle \implies \Gamma_2.} \tag{T-Cast}$$

It is easy to observe that $[\![\Gamma_1 \trianglelefteq \Gamma_2]\!]$ is defined if $\Gamma_1 \trianglelefteq \Gamma_2$ holds.

The following property holds for a cast instruction.

Lemma 1. *If $\Gamma_1 \trianglelefteq \Gamma_2$, then $\Gamma_1 \vdash_\Theta [\![\Gamma_1 \trianglelefteq \Gamma_2]\!] \implies \Gamma_2$.*

3.2 Constraints

Figure 10 defines the syntax of constraints. By abusing notation, we use meta-variables f and τ for expressions used in constraints; f for expressions for ownerships and τ for expressions for types. We use a meta-variable q for the elements of $\{x \in \mathbb{Q} \mid 0 \leq x \leq 1\}$. We also use the symbol $\trianglelefteq$ for constraints. We designate the set of countably infinite set **OVar** for *ownership variables*, unknowns for ownerships in constraints; the set is ranged over by φ. We write $\mathbf{FOV}(c)$ and $\mathbf{FOV}(s)$ for the set of ownership variables that appear in c and s respectively. we write $\mathbf{FOV}(C)$ for $\bigcup_{c \in C} \mathbf{FOV}(c)$.

In order to keep the type inference simple, we designate *type templates*; every reference type is assumed to be of the form $(\mu\alpha.\alpha\ \mathbf{ref}_f)\ \mathbf{ref}_{f'}$. The algorithm could be extended so that it deals with more complex templates (see Section 3.5.)

A *model* θ is a substitution of $\{x \in \mathbb{Q} \mid 0 \leq x \leq 1\}$ to **OVar**. We write $\theta \models c$ if θc is valid: $\theta \models \tau_1 \trianglelefteq \tau_2$ if and only if $\theta\tau_1 \trianglelefteq \theta\tau_2$; $\theta \models f_1 \leq f_2$ if and only if $\theta f_1 \leq \theta f_2$; and $\theta \models c_1 \implies c_2$ if and only if $\theta \not\models c_1$ or $\theta \models c_2$. We write $\theta \models C$ if $\theta \models c$ for any $c \in C$.

3.3   Algorithm

The transformation algorithm $\mathcal{L}(\langle D, s\rangle)$ is defined as follows:

$$\mathcal{L}(\langle D, s\rangle) =$$
$$\quad \textbf{let}\ \langle D', s'\rangle = \mathcal{I}(\langle D, s\rangle) \qquad (\text{* insertion of casts *})$$
$$\quad \textbf{let}\ C = \mathcal{C}^{prog}(\langle D', s'\rangle) \qquad (\text{* constraint generation *})$$
$$\quad \textbf{if}\ C\ \text{is unsatisfiable}\ \textbf{then fail}$$
$$\quad \textbf{else let}\ \theta\ \text{be a model s.t.}\ \theta \models C\ (\text{* model extraction*})$$
$$\quad [\![\langle \theta D, \theta s\rangle]\!]. \qquad (\text{* reduction of casts *})$$

The algorithm $\mathcal{L}$ first inserts a cast instruction to every program point with the algorithm $\mathcal{I}$ introduced later. Then, $\mathcal{L}$ generates a set of constraints C following the typing rules in Figure 7. If C is satisfiable, $\mathcal{L}$ extracts a model θ, applies it to the program, and then reduces every cast according to the definition in Figure 9.

We present each step in more detail in the rest of this section. The explanation is followed by soundness and completeness of $\mathcal{L}$.

Cast Insertion Algorithm. Given a statement, the algorithm $\mathcal{L}$ first inserts a cast template (i.e., a cast that contains type templates) at every location. $\mathcal{I}(\langle D, s\rangle)$ in Figure 11 defines the algorithm to insert cast templates. Let $templT()$ be a procedure that outputs a fresh type template $\mu\alpha.\alpha\ \mathbf{ref}_\varphi\ \mathbf{ref}_{\varphi'}$ such that φ and φ' are fresh ownership variables. Then, the procedure $templTE(S)$, where S is a set of variables, outputs a type environment $\bigcup_{x \in S} \{x \mapsto templTE()\}$.

The definition of $\mathcal{I}$ is kept redundant deliberately: resulting programs in general contain two or more adjacent casts, although two or more subsequent casts could be collapsed to one. We, however, use the current definition because it makes the proof of completeness easier.

Constraint-Generation Algorithm. Figure 12 defines the constraint-generation function $\mathcal{C}_\Theta$ for statements. The algorithm takes a statement s and a

$$\mathcal{I}(\langle \widetilde{d}, s \rangle) = \langle \widetilde{\mathcal{I}(d)}, \mathcal{I}(s, \emptyset) \rangle$$
$$\mathcal{I}((\widetilde{x})s) = (\widetilde{x})\mathcal{I}(s, \{\widetilde{x}\}); \langle templTE(\{\widetilde{x}\}) \trianglelefteq templTE(\{\widetilde{x}\}) \rangle$$

$$\mathcal{I}(\mathbf{skip}, S) = \langle templTE(S) \trianglelefteq templTE(S) \rangle$$
$$\mathcal{I}(s_1; s_2, S) = \mathcal{I}(s_1, S); \mathcal{I}(s_2, S)$$
$$\mathcal{I}(\mathbf{let}\ x = v\ \mathbf{in}\ s, S) =$$
$$\quad \langle templTE(S) \trianglelefteq templTE(S) \rangle;$$
$$\quad \mathbf{let}\ x = v\ \mathbf{in}\ \mathcal{I}(s, \{x\} \cup S); \langle templTE(\{x\} \cup S) \trianglelefteq templTE(\{x\} \cup S) \rangle$$
$$\mathcal{I}(F(x_1, \ldots, x_n), S) = \langle templTE(S) \trianglelefteq templTE(S) \rangle; F(x_1, \ldots, x_n)$$
$$\mathcal{I}(\mathbf{let}\ x = \mathbf{malloc}()\ \mathbf{in}\ s, S) =$$
$$\quad \langle templTE(S) \trianglelefteq templTE(S) \rangle;$$
$$\quad \mathbf{let}\ x = \mathbf{malloc}()\ \mathbf{in}\ (\mathcal{I}(s, \{x\} \cup S); \langle templTE(\{x\} \cup S) \trianglelefteq templTE(\{x\} \cup S) \rangle)$$
$$\mathcal{I}(\mathbf{free}(x), S) = \langle templTE(S) \trianglelefteq templTE(S) \rangle; \mathbf{free}(x)$$
$$\mathcal{I}(\mathbf{let}\ x = *y\ \mathbf{in}\ s, S) =$$
$$\quad \langle templTE(S) \trianglelefteq templTE(S) \rangle;$$
$$\quad \mathbf{let}\ x = *y\ \mathbf{in}\ (\mathcal{I}(s, \{x\} \cup S); \langle templTE(\{x\} \cup S) \trianglelefteq templTE(\{x\} \cup S) \rangle)$$
$$\mathcal{I}(*x \leftarrow y, S) = \langle templTE(S) \trianglelefteq templTE(S) \rangle; *x \leftarrow y$$
$$\mathcal{I}(\mathbf{ifnull}\ x\ \mathbf{then}\ s_1\ \mathbf{else}\ s_2, S) =$$
$$\quad \langle templTE(S) \trianglelefteq templTE(S) \rangle;$$
$$\quad \mathbf{ifnull}\ x\ \mathbf{then}$$
$$\qquad \mathcal{I}(s_1, S); \langle templTE(S) \trianglelefteq templTE(S) \rangle$$
$$\quad \mathbf{else}$$
$$\qquad \mathcal{I}(s_2, S); \langle templTE(S) \trianglelefteq templTE(S) \rangle$$
$$\mathcal{I}(\mathbf{assert}(x = y), S) = \langle templTE(S) \trianglelefteq templTE(S) \rangle; \mathbf{assert}(x = y)$$
$$\mathcal{I}(\mathbf{assert}(x = *y), S) = \langle templTE(S) \trianglelefteq templTE(S) \rangle; \mathbf{assert}(x = *y)$$

Fig. 11. Insertion of casts

post type environment Γ' as input, and returns a pre type environment Γ and a set of constraints C that is imposed to make $\Gamma \vdash_\Theta s \Longrightarrow \Gamma'$ correct. The procedure $newtempl()$ outputs a pair of a fresh type template τ and the constraint set $\mathbf{wf}(\tau)$. The algorithm $\mathcal{C}_\Theta$ is used in the constraint generation for function definitions and programs; the definition of these cases are in Figure 13.

The constraint-generation algorithm follows the standard design of constraint-based type inference [15]; the algorithm constructs a derivation tree following the rules in Figure 7. Concretely, $\mathcal{C}_\Theta$ is designed so that the following property holds.

Lemma 2. *Suppose s is an output of the algorithm $\mathcal{I}$. Then, if $(\Gamma, C) = \mathcal{C}_\Theta(s, \Gamma')$ and $\theta \models C$, then $\mathbf{dom}(\Gamma) = \mathbf{dom}(\Gamma')$ and $\theta\Gamma \vdash_{\theta\Theta} \theta s \Longrightarrow \theta\Gamma'$.*

Solving Constraints. The last step of the algorithm $\mathcal{L}$ is to solve the constraints generated by $\mathcal{C}$. First, the constraints of the shape $\tau_1 \trianglelefteq \tau_2$ is reduced into linear inequalities over ownership variables.

$\mathcal{C}_\Theta(\mathbf{skip}, \Gamma) = (\Gamma, \emptyset)$

$\mathcal{C}_\Theta(s_1; s_2, \Gamma_2) = (\Gamma_1, C_1 \cup C_2)$
     where $(\Gamma, C_1) = \mathcal{C}_\Theta(s_2, \Gamma_2)$ $(\Gamma_1, C_2) = \mathcal{C}_\Theta(s_1, \Gamma)$

$\mathcal{C}_\Theta(\mathbf{let}\ x = y\ \mathbf{in}\ s, \Gamma') = (\Gamma \cup \{y : \tau_1 + \tau_2\}, C_1)$
     where $(\Gamma_1, C_1) = \mathcal{C}_\Theta(s, \Gamma' \cup \{x : \mathbf{0}\})$ $\Gamma = \Gamma_1 \backslash \{x, y\}$ $\tau_1 = \Gamma_1(x)$ $\tau_2 = \Gamma_1(y)$

$\mathcal{C}_\Theta(\mathbf{let}\ x = \mathbf{null}\ \mathbf{in}\ s, \Gamma') = (\Gamma, C_1)$
     where $(\Gamma_1, C_1) = \mathcal{C}_\Theta(s, \Gamma' \cup \{x : \mathbf{0}\})$ $\Gamma = \Gamma_1 \backslash \{x\}$

$\mathcal{C}_\Theta(F(x_1, \ldots, x_n), \Gamma') = (\Gamma \cup \{x_1 : \tau_1, \ldots, x_n : \tau_n\}, C_1)$
     where $(\tau_1, \ldots, \tau_n) \to (\tau'_1, \ldots, \tau'_n) = \Theta(F)$
       $\Gamma = \Gamma' \backslash \{x_1, \ldots, x_n\}$ $C_1 = \bigcup_i (\Gamma'(x_i) = \tau'_i)$

$\mathcal{C}_\Theta(\mathbf{let}\ x = \mathbf{malloc}()\ \mathbf{in}\ s, \Gamma') = (\Gamma, C_1 \cup C_2)$
     where $(\Gamma_1, C_1) = \mathcal{C}_\Theta(s, \Gamma' \cup \{x : \mathbf{0}\})$ $\Gamma = \Gamma_1 \backslash x$
       $(\mu\alpha.\alpha\ \mathbf{ref}_{f'})\ \mathbf{ref}_f = \Gamma_1(x)$ $C_2 = (f = 1) \cup (f' = 0)$

$\mathcal{C}_\Theta(\mathbf{free}(x), \Gamma_1) = (\Gamma \cup \{x : \mathbf{0}\ \mathbf{ref}_1\}, C_1)$
     where $\Gamma = \Gamma_1 \backslash x$ $\tau = \Gamma_1(x)$ $C_1 = \mathbf{empty}(\tau)$

$\mathcal{C}_\Theta(\mathbf{let}\ x = *y\ \mathbf{in}\ s, \Gamma') = (\Gamma \cup \{y : (\mu\alpha.\alpha\ \mathbf{ref}_{f_1 + f_2})\ \mathbf{ref}_{f'_2}\}, C_1 \cup C_2)$
     where $(\Gamma_1, C_1) = \mathcal{C}_\Theta(s, \Gamma' \cup \{x : \mathbf{0}\})$ $\Gamma = \Gamma_1 \backslash \{x, y\}$ $C_2 = (f'_2 > 0) \cup (f_1 = f'_1)$
       $(\mu\alpha.\alpha\ \mathbf{ref}_{f_1})\ \mathbf{ref}_{f'_1} = \Gamma_1(x)$ $(\mu\alpha.\alpha\ \mathbf{ref}_{f_2})\ \mathbf{ref}_{f'_2} = \Gamma_1(y)$

$\mathcal{C}_\Theta(*x \leftarrow y, \Gamma') = ((\Gamma' \backslash \{x, y\}) \cup \{x : \mathbf{0}\ \mathbf{ref}_1, y : (\mu\alpha.\alpha\ \mathbf{ref}_{f_1 + f_2})\ \mathbf{ref}_{f_1 + f'_2}\}, f'_1 = 1)$
     where $(\mu\alpha.\alpha\ \mathbf{ref}_{f_1})\ \mathbf{ref}_{f'_1} = \Gamma'(x)$ $(\mu\alpha.\alpha\ \mathbf{ref}_{f_2})\ \mathbf{ref}_{f'_2} = \Gamma'(y)$

$\mathcal{C}_\Theta(\mathbf{ifnull}\ x\ \mathbf{then}\ s_1\ \mathbf{else}\ s_2, \Gamma') = (\Gamma_2, C_1 \cup C_2 \cup C_3)$
     where $(\Gamma_1, C_1) = \mathcal{C}_\Theta(s_1, \Gamma')$ $(\Gamma_2, C_2) = \mathcal{C}_\Theta(s_2, \Gamma')$ $\Gamma'_1 = \Gamma_1 \backslash x$ $\Gamma'_2 = \Gamma_2 \backslash x$
       $C_3 = \bigcup_{y \in \mathbf{dom}(\Gamma'_1)} (\Gamma'_1(y) = \Gamma'_2(y))$

$\mathcal{C}_\Theta(\mathbf{assert}(x = y), \Gamma') = (\Gamma \cup \{x : \tau_1, y : \tau_2\}, C_1 \cup C_2 \cup C_3)$
     where $\Gamma = \Gamma' \backslash \{x, y\}$ $((\tau_1, C_1), (\tau_2, C_2)) = (newtempl(), newtempl())$
       $C_3 = (\tau_1 + \tau_2 = \Gamma'(x) + \Gamma'(y))$

$\mathcal{C}_\Theta(\mathbf{assert}(x = *y), \Gamma') = (\Gamma \cup \{x : (\mu\alpha.\alpha\ \mathbf{ref}_{\varphi_1})\ \mathbf{ref}_{\varphi'_1}, y : (\mu\alpha.\alpha\ \mathbf{ref}_{\varphi_2})\ \mathbf{ref}_{f'_2}\}, C)$
     where $\Gamma = \Gamma' \backslash \{x, y\}$ $C = C_1$
       $((\mu\alpha.\alpha\ \mathbf{ref}_{f_1})\ \mathbf{ref}_{f'_1}, (\mu\alpha.\alpha\ \mathbf{ref}_{f_2})\ \mathbf{ref}_{f'_2}) = (\Gamma'(x), \Gamma'(y))$
       $\varphi_1, \varphi'_1, \varphi_2 = newovar(), newovar(), newovar()$
       $C_1 = (f'_2 > 0) \cup (\varphi_1 + \varphi_2 = f_1 + f_2) \cup (\varphi'_1 + \varphi_2 = f'_1 + f_2)$

$\mathcal{C}_\Theta(\langle \Gamma_1 \trianglelefteq \Gamma_2 \rangle, \Gamma') = (\Gamma_1, C_1)$
     where $C_1 = \bigcup_{x \in \mathbf{dom}(\Gamma')} (\Gamma'(x) = \Gamma_2(x)) \cup \bigcup_{x \in \mathbf{dom}(\Gamma_1)} (\Gamma_1(x) \trianglelefteq \Gamma_2(x))$

Fig. 12. Constraint generation for statements

$$\mathcal{C}_\Theta^{def}((x_1,\ldots,x_n)s,(\tau_1,\ldots,\tau_n) \to (\tau_1',\ldots,\tau_n')) = C_1 \cup C_2$$
$$\text{where } (\Gamma, C_1) = \mathcal{C}_\Theta(s, \{x_1 : \tau_1', \ldots, x_n : \tau_n'\})$$
$$C_2 = \bigcup_{i \in \{1,\ldots,n\}}(\Gamma(x_i) = \tau_i)$$

$$\mathcal{C}^{prog}(\langle D, s \rangle) = C \cup C'$$
$$\text{where } ((\tau_1^{F_d}, C_1^{F_d}), \ldots, (\tau_n^{F_d}, C_n^{F_d})) = (newtempl(), \ldots, newtempl())$$
$$((\tau_1^{F_c}, C_1^{F_c}), \ldots, (\tau_n^{F_c}, C_n^{F_c})) = (newtempl(), \ldots, newtempl())$$
$$\text{for each } (F \mapsto (x_1, \ldots, x_n)s) \in D$$
$$\Theta = \bigcup_{F \in \mathbf{dom}(D)}\{F : (\tau_1^{F_d}, \ldots, \tau_n^{F_d}) \to (\tau_1^{F_c}, \ldots, \tau_n^{F_c})\}$$
$$C = \bigcup_{F \in \mathbf{dom}(D)} \mathcal{C}_\Theta^{def}(D(F), \Theta(F)) \cup \bigcup_{1 \le i \le n}(C_i^{F_d} \cup C_i^{F_c})$$
$$C' = \mathcal{C}_\Theta(s, \emptyset)$$

Fig. 13. Constraint generation for function definitions and programs

Concretely, a set of constraints C is converted to the following formula F_C:

$$\bigwedge_{\varphi \in \mathbf{FOV}(C)} 0 \le \varphi \le 1 \wedge \bigwedge_{f_1 \le f_2 \in C}(f_1 \le f_2)$$
$$\wedge \bigwedge_{(\mu\alpha.\alpha \, \mathbf{ref}_f) \, \mathbf{ref}_{f_1} \trianglelefteq (\mu\alpha.\alpha \, \mathbf{ref}_{f'}) \, \mathbf{ref}_{f_1'} \in C}(Sub(f, f_1, f', f_1')),$$

where $Sub(f, f_1, f', f_1')$ is defined as follows:

$$Sub(f, f_1, f', f_1') :=$$
$$(f = f' \wedge f_1 = f_1')$$
$$\vee (f = 0 \wedge f_1 = 1 \wedge f' = 0 \wedge f_1' = 0)$$
$$\vee ((f = f' \vee (f = 1 \wedge f' = 0)) \wedge f_1 = f_1' \wedge f_1 > 0)$$
$$\vee (f = 1 \wedge f_1 = 1 \wedge f' = 0 \wedge f_1' = 0).$$

The formula $Sub(f, f_1, f', f_1')$ is equivalent to the disjunction of four cases in Figure 8.

Lemma 3. $\theta \models F_C$ if and only if $\theta \models C$.

Then, this reduced constraint is solved by an off-the-shelf solver such as an SMT solver. Notice that the reduced constraint is decidable because the constraint set C is a Boolean combination of linear inequalities.

After solving the constraints, the algorithm applies the obtained model to the program. Then, every cast can be replaced with its interpretation.

3.4 Soundness and Completeness

$\mathcal{L}$ is sound with respect to the type system in Section 2.2:

Theorem 2 (Soundness of $\mathcal{L}$). If $\mathcal{L}(\langle D, s \rangle) = \langle D', s' \rangle$, then $\vdash_\Theta \langle D', s' \rangle$.

We have completeness of $\mathcal{L}$ in the following sense. Let us write $\mathcal{F}(s)$, where s is cast-free, for the statement obtained by replacing all the **free**(x) with **skip**. The program $\mathcal{F}(\langle D, s\rangle)$ is defined in the same way. If s can be made well-typed within the types of the form $(\mu\alpha.\alpha\ \mathbf{ref}_f)\ \mathbf{ref}_{f'}$ by inserting memory-deallocating instructions, then $\mathcal{L}$, with the help of a smart-enough SMT solver, successfully finds a way to insert those instructions.

Lemma 4. *If there is a derivation of* $\theta' \Gamma_1 \vdash_\Theta \theta' s \implies \theta' \Gamma_2$ *with the types of the shape* $(\mu\alpha.\alpha\ \mathbf{ref}_f)\ \mathbf{ref}_{f'}$, *then there are* Γ_1' *and* θ *such that* $(\Gamma_1', C) = \mathcal{C}_\Theta(\mathcal{I}(\mathcal{F}(s), \mathrm{dom}(\Gamma_2)), \Gamma_2)$ *and* $\theta \models C$ *and* $\Gamma_1 = \theta\Gamma_1'$.

Theorem 3 (Completeness of $\mathcal{L}$).
If there is a derivation of $\vdash \langle D, s\rangle$ *with the types of the shape* $(\mu\alpha.\alpha\ \mathbf{ref}_f)\ \mathbf{ref}_{f'}$, *then there is* $\langle D', s'\rangle$ *such that* $\langle D', s'\rangle = \mathcal{L}(\mathcal{F}(\langle D, s\rangle))$ *and* $\vdash \langle D', s'\rangle$.

Remark 4. We need to prove that $\mathcal{L}(s)$ is somewhat equivalent to s (e.g., in the sense of termination). We leave it as future work, which we do not expect to be difficult.

Remark 5. Notice that $\mathcal{L}$ is in general non-deterministic due to the choice of models for generated constraints. The current experimental implementation arbitrarily picks up a model returned by an SMT solver (Z3 [6] in the current implementation). However, it would be more plausible if we can pick up a "better" models. Investigation of a measure for a better model (e.g., worst or average memory consumption) is an interesting direction of future work.

3.5 Extension

We can make the algorithm described so far more powerful by using more expressive templates. One of such templates is $(\mu\alpha.\alpha\ \mathbf{ref}_f)\ \mathbf{ref}_{f_1,\ldots,f_n}$ where $\tau\ \mathbf{ref}_{f_1,\ldots,f_n}$ is an abbreviation for $\tau\ \mathbf{ref}_{f_1}\ldots\mathbf{ref}_{f_n}$. The cast insertion for the extended templates is the same as $\mathcal{I}$ except for the definition of $templTE(S)$ that returns a type template of the form $\tau\ \mathbf{ref}_{f_1,\ldots,f_n}$. The extension of the constraint generation $\mathcal{C}$ is straightforward. The SMT formula F_C is extended as follows:

$$\bigwedge_{\varphi\in\mathbf{FOV}(C)} 0 \leq \varphi \leq 1 \wedge \bigwedge_{f_1 \leq f_2 \in C} (f_1 \leq f_2) \wedge \bigwedge_{\tau \trianglelefteq \tau' \in C} Sub(\tau, \tau')$$

where $Sub(\tau, \tau')$ is defined by

$$
\begin{aligned}
Sub(&(\mu\alpha.\alpha\ \mathbf{ref}_f)\ \mathbf{ref}_{f_1}, (\mu\alpha.\alpha\ \mathbf{ref}_{f'})\ \mathbf{ref}_{f_1'}) = \\
&(f = f' \wedge f_1 = f_1') \\
&\vee (f = 0 \wedge f_1 = 1 \wedge f' = 0 \wedge f_1' = 0) \\
&\vee ((f = f' \vee (f = 1 \wedge f' = 0)) \wedge f_1 = f_1' \wedge f_1 > 0) \\
&\vee (f = 1 \wedge f_1 = 1 \wedge f' = 0 \wedge f_1' = 0). \\
Sub(&(\mu\alpha.\alpha\ \mathbf{ref}_f)\ \mathbf{ref}_{f_1,\ldots,f_{n+1}}, (\mu\alpha.\alpha\ \mathbf{ref}_{f'})\ \mathbf{ref}_{f_1',\ldots,f_{n+1}'}) = \\
&Sub(f_n, f_{n+1}, f_n', f_{n+1}') \wedge \qquad\qquad (*\ Sub\ in\ Section\ 3.3\ *) \\
&Sub((\mu\alpha.\alpha\ \mathbf{ref}_f)\ \mathbf{ref}_{f_1,\ldots,f_n}, (\mu\alpha.\alpha\ \mathbf{ref}_{f'})\ \mathbf{ref}_{f_1',\ldots,f_n'}).
\end{aligned}
$$

4   Related Work

Our algorithm is designed on top of the type system by Suenaga and Kobayashi [23]. For relevant related work on memory-leak freedom verification, we refer readers to [23]. We discuss related work on automated error correction in what follows.

Khedker, Sanyal, and Karkare [12] propose a program transformation algorithm for improving memory efficiency of Java programs. Their algorithm analyzes liveness of references and nullifies them at a program point where they are not live any more. Such nullification of a reference makes it possible for a garbage collector, which approximates memory-cell liveness by reachability from root variables [18, 19], to reclaim more memory cells. They also present how their technique can be applied to C and C++ programs, in which they apply memory-deallocating instructions in place of nullification.

For this purpose, they use an *access graph* that summarizes how each reference in a program is used. Our types are analogous to access graphs in the sense that both approximate the usage of a pointer in a program. Although we need to further investigate the technical difference between access graphs and our types, one possible comparison would be the property guaranteed: They only guarantee that their program transformation does not introduce more null-pointer exceptions, which is an analogue of our Theorem 1 and 2. Memory-leak freedom in our sense is out of the scope of their work although memory efficiency is demonstrated empirically.

Ajiro, Ueda, and Cho [1] propose automated mode-error correction for a concurrent logic programming language. Their algorithm generates *moding constraints* (i.e., constraints on the direction of information flow of each variable occurrence); if the generated constraints are unsatisfiable, the algorithm suggests correction analyzing a minimal unsatisfiable subset of the constraints. They intend their algorithm to be an aid for debugging; thus, they do not need to guarantee that their transformation generates a program that follows the intention of a programmer. We do need to guarantee correctness because the algorithm proposed in the current paper is for verification; it is indeed possible because we focus only on memory-leak freedom.

Singh, Gulwani, and Solar-Lezama [20] propose a feedback-making algorithm for programming classes. The algorithm finds a correction to a program submitted by students. A tutor provides a reference implementation and an *error model*, a set of probable errors made by students, for each programming task. Their system is supposed to be used in programming classes where the specification of submitted programs are known completely and a set of probable errors is quite limited. Though we do not make such assumptions, their idea might be useful for our algorithm in choosing a model from multiple candidates.

Könighofer and Bloem [13] propose a method for localization and automated correction. Their approach is based on model-based diagnosis [5, 16] and concolic execution [7, 17]. Their algorithm first finds the set of statements that may be corrected using an SMT solver and attempts to correct expressions in these statements by template-based synthesis (e.g., [4]). Their approach cannot be directly applied to our problem because the former phase, in our setting, requires an appropriate handling of aliases; our algorithm addresses this issue with ownerships.

5 Conclusion

We have proposed a program transformation that correctly inserts memory-deallocating instructions to a program. The transformation is based on the ownership-based type system by Suenaga and Kobayashi [23]; it is extended with subtyping to capture ownership disposal. The transformation conducts type inference for the extended type system to detect where to insert deallocating-instructions.

Although we have an experimental implementation of the proposed transformation, our translator currently deals with only the toy language in Section 2. We plan to implement a translator for full-fledged C by extending FreeSafeTy [23]. We also plan to extend our transformation with concurrency following the idea by Suenaga et al. [22].

References

1. Ajiro, Y., Ueda, K., Cho, K.: Error-correcting source code. In: Maher, M.J., Puget, J.-F. (eds.) CP 1998. LNCS, vol. 1520, pp. 40–54. Springer, Heidelberg (1998)
2. Boyland, J.: Checking interference with fractional permissions. In: Cousot, R. (ed.) SAS 2003. LNCS, vol. 2694, pp. 55–72. Springer, Heidelberg (2003)
3. Clarke, D.G., Potter, J., Noble, J.: Ownership types for flexible alias protection. In: Freeman-Benson, B.N., Chambers, C. (eds.) OOPSLA, pp. 48–64. ACM (1998)
4. Colón, M.A., Sankaranarayanan, S., Sipma, H.B.: Linear invariant generation using non-linear constraint solving. In: Hunt Jr., W.A., Somenzi, F. (eds.) CAV 2003. LNCS, vol. 2725, pp. 420–432. Springer, Heidelberg (2003)
5. de Kleer, J., Williams, B.C.: Diagnosing multiple faults. Artif. Intell. 32(1), 97–130 (1987)
6. de Moura, L., Bjørner, N.: Z3: An efficient SMT solver. In: Ramakrishnan, C.R., Rehof, J. (eds.) TACAS 2008. LNCS, vol. 4963, pp. 337–340. Springer, Heidelberg (2008)
7. Godefroid, P., Klarlund, N., Sen, K.: DART: directed automated random testing. In: Sarkar, V., Hall, M.W. (eds.) PLDI, pp. 213–223. ACM (2005)
8. Gotsman, A., Berdine, J., Cook, B., Rinetzky, N., Sagiv, M.: Local reasoning for storable locks and threads. Technical Report MSR-TR-2007-39, Microsoft Research (2007)
9. Hastings, R., Joyce, B.: Purify: Fast detection of memory leaks and access errors. In: Proc. of the Winter 1992 USENIX Conference, San Francisco, California, pp. 125–138 (1991)
10. Heine, D.L., Lam, M.S.: A practical flow-sensitive and context-sensitive C and C++ memory leak detector. In: Cytron, R., Gupta, R. (eds.) PLDI, pp. 168–181. ACM (2003)
11. Kernighan, B.W., Ritchie, D.: The C Programming Language, 2nd edn. Prentice-Hall (1988)

12. Khedker, U.P., Sanyal, A., Karkare, A.: Heap reference analysis using access graphs (2007)
13. Könighofer, R., Bloem, R.: Automated error localization and correction for imperative programs. In: Bjesse, P., Slobodová, A. (eds.) FMCAD, pp. 91–100. FMCAD Inc. (2011)
14. Nethercote, N., Seward, J.: Valgrind: A framework for heavyweight dynamic binary instrumentation. In: Ferrante, J., McKinley, K.S. (eds.) PLDI, pp. 89–100. ACM (2007)
15. Nielson, F., Nielson, H.R., Hankin, C.: Principles of program analysis (2. corr. print). Springer (2005)
16. Reiter, R.: A theory of diagnosis from first principles. Artif. Intell. 32(1), 57–95 (1987)
17. Sen, K., Marinov, D., Agha, G.: CUTE: A concolic unit testing engine for C. In: Wermelinger, M., Gall, H. (eds.) ESEC/SIGSOFT FSE, pp. 263–272. ACM (2005)
18. Shaham, R., Kolodner, E.K., Sagiv, S.: Heap profiling for space-efficient java. In: Burke, M., Soffa, M.L. (eds.) PLDI, pp. 104–113. ACM (2001)
19. Shaham, R., Kolodner, E.K., Sagiv, S.: Estimating the impact of heap liveness information on space consumption in java. In: Boehm, H., Detlefs, D. (eds.) MSP/ISMM, pp. 171–182. ACM (2002)
20. Singh, R., Gulwani, S., Solar-Lezama, A.: Automated feedback generation for introductory programming assignments. In: Boehm, H.-J., Flanagan, C. (eds.) PLDI, pp. 15–26. ACM (2013)
21. Stroustrup, B.: The C++ programming language - special edition, 3rd edn. Addison-Wesley (2007)
22. Suenaga, K., Fukuda, R., Igarashi, A.: Type-based safe resource deallocation for shared-memory concurrency. In: Leavens, G.T., Dwyer, M.B. (eds.) OOPSLA, pp. 1–20. ACM (2012)
23. Suenaga, K., Kobayashi, N.: Fractional ownerships for safe memory deallocation. In: Hu, Z. (ed.) APLAS 2009. LNCS, vol. 5904, pp. 128–143. Springer, Heidelberg (2009)
24. Terauchi, T.: Checking race freedom via linear programming. In: Proc. of PLDI, pp. 1–10 (2008)

The Essence of Ruby*

Katsuhiro Ueno, Yutaka Fukasawa**,
Akimasa Morihata***, and Atsushi Ohori

Research Institute of Electric Communication, Tohoku University, Japan
{katsu,fukasawa,morihata,ohori}@riec.tohoku.ac.jp

Abstract. Ruby is a dynamic, object-oriented language with advanced features such as `yield` operator and dynamic class manipulation. They make Ruby a popular, highly productive scripting language, but they also make the semantics of Ruby complicated and difficult to understand. Even the JIS/ISO standard of Ruby seems to contain some ambiguities. For Ruby to be established as a reliable scripting language, it should have a rigorous semantics. To meet this challenge, we present a formal operational semantics that can serve as a high-level specification for both the users and implementers. The key insight underlying the semantics is that various elaborate features of Ruby can be cleanly represented as a composition of two orthogonal calculi: one for objects and classes and the other for representing control. The presented semantics leads straightforwardly to a reference implementation. Initial evaluation of our implementation confirms that the presented semantics conforms to commonly accepted Ruby behavior.

Keywords: Ruby, operational semantics, iterator, dynamic language.

1 Introduction

Ruby is a dynamic object-oriented language. Its design rationale is to provide the programmer a language that is easy and natural to write programs with maximum freedom. Its rich set of control abstractions such as *iterator* with `yield` operator enable the programmer to write sophisticated programs succinctly and efficiently, and its flexible dynamic semantics allows the programmer to configure evaluation environment including classes and their method suites. These features make Ruby a popular, highly productive scripting language. These features, however, make the semantics of Ruby complicated and difficult to understand. Clear and formal understanding of the semantics is essential for reasoning, verification, and thereby developing reliable software.

To address this issue, the designers and the user communities have been trying to define the standard of the language. The efforts have culminated to the

---

* The first author has been partially supported by JSPS KAKENHI Grant Number 24700021. The first and fourth author has been partially supported by JSPS KAKENHI Grant Number 25280019.

** The second author's current affiliation: Marvelous Inc.

*** The third author's current affiliation: The University of Tokyo.

J. Garrigue (Ed.): APLAS 2014, LNCS 8858, pp. 78–98, 2014.

JIS (Japanese Industrial Standard) standard [10] of Ruby followed by the ISO standard [8]. We based our research on the original JIS standard [10] written in Japanese; the ISO counterpart [8] is essentially the same. This 226 pages document defines the syntax and the semantics of Ruby in details by defining global run-time states including 7 independent run-time stacks, and specifying how each syntax of Ruby mutates the run-time states.

Studying the details of this document, we find it admirable to have completed the detailed descriptions of the evaluation process of all the language constructs. It can certainly serve as a guideline for a particular style of Ruby implementations, including the widely used CRuby interpreter [15]. As a specification of the semantics of Ruby, however, there seem to contain certain amount of ambiguities in its descriptions of the interactions of some of the elaborate language features. As a concrete example, let us consider the following Ruby program.

```ruby
def foo ; yield ; print "foo" ; end
def bar ; foo { yield } ; print "bar" ; end
bar { break }
print "end"
```

yield calls a block (a form of a lambda term written as {···}) passed as an argument to a method. The block { break } will be called from the yield in the first line through nested yield evaluations. The effect of the entire code should be to reset the run-time environment to those just before the execution of the third line and to jump to the forth line, according to a common informal understanding of yield with break. So this program only prints "end". We have to say that the standard is ambiguous in specifying the precise meanings of such codes. The document suggests some complication in evaluation of (nested) yields with control effects in its informal statement such as "possibly affected execution context", whose precise meanings remain to be clarified.

In principle, the specification could be refined to the point that the evaluation process is completely specified, but such a refinement would result in too detailed and too low-level descriptions to understand the semantics of Ruby, let alone to reason about it. A rigorous high-level specification of Ruby should ideally be structured as a simple composition of well-structured components, each of which is a straightforward specification of individual language feature. However, decomposing Ruby into such components is not trivial since Ruby's features are deeply interwoven with each other due to its dynamic nature with sophisticated control operations such as yields.

To meet this challenge, in this paper, we construct a big-step operational semantics (in the style of natural semantics [11]) of Ruby based on our following observations: the features of Ruby can be categorized as two disjoint subsets, one for object managements and another for control operations, and each of the two categories can be defined as a separate simple term calculus by abstracting the intersections between the two calculi as oracle relations. The object counterpart is *the object calculus* that accounts for dynamic behavior of instance variables, method look-up, and class manipulation. The control counterpart is *the control calculus* that describes local variable binding, method invocation, and Ruby's blocks with global control effects.

Our approach is inspired by the work of Guha et. al. [7], where a single calculus of JavaScript is explained through its two aspects of object and control operations. A novel contribution of the present paper is to show that these two aspects are presented as independent two calculi and the entire calculus is obtained by composing the two. This approach of modeling a dynamic language by composition of multiple calculi would be beneficial to understanding its semantic structure.

Each calculus can be further decomposed into its essential core part and extensions to the core. Each small component of this decomposition represents individual Ruby feature with an effectively small syntax and evaluation rules. The two core calculi and their extensions are combined straightforwardly into the Ruby calculus that represents the essential core of Ruby. The real Ruby is obtained by introducing a syntax elaboration phase that translates a number of context-dependent implicit constructs into explicit terms in the Ruby calculus. The composition of the syntax elaboration and the semantics of the Ruby calculus defines the semantics of the real Ruby language. The resulting semantics serves as a high-level specification of Ruby. Since the big-step semantics directly corresponds to an interpreter implementation, it also straightforwardly yields a reference implementation in a functional language with generative exceptions. We have implemented the semantics in Standard ML and have conducted initial evaluation against a subset of Ruby test programs, which we believe cover typical cases of Ruby's dynamic features and unique control structures. The results confirm that the presented semantics with respect to blocks and yields conforms to commonly accepted Ruby behavior.

In a wider perspective, the results shown in this paper can be regarded as a case study of developing a sophisticated dynamic language in a formal and clear way. Recent programming languages have complex control operators and flexible dynamic features which are considered practical but dirty. In addition, such languages evolve rapidly with drastic changes according to the needs of software developers. To prevent the specifications of such languages from becoming obsolete quickly, the construction of each specification as well as the specification itself must be clear and concise. Our developments shown in this paper suggest that this requirement can be satisfied by dividing their complex features into simple and nearly orthogonal subsets.

The rest of this paper is organized as follows. Section 2 overviews the syntax of Ruby and describes our strategy in defining the operational semantics. Section 3 defines the two calculi with their operational semantics, and combines the two calculi to form the essential core of Ruby. Section 4 extends the two calculi to represent the full functionality of Ruby. Section 5 defines the Ruby calculus. Section 6 describes the syntactic elaboration from real Ruby to the Ruby calculus. Section 7 describes our implementation and reports its evaluation results against crucial test cases. Sections 8 discusses related works. Sections 9 concludes the paper. The detailed definitions of the calculi presented in this paper is given in the Appendix which is available from the support web page of this paper, http://www.pllab.riec.tohoku.ac.jp/papers/the-essence-of-ruby/.

2 Overview of Ruby and Our Strategies

Ruby is a class-based "pure" object-oriented language, where all data elements are objects, and all the computations are done through method invocations on receiver objects. For example, 1 + 2 invokes the + method on an instance 1 of class Integer with an argument object 2.

Each object belongs to a single class. A class itself is also an object, which maintains a mutable set of methods for its instance objects. The system maintains the class hierarchy tree induced by the inheritance relation. Each object has identity and a set of mutable instance variables. Instance variables are dynamically generated in each object when they are initially assigned to some value. The following is a simple example of cons cell for lists.

```
class Cons
  def setcar(x) ; @car = x ; end     # define "Cons" class.
  def setcdr(x) ; @cdr = x ; end     # define "setcar" method in Cons.
                                     # define "setcdr" method in Cons.
  def car ; @car ; end               # define "car" method to Cons.
  def cdr ; @cdr ; end               # define "cdr" method to Cons.
end
```

@car is an instance variable. When setcar is called on a Cons object at the first time, this instance variable is generated in the receiver object.

Another feature that distinguishes Ruby from other object-oriented languages is its control mechanism called *block*, which is a piece of code that takes a parameter and returns a value. A block is passed as an optional parameter to a method. The passed block is invoked through an expression of the form yield(e) occurring in the body of the method. This expression *yields* the value denoted by e to the invoked block i.e. evaluates the block with the value. As an example, suppose we want to enrich the Cons class by adding an enumeration method each. With yield, this can be done by writing the following code just after the previous definitions of Cons class.

```
class Cons
  def each                           # add "each" method to Cons.
    yield(@car)                      # call the given block.
    @cdr.each { |x| yield(x) } if @cdr   # call "each" with a block.
  end
end
```

Since class and method definitions are statements whose effects are mutations to the class object, this code adds each method to the Cons class previously defined. This each method takes a block implicitly and calls the block with a cons cell value by the yield(@car) expression. Then it calls itself for the following cons cells with a block { |x| yield(x) } which propagates the given block to the recursive call. As a result, each method calls the given block with each cons cell value. For example, if l is an instance of Cons then l.each { |x| print x } prints each elements in l.

So far, blocks act just like lambda abstractions. The real strength of Ruby comes from the combination of blocks and a rich collection of non-local control statements such as break that breaks out of either an iteration or a block. This feature allows users to define various iteration abstractions in a concise and intuitive manner, as witnessed in the left-hand code below, which has the same structure and the intuitive meaning as the corresponding imperative one on the right:

using the each iterator:

```
sum = 0
l.each { |i|
   break if i == 0
   sum = sum + i
}
```

using while loop:

```
sum = 0
i = 1
while i do
   break if i.car == 0
   sum = sum + i.car
   i = i.cdr
end
```

Both the above programs accumulate values in the cons list l to variable sum until they meet zero. In both programs, break is used to terminate the iteration on l regardless of the form of the loop. Thanks to this feature, skillful Ruby programmers can write high-level object-oriented codes in a natural, intuitive, and efficient way.

As overviewed above, major features of Ruby are classified into two categories. The first is the *object structure* to represent dynamic behavior of objects and classes. The second is the *control structure* to support blocks with non-local control. The key observation underlying our construction of the semantics of Ruby is that these two structures can be cleanly represented by two independent sub-calculi, which we call *the object calculus* and *the control calculus*. The object calculus accounts for various dynamic features of objects including instance variables and dynamic method bindings. The control calculus realizes the mechanism of yield-ing a value to a block with a rich set of non-local control statements including break. This calculus accounts for Ruby's subtle control flow in a simple and precise manner.

After this separation, the object calculus can be defined relatively easily as a variant of dynamic object calculi extensively studied in literature (see [1] for a survey). In contrast, defining the control calculus requires to describe control flows that the combination of blocks and non-local jumps produce. James and Sabry [9] proposed a continuation-based approach to describe a generalized yield operator. However, continuation is not preferable to reveal the essential core of Ruby, which must looks like a subset of Ruby language, since it does not directly correspond to the commonly understood Ruby's control primitives and the Ruby implementations.

Our observation is that ML-style generative exception provides just enough power to represent these non-local jump statements. ML-style exceptions are generative in the sense that an exception definition dynamically generates a fresh exception tag every time it is evaluated at runtime, in contrast to other statically typed languages, such as C++ and Java, which uses statically declared types or classes as exception tags. The following example written in Standard ML shows the characteristics of the generative exceptions.

```
fun f () = let exception E
            in (fn () => raise E, fn g => g () handle E => ())
            end
val (r1, h1) = f ()
and (r2, h2) = f ()
val _ = h1 r2;  (* this causes uncaught exception *)
```

It defines function f, which creates a pair of functions that raises and handles exception E, and then calls f twice to obtain four functions: r1 and r2 which raise E, and h1 and h2 which handle E. Although they seem to deal with identical exception E, h1 handles only exceptions raised by r1 since two calls of f generates different exception tags for E. So function application h1 r2 causes uncaught exception error.

By including generative exception tags in the evaluation context, the evaluation relation precisely models Ruby's subtle behavior. Generativity is essential. To see this, consider the following example.

```
def foo(x)
  print "E#{x} "
  if x >= 5 then yield
  else foo(x+1) { print "B#{x} " ; if x <= 2 then break else yield end }
  end
  print "L#{x} "
end
foo(1)
```

Method foo recursively calls itself until x becomes 5, at which point the block is called from the yield statement in the body of foo method. The called block then executes yield inside of the block, resulting in calling the blocks of the previous invocations of foo until the one with the parameter 2. This block executes break whose effect is to jump to the statement print "L#{x} " of the method body of foo at the method invocation foo(2). As a result, this code produces the following output: E1 E2 E3 E4 E5 B4 B3 B2 L2 L1. As seen in this example, destinations of breaks cannot be statically labeled. This situation can be cleanly represented by generating a new exception tag for each execution of method call with a block and handling the generated exception.

By carefully constructing the two calculi in such a way that each calculus treats the features that are external to the calculus as oracles (primitives), the composition of the two calculi can be trivially done, yielding the Ruby calculus representing the essence of Ruby. By introducing syntax elaboration and various primitive classes, the combined calculus extends to full Ruby.

3   The Essential Core of Ruby

Following the strategy described in the previous section, we define two sub-calculi, the object calculus for object management, and the control calculus for control flows. These two sub-calculi are orthogonal except method invocation that is the point they intersect with each other. The intersection point of two calculi is explicitly specified by a pair of oracle relations. By combining two sub-calculi at the intersection point, the Ruby calculus is obtained. In this section, we define the essential core part of two calculi and combine them into the core Ruby calculus, which captures fundamentals of Ruby.

To define the calculi, we introduce some notations. {} is an empty map. $\text{dom}(F)$ is the domain of a function F. For a function F, $F \oplus \{x \mapsto v\}$ is the function F' such that $\text{dom}(F') = \text{dom}(F) \cup \{x\}$, $F'(x) = v$, and $F'(y) = F(y)$ for any $y \in \text{dom}(F')$ such that $x \neq y$. We also define $F \oplus G$ by extending the definition of $\oplus$ to any function G. $F \ni \{x \mapsto v\}$ indicates that $x \in \text{dom}(F)$ and $F(x) = v$. $[\,]$ is empty list and $[x]$ is a singleton list of an item x. $l_1 + l_2$ is the concatenation of two lists l_1 and l_2. We use list comprehension of the form $[F(x) \mid x \in l, P(x)]$ to generate a list in order from input list l where $P(x)$ is a predicate on an input item x and $F(x)$ is the output item corresponding to x. We define a big operator on lists $\bigoplus$ that fold the given list of maps by $\oplus$.

3.1 The Core Object Calculus

We let k, i and m range over the given set of *class identifiers*, *instance variable identifiers*, and *method identifiers*, respectively. We assume that there is a given set of *method entities* ranged over by ξ. In the object calculus, it is enough to treat a method entity as an atomic language construct.

The syntax of the core object calculus is given below.

$$e ::= k \mid e.i \mid e.i = e \mid e.m \mid \texttt{alloc } e \mid \texttt{new\_class } e \mid \texttt{def } e \# m = \xi$$

$e.i$ accesses instance variable i. $e_1.i = e_2$ assigns object e_2 to instance variable i of object e_1. They require to specify the object e to which i belongs, while in Ruby it is always the object bound to $\texttt{self}$ and omitted. $e.m$ looks up method m of an object e. We note that this calculus focuses only on object operations, and does not define how methods are invoked and how argument values are passed. $\texttt{alloc } e$ allocates an instance object of class e, which corresponds to $\texttt{Class\#new}$ method of Ruby. $\texttt{new\_class } e$ dynamically creates a new direct subclass of a class e. $\texttt{def } e \# m = \xi$ binds m to ξ in class e.

For this calculus, we define semantic structures necessary to evaluate this calculus as follows.

A class consists of its method binding and its direct super class. Let $\mathcal{M}$ range over *method bindings*, which are finite functions form method names to method entities. An *instance method context*, ranged over by M, is a finite function from class identifiers to method bindings. A *class inheritance context*, ranged over by K, is a finite function over class identifiers that associates a class to its direct super class. We refers to a pair (K, M) of the above two contexts as *class context* ranged over by $\mathcal{K}$. We say that K is well-formed if the transitive closure of K is irreflexive. This well-formedness condition means that no class inherits itself. We define *ancestors of k in K*, referred to as $ancestors(K, k)$, as follows.

$$ancestors(K, k) = \begin{cases} \epsilon & \text{if } k \notin \text{dom}(K) \\ ancestors(K, k') + [k] & \text{if } K \ni \{k \mapsto k'\} \end{cases}$$

Note that $ancestors(K, k)$ is the list of the ancestor classes in the reverse order, i.e. the front of the list is the farthest ancestor. If K is well-formed, the ancestors list of any k in K is always finite. As we shall see, all the rules we shall define preserve well-formedness of K. We define function $methods(\mathcal{K}, k)$ that computes the map of available instance methods of class k in $\mathcal{K}$ as follows.

$$methods((K, M), k) = \bigoplus [M(x) \mid x \in ancestors(K, k)]$$

In Ruby, there are several built-in classes that require special constructors to allocate those instances. To prevent allocating instances of such classes by the generic constructor **alloc**, we define *Special* as the set of the class identifiers of such built-in classes. we let *Special* be $\{\texttt{Class}, \texttt{Module}, \texttt{Proc}\}$ in this paper.

Let v range over the given countably infinite set of *object identifiers*, or *values*. As we mentioned, all data including classes are objects in Ruby, so a Ruby expression always denotes an object identifier. We let a range over the set of non-class object identities. So v is either k or a.

Any object in Ruby has its own instance variables and belongs to a class. Let $\mathcal{I}$ range over *instance variable bindings*, which are finite functions from instance variable names to object identifiers. An *object entity* is a pair $(\mathcal{I}, k)$ of an instance variable binding $\mathcal{I}$ and its class k. An *object heap*, ranged over by I, is a finite function from object identifiers to object entities.

The operational semantics of the object calculus is defined as a set of rules to derive the *evaluation relation* of the form $I, \mathcal{K} \vdash e \Downarrow r, I', \mathcal{K}'$ indicating the fact that, under the context I and $\mathcal{K}$, an expression e evaluates to a result r, and produces a new context I' and $\mathcal{K}'$. We note that due to the dynamic nature of Ruby, a class context $\mathcal{K}$ also acts as another mutable store in addition to an object heap I. A result r is either a value v or *wrong*. *wrong* indicates run-time failure.

As we mentioned above, we do not specify the structure of method entity in this calculus. To define a rule for method look-up term $e.m$, we assume that there is an oracle evaluation relation $I, \mathcal{K} \vdash \xi \rightsquigarrow r, I', \mathcal{K}'$ to convert a found method entity ξ to a result r and to return a new context I' and $\mathcal{K}'$ under the context I and $\mathcal{K}$. This oracle shall be replaced by the control calculus we shall define below.

Figure 1 shows the set of evaluation rules that derives the evaluation relation. We note that the above set of rules, and all the rules we shall define in the sequel, should be taken with the following implicit rules leading *wrong*: if any of the conditions in the premises are not satisfied, or evaluation of any component of a term yields *wrong*, then the entire evaluation will yield *wrong*.

3.2   The Core Control Calculus

Let x and b range over a given countable set of *local variable identifiers* and *block identifiers*, respectively. The set of the control calculus is given by the following syntax.

$$e ::= \texttt{bind } x = e \texttt{ in } e \mid x \mid \texttt{update } x = e \mid \texttt{proc } \{ |x| \ e \} \texttt{ as } b \texttt{ in } e$$

86   K. Ueno et al.

$$\text{CLASS} \quad \frac{(K,M) = \mathcal{K} \quad k \in \mathrm{dom}(K) \cap \mathrm{dom}(M)}{I, \mathcal{K} \vdash k \Downarrow k, \mathcal{K}}$$

$$\text{IVAR} \quad \frac{I, \mathcal{K} \vdash e \Downarrow v, I', \mathcal{K}' \quad I' \ni \{v \mapsto (\mathcal{I}, k)\} \quad \mathcal{I} \ni \{i \mapsto v'\}}{I, \mathcal{K} \vdash e.i \Downarrow v', I', \mathcal{K}'}$$

$$\text{ISTORE} \quad \frac{I, \mathcal{K} \vdash e_1 \Downarrow v_1, I', \mathcal{K}' \quad I', \mathcal{K}' \vdash e_2 \Downarrow v_2, I'', \mathcal{K}'' \quad I'' \ni \{v_1 \mapsto (\mathcal{I}, k)\}}{I, \mathcal{K} \vdash e_1.i = e_2 \Downarrow v_2, I'' \oplus \{v_1 \mapsto (\mathcal{I} \oplus \{i \mapsto v_2\}, k)\}, \mathcal{K}''}$$

$$\text{CALL} \quad \frac{\begin{array}{c} I, \mathcal{K} \vdash e \Downarrow v, I', \mathcal{K}' \quad I' \ni \{v \mapsto (\mathcal{I}, k)\} \quad methods(\mathcal{K}', k) \ni \{m \mapsto \xi\} \\ I', \mathcal{K}' \vdash \xi \leadsto r, I'', \mathcal{K}'' \end{array}}{I, \mathcal{K} \vdash e.m \Downarrow r, I'', \mathcal{K}''}$$

$$\text{ALLOC} \quad \frac{I, \mathcal{K} \vdash e \Downarrow k, I', \mathcal{K}' \quad k \notin Special \quad a \text{ fresh}}{I, \mathcal{K} \vdash \texttt{alloc } e \Downarrow a, I' \oplus \{a \mapsto (\{\}, k)\}, \mathcal{K}'}$$

$$\text{NEWCLASS} \quad \frac{I, \mathcal{K} \vdash e \Downarrow k', I', (K', M') \quad k \text{ fresh}}{\begin{array}{c} I, \mathcal{K} \vdash \texttt{new\_class } e \Downarrow k, I' \oplus \{k \mapsto (\{\}, \texttt{Class})\}, \\ (K' \oplus \{k \mapsto k'\}, M' \oplus \{k \mapsto \{\}\}) \end{array}}$$

$$\text{DEF} \quad \frac{I, \mathcal{K} \vdash e \Downarrow k, (K', M') \quad M' \ni \{k \mapsto \mathcal{M}\}}{I, \mathcal{K} \vdash \texttt{def } e\#m = \xi \Downarrow k, I, (K', M' \oplus \{k \mapsto \mathcal{M} \oplus \{m \mapsto \xi\}\})}$$

Fig. 1. Evaluation rules of the object calculus

$$\mid \texttt{yield } e \texttt{ to } b \mid e.m(e, \&b) \mid e; e \mid j\, e$$
$$j ::= \texttt{return} \mid \texttt{break} \mid \texttt{next}$$

bind $x = e_1$ in e_2 introduces local variable binding x in e_2. update $x = e$ destructively assigns value e to x. In Ruby, the standard syntax for assignments x = e is overloaded with variable definition (corresponding to bind) or variable update (corresponding to update), dependent on its context. As we shall mention in Section 6, this overloaded syntax can be supported by syntactic elaboration. proc $\{\,|x|\ e_1\,\}$ as b in e_2 binds b to block $\{\,|x|\ e_1\,\}$ in e_2. yield e to b calls block b with an argument e. $e_1.m(e_2, \&b)$ calls method m of object e_1 with an argument e_2 and a block b. $e_1; e_2$ is sequential execution. $j\, e$ performs non-local jumps of the three kinds. return e breaks out of the currently executing method. break e breaks out of the method invocation with the currently executing block. next e breaks out of the currently executing block. We refer to j as a *jump kind* in what follows. Ruby syntactically prohibits some of meaningless breaks. For simplicity, we do not introduce syntax restriction here. Instead, meaningless break is represented as *wrong*.

We define the semantic structure to evaluate this calculus as follows.

Non-local jumps performed by $j\ e$ are realized by meta-level exceptions. We follow a Standard ML style approach in representing exceptions [13], which is well studied in literature. Let t range over a given countably infinite set of (meta-level) *exception tags*. Let T be an *exception context*, which is a finite function from jump kinds to exception tags. A *packed value* $[v]^t$ is a pair of value v and an exception tag t, representing a raised exception with tag t and a parameter value v. The *result*, ranged over by r, is either a value v, packed value $[v]^t$, or *wrong*.

Different from the object calculus, a method entity ξ is defined to be a triple (x, b, e) of a variable x and a block b for formal parameters and an expression e for the method body. To represent a mutable variable, we introduce a *variable store* ranged over by S. Let s range over a given countably infinite set of *variable references*. A variable store S is a finite function from variable references to values. In the control calculus, we treat a value v as an atomic entity. A *variable environment* E is a finite function from variables to variable references. A *block entity* ranged over by ρ is a tuple (E, T, x, e) consisting of evaluation contexts E and T, a formal parameter variable x, and a block body e. Let B range over *block contexts*, which are finite maps from block identifiers to block entities.

The evaluation relation is defined by a set of rules to derive either of the forms $S, B, E, T \vdash e \Downarrow r, S'$ or $S, B, E, T \vdash e$ handle $t \Downarrow r, S'$. The former is the standard form indicating the fact that under the evaluation context S, B, E and T, e evaluates to r and produces S'. In this case, an exception raised during the evaluation of e is propagated. The latter catches exceptions with tag t raised during the evaluation of e.

To define a rule for method invocation term $e_1.m(e_2, \&p)$ in this calculus, we use an oracle relation $S, B, E, T \vdash e.m \rightsquigarrow \xi, S'$ to look up a method entity specified by $e.m$, in contrast to the object calculus which uses oracle to invoke methods. This oracle shall be replaced by the object calculus.

Figure 2 shows the set of the evaluation rules. This set of rules should be taken with implicit rules for *wrong* as before. In addition, each rule in the standard form comes with an exception propagation rule: if a component yields an unexpected raised exception then cancel any subsequent evaluation of other components and the entire term will yield the raised exception. The top-level evaluation does not expect any raised exception.

3.3   The Core Ruby Calculus

The object calculus and the control calculus are mostly orthogonal, and merges straightforwardly into the core Ruby calculus, representing the essence of Ruby; the semantics of all language constructs of Ruby shall be described as either extensions or syntactic elaborations to the Ruby calculus.

In the Ruby calculus, the contexts I and $\mathcal{K}$ of the object calculus and the context S of the control calculus are all mutable stores. We let H range over *Ruby heaps*, which is a tuple of of I, $\mathcal{K}$ and S. The notation $H \oplus \{x \mapsto y\}$ and $H \ni \{x \mapsto y\}$ affect the corresponding part of H. We also naturally extend the function $methods(\mathcal{K}, k)$ to $methods(H, k)$.

The evaluation relation of the merged calculus is of the form $H, B, E, T \vdash e \Downarrow r, H'$. The evaluation rules for the Ruby calculus are obtained by changing the rules so that each rules preserves non-attractive parts of given heap H in the returned heap. The only exception is the case for CALL. The case of CALL in the core Ruby calculus is obtained by combining two CALL rules as if each oracle relation $\rightsquigarrow$ is replaced with the counterpart provided by other calculus.

$$\frac{\begin{array}{c} S,B,E,T \vdash e_1 \Downarrow v, S' \\ S' \oplus \{s \mapsto v\}, E \oplus \{x \mapsto s\}, T \vdash e_2 \Downarrow r, S'' \ (s \text{ fresh}) \end{array}}{S,B,E,T \vdash \mathbf{bind}\ x = e_1\ \mathbf{in}\ e_2 \Downarrow r, S''} \quad \text{BIND}$$

$$\frac{E \ni \{x \mapsto s\} \quad S \ni \{s \mapsto v\}}{S,B,E,T \vdash x \Downarrow v, S} \quad \text{VAR}$$

$$\frac{E \ni \{x \mapsto s\} \quad S,B,E,T \vdash e \Downarrow v, S'}{S,B,E,T \vdash \mathbf{update}\ x = e \Downarrow v, S' \oplus \{s \mapsto v\}} \quad \text{UPDATE}$$

$$\frac{S,B \oplus \{b \mapsto (E,T \oplus \{\mathbf{break} \mapsto t\}, x, e_1)\}, E,T \vdash e_2\ \mathbf{handle}\ t \Downarrow v, S'}{S,B,E,T \vdash \mathbf{proc}\ \{\,|x|\ e_1\,\}\ \mathbf{as}\ b\ \mathbf{in}\ e_2 \Downarrow v, S'} \quad (t \text{ fresh}) \quad \text{PROC}$$

$$\frac{\begin{array}{c} S,B,E,T \vdash e \Downarrow v, S' \quad B \ni \{b \mapsto (E',T',x,e)\} \\ S' \oplus \{s \mapsto v\}, \emptyset, E' \oplus \{x \mapsto s\}, T' \oplus \{\mathbf{next} \mapsto t\} \vdash e\ \mathbf{handle}\ t \Downarrow r, S'' \end{array}}{S,B,E,T \vdash \mathbf{yield}\ e\ \mathbf{to}\ b \Downarrow r, S''} \quad (s,t \text{ fresh}) \quad \text{YIELD}$$

$$\frac{\begin{array}{c} S,B,E,T \vdash e_1.m \rightsquigarrow (x,b',e), S' \quad S',B,E,T \vdash e_2 \Downarrow v, S'' \\ B \ni \{b \mapsto \rho\} \\ S'' \oplus \{s \mapsto v\}, \{b' \mapsto \rho\}, \{x \mapsto s\}, \{\mathbf{return} \mapsto t\} \vdash e\ \mathbf{handle}\ t \Downarrow r, S''' \end{array}}{S,B,E,T \vdash e_1.m(e_2, \&b) \Downarrow r, S'''} \quad (s,t \text{ fresh}) \quad \text{CALL}$$

$$\frac{S,B,E,T \vdash e_1 \Downarrow v, S' \quad S',B,E,T \vdash e_2 \Downarrow r, S''}{S,B,E,T \vdash e_1;\ e_2 \Downarrow r, S''} \quad \text{SEQ}$$

$$\frac{S,B,E,T \vdash e \Downarrow v, S' \quad T \ni \{j \mapsto t\}}{S,B,E,T \vdash j\ e \Downarrow [v]^t, S'} \quad \text{JUMP}$$

$$\frac{S,B,E,T \vdash e \Downarrow v, S'}{S,B,E,T \vdash e\ \mathbf{handle}\ t \Downarrow v, S'} \quad \text{HANDLE} \qquad \frac{S,B,E,T \vdash e \Downarrow [v]^t, S'}{S,B,E,T \vdash e\ \mathbf{handle}\ t \Downarrow v, S'} \quad \text{CATCH}$$

Fig. 2. Evaluation rules of the control calculus

The resulting CALL rule of this construction is as follows:

$$\frac{\begin{array}{c} H,B,E,T \vdash e_1 \Downarrow v_1, H' \quad H' \ni \{v_1 \mapsto (\mathcal{I},k)\} \\ methods(H',k) \ni \{m \mapsto (x,b',e)\} \quad H',B,E,T \vdash e_2 \Downarrow v_2, H'' \quad B \ni \{b \mapsto \rho\} \\ H'' \oplus \{s \mapsto v_2\}, \{b' \mapsto \rho\}, \{x \mapsto s\}, \{\mathbf{return} \mapsto t\} \vdash e\ \mathbf{handle}\ t \Downarrow r, H''' \end{array}}{H,B,E,T \vdash e_1.m(e_2, \&b) \Downarrow r, H'''} \quad (s,t \text{ fresh})$$

The complete definition of the core Ruby calculus is given in Appendix.

4 Extension to the Core Calculi

To obtain the full Ruby calculus that embodies all of the Ruby's sophisticated language features, this section extends the core calculi with most of Ruby's features. Due to space limitations, this section presents brief summary of each extension. The definitions of the extended calculi are given in Appendix.

Modules and Mix-ins. A *module* in Ruby is a structure consisting of a mutable set of methods to be included in a class. By including modules in a class, Ruby supports full-fledged mix-in without any additional machinery other than dynamic method look-up mechanism.

We introduce the following terms to the object calculus: `new_module`, which creates a new module with empty set of methods, and `append_feature` e_1 to e_2 which mixes module e_1 in class (or module) e_2. We use the def $e\#m$ = ξ syntax to define method m in a module e as well as in a class.

We define the semantic structure of modules by reusing those of classes. Let d range over a given countably infinite set of *module identifiers*. Let δ range over the union of module identifiers and class identifiers, that shall be used for the common behavior between modules and classes. We refer to the union set as *class-module identifiers*.

In Ruby, every class or module has a mutable list of modules included in the class or module. Unlike class inheritance, the relation on module inclusions is not transitive; all affective included modules of a class or module are flatly listed in the included module list. To represent this list, we introduce an *included module list context*, ranged over by L, as a function from class-module identifiers to lists of module identifiers. As in the class inheritance context, we introduce the well-formedness condition on L as follows: for any $\delta' \in \mathrm{dom}(L)$, no identical δ occurs twice in $[\delta'] + L(\delta')$. This prevents circular and doubled inclusion of modules. We note that mutual inclusion of modules is allowed and it does not arise any circular references since module inclusions are not transitive. The only case causing circular references is the case that a module includes itself. The above well-formedness condition clearly prevents this.

A class context $\mathcal{K}$ is redefined to be a *class-module context* of the form (K, L, M) to represent the included modules in each class. We also redefine the structure of a method binding M to be a function from class-module identifiers. Since modules are mutable values, a value v can be a module identifier d. We can define evaluation rules for the mix-in terms by the above preparation.

Implicit Destinations of Method Definitions. In the actual Ruby, the destination class or module of a def is implicitly given through a `class` or `module` surrounding the method definition. However, the destination cannot be made up for by syntactic elaboration since def can be nested and combined with some reflection primitives. To see the subtle difficulty, consider the following example.

```
class Foo
  def define_bar(c)
    c.hoge { def bar ; "bar" ; end }   # where to define "bar" method?
  end
end
```

The destination of def bar $\cdots$ end depends on the run-time context. As an uncommon case, if c is a module object and `hoge` is an alias to `Module#class_eval` then bar is defined in the module denoted by c. Otherwise, it is defined in Foo.

To specify this behavior of the def in our calculi, we extend the object calculus with the feature to keep track of the current destination of def terms. We introduce the following new syntax: module e_1; e_2; end which specifies an existing class or module e_1 as the current destination of defs in e_2, and current_module which gets out the current destination as a value. For the semantics of these new constructs, we introduce a new evaluation context, *class-module list*, denoted by C, as a list of class-module identifiers. The evaluation relation becomes $H, C \vdash e \Downarrow r, H'$. To keep a class-module list along with each method entity, we introduce a *method closure*, ranged over by ζ, as a pair (C, ξ). We extend a method binding M to be a function to the method closures. Due to this extension, the CALL rule is modified so that the class-module list in a method closure is resumed when evaluating its method body.

Constants and Class-Variables. Let c range over the set of *constant identifiers*. Any Ruby construct that refers to a constant can be represented with the following two expressions: one is just c, which looks up a given constant from the current class-module list, and another is $e :: c$ that looks up c from specified module e. Mutations of constants can be essentially represented as single expression of the form $e_1 :: c = e_2$ which binds c to value e_2 in module e_1.

We extend the class-module context for constants as follows. Let $\mathcal{J}$ be a *constant bindings* as a finite function from constant identifiers to values. Let J be a *constant heap* as a function from class-module identifiers to constant bindings. Then a class-module context $\mathcal{K}$ is extended to be a tuple (J, K, L, M). To define the rule of constant look-ups, a function is needed to compute available constant bindings. This can be defined similarly to the *methods* function according to the standard constant look-up rules. We can define the terms and rules for class variables by introducing class variable identifiers, contexts and look-up mechanisms similarly to the constants.

Method Visibility and super Method Calls. Every method in Ruby has its own visibility, which is one of public, protected or private. The visibility controls method lookup of visibility conscious method invocations. In addition, there are two special forms of method invocations in Ruby: $m()$ for self method calls and super for calling a method bound in a super class. Any of these method invocations can be characterized by how they search for the method to be invoked. To support all variations of Ruby's method invocations, we add two method call terms of the form send $e.m$ for visibility conscious method lookup and super m for method lookup from super classes. The evaluation rules of these can be derived from the CALL rule by replacing the computation of available method bindings. To deal with the method visibility, we extend the class-module context $\mathcal{K}$ with a *visibility binding*, that is a map from method identifiers to method visibilities. Visibilities of the available methods can be computed by folding the ancestors list with visibility binding composition. We can obtain a visibility conscious available method binding by filtering out invisible methods from the available method binding.

Singleton Classes. A *singleton class* is a mechanism to associate a particular method to an object. In Ruby, a singleton class is a class with several minor limitations. Here we only list some of them: they cannot have any instance objects, they cannot be inherited (the standard says *unspecified*), and the visibility of their **protected** methods are unspecified. Exact conformity to all these details requires the operational semantics to distinguish singleton classes from ordinary classes, and re-define class manipulation rules for singleton classes. By omitting these details for simplicity, the singleton classes can be taken into account by extending the object entity to be a triple $(\mathcal{I}, k, k')$ where k' is its singleton class and adding a term for accessing to this k'. The ALLOC and CALL rules are also modified to be conscious of singleton classes along with these extensions.

Miscellaneous Control Constructs. Ruby has a variety of control flow constructs other than method calls and blocks such as **if** and **unless** expressions, **while** and **until** loops, and user-level exceptions. It is straightforward to incorporate these constructs to the control calculus by representing their control flows in meta-level exceptions. Here we present a set of primitive constructs sufficient for representing Ruby's control flows defined as follows

$$e ::= \cdots \mid \textbf{if } e \textbf{ then } e \textbf{ else } e \textbf{ end} \mid n{:}\{\, e \,\} \mid e \textbf{ rescue } x.e \mid e \textbf{ ensure } e$$
$$j ::= \cdots \mid \textbf{redo}_n \mid \textbf{break}_n \mid \textbf{raise}$$

where n ranges over the set of natural numbers, each of which is used as a loop label. $n{:}\{\, e \,\}$ indicates a loop labeled with n. $\textbf{redo}_n$ jumps to the beginning of the inner-most loop labeled with n. $\textbf{break}_n$ breaks out of the inner-most n-labeled loop. These primitives corresponds to Ruby's **while** or **until** and their **break**, **next** and **redo** statements. **rescue**, **ensure** and **raise** are for user-level exceptions. The evaluation rules for these constructs are trivial and we omit them. Actual Ruby's control flow constructs are introduced by the syntactic elaboration to these primitives.

5 The Ruby Calculus

The extended two calculi combine into a calculus in the same way as the core Ruby calculus. The full Ruby calculus is obtained by adding the following three features to the combined calculus: **Proc** objects, reflections, and error handling.

Proc Objects. In Ruby, a block is not only a control structure but a first-class value. It is straightforward to incorporate this feature to the Ruby calculus by adding block identifiers b to the set of values. The constructs for blocks are modified so that they generate and consume a block value. This is done by replacing the block identifier b in **proc** $\{\, |x| \; e_1 \,\}$ **as** b **in** e_2 with variable x and those in **yield** e **to** b and $e_1.m(e_2, \&b)$ with expression e.

Since blocks are first-class values and block values are represented by block identifiers, a block context B must be included in H. In addition, due to the introduction of class-module list mentioned in Section 4, a block entity ρ is extended to be a tuple (E, T, C, x, e). The evaluation relation of the resulting

Ruby calculus is of the form $H, E, T, C \vdash e \Downarrow r, H'$. The evaluation rules of the new proc and yield constructs are given below.

$$\frac{\begin{array}{c} H \oplus \{b \mapsto (E, T \oplus \{\text{break} \mapsto t\}, C, x_1, e_1)\} \oplus \{b \mapsto (\{\}, \text{Proc})\} \oplus \{s \mapsto b\}, \\ E \oplus \{x_2 \mapsto s\}, T, C \vdash e_2 \text{ handle } t \Downarrow r, H' \qquad\qquad (s, t \text{ fresh}) \end{array}}{H, E, T, C \vdash \text{proc } \{\,|x_1|\; e_1\,\} \text{ as } x_2 \text{ in } e_2 \Downarrow r, H'}$$

$$\frac{\begin{array}{c} H, E, T, C \vdash e_2 \Downarrow b, H' \qquad H' \ni \{b \mapsto (E', T', C', x, e)\} \\ H', E, T, C \vdash e_1 \Downarrow v, H'' \\ H'' \oplus \{s \mapsto v\}, E' \oplus \{x \mapsto s\}, T' \oplus \{\text{next} \mapsto t\}, C' \vdash e \text{ handle } t \Downarrow r, H''' \\ \qquad\qquad\qquad (s, t \text{ fresh}) \end{array}}{H, E, T, C \vdash \text{yield } e_1 \text{ to } e_2 \Downarrow r, H'''}$$

The CALL rule is also modified so that it obtains a block parameter through evaluating an expression. This modification is straightforward and we omit it.

Built-in Primitives for Reflections. Ruby provides a set of built-in primitives for reflecting and reifying evaluation context. The Ruby calculus can readily support these meta-level primitives uniformly. In most compiled languages, a large part of evaluation contexts are static and are consumed away by the compiler. We observe that this is the major source of difficulties in providing meta-level primitives in static languages. In contrast, the operational semantics of our Ruby calculus retains most of meta-level information in its evaluation context, particularly, in heap H. It is then a simple matter to provide reflection functionalities as primitives to examine and modify the current evaluation context. We have studied the meta-level primitives specified in the standard of Ruby and confirmed that in most cases this is indeed the case. In the following, we list typical Ruby's primitive methods and the required primitive constructs in the Ruby calculus.

1. Primitives to access module and class information, such as Module#instance _methods and Module#private. Since all the information on modules are in the heap, these methods are easily supported by introducing primitives to access to the class-module context in the heap.
2. Primitives to reify the current run-time environment, such as Kernel.local_ variables and Kernel.block_given?. These methods refer to the evaluation context of the caller. Since they do not modify the context, they can be supported through corresponding primitives in the Ruby calculus.
3. Primitives to manipulate the callers' run-time environment, such as Module# public and String#=~. To support these methods, we first introduce reserved local variables such as $~ and introduce primitives for manipulating the reserved variables. We note that the standard requires that regular expression matching method dynamically create a local variable binding named ~ in the callers' context. We would say this is unnatural, and this is neither the case in the widely-accepted Ruby implementations. Although approach mentioned above is not strictly compilant with the standard, it would more naturally describe the intuitive meaning of the reserved variables.

4. Primitives to evaluating program texts such as `Kernel.require` and `Kernel.eval`. These allow to execute arbitrary program codes. However, since the results do not affect the caller except for the modification to the heap, they can be supported similarly to the previous case by introducing new primitives.

These reflection mechanisms can be provided through primitive methods. Since primitive methods are themselves possible targets of reflection, the user code can manipulate them. This situation can be dealt with by materializing primitive methods as semantic objects, and separate the evaluation rule of primitive method calls from that of ordinary method calls.

Error Handling. The operational semantics of our Ruby calculus may get stuck, yielding *wrong*. In Ruby, however, program never stuck except for uncaught exception. Erroneous cases are reported to the user code through either user-level exceptions, fallback method calls, or default values. If the conformity to this specification is really desired, then it is straightforwardly achieved by introducing appropriate exception for each erroneous case and making all the cases that yield *wrong* in the Ruby calculus as explicit rules that raise the corresponding exception.

The only subtle case is Ruby's `LocalJumpError` exception. This exception is raised when a non-local jump cannot find appropriate jump destinations. This situation mainly occurs in the case where `break` is evaluated in a `Proc` object detached from the evaluation context. In this case, the operational semantics needs to maintain the set of effective exception tags in the evaluation context.

Corner Cases Requiring Extensions. As we have discussed in this section, our conclusion is that the Ruby calculus so far defined provides sufficient basis for a complete specification of the full real Ruby language. The remaining works towards the complete specification is to define semantic objects and evaluation rules for each of the minor details and corner cases that we does not cover in this paper. We list below some of those we found important during our close scrutiny of the standard of Ruby.

– To deal with `Symbol` objects, identifiers should be treated as values.
– `undef` can be dealt with a new "undefined" state in method closures.
– Global variables can be added by introducing a new environment.
– `self` can be treated as a local variable implicitly appearing in the parameter list of a method definition. To pass `self` along with user-specified arguments, methods should be extended to multiple arguments.
– Multiple assignments and multiple arguments can be dealt with by incorporating `Array` objects and their primitives to the semantics.

6   Elaborating Ruby to the Ruby Calculus

Ruby allows a number of shorthands and implicit references to various entities, resulting in syntactic ambiguities. The Ruby standard specifies how the ambiguities be resolved during the interpretation of the (abstract) syntax tree.

A systematic way to incorporate this ambiguity resolution is the introduction of syntactic elaboration, which translates the real Ruby syntax to terms in the Ruby calculus. We have designed the elaboration algorithm for major Ruby constructs as a series of functions of the form $[\![M]\!]^{\kappa}_{\mathcal{E}}$ that translates Ruby program M into a Ruby calculus term under given elaboration context $\mathcal{E}$, where κ is a name of an elaboration function. The structure of an elaboration context $\mathcal{E}$ is specific to each κ. In this paper, we pick up below some highlights of the elaboration algorithm that demonstrates how it resolves the Ruby's syntactic ambiguities.

Local Variable Scopes. In Ruby, variable identifiers in reference position are either local variable references or private method calls with no argument. Assignment syntax such as x = M implicitly declares that variable x is bound in certain (possibly nested) scope. This syntactic ambiguity is resolved by Ruby's scoping rules. Since the scoping rules are all syntactic, this resolution process can be factored into the elaboration algorithm.

We resolve this ambiguity in two steps. At first, we resolve the ambiguity of identifiers by adding explicit empty argument lists to private method calls. This step is defined as a context-sensitive Ruby-to-Ruby translation $[\![M]\!]^{\mathsf{pre}}_V$, where V is the set of identifiers that are decided as variable references. We show a few cases of $[\![M]\!]^{\mathsf{pre}}_V$ below

$$[\![x]\!]^{\mathsf{pre}}_V = \begin{cases} x & \text{if } x \in V \\ x() & \text{if } x \notin V \end{cases} \qquad [\![m \ \{ \ |x| \ M \ \}]\!]^{\mathsf{pre}}_V = m \ \{ \ |x| \ [\![M]\!]^{\mathsf{pre}}_{\{x\}} \ \}$$

$$[\![\text{for } x \text{ in } M_1 \text{ do } M_2 \text{ end}]\!]^{\mathsf{pre}}_V = \text{for } x \text{ in } [\![M_1]\!]^{\mathsf{pre}}_{V \cup \{x\}} \text{ do } [\![M_2]\!]^{\mathsf{pre}}_{V \cup \{x\} \cup \mathrm{BV}(M_1)} \text{ end}$$

where $\mathrm{BV}(M)$ is the set of bound variables occurring in M, some of whose cases are defined as follows.

$$\mathrm{BV}(x = M) = \{x\} \cup \mathrm{BV}(M) \qquad\qquad \mathrm{BV}(m \ \{ \ |x| \ M \ \}) = \emptyset$$
$$\mathrm{BV}(\text{for } x \text{ in } M_1 \text{ do } M_2 \text{ end}) = \{x\} \cup \mathrm{BV}(M_1) \cup \mathrm{BV}(M_2)$$

The second step is the function $[\![M]\!]^{\mathsf{top}}_V$ that decides the set V of bound variables for each local variable scope and insert **bind** of the Ruby calculus to make the scope explicit. Some cases of this algorithm are as follows

$$[\![m \ \{ \ |x| \ M \ \}]\!]^{\mathsf{top}}_V = m \ \{ \ |x| \ bind \ \mathrm{BV}(M) \setminus (\{x\} \cup V) \ in \ [\![M]\!]^{\mathsf{block}}_{V \cup \mathrm{BV}(M) \cup \{x\}} \ \}$$

$$[\![\text{for } x \text{ in } M_1 \text{ do } M_2 \text{ end}]\!]^{\mathsf{top}}_V =$$
$$[\![M_1]\!]^{\mathsf{top}}_V.\text{each} \ \{ \ |x'| \ (\text{update } x = x'; \ [\![M_2]\!]^{\mathsf{block}}_V) \ \} \quad (x' \text{ fresh})$$

where $bind \ V \ in \ \cdots$ is the sequence of **bind** $x = \texttt{nil}$ **in** $\cdots$ for all x in V.

Overloaded Constructs. Ruby contains many overloaded constructs so that the user can enjoy productive programming with less keywords. Some of the overloaded constructs are resolved by their syntactic context. The elaboration phase is adequate to perform this kind of resolution. Typical examples include **break** and **next** which break out of either **while** loops or blocks. The resolution is expressed as follows.

$$[\![\texttt{while } e_1 \texttt{ do } e_2 \texttt{ end}]\!]_{\mathcal{E}}^{\text{top}} = 1{:}\{\texttt{ if } [\![e_1]\!]_{\mathcal{E}}^{\text{while}} \texttt{ then } ([\![e_2]\!]_{\mathcal{E}}^{\text{while}}; \texttt{ redo}_1) \texttt{ else nil }\}$$

$$[\![\texttt{break}]\!]_{\mathcal{E}}^{\text{while}} = \texttt{break}_1 \texttt{ nil} \qquad\qquad [\![\texttt{break}]\!]_{\mathcal{E}}^{\text{block}} = \texttt{break nil}$$

$$[\![\texttt{next}]\!]_{\mathcal{E}}^{\text{while}} = \texttt{redo}_1 \texttt{ nil} \qquad\qquad [\![\texttt{next}]\!]_{\mathcal{E}}^{\text{block}} = \texttt{next nil}$$

For other overloaded constructs, their behavior is selected at run-time. A typical example of this kind is class statement in Ruby, which creates a new class or denotes an existing class. There are two design choices to represent this kind of resolution; one is to introduce a new primitive, and the other is to elaborate the class statement to a combination of primitives. We choose the latter since this yields a simpler calculus. We show the elaboration rule of class statement below

$$
\begin{aligned}
&[\![\texttt{class } c < e_1;\ e_2;\ \texttt{end}]\!]_{\mathcal{E}}^{\text{top}} = \\
&\quad \texttt{bind } x_1 = [\![e_1]\!]_{\mathcal{E}}^{\text{top}} \texttt{ in} \\
&\quad \texttt{bind } x = \texttt{if defined\_const?}(c) \\
&\qquad\qquad \texttt{then if } \text{eq}(\text{superclass\_of}(c), x_1) \texttt{ then } c \\
&\qquad\qquad\qquad\qquad\qquad \texttt{else raise TypeError} \\
&\qquad\qquad \texttt{else current\_module} :: c = \texttt{new\_class } x_1 \\
&\quad \texttt{in module } x;\, [\![e_2]\!]_{\mathcal{E}}^{\text{top}};\, \texttt{end} \qquad\qquad\qquad\qquad (x_1, x \text{ fresh})
\end{aligned}
$$

where $\texttt{defined\_const?}(c)$, $\texttt{superclass\_of}(e)$ and $\text{eq}(e_1, e_2)$ are built-in reify primitives. $\texttt{defined\_const?}(c)$ returns true if look-up of constant c is succeeded in current context. $\texttt{superclass\_of}(e)$ returns the direct super class of class e. $\text{eq}(e_1, e_2)$ returns true if two object e_1 and e_2 are identical.

7 Conformity Evaluation

In order to evaluate conformity of our formalism to the actual Ruby language, we developed a prototype Ruby interpreter and carried out an experiment.

Our interpreter is written in Standard ML. Since exceptions in Standard ML are generative, our implementation is a straightforward coding of the evaluation relations so far defined as a recursive evaluation function. We have implemented all of the core Ruby calculus presented in Section 3.3, the large part of extensions presented in Section 4 and 5, and the syntactic elaboration phase described in Section 6. Our prototype interpreter also includes several built-in classes and methods including Array and String.

We collected test cases from the test case suite distributed with CRuby (a.k.a., MRI, Matz Ruby Implementation) [15] version 1.9.3. CRuby is a de facto standard implementation of Ruby. We selected this test suite on considering that the JIS/ISO standard is largely based on CRuby version 1.8 and 1.9. This test suite consists of 2,729 test cases for both language features and built-in class libraries. We picked up all the test cases for behaviors of blocks and jumps as follows. Firstly, we excluded test cases essentially not for blocks but for methods that use blocks. Secondly, some of test cases use functionalities that our implementation does not support; hence, we modified them so as to conform to our implementation without changing their objectives. For example, we modify methods that take more than one arguments to those that take an array of arguments. Lastly, we had to omit a few test cases, such as those that heavily use variable-length arguments and hashes. This selection and modification gave us 28 test cases.

Our implementation passed 26 out of 28 test cases. The two failures are caused because of the following reasons. One is the case of `LocalJumpError` we discussed in Section 5. This is an expected case; this case can be treated by extending the operational semantics according to the strategy described in Section 5. The other one is a block that takes a block as its argument as follows.

```
Proc.new { |&b| b.call(10) }.call { |x| x }
```

Actually, this program does not follow the JIS/ISO standard, while this feature is available in CRuby from version 1.8.7. Our implementation can support it by a multiple-argument extension, which can certainly be incorporated.

We have seen that the behavior of our implementation is nearly the same as an actual Ruby implementation, and moreover, the exceptional differences can be fixed by small modifications. This result shows promise of our approach.

8 Related Works

We owe much of this work to the JIS/ISO standard of Ruby [10,8] written by the designers and developers of the language. As we mentioned, although it is not a formal specification and it is presented as a description of an abstract machine in a particular implementation style in mind, it provides detailed description of the language. Apart from this document, a few works have been done toward rigorous specification of Ruby. James and Sabry [9] proposed a continuation-based encoding of a generalized `yield` operator similar to the one found in Ruby. This account provides an interesting insight into general nature of iterators with `yield` operator. As we have shown in our development, Ruby's control structure including `yield` is directly represented by generative exceptions rather than continuations, and this scales to various other features of Ruby. Furr et. al. and An et. al. investigated static typing and type inference for a subset of Ruby [4,6,2,3] using their Ruby program analysis framework [5]. These works assume a simplified calculus with the features similar to Ruby. We expect that a formal operational semantics we have worked out in this paper should be beneficial for extending these works on the full set of Ruby.

Our work can be regarded as an attempt to develop a formal semantics of dynamic languages. In this general perspective, a number of works have been done on dynamic scripting languages, including JavaScript such as [12,7], and Python such as [14], to mention a few. Our approach of modeling a dynamic scripting language as a combination of multiple calculi would shed some light on understanding semantic structures of scripting languages.

9 Conclusions

We have developed a formal operational semantics for Ruby based on the observation that Ruby's dynamic behaviors can be cleanly represented by the composition of two calculi: the object calculus that represent dynamic structures of objects, and the control calculus that accounts for Ruby's control operators including `yields`. By constructing each of the two calculi in such a way that the features external to the calculus are represented as oracle primitives, two calculi combine trivially to yield the Ruby calculus that represents the essence of Ruby. This combined calculus scales up to the full Ruby specified in the JIS/ISO standard. The construction of the calculus straightforwardly leads to an implementation in a functional language with generative exceptions. Our evaluation using the implementation indicates that the presented semantics with respect to blocks and `yields` conforms to commonly accepted Ruby behavior. we plan to make a complete formal specification of Ruby according to the strategy described in Section 5 and present it elsewhere.

An interesting future work is to develop a general framework for specifying a complex language as a composition of multiple orthogonal calculi. Since many existing dynamic languages tend to contain various features, the approach shown in this paper would shade some light toward this direction.

References

1. Abadi, M., Cardelli, L.: A Theory of Objects. Springer, Heidelberg (1996)
2. An, J.-H., Chaudhuri, A., Foster, J.S.: Static typing for Ruby on Rails. In: IEEE/ACM International Conference on Automated Software Engineering, pp. 590–594 (2009)
3. An, J.-H., Chaudhuri, A., Foster, J.S., Hicks, M.: Dynamic inference of static types for Ruby. In: ACM SIGPLAN-SIGACT Symposium on Principles of Programming Languages, pp. 459–472 (2011)
4. Furr, M., An, J.-H., Foster, J.S.: Profile-guided static typing for dynamic scripting languages. In: ACM SIGPLAN Conference on Object Oriented Programming Systems Languages and Applications, pp. 283–300 (2009)
5. Furr, M., An, J.-H., Foster, J.S., Hicks, M.: The Ruby intermediate language. In: Symposium on Dynamic Languages, pp. 89–98 (2009)
6. Furr, M., An, J.-H., Foster, J.S., Hicks, M.: Static type inference for Ruby. In: ACM Symposium on Applied Computing, pp. 1859–1866 (2009)
7. Guha, A., Saftoiu, C., Krishnamurthi, S.: The essence of JavaScript. In: D'Hondt, T. (ed.) ECOOP 2010. LNCS, vol. 6183, pp. 126–150. Springer, Heidelberg (2010)
8. ISO/IEC 30170:2012, Information technology – Programming languages – Ruby (2012)
9. James, R.P., Sabry, A.: Yield: Mainstream delimited continuations. In: Workshop on the Theory and Practice of Delimited Continuations, pp. 20–32 (2011)
10. JIS X 3017:2011, Programming languages – Ruby (2011)
11. Kahn, G.: Natural semantics. In: Brandenburg, F.J., Vidal-Naquet, G., Wirsing, M. (eds.) STACS 1987. LNCS, vol. 247, pp. 22–39. Springer, Heidelberg (1987)

12. Maffeis, S., Mitchell, J.C., Taly, A.: An operational semantics for JavaScript. In: Ramalingam, G. (ed.) APLAS 2008. LNCS, vol. 5356, pp. 307–325. Springer, Heidelberg (2008)
13. Milner, R., Tofte, M., MacQueen, D.: The Definition of Standard ML. MIT Press (1997)
14. Politz, J.G., Martinez, A., Milano, M., Warren, S., Patterson, D., Li, J., Chitipothu, A., Krishnamurthi, S.: Python: the full monty. In: ACM SIGPLAN International Conference on Object Oriented Programming Systems Languages and Applications, pp. 217–232 (2013)
15. Ruby programming language, http://www.ruby-lang.org/en/

Types for Flexible Objects

Zachary Palmer, Pottayil Harisanker Menon,
Alexander Rozenshteyn, and Scott Smith

Department of Computer Science,
The Johns Hopkins University, USA
{zachary.palmer,pharisa2,arozens1,scott}@jhu.edu

Abstract. Scripting languages are popular in part due to their extremely flexible objects. Features such as dynamic extension, mixins, and first-class messages improve programmability and lead to concise code. But attempts to statically type these features have met with limited success. Here we present TinyBang, a small typed language in which flexible object operations can be encoded. We illustrate this flexibility by solving an open problem in OO literature: we give an encoding where objects can be extended after being messaged without compromising the expressiveness of subtyping. TinyBang's subtype constraint system ensures that all types are completely inferred; there are no data declarations or type annotations. We formalize TinyBang and prove the type system is sound and decidable; all examples in the paper run in our most recent implementation.

1 Introduction

Modern scripting languages such as Python and JavaScript have become popular in part due to the flexibility of their object semantics. In addition to supporting traditional OO operations such as inheritance and polymorphic dispatch, scripting programmers can add or remove members from existing objects, arbitrarily concatenate objects, represent messages as first-class data, and perform transformations on objects at any point during their lifecycle.

While a significant body of work has focused on statically typing flexible object operations [BF98,RS02,BBV11], the solutions proposed place significant restrictions on how objects can be used. The fundamental tension lies in supporting self-referentiality. For an object to be extensible, "self" must be exposed in some manner equivalent to a function abstraction $\lambda self \ldots$ so that different "self" values may be used in the event of extension. But exposing "self" in this way puts it in a contravariant position; as a result, subtyping on objects is invalid. The above systems create compromises; [BF98], for instance, does not permit objects to be extended after they are messaged.

Along with the problem of contravariant self, it is challenging to define a fully first-class object concatenation operation with pleasing typeability properties. The aforementioned type systems do not support concatenation of arbitrary objects. In the related space of typed record concatenation, previous work [Pot00] has shown that general record concatenation may be typed but requires considerable machinery including presence/absence types and conditional constraints.

J. Garrigue (Ed.): APLAS 2014, LNCS 8858, pp. 99–119, 2014.

In this paper, we present a new programming language calculus, TinyBang, which aims for significant flexibility in statically typing flexible object operations. In particular, we support object extension without restrictions, and we have simple type rules for a first-class concatenation operation.

TinyBang achieves its expressiveness with very few primitives: the core expressions include only labeled data, concatenation, higher-order functions, and pattern matching. Classes, objects, inheritance, object extension, overloading, and switch/case can be fully and faithfully encoded with these primitives. TinyBang also has full type inference for ease and brevity of programming. It is not intended to be a programming language for humans; instead, it aims to serve as a conceptual core for such a language.

1.1   Key Features of TinyBang

TinyBang's type system is grounded in subtype constraint type theory [AWL94], with a series of improvements to both expression syntax and typing to achieve the expressiveness needed for flexible object encodings.

Type-indexed records supporting asymmetric concatenation   TinyBang uses type-indexed records: records for which content can be projected based on its type [SM01]. For example, consider the type-indexed record `{foo = 45; bar = 22; 13}`: the untagged element 13 is implicitly tagged with type `int`, and projecting `int` from this record would yield 13. Since records are type-indexed, we do not need to distinguish records from non-records; 22, for example, is a type-indexed record of one (integer) field. Variants are also just a special case of 1-ary records of labeled data, so `'Some 3` expresses the ML `Some(3)`. Type-indexed records are thus a universal data type and lend themselves to flexible programming patterns in the same spirit as Lisp lists and Smalltalk objects.

TinyBang records support asymmetric concatenation via the `&` operator; informally, `{foo = 45; bar = 22; 13} & {baz = 45; bar = 10; 99}` results in `{foo = 45; bar = 22; baz = 45; 13}` since the left side is given priority for the overlap. Asymmetric concatenation is key for supporting flexible object concatenation, as well as for standard notions of inheritance. We term the `&` operation *onioning*.

Dependently typed first-class cases   TinyBang's first-class functions are written "*pattern -> expression*". In this way, first-class functions are also first-class *case clauses*. We permit the concatenation of these clauses via `&` to give multiple dispatch possibilities. TinyBang's first-class functions generalize the first-class cases of [BAC06].

Additionally, we define a novel notion of union elimination, a *slice*, which allows the type of bindings in a case arm to be refined based on which pattern was matched. Dependently typed first-class cases are critical for typing our object encodings, a topic we discuss in the next section.

Outline In the next section, we give an overview of TinyBang and how it can encode object features. In Section 3, we show the operational semantics and type system for a core subset of TinyBang, trimmed to the key features for readability; we prove soundness and decidability for this system in the appendices. Related work is in Section 4 and we conclude in Section 5.

2   Overview

This section gives an overview of the TinyBang language and of how it supports flexible object operations and other scripting features.

2.1   Language Features for Flexible Objects

The TinyBang expression syntax used in this section appears in Figure 1.

$$e ::= x \mid () \mid \mathbb{Z} \mid l\ e \mid \textbf{ref}\ e \mid !\ e \mid e\ \&\ e \mid \phi \texttt{->}e \mid e\ \boxdot\ e \mid e\ e \mid \texttt{let}\ x = e\ \texttt{in}\ e \mid x := e\ \texttt{in}\ e$$
$$\phi ::= x \mid () \mid \texttt{int} \mid l\ \phi \mid \phi\ \&\ \phi \qquad\qquad\qquad\qquad\qquad\qquad\qquad\qquad\qquad\textit{patterns}$$
$$\boxdot ::= \texttt{+} \mid \texttt{-} \mid \texttt{==} \mid \texttt{<=} \mid \texttt{>=} \qquad\qquad\qquad\qquad\qquad\qquad\qquad\qquad\qquad\textit{operators}$$
$$l ::= \text{`}\textit{(alphanumeric)} \qquad\qquad\qquad\qquad\qquad\qquad\qquad\qquad\qquad\qquad\qquad\textit{labels}$$

Fig. 1. TinyBang Syntax

Program types take the form of a set of subtype constraints [AWL94]. For the purposes of this Overview we will be informal about type syntax. For example, the informal `int` ∪ `bool` is in fact be expressed via constraints `int` <: α and `bool` <: α. The details of the type system are presented in Section 3.3.

Simple functions as methods We begin by considering the oversimplified case of an object with a single method and no fields or self-awareness. In the variant encoding, such an object is represented by a function which pattern-matches on the message identifying that single method. We see in Figure 1 that all TinyBang functions are written ϕ -> e, with ϕ being a *pattern* to match against the function's argument. Each function has only one pattern; we call these one-clause pattern-matching functions *simple functions*. For instance, consider the following object and its invocation:

```
ı let obj = ('twice x -> x + x) in obj ('twice 4)
```

The syntax `'twice 4` is a label constructor similar to an OCaml polymorphic variant or Haskell **newtype**; like these languages, the expression `'twice 4` has type `'twice int`. The simple function `'twice x -> x + x` is a function which matches on any argument containing a `'twice` label and binds its contents to the variable x. Note that the expression `'twice 4` is a first-class message.

A simple function is only capable of matching one pattern; to express general pattern matching, functions are concatenated via the *onion* operation & to give *compound functions*. Given two function expressions e1 and e2, the expression (e1 & e2) conjoins them to make a compound function. (e1 & e2) arg will apply the function which has a pattern matching arg; if both patterns match arg, the leftmost function (e.g. e1) is given priority. For example:

```
1  let obj = ('twice x -> x + x) & ('isZero x -> x == 0) in obj 'twice 4
```

The above shows that traditional **match** expressions can be encoded using the & operator to join a number of simple functions: one for each case. Because these functions are values, TinyBang's function conjunction generalizes the first-class cases of [BAC06]; that work does not support "override" of existing clauses or heterogeneously typed case branches.

Dependent pattern types The above shows the encoding of a simple object with two methods, no fields, and no self-awareness, but this function conjunction approach presents some typing challenges. Consider the analogous OCaml match/-case expression:

```
1  let obj m = (match m with | 'twice x -> x + x
2                            | 'isZero x -> x == 0) in ...
```

This will not typecheck, since the same type must be returned for all branches.[1] We resolve this in TinyBang by giving the function a dependent pattern type ('twice int → int) & ('isZero int → bool). If the function is applied in the context where the type of message is known, the appropriate result type is inferred; for instance, invoking this method with 'isZero 0 always produces type **bool** and not type int ∪ bool. When we present the formal type system below, we show how these dependent pattern types extend the expressiveness of conditional constraint types [AWL94,Pot00] in a dimension critical for typing objects.

This need for dependent typing arises largely from our desire to accurately type a variant-based object model; a record-based encoding of objects would not have this problem. We choose a variant-based encoding because it greatly simplifies encodings such as self-passing and overloading, which we describe below.

Onions are records There is no record syntax in TinyBang; instead, it suffices to use concatenation (&) on labeled values. We informally call these records *onions* to signify these properties. Here is an example of how multi-argument methods can be defined:

```
1  let obj = ('sum ('x x & 'y y) -> x + y)
2          & ('equal ('x x & 'y y) -> x == y)
3  in obj ('sum ('x 3 & 'y 2))
```

The 'x 3 & 'y 2 amounts to a two-label record. This 'sum-labeled onion is passed to the pattern 'x x & 'y y. (We highlight the pattern & differently than the onioning & because the former is a *pattern conjunction* operator: the value must match both subpatterns.) Also observe from this example how there is no hard distinction in TinyBang between records and variants: there is only one class of label. This means that the 1-ary record 'sum 4 is the same as the 1-ary variant 'sum 4.

---

[1] The recent OCaml 4 GADT extension mitigates this difficulty but requires an explicit type declaration, type annotations, and only works under a closed world assumption.

2.2   Self-awareness and Resealable Objects

Up to this point, objects have no self-awareness: they cannot invoke their own methods. Encoding a runtime model of self-awareness is simple; for instance, dynamic dispatch can be accomplished simply by transforming each method invocation (e.g. obj.m(arg)) into a function call in which the object is passed to itself (e.g. obj ('self obj & 'm arg)). But while this model exhibits appropriate runtime behavior, it does not typecheck properly in the presence of subtyping. Consider the code in Figure 2 and the Java statement A obj = new B();. The encoding of obj.foo() here would fail to typecheck; the B implementation of foo expects this to have a bar method, but the weakened obj cannot guarantee this. Although this example uses Java type annotations to weaken the variable's type, similar weakening eventually occurs with any decidable type inference algorithm. We also observe that the same problem arises if, rather than self-passing at the call site, we encode the object to carry itself in a field.

```
class A {                    class B extends A {
   int foo() { return 4; }      int foo() { return this.bar(); }
}                               int bar() { return 8; }
                             }
```

Fig. 2. Self-Encoding Example Code

The simple approach shown above fails because, informally, the object does not know its own type. To successfully typecheck dynamic dispatch, we must keep an *internal* type for the object separate from the *external* type it has in any particular context; that is, in the above example, the object must remember that it is a B-typed object even when it is generalized e.g. in an A-typed variable. One simple approach to this is to capture an appropriate self-type in closure, similar to how functions can recurse via self-passing:

```
1 let obj0 = self -> ('foo _ & 'self self -> self self ('bar _ & 'self self)) &
2                    ('bar _ & 'self self -> 8) in
3 let obj = obj0 obj0 in ...
```

The initial passing of obj0 to itself bootstraps the self-passing mechanism; obj becomes a function with obj0 captured in closure as self; thus, any message passed to obj uses the type of obj0 at the time obj was created rather than relying on its type in context. While this approach is successful in creating a self-aware object, it interferes with extensibility: the type of self is fixed, preventing additional methods from being added or overridden.

To create an extensible encoding of dynamically dispatched objects, we build on the work of [BF98]. In that work, an object exists in one of two states: as a prototype, which can be extended but not messaged, or as a "proper" object, which can be messaged but not extended. Prototypes cannot be messaged because they do not yet have a notion of their own type. A prototype may be "sealed" to transform it into a proper object, capturing the object's type in a fashion similar to the above. A sealed object may not be extended for the same reason as the above: there exists no mechanism to modify or specialize the captured self-type.

The work we present here extends [BF98] with two notable refinements. First, that work presents a calculus in which objects are primitives; in TinyBang, however, objects and the sealing process itself are encoded using simple functions and conjunction. Second, TinyBang admits a limited context in which sealed objects may be extended and then *resealed*, thus relaxing the sharp phase distinction between prototypes and proper objects. All object extension below will be performed on sealed objects. Object sealing is accomplished by a TinyBang function `seal`:

```
1 let fixpoint = f -> (w -> w w) (t -> a -> f (t t) a) in
2 let seal = fixpoint (seal -> obj ->
3                      (msg -> obj (msg & 'self (seal obj))) & obj) in
4 let obj = ('twice x -> x + x) &
5            ('quad x & 'self self -> self ('twice x) + self ('twice x))
6 let sObj = seal obj in
7 let twenty = sObj 'quad 5 in          // returns 20
```

Here, `fixpoint` is simply the Y-combinator. The `seal` function operates by adding a message handler which captures *every* message sent to `obj`. (We still add `& obj` to this message handler to preserve the non-function parts of the object.) This message handler captures the type of `obj` in the closure of a function; thus, later invocations of this message handler will continue to use the type at seal-time even if the types of variables containing the object are weakened. The message handler adds a `'self` component containing the sealed object to the right of the message and then passes it to the original object. We require `fixpoint` to ensure that this self-reference is also sealed. So, every message sent to `sObj` will be sent on to `obj` with `'self sObj` added to the right. Note that the `'twice` method does not require a `'self` pattern component: due to structural subtyping, any message with a `'twice` label (whether it also includes a `'self` or not) will do.

The key to preserving extensibility with this approach is the fact that, while the `seal` function has captured the type of `obj` in closure, the `self` value is still sent to the original object as an argument. We now show how this permits extension of sealed objects in certain contexts.

Extending previously sealed objects In the definition of `seal` above, the catch-all message handler adds a `'self` label to the *right* of the message; thus, if any `'self` label already existed in the message, it would be given priority over the one added by `seal`. We can take advantage of this behavior in order to extend a sealed object and then *reseal* it, refining its `self`-type. Consider the following continuation of the previous code:

```
1 let sixteen = sObj 'quad 4 in         // returns 16
2 let obj2 = ('twice x -> x) & sObj in
3 let sObj2 = seal obj2 in
4 let eight = sObj2 'quad 4 in ...      // returns 8
```

We can extend `sObj` after messaging it, here overriding the `'twice` message; `sObj2` represents the (re-)sealed version of this new object. `sObj2` properly knows its "new" self due to the resealing, evidenced here by how `'quad` invokes the new 'twice. To see why this works let us trace the execution. Expanding the sealing of sObj2, sObj2 ('quad 4) has the same effect as obj2 ('quad 4 & 'self sObj2), which has the same effect as sObj ('quad 4 & 'self sObj2). Recall sObj is also a sealed object which adds a 'self component to the *right*; thus this has the same effect as obj ('quad 4 & 'self sObj2 & 'self sObj). Because the leftmost 'self has priority, the 'self is properly sObj2 here. We see from the original definition of obj that it sends a 'twice message to the contents of self, which then follows the same pattern as above until obj ('twice 4 & 'self sObj2 & 'self sObj) is invoked (two times – once for each side of +).

Sealed and resealed objects obey the desired object subtyping laws because we "tie the knot" on self using seal, meaning there is no contravariant self parameter on object method calls to invalidate object subtyping. Additionally, our type system includes parametric polymorphism and so sObj and the re-sealed sObj2 do not have to share the same self type, and the fact that & is a *functional* extension operation means that there will be no pollution between the two distinct self types. Key to the success of this encoding is the asymmetric nature of &: it allows us to override the default 'self parameter. This self resealing is possible in the record model of objects, but is much more convoluted; this is a reason that we switched to a variant model.

It should be noted that this resealing approach is limited to contexts in which no type information has yet been lost regarding the sealed object. Using the example from Figure 2, typechecking would likely fail if one were to seal a B, weaken its type to an A, extend it, and then reseal the result: the new self-type would be derived from A, not B, and so would still lack knowledge of the bar method. The runtime behavior is always correct, and typechecking would also succeed if the extension provided its own override of the bar method for the newly-sealed object to use.

Onioning it all together Onions also provide a natural mechanism for including fields; we simply concatenate them to the functions that represent the methods. Consider the following object which stores and increments a counter:

```
1 let obj = seal ('x (ref 0) &
2           ('inc _ & 'self self -> ('x x -> x := !x + 1 in !x) self))
3 in obj 'inc ()
```

Observe how obj is a heterogeneous "mash" of a record field (the 'x) and a function (the handler for 'inc). This is sound because onions are *type-indexed* [SM01], meaning that they use the types of the values themselves to identify data. For this particular example, invocation obj 'inc () (note () is an empty onion, a 0-ary conjunction) correctly increments in spite of the presence of the 'x label in obj.

The above counter object code is quite concise: it defines a self-referential, mutable counter object using no syntactic sugar whatsoever in a core language with no explicit object syntax. But as we said before, we do not expect programmers to write directly in TinyBang under normal circumstances. Here are a few syntactic sugarings used in subsequent examples. (A "real" language built

on these ideas would include sugarings for each of the features we are about to
mention as well.)

```
o.x                      ≅ ('x x -> x) o
o.x = e₁ in e₂           ≅ ('x x -> x = e₁ in e₂) o
if e₁ then e₂ else e₃    ≅ (('True _ -> e₂) & ('False _ -> e₃)) e₁
e₁ and e₂                ≅ (('True _ -> e₂) & ('False _ -> 'False ())) e₁
```

2.3 Flexible Object Operations

We now cover how TinyBang supports a wealth of flexible object operations,
expanding on the first-class messages and flexible extension operations covered
above. We show encodings in terms of objects rather than classes for simplicity;
applying these concepts to classes is straightforward.

Default arguments TinyBang can easily encode optional arguments that take on
a default value if missing. For instance, consider:

```
1 let obj = seal ( ('add ('x x & 'y y) -> x + y)
2                & ('sub ('x x & 'y y) -> x - y) ) in
3 let dflt = obj -> ('add a -> obj ('add (a & 'x 1))) & obj in
4 let obj2 = dflt obj in
5 obj2 ('add ('y 3)) + obj2 ('add ('x 7 & 'y 2))  // 4 + 9
```

Object `dflt` overrides `obj`'s 'add to make 1 the default value for 'x. Because
the 'x 1 is onioned onto the right of a, it will have no effect if an 'x is explicitly
provided in the message.

Overloading The pattern-matching semantics of functions also provide a simple
mechanism whereby multi-functions can be defined to overload their behavior.
We might originally define negation on the integers as

```
1 let neg = x & int -> 0 - x in ...
```

Here, the conjunction pattern x & int will match the argument with int and
also bind it to the variable x. Later code could then extend the definition of
negation to include boolean values. Because multi-functions assign new meaning
to an existing symbol, we redefine neg to include all of the behavior of the old
neg as well as new cases for 'True and 'False:

```
1 let neg = ('True _ -> 'False ()) & ('False _ -> 'True ()) & neg in ...
```

Negation is now overloaded: neg 4 evaluates to -4, and neg 'True () evaluates
to 'False () due to how application matches function patterns.

Mixins The following example shows how a simple two-dimensional point object
can be combined with a mixin providing extra methods:

```
1 let point = seal ('x (ref 0) & 'y (ref 0)
2               & ('ll _ & 'self self -> self.x + self.y)
3               & ('isZero _ & 'self self -> self.x == 0 and self.y == 0)) in
4 let mixin = 'near _ & 'self self -> self 'll ()) < 4) in
5 let mixPt = seal (point & mixin) in mixPt 'near ()
```

Here `mixin` is a function which invokes the value passed as `self`. Because an object's methods are just functions onioned together, onioning `mixin` into `point` is sufficient to produce a properly functioning `mixPt`.

The above example typechecks in TinyBang; parametric polymorphism is used to allow `point`, `mixin`, and `mixPt` to have different self-types. The `mixin` variable has the approximate type "('near unit & 'self α) $\rightarrow$ bool where α is an object capable of receiving the '11 message and producing an int". `mixin` can be onioned with any object that satisfies these properties. If the object does not have these properties, a type error will result when the 'near message is passed; for instance, (seal mixin) ('near ()) is not typeable because `mixin`, the value of `self`, does not have a function which can handle the '11 message.

TinyBang mixins are first-class values; the actual mixing need not occur until runtime. For instance, the following code selects a weighting metric to mix into a point based on some runtime condition `cond`.

```
1 let cond = (runtime boolean) in let point = (as above) in
2 let w1 =
3 ('weight _ & 'self self -> self.x + self.y) in
4 let w2 = ('weight _ & 'self self -> self.x - self.y) in
5 let mixPt = seal (point & (if cond then w1 else w2)) in
6 mixPt 'weight ()
```

Inheritance, classes, and subclasses Typical object-oriented constructs can be defined similarly to the above. Object inheritance is similar to mixins, but a variable `super` is also bound to the original object and captured in the closure of the inheriting objects methods, allowing it to be reached for static dispatch. The flexibility of the `seal` function permits us to ensure that the inheriting object is used for future dispatches even in calls to overridden methods. Classes are simply objects that generate other objects, and subclasses are extensions of those object generating objects. We forgo examples here for brevity.

3   Formalization

Here we give formal semantics to TinyBang. For clarity, features which are not unique to our semantics – integers, state, etc. – are omitted. We first translate TinyBang programs to A-normal form; Section 3.2 defines the operational semantics of the A-normalized version of restricted TinyBang. Section 3.3 defines the type system and soundness and decidability properties. The full technical report [MPRS14b] shows how the omitted features are handled.

Notation For a given construct g, we let $[g_1, \ldots, g_n]$ denote an n-ary list of g, often using the equivalent shorthand $\overrightarrow{g}^n$. We elide the n when it is unnecessary. Operator $\|$ denotes list concatenation. For sets, we use similar notation: $\overset{n}{\underset{\smile}{g}}$ abbreviates $\{g_1, \ldots, g_n\}$ for some arbitrary ordering of the set.

3.1   A-Translation

In order to simplify our formal presentation, we convert TinyBang into A-normal form; this brings expressions, patterns, and types into close syntactic alignment which greatly simplifies the proofs. The grammar of our A-normalized language appears in Figure 3. For the purposes of discussion, we will refer to the restriction of the language presented in Section 2 as the *nested* language and to the language appearing in Figure 3 as the *ANF* language.

$$
\begin{array}{llll}
e ::= \vec{s} & expressions & \phi ::= \overrightarrow{x = \mathring{v}} & patterns \\
s ::= x = v \mid x = x \mid x = x\ x & clauses & & \\
E ::= \overrightarrow{x = v} & environment & B ::= \overrightarrow{x = x} & bindings \\
v ::= \mathbb{Z} \mid () \mid l\ x \mid x\,\&\,x \mid \phi \text{->} e & values & \mathring{v} ::= \texttt{int} \mid () \mid l\ x \mid x\,\&\,x & pattern\ vals \\
l ::= {}^{\backprime}\ (alphanumeric) & labels & x ::= (alphanumeric) & variables
\end{array}
$$

Fig. 3. TinyBang ANF Grammar

Observe how expression and pattern grammars are nearly identical. We require that both expressions and patterns declare each variable at most once; expressions and patterns which do not have this property must be α-renamed such that they do. The constructions E and B are not directly used in the A-translation; they define the environment and bindings in the semantics.

We define the A-translation function $\langle e \rangle_x$ in Figure 4. Here, e is a nested TinyBang expression; the result is the A-normalized form $\vec{s}$ in which the final declared variable is x. We overload this notation to patterns as well. We use y and z to range over fresh variables unique to that invocation of $\langle - \rangle_-$; different recursive invocations use different fresh variables y and z.

$$
\begin{array}{ll}
\textbf{Expressions} & \textbf{Patterns} \\[4pt]
\langle () \rangle_x = [x = ()] & \langle () \rangle_x = [x = ()] \\
\langle l\ e \rangle_x = \langle e \rangle_y \,\|\, [x = l\ y] & \langle l\ \phi \rangle_x = \langle \phi \rangle_y \,\|\, [x = l\ y] \\
\langle e_1\,\&\,e_2 \rangle_x = \langle e_1 \rangle_y \,\|\, \langle e_2 \rangle_z \,\|\, [x = y\,\&\,z] & \langle \phi_1\,\&\,\phi_2 \rangle_x = \langle \phi_1 \rangle_y \,\|\, \langle \phi_2 \rangle_z \,\|\, [x = y\,\&\,z] \\
\langle \phi \text{->} e \rangle_x = [x = \langle \phi \rangle_y \text{->} \langle e \rangle_z] & \langle x_2 \rangle_{x_1} = [x_2 = ()] \\
\langle e_1\ e_2 \rangle_x = \langle e_1 \rangle_y \,\|\, \langle e_2 \rangle_z \,\|\, [x = y\ z] & \\
\langle \texttt{let}\ x_1 = e_1\ \texttt{in}\ e_2 \rangle_{x_2} = \langle e_1 \rangle_{x_1} \,\|\, \langle e_2 \rangle_{x_2} & \\
\langle x_2 \rangle_{x_1} = [x_1 = x_2] &
\end{array}
$$

Fig. 4. TinyBang A-Translation

Notice that A-translation of patterns is in perfect parallel with the expressions in the above; for example, the expression ${}^{\backprime}\texttt{A x -> x}$ translates to $[y_1 = ([x = (), y_3 = {}^{\backprime}\texttt{A x}] \text{-> } [y_2 = x])]$. Using the same A-translation for patterns and expressions greatly aids the formal development, but it takes some practice to read these A-translated patterns. Variables matched against empty onion ($x = ()$ here) are unconstrained and represent bindings that can be used in the body. Variables matched against other pattern clauses (such as y_3) are not bindings; clause $y_3 = {}^{\backprime}\texttt{A x}$ constrains the argument to match a ${}^{\backprime}\texttt{A}$-labeled value. The last binding in the pattern, here $y_3 = {}^{\backprime}\texttt{A x}$, is taken to match the argument when the function is applied; this is in analogy to how the variable in the last clause of an expression is the final value. Variable binding takes place on $()$

(wildcard) definitions: every pattern clause x = () binds x in the function body. In clause lists, each clause binds the defining variable for all clauses appearing after it; nested function clauses follow the usual lexical scoping rules. For the remainder of the paper, we assume expressions are closed unless noted.

3.2 Operational Semantics

Next, we define an operational semantics for ANF TinyBang. The primary complexity of these semantics is pattern matching, for which several auxiliary definitions are needed.

Compatibility. The first basic relation we define is *compatibility*: is a value accepted by a given pattern? We define compatibility using a constructive failure model for reasons of well-foundedness which are discussed below. We use the symbol $\odot$ to range over the two symbols $\bullet$ and $\bigcirc$, which indicate compatibility and incompatibility, respectively, and order them: $\bigcirc < \bullet$.

We write $x \mathbin{\overset{\odot}{\underset{E}{\preceq}}}{}^B_\phi x'$ to indicate that the value x is compatible (if $\odot = \bullet$) or incompatible (if $\odot = \bigcirc$) with the pattern x'. E represents the environment in which to interpret the value x while ϕ represents the environment in which to interpret the pattern x'. B dictates how, upon a successful match, the values from E will be bound to the pattern variables in ϕ. Compatibility is the least relation satisfying the rules in Figure 5.

EMPTY ONION
$$\frac{x_0 = v \in E \quad x_0' = () \in \phi \quad B = [x_0' = x_0]}{x_0 \mathbin{\overset{\bullet}{\underset{E}{\preceq}}}{}^B_\phi x_0'}$$

LABEL
$$\frac{x_0 = l\ x_1 \in E \quad x_0' = l\ x_1' \in \phi \quad x_1 \mathbin{\overset{\odot}{\underset{E}{\preceq}}}{}^B_\phi x_1'}{x_0 \mathbin{\overset{\odot}{\underset{E}{\preceq}}}{}^B_\phi x_0'}$$

CONJUNCTION PATTERN
$$\frac{x_0' = x_1' \,\&\, x_2' \in \phi \quad x_0 \mathbin{\overset{\odot_1}{\underset{E}{\preceq}}}{}^{B_1}_\phi x_1' \quad x_0 \mathbin{\overset{\odot_2}{\underset{E}{\preceq}}}{}^{B_2}_\phi x_2'}{x_0 \mathbin{\overset{\min(\odot_1, \odot_2)}{\underset{E}{\preceq}}}{}^{B_1 \,\|\, B_2}_\phi x_0'}$$

ONION VALUE LEFT
$$\frac{x_0 = x_1 \,\&\, x_2 \in E \quad x_1 \mathbin{\overset{\bullet}{\underset{E}{\preceq}}}{}^B_\phi x_0'}{x_0 \mathbin{\overset{\bullet}{\underset{E}{\preceq}}}{}^B_\phi x_0'}$$

ONION VALUE RIGHT
$$\frac{x_0 = x_1 \,\&\, x_2 \in E \quad x_0' = x_1' \,\&\, x_2' \notin \phi \quad x_1 \mathbin{\overset{\bigcirc}{\underset{E}{\preceq}}}{}^{B'}_\phi x_0' \quad x_2 \mathbin{\overset{\odot}{\underset{E}{\preceq}}}{}^B_\phi x_0'}{x_0 \mathbin{\overset{\odot}{\underset{E}{\preceq}}}{}^B_\phi x_0'}$$

LABEL MISMATCH
$$\frac{x_0 = l\ x_1 \in E \quad x_0' = \hat{v} \in \phi \quad \hat{v} = l'\ x_2 \text{ only if } l \neq l' \quad \hat{v} \text{ not of the form } x' \,\&\, x'' \text{ or } ()}{x_0 \mathbin{\overset{\bigcirc}{\underset{E}{\preceq}}}{}^{[]}_\phi x_0'}$$

Fig. 5. Pattern compatibility rules

The compatibility relation is key to TinyBang's semantics and bears some explanation. As mentioned above, every clause $x = ()$ appearing in the pattern binds the variable x; the Empty Onion rule ensures this by adding a binding clause to B. The Label rule simply recurses when the value is a label and the pattern matches that label; the Label Mismatch rule (which is the base case for failure) applies when the pattern does not match that label. Conjunction is relatively self-evident; min is used here as a logical "and" over the two recursive premises. The onion rules reflect TinyBang's asymmetric concatenation semantics. Given a value $x_1 \,\&\, x_2$, it is possible that both x_1 and x_2 match the pattern.

If so, we must ensure that we take the bindings from the compatibility of x_1. The Onion Value Left rule applies when the left side matches. The Onion Value Right rule only applies only if the left side *doesn't* match; that is, a proof of compatibility may recursively depend on a proof of *incompatibility*. This is the reason that our relation is defined to be constructive for both success and failure: it is necessary to show that the relation is inductively well-founded.

For an example, consider matching the pattern 'A a & 'B b against the value 'A () & 'B (). The A-translations of these expressions are, respectively, the first and second columns below. Compatibility $v5 \underset{E \preceq \phi}{\bullet \preceq^B}$ p3 holds with the bindings B shown in the third column.

E	ϕ	B
v1 = ()	a = ()	a = v1
v2 = 'A v1	p1 = 'A a	
v3 = ()	b = ()	b = v3
v4 = 'B v3	p2 = 'B b	
v5 = v2 & v4	p3 = p1 & p2	

Matching. Compatibility determines if a value matches a *single* pattern; we next define a matching relation to check if a series of pattern clauses match. In TinyBang, recall that individual pattern clauses *pattern -> body* are simple functions $\phi -> e$ and a series simple functions onioned together expresses a multi-clause pattern match. So, we define an application matching relation $x_0\ x_1\ ^{\odot}\rightsquigarrow_E e$ to determine if an onion of pattern clauses x_0 can be applied to argument x_1. This relation is constructive on failure in the same fashion as compatibility.We define matching as the least relation satisfying the rules in Figure 6. The helper function RV extracts the return variable from a value, defined as follows: $\mathrm{RV}(e\,\|\,[x = ...]) = x$ and $\mathrm{RV}(e\,\|\,[x = \mathring{v}]) = x$.

FUNCTION
$$\frac{x_0 = (\phi -> e) \in E \quad x_1\ ^{\odot}\underset{E \preceq \phi}{\preceq^B}\ \mathrm{RV}(\phi)}{x_0\ x_1\ ^{\odot}\rightsquigarrow_E B\,\|\,e}$$

NON-FUNCTION
$$\frac{x_0 = (\phi -> e) \notin E \quad x_0 = x_2 \& x_3 \notin E}{x_0\ x_1\ ^{\odot}\rightsquigarrow_E e}$$

ONION LEFT
$$\frac{x_0 = x_2 \& x_3 \in E \quad x_2\ x_1\ ^{\bullet}\rightsquigarrow_E e}{x_0\ x_1\ ^{\bullet}\rightsquigarrow_E e}$$

ONION RIGHT
$$\frac{x_0 = x_2 \& x_3 \in E \quad x_2\ x_1\ ^{\circ}\rightsquigarrow_E e' \quad x_3\ x_1\ ^{\odot}\rightsquigarrow_E e}{x_0\ x_1\ ^{\odot}\rightsquigarrow_E e}$$

Fig. 6. Application matching rules

The Function rule is the base case of a simple function application: the argument value x_1 must be compatible with the pattern ϕ, and if so insert the resulting bindings B at the top of the function body e. The Onion Left/Right rules are the inductive cases; notice that the Onion Right rule can only match successfully if the (higher priority) left side has failed to match. The Non-Function rule is the base case for application of a non-function, which fails but in a way which permits dispatch to continue through the onion.

Operational Semantics. Using the compatibility and matching relations from above, we now define the operational semantics of TinyBang as a small step relation $e \longrightarrow^1 e'$. Our definition uses an environment-based semantics; it proceeds by acting on the first unevaluated clause of e. We use an environment-based semantics (rather than a substitution-based semantics) due to its suitability to ANF and because it aligns well with the type system presented in the next section.

We must freshen variables as they are introduced to the expression to preserve the invariant that the ANF TinyBang expression uniquely defines each variable; to do so, we take $\alpha(e)$ to be an α-renaming function which freshens all variables in e which are not free. We then define the small step relation as the least relation satisfying the rules given by Figure 7.

VARIABLE LOOKUP
$$\frac{x_1 = v \in E}{E \,\|\, [x_2 = x_1] \,\|\, e \longrightarrow^1 E \,\|\, [x_2 = v] \,\|\, e}$$

APPLICATION
$$\frac{x_0 \; x_1 \;\overset{\bullet}{\rightsquigarrow}_E\; e' \quad \alpha(e') = e''}{E \,\|\, [x_2 = x_0 \; x_1] \,\|\, e \longrightarrow^1 E \,\|\, e'' \,\|\, [x_2 = \mathrm{RV}(e'')] \,\|\, e}$$

Fig. 7. The operational semantics small step relation

The application rule simply inlines the freshened function body e'' in the event there was a match. We define $e_0 \longrightarrow^* e_n$ to hold when $e_0 \longrightarrow^1 \ldots \longrightarrow^1 e_n$ for some $n \geq 0$. Note that $e \longrightarrow^* E$ means that computation has resulted in a final value. We write $e \not\longrightarrow^1$ iff there is no e' such that $e \longrightarrow^1 e'$; observe $E \not\longrightarrow^1$ for any E. When $e \not\longrightarrow^1$ for some e not of the form E, we say that e is *stuck*.

3.3   Type System

We base TinyBang's type system on subtype constraint systems, which have been shown to be expressive [AWL94] and suitable for complex pattern matching [Pot00] and object-orientation [WS01]. We begin by aligning expressions and types (an operation made easy by our choice of ANF expression syntax); we then define type system relations which parallel those from the operational semantics, including a deductive constraint closure which parallels the small step relation itself. Our proof of soundness proceeds by showing a simulation property that programs stay aligned with their types as they execute, and stuck programs correspond to inconsistent constraint sets.

Initial Alignment. Figure 8 presents the type system grammar. Note the close alignment between expression and type grammar elements; E has type V, and variable bindings B have the type analog F. Expressions e have types $\alpha \backslash C$; expressions and type grammars are less different than they appear, since the expression clauses are a list where the last variable contains the final value implicitly whereas in the type the final type location α must be explicit. Both v and $\mathring{v}$ have type τ.

We formalize this initial alignment step as a function $[\![e]\!]_E$ which produces a constrained type $\alpha \backslash C$; see Figure 9. Initial alignment over a given e picks a single fresh type variable for each program variable in e; for the variable x_0, we denote this fresh type variable as $\mathring{\alpha}_0$.

$$C ::= \overleftrightarrow{c} \qquad \text{constraint sets}$$
$$V ::= \overrightarrow{\tau <: \alpha} \qquad \text{constraint value sets}$$
$$F ::= \overleftrightarrow{\alpha <: \alpha} \qquad \text{constraint flow sets}$$

$$c ::= \tau <: \alpha \mid \alpha <: \alpha \mid \alpha\,\alpha <: \alpha \qquad \text{constraint}$$
$$\tau ::= () \mid l\,\alpha \mid \alpha\,\&\,\alpha \mid \alpha \backslash V \to \alpha \backslash C \qquad \text{types}$$
$$\alpha \qquad \text{type variables}$$

Fig. 8. The TinyBang type grammar

$$[\![\overrightarrow{s}^n]\!]_{\mathrm{E}} = \alpha_n \backslash \overrightarrow{c}^n \text{ where } \forall i \in \{1..n\}.[\![s_i]\!]_{\mathrm{S}} = \alpha_i \backslash c_i$$
$$[\![\overrightarrow{x = \hat{v}}^n]\!]_{\mathrm{P}} = \alpha_n \backslash \overrightarrow{c}^n \text{ where } \forall i \in \{1..n\}.[\![x_i = \hat{v}_i]\!]_{\mathrm{\check{S}}} = \alpha_i \backslash c_i$$

$$[\![x_0 = \mathbb{Z}]\!]_{\mathrm{S}} = \mathring{\alpha}_0 \backslash \text{ int} <: \mathring{\alpha}_0$$
$$[\![x_0 = ()]\!]_{\mathrm{S}} = \mathring{\alpha}_0 \backslash \; () <: \mathring{\alpha}_0$$
$$[\![x_0 = l\,x_1]\!]_{\mathrm{S}} = \mathring{\alpha}_0 \backslash \; l\,\mathring{\alpha}_1 <: \mathring{\alpha}_0$$
$$[\![x_0 = x_1\,\&\,x_2]\!]_{\mathrm{S}} = \mathring{\alpha}_0 \backslash \; \mathring{\alpha}_1\,\&\,\mathring{\alpha}_2 <: \mathring{\alpha}_0$$
$$[\![x_0 = \phi \text{->} e]\!]_{\mathrm{S}} = \mathring{\alpha}_0 \backslash \; [\![\phi]\!]_{\mathrm{P}} \to [\![e]\!]_{\mathrm{E}} <: \mathring{\alpha}_0$$
$$[\![x_0 = x_1]\!]_{\mathrm{S}} = \mathring{\alpha}_0 \backslash \; \mathring{\alpha}_1 <: \mathring{\alpha}_0$$
$$[\![x_0 = x_1\,x_2]\!]_{\mathrm{S}} = \mathring{\alpha}_0 \backslash \; \mathring{\alpha}_1\,\mathring{\alpha}_2 <: \mathring{\alpha}_0$$

$$[\![x_0 = \text{int}]\!]_{\mathrm{\check{S}}} = \mathring{\alpha}_0 \backslash \text{ int} <: \mathring{\alpha}_0$$
$$[\![x_0 = ()]\!]_{\mathrm{\check{S}}} = \mathring{\alpha}_0 \backslash \; () <: \mathring{\alpha}_0$$
$$[\![x_0 = l\,x_1]\!]_{\mathrm{\check{S}}} = \mathring{\alpha}_0 \backslash \; l\,\mathring{\alpha}_1 <: \mathring{\alpha}_0$$
$$[\![x_0 = x_1\,\&\,x_2]\!]_{\mathrm{\check{S}}} = \mathring{\alpha}_0 \backslash \; \mathring{\alpha}_1\,\&\,\mathring{\alpha}_2 <: \mathring{\alpha}_0$$

Fig. 9. Initial alignment

Slicing. When defining type compatibility in TinyBang, a subtle problem arises which did not appear in the evaluation system. In the evaluation system, each variable is guaranteed to have a single assignment; thus, a premise of value compatibility in Figure 5 such as "$x_1 = l\,x_0 \in E$" is unambiguous. This is not so in the type system: a single type variable may have multiple lower bounds. Such type variables represent union types and present subtle challenges. For instance, consider a direct translation of Figure 5 to the type system (replacing all x with α, all B with F, all ϕ with V, and so on). In the resulting relation, the informal type `A $\alpha \cup$ `B α would appear to match the pattern `A _ & `B _: we can prove that the argument type variable has a `A lower bound and, independently, we can prove that it has a `B lower bound. This is an instance of the well-known *union elimination* problem: we must be consistent in our view of how case analysis on unions is performed. Because TinyBang's dispatch on functions has weak dependent typing properties, this imprecision would be unsound if not addressed: if the type system erroneously concludes that the argument matches the `A _ & `B _ pattern, this imprecision may cause it not to consider a lower priority function which is actually invoked at runtime.

We solve this problem by defining a *slicing* relation to eliminate unions before checking compatibility. This ensures that our union eliminations are consistent (because they are performed before, not during, compatibility checking) and additionally provides us with a refined form of the argument to use in typechecking the function body. Slicing eliminates the above soundness concern because the argument is first separated into the distinct `A $\alpha$ and `B α slices and compatibility is checked for each of them separately. Note that union elimination must be complete up to the depth of the pattern; otherwise, union alignment problems will begin where the elimination stopped.

We write $\alpha \backslash V \ll \alpha' \backslash C$ to indicate that $\alpha \backslash V$ is a slice of the constrained type $\alpha' \backslash C$; this relation is defined as follows:

$$\frac{\text{LEAF}}{\alpha \notin V} \qquad \frac{\text{ATOMIC} \quad \tau \text{ not of the form } l\,\alpha_1 \text{ or } \alpha_1 \,\&\, \alpha_2 \quad \tau <: \alpha \in V \quad \tau <: \alpha' \in C}{\alpha \backslash V \ll \alpha' \backslash C}$$

$$\frac{\text{LABEL}}{l\,\alpha_1 <: \alpha_0 \in V \quad l\,\alpha_1' <: \alpha_0' \in C \quad \alpha_1 \backslash V \ll \alpha_1' \backslash C}{\alpha_0 \backslash V \ll \alpha_0' \backslash C}$$

$$\frac{\text{ONION}}{\alpha_1 \,\&\, \alpha_2 <: \alpha_0 \in V \quad \alpha_1' \,\&\, \alpha_2' <: \alpha_0' \in C \quad \alpha_1 \backslash V \ll \alpha_1' \backslash C \quad \alpha_2 \backslash V \ll \alpha_2' \backslash C}{\alpha_0 \backslash V \ll \alpha_0' \backslash C}$$

Fig. 10. The slice relation for union elimination

Definition 1. $\alpha \backslash V \ll \alpha' \backslash C$ *is the least relation defined by the rules in Figure 10. Slices* $\alpha \backslash V$ *of* $\alpha' \backslash C$ *additionally must always be*

- well-formed: *each* α'' *in* V *has at most one lower bound in* V,
- disjoint: $\tau <: \alpha'' \in V$ *implies that* α'' *does not appear in* C, *and*
- minimal: *every upper-bounding* α'' *in* V *is either* α *or appears in a lower bound in* V.
- acyclic: *there exists a preorder on type variables in* V *s.t.* $\alpha_1 < \alpha_2$ *when* $\tau <: \alpha_2 \in V$ *and* α_1 *appears in* τ

One nuance of slicing is that the Leaf rule can allow slicing to stop at an arbitrary point - in practice the data is sliced as deep as the pattern requires it, but it is possible to slice too shallowly by this relation, in which case a *partial* match is all that is obtained, a topic discussed below.

Compatibility. Using the above slicing relation, we can now define the type compatibility relation. Because a slice is a union-free representation of a type up to some depth, we can define compatibility in much the same way as we did in the evaluation system. As mentioned above, however, slicing may stop at an arbitrary point.

To handle partial slices, we define the type compatibility relation to filter out slices which are too shallow. In addition to being compatible ($\bullet$) or incompatible ($\bigcirc$), type compatibility may show that a slice and a pattern are *partially* compatible ($\bullet$), meaning that the slice lines up with the pattern correctly but is insufficiently deep. We use the metavariable $\circledcirc$ to range over this extension to the $\odot$ grammar. As in value compatibility, we view these symbols as ordered: $\bigcirc < \bullet < \bullet$. We define type system compatibility as the least relation satisfying the rules appearing in Figure 11.

Figure 12 shows an example of slicing and compatibility on a recursive type: Peano integers. Here, α is a union type between a successor and a zero. We consider matching Peano integers against two patterns (written here in nested form): 'z () and 's 's (). (Recall that () in patterns means "match anything.") The topmost slice matches the first pattern directly. The middle slice is partial after a single 's: it fails to match the 'z () pattern (we elide that arrow for visual clarity) and *partially* matches the second pattern. The middle slice is

PARTIAL
$$\frac{\sharp \tau . \tau <: \alpha_0 \in V}{\alpha_0 \; {}_V^{\bigcirc}\preceq_{V'}^{\emptyset} \; \alpha_0'}$$

EMPTY ONION
$$\frac{\tau <: \alpha_0 \in V \quad () <: \alpha_0' \in V' \quad F = \{\alpha_0 <: \alpha_0'\}}{\alpha_0 \; {}_V^{\bullet}\preceq_{V'}^{F} \; \alpha_0'}$$

LABEL
$$\frac{l \; \alpha_1 <: \alpha_0 \in V \quad l \; \alpha_1' <: \alpha_0' \in V' \quad \alpha_1 \; {}_V^{\bigcirc}\preceq_{V'}^{F} \; \alpha_1'}{\alpha_0 \; {}_V^{\bigcirc}\preceq_{V'}^{F} \; \alpha_0'}$$

CONJUNCTION PATTERN
$$\frac{\alpha_1' \& \alpha_2' <: \alpha_0' \in V' \quad \alpha_0 \; {}_V^{\bigcirc_1}\preceq_{V'}^{F_1} \; \alpha_1' \quad \alpha_0 \; {}_V^{\bigcirc_2}\preceq_{V'}^{F_2} \; \alpha_2'}{\alpha_0 \; {}_V^{\min(\bigcirc_1,\bigcirc_2)}\preceq_{V'}^{F_1 \cup F_2} \; \alpha_0'}$$

ONION VALUE LEFT
$$\frac{\alpha_1 \& \alpha_2 <: \alpha_0 \in V \quad \alpha_1 \; {}_V^{\bigcirc}\preceq_{V'}^{F} \; \alpha_0' \quad \bigcirc \neq \bigcirc}{\alpha_0 \; {}_V^{\bigcirc}\preceq_{V'}^{F} \; \alpha_0'}$$

ONION VALUE RIGHT
$$\frac{\alpha_1 \& \alpha_2 <: \alpha_0 \in V \quad \alpha_1' \& \alpha_2' <: \alpha_0' \notin V' \quad \alpha_1 \; {}_V^{\bigcirc}\preceq_{V'}^{F'} \; \alpha_0' \quad \alpha_2 \; {}_V^{\bigcirc}\preceq_{V'}^{F} \; \alpha_0'}{\alpha_0 \; {}_V^{\bigcirc}\preceq_{V'}^{F} \; \alpha_0'}$$

LABEL MISMATCH
$$\frac{l \; \alpha_1 <: \alpha_0 \in V}{\tau <: \alpha_0' \in V' \quad \tau = l' \; \alpha_2 \text{ only if } l \neq l' \quad \tau \text{ not of the form } \alpha' \& \alpha'' \text{ or } ()}{\alpha_0 \; {}_V^{\bigcirc}\preceq_{V'}^{\emptyset} \; \alpha_0'}$$

Fig. 11. Type compatibility: does a type match a pattern?

insufficiently deep, indicating neither success nor failure. The bottommost slice matches the second pattern completely; although it is also a partial slice, it is deep enough that we can assert it would match that pattern regardless of how it might be further expanded. In general, there is always a point at which we can stop slicing: patterns are of fixed, finite depth, so every slice fixes as either compatible or incompatible after a certain depth.

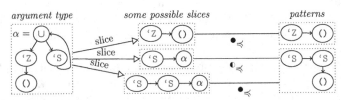

Fig. 12. Type compatibility example

Other than the additional concern of partial slices, type compatibility is much like value compatibility; so, see Section 3.2 for more explanation of compatibility.

Matching. Type matching directly parallels expression matching. As in the evaluation system, type matching propagates the result of compatibility and uses the $\bigcirc$ place to enforce left precedence of dispatch. Matching $\alpha_0 \; \alpha_1 \; {}_{V_0}^{\bigcirc}\leadsto_{V_1} \; \alpha_2 \backslash C'$ is defined as the least relation satisfying the clauses in Figure 13.

Constraint Closure. Constraint closure can now be defined; each step of closure represents one forward propagation of constraint information and abstractly

FUNCTION
$$\frac{(\alpha'\backslash V' \to \alpha\backslash C) <: \alpha_0 \in V_0 \quad \alpha_1 \, {}_{V_1}^{©}\!\preceq^F_{V'} \alpha'}{\alpha_0 \, \alpha_1 \, {}_{V_0}^{©}\!\leadsto_{V_1} \alpha\backslash C \cup F}$$

NON-FUNCTION
$$\frac{(\alpha'\backslash V' \to \alpha\backslash C) <: \alpha_0 \notin V_0 \quad \alpha_2 \,\&\, \alpha_3 <: \alpha_0 \notin V_0}{\alpha_0 \, \alpha_1 \, {}_{V_0}^{○}\!\leadsto_{V_1} \alpha\backslash C}$$

ONION LEFT
$$\frac{\alpha_2 \,\&\, \alpha_3 <: \alpha_0 \in V_0 \quad \alpha_2 \, \alpha_1 \, {}_{V_0}^{©}\!\leadsto_{V_1} \alpha\backslash C \quad © \neq ○}{\alpha_0 \, \alpha_1 \, {}_{V_0}^{©}\!\leadsto_{V_1} \alpha\backslash C}$$

ONION RIGHT
$$\frac{\alpha_2 \,\&\, \alpha_3 <: \alpha_0 \in V_0 \quad \alpha_2 \, \alpha_1 \, {}_{V_0}^{○}\!\leadsto_{V_1} \alpha'\backslash C' \quad \alpha_3 \, \alpha_1 \, {}_{V_0}^{©}\!\leadsto_{V_1} \alpha\backslash C}{\alpha_0 \, \alpha_1 \, {}_{V_0}^{©}\!\leadsto_{V_1} \alpha\backslash C}$$

Fig. 13. Type application matching

models a single step of the operational semantics. This closure is implicitly defined in terms of an abstract polymorphism framework defined by two functions. The first, Φ, is analogous to the $\alpha(-)$ freshening function of the operational semantics. For decidability, however, we do not want Φ to freshen *every* variable uniquely; it only performs *some* α-substitution on the constrained type. We write $\Phi(C, \alpha)$ to indicate the freshening of the variables in C. The additional parameter α describes the call site at which the polyinstantiation took place; this is useful for some polymorphism models.

The second function, Υ, unifies type variables by producing type variable equivalence relations. In particular, each of the above relations – slicing, compatibility, and matching – is actually defined to take an equivalence relation as an implicit parameter. In their definitions, we consider type variables in sets up to their equivalences by this relation; for instance, we read $\tau <: \alpha \notin V$ as $\nexists \alpha'. \tau <: \alpha' \in V \wedge \alpha \cong \alpha'$. For simplicity, readers may consider the monomorphic system given by $\Phi_{\mathrm{Mono}}(C, \alpha) = C$ and where the equivalence relation given by $\Upsilon_{\mathrm{Mono}}(-)$ is always equality; in this case, the definitions above can be read as they are presented. We discuss our concrete choice of polymorphism model for TinyBang in a Technical Report [MPRS14b].

We write $C \Longrightarrow^1 C'$ to indicate a single step of constraint closure. This relation is defined as the least such that the rules in Figure 14 are satisfied. This relation defines the equivalence to be used by the relations in its premises: at each constraint closure step $C \Longrightarrow^1 C'$, we take the type variable equivalence relation to be $\Upsilon(C)$. We write $C_0 \Longrightarrow^* C_n$ to indicate $C_0 \Longrightarrow^1 \ldots \Longrightarrow^1 C_n$.

APPLICATION

TRANSITIVITY
$$\frac{\{\tau <: \alpha_1, \alpha_1 <: \alpha_2\} \subseteq C}{C \Longrightarrow^1 C \cup \{\tau <: \alpha_2\}} \qquad \frac{\alpha_0 \, \alpha_1 <: \alpha_2 \in C \quad \alpha_0'\backslash V_0 \ll \alpha_0\backslash C \quad \alpha_1'\backslash V_1 \ll \alpha_1\backslash C \quad \alpha_0' \, \alpha_1' \, {}_{V_0}^{●}\!\leadsto_{V_1} \alpha'\backslash C' \quad \alpha''\backslash C'' = \Phi(\alpha'\backslash C', \alpha_2)}{C \Longrightarrow^1 C \cup V_1 \cup C'' \cup \{\alpha'' <: \alpha_2\}}$$

Fig. 14. Type constraint closure single-step relation

The operational semantics has a definition for a "stuck" expression; the type system analogue is the inconsistent constraint set, which we define as follows:

Definition 2 (Inconsistency). *A constraint set C is* inconsistent *iff, under the equivalence $\Upsilon(C)$, there exists some $\alpha_0 \; \alpha_1 <: \alpha_2 \in C$ and $\alpha_0'\backslash V_0 \ll \alpha_1\backslash C$ and $\alpha_1'\backslash V_1 \ll \alpha_1\backslash C$ such that $\alpha_0' \; \alpha_1' \; {\overset{\circ}{V_0}}{\leadsto}_{V_1} \; \alpha'\backslash C'$. A constraint set which is not* inconsistent *is* consistent.

Informally, inconsistency captures the cases in which an expression can get stuck.

Given the above, we define what it means for a program to be type correct:

Definition 3 (Typechecking). *A closed expression e* typechecks *iff $[\![e]\!]_{\mathrm{E}} = \alpha\backslash C$ and $C \Longrightarrow^* C'$ implies that C' is consistent.*

Formal Properties. We now state formal assertions regarding our type system. For reasons of space, we give proofs for each of these statements in [MPRS14b]. We begin with soundness which we prove by simulation: the A-translation of the program and the careful alignment between each of the relations in the system makes simulation a natural choice. We may state soundness as follows:

Theorem 1 (Soundness). *If $e \longrightarrow^* e'$ for stuck e' then e doesn't typecheck.*

This result is proven in Appendix A of [MPRS14b].

We must also show typechecking to be decidable. Our strategy is to demonstrate that the constraint closure of a finite constraint set C forms a subset inclusion lattice and that it is sufficient (and computable) to check the consistency of the top of that lattice. Because constraint closure is parametric in the polymorphism model, we must impose some requirements on the model. First, it must be *finitely freshening*: Φ must introduce finitely many variables into any produced constraint set given an initial constraint set. Second, to ensure convergence, polymorphism must be *equivalence monotone*: a constraint superset must induce monotonically more equivalences in Υ. See [MPRS14b] for the definition of a flexible polymorphism model with these properties.

Although the above restricts the polymorphism model to introduce finitely many variables to constraint closure, we have not bounded the number of variables introduced by slicing. The type system presented in this paper is oversimplified for legibility and does not bound the number of slice variables introduced; it is therefore undecidable. The solution to this problem is to introduce an occurrence check in slicing to prevent a single slice from making the same decision for the same variable at the same pattern multiple times. This approach is similar to determining whether the intersection of two regular trees is empty. While the type system is very slightly weakened by this modiciation, the examples in this paper are unaffected and the resulting system is intuitive and decidable.

Theorem 2 (Decidability). *Typechecking with the above modification and a finitely freshening, equivalence monotone polymorphism model is decidable.*

4   Related Work

TinyBang's object resealing is inspired by the Bono-Fisher object calculus [BF98], in which mixins and other higher-order object transformations are written as functions. Objects in this calculus must be "sealed" before they are messaged; unlike our resealing, sealed objects cannot be extended. Some related works relax this restriction but add others [RS02,BBV11].

Typed multimethods [MC99] perform a dispatch similar to TinyBang's dispatch on compound functions, but multimethod dispatch is *nominally* typed while compound function dispatch is *structurally* typed. First-class cases [BAC06] allow composition of case branches much like TinyBang. In [BAC06], however, general case concatenation requires case branches to be written in CPS and requires a phase distinction between constructing a case and matching with it. TinyBang has a form of dependent type which allows different case branches to return different types; this generalizes the expressiveness of conditional constraints [AWL94,Pot00] and is related to support for typed first-class messages *a la* [Nis98,Pot00] – first-class messages are just labeled data in our encoding.

TinyBang shares several features and goals with CDuce [CNX+14]: both aim to be flexible languages built around constraint subtyping. CDuce supports dependently-typed case results as we do, but it does not slice on the pattern side and so does not bind refined types. CDuce lacks a typed record append operation and so the object encodings of this paper are not possible there. CDuce takes a local type inference approach; this has the advantage of being modular but the disadvantage of not being complete, requiring type annotations in some cases, and the decidability of their inference algorithm remains open.

TinyBang's onions are unusual in that they are a form of record supporting typed asymmetric concatenation. The bulk of work on typing record extension addresses symmetric concatenation only [Rémy94]. Standard typed record-based encodings of inheritance [BCP99] avoid the problem of typing first-class concatenation by reconstructing records rather than extending them, but this requires the superclass to be fixed statically. A combination of conditional constraints and row types can be used to type record extension [Pot00]; TinyBang uses a different approach that does not need row types.

There have been many attempts to bring static typing to existing scripting languages; two of the more recent systems include [CRJ12,FAFH09]. The majority of such systems require some explicit type annotations, and invariably are incomplete since an uncomputable problem is being solved: the languages contain too many fundamentally dynamic operations (e.g. mutable object extension). Once a type system loses information on a dynamic operation, it is difficult to recover. One primary tenant of this project's design philosophy is to build a language from the beginning with flexible but fully static typing; this way, there will never be a need to attempt such recovery.

5   Conclusions

We presented TinyBang, a core language with a static type inference system that types such flexible operations without onerous false type errors or the need for manual programmer annotation. We believe TinyBang solves a longstanding open problem: it infers types for object-oriented programs without compromising the expressiveness of object subtyping or of object extension. This is possible due to a combination of novel features in TinyBang: asymmetric concatenation, first-class dependently-typed cases, slicing for type refinement, and a flexible non-let-based polymorphism model.

TinyBang is proved type sound; the proofs are found in the supplementary appendices. We have implemented the type inference algorithm and interpreter for TinyBang to provide a cross-check on the soundness of our ideas; the implementation can be downloaded from [MPRS14a]. Type inference is decidable but not provably polynomial for the same reason that let-polymorphism is not: artificial programs exist which will exhibit exponential runtimes. However, all of the examples in Section 2 typecheck in our implementation without exponential blowup, and we have designed the polymorphism model with practical performance in mind. We do not expect programmers to write in TinyBang. Instead, programmers would write in BigBang, a language we are developing which includes syntax for objects, classes, and so on, and which desugars to TinyBang.

TinyBang infers extremely precise types, especially in conjunction with the context-sensitive polymorphism model described in [MPRS14b]. While powerful, these types are by nature difficult to read and defy modularization. Addressing the problem of readability is part of our broader research agenda.

References

AWL94.   Aiken, A., Wimmers, E.L., Lakshman, T.K.: Soft typing with conditional types. In: POPL 21, pp. 163–173 (1994)

BAC06.   Blume, M., Acar, U.A., Chae, W.: Extensible programming with first-class cases. In: ICFP, pp. 239–250 (2006)

BBV11.   Bettini, L., Bono, V., Venneri, B.: Delegation by object composition. Science of Computer Programming 76, 992–1014 (2011)

BCP99.   Bruce, K.B., Cardelli, L., Pierce, B.C.: Comparing object encodings. Information and Computation 155(1-2), 108–133 (1999)

BF98.   Bono, V., Fisher, K.: An imperative, first-order calculus with object extension. In: Jul, E. (ed.) ECOOP 1998. LNCS, vol. 1445, pp. 462–497. Springer, Heidelberg (1998)

CNX+14.   Castagna, G., Nguyen, K., Xu, Z., Im, H., Lenglet, S., Padovani, L.: Polymorphic functions with set-theoretic types. Part 1: Syntax, semantics, and evaluation. In: POPL (2014)

CRJ12.   Chugh, R., Rondon, P.M., Jhala, R.: Nested refinements: A logic for duck typing. In: POPL (2012)

FAFH09.   Furr, M., (David) An, J.-H., Foster, J.S., Hicks, M.: Static type inference for Ruby. In: SAC (2009)

MC99.   Millstein, T.D., Chambers, C.: Modular statically typed multimethods. In: Guerraoui, R. (ed.) ECOOP 1999. LNCS, vol. 1628, pp. 279–303. Springer, Heidelberg (1999)

MPRS14a. Menon, P.H., Palmer, Z., Rozenshteyn, A., Smith, S.: Tinybang implementation (March 2014),
          http://pl.cs.jhu.edu/big-bang/tiny-bang_2014-03-01.tgz

MPRS14b. Menon, P.H., Palmer, Z., Rozenshteyn, A., Smith, S.: Types for flexible objects. Technical report, The Johns Hopkins University Programming Languages Laboratory (March 2014), `http://pl.cs.jhu.edu/big-bang/types-for-flexible-objects_2014-03-25.pdf`

Nis98.   Nishimura, S.: Static typing for dynamic messages. In: POPL (1998)

Pot00.   Pottier, F.: A versatile constraint-based type inference system. Nordic J. of Computing 7(4), 312–347 (2000)

Rémy94.   Rémy, D.: Type inference for records in a natural extension of ML. In: Theoretical Aspects of Object-Oriented Programming. MIT Press (1994)

RS02.   Riecke, J.G., Stone, C.A.: Privacy via subsumption. Inf. Comput. 172(1), 2–28 (2002)

SM01.   Shields, M., Meijer, E.: Type-indexed rows. In: POPL, pp. 261–275 (2001)

WS01.   Wang, T., Smith, S.F.: Precise constraint-based type inference for Java. In: Lindskov Knudsen, J. (ed.) ECOOP 2001. LNCS, vol. 2072, pp. 99–177. Springer, Heidelberg (2001)

A Translation of Intersection and Union Types for the $\lambda\mu$-Calculus

Kentaro Kikuchi[1] and Takafumi Sakurai[2]

[1] RIEC, Tohoku University, Sendai, Japan
[2] Department of Mathematics and Informatics, Chiba University, Japan

Abstract. We introduce an intersection and union type system for the $\lambda\mu$-calculus, which includes a restricted version of the traditional union-elimination rule. We give a translation from intersection and union types into intersection and product types, which is a variant of negative translation from classical logic to intuitionistic logic and naturally reflects the structure of strict intersection and union types. It is shown that a derivation in our type system can be translated into a derivation in the type system of van Bakel, Barbanera and de'Liguoro. As a corollary, the terms typable in our system turn out to be strongly normalising. We also present an intersection and union type system in the style of sequent calculus, and show that the terms typable in the system coincide with the strongly normalising terms of the $\overline{\lambda}\mu$-calculus, a call-by-name fragment of Curien and Herbelin's $\overline{\lambda}\mu\tilde{\mu}$-calculus.

1 Introduction

Since Griffin's seminal work [14], the Curry-Howard correspondence for classical logic has been extensively studied and has yielded various term systems, e.g. the calculi in [7,19,9]. Some of those systems can be considered as calculi with control operators which deal with first-class continuations. Parigot's $\lambda\mu$-calculus [19] is one of such systems, and since it is a syntactical extension of the usual λ-calculus, the type-free version of the calculus, called pure $\lambda\mu$-calculus in [19], has also been studied.

As a type assignment system for type-free $\lambda\mu$-terms, van Bakel, Barbanera and de'Liguoro [5] recently introduced an intersection type system to develop model theory of the calculus. The system includes not only intersection types but also product types, and so looks involved at first sight. However, the system can be naturally understood in the light of the negative translation used in [21], and indeed the simply typed part of the $\lambda\mu$-calculus is interpreted by the systems with intersection and product types in [5,6].

Another approach to providing a type assignment system for type-free $\lambda\mu$-terms is to employ a system with intersection and union types. In this approach, simple types inhabited by some terms correspond to implicational formulas that are provable in classical logic, and union types are used for continuations to have more than one type. There are two intersection and union type systems for the $\lambda\mu$-calculus in the literature [18,3]. In this paper we introduce another

J. Garrigue (Ed.): APLAS 2014, LNCS 8858, pp. 120–139, 2014.

intersection and union type system where, unlike in the systems of [18,3], union-introduction and elimination rules correspond to the usual or-introduction and elimination rules in natural deduction. It is well-known in the context of λ-calculus that the presence of such a standard union-elimination rule causes difficulties for the subject reduction property (cf. [8]). So we impose some restrictions on terms in the premisses of the union-elimination rule, expecting that the system enjoys the subject reduction property (though in this paper we focus on translations between systems and leave a proof of it for future work).

To clarify the relation between the two kinds of type systems, we introduce a translation from intersection and union types to intersection and product types. As in the previous systems [18,3], the types occurring in our system are the strict version of intersection and union types (cf. [1,4]). Our translation is defined along the structure of this class of types. Using the translation, we show that each derivation in our system can be transformed into a derivation in the system of [6]. This implies strong normalisation of terms typable in our system. Since strong normalisation has not been treated in [18,3], this is a new result on intersection and union type systems for the $\lambda\mu$-calculus.

In the latter half of the paper, we introduce and study an intersection and union type system for a call-by-name fragment of Curien and Herbelin's $\overline{\lambda}\mu\tilde{\mu}$-calculus [9]. It is shown that the system enjoys both the subject reduction property and the characterisation of strong normalisation by means of typability. To prove one direction of the characterisation, we use the strong normalisation result mentioned above, together with a transformation from derivations in the type system into derivations in the above type system for the $\lambda\mu$-calculus and simulation of each reduction step in the calculus by at least one reduction step in the $\lambda\mu$-calculus. The transformation of derivations clarifies the relation between the type systems (in particular, the left-union and the union-elimination rules).

One of the reasons to study systems based on sequent calculus, such as the $\overline{\lambda}\mu\tilde{\mu}$-calculus, is that they embody both logical and computational duality more explicitly than systems based on natural deduction. Since union types are thought to be dual to intersection types, a system with both types was proposed in [10,11] for the $\overline{\lambda}\mu\tilde{\mu}$-calculus. The system employs *definite* types in type environments whereas our system uses strict types similarly to the systems for the $\lambda\mu$-calculus. Restricting types to definite ones is, however, not enough to satisfy the subject reduction property, even in the case of call-by-name or call-by-value reduction, as pointed out in [12,2]. The system in [12], which uses intersection types and an involution operator rather than union types, does not satisfy subject reduction either, as illustrated in Section 8 of [2].

To recover the subject reduction property of an intersection and union type system for the $\overline{\lambda}\mu\tilde{\mu}$-calculus, another restriction is required. A crucial restriction is given in Definition 23(i) of [2] for the case of call-by-name reduction, which is also thought to be dual to the value restriction in call-by-value functional languages (for the second-order quantification case). Since the calculus we study in this paper does not have the $\tilde{\mu}$-operator, the restriction is automatically satisfied. Our result seems to be the first characterisation of strong normalisation of (a fragment of) the $\overline{\lambda}\mu\tilde{\mu}$-calculus by means of typability in an intersection and union type system that enjoys the subject reduction property.

The organisation of the paper is as follows. In Section 2 we discuss type systems for the $\lambda\mu$-calculus and their relationships. In Section 3 we introduce a type system for a call-by-name fragment of the $\overline{\lambda}\mu\tilde{\mu}$-calculus and study its properties. In Section 4 we conclude and give suggestions for further work.

To save space we omit some of the details in proofs, but a longer paper [17] is available at http://www.nue.riec.tohoku.ac.jp/user/kentaro/.

2   Intersection and Union Types for the $\lambda\mu$-Calculus

In this section we introduce a new intersection and union type system for the $\lambda\mu$-calculus, and discuss the relationships to systems in previous work.

2.1   The $\lambda\mu$-Calculus

First we introduce the syntax of Parigot's pure $\lambda\mu$-calculus [19].

Definition 1 (Grammar of $\lambda\mu$). *The sets of* terms *and* commands *are defined inductively by the following grammar:*

$$M, N ::= x \mid \lambda x.M \mid MN \mid \mu\alpha.C \quad \text{(terms)}$$
$$C ::= [\alpha]M \qquad\qquad\qquad \text{(commands)}$$

where x and α range over denumerable sets of λ-variables and μ-variables, respectively.

The notions of free and bound variables are defined as usual, with both λ and μ as binders. The sets of free λ-variables and μ-variables of a term M are denoted by $\mathsf{FV}_\lambda(M)$ and $\mathsf{FV}_\mu(M)$, respectively. We identify α-convertible terms and use $\equiv$ to denote syntactic equality modulo α-conversion.

Definition 2 (Reduction System of $\lambda\mu$). *The reduction rules are:*

$$(\beta) \quad (\lambda x.M)N \to M[x := N]$$
$$(\mu) \quad (\mu\alpha.C)N \to \mu\alpha.C[\alpha \Leftarrow N]$$

where $[x := N]$ is usual capture-free substitution, and $[\alpha \Leftarrow N]$ in the rule (μ) replaces inductively each occurrence in C of the form $[\alpha]P$ by $[\alpha](PN)$.

The reduction relation $\longrightarrow_{\beta,\mu}$ is defined by the contextual closure of the rules (β) and (μ). We use $\longrightarrow^+_{\beta,\mu}$ for its transitive closure, and $\longrightarrow^*_{\beta,\mu}$ for its reflexive transitive closure. A term M is said to be *strongly normalising* if there is no infinite β, μ-reduction sequence out of M. The set of strongly normalising terms is denoted by $\mathsf{SN}^{\beta,\mu}$. These kinds of notations are also used for the notions of other reductions in this paper.

2.2 An Intersection and Union Type System for the $\lambda\mu$-Calculus

In this subsection we introduce an intersection and union type system for the $\lambda\mu$-calculus. The types we consider here can be seen as an extension of strict intersection types [1,4]. We distinguish three kinds of types, following the definition in [18] (without the empty intersection).

Definition 3. *The sets* $\mathcal{T}_A, \mathcal{T}_I$ *and* $\mathcal{T}_U$ *of three kinds of types are defined inductively by the following grammar:*

$$
\begin{aligned}
\mathcal{T}_A : \quad & A, B ::= \varphi \mid I \to U & \text{(arrow types)} \\
\mathcal{T}_I : \quad & I, J ::= U \mid I \cap J & \text{(intersection types)} \\
\mathcal{T}_U : \quad & U, V ::= A \mid U \cup V & \text{(union types)}
\end{aligned}
$$

where φ ranges over a denumerable set of type variables. We identify types modulo associativity and commutativity of $\cap$ and $\cup$, and use $\equiv$ to denote the equivalence.

The type assignment system $\lambda\mu_{\cap\cup}$ is defined by the rules in Figure 1. A *type environment*, ranged over by Γ, is defined as a finite set of pairs $\{x_1 : I_1, \ldots, x_n : I_n\}$ where the λ-variables are pairwise distinct. The type environment $\Gamma, x : I$ denotes the union $\Gamma \cup \{x : I\}$ where x does not appear in Γ. Similarly for type environments with μ-variables $\{\alpha_1 : U_1, \ldots, \alpha_n : U_m\}$, ranged over by Δ, except that the types are restricted to union types. We write $\Gamma \vdash_{\cap\cup} M : I \mid \Delta$ if $\Gamma \vdash M : I \mid \Delta$ is derivable with the rules in Figure 1.

$$\frac{}{\Gamma, x : I \vdash x : I \mid \Delta} \ (\mathsf{Ax})$$

$$\frac{\Gamma \vdash M : U \mid \alpha : U, \Delta}{\Gamma \vdash \mu\alpha.[\alpha]M : U \mid \Delta} \ (\mu_1) \qquad \frac{\Gamma \vdash M : V \mid \alpha : U, \gamma : V, \Delta}{\Gamma \vdash \mu\alpha.[\gamma]M : U \mid \gamma : V, \Delta} \ (\mu_2)$$

$$\frac{\Gamma, x : I \vdash M : U \mid \Delta}{\Gamma \vdash \lambda x.M : I \to U \mid \Delta} \ (\to \mathsf{I}) \qquad \frac{\Gamma \vdash M : I \to U \mid \Delta \quad \Gamma \vdash N : I \mid \Delta}{\Gamma \vdash MN : U \mid \Delta} \ (\to \mathsf{E})$$

$$\frac{\Gamma \vdash M : I \mid \Delta \quad \Gamma \vdash M : J \mid \Delta}{\Gamma \vdash M : I \cap J \mid \Delta} \ (\cap \mathsf{I})$$

$$\frac{\Gamma \vdash M : I \cap J \mid \Delta}{\Gamma \vdash M : I \mid \Delta} \ (\cap \mathsf{E}) \qquad \frac{\Gamma \vdash M : I \cap J \mid \Delta}{\Gamma \vdash M : J \mid \Delta} \ (\cap \mathsf{E})$$

$$\frac{\Gamma \vdash M : U \mid \Delta}{\Gamma \vdash M : U \cup V \mid \Delta} \ (\cup \mathsf{I}) \qquad \frac{\Gamma \vdash M : V \mid \Delta}{\Gamma \vdash M : U \cup V \mid \Delta} \ (\cup \mathsf{I})$$

$$\frac{\Gamma \vdash M : U \cup V \mid \Delta \quad \Gamma, x : U \vdash xN : I \mid \Delta \quad \Gamma, x : V \vdash xN : I \mid \Delta}{\Gamma \vdash MN : I \mid \Delta} \ (\cup \mathsf{E})$$

where $x \notin \mathsf{FV}_\lambda(N)$

Fig. 1. Type assignment system $\lambda\mu_{\cap\cup}$

The rule $(\cup E)$ in Figure 1 is a rather restricted version of the traditional union-elimination rule that would have the form:

$$\frac{\Gamma \vdash M : U \cup V \mid \Delta \quad \Gamma, x : U \vdash N : I \mid \Delta \quad \Gamma, x : V \vdash N : I \mid \Delta}{\Gamma \vdash N[x := M] : I \mid \Delta}$$

This general version causes the subject-reduction problem as in the case of an intersection and union type system for λ-terms (cf. [8]). Though our rule $(\cup E)$ might look too restrictive, the system $\lambda\mu_{\cap\cup}$ is more general than the intersection and union type systems proposed in [18] and [3] in the sense that if a term is typable in one of their systems without the empty intersection then it is typable in $\lambda\mu_{\cap\cup}$ (cf. Subsection 2.4). An example of a judgement that is derivable in $\lambda\mu_{\cap\cup}$ but not in the systems in [18,3] is $x : \varphi_1 \vdash x : \varphi_1 \cup \varphi_2 \mid$.

Example 1. The term $(\mu\alpha.[\alpha](\lambda y.\mu\gamma.[\alpha]y))z$ is typable in the system $\lambda\mu_{\cap\cup}$ as follows. Let $A \equiv \varphi_1 \to \varphi_2$ and $\Gamma = \{z : \varphi_1 \cap A\}$, and let D_1 be the following derivation:

$$\frac{\dfrac{\dfrac{\dfrac{\dfrac{\dfrac{\overline{\Gamma, y : A \vdash y : A \mid \gamma : \varphi_3, \alpha : A \cup (A \to \varphi_3)}}{\Gamma, y : A \vdash y : A \cup (A \to \varphi_3) \mid \gamma : \varphi_3, \alpha : A \cup (A \to \varphi_3)} \text{(Ax)}}{\Gamma, y : A \vdash \mu\gamma.[\alpha]y : \varphi_3 \mid \alpha : A \cup (A \to \varphi_3)} \text{(}\cup\text{I)}}{\Gamma \vdash \lambda y.\mu\gamma.[\alpha]y : A \to \varphi_3 \mid \alpha : A \cup (A \to \varphi_3)} \text{(}\mu_2\text{)}}{\Gamma \vdash \lambda y.\mu\gamma.[\alpha]y : A \cup (A \to \varphi_3) \mid \alpha : A \cup (A \to \varphi_3)} \text{(}\to\text{I)}}{\Gamma \vdash \mu\alpha.[\alpha](\lambda y.\mu\gamma.[\alpha]y) : A \cup (A \to \varphi_3) \mid} \text{(}\cup\text{I)}} \quad (\mu_1)$$

Let D_2 be the following derivation:

$$\frac{\dfrac{\overline{\Gamma, x : A \vdash x : A \mid} \text{(Ax)} \quad \dfrac{\dfrac{\overline{\Gamma, x : A \vdash z : \varphi_1 \cap A \mid}}{\Gamma, x : A \vdash z : \varphi_1 \mid} \text{(}\cap\text{E)}}{} \text{(Ax)}}{\Gamma, x : A \vdash xz : \varphi_2 \mid} \text{(}\to\text{E)}}{\Gamma, x : A \vdash xz : \varphi_2 \cup \varphi_3 \mid} \text{(}\cup\text{I)}$$

Let D_3 be the following derivation:

$$\frac{\dfrac{\overline{\Gamma, x : A \to \varphi_3 \vdash x : A \to \varphi_3 \mid} \text{(Ax)} \quad \dfrac{\dfrac{\overline{\Gamma, x : A \to \varphi_3 \vdash z : \varphi_1 \cap A \mid}}{\Gamma, x : A \to \varphi_3 \vdash z : A \mid} \text{(}\cap\text{E)}}{} \text{(Ax)}}{\Gamma, x : A \to \varphi_3 \vdash xz : \varphi_3 \mid} \text{(}\to\text{E)}}{\Gamma, x : A \to \varphi_3 \vdash xz : \varphi_2 \cup \varphi_3 \mid} \text{(}\cup\text{I)}$$

Then by applying the rule $(\cup E)$ to the conclusions of D_1, D_2 and D_3, we obtain a derivation of $\Gamma \vdash (\mu\alpha.[\alpha](\lambda y.\mu\gamma.[\alpha]y))z : \varphi_2 \cup \varphi_3 \mid$. Note that this term is not typable without using the rules for $\cup$. $\qquad\square$

Lemma 1.

1. If $\Gamma \vdash_{\cap\cup} t : I \mid \Delta$ and x is a fresh λ-variable then $\Gamma, x : J \vdash_{\cap\cup} t : I \mid \Delta$.

2. *If $\Gamma \vdash_{\cap\cup} t : I \mid \Delta$ and α is a fresh μ-variable then $\Gamma \vdash_{\cap\cup} t : I \mid \alpha : U, \Delta$.*

Proof. By induction on the derivations. ☐

Lemma 2. *The following rule is admissible in the system $\lambda\mu_{\cap\cup}$.*

$$\frac{\Gamma \vdash M : U_1 \cup \cdots \cup U_n \mid \Delta \quad \Gamma, x : U_1 \vdash xN : I \mid \Delta \quad \cdots \quad \Gamma, x : U_n \vdash xN : I \mid \Delta}{\Gamma \vdash MN : I \mid \Delta} \ (\cup\mathsf{E})^n$$

where $n \geq 2$ and $x \notin \mathsf{FV}_\lambda(N)$.

2.3   The Type System of van Bakel, Barbanera and de'Liguoro

In this subsection we briefly recall the intersection type system in [6] which also uses product types. The system is a modification of the system in [5], which was inspired by denotational semantics developed in [21].

The intersection-free part of the system can be seen as the image of negative translation from the implication fragment of classical logic into the conjunction and negation fragment of intuitionistic logic (viewing $\times$ as conjunction and $\rightarrow \nu$ as negation). However, unlike in a CPS-translation, only types are translated in the image while terms are not changed from those in the $\lambda\mu$-calculus.

Definition 4. *The sets $\mathcal{T}_D$ of term types and $\mathcal{T}_C$ of continuation-stack types are defined inductively by the following grammar:*

$$\begin{aligned}\mathcal{T}_D : \quad & \delta ::= \nu \mid \omega \rightarrow \nu \mid \kappa \rightarrow \nu \mid \delta \wedge \delta \\ \mathcal{T}_C : \quad & \kappa ::= \delta \times \omega \mid \delta \times \kappa \mid \kappa \wedge \kappa\end{aligned}$$

where ν and ω are type constants. Elements of $\mathcal{T}_D \cup \mathcal{T}_C$ are ranged over by σ, τ, ρ.

The relations $\leq_D$ and $\leq_C$ on $\mathcal{T}_D$ and $\mathcal{T}_C$, respectively, are defined by the rules in Figure 2, where $\leq_A$ denotes either $\leq_D$ or $\leq_C$.

$$\overline{\sigma \leq_A \sigma} \quad \overline{\sigma \wedge \tau \leq_A \sigma} \quad \overline{\sigma \wedge \tau \leq_A \tau}$$

$$\overline{\nu \leq_D \omega \rightarrow \nu} \quad \overline{\omega \rightarrow \nu \leq_D \nu} \quad \overline{\delta_1 \times \delta_2 \times \omega \leq_C \delta_1 \times \omega}$$

$$\overline{(\delta_1 \times \omega) \wedge (\delta_2 \times \kappa) \leq_C (\delta_1 \wedge \delta_2) \times \kappa} \quad \overline{(\delta_1 \times \kappa_1) \wedge (\delta_2 \times \kappa_2) \leq_C (\delta_1 \wedge \delta_2) \times (\kappa_1 \wedge \kappa_2)}$$
$$\text{where } \kappa_1 \neq \omega \text{ and } \kappa_2 \neq \omega$$

$$\frac{\sigma \leq_A \rho \quad \rho \leq_A \tau}{\sigma \leq_A \tau} \quad \frac{\sigma \leq_A \tau_1 \quad \sigma \leq_A \tau_2}{\sigma \leq_A \tau_1 \wedge \tau_2}$$

$$\frac{\delta_1 \leq_D \delta_2}{\delta_1 \times \omega \leq_C \delta_2 \times \omega} \quad \frac{\delta_1 \leq_D \delta_2 \quad \kappa_1 \leq_C \kappa_2}{\delta_1 \times \kappa_1 \leq_C \delta_2 \times \kappa_2} \quad \frac{\kappa_2 \leq_C \kappa_1}{\kappa_1 \rightarrow \nu \leq_D \kappa_2 \rightarrow \nu}$$

Fig. 2. Relations $\leq_D$ and $\leq_C$

$$\frac{}{\Gamma, x : \delta \vdash x : \delta \mid \Delta} \text{ (Ax)}$$

$$\frac{\Gamma \vdash M : \kappa \to \nu \mid \alpha : \kappa, \Delta}{\Gamma \vdash \mu\alpha.[\alpha]M : \kappa \to \nu \mid \Delta} \ (\mu_1^\nu) \qquad \frac{\Gamma \vdash M : \kappa' \to \nu \mid \alpha : \kappa, \gamma : \kappa', \Delta}{\Gamma \vdash \mu\alpha.[\gamma]M : \kappa \to \nu \mid \gamma : \kappa', \Delta} \ (\mu_2^\nu)$$

$$\frac{\Gamma, x : \delta \vdash M : \kappa \to \nu \mid \Delta}{\Gamma \vdash \lambda x.M : \delta \times \kappa \to \nu \mid \Delta} \ \text{(Abs)} \qquad \frac{\Gamma \vdash M : \delta \times \kappa \to \nu \mid \Delta \quad \Gamma \vdash N : \delta \mid \Delta}{\Gamma \vdash MN : \kappa \to \nu \mid \Delta} \ \text{(App)}$$

where κ is either a type in $\mathcal{T}_C$ or ω where κ is either a type in $\mathcal{T}_C$ or ω

$$\frac{\Gamma \vdash M : \delta \mid \Delta \quad \Gamma \vdash M : \delta' \mid \Delta}{\Gamma \vdash M : \delta \wedge \delta' \mid \Delta} \ (\wedge) \qquad \frac{\Gamma \vdash M : \delta \mid \Delta \quad \delta \leq_D \delta'}{\Gamma \vdash M : \delta' \mid \Delta} \ (\leq)$$

Fig. 3. Type assignment system $\lambda\mu_{\wedge\times}$

Lemma 3. $(\delta_1 \wedge \cdots \wedge \delta_n) \times (\kappa_1 \wedge \cdots \wedge \kappa_n) \leq_C (\delta_1 \times \kappa_1) \wedge \cdots \wedge (\delta_n \times \kappa_n).$

Proof. By $\delta_1 \wedge \cdots \wedge \delta_n \leq_D \delta_i$ and $\kappa_1 \wedge \cdots \wedge \kappa_n \leq_C \kappa_i$, we have $(\delta_1 \wedge \cdots \wedge \delta_n) \times (\kappa_1 \wedge \cdots \wedge \kappa_n) \leq_C \delta_i \times \kappa_i$ for each $i \in \{1, \ldots, n\}$. Hence $(\delta_1 \wedge \cdots \wedge \delta_n) \times (\kappa_1 \wedge \cdots \wedge \kappa_n) \leq_C (\delta_1 \times \kappa_1) \wedge \cdots \wedge (\delta_n \times \kappa_n)$. $\square$

The type assignment system $\lambda\mu_{\wedge\times}$ is defined by the rules in Figure 3. We write $\Gamma \vdash_{\wedge\times} M : \delta \mid \Delta$ if $\Gamma \vdash M : \delta \mid \Delta$ is derivable with the rules of Figure 3.

In [6], it was shown that strongly normalising terms are characterised by means of typability in the system $\lambda\mu_{\wedge\times}$. The following is one direction of the characterisation theorem.

Theorem 1 ([6]). *If $\Gamma \vdash_{\wedge\times} M : \delta \mid \Delta$ for some Γ, δ and Δ, then $M \in \mathsf{SN}^{\beta,\mu}$.*

2.4   A Translation of Intersection and Union Types

Now we introduce a translation of intersection and union types into intersection and product types, extending the translation of simple types in [6]. The translation is defined along the structure of the three kinds of types in Definition 3. The aim is to prove strong normalisation of terms typable in $\lambda\mu_{\cap\cup}$, using this translation and the strong normalisation result of terms typable in $\lambda\mu_{\wedge\times}$.

Definition 5. *The mappings $(\cdot)^D : \mathcal{T}_I \to \mathcal{T}_D$ and $(\cdot)^C : \mathcal{T}_U \to \mathcal{T}_C$ are defined inductively as follows:*

$$\varphi^C := \nu \times \omega$$
$$(I \to U)^C := I^D \times U^C$$
$$(U \cup V)^C := U^C \wedge V^C$$

$$U^D := U^C \to \nu$$
$$(I \cap J)^D := I^D \wedge J^D$$

It can be easily verified that the above mappings are well-defined. We extend the mappings to type environments by $\Gamma^D := \{x : I^D \mid x : I \in \Gamma\}$ and $\Delta^C := \{\alpha : U^C \mid \alpha : U \in \Delta\}$.

Proving the preservation of derivability in $\lambda\mu_{\cap\cup}$ by the translation requires some observations on the system $\lambda\mu_{\wedge\times}$. We give a detailed proof of it in [17]. Here we instead show the preservation of derivability in the system that is obtained from $\lambda\mu_{\cap\cup}$ by replacing the rules ($\to$ E) and ($\cup$ E) with the following one:

$$\frac{\Gamma \vdash M : (I_1{\to}U_1) \cup \cdots \cup (I_n{\to}U_n) \mid \Delta \quad \Gamma \vdash N : I_1 \mid \Delta \quad \cdots \quad \Gamma \vdash N : I_n \mid \Delta}{\Gamma \vdash MN : U_1 \cup \cdots \cup U_n \mid \Delta} \ (\to\mathsf{E})'$$

where $n \geq 1$. This rule is the same as one of the rules of the intersection and union type system in [3]. A similar rule also appeared in [18]. We write $\Gamma \vdash_{\cap\cup'} M : \delta \mid \Delta$ if $\Gamma \vdash M : \delta \mid \Delta$ is derivable in this alternative system. By using the rule ($\cup$ E)^n in Lemma 2, we see that the rule ($\to$ E)$'$ is derivable in the original system $\lambda\mu_{\cap\cup}$, so $\Gamma \vdash_{\cap\cup'} M : \delta \mid \Delta$ implies $\Gamma \vdash_{\cap\cup} M : \delta \mid \Delta$.

Theorem 2. *If $\Gamma \vdash_{\cap\cup'} M : I \mid \Delta$ then $\Gamma^D \vdash_{\wedge\times} M : I^D \mid \Delta^C$.*

Proof. By induction on the derivation of $\Gamma \vdash_{\cap\cup'} M : I \mid \Delta$. Here we consider some cases.

- $$\frac{\Gamma \vdash M : V \mid \alpha : U, \gamma : V, \Delta}{\Gamma \vdash \mu\alpha.[\gamma]M : U \mid \gamma : V, \Delta} \ (\mu_2)$$

  By the induction hypothesis, we have $\Gamma^D \vdash_{\wedge\times} M : V^D \mid \alpha : U^C, \gamma : V^C, \Delta^C$ where $V^D \equiv V^C \to \nu$. Then by the rule (μ_2^ν), we obtain $\Gamma^D \vdash_{\wedge\times} \mu\alpha.[\gamma]M : U^C \to \nu \mid \gamma : V^C, \Delta^C$.

- $$\frac{\Gamma, x : I \vdash M : U \mid \Delta}{\Gamma \vdash \lambda x.M : I \to U \mid \Delta} \ (\to \mathsf{I})$$

  By the induction hypothesis, we have $\Gamma^D, x : I^D \vdash_{\wedge\times} M : U^D \mid \Delta^C$ where $U^D \equiv U^C \to \nu$. Then by the rule (Abs), we obtain $\Gamma^D \vdash_{\wedge\times} \lambda x.M : I^D \times U^C \to \nu \mid \Delta^C$ where $I^D \times U^C \to \nu \equiv (I \to U)^C \to \nu \equiv (I \to U)^D$.

- $$\frac{\Gamma \vdash M : U \mid \Delta}{\Gamma \vdash M : U \cup V \mid \Delta} \ (\cup\mathsf{I})$$

  By the induction hypothesis, we have $\Gamma^D \vdash_{\wedge\times} M : U^D \mid \Delta^C$ where $U^D \equiv U^C \to \nu$. From the definition of $\leq_D$, we have $U^C \to \nu \leq_D U^C \wedge V^C \to \nu$. Hence by the rule ($\leq$), we obtain $\Gamma^D \vdash_{\wedge\times} M : U^C \wedge V^C \to \nu \mid \Delta^C$ where $U^C \wedge V^C \to \nu \equiv (U \cup V)^C \to \nu \equiv (U \cup V)^D$.

- $$\frac{\Gamma \vdash M : (I_1{\to}U_1) \cup \cdots \cup (I_n{\to}U_n) \mid \Delta \quad \Gamma \vdash N : I_1 \mid \Delta \quad \cdots \quad \Gamma \vdash N : I_n \mid \Delta}{\Gamma \vdash MN : U_1 \cup \cdots \cup U_n \mid \Delta} \ (\to\mathsf{E})'$$

  By the induction hypothesis, we have $\Gamma^D \vdash_{\wedge\times} M : ((I_1 \to U_1) \cup \cdots \cup (I_n \to U_n))^D \mid \Delta^C$ and, for all $i \in \{1, \ldots, n\}$, $\Gamma^D \vdash_{\wedge\times} N : I_i^D \mid \Delta^C$. Then by the rule ($\wedge$), we have $\Gamma^D \vdash_{\wedge\times} N : I_1^D \wedge \cdots \wedge I_n^D \mid \Delta^C$. Now

$$
\begin{aligned}
((I_1 \to U_1) \cup \cdots \cup (I_n \to U_n))^D &\equiv ((I_1 \to U_1) \cup \cdots \cup (I_n \to U_n))^C \to \nu \\
&\equiv (I_1 \to U_1)^C \wedge \cdots \wedge (I_n \to U_n)^C \to \nu \\
&\equiv (I_1^D \times U_1^C) \wedge \cdots \wedge (I_n^D \times U_n^C) \to \nu \\
&\leq_D (I_1^D \wedge \cdots \wedge I_n^D) \times (U_1^C \wedge \cdots \wedge U_n^C) \to \nu \\
&\qquad\qquad\qquad\qquad\qquad\qquad\qquad \text{(by Lemma 3)}
\end{aligned}
$$

Hence by the rules ($\leq$) and (App), we obtain $\Gamma^D \vdash_{\wedge\times} MN : (U_1^C \wedge \cdots \wedge U_n^C) \to \nu \mid \Delta^C$ where $(U_1^C \wedge \cdots \wedge U_n^C) \to \nu \equiv (U_1 \cup \cdots \cup U_n)^C \to \nu \equiv (U_1 \cup \cdots \cup U_n)^D$. $\qquad\square$

Corollary 1. *If $\Gamma \vdash_{\cap\cup'} M : I \mid \Delta$ for some Γ, I and Δ, then $M \in \mathsf{SN}^{\beta,\mu}$.*

Proof. By Theorems 1 and 2. $\qquad\square$

The above corollary is enough to show strong normalisation of terms typable in the systems (without the type constants) of [18] and [3]. We can also prove the same result for the full system $\lambda\mu_{\cap\cup}$. (See [17].)

Theorem 3. *If $\Gamma \vdash_{\cap\cup} M : I \mid \Delta$ then $\Gamma^D \vdash_{\wedge\times} M : I^D \mid \Delta^C$.*

Corollary 2. *If $\Gamma \vdash_{\cap\cup} M : I \mid \Delta$ for some Γ, I and Δ, then $M \in \mathsf{SN}^{\beta,\mu}$.*

3   Intersection and Union Types for the $\overline{\lambda}\mu$-Calculus

In the remainder of the paper, we are concerned with the $\overline{\lambda}\mu$-calculus, a call-by-name fragment of Curien and Herbelin's $\overline{\lambda}\mu\tilde{\mu}$-calculus [9]. We present an intersection and union type system that enjoys both the subject reduction property and the characterisation of strongly normalising terms by means of typability. The strong normalisation result in the previous section is used to prove one direction of the characterisation theorem.

There are two main reasons to study here systems based on sequent calculus instead of the $\lambda\mu$-calculus based on natural deduction. One is that they embody the duality between call-by-name and call-by-value more explicitly than the $\lambda\mu$-calculus does. Though we only deal with a call-by-name calculus in the present paper, this leads to future investigations into call-by-value calculi. The other is a more technical reason. In the presence of the syntactic category of contexts, we can treat operation concerning μ-variables (i.e. $[\alpha \Leftarrow N]$ in Definition 2) as usual capture-free substitution (i.e. $[\alpha := e]$ in Definition 7). This allows us to prove properties of the systems, such as subject reduction, in a smoother way.

3.1   The $\overline{\lambda}\mu$-Calculus

The $\overline{\lambda}\mu$-calculus was originally introduced in [16] as an extension of the $\overline{\lambda}$-calculus [15,16]. Here we study a version in [9] that is a call-by-name fragment of the $\overline{\lambda}\mu\tilde{\mu}$-calculus.

Definition 6 (Grammar of $\overline{\lambda}\mu$). *The sets of* terms, contexts *and* commands *are defined inductively by the following grammar:*

$$
\begin{aligned}
t, s &::= x \mid \lambda x.t \mid \mu\alpha.c & \text{(terms)} \\
e &::= \alpha \mid t \cdot e & \text{(contexts)} \\
c &::= \langle t \mid e \rangle & \text{(commands)}
\end{aligned}
$$

where x and α range over denumerable sets of λ-variables and μ-variables, respectively.

The syntax has three kinds of expressions: terms, contexts and commands. Contexts are typically constructed from a μ-variable using the constructor '·'. They can also be considered to have a hole in the position of the head variable. So the command $\langle t \mid e \rangle$ is read as the result of filling the hole of e with a term t.

Definition 7 (Reduction System of $\overline{\lambda}\mu$). *The reduction rules are:*

$$
\begin{aligned}
(\overline{\beta}) &\quad \langle \lambda x.t \mid s \cdot e \rangle \to \langle t[x := s] \mid e \rangle \\
(\overline{\mu}) &\quad \langle \mu\alpha.c \mid e \rangle \to c[\alpha := e]
\end{aligned}
$$

where both $[x := s]$ and $[\alpha := e]$ are usual capture-free substitution.

The rule $(\overline{\beta})$ corresponds to (β) of the $\lambda\mu$-calculus, while the rule $(\overline{\mu})$ corresponds to consecutive applications of the rule (μ). A more precise correspondence is shown in Theorem 6.

3.2   An Intersection and Union Type System for the $\overline{\lambda}\mu$-Calculus

The type assignment system $\overline{\lambda}\mu_{\cap\cup}$ is defined by the rules in Figure 4. This type system is a sequent calculus based on three kinds of judgements: $\Gamma \vdash t : I \mid \Delta$, $\Gamma \mid e : I \vdash \Delta$ and $\langle t \mid e \rangle : (\Gamma \vdash \Delta)$. In the judgement $\Gamma \mid e : I \vdash \Delta$, the type I represents the type of the hole of the context e. So in the rule $(\mathsf{L} \to)$, the hole with type U in the right premiss is replaced, in the conclusion, by the hole with type $I \to U$ applied to the term t which is typed with I in the left premiss.

We write $\Gamma \vdash_{\cap\cup} t : I \mid \Delta$ (resp. $\Gamma \mid e : I \vdash_{\cap\cup} \Delta$ and $\langle t \mid e \rangle : (\Gamma \vdash_{\cap\cup} \Delta)$) if $\Gamma \vdash t : I \mid \Delta$ (resp. $\Gamma \mid e : I \vdash \Delta$ and $\langle t \mid e \rangle : (\Gamma \vdash \Delta)$) is derivable with the rules in Figure 4.

One of the differences from the systems in [10,11,2] is that they use *definite* types in type environments while we use the types in Definition 3. Definite types are, roughly speaking, those which allow neither union types in the (immediate) components of an intersection type nor intersection types in the (immediate) components of a union type.

The next example shows that the command $\langle \mu\alpha.\langle \lambda y.\mu\gamma.\langle y \mid \alpha \rangle \mid \alpha \rangle \mid z \cdot \delta \rangle$ is typable in the system $\overline{\lambda}\mu_{\cap\cup}$. Through the translation in the next subsection, this command corresponds to $[\delta]((\mu\alpha.[\alpha](\lambda y.\mu\gamma.[\alpha]y))z)$ in the $\lambda\mu$-calculus, where the subterm $(\mu\alpha.[\alpha](\lambda y.\mu\gamma.[\alpha]y))z$ is the term treated in Example 1.

$$\frac{}{\Gamma, x : I_1 \cap \cdots \cap I_n \vdash x : I_i \mid \Delta} \text{ (Ax)}$$
where $i \in \{1, \ldots, n\}$

$$\frac{}{\Gamma \mid \alpha : U_i \vdash \alpha : U_1 \cup \cdots \cup U_n, \Delta} \text{ (Ax)}$$
where $i \in \{1, \ldots, n\}$

$$\frac{\Gamma \vdash t : I \mid \Delta \quad \Gamma \mid e : I \vdash \Delta}{\langle t \mid e \rangle : (\Gamma \vdash \Delta)} \text{ (Cut)}$$

$$\frac{c : (\Gamma \vdash \alpha : U, \Delta)}{\Gamma \vdash \mu\alpha.c : U \mid \Delta} \text{ (MuAbs)}$$

$$\frac{\Gamma \vdash t : I \mid \Delta \quad \Gamma \mid e : U \vdash \Delta}{\Gamma \mid t \cdot e : I \to U \vdash \Delta} \text{ (L}\to\text{)}$$

$$\frac{\Gamma, x : I \vdash t : U \mid \Delta}{\Gamma \vdash \lambda x.t : I \to U \mid \Delta} \text{ (R}\to\text{)}$$

$$\frac{\Gamma \mid e : I_i \vdash \Delta}{\Gamma \mid e : I_1 \cap I_2 \vdash \Delta} \text{ (L}\cap\text{)}$$
where $i \in \{1, 2\}$

$$\frac{\Gamma \vdash t : I \mid \Delta \quad \Gamma \vdash t : J \mid \Delta}{\Gamma \vdash t : I \cap J \mid \Delta} \text{ (R}\cap\text{)}$$

$$\frac{\Gamma \mid e : U \vdash \Delta \quad \Gamma \mid e : V \vdash \Delta}{\Gamma \mid e : U \cup V \vdash \Delta} \text{ (L}\cup\text{)}$$

$$\frac{\Gamma \vdash t : U_i \mid \Delta}{\Gamma \vdash t : U_1 \cup U_2 \mid \Delta} \text{ (R}\cup\text{)}$$
where $i \in \{1, 2\}$

Fig. 4. Type assignment system $\overline{\lambda}\mu_{\cap\cup}$

Example 2. The command $\langle \mu\alpha.\langle \lambda y.\mu\gamma.\langle y \mid \alpha \rangle \mid \alpha \rangle \mid z \cdot \delta \rangle$ is typable in the system $\overline{\lambda}\mu_{\cap\cup}$ as follows. Let $A \equiv \varphi_1 \to \varphi_2$, $\Gamma = \{z : \varphi_1 \cap A\}$ and $\Delta = \{\alpha : A \cup (A \to \varphi_3), \delta : \varphi_2 \cup \varphi_3\}$, and let D_1 be the following derivation:

$$\frac{\dfrac{\dfrac{\overline{\Gamma, y : A \vdash y : A \mid \gamma : \varphi_3, \Delta} \text{ (Ax)} \quad \overline{\Gamma, y : A \mid \alpha : A \vdash \gamma : \varphi_3, \Delta} \text{ (Ax)}}{\langle y \mid \alpha \rangle : (\Gamma, y : A \vdash \gamma : \varphi_3, \Delta)} \text{ (Cut)}}{\dfrac{\Gamma, y : A \vdash \mu\gamma.\langle y \mid \alpha \rangle : \varphi_3 \mid \Delta}{\Gamma \vdash \lambda y.\mu\gamma.\langle y \mid \alpha \rangle : A \to \varphi_3 \mid \Delta} \text{ (}\to\text{I)} \quad \overline{\Gamma \mid \alpha : A \to \varphi_3 \vdash \Delta} \text{ (Ax)}} \text{ (MuAbs)}}{\dfrac{\langle \lambda y.\mu\gamma.\langle y \mid \alpha \rangle \mid \alpha \rangle : (\Gamma \vdash \Delta)}{\Gamma \vdash \mu\alpha.\langle \lambda y.\mu\gamma.\langle y \mid \alpha \rangle \mid \alpha \rangle : A \cup (A \to \varphi_3) \mid \delta : \varphi_2 \cup \varphi_3} \text{ (MuAbs)}} \text{ (Cut)}$$

Let $\Delta' = \{\delta : \varphi_2 \cup \varphi_3\}$, and let D_2 be the following derivation:

$$\frac{\dfrac{\overline{\Gamma \vdash z : \varphi_1 \mid \Delta'} \text{ (Ax)} \quad \overline{\Gamma \mid \delta : \varphi_2 \vdash \Delta'} \text{ (Ax)}}{\Gamma \mid z \cdot \delta : A \vdash \Delta'} \text{ (L}\to\text{)} \quad \dfrac{\overline{\Gamma \vdash z : A \mid \Delta'} \text{ (Ax)} \quad \overline{\Gamma \mid \delta : \varphi_3 \vdash \Delta'} \text{ (Ax)}}{\Gamma \mid z \cdot \delta : A \to \varphi_3 \vdash \Delta'} \text{ (L}\to\text{)}}{\Gamma \mid z \cdot \delta : A \cup (A \to \varphi_3) \vdash \Delta'} \text{ (L}\cup\text{)}$$

Then by applying the rule (Cut) to the conclusions of D_1 and D_2, we obtain a derivation of $\langle \mu\alpha.\langle \lambda y.\mu\gamma.\langle y \mid \alpha \rangle \mid \alpha \rangle \mid z \cdot \delta \rangle : (\Gamma \vdash \Delta')$. □

In the following we show some lemmas on properties of the system $\overline{\lambda}\mu_{\cap\cup}$.

Lemma 4.

1. If $\Gamma \vdash_{\cap\cup} t : I_1 \cap \cdots \cap I_n \mid \Delta$ then $\Gamma \vdash_{\cap\cup} t : I_i \mid \Delta$ for any $i \in \{1, \ldots, n\}$.
2. If $\Gamma \mid e : U_1 \cup \cdots \cup U_n \vdash_{\cap\cup} \Delta$ then $\Gamma \mid e : U_i \vdash_{\cap\cup} \Delta$ for any $i \in \{1, \ldots, n\}$.

Proof. By induction on the derivations. Note that if the last applied rule of the derivation of $\Gamma \vdash_{\cap\cup}^{-} t : I_1 \cap \cdots \cap I_n \mid \Delta$ is (MuAbs), (R $\rightarrow$) or (R $\cup$), then $n = 1$, and that the last applied rule of the derivation of $\Gamma \mid e : U_1 \cup \cdots \cup U_n \vdash_{\cap\cup}^{-} \Delta$ is not (L $\cap$).   □

Lemma 5 (Term Substitution Lemma). *Let $\Gamma \vdash_{\cap\cup}^{-} s : I \mid \Delta$.*

1. *If $\Gamma, x : I \vdash_{\cap\cup}^{-} t : J \mid \Delta$ then $\Gamma \vdash_{\cap\cup}^{-} t[x := s] : J \mid \Delta$.*
2. *If $\Gamma, x : I \mid e : J \vdash_{\cap\cup}^{-} \Delta$ then $\Gamma \mid e[x := s] : J \vdash_{\cap\cup}^{-} \Delta$.*
3. *If $c : (\Gamma, x : I \vdash_{\cap\cup}^{-} \Delta)$ then $c[x := s] : (\Gamma \vdash_{\cap\cup}^{-} \Delta)$.*

Proof. By simultaneous induction on the derivations. In the case where $\Gamma, x : I \vdash_{\cap\cup}^{-} t : J \mid \Delta$ is an axiom with $t \equiv x$, then we use Lemma 4(1).   □

Lemma 6 (Context Substitution Lemma). *Let $\Gamma \mid e : U \vdash_{\cap\cup}^{-} \Delta$.*

1. *If $\Gamma \vdash_{\cap\cup}^{-} t : I \mid \alpha : U, \Delta$ then $\Gamma \vdash_{\cap\cup}^{-} t[\alpha := e] : I \mid \Delta$.*
2. *If $\Gamma \mid e' : I \vdash_{\cap\cup}^{-} \alpha : U, \Delta$ then $\Gamma \mid e'[\alpha := e] : I \vdash_{\cap\cup}^{-} \Delta$.*
3. *If $c : (\Gamma \vdash_{\cap\cup}^{-} \alpha : U, \Delta)$ then $c[\alpha := e] : (\Gamma \vdash_{\cap\cup}^{-} \Delta)$.*

Proof. By simultaneous induction on the derivations. In the case where $\Gamma \mid e' : I \vdash_{\cap\cup}^{-} \alpha : U, \Delta$ is an axiom with $e' \equiv \alpha$, then we use Lemma 4(2).   □

Lemma 7 (Generation Lemma)

1. *If $\Gamma \mid e : I \vdash_{\cap\cup}^{-} \Delta$ then $I \equiv U_1 \cap \cdots \cap U_n$ and $\Gamma \mid e : U_i \vdash_{\cap\cup}^{-} \Delta$ for some U_i $(i \in \{1, \ldots, n\})$.*
2. *If $\Gamma \vdash_{\cap\cup}^{-} \lambda x.t : U \mid \Delta$ then $U \equiv A_1 \cup \cdots \cup A_n$ and $\Gamma, x : I \vdash_{\cap\cup}^{-} t : V \mid \Delta$ for some $A_i \equiv I \rightarrow V$ $(i \in \{1, \ldots, n\})$.*
3. *If $\Gamma \vdash_{\cap\cup}^{-} \mu\alpha.c : U \mid \Delta$ then $U \equiv U_1 \cup \cdots \cup U_n$ and $c : (\Gamma \vdash_{\cap\cup}^{-} \alpha : U_i, \Delta)$ for some U_i $(i \in \{1, \ldots, n\})$.*
4. *If $\Gamma \mid t \cdot e : U \vdash_{\cap\cup}^{-} \Delta$ then $U \equiv (I_1 \rightarrow V_1) \cup \cdots \cup (I_n \rightarrow V_n)$, $\Gamma \vdash_{\cap\cup}^{-} t : I_i \mid \Delta$ and $\Gamma \mid e : V_i \vdash_{\cap\cup}^{-} \Delta$ for any $I_i \rightarrow V_i$ $(i \in \{1, \ldots, n\})$.*

Proof. By induction on the derivations.   □

We are now in a position to show that the system $\overline{\lambda}\mu_{\cap\cup}$ satisfies the subject reduction property. First we prove the case where the reduction is at the root.

Lemma 8

1. *If $\langle \mu\alpha.c \mid e \rangle : (\Gamma \vdash_{\cap\cup}^{-} \Delta)$ then $c[\alpha := e] : (\Gamma \vdash_{\cap\cup}^{-} \Delta)$.*
2. *If $\langle \lambda x.t \mid s \cdot e \rangle : (\Gamma \vdash_{\cap\cup}^{-} \Delta)$ then $\langle t[x := s] \mid e \rangle : (\Gamma \vdash_{\cap\cup}^{-} \Delta)$.*

Proof. 1. Let $\langle \mu\alpha.c \mid e \rangle : (\Gamma \vdash_{\cap\cup}^{-} \Delta)$. Then there exists $I \equiv U_1 \cap \cdots \cap U_n$ such that $\Gamma \vdash_{\cap\cup}^{-} \mu\alpha.c : I \mid \Delta$ and $\Gamma \mid e : I \vdash_{\cap\cup}^{-} \Delta$. By Lemma 7(1), there exists U_i such that $\Gamma \mid e : U_i \vdash_{\cap\cup}^{-} \Delta$, and by Lemma 4(1), $\Gamma \vdash_{\cap\cup}^{-} \mu\alpha.c : U_i \mid \Delta$. So by Lemma 7(3), $U_i \equiv U_{i_1} \cup \cdots \cup U_{i_m}$ and $c : (\Gamma \vdash_{\cap\cup}^{-} \alpha : U_{i_k}, \Delta)$ for some U_{i_k}. Then by Lemma 4(2), $\Gamma \mid e : U_{i_k} \vdash_{\cap\cup}^{-} \Delta$. Hence by Lemma 6(3), we have $c[\alpha := e] : (\Gamma \vdash_{\cap\cup}^{-} \Delta)$.

2. Let $\langle \lambda x.t \,|\, s \cdot e \rangle : (\Gamma \vdash_{\cap U}^- \Delta)$. Then there exists $I \equiv U_1 \cap \cdots \cap U_n$ such that $\Gamma \vdash_{\cap U}^- \lambda x.t : I \,|\, \Delta$ and $\Gamma \,|\, s \cdot e : I \vdash_{\cap U}^- \Delta$. By Lemma 7(1), there exists U_i such that $\Gamma \,|\, s \cdot e : U_i \vdash_{\cap U}^- \Delta$, and by Lemma 4(1), $\Gamma \vdash_{\cap U}^- \lambda x.t : U_i \,|\, \Delta$. So by Lemma 7(2), $U_i \equiv A_{i_1} \cup \cdots \cup A_{i_m}$ and $\Gamma, x : J \vdash_{\cap U}^- t : V \,|\, \Delta$ for some $A_{i_k} \equiv J \to V$. Then by Lemma 7(4), $\Gamma \vdash_{\cap U}^- s : J \,|\, \Delta$ and $\Gamma \,|\, e : V \vdash_{\cap U}^- \Delta$. Now by Lemma 5(1), we have $\Gamma \vdash_{\cap U}^- t[x := s] : V \,|\, \Delta$. Hence by the rule (Cut), we obtain $\langle t[x := s] \,|\, e \rangle : (\Gamma \vdash_{\cap U}^- \Delta)$.   □

Theorem 4 (Subject Reduction)

1. *If* $\Gamma \vdash_{\cap U}^- t : I \,|\, \Delta$ *and* $t \longrightarrow_{\overline{\beta},\overline{\mu}} t'$ *then* $\Gamma \vdash_{\cap U}^- t' : I \,|\, \Delta$.
2. *If* $\Gamma \,|\, e : I \vdash_{\cap U}^- \Delta$ *and* $e \longrightarrow_{\overline{\beta},\overline{\mu}} e'$ *then* $\Gamma \,|\, e' : I \vdash_{\cap U}^- \Delta$.
3. *If* $c : (\Gamma \vdash_{\cap U}^- \Delta)$ *and* $c \longrightarrow_{\overline{\beta},\overline{\mu}} c'$ *then* $c' : (\Gamma \vdash_{\cap U}^- \Delta)$.

Proof. By simultaneous induction on the derivations. If the reduction is at the root, then we use Lemma 8.   □

3.3 Translating $\overline{\lambda}\mu_{\cap U}$ into $\lambda\mu_{\cap U}$

In this subsection we show that typing derivations in the system $\overline{\lambda}\mu_{\cap U}$ can be translated into ones in the system $\lambda\mu_{\cap U}$ in an appropriate way. To do so, we employ an equivalent formulation to $\lambda\mu_{\cap U}$ that has the following rules instead of (μ_1) and (μ_2):

$$\frac{\Gamma \vdash M : U \,|\, \alpha : U, \Delta}{[\alpha]M : (\Gamma \vdash \alpha : U, \Delta)} \; \text{(Nam)} \qquad \frac{C : (\Gamma \vdash \alpha : U, \Delta)}{\Gamma \vdash \mu\alpha.C : U \,|\, \Delta} \; \text{(MuAbs)}$$

The rule (Nam) introduces a new form of judgement $C : (\Gamma \vdash \Delta)$, which should be immediately followed by the rule (MuAbs). So the derivability of judgements of the form $\Gamma \vdash M : I \,|\, \Delta$ is not changed from that in the original $\lambda\mu_{\cap U}$. We write $C : (\Gamma \vdash_{\cap U} \Delta)$ if $C : (\Gamma \vdash \Delta)$ is derivable in this alternative formulation.

Also, we add the following to the reduction rules of the $\lambda\mu$-calculus:

$$(\rho) \quad [\alpha](\mu\gamma.C) \to C[\gamma := \alpha]$$

The translation from the terms in the $\overline{\lambda}\mu$-calculus to those in the $\lambda\mu$-calculus is given in Figure 5.

$$
\begin{aligned}
\Theta(x) &:= x \\
\Theta(\lambda x.t) &:= \lambda x.\Theta(t) \\
\Theta(\mu\alpha.c) &:= \mu\alpha.\Theta'(c) \\
\Theta'(\langle t \,|\, e \rangle) &:= \Theta''(\Theta(t), e) \\
\Theta''(M, \alpha) &:= [\alpha]M \\
\Theta''(M, t \cdot e) &:= \Theta''(M\Theta(t), e)
\end{aligned}
$$

Fig. 5. Translation from $\overline{\lambda}\mu$ to $\lambda\mu$

The following two technical lemmas are useful for proving Theorem 5.

Lemma 9. *If $\Gamma \mid \alpha : U \vdash_{\bar{\cap}\cup} \Delta$ then there exists $\alpha : V \in \Delta$ such that $V \equiv U \cup V_1 \cup \cdots \cup V_n$ $(n \geq 0)$.*

Proof. By induction on the derivation, assuming the commutativity of $\cup$.   ☐

Lemma 10. *Let $\Gamma \mid t\cdot e : (I_1 \to U_1)\cup\cdots\cup(I_n \to U_n) \vdash_{\bar{\cap}\cup} \Delta$ with its derivation length k. Then, for any $i \in \{1,\ldots,n\}$, $\Gamma \vdash_{\bar{\cap}\cup} t : I_i \mid \Delta$ with its derivation length less than k, and $\Gamma \mid e : U_1 \cup \cdots \cup U_n \vdash_{\bar{\cap}\cup} \Delta$ with its derivation length $k-1$.*

Proof. As in Lemma 7(4), we have $\Gamma \vdash_{\bar{\cap}\cup} t : I_i \mid \Delta$ and $\Gamma \mid e : U_i \vdash_{\bar{\cap}\cup} \Delta$ for all $i \in \{1,\ldots,n\}$, whose derivations are subderivations of the given derivation. Then we can construct a derivation of $\Gamma \mid e : U_1 \cup \cdots \cup U_n \vdash \Delta$ with its length $k-1$ by replacing each judgement for $t \cdot e$ and $(I_i \to U_i)$'s in the original derivation by a corresponding judgement for e and U_i's.   ☐

Now we prove that the translation Θ preserves types. This explains how the rules of $\overline{\lambda}\mu_{\cap\cup}$ corresponds to the rules of $\lambda\mu_{\cap\cup}$.

Theorem 5

1. *If $\Gamma \vdash_{\bar{\cap}\cup} t : I \mid \Delta$ then $\Gamma \vdash_{\cap\cup} \Theta(t) : I \mid \Delta$.*
2. *If $\Gamma \mid e : I \vdash_{\bar{\cap}\cup} \Delta$ then $\Theta''(M,e) : (\Gamma \vdash_{\cap\cup} \Delta)$ for any M such that $\Gamma \vdash_{\cap\cup} M : I \mid \Delta$.*
3. *If $c : (\Gamma \vdash_{\bar{\cap}\cup} \Delta)$ then $\Theta'(c) : (\Gamma \vdash_{\cap\cup} \Delta)$.*

Proof. We prove 1, 2 and 3 by simultaneous induction on the lengths of the derivations. We consider here some of the cases in 2.

- $$\frac{}{\Gamma \mid \alpha : U_i \vdash \alpha : U_1 \cup \cdots \cup U_n, \Delta} \text{ (Ax)}$$

  Let $\Gamma \vdash_{\cap\cup} M : U_i \mid \alpha : U_1 \cup \cdots \cup U_n, \Delta$. Then by the rules (R$\cup$) and (Nam), we have $[\alpha]M : (\Gamma \vdash_{\cap\cup} \alpha : U_1 \cup \cdots \cup U_n, \Delta)$ where $[\alpha]M \equiv \Theta''(M,\alpha)$.

- $$\frac{\Gamma \vdash t : I \mid \Delta \quad \Gamma \mid e : U \vdash \Delta}{\Gamma \mid t\cdot e : I \to U \vdash \Delta} \text{ (L} \to\text{)}$$

  Let $\Gamma \vdash_{\cap\cup} M : I \to U \mid \Delta$. By the induction hypothesis, we have $\Gamma \vdash_{\cap\cup} \Theta(t) : I \mid \Delta$. Then again by the induction hypothesis, we have $\Theta''(M\Theta(t), e) : (\Gamma \vdash_{\cap\cup} \Delta)$ where $\Theta''(M\Theta(t), e) \equiv \Theta''(M, t \cdot e)$.

- $$\frac{\Gamma \mid e : U \vdash \Delta \quad \Gamma \mid e : V \vdash \Delta}{\Gamma \mid e : U \cup V \vdash \Delta} \text{ (L}\cup\text{)}$$

  First we show the case where $e \equiv \alpha$. Then by Lemma 9, there exists $\alpha : W \in \Delta$ such that $W \equiv U \cup V \cup W_1 \cup \cdots \cup W_n$ $(n \geq 0)$. Let $\Gamma \vdash_{\cap\cup} M : U \cup V \mid \Delta$. Then by the rules (R$\cup$) and (Nam), we have $[\alpha]M : (\Gamma \vdash_{\cap\cup} \Delta)$ where $[\alpha]M \equiv \Theta''(M,\alpha)$.

  Next we show the case where $e \equiv t \cdot e'$. Then by Lemmas 7(4), $U \cup V \equiv (I_1 \to U_1)\cup\cdots\cup(I_n \to U_n)$, and by Lemma 10, for all $i \in \{1,\ldots,n\}$, $\Gamma \vdash_{\bar{\cap}\cup} t : I_i \mid \Delta$

and $\Gamma \mid e' : U_1 \cup \cdots \cup U_n \vdash^-_{\cap \cup} \Delta$ with their derivation lengths less than that of $\Gamma \mid e : U \cup V \vdash \Delta$. Hence by the induction hypothesis, we have $\Gamma \vdash_{\cap \cup} \Theta(t) : I_i \mid \Delta$ for each $i \in \{1, \ldots, n\}$. Now let $\Gamma \vdash_{\cap \cup} M : U \cup V \mid \Delta$, and consider the following derivation:

$$
\cfrac{\cfrac{}{\Gamma, x : I_i \to U_i \vdash x : I_i \to U_i \mid \Delta}\ (\mathsf{Ax}) \qquad \cfrac{\vdots \\ \Gamma \vdash \Theta(t) : I_i \mid \Delta}{\Gamma, x : I_i \to U_i \vdash \Theta(t) : I_i \mid \Delta}\ \text{Lemma 1}}{\cfrac{\Gamma, x : I_i \to U_i \vdash x\Theta(t) : U_i \mid \Delta}{\Gamma, x : I_i \to U_i \vdash x\Theta(t) : U_1 \cup \cdots \cup U_n \mid \Delta}\ (\cup\mathsf{I})}\ (\to \mathsf{E})
$$

where x is a fresh λ-variable. Then by applying the rule $(\cup\mathsf{E})^n$ in Lemma 2, we have $\Gamma \vdash_{\cap \cup} M\Theta(t) : U_1 \cup \cdots \cup U_n \mid \Delta$. Hence by the induction hypothesis for the derivation of $\Gamma \mid e' : U_1 \cup \cdots \cup U_n \vdash \Delta$, we obtain $\Theta''(M\Theta(t), e') : (\Gamma \vdash_{\cap \cup} \Delta)$ where $\Theta''(M\Theta(t), e') \equiv \Theta''(M, t \cdot e')$.   □

Next we show that reduction in the $\bar{\lambda}\mu$-calculus is simulated in the $\lambda\mu$-calculus through the translation Θ. This is used to prove one direction of the characterisation theorem of strong normalisation.

Lemma 11

1. $\Theta(t[x := s]) \equiv \Theta(t)[x := \Theta(s)]$.
2. $\Theta'(c[x := s]) \equiv \Theta'(c)[x := \Theta(s)]$.
3. $\Theta''(M[x := \Theta(s)], e[x := s]) \equiv \Theta''(M, e)[x := \Theta(s)]$.

Proof. By simultaneous induction on the structure of t, e or c.   □

In the following we abbreviate $M[\alpha \Leftarrow N_1] \cdots [\alpha \Leftarrow N_k]$ as $M[\alpha \Leftarrow N_1, \cdots, N_k]$.

Lemma 12. Let $e \equiv s_1 \cdot \cdots \cdot s_n \cdot \alpha$ and $\bar{N} \equiv \Theta(s_1), \cdots, \Theta(s_n)$.

1. $\Theta(t[\alpha := e]) \equiv \Theta(t)[\alpha \Leftarrow \bar{N}]$.
2. $\Theta'(c[\alpha := e]) \equiv \Theta'(c)[\alpha \Leftarrow \bar{N}]$.
3. $\Theta''(M[\alpha \Leftarrow \bar{N}], e'[\alpha := e]) \equiv \Theta''(M, e')[\alpha \Leftarrow \bar{N}]$.

Proof. By simultaneous induction on the structure of t, e or c.   □

Lemma 13

1. $\Theta(t[\alpha := \gamma]) \equiv \Theta(t)[\alpha := \gamma]$.
2. $\Theta'(c[\alpha := \gamma]) \equiv \Theta'(c)[\alpha := \gamma]$.
3. $\Theta''(M[\alpha := \gamma], e[\alpha := \gamma]) \equiv \Theta''(M, e)[\alpha := \gamma]$.

Proof. By simultaneous induction on the structure of t, e or c.   □

Now we are in a position to show the simulation theorem.

Theorem 6

1. If $t \longrightarrow_{\overline{\beta},\overline{\mu}} t'$ then $\Theta(t) \longrightarrow^+_{\beta,\mu,\rho} \Theta(t')$.
2. If $c \longrightarrow_{\overline{\beta},\overline{\mu}} c'$ then $\Theta'(c) \longrightarrow^+_{\beta,\mu,\rho} \Theta'(c')$.
3. If $e \longrightarrow_{\overline{\beta},\overline{\mu}} e'$ then $\Theta''(M,e) \longrightarrow^+_{\beta,\mu,\rho} \Theta''(M,e')$.

Proof. By simultaneous induction on the structure of t, e or c. We prove the case where the reduction is at the root.

- $\langle \lambda x.t \mid s \cdot e \rangle \to \langle t[x := s] \mid e \rangle$.
  We have $\Theta'(\langle \lambda x.t \mid s \cdot e \rangle) \equiv \Theta''(\Theta(\lambda x.t), s \cdot e) \equiv \Theta''((\lambda x.\Theta(t))\Theta(s), e) \longrightarrow_\beta$
  $\Theta''(\Theta(t)[x := \Theta(s)], e)$ and $\Theta'(\langle t[x := s] \mid e \rangle) \equiv \Theta''(\Theta(t[x := s]), e)$. Therefore, by Lemma 11, we have $\Theta'(\langle \lambda x.t \mid s \cdot e \rangle) \longrightarrow^+_{\beta,\mu,\rho} \Theta'(\langle t[x := s] \mid e \rangle)$.
- $\langle \mu\alpha.c \mid e \rangle \to c[\alpha := e]$.
  We have $\Theta'(\langle \mu\alpha.c \mid e \rangle) \equiv \Theta''(\Theta(\mu\alpha.c), e) \equiv \Theta''(\mu\alpha.\Theta'(c), e)$. Let $e \equiv s_1 \cdot$
  $\cdots s_n \cdot \gamma$ and $\bar{N} \equiv \Theta(s_1), \cdots, \Theta(s_n)$. Then, we have $\Theta''(\mu\alpha.\Theta'(c), e) \equiv$
  $\Theta''((\mu\alpha.\Theta'(c))\Theta(s_1) \cdots \Theta(s_n), \gamma) \equiv [\gamma]((\mu\alpha.\Theta'(c))\Theta(s_1) \cdots \Theta(s_n)) \longrightarrow^*_\mu$
  $[\gamma](\mu\alpha.\Theta'(c)[\alpha \Leftarrow \bar{N}]) \longrightarrow_\rho \Theta'(c)[\alpha \Leftarrow \bar{N}][\alpha := \gamma]$. Let $e' \equiv s_1 \cdots s_n \cdot \alpha$.
  Then, by Lemma 12, we have $\Theta'(c[\alpha := e']) \equiv \Theta'(c)[\alpha \Leftarrow \bar{N}]$, and so, by
  Lemma 13, we have $\Theta'(c[\alpha := e'][\alpha := \gamma]) \equiv \Theta'(c[\alpha := e'])[\alpha := \gamma] \equiv$
  $\Theta'(c)[\alpha \Leftarrow \bar{N}][\alpha := \gamma]$. Since $\Theta'(c[\alpha := e]) \equiv \Theta'(c[\alpha := e'][\alpha := \gamma])$, we have
  $\Theta'(\langle \mu\alpha.c \mid e \rangle) \longrightarrow^+_{\beta,\mu,\rho} \Theta'(c[\alpha := e])$.
  $\square$

Now we can prove that all terms typable in $\overline{\lambda}\mu_{\cap\cup}$ are strongly normalising.

Corollary 3

1. If $\Gamma \vdash^-_{\cap\cup} t : I \mid \Delta$ for some Γ, I and Δ, then $t \in \mathsf{SN}^{\overline{\beta},\overline{\mu}}$.
2. If $\Gamma \mid e : U \vdash^-_{\cap\cup} \Delta$ for some Γ, U and Δ, then $e \in \mathsf{SN}^{\overline{\beta},\overline{\mu}}$.
3. If $c : (\Gamma \vdash^-_{\cap\cup} \Delta)$ for some Γ and Δ, then $c \in \mathsf{SN}^{\overline{\beta},\overline{\mu}}$.

Proof. By Theorems 5 and 6, Corollary 2, and the fact that $\mathsf{SN}^{\beta,\mu} = \mathsf{SN}^{\beta,\mu,\rho}$. The last equality follows from (i) for any term M of the $\lambda\mu$-calculus, $M \in \mathsf{SN}^\rho$ and (ii) if $M \longrightarrow_\rho M' \longrightarrow_{\beta,\mu} N$ then there exists M'' such that $M \longrightarrow_{\beta,\mu} M'' \longrightarrow^*_\rho N$.
$\square$

3.4   Characterisation of Strongly Normalising Terms

By Corollary 3, we see that any term typable in $\overline{\lambda}\mu_{\cap\cup}$ is strongly normalising. However, it is not yet clear how many terms are typable in $\overline{\lambda}\mu_{\cap\cup}$. In this subsection we show that $\overline{\lambda}\mu_{\cap\cup}$ is powerful enough to type all strongly normalising terms. Although this is a typical property in intersection type systems for the usual λ-calculus, it has not been proved for the $\overline{\lambda}\mu$-calculus (or a fragment of the $\overline{\lambda}\mu\tilde{\mu}$-calculus) in a type system that enjoys the subject reduction property.

First we introduce notations on type environments.

Definition 8. *1. The type environment $\Gamma \cap \Gamma'$ is defined by*

$$\Gamma \cap \Gamma' := \{x : I \cap I' \mid x : I \in \Gamma \text{ and } x : I' \in \Gamma'\}$$
$$\cup \{x : I \mid x : I \in \Gamma \text{ and } x \text{ does not appear in } \Gamma'\}$$
$$\cup \{x : I' \mid x : I' \in \Gamma' \text{ and } x \text{ does not appear in } \Gamma\}.$$

2. The type environment $\Delta \cup \Delta'$ is defined by

$$\Delta \cup \Delta' := \{x : U \cup U' \mid x : U \in \Delta \text{ and } x : U' \in \Delta'\}$$
$$\cup \{x : U \mid x : U \in \Delta \text{ and } x \text{ does not appear in } \Delta'\}$$
$$\cup \{x : U' \mid x : U' \in \Delta' \text{ and } x \text{ does not appear in } \Delta\}.$$

Lemma 14

1. *If $\Gamma \vdash_{\cap\cup}^{-} t : I \mid \Delta$ then $\Gamma \cap \Gamma' \vdash_{\cap\cup}^{-} t : I \mid \Delta \cup \Delta'$.*
2. *If $\Gamma \mid e : I \vdash_{\cap\cup}^{-} \Delta$ then $\Gamma \cap \Gamma' \mid e : I \vdash_{\cap\cup}^{-} \Delta \cup \Delta'$.*
3. *If $c : (\Gamma \vdash_{\cap\cup}^{-} \Delta)$ then $c : (\Gamma \cap \Gamma' \vdash_{\cap\cup}^{-} \Delta \cup \Delta')$.*

Proof. By simultaneous induction on the derivations. □

Next we prove crucial lemmas about type-checking in the system $\overline{\lambda}\mu_{\cap\cup}$.

Lemma 15 (Term Inverse Substitution Lemma). *Let $\Gamma \vdash_{\cap\cup}^{-} s : I \mid \Delta$.*

1. *If $\Gamma \vdash_{\cap\cup}^{-} t[x := s] : J \mid \Delta$ then there exists I' such that $\Gamma, x : I' \vdash_{\cap\cup}^{-} t : J \mid \Delta$ and $\Gamma \vdash_{\cap\cup}^{-} s : I' \mid \Delta$.*
2. *If $\Gamma \mid e[x := s] : J \vdash_{\cap\cup}^{-} \Delta$ then there exists I' such that $\Gamma, x : I' \mid e : J \vdash_{\cap\cup}^{-} \Delta$ and $\Gamma \vdash_{\cap\cup}^{-} s : I' \mid \Delta$.*
3. *If $c[x := s] : (\Gamma \vdash_{\cap\cup}^{-} \Delta)$ then there exists I' such that $c : (\Gamma, x : I' \vdash_{\cap\cup}^{-} \Delta)$ and $\Gamma \vdash_{\cap\cup}^{-} s : I' \mid \Delta$.*

Proof. By simultaneous induction on the structure of t, e or c. The non-trivial cases are the following two cases.

- $e \equiv t \cdot e'$
  Suppose $\Gamma \mid (t \cdot e')[x := s] : J \vdash_{\cap\cup}^{-} \Delta$. By Lemma 7(1), there exist $U_1 \ldots, U_n$ such that $J \equiv U_1 \cap \cdots \cap U_n$ and $\Gamma \mid (t \cdot e')[x := s] : U_i \vdash_{\cap\cup}^{-} \Delta$ for some $i \in \{1, \ldots, n\}$. Then, fixing one such i and applying Lemma 7(4), there exist $I_1, V_1, \ldots, I_m, V_m$ such that $U_i \equiv (I_1 \to V_1) \cup \cdots \cup (I_m \to V_m)$, and $\Gamma \vdash_{\cap\cup}^{-} t[x := s] : I_j \mid \Delta$ and $\Gamma \mid e'[x := s] : V_j \vdash_{\cap\cup}^{-} \Delta$ for any $j \in \{1, \ldots, m\}$. So, for each $j \in \{1, \ldots, m\}$, there exists I'_j such that $\Gamma, x : I'_j \vdash_{\cap\cup}^{-} t : I_j \mid \Delta$ and $\Gamma \vdash_{\cap\cup}^{-} s : I'_j \mid \Delta$, and there exists I''_j such that $\Gamma, x : I''_j \mid e' : V_j \vdash_{\cap\cup}^{-} \Delta$ and $\Gamma \vdash_{\cap\cup}^{-} s : I''_j \mid \Delta$, by the induction hypothesis. By Lemma 14 and (L $\to$), we have $\Gamma, x : I'_j \cap I''_j \mid t \cdot e' : I_j \to V_j \vdash_{\cap\cup}^{-} \Delta$. Let $I' \equiv (I'_1 \cap I''_1) \cap \cdots \cap (I'_m \cap I''_m)$. By Lemma 14 and (L $\cup$), we have $\Gamma, x : I' \mid t \cdot e' : U_i \vdash_{\cap\cup}^{-} \Delta$, and, by (L $\cap$), we have $\Gamma, x : I' \mid t \cdot e' : J \vdash_{\cap\cup}^{-} \Delta$. We also have $\Gamma \vdash_{\cap\cup}^{-} s : I' \mid \Delta$ by (R $\cap$).
- $c \equiv \langle t \mid e' \rangle$
  This case can be proved dually to the same case of the proof of Lemma 16.

□

Lemma 16 (Context Inverse Substitution Lemma). *Let $\Gamma \mid e : U \vdash_{\cap\cup}^{-} \Delta$.*

1. *If $\Gamma \vdash_{\cap\cup}^{-} t[\alpha := e] : I \mid \Delta$ then there exists U' such that $\Gamma \vdash_{\cap\cup}^{-} t : I \mid \alpha : U', \Delta$ and $\Gamma \mid e : U' \vdash_{\cap\cup}^{-} \Delta$.*
2. *If $\Gamma \mid e'[\alpha := e] : I \vdash_{\cap\cup}^{-} \Delta$ then there exists U' such that $\Gamma \mid e' : I \vdash_{\cap\cup}^{-} \alpha : U', \Delta$ and $\Gamma \mid e : U' \vdash_{\cap\cup}^{-} \Delta$.*
3. *If $c[\alpha := e] : (\Gamma \vdash_{\cap\cup}^{-} \Delta)$ then there exists U' such that $c : (\Gamma \vdash_{\cap\cup}^{-} \alpha : U', \Delta)$ and $\Gamma \mid e : U' \vdash_{\cap\cup}^{-} \Delta$.*

Proof. By simultaneous induction on the structure of t, e or c. The non-trivial cases are the following two cases.

- $e \equiv t \cdot e'$
  This case can be proved dually to the same case of the proof of Lemma 15.
- $c \equiv \langle t \mid e' \rangle$
  Suppose $\langle t \mid e' \rangle[\alpha := e] : (\Gamma \vdash_{\cap\cup}^{-} \Delta)$. Then, there exists I such that $\Gamma \vdash_{\cap\cup}^{-} t[\alpha := e] : I \mid \Delta$ and $\Gamma \mid e'[\alpha := e] : I \vdash_{\cap\cup}^{-} \Delta$. By the induction hypothesis, there exists V' such that $\Gamma \vdash_{\cap\cup}^{-} t : I \mid \alpha : V', \Delta$ and $\Gamma \mid e : V' \vdash_{\cap\cup}^{-} \Delta$, and there exists V'' such that $\Gamma \mid e' : I \vdash_{\cap\cup}^{-} \alpha : V'', \Delta$ and $\Gamma \mid e : V'' \vdash_{\cap\cup}^{-} \Delta$. Let $U' \equiv V' \cup V''$. By Lemma 14 and (Cut), we have $\langle t \mid e' \rangle : (\Gamma \vdash_{\cap\cup}^{-} \alpha : U', \Delta)$, and by (L $\cup$), we have $\Gamma \mid e : U' \vdash_{\cap\cup}^{-} \Delta$. $\square$

Now we prove the characterisation theorem of strongly normalising terms.

Theorem 7

1. *$t \in \mathsf{SN}^{\overline{\beta},\overline{\mu}}$ if and only if $\Gamma \vdash_{\cap\cup}^{-} t : I \mid \Delta$ for some Γ, I and Δ.*
2. *$e \in \mathsf{SN}^{\overline{\beta},\overline{\mu}}$ if and only if $\Gamma \mid e : U \vdash_{\cap\cup}^{-} \Delta$ for some Γ, U and Δ.*
3. *$c \in \mathsf{SN}^{\overline{\beta},\overline{\mu}}$ if and only if $c : (\Gamma \vdash_{\cap\cup}^{-} \Delta)$ for some Γ and Δ.*

Proof. The right to left implications are by Corollary 3. For the converses, we prove 1, 2 and 3 simultaneously by main induction on the maximal length of all $\overline{\beta}, \overline{\mu}$-reduction sequences out of t, e or c, and subinduction on the structure of t, e or c. We analyse the possible cases according to the shape of t, e or c.

- $t \equiv x$ for some λ-variable x. In this case we just have to take $x : I \vdash x : I \mid$ which is an axiom.
- $e \equiv \alpha$ for some μ-variable α. Similar, taking an axiom $\mid \alpha : U \vdash \alpha : U$.
- $t \equiv \lambda x.s$. By the subinduction hypothesis, there exist Γ, I and Δ such that $\Gamma \vdash_{\cap\cup}^{-} s : I \mid \Delta$. Let $I \equiv U_1 \cap \cdots \cap U_n$. Then by Lemma 4(1), we have $\Gamma \vdash_{\cap\cup}^{-} s : U_i \mid \Delta$ for any $i \in \{1, \ldots, n\}$. Hence, if $x : J \in \Gamma$ then we have $\Gamma \setminus \{x : J\} \vdash_{\cap\cup}^{-} \lambda x.s : J \to U_i \mid \Delta$. Otherwise, using Lemma 14(1), we have $\Gamma \vdash_{\cap\cup}^{-} \lambda x.s : J \to U_i \mid \Delta$ for some J.
- The cases $t \equiv \mu\alpha.c$, $e \equiv t \cdot e'$, $c \equiv \langle x \mid e \rangle$ and $c \equiv \langle \lambda x.s \mid \alpha \rangle$ are proved using the subinduction hypothesis and Lemma 14.

The last two cases require us to use the main induction hypothesis.

- $c \equiv \langle \mu\alpha.c' \,|\, e \rangle$. By the main induction hypothesis, there exist Γ and Δ such that $c'[\alpha := e] : (\Gamma \vdash_{\bar{\cap}\cup} \Delta)$. By the subinduction hypothesis, there exist Γ', U and Δ' such that $\Gamma' \,|\, e : U \vdash_{\bar{\cap}\cup} \Delta'$. Then by Lemmas 14 and 16(3), there exists U' such that $c' : (\Gamma \cap \Gamma' \vdash_{\bar{\cap}\cup} \alpha : U', \Delta \cup \Delta')$ and $\Gamma \cap \Gamma' \,|\, e : U' \vdash_{\bar{\cap}\cup} \Delta \cup \Delta'$. From the former, we have $\Gamma \cap \Gamma' \vdash_{\bar{\cap}\cup} \mu\alpha.c' : U' \,|\, \Delta \cup \Delta'$. Hence by the rule (Cut), we obtain $\langle \mu\alpha.c' \,|\, e \rangle : (\Gamma \cap \Gamma' \vdash_{\bar{\cap}\cup} \Delta \cup \Delta')$.

- $c \equiv \langle \lambda x.t \,|\, s \cdot e \rangle$. By the main induction hypothesis, there exist Γ and Δ such that $\langle t[x := s] \,|\, e \rangle : (\Gamma \vdash_{\bar{\cap}\cup} \Delta)$. Then there exists J such that $\Gamma \vdash_{\bar{\cap}\cup} t[x := s] : J \,|\, \Delta$ and $\Gamma \,|\, e : J \vdash_{\bar{\cap}\cup} \Delta$. By the subinduction hypothesis, there exist Γ', I and Δ' such that $\Gamma' \vdash_{\bar{\cap}\cup} s : I \,|\, \Delta'$. Hence by Lemmas 14 and 15(1), there exists I' such that $\Gamma \cap \Gamma', x : I' \vdash_{\bar{\cap}\cup} t : J \,|\, \Delta \cup \Delta'$ and $\Gamma \cap \Gamma' \vdash_{\bar{\cap}\cup} s : I' \,|\, \Delta \cup \Delta'$. From the former, we have $\Gamma \cap \Gamma' \vdash_{\bar{\cap}\cup} \lambda x.t : I' \to J \,|\, \Delta \cup \Delta'$. From the latter and $\Gamma \,|\, e : J \vdash_{\bar{\cap}\cup} \Delta$, we have $\Gamma \cap \Gamma' \,|\, s \cdot e : I' \to J \vdash_{\bar{\cap}\cup} \Delta \cup \Delta'$. Hence by the rule (Cut), we obtain $\langle \lambda x.t \,|\, s \cdot e \rangle : (\Gamma \cap \Gamma' \vdash_{\bar{\cap}\cup} \Delta \cup \Delta')$. □

4 Conclusion

We have presented a translation from intersection and union types into intersection and product types. Using the translation, we have shown that our intersection and union type system for the $\lambda\mu$-calculus can be embedded into the type system of [6], which yields strong normalisation of terms typable by our system. We have also presented an intersection and union type system for the $\bar{\lambda}\mu$-calculus, and proved the subject reduction property and the characterisation theorem of strong normalisation.

It is expected that our type system for the $\lambda\mu$-calculus enjoys the subject reduction property. This is plausible since, by the side condition of the union-elimination rule, the variable to be discharged can occur only once in each premiss, in which case known counter examples do not emerge. It is also expected that all strongly normalising terms in the $\lambda\mu$-calculus are typable in our system. These problems are to be investigated in future work.

Another direction for future work is to design intersection and union type systems for call-by-value languages based on duality in sequent calculus. For languages without control operators, some natural deduction style systems have been proposed [13,20]. To give a uniform perspective, however, we consider the sequent calculus approach to be promising.

Acknowledgements. We would like to thank the anonymous referees for detailed comments and useful suggestions. The figures of the derivations have been drawn using Makoto Tatsuta's `proof.sty` macros. The second author was supported by JSPS KAKENHI Grant Numbers 24650002 and 25280025.

References

1. van Bakel, S.: Complete restrictions of the intersection type discipline. Theor. Comput. Sci. 102(1), 135–163 (1992)
2. van Bakel, S.: Completeness and partial soundness results for intersection and union typing for $\overline{\lambda}\mu\tilde{\mu}$. Ann. Pure Appl. Logic 161(11), 1400–1430 (2010)
3. van Bakel, S.: Sound and complete typing for $\lambda\mu$. In: Proc. ITRS 2010. EPTCS, vol. 45, pp. 31–44 (2011)
4. van Bakel, S.: Strict intersection types for the lambda calculus. ACM Comput. Surv. 43(3) (2011)
5. van Bakel, S., Barbanera, F., de'Liguoro, U.: A filter model for the $\lambda\mu$-calculus. In: Ong, L. (ed.) TLCA 2011. LNCS, vol. 6690, pp. 213–228. Springer, Heidelberg (2011)
6. van Bakel, S., Barbanera, F., de'Liguoro, U.: Characterisation of strongly normalising $\lambda\mu$-terms. In: Proc. ITRS 2012. EPTCS, vol. 121, pp. 1–17 (2013)
7. Barbanera, F., Berardi, S.: A symmetric lambda calculus for classical program extraction. Inform. and Comput. 125(2), 103–117 (1996)
8. Barbanera, F., Dezani-Ciancaglini, M., de'Liguoro, U.: Intersection and union types: Syntax and semantics. Inform. and Comput. 119(2), 202–230 (1995)
9. Curien, P.-L., Herbelin, H.: The duality of computation. In: Proc. ICFP 2000, pp. 233–243 (2000)
10. Dougherty, D., Ghilezan, S., Lescanne, P.: Characterizing strong normalization in a language with control operators. In: Proc. PPDP 2004, pp. 155–166 (2004)
11. Dougherty, D., Ghilezan, S., Lescanne, P.: Intersection and union types in the $\overline{\lambda}\mu\tilde{\mu}$-calculus. Electr. Notes Theor. Comput. Sci. 136, 153–172 (2005)
12. Dougherty, D., Ghilezan, S., Lescanne, P.: Characterizing strong normalization in the Curien-Herbelin symmetric lambda calculus: Extending the Coppo-Dezani heritage. Theor. Comput. Sci. 398(1-3), 114–128 (2008)
13. Dunfield, J., Pfenning, F.: Type assignment for intersections and unions in call-by-value languages. In: Gordon, A.D. (ed.) FOSSACS 2003. LNCS, vol. 2620, pp. 250–266. Springer, Heidelberg (2003)
14. Griffin, T.: A formulae-as-types notion of control. In: Proc. POPL 1990, pp. 47–58 (1990)
15. Herbelin, H.: A λ-calculus structure isomorphic to Gentzen-style sequent calculus structure. In: Pacholski, L., Tiuryn, J. (eds.) CSL 1994. LNCS, vol. 933, pp. 61–75. Springer, Heidelberg (1995)
16. Herbelin, H.: Séquents qu'on calcule. Thèse de Doctorat, Université Paris 7 (1995)
17. Kikuchi, K., Sakurai, T.: A translation of intersection and union types for the $\lambda\mu$-calculus (long version), http://www.nue.riec.tohoku.ac.jp/user/kentaro/
18. Laurent, O.: On the denotational semantics of the untyped lambda-mu calculus. Unpublished note (January 2004)
19. Parigot, M.: $\lambda\mu$-calculus: An algorithmic interpretation of classical natural deduction. In: Voronkov, A. (ed.) LPAR 1992. LNCS, vol. 624, pp. 190–201. Springer, Heidelberg (1992)
20. Riba, C.: On the values of reducibility candidates. In: Curien, P.-L. (ed.) TLCA 2009. LNCS, vol. 5608, pp. 264–278. Springer, Heidelberg (2009)
21. Streicher, T., Reus, B.: Classical logic, continuation semantics and abstract machines. J. Funct. Program. 8(6), 543–572 (1998)

A Formalized Proof of Strong Normalization for Guarded Recursive Types

Andreas Abel and Andrea Vezzosi

Computer Science and Engineering, Chalmers and Gothenburg University,
Rännvägen 6, 41296 Göteborg, Sweden
andreas.abel@gu.se, vezzosi@chalmers.se

Abstract. We consider a simplified version of Nakano's guarded fixed-point types in a representation by infinite type expressions, defined coinductively. Small-step reduction is parametrized by a natural number "depth" that expresses under how many guards we may step during evaluation. We prove that reduction is strongly normalizing for any depth. The proof involves a typed inductive notion of strong normalization and a Kripke model of types in two dimensions: depth and typing context. Our results have been formalized in Agda and serve as a case study of reasoning about a language with coinductive type expressions.

1 Introduction

In untyped lambda calculus, fixed-point combinators can be defined using self-application. Such combinators can be assigned recursive types, albeit only negative ones. Since such types introduce logical inconsistency, they are ruled out in Martin-Löf Type Theory and other systems based on the Curry-Howard isomorphism. Nakano (2000) introduced *a modality for recursion* that allows a stratification of negative recursive types to recover consistency. In essence, each negative recursive occurrence needs to be *guarded* by the modality; this coined the term *guarded recursive types* (Birkedal and Møgelberg, 2013).[1] Nakano's modality has found applications in functional reactive programming (Krishnaswami and Benton, 2011b) where it is referred to as *later* modality.

While Nakano showed that every typed term has a weak head normal form, in this paper we prove *strong normalization* for our variant $\lambda^{\blacktriangleright}$ of Nakano's calculus. To this end, we make the introduction rule for the later modality explicit in the terms by a constructor next, following Birkedal and Møgelberg (2013) and Atkey and McBride (2013). By allowing reduction under finitely many nexts, we establish termination irrespective of the reduction strategy. Showing strong normalization of $\lambda^{\blacktriangleright}$ is a first step towards an operationally well-behaved type theory with guarded recursive types, for which Birkedal and Møgelberg (2013) have given a categorical model.

Our proof is fully formalized in the proof assistant Agda (2014) which is based on intensional Martin-Löf Type Theory.[2] One key idea of the formalization is to represent

---

[1] Not to be confused with *Guarded Recursive Datatype Constructors* (Xi et al., 2003).

[2] A similar proof could be formalized in other systems supporting mixed induction-coinduction, for instance, in Coq.

J. Garrigue (Ed.): APLAS 2014, LNCS 8858, pp. 140–158, 2014.

the recursive types of $\lambda^{\blacktriangleright}$ as infinite type expressions in form of a coinductive definition. For this, we utilize Agda's new *copattern* feature (Abel et al., 2013). The set of strongly normalizing terms is defined inductively by distinguishing on the shape of terms, following van Raamsdonk et al. (1999) and Joachimski and Matthes (2003). The first author has formalized this technique before in Twelf (Abel, 2008); in this work we extend these results by a proof of equivalence to the standard notion of strong normalization.

Due to space constraints, we can only give a sketch of the formalization; a longer version and the full Agda proofs are available online (Abel and Vezzosi, 2014). This paper is extracted from a literate Agda file; all the colored code in displays is necessarily type-correct.

2   Guarded Recursive Types and Their Semantics

Nakano's type system (2000) is equipped with subtyping, but we stick to a simpler variant without, a simply-typed version of Birkedal and Møgelberg (2013), which we shall call $\lambda^{\blacktriangleright}$. Our rather minimal grammar of types includes product $A \times B$ and function types $A \to B$, delayed computations $\blacktriangleright A$, variables X and explicit fixed-points $\mu X A$.

$$A, B, C ::= A \times B \mid A \to B \mid \blacktriangleright A \mid X \mid \mu X A$$

Base types and disjoint sum types could be added, but would only give breadth rather than depth to our formalization. As usual, a dot after a bound variable shall denote an opening parenthesis that closes as far to the right as syntactically possible. Thus, $\mu X . X \to X$ denotes $\mu X (X \to X)$, while $\mu X X \to X$ denotes $(\mu X . X) \to X$ (with a free variable X).

Formation of fixed-points $\mu X A$ is subject to the side condition that X is guarded in A, i.e., X appears in A only under a *later* modality $\blacktriangleright$. This rules out all unguarded recursive types like $\mu X . A \times X$ or $\mu X . X \to A$, but allows their variants $\mu X . \blacktriangleright (A \times X)$ and $\mu X . A \times \blacktriangleright X$, and $\mu X . \blacktriangleright (X \to A)$ and $\mu X . \blacktriangleright X \to A$. Further, fixed-points give rise to an equality relation on types induced by $\mu X A = A[\mu X A / X]$.

$$\frac{\Gamma(x) = A}{\Gamma \vdash x : A} \qquad \frac{\Gamma, x : A \vdash t : B}{\Gamma \vdash \lambda x . t : A \to B} \qquad \frac{\Gamma \vdash t : A \to B \qquad \Gamma \vdash u : A}{\Gamma \vdash t u : B}$$

$$\frac{\Gamma \vdash t_1 : A_1 \qquad \Gamma \vdash t_2 : A_2}{\Gamma \vdash (t_1, t_2) : A_1 \times A_2} \qquad \frac{\Gamma \vdash t : A_1 \times A_2}{\Gamma \vdash \mathsf{fst}\, t : A_1} \qquad \frac{\Gamma \vdash t : A_1 \times A_2}{\Gamma \vdash \mathsf{snd}\, t : A_2}$$

$$\frac{\Gamma \vdash t : A}{\Gamma \vdash \mathsf{next}\, t : \blacktriangleright A} \qquad \frac{\Gamma \vdash t : \blacktriangleright (A \to B) \qquad \Gamma \vdash u : \blacktriangleright A}{\Gamma \vdash t * u : \blacktriangleright B} \qquad \frac{\Gamma \vdash t : A \qquad A = B}{\Gamma \vdash t : B}$$

Fig. 1. Typing rules

Terms are lambda-terms with pairing and projection plus operations that witness *applicative functoriality* of the later modality (Atkey and McBride, 2013).

$$t,u ::= x \mid \lambda x t \mid t\,u \mid (t_1,t_2) \mid \mathsf{fst}\,t \mid \mathsf{snd}\,t \mid \mathsf{next}\,t \mid t * u$$

Figure 1 recapitulates the static semantics. The dynamic semantics is induced by the following *contractions*:

$$
\begin{aligned}
(\lambda x.\,t)\,u &\mapsto t[u/x] \\
\mathsf{fst}\,(t_1,t_2) &\mapsto t_1 \\
\mathsf{snd}\,(t_1,t_2) &\mapsto t_2 \\
(\mathsf{next}\,t) * (\mathsf{next}\,u) &\mapsto \mathsf{next}\,(t\,u)
\end{aligned}
$$

If we conceive our small-step reduction relation $\longrightarrow$ as the compatible closure of $\mapsto$, we obtain a non-normalizing calculus, since terms like $\Omega = \omega\,(\mathsf{next}\,\omega)$ with $\omega = (\lambda x.\,x * (\mathsf{next}\,x))$ are typeable.[3] Unrestricted reduction of Ω is non-terminating: $\Omega \longrightarrow \mathsf{next}\,\Omega \longrightarrow \mathsf{next}\,(\mathsf{next}\,\Omega) \longrightarrow \ldots$ If we let next act as delay operator that blocks reduction inside, we regain termination. In general, we preserve termination if we only look under delay operators up to a certain depth. This can be made precise by a family $\longrightarrow_n$ of reduction relations indexed by a depth $n \in \mathbb{N}$, see Figure 2.

$$
\frac{t \mapsto t'}{t \longrightarrow_n t'}
\qquad
\frac{t \longrightarrow_n t'}{\lambda x.\,t \longrightarrow_n \lambda x.\,t'}
\qquad
\frac{t \longrightarrow_n t'}{t\,u \longrightarrow_n t'\,u}
\qquad
\frac{u \longrightarrow_n u'}{t\,u \longrightarrow_n t\,u'}
$$

$$
\frac{t \longrightarrow_n t'}{(t,u) \longrightarrow_n (t',u)}
\qquad
\frac{u \longrightarrow_n u'}{(t,u) \longrightarrow_n (t,u')}
\qquad
\frac{t \longrightarrow_n t'}{\mathsf{fst}\,t \longrightarrow_n \mathsf{fst}\,t'}
\qquad
\frac{t \longrightarrow_n t'}{\mathsf{snd}\,t \longrightarrow_n \mathsf{snd}\,t'}
$$

$$
\boxed{\frac{t \longrightarrow_n t'}{\mathsf{next}\,t \longrightarrow_{n+1} \mathsf{next}\,t'}}
\qquad
\frac{t \longrightarrow_n t'}{t * u \longrightarrow_n t' * u}
\qquad
\frac{u \longrightarrow_n u'}{t * u \longrightarrow_n t * u'}
$$

Fig. 2. Reduction

We should note that for a fixed depth n the relation $\longrightarrow_n$ is not confluent. In fact the term $(\lambda z.\,\mathsf{next}^{n+1}\,z)(\mathsf{fst}\,(u,t))$ reduces to two different normal forms, $\mathsf{next}^{n+1}\,(\mathsf{fst}\,(u,t))$ and $\mathsf{next}^{n+1}\,u$. We could remedy this situation by making sure we never hide redexes under too many applications of next and instead store them in an explicit substitution where they would still be accessible to $\longrightarrow_n$. Our problematic terms would then look like $\mathsf{next}^n\,((\mathsf{next}\,z)[\mathsf{fst}\,(u,t)/z])$ and $\mathsf{next}^n\,((\mathsf{next}\,z)[u/z])$ and the former would reduce to the latter. However, we are not bothered by the non-confluence since our semantics at level n (see below) does not distinguish between $\mathsf{next}^{n+1}\,u$ and $\mathsf{next}^{n+1}\,u'$ (as in $u' = \mathsf{fst}\,(u,t)$); neither u nor u' is required to terminate if buried under more than n nexts.

To show termination, we interpret types as sets $\mathscr{A}, \mathscr{B}, \mathscr{C}$ of depth-n strongly normalizing terms. We define semantic versions $[\![\times]\!]$, $[\![\to]\!]$, and $[\![\blacktriangleright]\!]$ of product, function

---

[3] $\vdash \Omega : A$ with $A = \mu X(\blacktriangleright X)$. To type ω, we use $x : \mu Y(\blacktriangleright(Y \to A))$.

space, and delay type constructor, plus a terminal (=largest) semantic type $[\![\top]\!]$. Then the interpretation $[\![A]\!]_n$ of closed type A at depth n can be given recursively as follows, using the Kripke construction at function types:

$$[\![A \times B]\!]_n = [\![A]\!]_n \, [\![\times]\!] \, [\![B]\!]_n \qquad \mathscr{A} \, [\![\times]\!] \, \mathscr{B} = \{t \mid \mathsf{fst}\, t \in \mathscr{A} \text{ and } \mathsf{snd}\, t \in \mathscr{B}\}$$

$$[\![A \to B]\!]_n = \bigcap\nolimits_{n' \le n}([\![A]\!]_{n'} \, [\![\to]\!] \, [\![B]\!]_{n'}) \qquad \mathscr{A} \, [\![\to]\!] \, \mathscr{B} = \{t \mid t\,u \in \mathscr{B} \text{ for all } u \in \mathscr{A}\}$$

$$[\![\blacktriangleright A]\!]_0 = [\![\blacktriangleright]\!] \, [\![\top]\!] \qquad [\![\top]\!] = \{t \mid t \text{ term}\}$$

$$[\![\blacktriangleright A]\!]_{n+1} = [\![\blacktriangleright]\!] \, [\![A]\!]_n \qquad [\![\blacktriangleright]\!] \, \mathscr{A} = \overline{\{\mathsf{next}\, t \mid t \in \mathscr{A}\}}$$

$$[\![\mu X A]\!]_n = [\![A[\mu X A/X]]\!]_n \qquad (\overline{\mathscr{A}} \text{ is weak head expansion closure of } \mathscr{A})$$

Due to the last equation (μ), the type interpretation is ill-defined for unguarded recursive types. However, for guarded types we only return to the fixed-point case after we have passed the case for $\blacktriangleright$, which decreases the index n. More precisely, $[\![A]\!]_n$ is defined by lexicographic induction on $(n, \mathrm{size}(A))$, where $\mathrm{size}(A)$ is the number of type constructor symbols $(\times, \to, \mu)$ that occur *unguarded* in A.

While all this sounds straightforward at an informal level, formalization of the described type language is quite hairy. For one, we have to enforce the restriction to well-formed (guarded) types. Secondly, our type system contains a conversion rule, getting us into the vincinity of dependent types which are still a challenge to a completely formal treatment (McBride, 2010). Our first formalization attempt used kinding rules for types to keep track of guardedness for formation of fixed-point, and a type equality relation, and building on this, inductively defined well-typed terms. However, the complexity was discouraging and lead us to a much more economic representation of types, which is described in the next section.

3   Formalized Syntax

In this section, we discuss the formalization of types, terms, and typing of $\lambda^{\blacktriangleright}$ in Agda. It will be necessary to talk about meta-level types, i. e., Agda's types, thus, we will refer to $\lambda^{\blacktriangleright}$'s type constructors as $\hat{\times}$, $\hat{\to}$, $\hat{\blacktriangleright}$, and $\hat{\mu}$.

3.1   Types Represented Coinductively

Instead of representing fixed-points as syntactic construction on types, which would require a non-trivial equality on types induced by $\hat{\mu} X A = A[\hat{\mu} X A / X]$, we use *meta-level* fixed-points, i. e., Agda's recursion mechanism.[4] Extensionally, we are implementing *infinite type expressions* over the constructors $\hat{\times}$, $\hat{\to}$, and $\hat{\blacktriangleright}$. The guard condition on recursive types then becomes an instance of Agda's "guard condition", i. e., the condition the termination checker imposes on recursive programs.

---

[4] An alternative to get around the type equality problem would be iso-recursive types, i. e., with term constructors for folding and unfolding of $\hat{\mu} X A$. However, we would still have to implement type variables, binding of type variables, type substitution, lemmas about type substitution etc.

Viewed as infinite expressions, guarded types are regular trees with an infinite number of $\blacktriangleright$-nodes on each infinite path. This can be expressed as the mixed coinductive(ν)-inductive(μ) (meta-level) type

$$\nu X \mu Y. \, (Y \times Y) + (Y \times Y) + X.$$

The first summand stands for the binary constructor $\hat{\times}$, the second for $\hat{\rightarrow}$, and the third for the unary $\hat{\blacktriangleright}$. The nesting of a least-fixed point (μ) inside a greatest fixed-point (ν) ensures that on each path, we can only take alternatives $\hat{\times}$ and $\hat{\rightarrow}$ a finite number of times before we have to choose the third alternative $\hat{\blacktriangleright}$ and restart the process.

In Agda 2.4, we represent this mixed coinductive-inductive type by a datatype Ty (inductive component) mutually defined with a record ∞Ty (coinductive component).

```
mutual
    data Ty : Set where
        _×̂_    : (a b : Ty)   → Ty
        _→̂_    : (a b : Ty)   → Ty
        ▶̂_     : (a∞ : ∞Ty)  → Ty

    record ∞Ty : Set where
        coinductive
        constructor delay_
        field        force_ : Ty
```

While the arguments a and b of the infix constructors $\hat{\times}$ and $\hat{\rightarrow}$ are again in Ty, the prefix constructor $\hat{\blacktriangleright}$ expects and argument $a\infty$ in ∞Ty, which is basically a wrapping[5] of Ty. The functions delay and force convert back and forth between Ty and ∞Ty so that both types are valid representations of the set of types of $\lambda^{\blacktriangleright}$.

$$\text{delay} : \text{Ty} \rightarrow \infty\text{Ty}$$
$$\text{force} : \infty\text{Ty} \rightarrow \text{Ty}$$

However, since ∞Ty is declared coinductive, its inhabitants are not evaluated until forced. This allows us to represent infinite type expressions, like top $= \hat{\mu}X(\blacktriangleright X)$.

```
top : ∞Ty
force top = ▶̂ top
```

Technically, top is defined by *copattern* matching (Abel et al., 2013); top is uniquely defined by the value of its only field, force top, which is given as $\hat{\blacktriangleright}$ top. Agda will use the given equation for its internal normalization procedure during type-checking. Alternatively, we could have tried to define top : Ty by top $= \hat{\blacktriangleright}$ delay top. However, Agda will rightfully complain here since rewriting with this equation would keep expanding top forever, thus, be non-terminating. In contrast, rewriting with the original equation is terminating since at each step, one application of force is removed.

The following two defined type constructors will prove useful in the definition of well-typed terms to follow.

---

[5] Similar to a newtype in the functional programming language Haskell.

$\blacktriangleright\_ : \mathsf{Ty} \to \mathsf{Ty}$
$\blacktriangleright a = \hat{\blacktriangleright}\ \mathsf{delay}\ a$

$\_\Rightarrow\_ : (a\infty\ b\infty : \infty\mathsf{Ty}) \to \infty\mathsf{Ty}$
$\mathsf{force}\ (a\infty \Rightarrow b\infty) = \mathsf{force}\ a\infty \mathbin{\hat{\to}} \mathsf{force}\ b\infty$

3.2 Well-Typed Terms

Instead of a raw syntax and a typing relation, we represent well-typed terms directly by an inductive family (Dybjer, 1994). Our main motivation for this choice is the beautiful inductive definition of strongly normalizing terms to follow in Section 5. Since it relies on a classification of terms into the three shapes *introduction*, *elimination*, and *weak head redex*, it does not capture all strongly normalizing raw terms, in particular "junk" terms such as fst (λxx). Of course, statically well-typed terms come also at a cost: for almost all our predicates on terms we need to show that they are natural in the typing context, i.e., closed under well-typed renamings. This expense might be compensated by the extra assistance Agda can give us in proof construction, which is due to the strong constraints on possible solutions imposed by the rich typing.

Our encoding of well-typed terms follows closely Altenkirch and Reus (1999); McBride (2006); Benton et al. (2012). We represent typed variables $x : \mathsf{Var}\ \Gamma\ a$ by de Brujin indices, i.e., positions in a typing context $\Gamma : \mathsf{Cxt}$, which is just a list of types.

$\mathsf{Cxt} = \mathsf{List}\ \mathsf{Ty}$

```
data Var : (Γ : Cxt) (a : Ty) → Set where
   zero : ∀{Γ a}                      → Var (a :: Γ) a
   suc  : ∀{Γ a b} (x : Var Γ a)  → Var (b :: Γ) a
```

Arguments enclosed in braces, such as Γ, a, and b in the types of the constructors zero and suc, are hidden and can in most cases be inferred by Agda. If needed, they can be passed in braces, either as positional arguments (e.g., $\{\Delta\}$) or as named arguments (e.g., $\{\Gamma = \Delta\}$). If $\forall$ prefixes bindings in a function type, the types of the bound variables may be omitted. Thus, $\forall\{\Gamma\ a\} \to \mathsf{A}$ is short for $\{\Gamma : \mathsf{Cxt}\}\{a : \mathsf{Ty}\} \to \mathsf{A}$.

Terms $t : \mathsf{Tm}\ \Gamma\ a$ are indexed by a typing context Γ and their type a, guaranteeing well-typedness and well-scopedness. In the following data type definition, $\mathsf{Tm}\ (\Gamma : \mathsf{Cxt})$ shall mean that all constructors uniformly take Γ as their first (hidden) argument.

```
data Tm (Γ : Cxt) : (a : Ty) → Set where
   var   : ∀{a}        (x : Var Γ a)                                        → Tm Γ a
   abs   : ∀{a b}      (t : Tm (a :: Γ) b)                                  → Tm Γ (a ⊸ b)
   app   : ∀{a b}      (t : Tm Γ (a ⊸ b)) (u : Tm Γ a)                      → Tm Γ b
   pair  : ∀{a b}      (t : Tm Γ a)        (u : Tm Γ b)                     → Tm Γ (a × b)
   fst   : ∀{a b}      (t : Tm Γ (a × b))                                   → Tm Γ a
   snd   : ∀{a b}      (t : Tm Γ (a × b))                                   → Tm Γ b
   next  : ∀{a∞}       (t : Tm Γ (force a∞))                                → Tm Γ (▶ a∞)
   _*_   : ∀{a∞ b∞}    (t : Tm Γ (▶(a∞ ⇒ b∞))) (u : Tm Γ (▶ a∞))            → Tm Γ (▶ b∞)
```

The most natural typing for next and $*$ would be using the defined $\blacktriangleright\_ : \mathsf{Ty} \to \mathsf{Ty}$:

$$\begin{array}{llll}
\mathsf{next} &: \forall\{a\} & (t : \mathsf{Tm}\ \Gamma\ a) & \to \mathsf{Tm}\ \Gamma\ (\blacktriangleright a) \\
\_*\_ &: \forall\{a\ b\} & (t : \mathsf{Tm}\ \Gamma\ (\blacktriangleright(a \mathbin{\hat{\to}} b)))\ (u : \mathsf{Tm}\ \Gamma\ (\blacktriangleright a)) & \to \mathsf{Tm}\ \Gamma\ (\blacktriangleright b)
\end{array}$$

However, this would lead to indices like $\blacktriangleright$ delay a and unification problems Agda cannot solve, since matching on a coinductive constructor like delay is forbidden—it can lead to a loss of subject reduction (McBride, 2009). The chosen alternative typing, which parametrizes over $a\infty\ b\infty : \infty\mathsf{Ty}$ rather than $a\ b : \mathsf{Ty}$, works better in practice.

3.3 Type Equality

Although our coinductive representation of $\lambda^{\blacktriangleright}$ types saves us from type variables, type substitution, and fixed-point unrolling, the question of type equality is not completely settled. The propositional equality $\equiv$ of Martin-Löf Type Theory is intensional in the sense that only objects with the same *code* (modulo definitional equality) are considered equal. Thus, $\equiv$ is adequate only for finite objects (such as natural numbers and lists) but not for infinite objects like functions, streams, or $\lambda^{\blacktriangleright}$ types.

However, we can define extensional equality or *bisimulation* on Ty as a mixed coinductive-inductive relation $\cong/\infty\cong$ that follows the structure of $\mathsf{Ty}/\infty\mathsf{Ty}$ (hence, we reuse the constructor names $\hat{\times}$, $\hat{\to}$, and $\blacktriangleright$).

```
mutual
  data _≅_ : (a b : Ty) → Set where
    _×̂_ : ∀{a a' b b'} (a≅ : a ≅ a') (b≅ : b ≅ b') → (a ×̂ b) ≅ (a' ×̂ b')
    _→̂_ : ∀{a a' b b'} (a≅ : a' ≅ a) (b≅ : b ≅ b') → (a →̂ b) ≅ (a' →̂ b')
    ▶̂_  : ∀{a∞ b∞} (a≅ : a∞ ∞≅ b∞)              → ▶̂ a∞ ≅ ▶̂ b∞

  record _∞≅_ (a∞ b∞ : ∞Ty) : Set where
    coinductive
    constructor ≅delay
    field       ≅force : force a∞ ≅ force b∞
```

Ty-equality is indeed an equivalence relation (we omit the standard proof).

$$\begin{array}{llll}
\cong\mathsf{refl} &: \forall\{a\} & & \to a \cong a \\
\cong\mathsf{sym} &: \forall\{a\ b\} & & \to a \cong b \to b \cong a \\
\cong\mathsf{trans} &: \forall\{a\ b\ c\} & & \to a \cong b \to b \cong c \to a \cong c
\end{array}$$

However, unlike for $\equiv$ we do not get a generic substitution principle for $\cong$, but have to prove it for any function and predicate on Ty. In particular, we have to show that we can cast a term in $\mathsf{Tm}\ \Gamma\ a$ to $\mathsf{Tm}\ \Gamma\ b$ if $a \cong b$, which would require us to build type equality at least into $\mathsf{Var}\ \Gamma\ a$. In essence, this would amount to work with setoids across all our development, which would add complexity without strengthening our result. Hence, we fall for the shortcut:

It is consistent to postulate that bisimulation implies equality, similarly to the functional extensionality principle for function types. This lets us define the function cast to convert terms between bisimilar types.

postulate ≅-to-≡ : ∀ {a b} → a ≅ b → a ≡ b

cast : ∀{Γ a b} (eq : a ≅ b) (t : Tm Γ a) → Tm Γ b

We shall require cast in uses of functorial application, to convert a type $c\infty$: ∞Ty into something that can be forced into a function type.

▶app : ∀{Γ c∞ b∞ a} (eq : c∞ ∞≅ (delay a ⇒ b∞))
$\qquad\qquad\qquad$ (t : Tm Γ (▶̂ c∞)) (u : Tm Γ (▶ a)) → Tm Γ (▶̂ b∞)
▶app eq t u = cast (▶̂ eq) t * u

3.4 Examples

Following Nakano (2000), we can adapt the Y combinator from the untyped lambda calculus to define a guarded fixed point combinator:

$$\text{fix} = \lambda f.\ (\lambda x.\ f\ (x * \text{next}\ x))\ (\text{next}\ (\lambda x.\ f\ (x * \text{next}\ x))).$$

We construct an auxiliary type Fix a that allows safe self application, since the argument will only be available "later". This fits with the type we want for the fix combinator, which makes the recursive instance y in fix $(\lambda y.t)$ available only at the next time slot.

fix : ∀{Γ a} → Tm Γ ((▶ a ⇀ a) ⇀ a)

Fix_ : Ty → ∞Ty
force (Fix a) = ▶̂ Fix a ⇀ a

selfApp : ∀{Γ a} → Tm Γ (▶̂ Fix a) → Tm Γ (▶ a)
selfApp x = ▶app (≅delay ≅refl) x (next x)

fix = abs (app L (next L))
$\quad$ where
$\qquad$ f = var (suc zero)
$\qquad$ x = var zero
$\qquad$ L = abs (app f (selfApp x))

Another standard example is the type of streams, which we can also define through corecursion.

mutual
$\quad$ Stream : Ty → Ty
$\quad$ Stream a = a ×̂ ▶ Stream∞ a

$\quad$ Stream∞ : Ty → ∞Ty
$\quad$ force (Stream∞ a) = Stream a

cons : ∀{Γ a} → Tm Γ a → Tm Γ (▶ Stream a) → Tm Γ (Stream a)
cons a s = pair a (cast (▶̂ (≅delay ≅refl)) s)

head : $\forall\{\Gamma\, a\} \to$ Tm Γ (Stream a) $\to$ Tm $\Gamma\, a$
head $s =$ fst s

tail : $\forall\{\Gamma\, a\} \to$ Tm Γ (Stream a) $\to$ Tm Γ ($\blacktriangleright$ Stream a)
tail $s =$ cast ($\hat{\blacktriangleright}$ ($\cong$delay $\cong$refl)) (snd s)

Note that tail returns a stream inside the later modality. This ensures that functions that transform streams have to be causal, i. e., can only have access to the first n elements of the input when producing the nth element of the output. A simple example is mapping a function over a stream.

mapS : $\forall\{\Gamma\, a\, b\} \to$ Tm Γ (($a \stackrel{.}{\to} b) \stackrel{.}{\to}$ (Stream $a \stackrel{.}{\to}$ Stream b))

Which is also better read with named variables.

$$\text{mapS} = \lambda f.\, \text{fix}\, (\lambda mapS.\, \lambda s.\, (f\, s,\, mapS * \text{tail}\, s))$$

4 Reduction

In this section, we describe the implementation of parametrized reduction $\longrightarrow_n$ in Agda. As a prerequisite, we need to define substitution, which in turn depends on renaming (Benton et al., 2012).

A *renaming* from context Γ to context Δ, written $\Delta \leq \Gamma$, is a mapping from variables of Γ to those of Δ of the same type a. The function rename lifts such a mapping to terms.

$\_\leq\_$: $(\Delta\, \Gamma :$ Cxt$) \to$ Set
$\_\leq\_$ $\Delta\, \Gamma = \forall\, \{a\} \to$ Var $\Gamma\, a \to$ Var $\Delta\, a$

rename : $\forall\, \{\Gamma\, \Delta :$ Cxt$\}\, \{a :$ Ty$\}\, (\eta : \Delta \leq \Gamma)\, (x :$ Tm $\Gamma\, a) \to$ Tm $\Delta\, a$

Building on renaming, we define well-typed parallel substitution. From this, we get the special case of substituting de Bruijn index 0.

subst0 : $\forall\, \{\Gamma\, a\, b\} \to$ Tm $\Gamma\, a \to$ Tm $(a :: \Gamma)\, b \to$ Tm $\Gamma\, b$

Reduction $t \longrightarrow_n t'$ is formalized as the inductive family $t\, \langle n\rangle{\Rightarrow}\beta\, t'$ with four constructors β... representing the contraction rules and one congruence rule cong to reduce in subterms.

data $\_\langle\_\rangle{\Rightarrow}\beta\_$ $\{\Gamma\} : \forall\, \{a\} \to$ Tm $\Gamma\, a \to N \to$ Tm $\Gamma\, a \to$ Set where

β : $\forall\, \{n\, a\, b\}\{t :$ Tm $(a :: \Gamma)\, b\}\{u\}$
     $\to$ app (abs t) $u\, \langle\, n\,\rangle{\Rightarrow}\beta$ subst0 $u\, t$

βfst : $\forall\, \{n\, a\, b\}\{t :$ Tm $\Gamma\, a\}\{u :$ Tm $\Gamma\, b\}$
     $\to$ fst (pair $t\, u$) $\langle\, n\,\rangle{\Rightarrow}\beta\, t$

βsnd : $\forall\, \{n\, a\, b\}\{t :$ Tm $\Gamma\, a\}\{u :$ Tm $\Gamma\, b\}$
     $\to$ snd (pair $t\, u$) $\langle\, n\,\rangle{\Rightarrow}\beta\, u$

$\beta\blacktriangleright$ $: \forall \{n\, a_\infty\, b_\infty\}\{t : \mathsf{Tm}\ \Gamma\ (\mathsf{force}\ a_\infty \mathbin{\dot\to} \mathsf{force}\ b_\infty)\}\{u : \mathsf{Tm}\ \Gamma\ (\mathsf{force}\ a_\infty)\}$
$\rightarrow (\mathsf{next}\ t * \mathsf{next}\ \{a_\infty = a_\infty\}\ u)\ \langle\, n\,\rangle{\Rightarrow}\beta\ (\mathsf{next}\ \{a_\infty = b_\infty\}\ (\mathsf{app}\ t\ u))$

cong $: \forall \{n\, n'\, \Delta\, a\, b\, t\, t'\, Ct\, Ct'\}\{C : \mathsf{N}\beta\mathsf{Cxt}\ \Delta\ \Gamma\ a\, b\, n\, n'\}$
$\quad\rightarrow (Ct\quad : Ct \equiv C\,[\,t\,])$
$\quad\rightarrow (Ct'\ : Ct' \equiv C\,[\,t'\,])$
$\quad\rightarrow (t{\Rightarrow}\beta\ : t\,\langle\, n\,\rangle{\Rightarrow}\beta\ t')$
$\quad\rightarrow Ct\,\langle\, n'\,\rangle{\Rightarrow}\beta\ Ct'$

The congruence rule makes use of shallow one hole contexts C, which are given by the following grammar

$$C ::= \lambda x_{\_} \mid \_u \mid t_{\_} \mid (t,\_) \mid (\_,u) \mid \mathsf{fst}\ \_ \mid \mathsf{snd}\ \_ \mid \mathsf{next}\_ \mid \_*u \mid t*\_ .$$

cong says that we can reduce a term, suggestively called Ct, to a term Ct', if (1) Ct decomposes into $C[t]$, a context C filled by t, and (2) Ct' into $C[t']$, and (3) t reduces to t'. As witnessed by relation $Ct \equiv C[t]$, context $C : \mathsf{N}\beta\mathsf{Cxt}\ \Gamma\ \Delta\ a\, b\, n\, n'$ produces a term $Ct : \mathsf{Tm}\ \Gamma\ b$ of depth n' if filled with a term $t : \mathsf{Tm}\ \Delta\ a$ of depth n. The depth is unchanged except for the case next, which increases the depth by 1. Thus, $t\,\langle n\rangle{\Rightarrow}\beta\ t'$ can contract every subterm that is under at most n many nexts.

$\mathsf{data}\ \mathsf{N}\beta\mathsf{Cxt} : (\Delta\ \Gamma : \mathsf{Cxt})\ (a\, b : \mathsf{Ty})\ (n\, n' : N) \rightarrow \mathsf{Set}\ \mathsf{where}$
$\quad\mathsf{abs}\ \ \ : \forall\{\Gamma\, n\, a\, b\}$ $\qquad\qquad\qquad\qquad\qquad \rightarrow \mathsf{N}\beta\mathsf{Cxt}\ (a :: \Gamma)\ \Gamma\ b\ (a \mathbin{\dot\to} b)\ n\, n$
$\quad\mathsf{appl}\ \ : \forall\{\Gamma\, n\, a\, b\}\ (u : \mathsf{Tm}\ \Gamma\ a)\ \qquad\quad \rightarrow \mathsf{N}\beta\mathsf{Cxt}\ \Gamma\ \Gamma\ (a \mathbin{\dot\to} b)\ b\ n\, n$
$\quad\mathsf{appr}\ : \forall\{\Gamma\, n\, a\, b\}\ (t\ : \mathsf{Tm}\ \Gamma\ (a \mathbin{\dot\to} b))\ \rightarrow \mathsf{N}\beta\mathsf{Cxt}\ \Gamma\ \Gamma\ a\, b\, n\, n$
$\quad\mathsf{pairl}\ : \forall\{\Gamma\, n\, a\, b\}\ (u : \mathsf{Tm}\ \Gamma\ b)\ \qquad\quad \rightarrow \mathsf{N}\beta\mathsf{Cxt}\ \Gamma\ \Gamma\ a\ (a \mathbin{\hat\times} b)\ n\, n$
$\quad\mathsf{pairr}\ : \forall\{\Gamma\, n\, a\, b\}\ (t\ : \mathsf{Tm}\ \Gamma\ a)\ \qquad\quad \rightarrow \mathsf{N}\beta\mathsf{Cxt}\ \Gamma\ \Gamma\ b\ (a \mathbin{\hat\times} b)\ n\, n$
$\quad\mathsf{fst}\ \ \ : \forall\{\Gamma\, n\, a\, b\}$ $\qquad\qquad\qquad\qquad\qquad \rightarrow \mathsf{N}\beta\mathsf{Cxt}\ \Gamma\ \Gamma\ (a \mathbin{\hat\times} b)\ a\, n\, n$
$\quad\mathsf{snd}\ \ : \forall\{\Gamma\, n\, a\, b\}$ $\qquad\qquad\qquad\qquad\qquad \rightarrow \mathsf{N}\beta\mathsf{Cxt}\ \Gamma\ \Gamma\ (a \mathbin{\hat\times} b)\ b\, n\, n$
$\quad\mathsf{next}\ : \forall\{\Gamma\, n\, a_\infty\}$ $\qquad\qquad\qquad\qquad\quad\ \rightarrow \mathsf{N}\beta\mathsf{Cxt}\ \Gamma\ \Gamma\ (\mathsf{force}\ a_\infty)\ (\blacktriangleright\, a_\infty)\ n\ (1+n)$
$\quad *l_{\_}\ \ : \forall\{\Gamma\, n\, a_\infty\, b_\infty\}\ (u : \mathsf{Tm}\ \Gamma\ (\blacktriangleright\, a_\infty)) \rightarrow \mathsf{N}\beta\mathsf{Cxt}\ \Gamma\ \Gamma\ (\blacktriangleright\, (a_\infty \Rightarrow b_\infty))\ (\blacktriangleright\, b_\infty)\ n\, n$
$\quad *r_{\_}\ \ : \forall\{\Gamma\, n\, a_\infty\, b_\infty\}$
$\qquad\qquad (t : \mathsf{Tm}\ \Gamma\ (\blacktriangleright\, (a_\infty \Rightarrow b_\infty)))\ \rightarrow \mathsf{N}\beta\mathsf{Cxt}\ \Gamma\ \Gamma\ (\blacktriangleright\, a_\infty)\ (\blacktriangleright\, b_\infty)\ n\, n$

$\mathsf{data}\ \_{\equiv}\_[\_]\ \{n : N\}\ \{\Gamma : \mathsf{Cxt}\} : \{n' : N\}\ \{\Delta : \mathsf{Cxt}\}\ \{b\ a : \mathsf{Ty}\} \rightarrow$
$\qquad \mathsf{Tm}\ \Gamma\ b \rightarrow \mathsf{N}\beta\mathsf{Cxt}\ \Delta\ \Gamma\ a\, b\, n\, n' \rightarrow \mathsf{Tm}\ \Delta\ a \rightarrow \mathsf{Set}$

5   Strong Normalization

Classically, a term is *strongly normalizing* (sn) if there's no infinite reduction sequence starting from it. Constructively, the tree of all the possible reductions from an sn term must be well-founded, or, equivalently, an sn term must be in the accessible part of the reduction relation. In our case, reduction $t\,\langle n\rangle{\Rightarrow}\beta\ t'$ is parametrized by a depth n, thus, we get the following family of sn-predicates.

$\mathsf{data}\ \mathsf{sn}\ (n : N)\ \{a\ \Gamma\}\ (t : \mathsf{Tm}\ \Gamma\ a) : \mathsf{Set}\ \mathsf{where}$
$\quad\mathsf{acc} : (\forall\ \{t'\} \rightarrow t\,\langle\, n\,\rangle{\Rightarrow}\beta\ t' \rightarrow \mathsf{sn}\ n\, t') \rightarrow \mathsf{sn}\ n\, t$

Van Raamsdonk et al. (1999) pioneered a more explicit characterization of strongly normalizing terms SN, namely the least set closed under introductions, formation of neutral (=stuck) terms, and weak head expansion. We adapt their technique from lambda-calculus to $\lambda^\blacktriangleright$; herein, it is crucial to work with well-typed terms to avoid junk like $\mathsf{fst}\,(\lambda x.x)$ which does not exist in pure lambda-calculus. To formulate a deterministic weak head evaluation, we make use of the *evaluation contexts* E : ECxt

$$E ::= \_\,u \mid \mathsf{fst}\,\_ \mid \mathsf{snd}\,\_ \mid \_*u \mid (\mathsf{next}\,t)*\_.$$

Since weak head reduction does not go into introductions which include λ-abstraction, it does not go under binders, leaving typing context Γ fixed.

```
data ECxt (Γ : Cxt) : (a b : Ty) → Set
data _≅_[_] {Γ : Cxt} : {a b : Ty} → Tm Γ b → ECxt Γ a b → Tm Γ a → Set
```

$Et \cong E[t]$ witnesses the splitting of a term Et into evaluation context E and hole content t. A generalization of $\_\cong\_[\_]$ is PCxt P which additionally requires that all terms contained in the evaluation context (that is one or zero terms) satisfy predicate P. This allows us the formulation of P-neutrals as terms of the form $\vec{E}[x]$ for some $\vec{E}[\_] = E_1[\ldots E_n[\_]]$ and a variable x where all immediate subterms satisfy P.

```
data PCxt {Γ} (P : ∀{c} → Tm Γ c → Set) :
          ∀ {a b} → Tm Γ b → ECxt Γ a b → Tm Γ a → Set where
  appl :  ∀ {a b t u}      (u : P u) → PCxt P (app t u) (appl u)  (t : (a ⌢ b))
  fst  :  ∀ {a b t}                  → PCxt P (fst t)    fst      (t : (a ⌢×  b))
  snd  :  ∀ {a b t}                  → PCxt P (snd t)    snd      (t : (a ⌢×  b))
  *l   :  ∀ {a∞ b∞ t u}    (u : P u) → PCxt P (t * (u : ▶ a∞) : ▶ b∞) (*l u) t
  *r   :  ∀ {a∞ b∞ t u}    (t : P (next {a∞ = a∞ ⇒ b∞} t))
                          → PCxt P ((next t) * (u : ▶ a∞) : ▶ b∞) (*r t) u
```

```
data PNe {Γ} (P : ∀{c} → Tm Γ c → Set) {b} : Tm Γ b → Set where
  var :  ∀  x                                  → PNe P (var x)
  elim : ∀  {a} {t : Tm Γ a} {E Et}
        → (n : PNe P t) (Et : PCxt P Et E t)  → PNe P Et
```

Weak head reduction (whr) is a reduction of the form $\vec{E}[t] \longrightarrow \vec{E}[t']$ where $t \mapsto t'$. It is well-known that weak head expansion (whe) does not preserve sn, e.g., $(\lambda x.y)\Omega$ is not sn even though it contracts to y. In this case, Ω is a *vanishing term* lost by reduction. If we require that all vanishing terms in a reduction are sn, weak head expansion preserves sn. In the following, we define P-whr where all vanishing terms must satisfy P.

```
data _/_⇒_ {Γ} (P : ∀{c} → Tm Γ c → Set) :
          ∀ {a} → Tm Γ a → Tm Γ a → Set where

  β    : ∀ {a b}{t : Tm (a :: Γ) b}{u}
        → (u : P u)
        → P / (app (abs t) u) ⇒ subst0 u t

  βfst : ∀ {a b}{t : Tm Γ a}{u : Tm Γ b}
        → (u : P u)
```

$$\to P \,/\, \mathsf{fst}\,(\mathsf{pair}\,t\,u) \Rightarrow t$$

$\beta\mathsf{snd}$: $\forall\,\{a\,b\}\{t : \mathsf{Tm}\,\Gamma\,a\}\{u : \mathsf{Tm}\,\Gamma\,b\}$
$\qquad\to (t : P\,t)$
$\qquad\to P \,/\, \mathsf{snd}\,(\mathsf{pair}\,t\,u) \Rightarrow u$

$\beta\blacktriangleright$: $\forall\,\{a\infty\,b\infty\}\{t : \mathsf{Tm}\,\Gamma\,(\mathsf{force}\,(a\infty \Rightarrow b\infty))\}\{u : \mathsf{Tm}\,\Gamma\,(\mathsf{force}\,a\infty)\}$
$\qquad\to P \,/\, (\mathsf{next}\,t \ast \mathsf{next}\,\{a\infty = a\infty\}\,u) \Rightarrow (\mathsf{next}\,\{a\infty = b\infty\}\,(\mathsf{app}\,t\,u))$

cong : $\forall\,\{a\,b\,t\,t'\,Et\,Et'\}\{E : \mathsf{ECxt}\,\Gamma\,a\,b\}$
$\qquad\to (Et \ \ : Et \cong E\,[\,t\,])$
$\qquad\to (Et' \ : Et' \cong E\,[\,t'\,])$
$\qquad\to (t\!\Rightarrow \ \ : P \,/\, t \Rightarrow t')$
$\qquad\to P \,/\, Et \Rightarrow Et'$

The family of predicates $\mathsf{SN}\,n$ is defined inductively by the following rules—we allow ourselves set-notation at this semi-formal level:

$$\frac{t \in \mathsf{SN}\,n}{\lambda x t \in \mathsf{SN}\,n} \qquad \frac{t_1, t_2 \in \mathsf{SN}\,n}{(t_1, t_2) \in \mathsf{SN}\,n} \qquad \frac{}{\mathsf{next}\,t \in \mathsf{SN}\,0} \qquad \frac{t \in \mathsf{SN}\,n}{\mathsf{next}\,t \in \mathsf{SN}\,(1+n)}$$

$$\frac{t \in \mathsf{SNe}\,n}{t \in \mathsf{SN}\,n} \qquad \frac{t' \in \mathsf{SN}\,n \qquad t\,\langle n\rangle \Rightarrow t'}{t \in \mathsf{SN}\,n}$$

The last two rules close SN under neutrals SNe, which is an instance of PNe with $P = \mathsf{SN}\,n$, and level-n *strong head expansion* $t\,\langle n\rangle \Rightarrow t'$, which is an instance of P-whe with also $P = \mathsf{SN}\,n$.

The SN-relations are antitone in the level n. This is one dimension of the Kripke worlds in our model (see next section).

mapSN : $\forall\,\{m\,n\} \to m \leq_N n \to \forall\,\{\Gamma\,a\}\{t : \mathsf{Tm}\,\Gamma\,a\} \to \mathsf{SN}\,n\,t \to \mathsf{SN}\,m\,t$

The other dimension of the Kripke worlds is the typing context; our notions are also closed under renaming (and even undoing of renaming). Besides $\mathsf{renameSN}$, we have analogous lemmata $\mathsf{renameSNe}$ and $\mathsf{rename}{\Rightarrow}$.

$\mathsf{renameSN}$: $\forall\,\{n\,a\,\Delta\,\Gamma\}\,(\rho : \Delta \leq \Gamma)\,\{t : \mathsf{Tm}\,\Gamma\,a\} \to$
$\qquad\qquad\quad \mathsf{SN}\,n\,t \to \mathsf{SN}\,n\,(\mathsf{rename}\,\rho\,t)$

$\mathsf{fromRenameSN}$: $\forall\{n\,a\,\Gamma\,\Delta\}\,(\rho : \Delta \leq \Gamma)\,\{t : \mathsf{Tm}\,\Gamma\,a\} \to$
$\qquad\qquad\qquad\quad \mathsf{SN}\,n\,(\mathsf{rename}\,\rho\,t) \to \mathsf{SN}\,n\,t$

A consequence of $\mathsf{fromRenameSN}$ is that $t \in \mathsf{SN}\,n$ iff $t\,x \in \mathsf{SN}\,n$ for some variable x. (Consider $t = \lambda y.t'$ and $t\,x\,\langle n\rangle \Rightarrow t'[y/x]$.) This property is essential for the construction of the function space on sn sets (see next section).

$\mathsf{absVarSN}$: $\forall\{\Gamma\,a\,b\,n\}\{t : \mathsf{Tm}\,(a :: \Gamma)\,(a \dot\to b)\} \to$
$\qquad\qquad\quad \mathsf{app}\,t\,(\mathsf{var}\,\mathsf{zero}) \in \mathsf{SN}\,n \to t \in \mathsf{SN}\,n$

6 Soundness

A well-established technique (Tait, 1967) to prove strong normalization is to model each type a as a set $\mathscr{A} = [\![a]\!]$ of sn terms. Each so-called semantic type $\mathscr{A}$ should contain the variables in order to interpret open terms by themselves (using the identity valuation). To establish the conditions of semantic types compositionally, the set $\mathscr{A}$ needs to be *saturated*, i. e., contain SNe (rather than just the variables) and be closed under strong head expansion (to entertain introductions).

As a preliminary step towards saturated sets we define sets of well-typed terms in an arbitrary typing context but fixed type, TmSet a. We also define shorthands for the largest set, set inclusion and closure under expansion.

$$\mathsf{TmSet} : (a : \mathsf{Ty}) \to \mathsf{Set}_1$$
$$\mathsf{TmSet}\ a = \{\Gamma : \mathsf{Cxt}\}\ (t : \mathsf{Tm}\ \Gamma\ a) \to \mathsf{Set}$$

$$[\top] : \forall\{a\} \to \mathsf{TmSet}\ a$$
$$[\top]\ t = \top$$

$$\_\subseteq\_ : \forall\{a\}\ (A\ A' : \mathsf{TmSet}\ a) \to \mathsf{Set}$$
$$A \subseteq A' = \forall\{\Gamma\}\{t : \mathsf{Tm}\ \Gamma\ \_\} \to A\ t \to A'\ t$$

$$\mathsf{Closed} : \forall\ (n : N)\ \{a\}\ (A : \mathsf{TmSet}\ a) \to \mathsf{Set}$$
$$\mathsf{Closed}\ n\ A = \forall\{\Gamma\}\{t\ t' : \mathsf{Tm}\ \Gamma\ \_\} \to t\langle n\rangle \Rightarrow t' \to A\ t' \to A\ t$$

For each type constructor we define a corresponding operation on TmSets. The product is simply pointwise through the use of the projections.

$$\_[\times]\_ : \forall\{a\ b\} \to \mathsf{TmSet}\ a \to \mathsf{TmSet}\ b \to \mathsf{TmSet}\ (a\ \hat{\times}\ b)$$
$$(\mathscr{A}\ [\times]\ \mathscr{B})\ t = \mathscr{A}\ (\mathsf{fst}\ t) \times \mathscr{B}\ (\mathsf{snd}\ t)$$

For function types we are forced to use a Kripke-style definition, quantifying over all possible extended contexts Δ makes $\mathscr{A}\ [\to]\ \mathscr{B}$ closed under renamings.

$$\_[\to]\_ : \forall\{a\ b\} \to \mathsf{TmSet}\ a \to \mathsf{TmSet}\ b \to \mathsf{TmSet}\ (a\ \dot{\to}\ b)$$
$$(\mathscr{A}\ [\to]\ \mathscr{B})\ \{\Gamma\}\ t = \forall\{\Delta\}\ (\rho : \Delta \le \Gamma) \to \forall\ \{u\} \to \mathscr{A}\ u \to \mathscr{B}\ (\mathsf{app}\ (\mathsf{rename}\ \rho\ t)\ u)$$

The TmSet for the later modality is indexed by the depth. The first two constructors are for terms in the canonical form next t, at depth zero we impose no restriction on t, otherwise we use the given set A. The other two constructors are needed to satisfy the properties we require of our saturated sets.

```
data [▶] {a∞} (A : TmSet (force a∞)) {Γ} : (n : N) → Tm Γ (▶ a∞) → Set where
  next0 : ∀ {t : Tm Γ (force a∞)}                        → [▶] A zero     (next t)
  next  : ∀ {n}{t : Tm Γ (force a∞)} (t : A t)           → [▶] A (suc n)  (next t)
  ne    : ∀ {n}{t : Tm Γ (▶ a∞)}         (n : SNe n t)   → [▶] A n        t
  exp   : ∀ {n}{t t' : Tm Γ (▶ a∞)}
          (t⇒ : t⟨n⟩⇒ t')                (t : [▶] A n t') → [▶] A n        t
```

The particularity of our saturated sets is that they are indexed by the depth, which in our case is needed to state the usual properties. In particular if a term belongs to a saturated set it is also a member of SN, which is what we need for strong normalization. In addition we require them to be closed under renaming, since we are dealing with terms in a context.

```
record IsSAT (n : N) {a} (A : TmSet a) : Set where
  field
    satSNe     : SNe n ⊆ A
    satSN      : A       ⊆ SN n
    satExp     : Closed n A
    satRename  : ∀ {Γ Δ} (ρ : Δ ≤ Γ) → ∀ {t} → A t → A (rename ρ t)

record SAT (a : Ty) (n : N) : Set₁ where
  field
    satSet  : TmSet a
    satProp : IsSAT n satSet
```

For function types we will also need a notion of a sequence of saturated sets up to a specified maximum depth n.

```
SAT≤ : (a : Ty) (n : N) → Set₁
SAT≤ a n = ∀ {m} → m ≤N n → SAT a m
```

To help Agda's type inference, we also define a record type for membership of a term into a saturated set.

```
record _∈_ {a n Γ} (t : Tm Γ a) (𝒜 : SAT a n) : Set where
  constructor [U+21BF]_
  field [U+21C3]_ : satSet 𝒜 t

_∈⟨_⟩_ : ∀ {a n Γ} (t : Tm Γ a) {m} (m≤n : m ≤N n) (𝒜 : SAT≤ a n) → Set
t ∈⟨ m≤n ⟩ 𝒜 = t ∈ 𝒜 m≤n
```

Given the lemmas about SN shown so far we can lift our operations on TmSet to saturated sets and give the semantic version of our term constructors.

For function types we need another level of Kripke-style generalization to smaller depths, so that we can maintain antitonicity.

```
_[→]_ : ∀ {n a b} (𝒜 : SAT≤ a n) (ℬ : SAT≤ b n) → SAT (a ⇾ b) n
𝒜 [→] ℬ = record
  { satSet = λ t → ∀ m (m≤n : m ≤N _) → (A m≤n [→] B m≤n) t
  ; satProp = record
    { satSN = CSN
  - etc.
    }
  }
  where
    module 𝒜 = SAT≤ 𝒜
    module ℬ = SAT≤ ℬ
    A = 𝒜.satSet
    B = ℬ.satSet
```

$$C \; : \; \mathsf{TmSet}\,(\_ \stackrel{\scriptscriptstyle\wedge}{\to} \_)$$
$$C\,t \; = \; \forall\, m\,(m{\le}n : m \le N \_\,) \to (A\; m{\le}n\; [{\to}]\; B\; m{\le}n)\,t$$

$$\mathsf{CSN} \; : \; C \subseteq \mathsf{SN}\, \_$$
$$\mathsf{CSN}\,t \; = \; \mathsf{fromRenameSN}\;\mathsf{suc}\,(\mathsf{absVarSN}$$
$$(\mathcal{B}.\mathsf{satSN} \le N.\mathsf{refl}\,(t\; \_\; \le N.\mathsf{refl}\;\mathsf{suc}\,(\mathcal{A}.\mathsf{satSNe} \le N.\mathsf{refl}\,(\mathsf{var}\;\mathsf{zero})))))$$
- etc.

The proof of inclusion into SN first derives that app (rename suc t) (var zero) is in SN through the inclusion of neutral terms into $\mathcal{A}$ and the inclusion of $\mathcal{B}$ into SN, then proceeds to strip away first (var zero) and then (rename suc), so that we are left with the original goal SN $n\,t$. Renaming t with suc is necessary to be able to introduce the fresh variable zero of type a.

The types of semantic abstraction and application are somewhat obfuscated because they need to mention the upper bounds and the renamings.

$$[\![\mathsf{abs}]\!] \; : \; \forall\; \{n\,a\,b\}\,\{\mathcal{A} : \mathsf{SAT}{\le}\,a\,n\}\,\{\mathcal{B} : \mathsf{SAT}{\le}\,b\,n\}\,\{\Gamma\}\,\{t : \mathsf{Tm}\,(a :: \Gamma)\,b\} \to$$
$$(\forall\;\{m\}\,(m{\le}n : m \le N\,n)\,\{\Delta\}\,(\rho : \Delta \le \Gamma)\,\{u : \mathsf{Tm}\,\Delta\,a\} \to$$
$$u \in \langle\, m{\le}n\,\rangle\,\mathcal{A} \to (\mathsf{subst0}\,u\,(\mathsf{subst}\,(\mathsf{lifts}\,\rho)\,t)) \in \langle\, m{\le}n\,\rangle\,\mathcal{B})$$
$$\to \; \mathsf{abs}\,t \in (\mathcal{A}\;[{\to}]\;\mathcal{B})$$
$$(\downarrow [\![\mathsf{abs}]\!]\,\{\mathcal{A} = \mathcal{A}\}\{\mathcal{B} = \mathcal{B}\}\,t)\,m\,m{\le}n\,\rho\,u =$$
$$\mathsf{SAT}{\le}.\mathsf{satExp}\;\mathcal{B}\;m{\le}n\,(\beta\,(\mathsf{SAT}{\le}.\mathsf{satSN}\;\mathcal{A}\;m{\le}n\,u))\,(\downarrow\,t\,m{\le}n\,\rho\,(\uparrow\,u))$$

$$[\![\mathsf{app}]\!] \; : \; \forall\,\{n\,a\,b\}\{\mathcal{A} : \mathsf{SAT}{\le}\,a\,n\}\{\mathcal{B} : \mathsf{SAT}{\le}\,b\,n\}\{\Gamma\}\{t : \mathsf{Tm}\,\Gamma\,(a \stackrel{\scriptscriptstyle\wedge}{\to} b)\}\{u : \mathsf{Tm}\,\Gamma\,a\}$$
$$\to t \in (\mathcal{A}\;[{\to}]\;\mathcal{B}) \to u \in \langle\, \le N.\mathsf{refl}\,\rangle\,\mathcal{A} \to \mathsf{app}\,t\,u \in \langle\, \le N.\mathsf{refl}\,\rangle\,\mathcal{B}$$
$$[\![\mathsf{app}]\!]\,\{\mathcal{B} = \mathcal{B}\}\,\{u = u\}\,(\uparrow t)\,(\uparrow u) = \equiv.\mathsf{subst}\,(\lambda\,t \to \mathsf{app}\,t\,u \in \langle\, \le N.\mathsf{refl}\,\rangle\,\mathcal{B})\;\mathsf{renId}$$
$$(\uparrow t\; \_\; \le N.\mathsf{refl}\;\mathsf{id}\,u)$$

The TmSet for product types is directly saturated, inclusion into SN uses a lemma to derive SN $n\,t$ from SN n (fst t), which follows from $\mathcal{A} \subseteq \mathsf{SN}$.

$$\_[\![\times]\!]\_ : \forall\,\{n\,a\,b\}\,(\mathcal{A} : \mathsf{SAT}\,a\,n)\,(\mathcal{B} : \mathsf{SAT}\,b\,n) \to \mathsf{SAT}\,(a \stackrel{\scriptscriptstyle\times}{\times} b)\,n$$
$$\mathcal{A}\;[\![\times]\!]\;\mathcal{B} = \mathsf{record}$$
$$\{\, \mathsf{satSet} = \mathsf{satSet}\;\mathcal{A}\;[\times]\;\mathsf{satSet}\;\mathcal{B}$$
- etc.

Semantic introduction $[\![\mathsf{pair}]\!] : t_1 \in \mathcal{A} \to t_2 \in \mathcal{B} \to \mathsf{pair}\,t_1\,t_2 \in (\mathcal{A}\;[\![\times]\!]\;\mathcal{B})$ and eliminations $[\![\mathsf{fst}]\!] : t \in (\mathcal{A}\;[\![\times]\!]\;\mathcal{B}) \to \mathsf{fst}\,t \in \mathcal{A}$ and $[\![\mathsf{snd}]\!] : t \in (\mathcal{A}\;[\![\times]\!]\;\mathcal{B}) \to \mathsf{snd}\,t \in \mathcal{B}$ for pairs are straightforward.

The later modality is going to use the saturated set for its type argument at the preceeding depth, we encode this fact through the type SATpred.

$$\mathsf{SATpred} : (a : \mathsf{Ty})\,(n : N) \to \mathsf{Set}_1$$
$$\mathsf{SATpred}\,a\,\mathsf{zero} \quad = \top$$
$$\mathsf{SATpred}\,a\,(\mathsf{suc}\,n) = \mathsf{SAT}\,a\,n$$

$$\mathsf{SATpredSet} : \{n : N\}\{a : \mathsf{Ty}\} \to \mathsf{SATpred}\,a\,n \to \mathsf{TmSet}\,a$$
$$\mathsf{SATpredSet}\,\{\mathsf{zero}\} \quad \mathcal{A} = [\top]$$
$$\mathsf{SATpredSet}\,\{\mathsf{suc}\,n\} \quad \mathcal{A} = \mathsf{satSet}\,\mathcal{A}$$

Since the cases for $[\blacktriangleright]\_$ are essentially a subset of those for SN, the proof of inclusion into SN goes by induction and the inclusion of $\mathscr{A}$ into SN.

$$[\blacktriangleright]\_ : \forall\{n\ a\infty\}\ (\mathscr{A} : \mathsf{SATpred}\ (\mathsf{force}\ a\infty)\ n) \to \mathsf{SAT}\ (\hat{\blacktriangleright}\ a\infty)\ n$$
$$[\blacktriangleright]\_ \{n\}\ \{a\infty\}\ \mathscr{A} = \mathsf{record}$$
$$\{\ \mathsf{satSet} = [\blacktriangleright]\ (\mathsf{SATpredSet}\ \mathscr{A})\ n$$
$$\text{- etc.}$$

Following Section 3 we can assemble the combinators for saturated sets into a semantics for the types of $\lambda^{\blacktriangleright}$. The definition of $[\![\_]\!]\_$ proceeds by recursion on the inductive part of the type, and otherwise by well-founded recursion on the depth. Crucially the interpretation of the later modality only needs the interpretation of its type parameter at a smaller depth, which is then decreasing exactly when the representation of types becomes coinductive and would no longer support recursion.

$$[\![\_]\!]^{\leq} : (a : \mathsf{Ty})\ \{n : N\} \to \forall\ \{m\} \to m \leq_N n \to \mathsf{SAT}\ a\ m$$

$$[\![\_]\!]\_ : (a : \mathsf{Ty})\ (n : N) \to \mathsf{SAT}\ a\ n$$
$$[\![\ a \stackrel{.}{\to} b\ ]\!]\ n = [\![\ a\ ]\!]^{\leq}\{n\}\ [\![\to]\!]\ [\![\ b\ ]\!]^{\leq}\{n\}$$
$$[\![\ a \stackrel{.}{\times} b\ ]\!]\ n = [\![\ a\ ]\!]\ n\quad [\![\times]\!]\quad [\![\ b\ ]\!]\ n$$
$$[\![\ \hat{\blacktriangleright}\ a\infty\ ]\!]\ n = [\blacktriangleright]\ P\ n$$
$$\text{where}$$
$$P : \forall\ n \to \mathsf{SATpred}\ (\mathsf{force}\ a\infty)\ n$$
$$P\ \mathsf{zero} = \_$$
$$P\ (\mathsf{suc}\ n) = [\![\ \mathsf{force}\ a\infty\ ]\!]\ n$$

Well-founded recursion on the depth is accomplished through the auxiliary definition $[\![\_]\!]^{\leq}$ which recurses on the inequality proof. It is however straightforward to convert in and out of the original interpretation, or between different upper bounds.

$$\mathsf{in}^{\leq} : \forall\ a\ \{n\ m\}\ (m{\leq}n : m \leq_N n) \to \mathsf{satSet}\ ([\![\ a\ ]\!]\quad m) \subseteq \mathsf{satSet}\ ([\![\ a\ ]\!]^{\leq}\ m{\leq}n)$$
$$\mathsf{out}^{\leq} : \forall\ a\ \{n\ m\}\ (m{\leq}n : m \leq_N n) \to \mathsf{satSet}\ ([\![\ a\ ]\!]^{\leq}\ m{\leq}n) \subseteq \mathsf{satSet}\ ([\![\ a\ ]\!]\ m)$$

$$\mathsf{coerce}^{\leq} : \forall\ a\ \{n\ n'\ m\}\ (m{\leq}n : m \leq_N n)\ (m{\leq}n' : m \leq_N n')$$
$$\to \mathsf{satSet}\ ([\![\ a\ ]\!]^{\leq}\ m{\leq}n) \subseteq \mathsf{satSet}\ ([\![\ a\ ]\!]^{\leq}\ m{\leq}n')$$

As will be necessary later for the interpretation of next, the interpretation of types is also antitone. For most types this follows by recursion, while for function types antitonicity is embedded in their semantics and we only need to convert between different upper bounds.

$$\mathsf{map}[\![\_]\!] : \forall\ a\ \{m\ n\} \to m \leq_N n \to \mathsf{satSet}\ ([\![\ a\ ]\!]\ n) \subseteq \mathsf{satSet}\ ([\![\ a\ ]\!]\ m)$$

Typing contexts are interpreted as predicates on substitutions. These predicates inherit antitonicity and closure under renaming. Semantically sound substitutions act as environments θ. We will need Ext to extend the environment for the interpretation of lambda abstractions.

$$[\_]C : \forall\, \Gamma\, \{n\} \to \forall\, \{\Delta\}\, (\sigma : \mathsf{Subst}\, \Gamma\, \Delta) \to \mathsf{Set}$$
$$[\![\, \Gamma\,]\!]C\, \{n\}\, \sigma = \forall\, \{a\}\, (x : \mathsf{Var}\, \Gamma\, a) \to \sigma\, x \in [\![\, a\,]\!]\, n$$

$$\mathsf{Map} : \forall\, \{m\, n\} \to (m{\le}n : m \le N\, n) \to$$
$$\qquad \forall\, \{\Gamma\, \Delta\}\, \{\sigma : \mathsf{Subst}\, \Gamma\, \Delta\}\, (\theta : [\![\, \Gamma\,]\!]C\, \{n\}\, \sigma) \to [\![\, \Gamma\,]\!]C\, \{m\}\, \sigma$$
$$\mathsf{Map}\, m{\le}n\, \theta\, \{a\}\, x = \mathsf{map}[\![\, a\,]\!] \in m{\le}n\, (\theta\, x)$$

$$\mathsf{Rename} : \forall\, \{n\, \Delta\, \Delta'\} \to (\rho : \mathsf{Ren}\, \Delta\, \Delta') \to$$
$$\qquad \forall\, \{\Gamma\}\{\sigma : \mathsf{Subst}\, \Gamma\, \Delta\}\, (\theta : [\![\, \Gamma\,]\!]C\, \{n\}\, \sigma) \to$$
$$\qquad [\![\, \Gamma\,]\!]C\, (\rho \bullet s\, \sigma) \to$$
$$\mathsf{Rename}\, \rho\, \theta\, \{a\}\, x = \text{[U+21BF]}\, \mathsf{satRename}\, ([\![\, a\,]\!]\, \_)\, \rho\, (\text{[U+21C3]}\, \theta\, x)$$

$$\mathsf{Ext} : \forall\, \{a\, n\, \Delta\, \Gamma\}\, \{t : \mathsf{Tm}\, \Delta\, a\} \to (t : t \in [\![\, a\,]\!]\, n) \to$$
$$\qquad \forall\, \{\sigma : \mathsf{Subst}\, \Gamma\, \Delta\}\, (\theta : [\![\, \Gamma\,]\!]C\, \sigma) \to [\![\, a :: \Gamma\,]\!]C\, (t ::s\, \sigma)$$
$$\mathsf{Ext}\, t\, \theta\, (\mathsf{zero}) = t$$
$$\mathsf{Ext}\, t\, \theta\, (\mathsf{suc}\, x) = \theta\, x$$

The soundness proof, showing that every term of $\lambda^{\blacktriangleright}$ is a member of our saturated sets and so a member of SN, is now a simple matter of interpreting each operation in the language to its equivalent in the semantics that we have defined so far.

$$\mathsf{sound} : \forall\, \{n\, a\, \Gamma\}\, (t : \mathsf{Tm}\, \Gamma\, a)\, \{\Delta\}\, \{\sigma : \mathsf{Subst}\, \Gamma\, \Delta\} \to$$
$$\qquad (\theta : [\![\, \Gamma\,]\!]C\, \{n\}\, \sigma) \to \mathsf{subst}\, \sigma\, t \in [\![\, a\,]\!]\, n$$
$$\mathsf{sound}\, (\mathsf{var}\, x)\, \theta = \theta\, x$$
$$\mathsf{sound}\, (\mathsf{abs}\, t)\, \theta = [\![\mathsf{abs}]\!]\, \{t = t\}\, \lambda\, m{\le}n\, \rho\, u \to$$
$$\quad \uparrow \mathsf{in}{\le}\, \_\, m{\le}n\, (\downarrow\, \mathsf{sound}\, t\, (\mathsf{Ext}\, (\uparrow \mathsf{out}{\le}\, \_\, m{\le}n\, (\downarrow\, u))\, (\mathsf{Rename}\, \rho\, (\mathsf{Map}\, m{\le}n\, \theta))))$$
$$\mathsf{sound}\, (\mathsf{app}\, t\, u)\, \theta = [\![\mathsf{app}]\!]\, (\mathsf{sound}\, t\, \theta)\, (\mathsf{sound}\, u\, \theta)$$
$$\mathsf{sound}\, (\mathsf{pair}\, t\, u)\, \theta = [\![\mathsf{pair}]\!]\, (\mathsf{sound}\, t\, \theta)\, (\mathsf{sound}\, u\, \theta)$$
$$\mathsf{sound}\, (\mathsf{fst}\, t)\quad \theta = [\![\mathsf{fst}]\!]\quad (\mathsf{sound}\, t\, \theta)$$
$$\mathsf{sound}\, (\mathsf{snd}\, t)\quad \theta = [\![\mathsf{snd}]\!]\quad (\mathsf{sound}\, t\, \theta)$$
$$\mathsf{sound}\, (t * u)\quad \theta = [\![*]\!]\quad (\mathsf{sound}\, t\, \theta)\, (\mathsf{sound}\, u\, \theta)$$
$$\mathsf{sound}\, \{\mathsf{zero}\}\, (\mathsf{next}\, t)\, \theta = \uparrow\, \mathsf{next0}$$
$$\mathsf{sound}\, \{\mathsf{suc}\, n\}\, (\mathsf{next}\, t)\, \theta = \uparrow\, (\mathsf{next}\, (\downarrow\, \mathsf{sound}\, t\, (\mathsf{Map}\, n{\le}sn\, \theta)))$$

The interpretation of next depends on the depth, at zero we are done, at suc n we recurse on the subterm at depth n, using antitonicity to Map the current environment to depth n as well. In fact without next we would not have needed antitonicity at all since there would have been no way to embed a term from a smaller depth into a larger one.

7 Conclusions

In this paper, we presented a family of strongly-normalizing reduction relations for simply-typed lambda calculus with Nakano's modality for recursion. Using a similar stratification, Krishnaswami and Benton (2011a) have shown weak normalization using hereditary substitutions, albeit for a system without recursive types.

Our Agda formalization uses a saturated sets semantics based on an inductive notion of strong normalization. Herein, we represented recursive types as infinite type expressions and terms as intrinsically well-typed ones.

Our treatment of infinite type expressions was greatly simplified by adding an extensionality axiom for the underlying coinductive type to Agda's type theory. This would not have been necessary in a more extensional theory such as *Observational Type Theory* (Altenkirch et al., 2007) as shown in (McBride, 2009). Possibly *Homotopy Type Theory* (UnivalentFoundations, 2013) would also address this problem, but there the status of coinductive types is yet unclear.

For the future, we would like to investigate how to incorporate guarded recursive types into a dependently-typed language, and how they relate to other approaches like coinduction with sized types, for instance.

Acknowledgments. Thanks to Lars Birkedal, Ranald Clouston, and Rasmus Møgelberg for fruitful discussions on guarded recursive types, and Hans Bugge Grathwohl, Fabien Renaud, and some anonymous referees for useful feedback on the Agda development and a draft version of this paper. The first author acknowledges support by Vetenskapsrådet framework grant 254820104 (Thierry Coquand). This paper has been prepared with Stevan Andjelkovic's Agda-to-LaTeX converter.

References

Agda Wiki. Chalmers and Gothenburg University, 2.4 edn. (2014),
   http://wiki.portal.chalmers.se/agda
Abel, A.: Normalization for the simply-typed lambda-calculus in Twelf. In: Logical Frameworks and Metalanguages (LFM 2004). Electronic Notes in Theoretical Computer Science, vol. 199C, pp. 3–16. Elsevier (2008)
Abel, A., Pientka, B., Thibodeau, D., Setzer, A.: Copatterns: Programming infinite structures by observations. In: The 40th Annual ACM SIGPLAN-SIGACT Symposium on Principles of Programming Languages, POPL 2013, Rome, Italy, January 23-25, pp. 27–38. ACM Press (2013)
Abel, A., Vezzosi, A.: A formalized proof of strong normalization for guarded recursive types (long version and Agda sources) (August 2014),
   http://www.cse.chalmers.se/~abela/publications.html#aplas14
Altenkirch, T., McBride, C., Swierstra, W.: Observational equality, now! In: Proceedings of the ACM Workshop Programming Languages meets Program Verification, PLPV 2007, Freiburg, Germany, October 5, pp. 57–68. ACM Press (2007)
Altenkirch, T., Reus, B.: Monadic presentations of lambda terms using generalized inductive types. In: Flum, J., Rodríguez-Artalejo, M. (eds.) CSL 1999. LNCS, vol. 1683, pp. 453–468. Springer, Heidelberg (1999)
Atkey, R., McBride, C.: Productive coprogramming with guarded recursion. In: Proc. of the 18th ACM SIGPLAN Int. Conf. on Functional Programming, ICFP 2013, pp. 197–208. ACM Press (2013)
Benton, N., Hur, C.K., Kennedy, A., McBride, C.: Strongly typed term representations in Coq. Journal of Automated Reasoning 49(2), 141–159 (2012)

Birkedal, L., Møgelberg, R.E.: Intensional type theory with guarded recursive types qua fixed points on universes. In: 28th Annual ACM/IEEE Symposium on Logic in Computer Science, LICS 2013, New Orleans, LA, USA, June 25-28, pp. 213–222. IEEE Computer Society Press (2013)

Dybjer, P.: Inductive families. Formal Aspects of Computing 6(4), 440–465 (1994)

Joachimski, F., Matthes, R.: Short proofs of normalization. Archive of Mathematical Logic 42(1), 59–87 (2003)

Krishnaswami, N.R., Benton, N.: A semantic model for graphical user interfaces. In: Proceeding of the 16th ACM SIGPLAN International Conference on Functional Programming, ICFP 2011, Tokyo, Japan, September 19-21, pp. 45–57. ACM Press (2011a)

Krishnaswami, N.R., Benton, N.: Ultrametric semantics of reactive programs. In: Proceedings of the 26th Annual IEEE Symposium on Logic in Computer Science, LICS 2011, Toronto, Ontario, Canada, June 21-24, pp. 257–266. IEEE Computer Society Press (2011b)

McBride, C.: Type-preserving renaming and substitution, unpublished draft (2006), http://strictlypositive.org/ren-sub.pdf

McBride, C.: Let's see how things unfold: Reconciling the infinite with the intensional (Extended abstract). In: Kurz, A., Lenisa, M., Tarlecki, A. (eds.) CALCO 2009. LNCS, vol. 5728, pp. 113–126. Springer, Heidelberg (2009)

McBride, C.: Outrageous but meaningful coincidences: Dependent type-safe syntax and evaluation. In: Proceedings of the ACM SIGPLAN Workshop on Generic Programming, WGP 2010, Baltimore, MD, USA, September 27-29, pp. 1–12. ACM Press (2010)

Nakano, H.: A modality for recursion. In: Proceedings of the 15th Annual IEEE Symposium on Logic in Computer Science (LICS 2000), Santa Barbara, California, USA, June 26-29, pp. 255–266. IEEE Computer Society Press (2000)

van Raamsdonk, F., Severi, P., Sørensen, M.H., Xi, H.: Perpetual reductions in lambda calculus. Information and Computation 149(2), 173–225 (1999)

Tait, W.W.: Intensional interpretations of functionals of finite type I. The Journal of Symbolic Logic 32(2), 198–212 (1967)

Univalent Foundations: Homotopy type theory: Univalent foundations of mathematics. Tech. rep. Institute for Advanced Study (2013), http://homotopytypetheory.org/book/

Xi, H., Chen, C., Chen, G.: Guarded recursive datatype constructors. In: Proceedings of the 30th ACM SIGPLAN Symposium on Principles of Programming Languages, New Orleans, pp. 224–235 (2003)

Functional Pearl: Nearest Shelters in Manhattan

Shin-Cheng Mu[1] and Ting-Wei Chen[2]

[1] Institute of Information Science, Academia Sinica, Taipei, Taiwan
[2] Dep. of Computer Science and Information Engineering,
National Taiwan University, Taipei, Taiwan

Abstract. Godzilla is attacking New York, and your task is to choose, for each shelter in the city, a nearest shelter to evacuate to. Luckily, distance between shelters is measured by Manhattan length, which allows us to complete the task in $O(n \log n)$ time. We present two algorithms: an algorithmic solution that solves the problem by a list-homomorphism, and a data structure based solution that exploits a "thinning" property.

Godzilla is awakened again, and is attacking New York this time. The citizens not evacuated in time are hiding in numerous shelters all over the city, which are currently the only places with water and food. In this functional pearl, you are given the set of coordinates of these shelters, and your task is to come up with an escape plan: for each shelter, in case it gets attacked, find a nearest shelter where people should evacuate to. Note that "being the nearest shelter" is not a symmetric relation: consider three shelters at coordinates $(0,0), (2,0), (3,0)$, where the shelter nearest to $(0,0)$ is $(2,0)$, while the one nearest to $(2,0)$ is $(3,0)$.

There is a good twist, however. Being in New York, where streets are grid-aligned, distances between buildings are measured by the so-called Manhattan distance — sum of the absolute differences of their coordinates. This allows us to compute the nearest shelters, for each of the n shelters, in $O(n \log n)$ time. In fact, we will present in this pearl two algorithms: an algorithmic approach using a list-homomorphism, and a data structure based approach that exploits a "thinning" property that allows logarithm-time looking-up.[1]

1 Specification

We adopt a Haskell-like notation, use xs, ys, etc., to denote sets and lists, and use x, y, etc. to denote their elements. Standard functions on lists such as (:), *map*, *filter*, etc., are overloaded to sets. We let X and Y coordinates increase toward the east (right) and north (top), thus when we say that (x_2, y_2) is to the northeast of (x_1, y_1), we mean $x_1 \leq x_2$ and $y_1 \leq y_2$.

---

[1] Haskell code accompanying this pearl can be fetched from http://www.iis.sinica.edu.tw/~scm/sw/nearest_shelters.zip .

J. Garrigue (Ed.): APLAS 2014, LNCS 8858, pp. 159–175, 2014.
© Springer International Publishing Switzerland 2014

To give a specification, we start with defining a function *allpairs*. Given a list of type $[a]$, it returns a set of pairs $\{(a, \{a\})\}$, such that each element in the input is paired with all elements other than itself:

$$
\begin{aligned}
&allpairs & :: \quad & [a] \rightarrow \{(a, \{a\})\} \\
&allpairs\;[] & = \quad & \{\} \\
&allpairs\;(x : xs) & = \quad & \{(x, xs)\} \cup map\;(id \times (x :))\;(allpairs\;xs),
\end{aligned}
$$

where $(f \times g)\;(x, y) = (f\;x, g\;y)$. For example, *allpairs* $[1, 2, 3] = \{(1, \{2, 3\}),$ $(2, \{1, 3\}), (3, \{1, 2\})\}$. One can easily see that we have

$$
map\;fst\;(allpairs\;xs) = setify\;xs, \tag{1}
$$

where $setify :: [a] \rightarrow \{a\}$ converts a list to a set. Note that the output of *allpairs* is a set, not a multiset. The input list is also meant to represent a set of points, and thus we assume that it contains no duplicates. The sets will be represented by concrete data structures, but we defer the decision until the choice is clear.

A shelter is identified with its coordinates:

type $Ptr = (Int, Int)$.

The task is to find, for each point, their nearest neighbours:

$$
\begin{aligned}
&nearall & :: \quad & [Ptr] \rightarrow \{(Ptr, Ptr)\} \\
&nearall & = \quad & map\;nearest \circ allpairs \\
& & \mathbf{where}\;\; & nearest\;(x, xs) = (x, min_{\leq_x}\;xs),
\end{aligned}
$$

where the relation $\leq_x$ compare points by their Manhattan distance from x,

$$
\begin{aligned}
y \leq_x z &= manhattan\;x\;y \leq manhattan\;x\;z\;\;, \\
manhattan\;(x_1, y_1)\;(x_2, y_2) &= |x_1 - x_2| + |y_1 - y_2|\;.
\end{aligned}
$$

Given a connected preorder $\trianglelefteq$,[2] the function $min_\trianglelefteq$ computes a minimum element under $\trianglelefteq$ in its input, while the binary minimum operator is denoted by $\sqcap_\trianglelefteq$. It will be specified later what $min_\trianglelefteq$ and $\sqcap_\trianglelefteq$ return in case of a tie, for $\trianglelefteq$ of our interest. For a concise presentation, we let $min_{\leq_x}\;\{\} = \top$, where $\top$ is a pseudo "furthest shelter" and an identity element of $\sqcap_{\leq_x}$. In the actual code it can be emulated by lifting Ptr to $Maybe\;Ptr$ and denoting $\top$ by Nothing.

It will turn out that we wish the input list to be sorted primarily by X-coordinates, then secondarily by Y, but we will bring up this constraint when it is motivated in Section 3.1. The output set will also be eventually represented by a list, and it might be sorted differently from the input. It often happens in algorithm design that finding an appropriate set representation is crucial to efficiency, and the decision should be postponed until its motivations and effects are clear.

---

[2] A *preorder* $\trianglelefteq$ on A is a relation (a subset of $A \times A$) that is reflexive and transitive. It is *connected* if for every x, y in A, at least one of $x \trianglelefteq y$ and $y \trianglelefteq x$ holds.

2 Looking Toward the Northeast

When tackling problems involving Manhattan distance, it is sometimes a useful strategy to first solve a subproblem in which we consider, for each point, only those points to its northeast. To see the motivation, let (x_2, y_2) be a point located to the northeast of (x_1, y_1), and consider the Manhattan distance between them:

$$\begin{aligned}
& |x_1 - x_2| + |y_1 - y_2| \\
= \; & \{ \text{ since } x_2 \geq x_1 \text{ and } y_2 \geq y_1 \ \} \\
& x_2 - x_1 + y_2 - y_1 \\
= \; & (x_2 + y_2) - (x_1 + y_1).
\end{aligned}$$

The distance is the difference between the sums of their coordinates. Given a point x, consider a set of points, all to the northeast of x. To choose the point nearest to x, we simply pick the one whose sum of coordinates is the smallest. To put it formally, if we define:

$$(x_1, y_1) \nearrow (x_2, y_2) = x_1 \leq x_2 \wedge y_1 \leq y_2,$$

such that $x \nearrow y$ yields *true* if y is to the northeast of x, we have

$$min_{\leq_x} \circ \mathit{filter}\ (x \nearrow) \; = \; min_{\leq_+} \circ \mathit{filter}\ (x \nearrow), \qquad (2)$$

where $(x_1, y_1) \leq_+ (x_2, y_2) = x_1 + y_1 \leq x_2 + y_2$. Given a point, we will refer to the sum of its X and Y coordinates simply as its "sum", when no confusion occurs.

Property (2) is useful because, while $min_{\leq_x}$ depends on x, $min_{\leq_+}$ does not. We have thus turned a local property into a global property. As we will see later, this allows us to reuse the result of $min_{\leq_+}$ when we consider nearest shelters of each points.

To compute *nearall*, we solve a subproblem in which we compute for every shelter the nearest shelter to its northeast:

$$\begin{aligned}
& nearall_{\nearrow} \; :: \; [Ptr] \rightarrow [(Ptr, Ptr)] \\
& nearall_{\nearrow} \; = \; map\ nearest_{\nearrow} \circ allpairs \\
& \quad \textbf{where } nearest_{\nearrow}\ (x, xs) \; = \; (x, min_{\leq_x}\ (\mathit{filter}\ (x \nearrow)\ xs)).
\end{aligned}$$

Nothing is lost by considering only the points to the northeast. The nearest shelters toward the northwest, for example, could be computed by reusing $nearall_{\nearrow}$, if we flip every point around the X-axis:

$$nearall_{\nwarrow} \; = \; map\ (\mathit{flipX} \times \mathit{flipX}) \circ nearall_{\nearrow} \circ map\ \mathit{flipX}\ ,$$

where $\mathit{flipX}\ (x, y) = (-x, y)$. Functions $nearall_{\swarrow}$ and $nearall_{\searrow}$ can be defined similarly, and *nearall* can be computed by searching toward each direction in turns before combining the results:

$$\begin{aligned}
& nearall\ xs \; = \; nearall_{\nearrow}\ xs \oplus nearall_{\nwarrow}\ xs \oplus nearall_{\searrow}\ xs \oplus nearall_{\swarrow}\ xs \\
& \quad \textbf{where } ys \oplus zs \; = \; \{(x, y \sqcap_{\leq_x} z) \mid x \in xs, (x, y) \in ys, (x, z) \in zs\}.
\end{aligned}$$

The rest of the pearl will be focusing on constructing efficient implementations of $nearall_{\nearrow}$.

3 A Divide-and-Conquer Approach

Aiming for an $O(n \log n)$-time algorithm, one naturally goes for a divide-and-conquer approach. Let us consider how $\mathit{allpairs}\ (xs \mathbin{+\!\!\!+} ys)$ can be computed in terms of $\mathit{allpairs}\ xs$ and $\mathit{allpairs}\ ys$:

$$
\begin{aligned}
\mathit{allpairs}\ [] \quad &= \quad \{\} \\
\mathit{allpairs}\ [x] \quad &= \quad \{(x, \{\})\} \\
\mathit{allpairs}\ (xs \mathbin{+\!\!\!+} ys) \quad &= \quad \mathit{map}\ (id \times (\cup ys'))\ xss \cup \mathit{map}\ (id \times (xs'\cup))\ yss \\
&\mathbf{where}\ (xss, yss) = (\mathit{allpairs}\ xs, \mathit{allpairs}\ ys) \\
&\qquad\quad (xs', ys') = (\mathit{setify}\ xs, \mathit{setify}\ ys)
\end{aligned}
$$

Note that, by (1), $(xs', ys') = (\mathit{map\ fst}\ xss, \mathit{map\ fst}\ yss)$. The function $\mathit{allpairs}$ thus turns out to be a list homomorphism, a common pattern used to describe divide-and-conquer algorithms on lists [9,7]. Our task now is to come up with a list-homomorphic definition of $\mathit{nearall}_\nearrow$.

3.1 Finding the Nearest Shelter in a List Homomorphism

We try to construct an inductive definition of $\mathit{nearall}_\nearrow$ by the typical unfold-fold transformation. The cases for empty and singleton lists are easy. The goal is to find some $\oplus$ such that $\mathit{nearall}_\nearrow\ (xs \mathbin{+\!\!\!+} ys) = \mathit{nearall}_\nearrow\ xs \oplus \mathit{nearall}_\nearrow\ ys$, and discover what constraints we need to impose on xs and ys. Some hints for the impatient readers: if we assume that the input is sorted by X-coordinate, the result of $\mathit{nearall}_\nearrow\ ys$ can be used as it is, while the result of $\mathit{nearall}_\nearrow\ xs$ will be updated by integrating those points in ys.

Assuming that xs and ys are non-empty, we reason:

$$
\begin{aligned}
&\mathit{nearall}_\nearrow\ (xs \mathbin{+\!\!\!+} ys) \\
=\ &(\mathit{map\ nearest}_\nearrow \circ \mathit{allpairs})\ (xs \mathbin{+\!\!\!+} ys) \\
=\ &\{\ \text{by definition, let}\ (xss, yss) = (\mathit{allpairs}\ xs, \mathit{allpairs}\ ys),\ \text{and} \\
&\qquad (xs', ys') = (\mathit{setify}\ xs, \mathit{setify}\ ys)\ \} \\
&\mathit{map\ nearest}_\nearrow\ (\mathit{map}\ (id \times (\cup ys'))\ xss \cup \mathit{map}\ (id \times (xs'\cup))\ yss) \\
=\ &\{\ \mathit{map}\ \text{fusion}\ \} \\
&\mathit{map}\ (\lambda(x, zs).(x, \min_{\leq_x}\ (\mathit{filter}\ (x\nearrow)\ (zs \cup ys'))))\ xss \cup \\
&\mathit{map}\ (\lambda(y, zs).(y, \min_{\leq_y}\ (\mathit{filter}\ (y\nearrow)\ (xs' \cup zs))))\ yss.
\end{aligned}
$$

Observe that, by (1), x and y in the λ expression are respectively members of xs and ys. If we assume that the input $xs \mathbin{+\!\!\!+} ys$ is sorted primarily by ascending X-coordinate and secondarily by ascending Y-coordinate, we have

$$
\begin{aligned}
x \nearrow y \ &\Leftrightarrow\ x \uparrow y \ \wedge \tag{3} \\
&\quad \neg(y \nearrow x)\ , \tag{4}
\end{aligned}
$$

$$\text{for all } x \in xs \text{ and } y \in ys,$$

where $x{\uparrow}y$ denotes that y is to the north of x, that is, $(x_1, y_1){\uparrow}(x_2, y_2) = y_1 \leq y_2$.

The right-hand side of $\cup$ (the last line of the derivation above) thus reduces to $nearall_{\nearrow}\ ys$:

$$map\ (\lambda(y, zs).(y, min_{\leq_y}\ (filter\ (y{\nearrow})\ (xs' \cup zs)))))\ yss$$

$=$ { (4) holds by assumption }

$$map\ (\lambda(y, zs).(y, min_{\leq_y}\ (filter\ (y{\nearrow})\ zs)))\ yss$$

$=$ { definitions of $nearest_{\nearrow}$ and $nearall_{\nearrow}$ }

$$nearall_{\nearrow}\ ys.$$

For the left-hand side of $\cup$, we calculate:

$$map\ (\lambda(x, zs).(x, min_{\leq_x}\ (filter\ (x{\nearrow})\ (zs \cup ys')))))\ xss$$

$=$ { $filter$ and min distributes into $\cup$ }

$$map\ (\lambda(x, zs).(x, min_{\leq_x}\ (filter\ (x{\nearrow})\ zs)\ \sqcap_{\leq_+}$$
$$min_{\leq_x}\ (filter\ (x{\nearrow})\ ys'))))\ xss$$

$=$ { map-fusion }

$$map\ (\lambda(x, z).(x, z\ \sqcap_{\leq_x}\ min_{\leq_x}\ (filter\ (x{\nearrow})\ ys')))$$
$$(map\ (\lambda(x, zs).(x, min_{\leq_x}\ (filter\ (x{\nearrow})\ zs)))\ xss)$$

$=$ { definition of $nearall_{\nearrow}$ }

$$map\ (\lambda(x, z).(x, z\ \sqcap_{\leq_x}\ min_{\leq_x}\ (filter\ (x{\nearrow})\ ys')))$$
$$(nearall_{\nearrow}\ xs)$$

$=$ { by (2) and (3) }

$$map\ (\lambda(x, z).(x, z\ \sqcap_{\leq_x}\ min_{\leq_+}\ (filter\ (x{\uparrow})\ ys')))$$
$$(nearall_{\nearrow}\ xs).$$

For brevity, we extract from the last line the following definition:

$$minWithin\ ys\ (x, z)\ =\ (x, z\ \sqcap_{\leq_x}\ min_{\leq_+}\ (filter\ (x{\uparrow})\ ys)).$$

In words, $minWithin\ ys\ (x, z)$ selects, from ys, those points that are to the north of x, find a point whose sum is minimum, before comparing it with z. We now have:

$$nearall_{\nearrow}\ []\quad\quad =\ \{\}$$
$$nearall_{\nearrow}\ [x]\quad\quad =\ \{(x, \top)\}$$
$$nearall_{\nearrow}\ (xs + ys)\ =$$
$$map\ (minWithin\ (setify\ ys))\ (nearall_{\nearrow}\ xs)\ \cup\ nearall_{\nearrow}\ ys.$$

By always splitting $xs + ys$ into two lists of roughly the same size, we get a $O(n \log n)$-time algorithm if we can compute $map\ (minWithin\ (setify\ ys))\ xs'$ in time linear to the sizes of ys and xs', where $xs' = nearall_{\nearrow}\ xs$.

3.2   Sweeping

In this section we develop an efficient way to compute the expression

$$map\ (minWithin\ (setify\ ys))\ (nearall_{\nearrow}\ xs)\ \cup\ nearall_{\nearrow}\ ys.$$

Again, some spoilers for the impatient readers: we will assume that the results of $nearall_\nearrow$ xs and $nearall_\nearrow$ ys are sorted by Y-coordinates, and merge them in a zip-like manner.

Consider map $(minWithin$ $ys')$ xs' (where, for brevity, $ys' = setify$ ys and $xs' = nearall_\nearrow$ xs). For each element (x, z) of xs' we apply $minWithin$ ys', that is, to filter out those points in ys' that are to the north of x and pick a minimum (before comparing with z). If the elements in xs' are processed in north-to-south order, we will filter out a successively larger subset of ys'. That allows us to reuse previously computed results of smaller subsets of ys'.

Since we typically process lists from right-to-left, to process $nearall_\nearrow$ xs in the order mentioned above, we would want to store it in a list such that the first components are sorted by *ascending* (left-to-right) Y-coordinates. The input and output of our main algorithm are thus sorted differently: the former is sorted primarily by X (a constraint discovered in Section 3.1), while the output is sorted by Y.

Define $snearall_\nearrow = sort_Y \circ nearall_\nearrow$, where $sort_Y$, of type $\{(Ptr, Ptr)\} \to [(Ptr, Ptr)]$, sorts the input set into a list of pairs of points such that the Y-coordinates of the first components are ascending. By distributing $sort_Y$ into $nearall_\nearrow$, one easily get:

$snearall_\nearrow$ $(xs \mathbin{+\mkern-8mu+} ys) =$
$\quad map$ $(minWithin$ $(setify$ $ys))$ $(snearall_\nearrow$ $xs)$ '$merge$' $snearall_\nearrow$ $ys,$

where $merge$ combines two sorted lists. To efficiently compute the subexpression map $(minWithin$ $(setify$ $ys))$ $(snearall_\nearrow$ $xs)$, we define:

$sweep$ $::$ $[(Ptr, Ptr)] \to [Ptr] \to ([(Ptr, Ptr)], Ptr)$
$sweep$ xs $ys = (map$ $(minWithin$ $(setify$ $ys))$ $xs, min_{\leq_+}$ $ys),$

which caches the results of the current minimum in the second component of the pair. Caching some reusable results in a pair to avoid redundant function calls is called "tupling" [3], a common technique in program derivation. If $sweep$ can be computed efficiently, $snearall_\nearrow$ $(xs \mathbin{+\mkern-8mu+} ys)$ can be computed by:

$snearall_\nearrow$ $(xs \mathbin{+\mkern-8mu+} ys) = fst$ $(sweep$ $(snearall_\nearrow$ $xs)$ $ys')$ '$merge$' zs
$\quad$ **where** $zs = snearall_\nearrow$ ys
$\qquad\quad\; ys' = map$ fst $zs.$

Note that $sweep$ assumes that both of its arguments are sorted by the Y-coordinate. We let $ys' = map$ fst zs to satisfy the demand that ys' is sorted.

Now we aim to construct an inductive definition of $sweep$. The cases when $xs := []$ or $ys := []$ are omitted. The more interesting case is $sweep$ $((x, z) : xs)$ $(y : ys)$, for which we distinguish between following two cases, where $\leq_Y$ compares the Y-coordinate:

Case $x >_Y y$. Since $(x, z) : xs$ is sorted by ascending Y, we have that for all $(x', z') \in ((x, z) : xs)$, $x' >_Y y$. That is, y is not in the northeast direction of any points in $((x, z) : xs)$ and can be dropped. Indeed we have

$$sweep\;((x, z) : xs)\;(y : ys) = (id \times (y \sqcap_{\leq_+}))\;(sweep\;((x, z) : xs)\;ys).$$

The equation above is best proved as a separate lemma

Lemma 1. *sweep xs* $(y : ys)$ = $(id \times (y \sqcap_{\leq_+}))$ *(sweep xs ys), if* $x >_Y y$ *for all* $(x, z) \in xs$.

Proof of the lemma is a routine induction on *xs*, shown in Appendix A.

Case $x \leq_Y y$. We reason:

$$sweep\ ((x, z) : xs)\ (y : ys)$$
$$= (map\ (minWithin\ (setify\ (y : ys)))\ ((x, z) : xs)),$$
$$min_{\leq_+}\ (y : ys))$$
$$= \quad \{\ \text{definitions of } map \text{ and } minWithin\ \}$$
$$((x, z \sqcap_{\leq_+} min_{\leq_+}\ (filter\ (x\uparrow)\ (y : ys)))\ :$$
$$map\ (minWithin\ (setify\ (y : ys)))\ xs,$$
$$min_{\leq_+}\ (y : ys))$$
$$= \quad \{\ \text{since } x \leq_Y y, \text{ and } y : ys \text{ ascending w.r.t } \leq_Y\ \}$$
$$((x, z \sqcap_{\leq_x} min_{\leq_+}\ (y : ys))\ :$$
$$map\ (minWithin\ (setify\ (y : ys)))\ xs,$$
$$min_{\leq_+}\ (y : ys))$$
$$= \quad \{\ \text{definition of } sweep\ \}$$
$$\mathbf{let}\ (zs, m) = sweep\ xs\ (y : ys)$$
$$\mathbf{in}\ ((x, z \sqcap_{\leq_x} m) : zs, m).$$

We have thus constructed *sweep*:

$$sweep\ []\ ys\ =\ ([], min_{\leq_+}\ ys)$$
$$sweep\ xs\ []\ =\ (xs, \infty)$$
$$sweep\ ((x, z) : xs)\ (y : ys)$$
$$\mid x >_Y y\ =\ (id \times (y \sqcap_{\leq_+}))\ (sweep\ ((x, z) : xs)\ ys$$
$$\mid x \leq_Y y\ =\ \mathbf{let}\ (zs, m) = sweep\ xs\ (y : ys)$$
$$\mathbf{in}\ ((x, z \sqcap_{\leq_x} m) : zs, m).$$

In fact, the structure of *sweep* resembles *merge*. We may further combine *sweep* and *merge*, to be a little bit more efficient. Define:

$$sweepmrg\ ::\ [(Ptr, Ptr)] \to [(Ptr, Ptr)] \to ([(Ptr, Ptr)], Ptr)$$
$$sweepmrg\ xs\ ys\ =\ \mathbf{let}\ (zs, m) = sweep\ xs\ (map\ fst\ ys)$$
$$\mathbf{in}\ (merge\ zs\ ys, m).$$

It takes a routine calculation to derive an inductive definition of *sweepmrg*:

$$sweepmrg\ []\ ys\ =\ (ys, min_{\leq_+}\ (map\ fst\ ys))$$
$$sweepmrg\ xs\ []\ =\ (xs, \infty)$$
$$sweepmrg\ ((x, z) : xs)\ ((y, w) : ys)$$
$$\mid x >_Y y\ =\ \mathbf{let}\ (zs, m) = sweepmrg\ ((x, z) : xs)\ ys$$
$$\mathbf{in}\ ((y, w) : zs, y \sqcap_{\leq_+} m)$$
$$\mid x \leq_Y y\ =\ \mathbf{let}\ (zs, m) = sweepmrg\ xs\ ((y, w) : ys)$$
$$\mathbf{in}\ ((x, z \sqcap_{\leq_x} m) : zs, m).$$

$$nearall_\nearrow \;::\; [Ptr] \to [(Ptr, Maybe\ Ptr)]$$
$$nearall_\nearrow \;=\; snearall_\nearrow \circ sort$$

$$snearall_\nearrow \quad::\; [Ptr] \to [(Ptr, Maybe\ Ptr)]$$
$$snearall_\nearrow\ [] \;=\; []$$
$$snearall_\nearrow\ [x] \;=\; [(x, \mathsf{Nothing})]$$
$$snearall_\nearrow\ xs \;=\; fst\ (sweepmrg\ (snearall_\nearrow\ ys)\ (snearall_\nearrow\ zs))$$
$$\textbf{where}\ (ys, zs) = splitAt\ ((length\ xs)\ `div`\ 2)\ xs$$

$$sweepmrg :: [(Ptr, Maybe\ Ptr)] \to [(Ptr, Maybe\ Ptr)] \to$$
$$([(Ptr, Maybe\ Ptr)], Maybe\ Ptr)$$
$$sweepmrg\ []\ ys = (ys, min_{\leq_+}\ (map\ fst\ ys))$$
$$sweepmrg\ xs\ [] = (xs, \mathsf{Nothing})$$
$$sweepmrg\ ((x, z) : xs)\ ((y, w) : ys)$$
$$|\ x >_Y y \qquad = \textbf{let}\ (zs, m) = sweepmrg\ ((x, z) : xs)\ ys$$
$$\textbf{in}\ ((y, w) : zs, \mathsf{Just}\ y \sqcap_{\leq_+} m)$$
$$|\ \textbf{otherwise} = \textbf{let}\ (zs, m) = sweepmrg\ xs\ ((y, w) : ys)$$
$$\textbf{in}\ ((x, z \sqcap_{\leq_+} m) : zs, m)$$

Fig. 1. Computing $nearall_\nearrow$ in a list-homomorphism

While $snearall_\nearrow$ may thus be defined as:

$$snearall_\nearrow\ [] \qquad\qquad = []$$
$$snearall_\nearrow\ [x] \qquad\qquad = [(x, \top)]$$
$$snearall_\nearrow\ (xs \mathbin{+\!\!+} ys) \;=\; fst\ (sweepmrg\ (snearall_\nearrow\ xs)\ (snearall_\nearrow\ ys)).$$

The key components of the actual code is summarised in Figure 1, where we lift Ptr to $Maybe\ Ptr$ and use $\mathsf{Nothing}$ to denote $\top$. To ensure that the input is sorted by X-coordinate, we compose $sort$ before $snearall_\nearrow$.

3.3 Complexity Analysis

We give a brief complexity analysis before we conclude discussion of this algorithm. In each recursive call of $sweepmrg$, the sum of the lengths of its arguments is decremented by one. Therefore the running time of $sweepmrg$ is clearly linear in the sum of lengths of its two arguments. In each recursive call to function $snearall_\nearrow$ cuts the length of its argument by half. The running time of $snearall_\nearrow$ can be estimated by $T(n) = n + 2 \times T(n/2)$. By standard analysis we may conclude that $T(n)$ is in $O(n \log n)$.

4 A Thinning Approach

The solution in the previous section achieves $O(n \log n)$ complexity by splitting the problem into at most $O(\log n)$ levels, while ensuring that each level can be processed in linear time. We now present a complementary approach, in which we make n queries into a data structure, time of each query bounded by $O(\log n)$. Interestingly, it turns out that to maintain the data structure, we have to keep "thinning" it, a technique often used to construct efficient algorithms for optimisation problems.

Following the development in Section 2, we focus on developing a fast algorithm for $nearall_\nearrow$, and also assume that the input list of points is sorted, with no duplication. Recall that $nearall_\nearrow = map\ nearest_\nearrow \circ allpairs$, where $nearest_\nearrow\ (x, xs) = (x, min_{\leq_x}\ (filter\ (x\nearrow)\ xs))$. This time, we attempt to compute $nearall_\nearrow$ by processing the input from right to left, that is, to express $nearall_\nearrow\ (x : xs)$ as a function of xs and $nearall_\nearrow\ xs$:

$$nearall_\nearrow\ (x : xs)$$
$$= \quad nearest_\nearrow\ (x, xs) : map\ (nearest_\nearrow \circ (id \times (x :)))\ (allpairs\ xs)$$
$$= \quad \{\ (x : xs)\ \text{sorted, and thus}\ \neg(y \nearrow x)\ \text{for all}\ y \in xs\ \}$$
$$\quad nearest_\nearrow\ (x, xs) : map\ nearest_\nearrow\ (allpairs\ xs)$$
$$= \quad \{\ \text{definition of}\ nearall_\nearrow\ \}$$
$$\quad nearest_\nearrow\ (x, xs) : nearall_\nearrow\ xs$$
$$= \quad \{\ \text{definition of}\ nearest_\nearrow, (2)\ \}$$
$$\quad (x, min_{\leq_+}\ (filter\ (x\nearrow)\ xs)) : nearall_\nearrow\ xs$$
$$= \quad \{\ x : xs\ \text{sorted by X}\ \}$$
$$\quad (x, min_{\leq_+}\ (filter\ (x\uparrow)\ xs)) : nearall_\nearrow\ xs$$

The second step is valid because one can easily show that $nearest_\nearrow\ (y, x : zs) = nearest_\nearrow\ (y, zs)$ if $\neg(y \nearrow x)$ for all x, y, zs. The last step is valid because, now that $x : xs$ is sorted primarily by X, to check for $(x\nearrow)$ reduces to checking for $(x\uparrow)$.

Given an input list of length n, for each tail $x : xs$, one can see $nearest_\nearrow$ as making a query: "among the points in xs that are to the north of x, which point has minimum sum?" A series of such queries are made, from right to left (or, east to west), on the n such tails of the input. Our wish is to ensure that each query can be completed in $O(\log n)$ time.

Some points in xs are redundant. Consider, for example, two points $y = (1, 2)$ and $z = (3, 1)$ in xs. A moment's thought reveals that we do not need to keep z, since for all x, if $x \nearrow z$, it must also be the case that $x \nearrow y$, and yet $y \leq_+ z$ — wherever z is chosen, it makes no harm to use y instead. Therefore, instead of querying into xs, we can keep only a "thinned" version of xs without such redundant elements.

The algorithm scans the input list right-to-left, while carrying a subset of the tail containing only those elements that are needed. In Section 4.1 we review some theories on such "thinned" sets, before we instantiate the theory to this particular problem and develop the main structure of the algorithm in Section 4.2. In Section 4.3 we develop the data structure used in the algorithm that allows efficient thinning and querying.

4.1   Minimum, Thinning, and Filtering

The idea, when computing some optimal solutions, of throwing away elements that are no longer needed has been called "thinning" [2], and has been applied to solve a number of optimisation problems [5,13,11], as well as deriving approximation algorithms [12]. In those contexts, the main purpose of thinning is to asymptotically reduce the number of potential solutions. Less addressed, however, is that thinning a set also reveals more structure that we may exploit to allow efficient access, which is what we need.

Thinning is typically described in a relational setting. In this section, we will try to give a minimal, not-so-relational account sufficient for readers to get an idea of the concept.

Assume some preorder $\preceq$ such that $y \preceq z$ captures the idea that z is no longer needed in the presence of y. Apparently, not all elements are comparable under $\preceq$. The non-redundant elements of a set are those minimal elements under $\preceq$. The operation $thin_{\preceq}\ ys$ yields a subset xs of ys, with some redundant elements possibly removed.

Our implementation of $thin_{\preceq}$, in fact, keeps only those minimal elements. To prove its properties, however, it is sufficient to assume a weaker specification: that $thin_{\preceq}$ does not throw away non-redundant elements. More precisely, if ys is a result of $thin_{\preceq}\ zs$, we demand merely that $ys \subseteq zs$ and [3]

$$(\forall z : z \in zs : (\exists y : y \in ys : y \preceq z)).$$

That is, while being a subset of zs, ys is large enough such that every element in zs is subsumed by some element in ys. Not over-specifying $thin_{\preceq}$ allows more flexibility and, by capturing only the essential constraints, makes some properties about $thin_{\preceq}$ easier to prove.

We will need the following two properties about $thin$. Firstly, we have

$$min_{\lhd} \circ thin_{\preceq} \subseteq min_{\lhd},$$
$$\text{if } y \preceq z \Rightarrow y \unlhd z. \tag{5}$$

The symbol $\subseteq$ denotes inclusion of relations, but we may roughly understand it as saying that "for all inputs, the output of the LHS is a legitimate output of the RHS." Therefore, (5) states that as long as $\preceq$ implies $\unlhd$, if we remove some redundant elements from a set by $thin_{\preceq}$ and take a minimum, the result is still a minimum of the original set.

The second property says that $thin$ and $filter$ commute:

$$filter\ p \circ thin_{\preceq} \subseteq thin_{\preceq} \circ filter\ p,$$
$$\text{if } y \preceq z \Rightarrow (p\ z \Rightarrow p\ y). \tag{6}$$

The antecedent ensures that if the lesser solution z is kept by $filter\ p$, so is y. Proof of (6) is given in Appendix B.

---

[3] $(\forall \bar{x} : R : P)$ is read "for all variable(s) $\bar{x}$ in range R, P is true." Similarly with $\exists$. The notation is suggested, among others, by Gries and Schneider [8].

4.2   Thinning the Set of Shelters

To describe the kind of thinning we perform, define

$$y \preceq z \quad \equiv \quad y \leq_+ z \wedge z \uparrow y.$$

By $y \preceq z$ we denote that y subsumes z and makes z redundant, that is, to compute the nearest shelter to the northeast of any x, we do not need z as long as y is around. The definition says that $y \preceq z$ if and only of the sum of y is no worse than z, while it is located no southerner than z. Indeed, it immediately follows from the definition that

$$y \preceq z \Rightarrow y \leq_+ z \quad \wedge$$
$$y \preceq z \Rightarrow (x \uparrow z) \Rightarrow (x \uparrow y) \quad \text{, for all } x,$$

which guarantee (5) and (6).

Back to $nearall_{\nearrow}$. The following calculation justifies defining it in terms of a function that passes a thinned set of shelters around. We have shown in the beginning of this section that $nearall_{\nearrow} \ (x : xs) = (x, min_{\leq_+} \ (filter \ (x \uparrow) \ xs)) : nearall_{\nearrow} \ xs$. Consider the second component of the pair:

$$
\begin{aligned}
& min_{\leq_+} \ (filter \ (x \uparrow) \ xs) \\
=\ & \{ \text{ by } (5) \ \} \\
& min_{\leq_+} \ (thin_{\preceq} \ (filter \ (x \uparrow) \ xs)) \\
=\ & \{ \text{ by } (6) \ \} \\
& min_{\leq_+} \ (filter \ (x \uparrow) \ (thin_{\preceq} \ xs)) \quad .
\end{aligned}
$$

That is, to find the point in xs nearest to x, it is sufficient to query into a thinned set $thin_{\preceq} \ xs$. To avoid recomputing $thin_{\preceq} \ xs$ from scratch, we perform tupling again by defining:

$$
\begin{aligned}
nearthin \quad & :: \ [Ptr] \to ([(Ptr, Ptr)], \{Ptr\}) \\
nearthin \ xs \ & = \ (nearall_{\nearrow} \ xs, thin_{\preceq} \ xs) \quad .
\end{aligned}
$$

If $nearthin$ can be computed efficiently, we may let

$$nearall_{\nearrow} = fst \circ nearthin.$$

A routine calculation yields:

$$
\begin{aligned}
nearthin \ [] \quad & = \ ([], \{\}) \\
nearthin \ (x : xs) & = \ \textbf{let} \ (zs, xs') = nearthin \ xs \\
& \quad \ \ \textbf{in} \ ((x, min_{\leq_+} \ (filter \ (x \uparrow) \ xs')) : zs, thinadd \ x \ xs'),
\end{aligned}
$$

where $thinadd \ x \ xs' = thin_{\preceq} \ (x : xs')$, that is, it adds x into xs', before removing redundant elements.

It remains to decide what data structure we may use to represent $\{Ptr\}$ to allow efficient implementation of $min_{\leq_+} \circ filter \ (x \uparrow)$ and $thinadd$.

4.3   A Splay Tree Representation

It often turns out that the key to constructing efficient algorithm is to find efficient representations of sets. Now let us consider how a fully thinned set, that is, one containing only minimal elements under $\preceq$, looks like.

- If two points have the same Y-coordinate, we only need to keep the one with a smaller sum. Thus for each Y value there needs to be at most one point.
- If y and z, with $y \uparrow z$, both remain in the fully thinned set, it must be the case that $y <_+ z$ — otherwise y would be dropped.
  That is, if we sort the elements of the fully thinned set of points by increasing Y-coordinates, the sums of these points must be increasing too.

Let xs be a thinned set. To perform $min_{\leq_+} \; (filter \; (x\uparrow) \; xs)$, one only need to find, among those points to the north of x, the one with the smallest Y-value, since its sum must be the smallest too! One could use some variation of binary search tree that allows logarithm look-up on Y. The operation $thinadd$ is trickier, since after inserting x, we have to remove elements that became redundant in the presence of x.

For advantages to be seen later, we will use splay trees [14], a well-known, self-adjusting binary search tree with amortised $O(\log n)$ look-up and insertion. One interesting property of splay tree is that the most recently accessed or inserted element is moved to the root. For our purpose it suffices to use an ordinary binary tree as the backbone:

data *Tree a* = Lf | Nd (*Tree a*) a (*Tree a*).

We implemented the following operations:

- *find* :: $(a \to a \to Ordering) \to a \to Tree \; a \to Zipper \; a$.[4] The function call *find cmp x t* tries to find x in t, using *cmp* for comparison. The trail it goes through is recorded in a zipper [10]:

  data *ZigZag a* = L a (*Tree a*) | R (*Tree a*) a,
  type *Zipper a* = (*Tree a*, [*ZigZag a*]).

  If the result is (Lf, *zs*), x is not found in t. Otherwise it returns (Nd u x' v, *zs*) such that *cmp x x'* = EQ, and *zs* is the path leading to the tree where x' is found. Once we have a zipper, a lot can be done to it.
- *lub* :: *Zipper a* $\to$ *Maybe a* takes a zipper (resulting from a search using *find cmp x t*) and returns the least element in t that is no smaller than x, if such an element exists.
- *splay* :: *Zipper a* $\to$ *Tree a* rolls the zipper back to a tree, while rotating the nodes all the way up such that the node accessed just now becomes the root.
- *insZip* :: $a \to (a \to a \to a) \to$ *Zipper a* $\to$ *Tree a*, defined in terms of *splay*, performs insertion. If $(u, zs) =$ *find cmp x t* is the result of searching for x in t, *insZip y f (u, zs)* inserts a value into where the search ended. If the

---

[4] **data** *Ordering* = LT | EQ | GT.

search failed ($u = $ Lf), the value y is inserted as it is. If the search succeeded ($u = $ Nd u x v), the value f y x is added in place of x. The newly inserted value is splayed to the root.

- For convenience, we also define $insert$ cmp x f t = $insZip$ x f ($find$ cmp x t), which performs insertion right after a search.

There are many ways these and similar operations can be implemented and the readers do not need to know a particular implementation to understand the algorithm. For the interested readers, however, our definitions are recorded in Figure 2. The main work is done in $splay$, whose last four clauses pattern-match against the two most recent steps of the zipper, to determine whether a zig-zig, or a zig-zag step, etc., should be performed. The two clauses where the zipper is a singleton list are respectively the zig and the zag case.

Given these operations, it is not hard to see that $min_{\leq_+}$ ($filter$ ($x{\uparrow}$) xs) can be implemented by first finding x using its Y-coordinate, then performing lub on the resulting zipper. We thus refine $nearthin$ to:

$$
\begin{array}{ll}
nearthin & :: [Ptr] \rightarrow ([(Ptr, Maybe\ Ptr)], Tree\ Ptr) \\
nearthin\ [] & = ([], \mathsf{Lf}) \\
nearthin\ (x : xs) & = \mathbf{let}\ (ys, t) = nearthin\ xs \\
& \qquad\quad zpr = find\ cmp_Y\ x\ t \\
& \quad \mathbf{in}\ ((x, lub\ zpr) : ys, thinadd\ x\ zpr),
\end{array}
$$

where cmp_Y compares the Y-coordinate. The function $thinadd$, on the other hand, inserts x into zpr before performing thinning using $thin$:

$$
\begin{array}{l}
thinadd :: Ptr \rightarrow Zipper\ Ptr \rightarrow Tree\ Ptr \\
thinadd\ x\ zpr = thin\ (insZip\ x\ const\ zpr).
\end{array}
$$

The parameter $const$ to $insZip$ means "when there is another point having the same Y-value, keep the newly inserted one."

How do we implement $thin$, then? Notice that the tree returned by $insZip$ must look like Nd t x u, where x is the newly inserted point and t contains all the points having a smaller Y-value than x. We aim to remove from t those points whose sums are greater than or equal to that of x. Luckily, the sums in t are also sorted! Therefore, we insert x into t, this time using cmp_S, a function comparing the sums:

$$
\begin{array}{ll}
thin\ (\mathsf{Nd}\ t\ x\ u) & = \mathbf{let}\ \mathsf{Nd}\ t'\ \_\ u' = insert\ cmp_S\ x\ const\ t \\
& \quad \mathbf{in}\ \mathsf{Nd}\ t'\ x\ u.
\end{array}
$$

In the resulting tree Nd t' $\_$ u', the omitted root must be x, the tree u' contains all the points whose sums are greater than that of x, while t' contains all the points with smaller sums. We simply get rid of u' and put back t'. All auxiliary functions we need for $nearthin$ are now in place.

4.4   Complexity Analysis

The main work is carried out by $nearthin$. Given an input of length n, it makes $2n$ calls to $find$, n calls to lub, and $2n$ calls to $insZip$. All these operations have amortised complexity $O(\log n)$. The algorithm thus runs in $O(n \log n)$ time.

```
find           :: (a → a → Ordering) → a → Tree a → Zipper a
find cmp x t = mkZIter t []
  where mkZIter Lf zs = (Lf, zs)
        mkZIter (Nd t y u) zs =
          case cmp x y of
              LT → mkZIter t (L y u : zs)
              EQ → (Nd t y u, zs)
              GT → mkZIter u (R t y : zs)


splay :: Zipper a → Tree a
splay (t, []) = t
splay (Lf, L x u : zs) = splay (Nd Lf x u, zs)
splay (Lf, R t x : zs) = splay (Nd t x Lf, zs)
splay (Nd t x u, [L y v]) = Nd t x (Nd u y v)
splay (Nd u x v, [R t y]) = Nd (Nd t y u) x v
splay (Nd t x u, L y v : L z w : zs) = splay (Nd t x (Nd u y (Nd v z w)), zs)
splay (Nd u y v, R t x : L z w : zs) = splay (Nd (Nd t x u) y (Nd v z w), zs)
splay (Nd u y v, L z w : R t x : zs) = splay (Nd (Nd t x u) y (Nd v z w), zs)
splay (Nd v z w, R u y : R t x : zs) = splay (Nd (Nd (Nd t x u) y v) z w, zs)


insert :: (a → a → Ordering) → a → (a → a → a) → Tree a → Tree a
insert cmp x f t = insZip x f (find cmp x t)


insZip :: a → (a → a → a) → Zipper a → Tree a
insZip x f (Lf, zs)       = splay (Nd Lf x Lf, zs)
insZip x f (Nd u x' v, zs) = splay (Nd u (f x x') v, zs)


lub            :: Zipper a → Maybe a
lub (Nd _ x _, _) = Just x
lub (Lf, cxt)     = lubCxt cxt
   where  lubCxt []            = Nothing
          lubCxt (L x _ : zs) = Just x
          lubCxt (R _ _ : zs) = lubCxt zs
```

Fig. 2. Splay Tree Operations

5   Conclusion

What have we achieved? We have developed two algorithms solving the nearest shelters problem. The first algorithm uses a list homomorphism to achieve $O(n \log n)$ complexity. It processes the inputs through the X-axis, while sweeps and combines the results of recursive calls through the Y-axis.

The second algorithm is a new application of thinning. Elements in the thinned set possess a familiar structure: for each Y we keep only the best sum, and the sum increases with Y. Sets maintained in a number of thinning algorithms often possess the same structure (a typical example being the knapsack problem [5]). In those cases, however, thinning is used to asymptotically reduce the number of solutions, allowing (pseudo) linear-time massive updates. For our problem, the same property is exploited to organise solutions in a tree, thus allowing logarithm time query and thinning. We are interested to see more examples like this.

Our derivations fit into the niche category of cute, little calculations suitable to be presented as functional pearls. For the program derivation community, it might be interesting since it relates existing techniques, such as list homomorphism and thinning, to a new problem. More complex solutions to more general problems have been studied in the algorithm community. Bentley, in his study of multidimensional divide-and-conquer [1], very briefly described in words a $O(n \log n)$ algorithm for finding, under Euclidean distance, nearest neighbours for all points on a two-dimensional plane. The algorithm is similar in structure to our first algorithm, although our sweeping and merging is much simplified by considering only Manhattan distance. Bentley claimed that the algorithm extends to k-dimensions with complexity $O(n \log^{k-1} n)$. Clarkson [4] and Gabow et al. [6] proposed $O(n \log \delta)$ deterministic algorithms, where δ is the ratio of maximum to minimum distances between the given points. Clarkson also proposed a $O(c^k n \log n)$ randomized algorithm, where k is the dimension and c is a constant. Vaidya [15] presented a deterministic algorithm that works for Minkowski distance — a generalisation of both Euclidean and Manhattan distance, with $O((ck)^k n \log n)$ worst-case complexity. The algorithms of Clarkson, Gabow and Vaidya make use of *cell trees*, which partitions the plane into square-sized cells, each cell storing information about useful neighbour cells, while allowing efficient querying. It remains to see whether these algorithms can be derived or proved in a calculational manner.

References

1. Bentley, J.L.: Multidimensional divide-and-conquer. Communications of the ACM 23(4), 214–229 (1980)
2. Bird, R.S., de Moor, O.: Algebra of Programming. International Series in Computer Science. Prentice Hall (1997)
3. Chin, W.-N., Hu, Z.: Towards a modular program derivation via fusion and tupling. In: Batory, D., Blum, A., Taha, W. (eds.) GPCE 2002. LNCS, vol. 2487, pp. 140–155. Springer, Heidelberg (2002)
4. Clarkson, K.L.: Fast algorithms for the all nearest neighbors problem. In: Synder, L. (ed.) Foundations of Computer Science, pp. 226–232. IEEE Computer Society Press (1983)
5. de Moor, O.: A generic program for sequential decision processes. In: Hermenegildo, M., Swierstra, S.D. (eds.) PLILP 1995. LNCS, vol. 982, pp. 1–23. Springer, Heidelberg (1995)
6. Gabow, H.N., Bentley, J.L., Tarjan, R.E.: Scaling and related techniques for geometry problems. In: DeMillo, R.A. (ed.) Theory of Computing, pp. 135–143. ACM Press (1984)
7. Gibbons, J.: The third homomorphism theorem. Journal of Functional Programming 6(4), 657–665 (1996)
8. Gries, D., Schneider, F.B.: A Logical Approach to Discrete Math. Springer (October 22, 1993)

9. Hu, Z., Iwasaki, H., Takeichi, M.: Construction of list homomorphisms via tupling and fusion. In: Penczek, W., Szałas, A. (eds.) MFCS 1996. LNCS, vol. 1113, pp. 407–418. Springer, Heidelberg (1996)
10. Huet, G.: The zipper. Journal of Functional Programming 7(5), 549–554 (1997)
11. Morihata, A., Koishi, M., Ohori, A.: Dynamic programming via thinning and incrementalization. In: Codish, M., Sumii, E. (eds.) FLOPS 2014. LNCS, vol. 8475, pp. 186–202. Springer, Heidelberg (2014)
12. Mu, S.-C., Lyu, Y.-H., Morihata, A.: Constructing datatype-generic fully polynomial-time approximation schemes using generalised thinning. In: Oliveira, B.C.d.S., Zalewski, M. (eds.) Workshop on Generic Programming, pp. 97–108. ACM Press (2010)
13. Sasano, I., Hu, Z., Takeichi, M., Ogawa, M.: Make it practical: A generic linear-time algorithm for solving maximum-weightsum problems. In: Odersky, M., Wadler, P. (eds.) International Conference on Functional Programming, pp. 137–149. ACM Press (2000)
14. Tarjan, R.E.: Amortized computational complexity. SIAM Journal on Algebraic and Discrete Methods 6(2), 306–318 (1985)
15. Vaidya, P.M.: An $O(n \log n)$ algorithm for the all-nearest-neighbors problem. Discrete and Computational Geometry 4(2), 101–115 (1989)

A Proof of Lemma 1

Lemma: If $x >_Y y$ for all $(x, z) \in xss$, we have

$$sweep\ xs\ (y : ys) = (id \times (y \sqcap_{\leq_+}))\ (sweep\ xs\ ys).$$

Proof. The proof is routine and we sketch an outline here. The main proof is:

$$
\begin{aligned}
& sweep\ xs\ (y : ys) \\
= \ & (map\ (minWithin\ (setify\ (y : ys)))\ xs, min_{\leq_+}\ (y : ys)) \\
= \ & \{\ \text{by (7), see below}\ \} \\
& (map\ (minWithin\ (setify\ ys))\ xs, min_{\leq_+}\ (y : ys)) \\
= \ & \{\ \text{definition of } min\ \} \\
& (map\ (minWithin\ (setify\ ys))\ xs, y \sqcap_{\leq_+} min_{\leq_+}\ ys) \\
= \ & \{\ \text{definition of } sweep\ \} \\
& (id \times (y \sqcap_{\leq_+}))\ (sweep\ xs\ ys).
\end{aligned}
$$

In the second step we need this property: if $x >_Y y$ for all $(x, z) \in xs$, we have

$$map\ (minWithin\ (setify\ (y : ys)))\ xs = map\ (minWithin\ (setify\ ys))\ xs, \quad (7)$$

which follows from a corresponding property for $minWithin$: for all x, y, z, and ys,

$$minWithin\ (setify\ (y : ys))\ (x, z) = minWithin\ (setify\ ys)\ (x, z), \qquad (8)$$

provided that $x >_Y y$. The proof of (8) goes:

$$minWithin \; (setify \; (y:ys)) \; (x,z)$$
$$= \; (x, z \sqcap_{\leq_x} min_{\leq_+} \; (filter \; (x\uparrow) \; (y:ys)))$$
$$= \quad \{ \text{ since } x >_Y y \; \}$$
$$(x, z \sqcap_{\leq_x} min_{\leq_+} \; (filter \; (x\uparrow) \; ys))$$
$$= \; minWithin \; (setify \; ys) \; (x,z).$$

B Proof of (6)

To formally prove (6), we need more machineries of relational calculus which we cannot fully explain here. Readers are referred to [2]. Relationally, *filter p* can be seen as lifting a coreflexive relation $p?$ to a function on sets, written $Ep?$ can bee The aim is to prove that $Ep? \circ thin \; Q \subseteq thin \; Q \circ Ep?$. According to the universal property of *thin*, we have $R \subseteq thin \; Q \circ ES$ if and only if

$$\in \circ R \; \subseteq \; S \circ \in \; \wedge$$
$$R \circ \ni \circ S^\circ \; \subseteq \; \ni \circ Q.$$

The two proof obligations are discharged below:

$$\in \circ \; Ep? \circ thin \; Q$$
$$= \quad \{ \text{ definition of } E \; \}$$
$$p? \circ \in \circ thin \; Q$$
$$\subseteq \quad \{ \text{ definition of } thin \; \}$$
$$p? \circ \in \circ \in\backslash\in$$
$$\subseteq \; p? \circ \in.$$

$$Ep? \circ thin \; Q \circ \ni \circ p?$$
$$\subseteq \quad \{ \text{ definition of } thin \; \}$$
$$Ep? \circ \ni \circ Q \circ p?$$
$$= \quad \{ \text{ definition of } E \; \}$$
$$\Lambda(p? \circ \in) \circ \ni \circ Q \circ p?$$
$$\subseteq \quad \{ \text{ since } Q \circ p? \subseteq p? \circ Q \; \}$$
$$\Lambda(p? \circ \in) \circ \ni \circ p? \circ Q$$
$$\subseteq \quad \{ \text{ since } \Lambda R \circ R^\circ \subseteq \ni \; \}$$
$$\ni \circ Q.$$

The property $Q \circ p? \subseteq p? \circ Q$ is a point-free way of saying that, for all x and y, $p \; y \wedge x \, Q \, y \; \Rightarrow \; p \; x$.

Suppl: A Flexible Language for Policies

Robert Dockins and Andrew Tolmach

Dept. of Computer Science Portland State University Portland, Oregon, USA

Abstract. We present the Simple Unified Policy Programming Language (Suppl), a domain-neutral language for stating, executing, and analyzing event-condition-action policies. Suppl uses a novel combination of pure logic programming and disciplined imperative programming features to make it easy for non-expert users to express common policy idioms. The language is strongly typed and moded to allow static detection of common programming errors, and it supports a novel logic-based static analysis that can detect internally inconsistent policies. Suppl has been implemented as a compiler to Prolog and used to build several network security applications in a Java framework.

1 Introduction

Many computing systems incorporate *policies* that specify how the system should respond to events. Policies are used to define, e.g., who may access protected web sites, how to categorize arriving emails, or what to do when the temperature in boiler #2 exceeds safe limits. Because policies change over time, designers often provide a mechanism to express them separately from the main body of implementation code. This mechanism might be simple, like configuration parameters accessed by a GUI (e.g., your email client); but it may be a non-trivial external language in its own right (e.g., configuration files for a Cisco router). A dedicated policy language allows relatively non-technical users to write and review policies without understanding the underlying code. It may also support automatic analysis of policies for properties such as consistency or completeness.

Many existing policy languages evolved in the context of particular applications or execution environments and hence are domain-specific, "baking in" concepts related to, say, networks or access control. However, policy languages often share common basic requirements and structures. This raises a natural challenge: can we define a *domain-neutral* policy language suitable for use in a wide variety of applications? Moreover, existing policy languages often appear very ad-hoc: they typically lack control abstractions, types, and support for modularity. This raises another challenge: can we improve on these languages by applying ideas from *programming language design*?

Suppl, the Simple Unified Policy Programming Language, is our attempt to address these challenges.[1] Suppl is designed to describe the large class of policies known as *event-condition-action (ECA)* policies. The ECA paradigm, originally

---

[1] http://web.cecs.pdx.edu/~rdockins/suppl/

J. Garrigue (Ed.): APLAS 2014, LNCS 8858, pp. 176–195, 2014.

developed in the context of active databases [10], is based on an event-handling loop. When an external stimulus generates an event, the policy evaluates conditions based on the current state of the world and its internal memory and decides what actions to take. SUPPL uses a novel combination of (pure) predicates from logic programming, used to describe conditions, and imperative event handlers, which generate actions. Both parts work together to make expressing common policy idioms simple and understandable. The SUPPL language is parameterized over the vocabulary of events and actions needed for a particular domain. These are provided by an ambient execution environment (coded in a conventional language) which triggers calls into SUPPL when an event occurs and interprets the action directives that SUPPL returns.

SUPPL is strongly typed, strongly moded, and locally stateless. These features are designed to make SUPPL programs easy to reason about and to facilitate the early detection of errors. Despite its locally stateless properties, SUPPL is capable of expressing stateful policies by making controlled use of *data tables* that provide a principled point of interaction between the stateless logic-programming core and the imperative event-handling language.

SUPPL is also designed to allow easy combination of distinct policy units, perhaps written by different people. Both predicates and event handlers can be easily extended by additional, textually separate, clauses. However, these features make it possible to write policies that are incoherent—for example, an access control policy might generate both "allow" and "deny" actions in response to a request event. To report such possible inconsistencies, we have developed a novel logic-based static analysis called *conflict detection*, which is only feasible because we have a carefully-designed language specifically for policies.

SUPPL has been implemented as a compiler generating Prolog code, which runs in a Java execution environment that provides the realizations of events and actions. On top of this implementation we have built two network security applications. The first is a prototype active network firewall built on the Linux netfilter stack, in which connection attempts are mediated by a SUPPL policy. The second is the SOUND platform [9], which uses active sensing to detect misbehavior on networks and introduction-based-routing [13] to control access. SUPPL can be used to define various aspects of policy in this system, for example, what remedial actions to take when misbehavior is detected.

The detailed contributions of this paper are as follows:

- A tutorial introduction to SUPPL from the viewpoint of a policy author, using a simple example (§2).
- A novel approach to integrating pure predicates and stateful event handlers (§3.1).
- The static type and mode system used for predicates, which is both simple and practical (§3.2).
- Conflict detection analysis, which combines control-flow analysis and automated provers to find potential inconsistencies in policies (§4).
- An implementation of SUPPL, using a Java-based runtime system (§5).

2   Suppl by Example

SUPPL is our attempt to build a general-purpose policy language as described in the introduction. It explicitly embraces the ECA paradigm; events and actions are primitive concepts in the language, and event handlers are the fundamental construct for initiating computation. Conditions are another bedrock concept: the main programming abstraction in SUPPL is the predicate, similar to that found in logic programming languages like Prolog. Unlike Prolog, the SUPPL predicate language is pure (no side effects), strongly typed and strongly moded. Event handlers are written in a separate imperative vocabulary designed to make expressing policy decisions as natural as possible.

To illustrate SUPPL, we will examine an extended example. Suppose we are writing a policy for a system that controls door locks in a secure facility. A person requests a door to open by using their keycard; the system decides to accept the request and open the door, or to deny the request and leave the door locked. The system is also capable of raising an alarm, which will cause security personnel to head to the area to investigate.

Primitives. We can model these concepts in SUPPL in a few lines; see Listing 1, lines 1–8. We declare person, scanner, location and door to be primitive types. These types will have some concrete implementation in the security system, but they are treated as opaque by SUPPL. We also declare an event open_door_request, indicating that someone has used a keycard scanner and requested a door to be opened, and two actions the system can take in response: open_door and dispatch_security. These declarations (together with the other primitive declarations) form the interface between the policy and the system being governed. Note that a policy may decide to do *nothing* in response to an event; for this door lock setting, this constitutes a request denial.

On line 10 we declare that the open_door and dispatch_security actions are in *conflict*. This is our way to state our intention that a single policy event should not elicit both actions. Conflict declarations will come into play when we discuss conflict analysis later.

To define any interesting policies regarding this security system, we need to have some operations that allow us to examine the properties of the opaque types. For example, we need to know which scanners govern which doors, where the scanners are, and the location to which the scanner gates access. Lines 12–14 of Listing 1 declare three functions from the opaque type scanner to doors and locations. It will eventually be the responsibility of the security system to implement these operations. Finally, we need to know who is allowed to be where. Line 16 introduces a *predicate*, authorized_loc, which represents a relation between persons and locations. For now, we leave unspecified how authorizations are determined; thus the predicate is declared primitive. The in keyword is related to the mode system and indicates that uses of this predicate must pass both arguments in; modes are discussed in more detail below.

```
1   primitive type person.
2   primitive type scanner.
3   primitive type location.
4   primitive type door.
5
6   event open_door_request(person, scanner).
7   action open_door(door).
8   action dispatch_security(location).
9
10  conflict open_door(_), dispatch_security(_).
11
12  primitive function scan_door(scanner) yields door.
13  primitive function scan_loc(scanner) yields location.
14  primitive function scan_gates(scanner) yields location.
15
16  primitive predicate authorized_loc(person in, location in).
17
18  handle open_door_request(?P, ?S) =>
19    query
20    | authorized_loc(P, scan_loc(S)) =>
21      query
22      | authorized_loc(P,scan_gates(S)) =>
             open_door(scan_door(S));
23      | _ => skip;
24      end;
25    | _ => dispatch_security(scan_loc(S));
26    end;
27  end.
```

Listing 1. A simple door security policy

Event Handler Now we can define a simple event handler for the security system (lines 18–27). This handler says how to respond to an open_door_request event. Like every event handler, it starts by naming the event to be handled and binding the event arguments; the ?P form indicates a variable binding. The main body of the handler consists of a query statement with two branches. Each branch consists of a logical query on the left of the => symbol and a list of statements on the right. The first branch is entered if the person P is authorized to be where they are now, i.e., in the location where the scanner is; otherwise the second branch is entered and security is dispatched to that location. In the first branch, another query is run to see if person P is allowed on the far side of the door. If so, the door is opened; otherwise, the request is denied. In general, a query construct may have many branches; the queries are attempted in order and (only) the first one to succeed is executed. The underscore represents a trivial query that always succeeds, and skip is a command that has no effect. If no branch of a query construct succeeds, nothing happens. Thus, the query branch on line 23 is redundant and could be eliminated without changing the meaning of the program.

Authorization. Suppose we want to define the predicate authorized_loc instead of making it a primitive. To do this, we remove the primitive keyword from its declaration and we specify rules that define when the predicate holds. The syntax for rules is quite similar to Prolog syntax. In particular, we adopt the Prolog lexical convention that variables begin with uppercase letters and program identifiers begin with lowercase letters.

Listing 2, lines 1–9, uses two rules to define the `authorized_loc` predicate in terms of some new, lower-level, primitives. (Note: for space reasons we have not repeated lines 1–14 of Listing 1.) A rule consists of a single predicate applied to some arguments followed by the : − symbol and a comma-separated list of clauses. A rule should be read as an implication from right to left. Thus, the rule `authorized_loc(P,L) :− public_space(L)` means that "for all P and L, if L is a public space then P is authorized to be in L." When multiple clauses are separated by a comma, all must hold. So the second rule means that P is authorized to be in L if P belongs to some group G that owns L. Finally, the meaning of the predicate `authorized_loc` is the disjunction of all the right-hand-sides of its rules. So, `authorized_loc` holds if either of its two rule bodies hold.

The overall effect of this policy will be to allow persons into and out of areas that are public or for which they are members of an owning group. If someone gets into an area for which they are not authorized (by tailgating someone else, say) then security will be notified if they try to leave by using a keycard scanner.

Detecting repeated failures. Now, suppose we want to prevent someone from doing a trial-and-error scan with their keycard; that is, we don't want people to be able to map out which doors are opened by a keycard by simply trying all of them and seeing which ones open. Such a pattern of use might occur if a keycard is stolen and the thief doesn't know what doors it opens. One way to mitigate this risk is to keep track of failed open attempts. If too many failed attempts happen within a short time frame, we want to dispatch security to investigate.

To do this, we need to keep some state about failed requests. SUPPL is, by design, locally stateless, so there are no mutable references or data structures we can manipulate within queries to keep track of this information. Instead, SUPPL includes a concept of *data tables*, which provide a principled way to implement stateful policies. From the point of view of the logic programming query language, tables are just another predicate that may be used in rules. However, the imperative event handling language has commands that insert and delete rows from tables.

Suppose we want to trigger an alarm if more than five failed attempts are made by a single person within an hour. To keep track of the required data, we set up a table and write an event handler to populate it (see Listing 2 lines 11–21). Table declarations are similar in most ways to predicate declarations; the columns of the table are given as an ordered tuple of types, just as for predicates. However, unlike predicates, tables behave much like the tables of a relational database: tuples are added and removed from tables explicitly rather than by defining rules. The `key` clause declares the table's primary key. The mode keywords following `key` indicate which columns form the table's primary key: columns declared with the mode `in` are in the primary key and those declared with mode `out` are not.

```
1  predicate authorized_loc(person in, location in).
2
3  authorized_loc(P,L)  :- public_space(L).
4  authorized_loc(P,L)  :- group_owns(G,L), group_member(P,G).
5
6  primitive type group.
7  primitive predicate public_space(location in).
8  primitive predicate group_owns(group in, location in).
9  primitive predicate group_member(person in, group out).
10
11 table failed_attempts(person, scanner, eventid)
12    key (in,in,in) lifetime 3600000.
13 index failed_attempts(in, out, out).
14
15 handle open_door_request(?P, ?S) =>
16   query
17   | authorized_loc(P, scan_gates(S)) => skip;
18   | _ => queue insert (P, S, current_event)
19            into failed_attempts;
20   end;
21 end.
22
23 predicate excessive_failures(person in).
24 excessive_failures(P)  :-
25   findall(EID,failed_attempts(P,_,?EID),RS), set_size(RS) >=
          5.
26
27 handle open_door_request(?P, ?S) =>
28   query
29   | authorized_loc(P, scan_loc(S)) =>
30     query
31     | authorized_loc(P, scan_gates(S)) =>
32         open_door(scan_door(S));
33     | excessive_failures(P) =>
34         dispatch_security(scan_loc(S));
35     end;
36   | _ => dispatch_security(scan_loc(S));
37   end;
38 end.
```

Listing 2. A more complicated door security policy

Every table will contain at most one row for the values in the primary key. If a new row is inserted with the same values for all primary key columns as a row already in the table, the old row will be evicted and the new row will replace it. Tables also have an optional lifetime argument that indicates how many milliseconds each row should remain in the table from the time it was inserted (3600000 milliseconds corresponds to one hour). The eventid type is a built-in type that is used to give a unique identifier to each event occurrence.

The index declaration indicates that we intend to query this table by supplying the first column as an argument; the index declaration both interacts with the mode system (described below) and also suggests to the implementation that building an index for this table on its first column would be worthwhile. Unlike the primary key, a table index does not impose any uniqueness constraints.

Despite the strong similarities between SUPPL tables and the relational tables of a typical RDBMS, their use cases are rather different. SUPPL tables are primarily intended to store short-term, "soft" data; the SUPPL runtime holds table data in memory and makes no persistence guarantees about it. Restarting the SUPPL runtime will clear all table data. It should be possible to have SUPPL data tables backed instead by a persistent RDBMS; however, a reasonable semantics for interacting with external RDBMSs seems to require distributed transaction support in the general case. We hope to examine these issues in future work.

Now we write an event handler that inserts a row into failed_attempts whenever an unauthorized person attempts to enter a gated area (Lines 15–21). It is normal in SUPPL to have more than one handler for a given event; when that event occurs, *all* its handlers will be run. The query illustrates the use of sequential evaluation to implement a form of negation. If the person is authorized, the first query branch succeeds and the handler does nothing; otherwise, the second branch is executed and the insertion is performed. The primitive current_event function returns the eventid corresponding to the event currently being handled. The result of this pattern is that we get a sliding window view of all the failed open attempts that have occurred in the last hour.

Note that the command to insert a row is written queue insert: this indicates that the insert does not happen immediately. Instead, it occurs after all handlers for the current event have completed. This is to ensure that there are no complicated and difficult-to-debug interactions between separately-defined event handlers. State changes are queued up and executed after all handers are finished, so that the next event that occurs will see the updated table state.

Now we can write the excessive_failures predicate that holds if a person has amassed too many failed attempts (lines 23–25). This predicate holds on a person P who has five or more distinct failed door-open event identifiers in the failed_attempts table. The excessive_failures predicate relies on the primitive findall construct, which calculates a set of all the solutions to a given query. Here we use it to get a result set whose size we can then calculate using the built-in set_size function. As used here, the findall can be rendered as "find all instances of EID such that P is related to EID (for some ignored scanner value) in the failed events table; place the result set in variable RS." In contrast to every other predicate construct, findall has explicit variable binding. Variables bound in the second argument (the search goal) may appear in the first argument. Using this predicate, we can now replace our original event handler (Listing 1 lines 17–27) with one that also responds to excessive_failures (Listing 2 lines 27–38).

3   Suppl in Detail

SUPPL's design attempts to balance competing objectives: simplicity, expressivity, support for early detection of errors, and ease of combining separately-written policies. The use of logic programming, for example, is driven both by the need for expressivity (realistic policy conditions are naturally expressed using logic programming rules) and to make it easy to combine policies. As compared to procedures or functions, it is easy to extend the functionality of predicates by adding new rules. In the interests of both simplicity and expressivity, we allow arbitrary recursive predicates to be written, which makes the language Turing-complete. Event handling is likewise easy to extend by adding new handlers—event handling logic does not have to be collected together in a single place.

A slightly simplified syntax for SUPPL is presented in Figure 1. For lack of space, we do not give full explanations of all the language's constructs, but instead focus on the most important and novel. There are four major syntactic classes: terms, clauses, handler bodies and declarations. Terms represent data values, clauses are used to define predicates, and handler bodies are used to implement handlers and procedures. A SUPPL program consists of a set of declarations, which are used both to provide static information to the compiler (declaring types and modes for predicates, functions, etc.) and to implement the policy (rules, event handlers, procedure definitions). Terms are quite similar to those of Prolog, with the addition of the variable binding form ?A (used inside handler bodies to make variable bindings explicit), and of tuple data structures. Clauses also take inspiration from Prolog; the main syntactic difference is that disjunction is written with a vertical bar rather than with the traditional semicolon. The operational semantics of the logic programming core of SUPPL can be understood in a standard way, as performing selective linear definite clause (SLD) resolution [18] with negation-as-failure [7]. The parts of SUPPL that cannot be understood by analogy to standard logic programming concepts are covered in further detail below.

3.1   Event Handlers

The primary interface between a SUPPL policy and the system it governs is defined by *events* and *actions*. These are declared as distinguished identifiers carrying some number of data arguments. Their meaning is determined entirely by the surrounding execution environment.

Program execution is always initiated by an event and events happen when the system being governed wishes to interrogate the policy. When an event occurs, every event handler in the program matching the event is executed and the set (possibly empty) of all resulting actions is collected together to be passed to the surrounding execution environment. The execution environment is responsible for executing these actions, as well as for implementing all declared primitive functions and predicates. The SUPPL semantics assumes that the execution of primitive functions and predicates is side-effect free. SUPPL is "locally stateless," which means the only state in SUPPL is in the data tables, and they do not change during the execution of the handlers for a single event. Instead, the effects of any queue insert or queue delete statements are delayed until after all handlers for the event have completed.

$d ::=$ Declaration

| primitive type $\langle$id$\rangle$.   prim type decl
| type $\langle$id$\rangle$:= t .   type decl
| data $\langle$id$\rangle$ ::= $\langle$id$\rangle(t_1, \cdots, t_m)$ | $\cdots$ | $\langle$id$\rangle(t_1, \cdots, t_n)$.   data type decl
| event $\langle$id$\rangle(t_1, \cdots, t_n)$.   event decl
| action $\langle$id$\rangle(t_1, \cdots, t_n)$.   action decl
| conflict $\langle$id$_1\rangle(t_1, \cdots, t_n), \langle$id$_2\rangle(t_1, \cdots, t_m)$ (=> c)? .   conflict decl
| procedure $\langle$id$\rangle(t_1, \cdots, t_n)$.   procedure decl
| primitive function$\langle$id$\rangle$ $(t_1, \cdots, t_n)$ yields t .   prim function decl
| (primitive)? predicate $\langle$id$\rangle(t_1\ o_1?, \cdots, t_n\ o_n?)$.   predicate decl
| mode $\langle$id$\rangle(o_1, \cdots, o_n)$.   mode decl
| table $\langle$id$\rangle(t_1, \cdots, t_n)$ key $(o_1, \cdots, o_n)$ (lifetime $\langle$int$\rangle$)? .   table decl
| index $\langle$id$\rangle(o_1, \cdots, o_n)$.   index decl
| g :- c .   rule
| handle $\langle$id$\rangle(?X_1, \cdots, ?X_n)$ => b end.   event handler
| define procedure $\langle$id$\rangle(?X_1, \cdots, ?X_n)$:= b end.   procedure defn
| axiom c .   axiom decl
| lemma c .   lemma decl

$b ::=$ Handler Body

| $b_1\ b_2$ sequence
| $\langle$id$\rangle(m_1, \cdots, m_n)$;   procedure or action
| queue insert$(m_1, \cdots, m_n)$ into $\langle$id$\rangle$;   table insert
| queue delete$(m_1, \cdots, m_n)$ from $\langle$id$\rangle$;   table delete
| skip;   noop
| query | c_1 => b_1 $\cdots$ | c_n => b_n end;   multibranch query
| foreach c => b end;   foreach query

$t ::=$ Type $o ::=$ Mode

| $\langle$id$\rangle$ named type | in | out | ignore
| $X, Y, Z, \cdots$ type variables
| list(t) list $g ::= \langle$id$\rangle(m_1, \cdots, m_n)$ Goal
| set(t) finite set
| map(t_1, t_2) finite map $m ::=$ Term
| $t_1 * \cdots * t_n$ tuple type
| number   numeric type | "literal", $\cdots$ strings
| string   string type | 10, 3.14, 2.9e8, $\cdots$ numbers
                                                           | $X, Y, Z, \cdots$ variables
                                                           | $?X, ?Y, ?Z, \cdots$ var bindings
$c ::=$ Clause | _   anonymous var
                                                           | $\langle$id$\rangle(m_1, \cdots, m_n)$ function call
| $m_1 = m_2$ | $m_1 <> m_2$ (dis)equality | $m_1 + m_2$ | $m_1 - m_2$ numeric ops
| $m_1 <= m_2$ | $m_1 < m_2$ comparisions | $m_1 * m_2$ | m_1/m_2
| $m_1 >= m_2$ | $m_1 > m_2$ | $\sim m$ negative
| $\langle$id$\rangle(m_1, \cdots, m_n)$ predicate | [ ]   empty list
| $c_1 | c_2$ disjunction | $[m_1, \cdots, m_n]$ concrete list
| c_1, c_2 conjunction | $[m_1 | m_2]$ list cons cell
| not c negation | $(m_1, \cdots, m_n)$ tuple
| c_1 -> c_2 implication
| findall(m, g, X) find all

Fig. 1. Simplified syntax of SUPPL

All program execution is event-driven, and the event handler serves as the entry point for Suppl programs. The body of an event handler is a sequence of statements, which may be actions, commands to manipulate data tables, query evaluations, or foreach invocations. Event handlers can also invoke user-defined procedures that abstract over common sequences of statements.

The query construct, illustrated by several examples in §2, consists of a series of branches, each guarded by a query into the core logic-programming part of the language; the branch corresponding to (just) the first successful query is executed. This behavior captures a common idiom that is inconvenient to express in pure logic programming (without cut).

The foreach construct foreach some_pred(A,?B)=> ... end; is an iterator: it asks the system to find all values for B such that some_pred(A,B) is true, and executes its body once for each instantiation found.

3.2   Predicates, Types, and Modes

Unlike Prolog, Suppl predicates are pure (they lack both side-effects and non-logical constructs, like cut), well-typed and well-moded. Types and modes are primarily intended to help with early detection of errors. They make large classes of "shallow" errors (e.g., mixing up argument order) detectable at compile time. A strong typing discipline also makes it easier to interface with SMT solvers for discovering deeper program properties (see §4). Our type and mode systems are similar to those of Mercury [22] and HAL [14], but significantly simpler.

Types built in to the system include number and string. There are also built-in polymorphic type operators list, (finite) set and (finite) map. Users may also declare recursive algebraic datatypes for generating arbitrary tree-shaped data structures. Every predicate in a Suppl program must be declared, giving the number and types of its arguments.

Modes indicate which arguments of a predicate are inputs and which are considered outputs. For example, the predicate call member([1,2,3,4], 2) asks the question: "does the list [1,2,3,4] contain the value 2?" Both arguments are used in input mode. On the other hand, the call member([1,2,3,4],N) asks the system to *find* all values for N (four in this case) that make the statement true. Here we are using the second argument in output mode. Not all modes make sense for a given predicate. The call member(L, 5) asks the system to find all lists L that contain value 5; there is no obvious algorithm for doing this, so member can not be used with its first argument in output mode.

As with types, the modes of all predicates in a Suppl program must be declared. For example, we can express the allowed modes for the member predicate by writing:

```
mode member(in, in).
mode member(in, out).
```

The rules of predicates are checked to ensure they respect the specified modes by reordering the body of each rule (if necessary) so that every variable is instantiated before it is used. Variables get instantiated by being passed in as formal arguments to a predicate rule, by being generated as outputs from predicate calls, or via the equality operator. Mode checking ensures that every predicate can be implemented as a nondeterministic program manipulating only ground data (i.e., containing no unbound variables) and ensures that "instantiation errors" (which can happen in an ill-moded Prolog program) never occur.

4   Conflict Detection

Problem. The extensibility of predicates and event handlers makes it easy to combine SUPPL code from multiple sources, but also makes it easy to write policies that are self-contradictory. The runtime environment must choose *some* action (even if that is to do nothing) in response to an incoherent policy outcome; but without further guidelines, any such choice is necessarily arbitrary.

Consider again the door-lock policy from section 2. The main event handler (see Listing 2 lines 27–38) opens the door if the requester is authorized both to be where he is *and* where he is going. Security is instead dispatched if the user is not authorized to be where he is. Now suppose we separately want to define a special class of persons that always have access to any door. One way to do this is to add the following predicate and handler. We assume the environment has some way to determine who currently has global privileges.

```
primitive predicate has_global_privileges(person in).

handle open_door_request(?P, ?S) =>
   query
   | has_global_privileges(P) => open_door(scan_gates(S));
   end;
end.
```

Each of these handlers make sense on their own, but in combination they can result in the policy both opening a door (because the requester has global access) and also dispatching security (because the requester is not authorized according to `authorized_loc`). Such a result is undesirable.

Solutions. One solution might be to layer an additional mechanism for dynamic conflict *resolution* on top of the basic policy language. For example, we might provide a way to assign priorities to actions, and say that higher-priority actions "win" in the event of a conflict. But the details of such an approach become complicated: it is hard to find a modular way to assign priorities (especially because ties must not be allowed), and it is not clear what to do about the actions that "lose." Dynamic conflict resolution can lead to fragile, inscrutable policies where minor-seeming changes have wide-ranging, poorly understood effects.

We would prefer instead to provide a tool that detects potential conflicts *statically*, so that the policy programmer can then use the existing facilities of the policy language to fix them before execution. Specifically, we focus on a static analysis that identifies control-flow paths through a policy that are initiated by the same event and lead to conflicting actions. The policy author declares what actions she considers conflicting by writing a conflict declaration, e.g., listing 1 line 10.

Let us examine the example conflict from above in more detail. For the conflict to occur there must be some event that triggers both handlers; thus, assume open_door_request(P,S) has occurred. The first handler must have control flow pass to one of the two branches that dispatches security. For now, let us consider only one of these, the one appearing in the outermost query construct. For this branch to activate, the previous branch must have failed, so authorized_location(P,scanner_loc(S)) is false. However, the proposition has_global_privileges(P) must hold for the other handler to issue the conflicting open_door verdict. To rule out this conflict, we must prove a contradiction under these assumptions. However, we cannot do this; nothing in the definition of authorized_location allows us to derive a contradiction. So our analysis should report a possible conflict between the two handlers.

We have developed a prototype conflict detection analysis for SUPPL that formalizes the line of reasoning outlined above. The analysis works in two phases. In the first phase, it identifies all the pairs of control-flow paths in the program that could possibly conflict. For each of these, it builds a formula in first-order logic that states what conditions would have to be true for the program to traverse both paths on a single event occurrence. In the second phase, these formulae are passed to an off-the-shelf SMT solver; we have experimented with Z3 [21], CVC4 [1] and Alt-Ergo [2]. If the solver can show the formula is unsatisfiable, we know the potential conflict cannot occur. Otherwise (if the solver finds a model or runs out of time), we report a potential conflict to the user.

We have designed the analysis to be sound, in the sense that it reports all potential conflicts. But to be useful in practice, it is crucial that the analysis also be as precise as possible, so that false positives are rare. Because SUPPL is Turing-complete, the analysis cannot be complete, in the sense that it only reports genuine conflicts: some false positives are inevitable. Moreover, the particular SMT solvers we use may have limitations that induce further imprecisions. However, although we are still in the early stages of working with our prototype, our initial results on precision are promising.

Generation of Conflict Formulae. The problem definitions that get fed to the external solver break down into two distinct parts. One part is the definition of predicates in the program, which we call the background theory. This theory is the same for all problem instances. The second part consists of a formula corresponding to a particular pair of potentially-conflicting control-flow paths.

Building the background theory follows well-known work in the semantics of logic programs with negation-as-failure. For each defined predicate, the analysis calculates the Clark completion [7], which is a standard way to render the semantics of a logic program into a formula of first-order logic. It essentially formalizes the idea that a predicate is defined by the disjunction of its rules, while taking care to bind variables in the places that give the desired meaning. In other words, the Clark completion defines a predicate to hold if and only if it is established by one of its rules. Primitive predicates are uninterpreted in the translation; that is, they are declared but not given any definition. The Clark completion procedure is sound (but not complete) with respect to Selective Linear Definite clause (SLD) resolution, the logical reasoning system underlying the operational semantics of Prolog and similar logic programming languages [18]. This means that every query answered by SLD resolution will be a model of the Clark completion. However, in some cases SLD resolution will fail to terminate even when the Clark completion has a model.

The soundness of Clark completion is sufficient for the soundness of our conflict analysis. Our analysis attempts to show that the Clark completion has *no* models corresponding to the control-flow paths in question; *a fortiori* a logic-programming language based on SLD resolution will fail to activate those control-flow paths. Consider, for example, the `authorized_loc` predicate, defined by the rules below.

```
authorized_loc(P,L)  :- public_space(L).
authorized_loc(P,L)  :- group_owns(G,L), group_member(P,G).
```

The Clark completion defines this predicate by the first-order formula below:

$$\forall P\ L.\ \texttt{authorized\_loc}(P, L) \leftrightarrow$$
$$\big(\texttt{public\_space}(L)\ \lor\ (\exists G.\ \texttt{group\_owns}(G, L) \land \texttt{group\_member}(P, G))\big)$$

Note that variables corresponding to the predicate arguments are quantified universally at the outside, whereas variables appearing only in the body are quantified existentially at the level of the rule. If a rule body contains a compound term instead of a variable, a new fresh variable is introduced and an equality is added to the rule body.

Next we examine the control-flow paths through the imperative event handlers so we can generate queries to send to an SMT solver. This is done via a recursive algorithm which, when given the syntax of a handler body, calculates a set of *potential conflicts*. A potential conflict consists of the following data: the name of the initiating event, the user-defined conflict clause that is involved, and control flow paths that lead from the initiating event to the conflicting actions. From a given control-flow path, we can determine what logical queries must have succeeded and failed for the control-flow path to be traversed. For example, if a control-flow path goes into a branch of a `query` construct, the logical predicates guarding that branch must hold; and furthermore, the logical predicates guarding any preceding branches in the `query` must fail.

For each potential conflict, we can construct a formula in first-order logic that represents the state of affairs that must exist for the potential conflict to actually occur. For the example above, the generated conflict formula is:

$$\exists P\ S.$$
$$\neg\texttt{authorized\_loc}(P, \texttt{scan\_loc}(S))\ \land\ \texttt{has\_global\_privileges}(P)$$

A potential conflict is *satisfiable* if the associated conflict formula is satisfiable, given the background theory of the associated logical predicates. Dually, a potential conflict is *unsatisfiable* if we can derive a contradiction by assuming the conflict formula; in other words, if it is logically impossible for the potential conflict to actually occur.

We have proved the soundness of our conflict analysis with respect to an idealized version of the semantics of SUPPL. In particular, we have proved that, for every actual conflict that occurs during the run of a SUPPL program, our analysis algorithm generates a satisfiable potential conflict. A straightforward corollary is: if all the potential conflicts generated by the conflict analysis are unsatisfiable, then the policy will produce no actual conflicts when executed. We lack here the space to discuss the conflict generation algorithm or its proof; details will appear in a forthcoming paper [23].

Asserting facts. Sometimes the conflict detection system will report a conflict where none exists because it has no way to analyze the policy primitives. Policy authors can communicate domain knowledge about the primitives to the analysis by using the `axiom` keyword. Any clause asserted as an axiom is assumed to be true and will be used by external provers during analysis. Of course, the user must be very careful only to assert axioms that actually hold; otherwise the correctness of the analysis will be compromised.

A policy author can also state a `lemma`; like axioms, lemmas are used by provers when trying to discharge proof obligations. However, the prover will also try to prove the lemma. In this way, the policy author can help guide provers toward finding useful facts they might not otherwise find in time, and also document the policy with properties that are expected to hold.

External Solver. To interface with back-end provers, we use the Why3 program verification system [4]. Why3 understands all the concepts we need to express SUPPL programs: first-order logic, recursive datatypes, parametric polymorphism, numbers, sets, etc. Why3 can translate all these concepts into forms that can be understood by back-end SMT solvers; in particular, Why3 knows how to perform the tricky transformations that are needed to remove parametric polymorphism, which is not supported natively by most SMT solvers (Alt-Ergo seems to be the sole exception [3]).

Once our conflict detection problems are exported in Why3 format, we can use the Why3 system to dispatch the problems to a variety of solvers, including: CVC4, Alt-Ergo, Z3, and many others. Problems may even be translated into a form suitable to manual proof in Coq or Isabelle/HOL, if desired.

Discussion. We cannot hope to have a complete procedure for finding conflicts, and false positives are inevitable. However, even if the problem were decidable, using SMT solvers means that, as a practical matter, we cannot expect to always get back answers in a reasonable amount of time. Nonetheless, our limited experience so far has given us promising results; CVC4 and Alt-Ergo both seem to do well at discharging the problem instances we build. We tested a number of different ways to resolve the conflict in our door lock policy from above (and for other similar policies); for each alternative we tried, a solver was able to prove the conflict could not occur using less than 1 second of runtime.

We do not yet have any data about how this analysis system scales to large policies. The number of potential conflicts is quadratic in the number of control-flow paths in a program, but this may be acceptable for realistic policies.

Conflict detection for policies is important in its own right. However, the potential applications for our analysis pipeline go further. For example, lemmas can be used simply to document properties of a policy that a user expects to be true; over time, as a policy is modified, if the lemma is falsified by some change, the analysis will indicate if the lemma can no longer be proved, indicating a problem. In future work we hope to explore other avenues for analysis, including liveness properties and data invariants.

5   Implementation

The implementation of SUPPL is divided into two parts: a compiler that translates SUPPL code into an executable Prolog policy; and a backend runtime system. The compiler is a standalone application written in Haskell, whereas the runtime is built on top of the tuProlog interpreter [11], which is written in Java. SUPPL is an open-source project; additional information may be found at the first author's home page.[2]

The most complicated tasks performed by the frontend compiler involve implementing the static type and mode disciplines. The type system is essentially a first-order variant of Hindley-Milner polymorphism. The type checking algorithm follows the main ideas of the classic type inference algorithm W [20].

The mode system is responsible for ensuring that each predicate defined in a policy respects its stated modes. Actually, the term "mode checking" is a slight misnomer, because each mode for a predicate causes different code to be generated. Mode checking works by literally rearranging the clauses of rules until data flows strictly from left to right. The mode checking algorithm is extremely naive—we simply explore all rearrangements of the rule body until we find one that satisfies the dataflow constraints. Although this takes worst-case time factorial in the number of clauses, it seems to perform well enough in practice.

As SUPPL is designed to be agnostic to the problem domain to which it is being applied, it is important that it be easy to extend the language with problem-specific programming facilities and to interface with an external system that generates the events and implements the actions returned by a SUPPL program. In order to make this interface as easy as possible and to support the basic logic-programming facilities need for SUPPL semantics, our runtime system for SUPPL is based on the tuProlog system [11], a Prolog interpreter written in Java, which has a well-designed external function interface. To implement SUPPL primitive functions and predicates simply requires writing a Java class containing methods with the correct names using the tuProlog's API, and arranging for the custom class to be loaded into the interpreter. The interpreter uses Java reflection to find the external functions and execute them as required.

---

[2] http://web.cecs.pdx.edu/~rdockins/suppl/

The executable part of SUPPL is deliberately quite similar to Prolog, and the mapping between SUPPL data structures and Prolog data structures is nearly trivial. The connection between the Java API and Prolog data structures is a little more distant, but the tuProlog API for manipulating Prolog terms is relatively easy to use. To get a flavor for the required interface programming, consider the following example file, which implements a simple primitive predicate named primOp at two different modes.

```
public class NewLibrary
    extends alice.tuprolog.Library {
    // in this case, the io mode implementation
    // also works for mode ii
    public boolean primOp_ii_2(Term arg1, Term arg2) {
      return primOp_io_2(arg1,arg2);
    }

    public boolean primOp_io_2(Term arg1, Term arg2) {
      arg1 = arg1.getTerm();

      // build some new term
      Struct x = new Struct("mkAsdf", arg1);

      // try to unify x with arg2
      return engine.unify(x, arg2);
    }
}
```

This Java code is sufficient to implement the following declared SUPPL primitive.

```
data asdf ::= mkAsdf(string).

primitive predicate primOp(string, asdf).
mode primOp(in,in).
mode primOp(in,out).
```

SUPPL data constructs, as well as action and event instances, are all represented directly as functor applications in Prolog; lists and numbers are handled natively by the Prolog system. Strings are interpreted in Prolog as atoms.

In the tuProlog API, the Struct class (a subclass of Term) represents atoms, lists and functor applications. Above, new Struct("mkAsdf",arg1) constructs a new Prolog functor instance with name mkAsdf and a single argument, represented by arg1. This maps directly onto a SUPPL term built using the mkAsdf data constructor. The class Number (also a Term subclass) is used to represent numeric values. Primitive SUPPL types can be represented by arbitrary Java objects. These objects will be passed around by reference inside the policy code; the runtime will make use only of basic Java Object methods, like equals and hashCode.

Using a Prolog interpreter in this way is a relatively heavyweight implementation strategy and will be unsuitable for applications requiring very frequent policy queries or which have tight real-time deadlines. So, it would almost certainly not be acceptable for, say, a firewall to query a SUPPL policy every time a packet arrives; however, it may be acceptable to query the policy every time a new connection is opened.

Here is some sample code showing how to set up the SUPPL runtime environment and load a custom library and interact with a loaded policy.

```
public static void main( String[] args )
  throws Exception {

    SupplEngine engine = RunPolicy.setupEngine();
    NewLibrary lib = new NewLibrary(engine);
    engine.loadLibrary(lib);
    RunPolicy.loadTheories(args, engine);

    Term[] evargs = new Term[] {
        new Struct( "string literal" ),
        new Int( 6 ) };
    Struct event = new Struct( "notification", evargs );

    List<Term> actions =
        RunPolicy.handleEvent(engine, event);

    for( Term t : actions ) {
      t = t.getTerm();
      System.out.println(t.toString());
    }
}
```

This sample code will load any compiled policy files given as command line arguments, feed a single synthetic event into the policy engine and print the resulting actions.

The result of this design is that it should be easy to integrate SUPPL-defined policies into existing Java applications whenever policy questions can be organized into the event-condition-action paradigm. In addition, only modest changes to the SUPPL compiler should be required to target other Prolog systems, which would allow SUPPL policies to integrate with applications written in languages other than Java.

6   Related Work

Here we survey existing work including both explicitly domain-neutral languages and languages that were designed for network security applications but can easily be generalized to broader domains.

Generic policy languages. The Policy Description Language (PDL) [19] is similar in many ways to SUPPL; it is based on the ECA policy paradigm, is influenced by logic programming ideas and is also designed with ease of analysis in mind. PDL has only one form of rule, which states that an event causes a particular action provided some condition holds. A significant difference from SUPPL is that PDL lacks any explicit notion of state; instead, time-varying policies can be written using rules that match on *event sets* that can examine events that occurred in the past. SUPPL event handlers can only examine the current event, but data tables allow a principled way to record information for later examination.

Ponder [8] is a language for expressing security policies interacting at various levels of the hardware/software stack: network firewalls, databases, Java runtime security. Ponder's approach to specifying policy is quite different to ours; it has a strongly-developed object model for roles, groups, membership, etc. and syntax for manipulating these objects. In contrast, SUPPL builds in nothing except primitive base types, and instead relies on the user (or a library author) to build a model of the problem domain in question.

Modern business rules management systems such as JRules [5] and Drools [17] include languages for defining arbitrary production rule systems that can be integrated into Java applications. While production rules have a declarative flavor, rule actions can actually contain arbitrary imperative code, and chaining among rules can cause complicated and opaque control flow logic. SUPPL enforces a more disciplined separation between conditions and actions.

Network security. The Authorization Specification Language (ASL) [16] is a language for expressing certain kinds of access control policies. Like SUPPL, it takes inspiration from logic programming constructs, and the primary act of programming in ASL involves writing various kinds of rules: authorization rules, access control rules, data integrity rules, etc. ASL allows users to express various kinds of conflict resolution metapolicies. ASL seems to lack any method for expressing stateful policies.

The Flow-based Management Language (FML) [15] is a declarative language for managing enterprise network configuration. An FML policy is expressed as a set of implication rules, based on nonrecursive DATALOG with negation. There is no internal notion of state. The language design is tailored to support efficient (linear time) evaluation. Conflicts can be resolved either by ordering rules or by assigning priorities to primitive actions.

Procera [24] is a domain specific language (embedded in Haskell) for expressing networking policy using the framework of functional reactive programming. In this framework, one defines a policy program (conceptually) as a time-varying function from an infinite stream of input events to a stream of output events. Aside from the quite different programming model, Procera's status as an embedded DSL makes it more difficult to build static analysis tools, as any analyses must be able to handle essentially all of the constructs of the host language, Haskell, a large general-purpose language in its own right.

Conflict detection and resolution. Conflict resolution has been studied in the context of PDL [6]. The PDL conflict resolution system allows users to declare the conditions under which a conflict occurs. At runtime, conflicts can be handled in a number of different ways by writing conflict monitors. These may resolve conflicts by choosing actions with higher priorities, by canceling all effects of the event causing the conflict, etc. Policy monitors are not expressible in PDL itself, but must be defined externally. SUPPL avoids the tricky issue of conflict *resolution* by passing it off instead to the external system we already assume must exist. Instead, we have concentrated our efforts on building a system to help users discover potential conflicts in their policies statically.

Dunlop et al. [12] present a system for both detecting and dynamically resolving policy conflicts. In their system, policies are stated using operators of deontic logic—in particular, modal operators for permission, prohibition and obligations. They propose a number of strategies for resolving conflicts at runtime (explicit priority values, new policy overrides old, specific policy overrides general, etc.) and suggest that no one strategy is appropriate for all uses.

7   Conclusion

SUPPL is a programming language designed from the ground up for expressing and reasoning about event-condition-action policies over arbitrary domains. It combines the power and simplicity of pure logic programming, used for describing conditions, with the flexibility and familiarity of imperative programming, used to connect events to actions. The language has been implemented and integrated into several Java-based network security applications. We are actively working to apply it in additional domains.

Perhaps the most important benefit of having a dedicated language for authoring policies is the opportunity to apply sophisticated static analyses to detect errors before a policy is fielded. We have developed a prototype of one such analysis, which discovers conflicts caused by inconsistent actions, making essential use of an external logic solver. As future work, we plan to extend this prototype—in particular, by improving the quality of feedback from the external solver to the programmer—and to apply the same approach to other static analyses, such as liveness or functional correctness.

Acknowledgments. This work was supported by the Air Force Research Laboratory under contract FA8650-11-C-7189. Any opinions, findings, and conclusions or recommendations expressed herein are those of the authors and do not necessarily reflect the views of the funding agency.

References

1. Barrett, C., Conway, C.L., Deters, M., Hadarean, L., Jovanović, D., King, T., Reynolds, A., Tinelli, C.: CVC4. In: Gopalakrishnan, G., Qadeer, S. (eds.) CAV 2011. LNCS, vol. 6806, pp. 171–177. Springer, Heidelberg (2011)
2. Bobot, F., Conchon, S., Contejean, E., Iguernelala, M., Lescuyer, S., Mebsout, A.: The Alt-Ergo automated theorem prover (2008), http://alt-ergo.lri.fr/
3. Bobot, F., Conchon, S., Contejean, E., Lescuyer, S.: Implementing Polymorphism in SMT solvers. In: Intl. Workshop on Satisfiability Modulo Theories (SMT). ACM International Conference Proceedings Series, vol. 367, pp. 1–5 (2008)

4. Bobot, F., Filliâtre, J.C., Marché, C., Paskevich, A.: Why3: Shepherd your herd of provers. In: Boogie 2011: Workshop on Intermediate Verification Languages, Wrocław, Poland, pp. 53–64 (August 2011)
5. Boyer, J., Mili, H.: Agile Business Rule Development. Springer (2011)
6. Chomicki, J., Lobo, J., Naqvi, S.: Conflict resolution using logic programming. IEEE Trans. on Knowl. and Data Eng. 15(1), 244–249 (2003)
7. Clark, K.L.: Negation as failure. In: Logic and Data Bases, pp. 293–322 (1977)
8. Damianou, N., Dulay, N., Lupu, E., Sloman, M.: The Ponder policy specification language. In: Sloman, M., Lobo, J., Lupu, E.C. (eds.) POLICY 2001. LNCS, vol. 1995, pp. 18–38. Springer, Heidelberg (2001)
9. DARPA: Safety On Untrusted Network Devices (SOUND) (2011), Mission-oriented Resilient Clouds (MRC) program: DARPA-BAA-11-55
10. Dayal, U., Hanson, E.N., Wisdom, J.: Active database systems. In: Modern Database Systems. ACM (1994)
11. Denti, E., Omicini, A., Ricci, A.: Multi-paradigm Java-Prolog integration in tuProlog. Sci. Comput. Program. 57(2), 217–250 (2005)
12. Dunlop, N., Indulska, J., Raymond, K.: Methods for conflict resolution in policy-based management systems. In: Intl. Conf. on Enterprise Distributed Object Computing. IEEE (2003)
13. Frazier, G., Duong, Q., Wellman, M.P., Petersen, E.: Incentivizing responsible networking via introduction-based routing. In: McCune, J.M., Balacheff, B., Perrig, A., Sadeghi, A.-R., Sasse, A., Beres, Y. (eds.) TRUST 2011. LNCS, vol. 6740, pp. 277–293. Springer, Heidelberg (2011)
14. Garcia de la Banda, M., Stuckey, P.J., Harvey, W., Marriott, K.: Mode checking in HAL. In: Lloyd, J. (ed.) CL 2000. LNCS (LNAI), vol. 1861, pp. 1270–1284. Springer, Heidelberg (2000)
15. Hinrichs, T.L., Gude, N.S., Casado, M., Mitchell, J.C., Shenker, S.: Practical declarative network management. In: Workshop on Research on Enterprise Networking, WREN 2009, pp. 1–10. ACM (2009)
16. Jajodia, S., Samarati, P., Subrahmanian, V.S.: A logical language for expressing authorizations. In: IEEE Symp. on Security and Privacy. IEEE (1997)
17. JBoss Drools Team: Drools documentation (2014), http://docs.jboss.org/drools/release/6.1.0.Final/drools-docs/html_single
18. Kowalski, R., Kuehner, D.: Linear resolution with selection function. Artificial Intelligence 2, 227–260 (1971)
19. Lobo, J., Bhatia, R., Naqvi, S.: A policy description language. In: AAAI Conf. on Artificial Intelligence. American Association for Artificial Intelligence (1999)
20. Milner, R.: A theory of type polymorphism in programming. J. Comput. Syst. Sci. 17, 348–375 (1978)
21. de Moura, L., Bjørner, N.: Z3: An efficient SMT solver. In: Ramakrishnan, C.R., Rehof, J. (eds.) TACAS 2008. LNCS, vol. 4963, pp. 337–340. Springer, Heidelberg (2008)
22. Somogyi, Z., Henderson, F., Conway, T.: The execution algorithm of Mercury: An efficient purely declarative logic programming language. Journal of Logic Programming 29(1-3), 17–64 (1996)
23. Trieu, A., Dockins, R., Tolmach, A.: Conflict analysis for SUPPL (in preparation, 2014)
24. Voellmy, A., Kim, H., Feamster, N.: Procera: A language for high-level reactive network control. In: HotSDN (2012)

A Method for Scalable and Precise Bug Finding Using Program Analysis and Model Checking

Manuel Valdiviezo, Cristina Cifuentes, and Padmanabhan Krishnan

Oracle Labs
Brisbane Australia
{manuel.valdiviezo,cristina.cifuentes,paddy.krishnan}@oracle.com

Abstract. This paper presents a technique for defect detection in large code bases called model-based analysis. It incorporates ideas and techniques from program analysis and model checking. Model checking, while very precise, is unable to handle large code bases that are in the millions of lines of code. Thus we create a number of abstract programs from the large code base which can all be model checked. In order to create these abstract programs, we first identify potential defects quickly via static analysis. Second we create a program slice containing one potential defect. Each slice is then abstracted using a combination of automatic data and predicate abstraction. This abstracted model is then model checked to verify the existence or absence of the defect. By applying model checking to a large number of small models instead of one single large model makes our approach scalable without compromising on precision.

We have applied our analysis to detect memory leaks and implemented it using aspects of the Parfait static code analysis tool and the SPIN model checker. Results show that our approach scales to large code bases and has good precision: the analysis runs over 1 million lines of non-commented C++ OpenJDK^{TM} source code in 1 hour and 19 minutes, with a precision of 84.5%. Further, our analysis found 62.2% more defects when compared to the dataflow approach used by Oracle Parfait's memory leak checker.

1 Introduction

In this paper we present a technique that combines abstraction and software model checking (SMC), which enables us to detect defects in large code bases. The motivation for this research is the need to develop automated defect finding techniques that are more accurate than purely static analysers and can be made to scale systems consisting of 1 million lines of uncommented code. The technique must also be able to report the results in a few hours on standard desktop machines. To be realistic, we do not demand completeness; thus the technique might miss a few defects. Hence we do *not* aim to verify the original program. But we require high precision (viz., a low false positive rate) as demanded by the consumers of our results. Our aim is to have a precision of more than 80%.

As we are looking for automated techniques, model checking is a potential starting point. Software model checking (SMC) technology is suitable for the

J. Garrigue (Ed.): APLAS 2014, LNCS 8858, pp. 196–215, 2014.
© Springer International Publishing Switzerland 2014

verification of small/medium code bases, up to the low thousands of lines of code. However, it cannot handle large code bases that have millions of lines of code [1].

The TACAS 2013 and 2014 competitions on software verification (http://sv-comp.sosy-lab.org/2013/results/ and http://sv-comp.sosy-lab.org/2014/results/) identify model-checkers that perform well on various benchmarks. All the benchmarks used in the competition are relatively small when compared with our needs. We were unable to use tools identified by them (such as LLBMC [2] or CBMC [3]) on our real code bases which have more than one million lines of uncommented code.

Abstraction [4,1] and bounded model checking [3] are two of the possible techniques to get a handle on such large code bases. In this paper we describe and demonstrate an effective abstraction (also called model generation) technique that can be combined with SMC. Our data and predicate abstraction is totally automatic unlike Bandera [4] which requires manual processing which is just not feasible on our large code bases. The main reason for the efficacy of our approach is the generation of multiple models for a given property. We ensure that each model has only one potential defect. Thus each model will be small enough to be verified using model checking very quickly. This is based on the observation that model checking works very well on small program and our aim is to run many invocations of the model checker on small models. To achieve this we use a defect-driven slicing and abstraction process.

The key steps in our approach are as follows.

1. Given a desired property, we identify all statements where a defect *could* occur. These statements form the list of potential defects.
2. For each potential defect we create a slice of the program that has only the relevant variables and conditions we want to check for.
3. Each slice is converted into a *specialised abstraction* using automatic data abstraction (i.e., discarding irrelevant values, or converting a range of values to a single value related to the property being checked for). Where automatic data abstraction is not possible, a suitable predicate abstraction (i.e., replacing predicates with boolean variables) is used. By using predicate abstraction only in limited contexts, we reduce the cost of predicate solving. This results in small models that are constructed quickly.
4. The resulting models are then verified against the desired property using a model checker.

The novel aspects in our approach include the use of automatic data and predicate abstraction to generate a number of, potentially small, models that can be model checked, and at the same time keeping sufficient information in the model so as to not require refinement based on any counter-example after the model-checking process.

While our approach is general, we use memory leaks as an example to demonstrate the generation of the set of abstractions. In order to handle other defect types, one has to specify a customised abstraction algorithm. This customisation can be based on our technique of using data and predicate abstraction.

The rest of the paper is organised as follows. In Section 2, we survey some related work. In Section 3, we present an example that illustrates our approach. In Section 4, we explain the technical details of our approach while in Section 5, we outline our implementation. In Section 6, we present our experimental results and conclude in Section 7.

2   Related Work

From a performance view point static analysers can be very effective at detecting defects; they often trade speed for accuracy. However, it is often the case that complex analyses are not scalable. ESP [5] represents a general techniques that could be applied to the detection of memory leaks. It uses property simulation to prune the number of paths explored by the analysis. It relies on encoding of temporal safety properties and, in principle, can be used to detect memory leaks. However, the results reported [6] appear to indicate that the approach is very sensitive to the input program. In the context of memory leaks, Sparrow [7] uses interprocedural but non-path-sensitive analysis. Sparrow took about 2 hours to process `binutils-2.13.1`, a small to medium sized program. Saber [8] uses sparse value-flow graph to represent def-use chains and value flows via assignments. Leaks are detected by performing a reachability analysis on this graph. The authors state that Saber is faster than Sparrow and also works on large systems such as `wine-0.9.24`. Unfortunately, these tools are not available and we have been unable to use them in our experimentation.

The idea of using slicing to reduce the complexity of analysis to speed up the verification process has been explored in recent times [9]. The scalability of such techniques is very much an open question, especially as they slice models which by definition are compact. Similarly [10] attempt to verify aspects of operating systems after code slicing. But they admit that they can use model checking only within a limited scope.

It is also possible to use SMT solvers on the slicing to remove false alarms (i.e., verify that the defect is not possible) [11]. However, the results provided by the authors indicate that SMT solvers are unlikely to scale. None of the programs considered are really large. In some cases the SMT solver did not terminate and in other cases it took more than 30 minutes. This appears to be related to the complexity of the path constraints that need to be solved.

SANTE [12] combines static and dynamic analysis to reduce the number of false positives. This is aimed mainly at test generation and they do not use model checking for defect detection. The key idea, like ours, is that slicing can reduce the size of the program that needs to be analysed.

There are numerous approaches to model checking and we summarise a few key ones here. Bandera is a SMC that allows the verification of user-defined properties in Java programs [4]. The checking process applies slicing to the program, user-guided data abstraction over the slice and the resulting abstracted version of the program is model checked. The major drawback of this approach is that user input is required for the data abstraction. Such a manual process is tedious and impossible to apply in practice in large code bases.

The Static Driver Verifier (SDV) [1], based on SLAM is an SMC for verifying user-defined properties on sequential C programs. C programs are abstracted using predicate abstraction with an initial set of predicates derived from the property. SDV then employs iterative counter-example guided abstraction refinement (CEGAR) to determine if the user-defined property is satisfied. However, the authors state that: "SLAM is unable to handle very large programs (with hundreds of thousands of lines of code)" [1].

Similar to SDV, the Berkeley Lazy Abstraction Software verification Tool (BLAST), is a SMC for verifying properties in C programs [13]. It applies a technique called lazy abstraction during the refinement process. While this improves the scalability of the CEGAR approach, we have been unable to use it for our work.

The C–Bounded Model Checker (CBMC) [3] and Low-level Bounded Model Checker (LLBMC) [2] verify properties in C programs via bounded model checking. In CBMC, the C program is abstracted once by unwinding the loop structures (including backward goto statements) according to the 'unwind' parameter. Function calls are also inlined. Optionally, slicing can be applied on the C program. LLBMC uses the bit code representation of the C program to perform bounded model checking.

The main drawback of such approaches is their sensitivity to the 'unwind' parameter. A small value can reduce the accuracy of the verification, but a large value can increase the runtime unnecessarily. Determining what is the best value needs significant experimentation and determining this value a-priori is not possible for large code bases.

3   Illustrative Example

Memory leak is a common defect in programs written in C. A memory leak happens when memory that has been previously allocated (via 'malloc' or similar memory allocation function in C), is not deallocated (via 'free' or similar) prior to the program ending.

Figure 1 shows a small C program for motivation purposes. At line 3, 128 bytes are allocated and the starting address of those 128 bytes is stored in pointer 'p'. At lines 14 and 19, memory pointed to by 'p' is deallocated. At lines 17–22, the memory pointed to by 'p' is deallocated only when 'retval' is equal to -1 and 'p' is not equal to NULL. Thus the case when 'retval' is equal to -2 is not taken into account and 'free' is not called. Therefore, memory leaks at the end of this function.

Figure 2 presents the control flow graph for the example C function using SSA form [14]. In SSA form, each variable is defined exactly once; existing variables are split into separate versions, and a 'phi' function is used at merge points. For example, variable 'retval' is assigned values at lines 5 and 10. Both of these constant values reach the 'end' basic block, therefore, the first intermediate statement in that basic block (statement 'P11') is the definition of 'retval' as the 'phi' function between values -1 and -2. 'P11' states that the value of 'retval' is either

```
 1   int foo {                        13      fclose(f);
 2      int retval = 0;               14      free(p);
 3      char *p = malloc(128);        15      return 0;
 4      if( p == NULL ) {             16   end:
 5         retval = -1;               17      if( retval == -1 ) {
 6         goto end;                  18         if( p != NULL ) {
 7      }                             19            free(p);
 8      FILE *f = fopen("test.c"      20            p = NULL;
             ,"ro");                  21         }
 9      if( f == NULL ) {             22      }
10         retval = -2;               23      return retval;
11         goto end;                  24   }
12      }
```

Fig. 1. Motivating Example with a Memory Leak

-1 or -2 depending on which path was followed. Other statements of interest include 'P0' which does the allocation of memory, 'P9' and 'P16' which do the deallocation of memory, and both 'P10' and 'P18' which are exit points for this function.

As part of our analysis we make use of program slicing [9]. A program slice is the set of statements in a program that may affect the value of a variable at some point of interest; commonly referred to as the slicing criterion. If we use 'P18' as our slicing criterion, we are interested in all statements that may affect the value of 'retval'.

The slice therefore includes the branches into 'bb7', namely 'P17', 'P15' and 'P13' and their dependencies, 'P11', 'P12' and 'P14', and the dependencies of these three basic blocks, namely, 'P3', 'P7', 'P13' and 'P15' (these last two already in the set), and so on.

In this case the slice contains all statements in the example except for those in the shaded basic block 'bb4'; i.e., the slice of slicing criterion 'P18' are all statements that are not shaded.

We now describe some of the key steps in the abstraction process for this example. As part of the data abstraction process for pointers, we use the values 'NULL_ADDR', 'MEM_ALLOC' and 'OTHER' to indicate a null pointer, a pointer pointing to an allocated block of memory and a pointer pointing to other addresses respectively. The slice in our example has 4 predicates: 'P1: p == NULL', 'P5: f == NULL', 'P12: retval == -1' and 'P14: p != NULL'. Three of the four predicates can be effectively represented using data abstraction, viz., using 'NULL_ADDR' . As a result, only one boolean variable (say 'b') needs to be created to keep track of the predicate 'retval == -1'. For this predicate, the instruction at 'P11' defines 'retval'. The instructions 'b = true' and 'b = false' are added to predecessor basic blocks 'bb' and 'bb3', respectively, prior to the last branching instruction, to abstract the incoming values of the phi function (-1 and -2, respectively). Thus by using data abstraction first, we reduce the number of extra variables that need to be introduced for predicate abstraction.

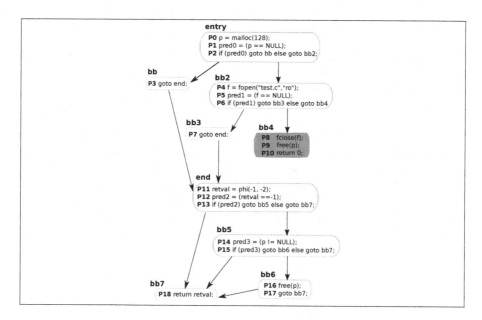

Fig. 2. Control Flow Graph in SSA Form for the Example of Figure 1

To handle the memory allocation at 'P0', two abstracted instructions are created. The first is a declaration of a variable that keeps track of the pointer 'p', and the second is noting that the result of invoking an external library function ('malloc') can return one of two values; the newly allocated address or NULL if there is not enough memory available. This indecisive result is expressed by using a non-deterministic selection statement which covers the two cases 'p = NULL' and 'p = MEM_ALLOC'. Similarly the call to 'fopen' at 'P4' defines the value of variable 'f'. We assume that the 'fopen' can only return either 'NULL' (which indicates failure) or 'OTHER' (which indicates success) since the return value is a pointer and there is no memory allocation involved.

Although, not present in the above example, we show how integer values are handled. For instance, a particular data abstraction rule could define that some integers can be abstracted to the range {'below1', 'between1&9', 'above9'}. Based on this, a control predicate 'x<1' can be expressed as 'x==below1'; therefore, 'x' can be data abstracted and no extra boolean variable needs to be added to the model. On the other hand, the control predicates like 'y==5' requires a new boolean variable since it cannot be represented using the earlier data abstraction rule. To reiterate, data abstraction followed by predicated abstraction reduces the introduction of extra variables.

In the next section we describe our analysis that combines program analysis and model checking techniques. The description of the specialised abstraction will explain how the values used in the above example arise.

In the next section we describe our analysis that combines program analysis and model checking techniques. The description of the specialised abstraction will explain how the values used in the above example arise.

4   Model-Based Analysis

Recall that the aim of our model-based analysis is to use model checking techniques to find defects such as memory leaks in large C code bases effectively. That is, the analysis should take only a few hours to complete code that has around a million lines. In contrast to most SMCs, where one model is generated per program, we generate multiple models per program. We use a specialised abstraction that aims to reduce the size of the models. Model checking is then performed separately over each model resulting in reduction in the search space.

Given a defect type (e.g., memory leak), we use a demand-driven approach to identify all statements in the program where that defect *may* happen. We call these locations "potential defects". The list of potential defects is created by using a static analyser that runs very quickly. For each potential defect, we create a model using a specialised abstraction that is checked by a model checker.

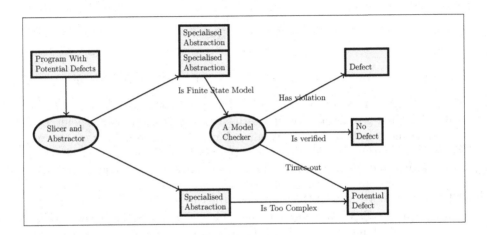

Fig. 3. Architecture of the Model-based Analysis Approach

Figure 3 illustrates our approach to model-based analysis: for each potential defect we first determine all the other statements in the program that are dependent on the statement of the potential defect; this step effectively creates a slice of the program starting at the potential defect statement, taking into account only variables and conditions that are relevant for the analysis to be applied. We then reduce the slice to a specialised abstraction which in turn is transformed into a finite state model that is fed into a model checker.

Automatic data abstraction is used to discard irrelevant ranges of values unrelated to the property to be checked. We also use predicate abstraction on statements when it is not possible to use data abstraction, resulting also in smaller abstracted models. This combination of data and predicate abstractions alleviates the expensive predicate solving, and reduces the complexity of the resulting model; again, improving performance of the analysis.

Owing to the use of automatic abstraction techniques it is possible that an abstraction proves too complex to transform into a model. In such cases the particular potential defect is not analysed further. The complex abstractions result because of the presence of unsupported operations for the data abstraction mechanism and also because of limitations in the predicate solver. In contrast to the CEGAR approach, where multiple iterations of generation of an abstraction may happen, we only abstract once. We generate simpler models by specialising the property (i.e., the defect type in our case) to be checked. Thus our technique is faster than CEGAR based approaches but less accurate. This tradeoff enables us to handle large code bases without reducing the value of the reported defects.

Once the model is run through the model checker, either a counterexample is generated; in which case the potential defect violates the property being checked for and is therefore a defect, or no property violation happens; in which case the potential defect is not a defect.

Algorithm 1. High Level Algorithm

---

procedure DEFECTSPECIFICMODELCHECK(program)
    potentialDefects := GETPOTENTIALDEFECTSLIST($program$)
    defects := $\emptyset$
    for each pd in potentialDefects **do**
        slice := SLICING($program, pd$)
        if $slice$ is executable **then**
            model := SPECIALISEDABSTRACTION($slice, pd$)
            if $model$ is not empty **then**
                result := MODELCHECK($model, fixedProperty$)
                if $fixedProperty$ is not satisfied **then**
                    defects := defects $\cup$ { pd }
                end if
                potentialDefects := potentialDefects $\setminus$ { pd }
            end if
        end if
    end for
    PRINT(defects)
end procedure

The Procedure DEFECTSPECIFICMODELCHECK in Algorithm 1 depicts our model-based analysis at a high level. First a list of 'potentialDefects' is generated for the program. This is a simple static analysis pass. For each potential defect, a slice of the code is obtained. If the resulting slice is a self-contained piece of code that can be executed, a model of it is generated via specialised abstraction. If a non-empty model is generated, it is run by a model checker and determined to be safe or unsafe; unsafe results are placed in the 'defects' list. Other cases lead to the potential defect remaining in the list of potential defects. The slicing and model checking components of the algorithm are standard. We explain our specialised abstraction in the next section.

4.1   Specialised Abstraction

As mentioned earlier, our specialised abstraction for defect types makes use of data abstraction and predicate abstraction. Procedure SPECIALISEDABSTRACTION in Algorithm 2 describes the specialised abstraction for a given slice 'slice' and a potential defect 'pd'. The algorithm keeps track of a set of boolean variables ('boolVariables') and a set of data variables ('dataVariables'), as well as a list of abstracted instructions ('model').

Algorithm 2. Specialised Abstraction Algorithm

---

function SPECIALISEDABSTRACTION(slice,pd)
    boolVariables := ∅; dataVariables := ∅
    predicates := GETCONTROLSTATEMENTPREDICATES(*slice*)
    for each *pred* in *predicates* **do**
        if *pred* cannot be expressed using DataAbstraction **then**
            boolVar := CREATEBOOLVARIABLE(*pred*)
            boolVariables := boolVariables ∪ { boolVar}
        end if
    end for
    model := <>
    for each *inst* in slice **do**
        modelInst, dataVariables := APPLYDEFECTSPECIFICABSTRACTION(*inst*,
            pd, boolVariables, dataVariables)
        if modelInst is empty **then**
          return empty
        else
          model := model ⌒ modelInst
        end if
    end for
    return model
end function

For a given slice, we first determine all predicates in the control statements. If the predicate cannot be expressed using the specific defect data abstraction, a boolean variable is created for it and added to the set 'boolVariables'.

Each instruction in the slice is processed by 'ApplyDefectSpecificAbstraction' to generate the abstracted instruction ('modelInst') and update the set of data variables 'dataVariables'. Predicate abstraction is applied to predicates associated with boolean variables (i.e., in the set 'boolVariables'). If the instruction is too complex for the abstraction at hand, an empty model is returned. Otherwise the model is extended (⌒ is just concatenation) with the model representing the current instruction (*inst*) being processed.

Next we explain the details of the data and predicate abstraction (denoted by 'ApplyDefectSpecificAbstraction') for finding memory leak defects. Recall that we will create one model per potential defect. We consider a potential memory leak a pair of memory allocation and return statements. Thus each model will have only one allocation that may leak at exactly one exit point. For memory leak detection, the 'dataVariables' of interest are pointers. A pointer value is represented by its abstracted address, address space and its offset. The abstracted address, used in the data abstraction process, can either be NULL ('NULL_ADDR'), point to the allocated memory in question ('MEM_ALLOC_ADDR'), or point elsewhere ('OTHER_ADDR'). The address space attribute keeps track of relevant information of the memory contained in the address of the pointer; there are three possible values. Pointers that point to memory containing an address to an allocated memory are marked as 'PARENT_ALLOC_ADDR'. For example, a double pointer 'p' (i.e.,'void **p') will be flagged as 'PARENT_ALLOC_ADDR' if the memory it points to (i.e.,'*p') includes a memory allocation (e.g., '*p = malloc(..)'). This information allows for the detection of indirect deallocations or escapes of 'MEM_ALLOC_ADDR'. In cases where a pointer address is reachable from outside the function being analysed (e.g., argument passed by reference), it is marked as 'ESCAPE_ ADDR'. This way it is possible to identify when the 'MEM_ ALLOC_ADDR' escapes. If the pointer does not point to a parent compound data type and does not escape, its value is 'NONE'. Last, the offset of the pointer is stored as an integer, which is needed for supporting arithmetic operations.

The arithmetic operations that can be represented by this abstraction are limited to additions and subtractions between pointers and integers. As a result, only the offset section of pointers is affected in these operations. In the case of logical operations, our approach only supports equals and not equals predicates. The address space attribute is ignored when computing comparisons as they do not represent the value of the address itself. The particular case of comparing between two pointers evaluating to 'OTHER_ADDR' is handled by assigning 'true or false' non-deterministically.

The address space attribute of pointers is modified as a side effect of definitions of external pointers, memory writes and memory copies. First, when a pointer is defined externally (e.g., a pointer returned by a library function), the address space of that pointer is set to 'ESCAPE_ADDR'. Secondly, we need to propagate the address space attribute when a 'child' pointer is stored in a memory pointed by a 'parent' pointer. The 'parent' pointer is flagged as 'PARENT_ALLOC_ADDR' if the 'child' pointer address is a memory allocation or it is marked as 'PARENT_ALLOC_ADDR'. On the other hand, the 'ESCAPE_ADDR' flag is propagated to the 'child' pointer from the 'parent' pointer if it is the case. Finally, memory copies (e.g., using memcpy(...)) sets the destination pointer as 'PARENT_ALLOC_ADDR' if the source pointer is marked as such. In all of the three cases stated above, our algorithm declares that memory leak is not possible and defines an end state in the model when a pointer address space needs to be set to 'PARENT_ALLOC_ADDR' and 'ESCAPE_ADDR' at the same time.

The address and address space abstractions are summarised in Figure 4.

$Address \in \{NULL\_ADDR,\ MEM\_ALLOC\_ADDR,\ OTHER\_ADDR\}$

$AddressSpace \in \{NONE,\ PARENT\_ALLOC\_ADDR,\ ESCAPE\_ADDR\}$

$Offset \in \mathbb{Z}$

Fig. 4. Address data abstraction

Concretely, we represent pointers as integers: the address, address space and offset of the abstracted representation of pointers. They are extracted by using arithmetic modulus operations as defined in Figure 5.

$pointerAddress(ptr) \equiv (|\ ptr\ |\ \mathrm{MOD}\ 10\ )\ \mathrm{MOD}\ 3$

$pointerAddressSpace(ptr) \equiv (|\ ptr\ |\!\!-\ \mathrm{MOD}\ 10\ )\ \mathrm{DIV}\ 3$

$pointerOffset(ptr) \equiv ptr\ \mathrm{DIV}\ 10$

Fig. 5. Operations to extract elements from pointers represented as integers

There are two limitations to using specialised abstraction. First, it does not support the analysis of user-defined properties, and second, the resulting model cannot be guaranteed to be non spurious. It may be inaccurate due to predicates that may be missing in the model. The first limitation results from the fact that each property needs a particular algorithm for the analysis. However, this is not a requirement in our case as we are interested in checking for known types of defects for which effective algorithms have been developed. To minimise the effects of the second limitation, the analysis accepts this fact and just leaves the potential defect as a potential defect, rather than attempting to generate a more accurate model.

4.2   Example Revisited

We now show the working of the memory leak abstraction technique on our running example presented in Figure 1. Recall that the slice for the criterion 'P18' is all the statements in non-shaded basic blocks. This slice has 4 predicates: 'P1: p == NULL', 'P5: f == NULL', 'P12: retval == -1' and 'P14: p != NULL'. Three of the four predicates can be effectively represented using our data abstraction, since 'NULL_ADDR' is a possible abstracted value. As indicated earlier, only one boolean variable needs to be created to keep track of the predicate 'retval == -1'.

We illustrate the processing of a couple of instructions. The instruction at 'P0' allocates memory via 'malloc' and stores the result in 'p'. This instruction is modelled by two abstracted instructions: a declaration of a variable that keeps track of the pointer 'p', and the result of invoking an external library function that can return one of two values; the newly allocated address or NULL if there is not enough memory available. This indecisive result is expressed by using a non-deterministic selection statement which covers the two cases 'p = NULL' and 'p = MEM_ALLOC'. This is shown in the first **if** – **fi** statement in Figure 6.

The instruction at 'P11' defines the variable 'retval'; this variable affects the boolean variable associated with predicate 'retval == -1'. Assume the boolean variable is named 'b'. The instructions 'b = true' and 'b = false' are added to basic blocks 'bb' and 'bb3', respectively, prior to the last branching instruction, to abstract the incoming values of the phi function (-1 and -2, respectively).

The instruction at 'P4' is a call to the library function 'fopen' and defines the value of variable 'f'. This instruction generates a non-deterministic selection statement to represent the result of 'fopen' and an assignment that makes 'f' an escape address. In the first construct, we assume that the 'fopen' can only return either 'OTHER' or 'NULL' since the return value is a pointer and there is no memory allocation involved. The address is flagged as 'ESCAPE_ADDR' for safety as we assume that this address can be potentially reached interprocedurally. This last statement is not relevant in this particular example as there is no memory write to this address. However, it prevents other cases from reporting false positives.

4.3   Function Summaries and Interprocedural Support

We conclude the discussion of our approach by noting our use of standard function summaries to handle interprocedural analysis [15]. That is, function summaries of each function are created and then used at each calling site. A function summary is a collection of pre and post conditions that encapsulates how the inputs and outputs of a function are affected in the context of a function call. These predicates can represent relevant effects for the memory leak detection analysis such as pointer escapes, memory copies, memory allocations and deallocations. The summaries of functions from external library functions can be defined in a configuration file. In particular, summaries of common functions of the C library, such as 'malloc' and 'free', are used in the analysis.

Whenever a function summary is missing for a given (external) function, the algorithm makes use of the worst case scenario for the defect at hand. For example, for memory leak defects, we can safely assume that every pointer input is escaped and that every pointer output is in an escaped abstracted address space. Further, the return value is non-deterministically defined in this case to avoid missing defects that are not directly related with such calls.

5   Implementation

We have implemented our model-based analysis for detecting memory leaks using the Parfait static code analysis tool [16] and the SPIN [17] model checker. Given our abstraction technique, the model checker we use need not have support for memory leaks.

Our slicing implementation is performed in two passes: a backward pass to calculate the control and data dependencies from the exit point back to the point of interest (the allocation), and a forward pass to track the uses of the allocation statement. This implementation makes use of Parfait's pointer alias analysis.

To implement predicate abstraction, we make use of Parfait's predicate module. When this module cannot determine the value of an abstracted boolean variable, e.g., the predicate is too complex for the module to solve, we assign a value non-deterministically. This module is fast but less precise than a theorem prover, again, as a tradeoff between precision and scalability.

Our implementation has some limitations in the abstraction and the interprocedural support. Our specialised abstraction method is occasionally unable to generate a model because of the use of a simple predicate solver. For instance, it is not able to express boolean variables, representing predicates, in terms of other boolean variables, and it cannot resolve predicates containing floating point values. Our interprocedural support is not complete. As explained in Section 4.3, we rely on Parfait's existing function summaries for detecting interprocedural defects. We have not extended Parfait to fully support our model-based analysis needs. So, some information is not considered in the generation of these summaries and, therefore, our algorithm can miss relevant information for the analysis.

We translate our specialised abstraction into the Promela which is the input language to the SPIN model checker. There are two features of the Promela language that deserve explanation as they differ from traditional programming languages. Promela's control flow is based on whether a statement is executable or not [17]. A statement is executable if it evaluates to a non-zero integer value; therefore, every statement in Promela returns a value. A statement can be an expression on its own, and expressions like '0;' are not executable as they do not evaluate to a non-zero value. We take advantage of this property of the language and use non-executable statements to specify end states. This combined with Promela's modelling of non-determinism using guarded statements enables us to represent different behaviours.

The generated Promela model for our memory leak example shown in Figure 1 is presented in Figure 6. It has been slightly modified to aid readability. The model contains only one active process, 'myProcess', which is enough for evaluating sequential properties such as memory leak. Two auxiliary global boolean variables are included in the construction of the model: 'memoryLeak' and 'exit'. The 'memoryLeak' variable will evaluate to true when the memory in question is allocated and has not been either freed nor escaped. The 'exit' variable is set to true in the block containing the exit statement in the potential defect. As a result, the logical temporal logic (LTL) property that expresses memory leak freedom is represented as [](exit -> !memoryLeak), which means "at any state in the model, if exit holds true, memoryLeak is false".

```
bool memoryLeak = false;              pred1 = addrSpace(f) == NULL;
bool exit = false;                    if
active proctype myProcess() {             :: (pred1) -> goto bb3;
int p; //pointer p                        :: else -> 0;
int f; //pointer f                    fi;
bool b; //representing                bb3: b = false; // retval = -2;
       //retval == -1                 goto end;
bool pred0, pred1;                    end:
bool pred2, pred3;                    pred2 = b;
entry:                                if
if                                        :: (pred2) -> goto bb5;
    :: true ->                            :: else -> goto bb7;
      memoryLeak = true;              fi;
      p = MEM_ALLOC;                  bb5: pred3 = addrSpace(p) != NULL;
    :: true -> p = NULL;              if
fi;                                       :: (pred3) -> goto bb6;
pred0 = addrSpace(p) == NULL;             :: else -> goto bb7;
if                                    fi;
    :: (pred0) -> goto bb;            bb6:
    :: else -> goto bb2;             if
fi;                                       :: addrSpace(p) == MEM_ALLOC ->
bb: b = true; // retval = -1;                memoryLeak = false; 0;
goto end;                                 :: else -> skip;
bb2:                                  fi;
if                                    goto bb7;
    ::true -> f = OTHER;              bb7: exit = true;
    ::true -> f = NULL;               0;
fi;                                   }
f = setAddrSpace(f, ESCAPE_ADDR);
```

Fig. 6. Promela model for example of Figure 1

The Promela model is then passed to SPIN to perform the model checking. If SPIN reports an error, the memory leak is reported as such. We make use of a timeout in case the SPIN processing time takes too long. In practice, test runs indicate that 10 seconds is sufficient time prior to timeout for the size and complexity of the models our analysis generates.

6   Experimental Results

We measure the effectiveness of our technique and report both precision and recall [18]. We evaluated our approach by running two sets of experiments. The first measured the precision and recall of the results against existing benchmarks from the program analysis community. The second measured precision and performance against a large open source code base. For this case it is not possible to measure recall as the list of all defects in the large code base is not known. We also compare the results produced by the LLBMC model-checker [2] and results produced by a purely static-analysis approach using Parfait [16]. We chose LLBMC because, unlike other model-checkers for C, it supports the detection of memory leaks.

6.1 Evaluation of Precision and Recall Against Benchmarks

We use the subset of memory leak benchmarks available in the NIST SA-MATE [19] suite and the Error Detection Test Suite from Iowa State University [20]. These suites contains small benchmarks (the average number of lines of code without comments/blank lines is also shown) with known memory leaks. Furthermore each program has one defect per benchmark. Knowing the location of the defect in the code allows us to determine whether the results of our analysis are correct (hence a true positive), incorrect (hence a false positive) or whether defects were missed all together (hence a false negative). Precision and recall are then computed based on these values. It should be noted that we are not including benchmarks with allocation to global pointers as our implementation does not consider those cases as memory leaks.

Table 1. Small Benchmark Results

Benchmark	Total Defects	Avg LOC	Tool	True +	False +	False -	Precision	Recall	Time (sec)
SAMATE	50	22	Model-based	44	0	6	100%	88%	34
			LLBMC	39	0	11	100%	86.67%	6.38
			Parfait	44	0	6	100%	88%	6.53
IOWA	25	35	Model-based	17	0	8	100%	68%	20.44
			LLBMC	22	0	3	100%	88%	7.67
			Parfait	13	0	12	100%	52%	1.05

Table 1 shows the results of this evaluation. For each benchmark suite we list the total number of defects in the benchmarks, the reported true positives, the number of false positives and false negatives, and compute the precision and recall for the analysis results. As can be seen, all reports produced by the analysis in both benchmarks are correct, hence a false positive rate of 0 and therefore precision of 100%.

The false negatives for the model-based approach in these benchmarks are mostly due to the incomplete function summaries. Thus, our algorithm is unable to process relevant statements or has to be more conservative when abstracting calls to those functions; e.g., assume that every parameter in the call escapes. LLBMC also suffers from a similar problem. More than half the number of false negatives are because LLBMC does not recognise strdup as allocating memory or because of exceptions. LLBMC ran out of memory on three of the programs in the SAMATE suite. In terms of runtime, our model-based approach will generate models for all potential memory leaks in the code, whereas the LLBMC approach will stop when it first encounters a memory leak defect.

Our model-based approach generates 125 potential defects for the various programs in SAMATE. For these 125 potential defects 122 models were generated, i.e., 3 models were too complex. The model-checking process is able to prove violations in 44 of the 122 models. Thus it missed finding 6 defects. Similarly, for the IOWA data set, our approach generates 37 potential defects for which 32 models were generated with 5 models being too complex. The model-checking process verified 17 out of the 32 models.

Parfait will also process all potential memory leaks in the program, however, it uses less expensive data flow techniques which have been optimised over the years. Thus its performance on small benchmarks is excellent both in terms of accuracy and run-time.

The main conclusion we wish to draw from this experiment is that model checking does work for small programs. There is no advantage in generating models on small programs as shown by the significantly larger time taken by the model-based analysis. The model checking process (using LLBMC) is effective although in the case of the benchmarks from the SAMATE set, Parfait is much better than LLBMC. The next section evaluates the effectiveness of slicing and the specialised abstraction technique as applied to a large system.

6.2   Evaluation Using OpenJDK

We ran our analysis over the OpenJDK 7 build 136, on a Sun Ultra24 machine with Core2Duo 3.3Ghz with 6GB RAM of memory. The OpenJDK version has more than 1.4 million lines of non-commented C/C++ code. We used version 5.2.2 of the SPIN model checker. For this system we compare our approach with only the dataflow analysis built into Parfait. Unfortunately LLBMC was unable to run successfully on the above system; thus we are unable to present any results for it. Also tools such as Sparrow and Saber were not available for our experimentation. So no comparison with their approaches can be made.

Although our implementation uses Parfait, the memory leak detection in Parfait is a separate pass that can be run in stand-alone mode. These features of Parfait are independent from each other and hence the comparison does not suffer from any internal biases.

Since neither us nor the authors of the code know where all memory leaks are in the OpenJDK code base, we can only measure precision of the results produced by the analysis, as measuring recall requires knowledge of the location of all memory leaks. Precision is measured by manually inspecting each report produced by the analysis and determining whether the report is correct (i.e., true positive) or incorrect (i.e., false positive). Given the industrial nature of the code base, and its size we used this code base to measure the runtime performance of the analysis.

Table 2. OpenJDK Benchmark Results

Tool	Total Reports	True Positive	False Positive	Relative False Negative	Precision	Performance
Parfait	38	37	1	25	97.37%	55 sec
Model-based	71	60	11	2	84.5%	1:19 hr

Table 2 shows the results of this evaluation. Of the 71 defects reported by the analysis, 60 are correct and 11 are false positives, leading to a precision of 84.5%. The precision in this case is less when compared to the SAMATE and IOWA benchmarks. This is because the latter benchmarks are small and not necessarily fully representative of real code, i.e., they lack in complexity of the code. The false positives included in this test were caused by limitation in the implementation of the slicing module. In some cases our slicing algorithm fails to include uses of parent pointers in the slice and, thus, relevant escapes are not added to the model. We also measure the *relative* false negative for both tools based on the true positive results. For each true positive, we determine whether the other tool reports it or not; if it does not, then it is a false negative. 35 reports were found by both tools. So Parfait missed 25 memory leaks reported by model-based analysis, whereas our approach only missed 2 reported by Parfait. That is, 62.2% more defects were correctly reported.

These results were expected as the model-based approach is more exhaustive and thus more computationally expensive than the data flow technique. The extra performance runtime is still within acceptable time for scaling the analysis to millions of lines of code.

Although the general algorithm reduces the number of model construction cancellations by making safe assumptions and using non-deterministic assignments, we are still forced to abandon the analysis in several of these cases. We also found some data and predicate abstraction clashes; e.g., operations composed of both predicate and data abstracted variables. These instances are handled by discarding predicate abstraction and applying data abstraction on the fly when possible. Otherwise the analysis is cancelled. For example for the OpenJDK code base, we only generate models for 67% of the potential defects.

We also examined the minimum, maximum and average number of states of the models generated by the analysis. The smallest model had 7 states while the largest model had close to 1.8 million states. The average size of the model was about 92,000 states. For models that had a defect, the smallest model had 12 states and the largest model had about 800,000 states and the average size was 14,000 states. Of the 4,186 models generated only 13 models timeout given the 10 second limit. We can therefore conclude that model checking was, in general, effective. We are investigating if there is any correlation between the number of states in the models and the overall performance. Intuitively, large models which do not have a defect lead to reduction in performance as all states need to be examined. However, a large model which has a defect that can be found without computing the entire space will not affect performance.

6.3   Threats to Validity

We now discuss a few threats to validity. The first is related to the selection of benchmarks. We have chosen IOWA and SAMATE as representative of small programs and OpenJDK for a large system. Experimenting with other systems may yield different results. In our evaluation we have converted the specialised abstraction to Promela and used the SPIN model checker. We could have translated the abstraction to C (and used CBMC [3]) or to LLVM bit code (and used LLBMC). While the exact timing will vary, in all these cases we do not think that this would change the overall validity of our approach. The initial list of the potential defects has a significant influence on the process. That is, larger the list the more abstractions that need to be created. If one can use a more sophisticated (and hence potentially more expensive) static analyser, our results could be improved. But the identification of the optimal point is an open question. Also we are using the function summaries from Parfait. This results in a fair comparison for OpenJDK but also points to an area that could be improved.

7   Conclusion and Future Work

In this paper we have presented our model-based analysis approach to finding defects, which makes use of model checking techniques in conjunction with program analysis. The aim of our approach was to develop a defect detection mechanism that can scale to thousands and millions of lines of code, without loss in precision, at the expense of missing some defects. Our approach has been applied to a version OpenJDK that has approximately 1.4 million lines of code which is much larger than programs used in the TACAS 2013 and 2014 benchmarks and tools such as Saber [8].

The key to our analysis is the use of a specialised abstraction that relies on both data and predicate abstraction and the use of multiple models (one per potential defect) to generate a number of small models each of which can be model checked. Thus we are able to leverage the strengths of program analysis and model checking. As our abstraction process limits the size of the models and hence could have false negatives.

Our implementation results for memory leak detection show that the analysis scales well to large code bases without detracting from precision, at the expense of missing some defects. When compared to data flow analysis, our analysis was much slower but reported 62% more defects. The runtime performance of our analysis is reasonable to include this analysis in a static code analysis tool that runs over millions of lines of code.

There are two main avenues for further research. The first is a more detailed comparison. For instance, we could compare our approach with other techniques developed for memory leak (e.g., if we get access to Saber). Second, we believe that our analysis can be applied to other types of defects which needs validation.

Acknowledgements. Initial work was conducted by the first author under Prof. Hayes's supervision. We thank Daniel Wainwright and Matthew Johnson for their assistance with our experiments.

References

1. Ball, T., Levin, V., Rajamani, S.K.: A decade of software model checking with SLAM. Communications of the ACM 54, 68–76 (2011)
2. Merz, F., Falke, S., Sinz, C.: LLBMC: Bounded model checking of C and C++ programs using a compiler IR. In: Joshi, R., Müller, P., Podelski, A. (eds.) VSTTE 2012. LNCS, vol. 7152, pp. 146–161. Springer, Heidelberg (2012)
3. Clarke, E., Kroning, D., Lerda, F.: A tool for checking ANSI-C programs. In: Jensen, K., Podelski, A. (eds.) TACAS 2004. LNCS, vol. 2988, pp. 168–176. Springer, Heidelberg (2004)
4. Corbett, J.C., Dwyer, M.B., Hatcliff, J., Laubach, S., Pasareanu, C.S., Robby, Hongjun, Z.: Bandera: Extracting finite-state models from Java source code. In: Proceedings of the International Conference on Software Engineering, pp. 439–448 (2000)
5. Das, M., Lerner, S., Seigle, M.: ESP: Path-sensitive program verification in polynomial time. In: Proceedings of the Conference on Programming Language Design and Implementation (PLDI), pp. 57–68. ACM Press (June 2002)
6. Dor, N., Adams, S., Das, M., Yang, Z.: Software validation via scalable path-sensitive value flow analysis. In: Proceedings of the ACM SIGSOFT International Symposium on Software Testing and Analysis (ISSTA), pp. 12–22. ACM (2004)
7. Jung, Y., Yi, K.: Practical memory leak detector based on parameterized procedural summaries. In: Proceedings of the 7th International Symposium on Memory Management (ISMM), pp. 131–140 (2008)
8. Sui, Y., Ye, D., Xue, J.: Static memory leak detection using full-sparse value-flow analysis. In: Proceedings of the 2012 International Symposium on Software Testing and Analysis (ISSTA), pp. 254–264. ACM (2012)
9. Yatapanage, N., Winter, K., Zafar, S.: Slicing behavior tree models for verification. In: Calude, C.S., Sassone, V. (eds.) TCS 2010. IFIP AICT, vol. 323, pp. 125–139. Springer, Heidelberg (2010)
10. Park, M., Byun, T., Choi, Y.: Property-based code slicing for efficient verification of OSEK/VDX operating systems. In: Proceedings of the First International Workshop on Formal Techniques for Safety-Critical Systems (FTSCS), pp. 69–84 (2012)
11. Kim, Y., Lee, J., Han, H., Choe, K.M.: Filtering false alarms of buffer overflow analysis using SMT solvers. Information and Software Technology 52(2), 210–219 (2010)
12. Chebaro, O., Kosmatov, N., Giorgetti, A., Julliand, J.: Program slicing enhances a verification technique combining static and dynamic analysis. In: Proceedings of the ACM Symposium on Applied Computing (SAC), pp. 1284–1291 (2012)
13. Henzinger, T.A., Jhala, R., Majumdar, R., Sutre, G.: Software verification with BLAST. In: Ball, T., Rajamani, S.K. (eds.) SPIN 2003. LNCS, vol. 2648, pp. 235–239. Springer, Heidelberg (2003)
14. Cytron, R., Ferrante, J., Rosen, B.K., Wegman, M.N., Zadeck, F.K.: Efficiently computing static single assignment form and the control dependence graph. ACM Transactions on Programming Languages and Systems 13(4), 451–490 (1991)
15. Hampapuram, H., Yang, Y., Das, M.: Symbolic path simulation in path-sensitive dataflow analysis. In: Proceeding of PASTE, pp. 52–58. ACM Press (2005)

16. Cifuentes, C., Keynes, N., Li, L., Hawes, N., Valdiviezo, M., Browne, A., Zimmermann, J., Craik, A., Teoh, D., Hoermann, C.: Static deep error checking in large system applications using Parfait. In: Proceedings of the 19th ACM SIGSOFT Symposium and the 13th European Conference on Foundations of Software Engineering, pp. 432–435. ACM (2011)
17. Holzmann, G.: The SPIN Model Checker: Primer and Reference Manual, 1st edn. Addison-Wesley Professional (2011)
18. Anderson, P.: The use and limitations of static-analysis tools to improve software quality. CrossTalk: The Journal of Defense Software Engineering, 18–21 (2008)
19. NIST: National Institute of Standards and Technology SAMATE Reference Dataset (SRD) project (January 2006), http://samate.nist.gov/SRD
20. Luecke, G.R., Coyle, J., Hoekstra, J., Kraeva, M., Li, Y., Taborskaia, O., Wang, Y.: A survey of systems for detecting serial run-time errors. Concurrency and Computation – Practice and Experience 18(15), 1885–1907 (2006)

Model-Checking for Android Malware Detection[*]

Fu Song[1] and Tayssir Touili[2]

[1] Shanghai Key Laboratory of Trustworthy Computing,
East China Normal University, P.R. China
fsong@sei.ecnu.edu.cn
[2] LIAFA, CNRS and Université Paris Diderot, France
touili@liafa.univ-paris-diderot.fr

Abstract. The popularity of Android devices results in a significant increase of Android malwares. These malwares commonly steal users' private data or do malicious tasks. Therefore, it is important to efficiently and automatically analyze Android applications and identify their malicious behaviors. This paper introduces an automatic and scalable approach to analyze Android applications and identify malicious applications. Our approach consists of modeling an Android application as a PushDown System (PDS), succinctly specifying malicious behaviors in Computation Tree Logic (CTL) or Linear Temporal Logic (LTL), and reducing the Android malware detection problem to CTL/LTL model-checking for PDSs. We implemented our techniques in a tool and applied it to analyze more than 1260 android applications. We obtained encouraging results. In particular, we discovered ten programs known as benign that are leaking private data.

1 Introduction

The rapid growth of Android's market results in a significant increase in Android malwares. Although Google introduced a security service *Bouncer* on the Android Play Store (Android Market) in February 2012, according to a recent report, the number of Android malwares has increased from 3063 to 51447 between the first and third quarters of 2012 [1]. These malwares usually steal users' private information such as phone identifiers, location information, or send overpriced messages, etc.

Researchers have done many efforts aimed at addressing these problems [2, 4, 7–10, 12–16, 19, 20, 22, 30]. All these works cannot directly analyze Dalvik codes to identify complicated malwares (Android applications are written in Java and compiled into Dalvik codes. Dalvik codes are a kind of assembly programs that run in Dalvik Virtual Machine, like Java bytecode run in Java Virtual Machine). In this work, we directly analyze Dalvik bytecode rather than translating it into Java and then using Java program analyzers. Indeed, several malwares are written directly in Dalvik. Moreover, decompilation from Android applications to Java does not always work, due to the fact

---

[*] This work was partially supported by STCSM Project (No. 14PJ1403200), NSFC Project (No. 61402179), SHMEC-SHEDF Project (No.13CG21), the Open Project of Shanghai Key Laboratory of Trustworthy Computing (No. 07dz22304201301), ANR grant (No.ANR-08-SEGI-006), SHEITC Project (No.130407), Shanghai Knowledge Service Platform for Trustworthy Internet of Things (No. ZF1213).

[1] http://www.f-secure.com.

J. Garrigue (Ed.): APLAS 2014, LNCS 8858, pp. 216–235, 2014.
© Springer International Publishing Switzerland 2014

that existing reverse engineering tools are prone to failure. We propose an efficient and automatic approach that directly analyzes Dalvik codes and can identify complicated malwares. Our approach consists of modeling an Android application as a Pushdown System (PDS) which is a natural model of sequential programs with potentially recursive procedure calls [11], and expressing malicious behaviors in SCTPL [25, 26] and SLTPL [27]. SCTPL (resp. SLTPL) is an extension of Computation Tree Logic (CTL) (resp. Linear Temporal Logic (LTL)) with variables, quantifiers and predicates over the stack that allows to succinctly describe malicious behaviors. The Android malware detection problem is reduced to SCTPL/SLTPL model-checking for PDSs which can be solved by [26, 27].

For instance, let us consider an Android application that intends to steal the IMSI ID of the phone by sending a text message to another phone. This application can obtain the IMSI ID by calling the *getSubscriberId* method whose return value is the IMSI ID. Later, it can call the *sendTextMessage* method with the IMSI ID as third parameter by which the IMSI ID is sent to another phone. Since the IMSI ID is users' private information, it is important to identify whether an Android application steals the IMSI ID or not. We can model the Android application as a PDS and specify this malicious behavior as the following SCTPL formula: $\mathbf{EF}\exists x(x = getSubscriberId() \wedge \mathbf{EF}sendTextMessage(-,-,x,-,-))$, where $-$ denotes the non-important parameters. This formula expresses that the return value of *getSubscriberId* (i.e., the IMSI ID) is assigned to a variable x. Later, *sendTextMessage* is called with x as third parameter. However, this formula is not robust enough and malwares could easily get around by some obfuscation techniques. For example, a malware could encrypt the IMSI ID such that the sent text (i.e., third parameter of *sendTextMessage*) does not have any explicit relation with the IMSI ID. E.g., the malware *Hongtoutou* uses the DES algorithm to encrypt the IMSI ID by the secret key 48734154. To overcome this problem, in this paper, we introduce a predicate *encode* to express the existence of a relation between two variables. More precisely, the predicate $y = encode(x,l)$ expresses that the value of y depends on the value of x at the control point l. Thus, the above malicious behavior can be specified in a more precise manner using the following SCTPL formula: $\mathbf{EF}\exists x\exists l(x = getSubscriberId() \wedge Loc(l) \wedge \mathbf{EF}\exists y(sendTextMessage(-,-,y,-,-) \wedge y = encode(x,l)))$. This formula specifies that the return value of *getSubscriberId* is assigned to a variable x at a control point l (i.e., $Loc(l)$ holds). Later, *sendTextMessage* is called with y as third parameter such that the value of y depends on the value of x at l.

However, it is not trivial to determine whether a configuration of the PDS model satisfies predicates of the form $y = encode(x,l)$ or not. To solve this problem, we propose an algorithm based on the saturation procedure of [11]. Our algorithm computes an *annotation function* from which we can infer whether a configuration satisfies $y = encode(x,l)$ or not. Thus, we can check whether an Android application has some malicious behaviors by applying SCTPL and SLTPL model-checking for PDSs.

We implemented our techniques in a tool and applied it to check 1260 Android malwares. We obtained interesting results. Our tool was able to detect all these malwares. We also applied our tool to check 71 applications from Android Compatibility Test Suite which are regarded as benign applications. We found that ten of them leak private data and three of them do some malicious behaviors such as record videos without the

```
1  class Myactivity extends Activity{
2    public String id;
3    public onCreate(){
4      TelephonyManager m = Context.getSystemService(''phone'');
5      id=m.getDeviceId();
6      return;    }
7
8    public onPause(){
9      SmsManager s=SmsManager.getDefault();
10     String text=encrypt(id, key);
11     s.sendTextMessage(''1'',''2'', text, intent, intent);
12     return;    }  }
```

Fig. 1. A simplified program that leaks the device ID of the phone via text message

users' knowledge. To our knowledge, the results we obtained for these 71 applications are previously unknown. Our approach could also be applied to detect other malicious programs, such as iOS programs, Windows programs, etc.

Outline: Section 2 presents the background of Android applications needed in this paper. Section 3 recalls the definition of PDSs and shows how to model an Android application as a PDS. Section 4 gives the definitions of SCTPL and SLTPL, and shows how to express malicious behaviors of Android applications in SCTPL/SLTPL. Section 5 proposes an algorithm computing the annotation function. Section 6 gives the experimental results. Section 7 shows related work. Due to lack of space, proofs are omitted. They can be found in the full version of this paper [28].

2   Android Applications

Android provides four base classes: *Activity, Service, Content Providers* and *Broadcast Receiver*, each of them consists of several methods that could be invoked by the Android operating system (OS) when its state is changed. These methods are called *callback methods*. For instance, the *Activity* class has two callback methods *onCreate* and *onPause* which will be invoked respectively by the Android OS when an *activity* is launched and is about to start resuming a previous activity. Also, there are other classes containing callback methods. E.g., the *OnClickListener* interface has the *onClick* method which will be called when the application is at the idle state and the corresponding button was clicked by the user. An Android application should define one or more classes that extend *Activity, Service, Content Providers* or *Broadcast Receiver* and the extended classes can override callback methods to implement their own functionalities. Moreover, an Android application does not necessarily have a *main* method (i.e., the entry point of a normal program). Instead, an application may have several entry points that are some callback methods of the four base classes. The Android OS can start an application by calling one of these callback methods. Malicious Android applications can also override the callback methods to execute a malicious task.

For example, Fig. 1 presents a simplified Android application that defines the *Myactivity* class which extends the *Activity* class. It overrides the *onCreate* and *onPause* methods. In the *onCreate* method, a *TelephonyManager* object m is obtained by calling the *getSystemService* method at line 4. It calls the *getDeviceId* method of the object m and assigns the return value to the variable *id* at line 5. The return value of *getDeviceId* is the unique device ID (called *IMEI*) of the phone which is private. In the *onPause* method, it calls the *getDefault* method to obtain a *SmsManager* object s at line 9. Then, it encrypts the obtained device ID (i.e., IMEI) by calling the *encrypt* method and assigns the result to the variable *text* at line 10. Finally, it sends the value in the variable *text* via a text message by invoking the *sendTextMessage* method of s at line 11. Note that this program will send the user's device ID to other phones via text messages. Thus, this program may be malicious. It is important to analyze Android applications and tell the user what the applications will do before installing them.

3 Program Model

We will use pushdown systems (PDSs) to model Android applications. PDSs are suitable to model sequential programs with (potentially recursive) procedure calls [11]. The translation from the code of an Android application to a PDS is different from the standard translation from sequential programs to PDSs as it has to take into account the specificity of Android applications such as the existence of callback methods, the way these methods are called, and the absence of the main function.

3.1 Pushdown Systems

A *Pushdown System* (PDS) is a tuple $\mathcal{P} = (P, \Gamma, \Delta)$, where P is a finite set of control locations, Γ is the finite stack alphabet and $\Delta \subseteq (P \times \Gamma) \times (P \times \Gamma^*)$ is a finite set of transition rules. A configuration of $\mathcal{P}$ is pair $\langle p, \omega \rangle$ with $p \in P$ and $\omega \in \Gamma^*$. If $((p, \gamma), (q, \omega)) \in \Delta$, we write $\langle p, \gamma \rangle \hookrightarrow \langle q, \omega \rangle$. W.l.o.g., for every $\langle p, \gamma \rangle \hookrightarrow \langle q, \omega \rangle \in \Delta$, we assume $|\omega| \leq 2$ [11].

The successor relation $\leadsto_{\mathcal{P}} \subseteq (P \times \Gamma^*) \times (P \times \Gamma^*)$ is defined as follows: if $\langle p, \gamma \rangle \hookrightarrow \langle q, \omega \rangle$, then $\langle p, \gamma\omega' \rangle \leadsto_{\mathcal{P}} \langle q, \omega\omega' \rangle$ for every $\omega' \in \Gamma^*$. If $\langle p, \gamma\omega' \rangle \leadsto_{\mathcal{P}} \langle q, \omega\omega' \rangle$, then $\langle q, \omega\omega' \rangle$ is a successor of $\langle p, \gamma\omega' \rangle$. A path is a sequence of configurations $c_0 c_1 ...$ such that for every $i \geq 0$, $c_i \leadsto_{\mathcal{P}} c_{i+1}$. Let $\leadsto_{\mathcal{P}}^* \subseteq (P \times \Gamma^*) \times (P \times \Gamma^*)$ be the transitive and reflexive relation of $\leadsto_{\mathcal{P}}$ such that for every $c, c' \in P \times \Gamma^*$, $c \leadsto_{\mathcal{P}}^* c$, and $c \leadsto_{\mathcal{P}}^* c'$ iff there exists $c'' \in P \times \Gamma^*$: $c \leadsto_{\mathcal{P}} c''$ and $c'' \leadsto_{\mathcal{P}}^* c'$. Let $post^* : 2^{P \times \Gamma^*} \longrightarrow 2^{P \times \Gamma^*}$ be the *successor function* such that for every $C \subseteq 2^{P \times \Gamma^*}$, $post^*(C) = \{c \in P \times \Gamma^* \mid \exists c' \in C : c' \leadsto_{\mathcal{P}}^* c\}$.

To finitely represent (potentially) infinite sets of configurations of PDSs, we use multi-automata.

Given a PDS $\mathcal{P} = (P, \Gamma, \Delta)$, a *Multi-Automaton* (MA) [3] is a tuple $\mathcal{M} = (Q, \Gamma, \delta, I, F)$, where Q is a finite set of states, $\delta : (Q \times \Gamma) \times Q$ is a finite set of transition rules, $I \subseteq Q$ is a set of initial states corresponding to the control locations P, $F \subseteq Q$ is a finite set of final states

Let $\rightarrow_\delta : Q \times \Gamma^* \times Q$ be the transition relation such that for every $q \in Q$: $q \xrightarrow{\epsilon}_\delta q$ and $q \xrightarrow{\gamma\omega}_\delta q'$ if there exists a state $q'' \in Q$ such that $(q, \gamma, q'') \in \delta$ and $q'' \xrightarrow{\omega}_\delta q'$. A configuration $\langle p, \omega \rangle \in P \times \Gamma^*$ is accepted by $\mathcal{M}$ iff $p \xrightarrow{\omega}_\delta q$ for some $q \in F$. A set of configurations $C \subseteq P \times \Gamma^*$ is *regular* iff there exists a MA $\mathcal{M}$ such that $\mathcal{M}$ exactly accepts the set of configurations C. Let $L(\mathcal{M})$ be the set of configurations accepted by $\mathcal{M}$.

3.2 Modeling Android Applications as PDSs

In this section, we show how to model an Android application as a PDS. Given an application with a set N of control points (excluding the control points of declaration statements, e.g., the control point 2 in Fig. 1.), we construct a PDS $\mathcal{P} = (\{p\}, N \cup \{\gamma_\perp\}, \Delta)$ with p as the unique control location and $N \cup \{\gamma_\perp\}$ as the stack alphabet, where $\gamma_\perp \notin N$ is used to handle entry points and callback methods. The PDS transition rules model the control flow of the application. (In our implementation, we use Smali[2], a disassembler for Android applications, to disassemble the application into control flow graphs.) Intuitively, the configuration $\langle p, \gamma_\perp \rangle$ is the initial configuration of the PDS model. It denotes that the run of the PDS is at the idle state (i.e., the application does not execute any statement). A configuration $\langle p, \gamma\omega \rangle$ such that $\gamma \in N$ denotes that the run of the application is at the control point γ and ω is the return addresses of the calling procedures (i.e., the procedures that have not returned yet). Formally, Δ is computed as follows: for every control point $\gamma \in N$ s.t. *stmt* is the statement at the control point γ:

1. If *stmt* is a function call $v = f(v_1, ..., v_m)$ and γ' is the next control point of γ, then $\langle p, \gamma \rangle \hookrightarrow \langle p, f_e\gamma' \rangle \in \Delta$, where f_e is the entry point of the procedure f and γ' is regarded as the return address of f;
2. If *stmt* is a return statement *return v*, then $\langle p, \gamma \rangle \hookrightarrow \langle p, \epsilon \rangle \in \Delta$, where ϵ is the empty word;
3. If *stmt* is neither a function call nor a return statement and γ' is the next control point of γ, then $\langle p, \gamma \rangle \hookrightarrow \langle p, \gamma' \rangle \in \Delta$;
4. Moreover, for every callback method *proc* in the application, $\langle p, \gamma_\perp \rangle \hookrightarrow \langle p, proc_e\gamma_\perp \rangle \in \Delta$, where $proc_e$ is the entry point of *proc*.

The first three items describe the standard construction of a PDS model from a sequential program as shown in [11]. The last item models the invoking of callback methods. As explained previously, an Android application can override the callback methods that are invoked by the Android OS. This implies that some callback methods may not be reachable if we only use the first three items, but they can be called by the Android OS. For example, let us consider the program shown in Fig. 1. The function *onCreate* is only called by the Android OS when the activity is launched and can be an entry point of the application. The *onClick* method of an *ok* button that implements the *OnClickListener* interface is called only when the *ok* button is clicked by the user. That is why we add the last item by which all the callback methods could be invoked in any order whenever the application is at an idle state, i.e., the PDS is at the configuration $\langle p, \gamma_\perp \rangle$. From the view point of the application, we associate all the function calls of callback methods to the control point $\gamma_\perp$. The resulting PDS model is a sound over-approximation of the application.

4 Android (Malicious) Behaviors Specifications

In this section, we recall the definition of the logics SLTPL [27] and SCTPL [26], and show how to use them to describe Android (malicious) behaviors.

---

[2] http://code.google.com/p/smali

Hereafter, we fix the following notations. Let $X = \{x_1, x_2, ...\}$ be a finite set of variables ranging over a finite domain $\mathcal{D}$. Let $B : X \cup \mathcal{D} \longrightarrow \mathcal{D}$ be an environment function that assigns a value $v \in \mathcal{D}$ to each variable $x \in X$ and such that $B(v) = v$ for every $v \in \mathcal{D}$. $B[x \leftarrow v]$ denotes the environment function such that $B[x \leftarrow v](x) = v$ and $B[x \leftarrow v](y) = B(y)$ for every $y \neq x$. Let AP be a finite set of atomic propositions, AP_X be a finite set of atomic predicates in the form of $a(\alpha_1, ..., \alpha_m)$ such that $a \in AP$, $\alpha_i \in X \cup \mathcal{D}$ for every $1 \leq i \leq m$, and $AP_\mathcal{D}$ be a finite set of atomic predicates of the form $a(\alpha_1, ..., \alpha_m)$ such that $a \in AP$, $\alpha_i \in \mathcal{D}$ for every $1 \leq i \leq m$.

4.1 The SCTPL Logic

SCTPL can be seen as an extension of CTL with variables, quantifiers and predicates over the stack. Variables are parameters of atomic predicates and can be quantified by the existential and universal quantifiers. Formally, the set of *SCTPL formulas* is given by (where $x \in X$ and $a(x_1, ..., x_m) \in AP_X$):

$$\varphi ::= a(x_1, ..., x_m) \mid \neg\varphi \mid \varphi \wedge \varphi \mid \forall x\, \varphi \mid \mathbf{EX}\varphi \mid \mathbf{EG}\varphi \mid \mathbf{E}[\varphi\mathbf{U}\varphi].$$

Given a PDS $\mathcal{P} = (P, \Gamma, \Delta)$, let $\lambda : AP_\mathcal{D} \to 2^{P \times \Gamma^*}$ be a labeling function that assigns to each predicate a regular set of configurations. Let $c \in P \times \Gamma^*$ be a configuration of $\mathcal{P}$. $\mathcal{P}$ satisfies a SCTPL formula ψ in c, denoted by $c \models_\lambda \psi$, iff there exists an environment B such that $c \models_\lambda^B \psi$, where $c \models_\lambda^B \psi$ is defined by induction as follows:

- $c \models_\lambda^B a(x_1, ..., x_m)$ iff $c \in \lambda\big(a(B(x_1), ..., B(x_m))\big)$.
- $c \models_\lambda^B \psi_1 \wedge \psi_2$ iff $c \models_\lambda^B \psi_1$ and $c \models_\lambda^B \psi_2$.
- $c \models_\lambda^B \forall x\, \psi$ iff $\forall v \in \mathcal{D}$, $c \models_\lambda^{B[x \leftarrow v]} \psi$.
- $c \models_\lambda^B \neg\psi$ iff $c \not\models_\lambda^B \psi$.
- $c \models_\lambda^B \mathbf{EX}\,\psi$ iff there exists a successor c' of c s.t. $c' \models_\lambda^B \psi$.
- $c \models_\lambda^B \mathbf{E}[\psi_1\mathbf{U}\psi_2]$ iff there exists a path $\pi = c_0 c_1...$ of $\mathcal{P}$ with $c_0 = c$ s.t. $\exists i \geq 0$, $c_i \models_\lambda^B \psi_2$ and $\forall 0 \leq j < i, c_j \models_\lambda^B \psi_1$.
- $c \models_\lambda^B \mathbf{EG}\psi$ iff there exists a path $\pi = c_0 c_1...$ of $\mathcal{P}$ with $c_0 = c$ s.t. $\forall i \geq 0: c_i \models_\lambda^B \psi$.

Intuitively, $c \models_\lambda^B \psi$ holds iff the configuration c satisfies ψ under the environment B. We will freely use the following abbreviations: $\mathbf{EF}\psi = \mathbf{E}[true\mathbf{U}\psi]$, $\mathbf{AG}\psi = \neg\mathbf{EF}(\neg\psi)$, and $\exists x\psi = \neg\forall x\neg\psi$.

Theorem 1. *[26] SCTPL model-checking for PDSs is decidable.*

4.2 The SLTPL Logic

Similarly, SLTPL can be seen as an extension of LTL with variables, quantifiers and predicates over the stack. The set of *SLTPL formulas* is given by (where $x \in X$ and $a(x_1, ..., x_m) \in AP_X$): $\varphi ::= a(x_1, ..., x_m) \mid \neg\varphi \mid \varphi \wedge \varphi \mid \forall x\, \varphi \mid \mathbf{X}\varphi \mid \varphi\mathbf{U}\varphi$.

Given a PDS $\mathcal{P} = (P, \Gamma, \Delta)$ and a path $\pi = c_0 c_1...$ of $\mathcal{P}$, let $\pi(i)$ denote c_i and π^i denote the *suffix* starting from $\pi(i)$. Let c be a configuration of $\mathcal{P}$. $\mathcal{P}$ satisfies a SLTPL formula ψ in c (denoted by $c \models_\lambda \psi$) iff there exists an environment B such that c satisfies ψ under B (denoted by $c \models_\lambda^B \psi$). $c \models_\lambda^B \psi$ holds iff there exists an execution π starting from c such that π satisfies ψ under B (denoted by $\pi \models_\lambda^B \psi$), where $\pi \models_\lambda^B \psi$ is defined by induction as follows:

- $\pi \models^B_\lambda a(x_1, ..., x_m)$ iff $\pi(0) \in \lambda\big(a(B(x_1), ..., B(x_m))\big)$;
- $\pi \models^B_\lambda \neg\psi_1$ iff $\pi \not\models^B_\lambda \psi_1$;
- $\pi \models^B_\lambda \psi_1 \wedge \psi_2$ iff $\pi \models^B_\lambda \psi_1$ and $\pi \models^B_\lambda \psi_2$;
- $\pi \models^B_\lambda \forall x \psi$ iff for every $v \in \mathcal{D}$, $\pi \models^{B[x \leftarrow v]}_\lambda \psi$;
- $\pi \models^B_\lambda \mathbf{X} \psi$ iff $\pi^1 \models^B_\lambda \psi$;
- $\pi \models^B_\lambda \psi_1 \mathbf{U} \psi_2$ iff there exists $i \geq 0$ s.t. $\pi^i \models^B_\lambda \psi_2$ and $\forall j,\ 0 \leq j < i : \pi^j \models^B_\lambda \psi_1$;

We will freely use the following abbreviations: $\mathbf{F}\psi = true \mathbf{U}\psi$, $\mathbf{G}\psi = \neg\mathbf{F}(\neg\psi)$ and $\exists x \psi = \neg\forall x \neg\psi$.

Theorem 2. *[27] SLTPL model-checking for PDSs is decidable.*

4.3   SLTPL and SCTPL for Android Applications

In the context of Android applications, usually AP consists of the method names. For the sake of readability, predicates such as $f(x_1, ..., x_n)$ in AP_X will sometimes be written as $x_1 = x_n.f(x_2, ..., x_{n-1})$ when x_1 denotes the return value of f and x_n denotes the object having the method f, where $x_2, ..., x_{n-1}$ are f's parameters. The labeling function λ is syntactically extracted from the application. For every function call $v = f(v_1, ..., v_m)$, every $\omega \in \Gamma^*$, $\langle p, \gamma\omega\rangle \in \lambda(v = f(v_1, ..., v_m))$ iff $v = f(v_1, ..., v_m)$ is called at the point γ.

Example 1. Consider the program shown in Fig. 1 and the following SCTPL formula: $\phi = \exists x_1 \exists x_2 \mathbf{EF}\big(x_1 = x_2.getDeviceId() \wedge (\mathbf{EF}\exists x_3 \exists x_4\ x_3 = encrypt(x_1, x_4) \wedge \exists x_5 \exists x_6 \exists x_7 \exists x_8 \exists x_9\ \mathbf{EF}x_5.sendTextMessage(x_6, x_7, x_3, x_8, x_9))\big)$, we have: $X = \{x_1, ..., x_9\}$ is the set of variables appearing in ϕ; $AP = \{getDeviceId, sendTextMessage, encrypt\}$ is the set of atomic propositions corresponding to method names (we only list the propositions that are used in ϕ); $AP_X = \{x_1 = x_2.getDeviceId(), x_3 = encrypt(x_1, x_4), x_5.sendTextMessage(x_6, x_7, x_3, x_8, x_9)\}$ is the set of predicates appearing in ϕ; $\mathcal{D} = \{m, id, s, key, "phone", text, "1", "2", intent\}$ is the set of variables and constants that appear in the program; $AP_{\mathcal{D}} = \{id = m.getDeviceId(), s.sendTextMessage("1", "2", text, intent, intent), text = encrypt(id, key)\}$ is the set of function calls; the labeling function λ is given as follows: $\lambda(id = m.getDeviceId()) = \{\langle p, l_5\omega\rangle \mid \omega \in \Gamma^*\}$, $\lambda(s.sendTextMessage("1", "2", text, intent, intent)) = \{\langle p, l_{10}\omega\rangle \mid \omega \in \Gamma^*\}$ and $\lambda(text = encrypt(id, key)) = \{\langle p, l_9\omega\rangle \mid \omega \in \Gamma^*\}$.

Simplified Formulas: A variable x is *non-important* in a formula if x is quantified by $\exists$ and occurs only in one atomic predicate. All the non-important variables will be replaced by "$-$". Let us consider the behavior that sends the IMEI (or an encrypted version of it so that it becomes difficult to check that the IMEI is sent) to other phones via text messages as shown in Fig. 1. We can specify this behavior in the SCTPL formula ϕ (in Example 1). ϕ states that there exist a *TelephonyManager* object x_2 and a variable x_1 such that the return value of the *getDeviceId* method of x_2 (i.e., IMEI) is assigned to x_1. Later, there exist a variable x_3 and a key x_4 such that *encrypt* is invoked with parameters x_1 and x_4, the return value is assigned to x_3 (i.e., the IMEI stored in x_1 is encrypted with the key x_3 and the encrypted IMEI is stored in x_3). Finally, there exist a *SmsManager* object x_5 and variables $x_6, ..., x_9$ such that the *sendTextMessage* method of x_5 is called with parameters x_6, x_7, x_3, x_8 and x_9 (i.e., the encrypted IMEI is sent by calling *sendTextMessage*). The variable x_2 is quantified by $\exists$ and only occurs in $x_1 = x_2.getDeviceId()$, then, we can simplify $x_1 = x_2.getDeviceId()$ as $x_1 = -.getDeviceId()$ which is written as $x_1 = getDeviceId(-)$. The same holds for the variables $x_4, .., x_9$. Thus, the formula is simplified as $\Phi_{id} = \exists x_1 \mathbf{EF}\big(x_1 = getDeviceId(-) \wedge (\mathbf{EF}\exists x_3 \; x_3 = encrypt(x_1, -) \wedge \mathbf{EF} sendTextMessage(-, -, x_3, -, -, -))\big)$.

4.4 Expressing Android (Malicious) Behaviors in SCTPL and SLTPL

In this section, we show how to use SCTPL/SLTPL to express malicious behaviors. We need a special predicate of the form $y = encode(x, l)$ to express that the value of y is computed by encrypting the value of x at the control point l and a predicate of the form $Loc(l)$ to denote that the control point is l, where a configuration $\langle p, \gamma\omega\rangle$ for every $\omega \in \Gamma^*$ satisfies $Loc(l)$ iff $l = \gamma$.

4.4.1 The Predicate *Encode*

The formula Φ_{id} given at the end of Section 4.3 is not robust enough for specifying the behavior that sends the device ID (which may be encrypted) to other phones via text messages. A malware writer could use other approaches to change the IMEI instead of calling the *encrypt* method. For example, a malware writer can replace the statements at lines 9 and 10 in Fig. 1 by the following code:

```
for(int i=0; i<id.length(); i++){
    String text=id.get(i);
    text=text+i;
    s.sendTextMessage(''1'',''2'', text, intent, intent);
}
```

where for every i from 0 upto the length $id.length()$ of the string id (i.e., the IMEI), first, a letter at position i in id is obtained by calling $id.get(i)$ which is assigned to the variable *text*, then the position number i is appended to the string stored in *text* (i.e., $text = text + i$). Finally, the string stored in *text* is sent by calling *sendTextMessage*. By doing this, the IMEI is sent one letter by one letter, and each letter is sent appended with its position. E.g., suppose the IMEI is the string *abcd*, then *a0*, *b1*, *c2* and *d3* are sent one by one. Thus, to make the behavior specification more robust, we introduce a new predicate *encode*. Intuitively, $y = encode(x, l)$ expresses that the value of the variable y depends on the value of the variable x at the control point l. Formally, a configuration $\langle p, \gamma\omega\rangle$ satisfies a predicate $y = encode(x, l)$ iff the run of the program starting from the entry point reaches the control point γ such that the value of y depends on the value of x at the control point l. We can specify the above behavior in a more precise way as follows: $\Psi_{id} = \mathbf{EF}\exists x_1 \exists l\big(x_1 = getDeviceId(-) \wedge Loc(l) \wedge$
$\mathbf{EF}\exists x_3 (sendTextMessage(-, -, x_3, -, -, -) \wedge x_3 = encode(x_1, l))\big)$. Ψ_{id} states that the return value of *getDeviceId* (i.e., IMEI) is assigned to a variable x_1 at the control point l. Later, *sendTextMessage* is called with x_3 as third parameter when the value of x_3 depends on the value of x_1 at l (i.e., the (encrypted) IMEI is sent via text messages).

Table 1. Privates data sources and sinks

Descriptions of source functions
The return value of *getLatitude* or *getlongitude* is the location of the phone
The first parameter of *onLocationChanged* contains the location data of the phone
The return value of *getDeviceId* is the IMEI id of the phone
The return value of *getSubscriberId* is the IMSI id of the phone
The return value of *getDeviceSoftwareVersion* is the IMSI/SV of the phone
The return value of *getLine1Number* is the phone number (PN)
The return value of *getNetworkCountryIso* is the Phone's Iso country code (ISOC)
The first parameter of *getNetworkCountryIso* is the incoming phone number (IPN)
The return value of *getResult* of *AccountManagerFuture* class contains the authentication token (AT) of the phone
The return value of *query* or *managedQuery* is the contact or calendar data (CC) of the phone
The second parameter of *setOutputFile* contains the media data (MD) of the phone
The return value of *getExternalStorageDirectory* contains the SD card (SDC) data of the phone
The return value of *getConnectionInfo* contains the WiFi network connection information of the phone
The return value of *getStringExtra* of the *Intent* class contains the data of an Intent object

Descriptions of sink functions
The third (resp. fourth) parameter of *sendTextMessage* (resp. *sendMultipartTextMessage*) leaks data via a text messages.
The first and second parameters of *d,e,i,v,w,wtf* leak data by writing into log files
The first and second parameters of *loadurl* leaks data via network connections
The first-fourth parameters of ⟨@1init⟩@1 in the *URL* class leak data via network connections
The fourth-eighth parameters of *set* in the *URL* class leak data via network connections
The first parameter of *setRequestProperty* leak data via network connections
The first and second parameters of *execute* in the *http* class can leak data via network connections
The first parameter of *write* or *println* leak data by writing data to files
The first parameter of ⟨*init*⟩ of the *Intent* class leak data to other applications or components

4.4.2   Malicious Behaviors in SCTPL or SLTPL

Information-Leaks: A *source function* is a function that will return a private data through a return value or a parameter. A *source port* is a variable that stores the private data of a source function. A *sink function* is a function which can leak some private data through some parameters of the function. A *sink port* is a parameter of a sink function that can leak some private data. An *information-leak* is the behavior where a sink function is called and its sink port stores some private data (usually got from a source function). This kind of malicious behavior could be specified in SCTPL as the pattern:

$$\mathbf{EF}\exists x\exists l(f_1(x) \wedge Loc(l) \wedge \mathbf{EF}\exists y(f_2(y) \wedge y = encode(x, l)))$$

where f_1 (resp. f_2) is a source (resp. sink) function and x (resp. y) is a source (resp. sink) port such that the value of y relies on the value of x at the control point l. E.g., the application shown in Fig. 1 has an information leak behavior that sends the IMEI of the phone to the other phone via text messages. The formula Ψ_{id} is an instance of the pattern, where *getDeviceId* and *sendTextMessage* are the source and sink functions, respectively. x_1 and x_3 are the source and sink ports. In Table 1, we give all the source and sink functions considered in this work.

Background Picture Taking: An application may take a picture using a camera of the phone without the user's knowledge. To take a picture, an application first creates a new *Camera* object to access a particular hardware camera by invoking the *open* method of the *Camera* class. Next, it calls the *setPreviewDisplay* or *setPreviewTexture* method with the *Camera* object as first parameter to set a surface to preview, and then calls the *takePicture* method with the *Camera* object to take a picture. Calling *setPreviewDisplay* or *setPreviewTexture* will inform the user about a camera access. But, without calling them before taking the picture (i.e., calling *takePicture*) after the • *Camera* object is created (i.e., calling *open*) will take a picture without informing the user. Thus, this behavior is malicious. We can specify this behavior in a SLTPL formula as follows: $\Psi_{bp} = \mathbf{F}\exists x_1 \exists l_1 \big(x_1 = open(-) \wedge Loc(l_1) \wedge \exists x_2(\neg((setPreviewDisplay(x_2, -) \vee setPreviewTexture(x_2, -)) \wedge x_2 = encode(x_1, l_1))$ **U** $\exists x_3\ takePicture(x_3) \wedge x_3 = encode(x_1, l_1))\big)$. The formula Ψ_{bp} states that a *Camera* object x_1 is created by calling *open* at l_1. Later, a picture is taken by calling *takePicture* with x_3 as its first parameter such that the value of x_3 is obtained from the value of x_1 at l_1 (i.e., $x_3 = encode(x_1, l_1)$), since the *Camera* object stored in x_1 can be assigned to another variable x_3. Between calling *open* and *takePicture*, there does not exist a variable x_2 such that *setPreviewDisplay* or *setPreviewTexture* is called with x_2 as first parameter and the value of x_2 is obtained from the value of x_1 at l_1 (i.e. $x_2 = encode(x_1, l_1)$). This means that a picture is taken without informing the user.

Background Video Recording: Android provides the *MediaRecorder* class to record a video using a camera of the phone. To do this, an application first creates a *MediaRecorder* object, then calls the *setVideoSource* method to choose a camera (a phone may have two cameras). The application should call the *setPreviewDisplay* method to set a surface to show a preview of the video. Thus, an application recording the video without calling *setPreviewDisplay*, i.e., informing the user, is malicious. We can specify this behavior in SCTPL as follows: $\Psi_{bv} = \exists x_1 \exists l_1 \mathbf{E}[\neg(setPreviewDisplay(x_1, -) \wedge Loc(l_1))$ **U** $\exists x_2 setVideoSource(x_2, -) \wedge x_2 = encode(x_1, l_1) \wedge \mathbf{AG}\neg \exists x_3 setVideoSource(x_3, -) \wedge x_3 = encode(x_1, l_1)]$. Ψ_{bv} states that there does not exist a *MediaRecorder* object x_1 such that the calling of *setVideoSource* with x_2 as its first parameter such that the value of x_2 depends on x_1 (i.e., $x_2 = encode(x_1, l_1)$) is not preceded by calling *setPreviewDisplay* with x_1 as its first parameter at l_1. Later, in all the future paths, *setVideoSource* will not be called with x_3 as its first parameter such that the value of x_3 is obtained from the value of x_1 at l_1 (i.e., $x_3 = (x_1, l_1)$).

Dynamically Loaded Code Execution: In Android, an application can dynamically load classes from libraries and call functions in these classes. To do this, it first calls *loadclass* to load a class from a library. Then, the return value is the class object. Later, it calls the *getMethod* method with the class object as its first parameter. This returns the method. Finally, it can call the method by calling *invoke* with the method as parameter. The loaded classes may perform malicious behaviors that cannot be identified by statically checking the application. Thus, it is important to tell the user whether an application executes some dynamically loaded code. To check this, we use the following SCTPL formulas: $\Psi_{dc} = \mathbf{EF}\exists x_1 \exists l_1 \big(x_1 = loadClass(-, -) \wedge Loc(l_1) \wedge \exists x_2 \exists x_3 \exists l_2 \mathbf{EF}(x_3 = getMethod(x_2, -) \wedge Loc(l_2) \wedge x_2 = encode(x_1, l_1) \wedge \exists x_4 \mathbf{EF} invoke(x_4, -, -) \wedge x_4 = encode(x_3, l_2))\big)$. Ψ_{dc} states that the x_1 class is dynamically loaded by calling *loadClass* at l_1. Next, *getMethod* is called with x_2 as first parameter such that the value of x_2 is obtained from the value of x_1 at l_1 (i.e., $x_2 = encode(x_1, l_1)$), since the class object stored in x_1 may be assigned to another variable x_2. Later, *invoke* is called at l_2 with x_4 as the first parameter such that the value of x_4 is obtained from the return value x_3 of the previous *getMethod* method call, i.e., $x_4 = encode(x_3, l_2)$ and the method stored in x_4 (x_3) is invoked by the application.

Harvesting Installed Applications: Android provides the *getInstalledPackages* method of the *PackageManager* class to access information of the installed applications, their components, and permissions. An application harvesting the installed applications is dangerous, as the installed applications are users' private data. To harvest the installed applications, an application can call *getInstalledPackages* which returns a list of installed applications. Then, the application can traverse this list using the *hasNext* function of the *Iterator* class or the *get* function of the *List* class. Since a conditional statement is modeled as two non-deterministic PDS transition rules when we model an application as a PDS, then, the traversing of the list which checks whether all the elements are visited will be an infinite loop. This is an over-approximation of the control flow of the application. We can specify this behavior in the following SLTPL formula: $\Psi_{hi} = \mathbf{F}\exists x_1 \exists l_1(x_1 = getInstalledPackages(-,-) \land Loc(l_1) \land \mathbf{GF}\exists x_2 \land (get(x_2,-) \lor hasNext(x_2)) \land x_2 = encode(x_1, l_1))$. Ψ_{hi} states that a list x_1 of installed applications is obtained by calling *getInstalledPackages* at l_1. Later, it will infinitely often access this list by calling *get* or *hasNext* with x_2 as first parameter such that the value of x_2 is obtained from the value of x_1 at l_1 (i.e., $x_2 = encode(x_1, l_1)$). Note that the always operator $\mathbf{G}$ specifies the infinite loop that traverses the list of installed applications.

Native Codes Execution: Android Applications have a way to execute native codes that are written in other languages such as C/C++. Applications can execute native libraries by calling the *loadLibrary* method (i.e., the Java Native Interface) or the *exec* method of the *Runtime* object. As these codes are not in Android assembly language and may contain malicious behaviors, it is crucial to tell the user whether an application will execute codes in native libraries. For this, we check whether the *loadLibrary* or *exec* is called or not by the following formula: $\Psi_{nc} = \mathbf{EF}(loadLibrary(-) \lor exec(-))$. Ψ_{nc} checks whether the function *loadLibrary* or *exec* is called.

Downloading Data from Servers: Many applications download payloads from servers. They may download malicious applications and the downloading costs network flow. Thus, it is important to check whether an application downloads data from some servers. An application can use the *getInputStream* method of the *URLConnection*, *HttpURLConnection* or *HttpsURLConnection* classes to obtain an *InputStream* object. The *InputStream* object allows the application to read data from the server by calling the *read* method of the *InputStream* class. By doing so, the data read from the *InputStream* object is put at the buffer pointed by the second parameter of the *read* method. Then, an application can write the data to a file by calling the *write* method of the *FileOutputStream* class with the buffer as second parameter. Thus, it is important to check whether an application reads data using an *InputStream* object and then writes this data into a file. We can express this behavior in a SCTPL formula as follows: $\Psi_{dd} = \mathbf{EF}\exists x_1 \exists l_1(x_1 = getInputStream(-) \land Loc(l_1) \land \mathbf{EF}\exists x_2 \exists x_3 \exists l_2(read(x_2, x_3) \land Loc(l_2) \land x_2 = encode(x_1, l_1) \land \mathbf{EF}\exists x_4 \ write(-, x_4, -, -) \land x_4 = encode(x_3, l_2)))$. Ψ_{dd} expresses that the return value of *getInputStream* is assigned to the variable x_1 (i.e., x_1 is an *InputStream* object) at l_1. Next, *read* is called at control point l_2 with x_2 and x_3 as its parameters such that the value of x_2 is obtained from the value of x_1 at l_1

(i.e., $x_2 = encode(x_1, l_1)$), since the *InputStream* object stored in x_1 may be assigned to another variable x_2. This means that the application reads data from a server by calling the *read* method of the *InputStream* object and the data is put at the buffer x_3. Later, *write* is called with x_4 as its second parameter whose value is obtained from the value of x_3 at l_2 which stores the data from the server.

Remark 1. Note that we need both SLTPL and SCTPL to be able to express the Android malicious behaviors. Indeed, the SCTPL formula Ψ_{bv} cannot be expressed in SLTPL, whereas the SLTPL formula Ψ_{hi} cannot be expressed in SCTPL.

5   Model-Checking Android Applications

As described previously, we model an Android application as a PDS and specify Android malicious behaviors in SCTPL/SLTPL. Then, to check whether an application contains a malicious behavior or not, it is sufficient to check whether the PDS model satisfies the SCTPL/SLTPL formula expressing the malicious behavior. However, it is non-trivial to decide whether or not a configuration $\langle p, \gamma\omega\rangle$ satisfies a predicate of the form $v_2 = encode(v_1, l)$, since one cannot easily determine whether the value of v_2 depends on the value of v_1 at the control point l or not. To solve this problem, in this section, we propose an approach to compute an *annotation function* that allows us to determine whether a configuration satisfies predicates of the form $v_2 = encode(v_1, l)$. Intuitively, the annotation function associates to each control point n of the program a *dependency function*, where the dependency function assigns to each variable x a set of pairs (y, l) expressing that the value of x at the control point n depends on the value of y at l. The annotation function is computed by an extension of the saturation procedure of [11] which computes all the reachable configurations represented by a MA of the PDS model. We assign to each transition of the MA a dependency function and update the dependency function during the saturation procedure according to the side-effects of the program statements. To distinguish variables in SCTPL/SLTPL formulas from those that appear in the applications, from now on, we will use x, y, z to denote variables in SCTPL/SLTPL formulas, and use $v, v_1, v_2...$ to denote variables in applications.

5.1   Annotating the Program with *encode* Predicates

Let us fix a PDS $\mathcal{P} = (P, \Gamma, \Delta)$ modeling a given Android application. For every $\gamma \in \Gamma$, let $Proc(\gamma)$ be the procedure that contains the control point γ. Let G be the set of global variables used in an application and L_{proc} be the set of local variables in the procedure *proc*. For each procedure *proc*, let R_{proc} be a local variable of the procedure *proc* which denotes the return value of *proc* after the return statement. The formal parameters $p_1, ..., p_m$ of each procedure are local variables of this procedure. Let L be the set of local variables used in the application. Let $\theta : G \cup L \longrightarrow 2^{(G \cup L) \times \Gamma}$ be a *dependence function* that assigns to each variable $v \in G \cup L$ a set of pairs (v', γ) such that v depends on the value of v' at the control point γ. Let Θ be the set of dependence functions. Let $\uplus : \Theta \times \Theta \longrightarrow \Theta$ be a function such that for every $\theta, \theta' \in \Theta$, every variable $v \in G \cup L: (\theta \uplus \theta')(v) = \theta(v) \cup \theta'(v)$.

Let $\mathcal{M} = (Q, \Gamma, \delta, I, F)$ be the MA where $Q = \{p, q_f\}$, $I = \{p\}$, $F = \{q_f\}$ and $\delta = \{(p, \gamma_\perp, q_f)\}$. $\mathcal{M}$ accepts the configuration $\langle p, \gamma_\perp \rangle$ (i.e., the initial configuration). We create a new MA $\mathcal{M}^* = (Q^*, \Gamma, \delta^*, I, F)$ with ϵ-transition rules and an annotation function $\rho : \delta^* \longrightarrow \Theta$ that associates each transition rule of $\mathcal{M}^*$ with a dependence function θ such that $L(\mathcal{M}^*) = post^*(L(\mathcal{M}))$, and for every control point γ, $\mathcal{M}^*$ has a transition rule $t = (p, \gamma, q_1)$ such that $q_1 \xrightarrow{\omega}_{\delta^*} q_f$ and $(v, l) \in \rho(t)(v')$ iff a configuration $\langle p, \gamma\omega' \rangle$ satisfies $v' = encode(v, l)$.

Let $Var(exp)$ be the set of variables used in the expression exp. The computation of $\mathcal{M}^*$ and ρ consists of two steps. First, we construct the MA $\mathcal{M}^*$ accepting $post^*(L(\mathcal{M}))$. Then, we annotate the transition rules of $\mathcal{M}^*$ with an adequate dependence function (i.e. compute ρ). We use the saturation procedure of [11] to compute $\mathcal{M}^*$ by adding a finite number of transition rules into $\mathcal{M}$ based on the following rules: Initially, $\mathcal{M}^*$ equals $\mathcal{M}$;

- For every transition rule $\langle p, \gamma \rangle \hookrightarrow \langle p', \gamma'\gamma'' \rangle \in \Delta$, add a new state $p'_{\gamma'}$, and a new transition rule $(p', \gamma', p'_{\gamma'})$ into $\mathcal{M}^*$;
- Add new transition rules into $\mathcal{M}^*$ according to the following saturation rules: for every $p \xrightarrow{\gamma}_{\delta^*} q$ in $\mathcal{M}^*$,
  - If $\langle p, \gamma \rangle \hookrightarrow \langle p', \gamma'\gamma'' \rangle \in \Delta$, we add a new transition rule $(p'_{\gamma'}, \gamma'', q)$ into $\mathcal{M}^*$;
  - If $\langle p, \gamma \rangle \hookrightarrow \langle p', \gamma' \rangle \in \Delta$, we add a new transition rule (p', γ', q) into $\mathcal{M}^*$;
  - If $\langle p, \gamma \rangle \hookrightarrow \langle p', \epsilon \rangle \in \Delta$, we add a new transition rule (p', ϵ, q) into $\mathcal{M}^*$;
  - If $(p', \epsilon, p) \in \delta^*$, we add a new transition rule (p', γ, q) into $\mathcal{M}^*$.

The annotation function ρ is computed according to the following rules:

β_0: For every transition rule $t = (p, \gamma, q)$ in $\mathcal{M}^*$, let $\rho(t)(v) = \emptyset$ for any $v \in G \cup L$;

β_1: For every transition $\langle p, \gamma \rangle \hookrightarrow \langle p', \gamma' \rangle \in \Delta$, every $t = (p, \gamma, q)$ and $t' = (p', \gamma', q)$ in $\mathcal{M}^*$, $\rho(t') = \rho(t') \uplus \theta$, where

  $\beta_{1.1}$: If the statement at the control point γ is an assignment $v = exp$, then, $\forall v' \in G \cup L \setminus \{v\}$: $\theta(v') = \rho(t)(v')$ and $\theta(v) = \{(v, \gamma)\} \cup \bigcup_{v' \in Var(exp)} \rho(t)(v')$;

  $\beta_{1.2}$: Otherwise, $\theta = \rho(t)$;

β_2: For every $\langle p, \gamma \rangle \hookrightarrow \langle p', \gamma'\gamma'' \rangle \in \Delta$ s.t. $v = f(v_1, ..., v_m)$ is called at γ, every $t = (p, \gamma, q)$, $t' = (p', \gamma', p'_{\gamma'})$ and $t'' = (p'_{\gamma'}, \gamma'', q)$ in $\mathcal{M}^*$:

  $\beta_{2.1}$: $\rho(t') = \rho(t') \uplus \theta$, where $\forall v' \in G$: $\theta(v') = \rho(t)(v')$, $\forall v' \in L_f$: $\theta(v') = \emptyset$ and $\forall i \in \{1, ..., m\}$: $\theta(p_i) = \{(p_i, \gamma')\} \cup \rho(t)(v_i)$ (note that $p_1, ..., p_m$ are formal parameters of f);

  $\beta_{2.2}$: $\rho(t'') = \rho(t'') \uplus \theta'$, where $\forall v' \in L_{Proc(\gamma)}$: $\theta'(v') = \rho(t)(v')$, $\forall v' \in G$: $\theta'(v') = \emptyset$ and $\theta'(v) = \{(v, \gamma)\} \cup \{(R_f, \gamma'')\}$; (Note that $Proc(\gamma)$ denotes the procedure that contains the control point γ, i.e., where $v = f(v_1, ..., v_m)$ is called.)

β_3: For every $\langle p, \gamma \rangle \hookrightarrow \langle p', \epsilon \rangle \in \Delta$ s.t. *return* v is the statement at the control point γ, every $t = (p, \gamma, q)$ and $t' = (p', \epsilon, q)$ in $\mathcal{M}^*$, $\rho(t') = \rho(t') \uplus \theta$, where $\forall v' \in G \cup L_{Proc(\gamma)}$: $\theta(v') = \rho(t)(v')$ and $\theta(R_{Proc(\gamma)}) = \{(v, \gamma)\} \cup \rho(t)(v)$;

β_4: For every $t = (p, \epsilon, q)$, $t' = (q, \gamma, q')$ and $t'' = (p, \gamma, q')$ in $\mathcal{M}^*$, $\rho(t'') = \rho(t'') \uplus \theta$, where $\forall v \in G$: $\theta(v) = \rho(t)(v)$; $\forall v \in L_{Proc(\gamma)}$: $\theta(v) = \rho(t')(v)$; moreover, $\forall v \in G \cup L_{Proc(\gamma)}$ s.t. $(R_f, \gamma) \in \rho(t')(v)$ where $\rho(t)(R_f) \neq \emptyset$: $\theta(v) = \rho(t')(v) \cup \rho(t)(R_f)$.

Item β_0 initializes the annotation function ρ such that the value of any variable v at each control point does not depend on any variable at any location. Then, by iteratively applying Items $\beta_1, ..., \beta_4$ until there does not exist any transition t in $\mathcal{M}^*$ such that $\rho(t)$ can be updated, we can get the annotation function ρ such that for every configuration $\langle p, \gamma\omega\rangle \in L(\mathcal{M}^*)$ with $\gamma \in \Gamma$, $\langle p, \gamma\omega\rangle$ satisfies $v' = encode(v, l)$ iff there exists a transition rule $t = (p, \gamma_0, q_1) \in \delta^*$ such that $(v, l) \in \rho(t)(v')$ and $q_1 \xrightarrow{\omega'}_{\delta^*} q_f$ for some $\omega' \in \Gamma^*$. The intuition behind these rules is explained as follows.

Item β_1 expresses that if $\langle p, \gamma\rangle \hookrightarrow \langle p', \gamma'\rangle$ is a transition of the PDS, $t = (p, \gamma, q)$ and $t' = (p', \gamma', q)$ are in $\mathcal{M}^*$, then, the procedure depends on whether the statement is an assignment or not. If $v = exp$ is the assignment statement at the control point γ (Item $\beta_{1.1}$), we associate the set of pairs $\{(v, \gamma)\} \cup \bigcup_{v' \in Var(exp)} \rho(t)(v')$ to the variable v in the dependence function of the transition rule t'. This means that after executing the $v = exp$ statement, the value of v at the control point γ' depends on the variables in $Var(exp)$ and on itself at γ. Moreover, the values of the other variables v' remain the same as at γ. Therefore, the set of variables they depend on remain the same as at γ, i.e., $\theta(v') = \rho(t)(v')$. Item $\beta_{1.2}$ states that if the statement at the control point γ does not change the value of any variable, we associate the dependence function $\rho(t') \uplus \rho(t)$ to the transition rule t'.

Item β_2 states that if $\langle p, \gamma\rangle \hookrightarrow \langle p', \gamma'\gamma''\rangle$ is a transition rule of the PDS such that $v = f(v_1, ..., v_m)$ is called at γ, $t = (p, \gamma, q)$, $t' = (p', \gamma', p'_{\gamma'})$ and $t'' = (p'_{\gamma'}, \gamma'', q)$ are transition rules in $\mathcal{M}^*$, then, we update the dependence functions of t' in Item $\beta_{2.1}$ and t'' in Item $\beta_{2.2}$, respectively. Note that γ' denotes the entry point of the procedure f and γ'' is its corresponding return address. Item $\beta_{2.1}$ updates the dependence function of t' (i.e., the control point γ') by setting $\rho(t') = \rho(t') \uplus \theta$ such that (1) for every global variable $v' \in G$, $\theta(v') = \rho(t)(v')$ (i.e., at the entry point γ' of the function f, the set of variables that v' depends on remain the same as in γ), (2) for every local variable $v' \in L_f$ of the procedure f: $\theta(v') = \emptyset$; (3) for every parameter p_i of f, $\theta(p_i) = \{(p_i, \gamma')\} \cup \rho(t)(v_i)$, since according to parameter passing p_i equals v_i and p_i at γ' also depends on its value at γ'. Item $\beta_{2.2}$ updates the dependence function of t'' (i.e., the control point γ'') by setting $\rho(t'') = \rho(t'') \uplus \theta'$ such that (1) for every local variable $v' \in L_{Proc(\gamma)}$: $\theta'(v') = \rho(t)(v')$, this records the set of variables on which the local variables of the procedure $Proc(\gamma)$ at the caller-site depend on. This information will be used when the procedure f returns, i.e., at the control point γ'', see Item β_4; (2) for every global variable $v' \in G$: $\theta'(v') = \emptyset$ (since global variables may be changed in the procedure f, we update these global variables when f returns, see Item β_4); (3) the variable v is associated with the specific variable R_f and control location γ'' which denotes that v depends on R_f at γ'' and the value of v at γ' depends on its value at γ i.e., $\theta'(v) = \{(v, \gamma)\} \cup \{(R_f, \gamma'')\}$. R_f will be replaced by the real return value of f when f returns, see Item β_4.

Item β_3 expresses that if $\langle p, \gamma\rangle \hookrightarrow \langle p', \epsilon\rangle$ is a transition rule of the PDS such that *return* v is the statement at the control point γ (w.l.o.g., we assume that each function will return a value), and $t = (p, \gamma, q)$ and $t' = (p', \epsilon, q)$ are transition rules in $\mathcal{M}^*$, then, we update the annotation function of the transition t' by setting $\rho(t') = \rho(t') \uplus \theta$ such that for every variable $v' \in G \cup L_{Proc(\gamma)}$, $\theta(v') = \rho(t)(v')$ (since the values of these variables remain the same as in γ), and since at this point the variable $R_{Proc(\gamma)}$ denoting the return value of the procedure $Proc(\gamma)$ is instantiated with v, it depends on the set of variables that v depends on at γ and on itself at γ. The transition rule $t' = (p', \epsilon, q)$ will be used in Item β_4 to pass the return value to the caller-side.

Item β_4 states that if $t = (p, \epsilon, q)$ denoting the return of a procedure f (see Item β_3), $t' = (q, \gamma, q')$ denoting that γ is the return address of the procedure f, and $t'' = (p, \gamma, q')$ denoting that the control point of the program is at the return address γ, are transition rules in $\mathcal{M}^*$, then, we update the annotation function of the transition t'' by setting $\rho(t'') = \rho(t'') \uplus \theta$ such that (1) for every global variable $v \in G$: $\theta(v) = \rho(t)(v)$ (i.e. at the return address γ, the program should use the values of the global variables of the procedure f); (2) for every local variable $v \in L_{Proc(\gamma)}$: $\theta(v) = \rho(t')(v)$ (i.e. the local variables of the procedure $Proc(\gamma)$ depend on the same set of variables at the caller-site in which the function f is called); (3) for every variable $v \in G \cup L_{Proc(\gamma)}$ that depends on the specific variable R_f (i.e. the return value of the procedure f) at γ: $\theta(v) = \rho(t')(v) \cup \rho(t)(R_f)$, since the variable v at γ depends on the same set of variables as R_f. Intuitively, the dependence function of the transition rule t' is updated in Item $\beta_{2.2}$ when a function call is made, thus, $\rho(t')$ records the sets of variables and locations that the local variables of $Proc(\gamma)$ depend on at the caller-side. The dependence function of t is updated in Item β_3 when the procedure f returns, this implies that $\rho(t)$ records the sets of variables and locations that the global variables and the return value R_f depend on at the return point. The transition rule t'' denotes that the control point is at the return address γ, thus, the update θ of the transition rule t'' uses the values of the global variables and R_f in $\rho(t)$ and uses the values of the local variables of $Proc(\gamma)$ in $\rho(t')$.

Complexity: Since the number of variables is bounded, the number of dependence functions is also bounded, at most $\mathbf{O}(|G| \cdot |L| \cdot 2^{|G| \cdot |L| \cdot |\Gamma|})$. The number of transition rules of $\mathcal{M}^*$ is at most $\mathbf{O}((|P| + k) \cdot |P| \cdot |\Delta|)$ where k is the number of pairs $(p', \gamma') \in P \times \Gamma$ such that $\langle p, \gamma \rangle \hookrightarrow \langle p', \gamma' \gamma'' \rangle \in \Delta$ for some $p \in P, \gamma, \gamma'' \in \Gamma$. Then, we can get ρ and $\mathcal{M}^*$ in time $\mathbf{O}((|P| + k) \cdot |P| \cdot |\Delta| \cdot |G| \cdot |L| \cdot 2^{|G| \cdot |L| \times |\Gamma|})$.

Theorem 3. *Given a PDS $\mathcal{P} = (P, \Gamma, \Delta)$ modeling a given application, we can compute a MA $\mathcal{M}^*$ and an annotation function ρ in time $\mathbf{O}((|P| + k) \cdot |P| \cdot |\Delta| \cdot |G| \cdot |L| \cdot 2^{|G| \cdot |L|})$, such that for every $\langle p, \gamma \rangle \in P \times \Gamma$, every $\omega \in \Gamma^*$: $\langle p, \gamma\omega \rangle$ satisfies $v' = encode(v, l)$ iff there exists a transition rule $t = (p, \gamma, q) \in \delta^*$ such that $(v, l) \in \rho(t)(v')$ and $q \xrightarrow{\omega}_{\delta^*} q_f$.*

5.2 SCTPL and SLTPL Model-Checking for Android Applications

By Theorem 3, we can determine each predicate of the form $v' = encode(v, l)$ from $\mathcal{M}^*$ and ρ, then, we can obtain the labeling function λ as follows: for every function call $v = f(v_1, ..., v_m)$, we let $\lambda(v = f(v_1, ..., v_m)) = \{\langle p, \gamma\omega \rangle \mid \omega \in \Gamma^*$ such that the call $v = f(v_1, ..., v_m)$ is made at the control point $\gamma\}$; for every predicate $Loc(l)$, $\lambda(Loc(l)) = \{\langle p, \gamma\omega \rangle \mid \omega \in \Gamma^* \wedge \gamma = l\}$; for every predicate $v' = encode(v, l)$, $\lambda(v' = encode(v, l)) = \{\langle p, \gamma\omega \rangle \mid t = (p, \gamma, q) \in \delta^* \wedge (v, l) \in \rho(t)(v') \wedge q \xrightarrow{\omega}_{\delta^*} q_f\}$ which is a regular set of configurations. By applying Theorems 1 and 2, we can get the following theorem.

Theorem 4. *Given a PDS modeling an Android application and a (malicious) behavior expressed in SCTPL/SLTPL formula, whether the PDS satisfies this behavior or not is decidable.*

Table 2. Results of checking information-leak formulas on the malicious applications

		Location	IMEI	IMSI	IMSI/SV	PN	ISOC	IPN	AT	CC	MD	SDC	WiFi	Intent	Sum$_2$
		Private Data													
Leak ways	TextMessage	2	74	20	0	0	0	0	0	3	0	0	0	1	100
	Log File	315	278	179	0	33	178	26	0	267	0	199	52	275	1802
	Network	138	345	165	9	67	11	23	0	82	0	163	10	439	1443
	File writer	90	424	219	18	27	19	5	0	61	0	331	2	14	1210
	Intent	105	1	0	0	0	0	12	0	7	0	167	5	9	306
Sum$_1$		348	685	480	18	114	204	48	0	288	0	352	52	529	
Avg. Time(s)		5.79	3.29	3.16	3.39	2.64	8.07	5.69	0	4.77	0	3.97	7.10	5.57	
Avg. Mem(MB)		76.6	63.8	56.3	50.1	48.3	68.8	81.1	0	61.4	0	67.8	61.5	63.8	

6   Experiments

We implemented a **model builder** based on the tool Smali, a disassembler for Android applications. Given an Android application as an *app* file which contains the application's Dalvik code, **model builder** automatically outputs a labeling function λ and a PDS modeling the application. We use the model-checking algorithms of [26, 27] to check whether the PDS model satisfies a given formula describing Android applications' (malicious) behaviors. We applied our tool to check 1331 applications which consists of 1260 confirmed real malwares from the dataset of [29], and 71 applications from the Android Compatibility Test Suite (CTS) [3] considered as benign applications. The size of malwares ranges from 13 KB to 15022 KB. The total size is 1.5 GB. While the size of CTS applications ranges from 2.7 KB to 26748 KB and its total size is 56.8 MB. We checked these applications against all the formulas presented in this paper. The analysis of each application costs only few seconds time and MB memory. This implies that our techniques are efficient and scalable. Our tool was able to detect all these malwares and several previously unknown malicious behaviors in the applications from CTS.

6.1   Information-Leak Android Applications

Table 2 gives the result of checking applications against information-leak formulas. **TextMessage, Log File, Network, File writer** and **Intent** denote different leaking ways that the private data can leak via text messages, log files, network connections, files and *Intent* object, respectively. **Location, IMEI, IMSI, IMSI/SV, PN, ISOC, IPN, AT, CC, MD, SDC, WiFi** and **Intent** are the private data we considered, denoting the location data, IMEI id, IMSI id, IMSI/SV id, phone number, Iso country code, incoming phone number, authentication token, contact or calendar data, mediate data, SD card data, WiFi connection information of the phone and the data stored in an Intent object, respectively. Our tool can check all the information-leak formulas for each application at the same time. Each cell in Table 2 except the rows **Avg. Time(s)**, **Avg. Mem(MB)**, **Sum$_1$** and the column **Sum$_2$**, gives the number of applications that leak the private data indicated by the column title via the (way) approach indicated by the row title. For instance, there are 345 applications in the benchmark leaking the IMEI of the phone

---

[3] http://developer.android.com

via network connections. The **Sum₁** row (resp. **Sum₂** column) shows the total number of applications that leak the private data indicated by the column title (resp. use the leaking approach indicated by the row title). The **Avg. Time(s)** (resp. **Avg. Mem(MB)**) row gives the average of time (resp. memory) consumption in seconds (resp. MB) used to detect all the applications that leak the private data indicated by the column title.

As shown in Table 2, 685 applications leaks the IMEI of the phone, most of them are leaked via Log files, files and networks. No application in our experiment leaks media data (MD) and authentication token (AT). The detection of these applications costs only several seconds. This implies that our techniques are efficient and scalable.

We checked all the benign programs from Android CTS against all the information leak formulas using only 2569 seconds. The average memory consumption is 13.6 MB. Our tool reports that there are ten benign programs leaking private data, 8 of them have the corresponding permissions which will inform users the use of the private data, while the other two applications (*CtsTelephonyTestCases* and *CtsWidgetTestCases*) do not have permissions to access the private data, i.e., the users do not know the use of the private data. *CtsTelephonyTestCases* accesses *WiFi connection information* by calling the method *getConnectionInfo* of the class *WifiManager* and sends the information to other applications by *Intent* object. *CtsTelephonyTestCases* accesses *Contact and Calender data* by calling the *query* of the class *ContentResolver* and writes the information into a log file.

6.2   Checking the Other Malicious Behaviors

We applied our tool to check the benchmark against the other SCTPL/SLTPL formulas shown in Section 4.4. Table 3 depicts the results of checking all the malicious applications. The **Number of Apps** row shows the number of applications that satisfy the corresponding formula indicated by the column title. The **Avg. Time(s)** (resp. **Avg. Mem(MB)**) row gives the average of time (resp. memory) consumption in seconds (resp. MB) used to detect all the applications that satisfy the corresponding formula, where the time consumption is the sum of the time for computing the MA $\mathcal{M}^*$ and the annotation function ρ and for model-checking. The memory consumption is the maximum of the memory for computing the MA $\mathcal{M}^*$ and the annotation function ρ and for model-checking. From Table 3, we can see that malicious applications rarely take pictures or record videos without users' knowledge. But, many malicious applications executes dynamically loaded codes, and harvest installed applications.

Table 3. Results of model-checking the malicious applications

	Ψ_{dd}	Ψ_{bp}	Ψ_{bv}	Ψ_{nc}	Ψ_{dc}	Ψ_{hi}
Number of Apps	491	0	1	679	185	793
Avg. Time(s)	40.04	0	21.77	16.44	11.8	17.51
Avg. Mem(MB)	86.3	0	59	41.1	23.8	78.9

The analysis of all the benign programs against all the SCTPL/SLTPL formulas (excepting information leak formulas) costs 3611.73 seconds. The average of memory consumption is 10.4 MB. 5 applications execute native codes, 2 applications record videos without the users' knowledge and 1 application harvests installed applications. During the analysis of benign programs, our tool automatically avoids to apply model-checking on an application against a SCTPL/SLTPL formula if no function of in SCTPL/SLTPL formula is called. This improves the efficiency of our tool.

7 Related Work

Many works such as [1, 8, 9, 13, 14, 16, 19] use dynamic and/or static data flow analysis to analyze Android malwares. However, these works consider only information-leak malwares, and do not consider more complicated malicious behaviors. [30] aims to mainly analyze known Android malwares and needs samples to extract behavioral signatures. However, the signature-based techniques can be easily gotten around by malware writers. [9] static analyzes Android applications by translating them (Dalvik codes) into Java source codes and applying existing static analyzers of Java programs. However, as we discussed in the introduction, known reverse engineering tools, such as dex2jar, ded [9] and Dare [21], fail in some cases and it is also possible for malicious developers to write malicious codes at the Dalvik bytecode level that makes the application hard to be retargeted.

[21] proposes a more precise tool translating Dalvik codes into Java. However, the resulting Java source codes may miss some malicious behaviors. In this work, we propose an efficient and automatic approach that directly analyzes Android Dalvik codes. Our approach can analyze information-leak malwares and other more complicated (malicious) behaviors beyond information-leaks.

[17] introduces CTPL to specify malicious behaviors. SCTPL is an extension of CTPL with predicates over the stack [25, 26]. SLTPL is first introduced in [27], to specify malicious behaviors of executable programs. [17, 25–27] do not consider Android malware specifications and cannot be applied to check Android malwares in a precise manner. Indeed, for Android applications, we need predicates of the form $y = encode(x, l)$ which cannot be determined in [17, 25–27]. Moreover, the translation from Android applications to PDSs extends the standard translation from sequential programs to PDSs [11] and the translation used in [25–27] cannot be applied in the Android context due to existence of callback methods, the way these methods are called, and the absence of the main function. Furthermore, the Android malicious behaviors described in this work were not considered in [17, 25–27]. Model-checking and static analysis such as [5, 6, 17, 24] have been applied to detect non Android malwares.

The saturation procedure proposed in this work is an extension of the saturation procedure of [11]. However, [11] does not consider how to compute the annotation function ρ, i.e., the dependence relation between variables. [23] extends PDSs with a weight domain (called weighted PDSs) and their saturation procedure computes the weights of reachable configurations. [18] introduces an extension of weighted PDSs, called extended weighted PDSs, and shows how to compute the weights of reachable configurations by a kind of a saturation procedure. We could define the dependence relation of variables as a weight domain and apply the approaches of [18, 23] to compute the weights of reachable configurations, where each transition rule of the resulting MA is associated with a function over variables. Then, to decide whether the value of a variable depends on some variable at some control point, we have to compose several functions over the weight domain multiple times which can be avoided using our approach. Indeed, we only need to query the transition rules of the MA $\mathcal{M}^*$ that are labeled by γ.

References

1. Arzt, S., Rasthofer, S., Fritz, C., Bodden, E., Bartel, A., Klein, J., Traon, Y.L., Octeau, D., McDaniel, P.: Flowdroid: Precise context, flow, field, object-sensitive and lifecycle-aware taint analysis for android apps. In: PLDI (2014)
2. Beresford, A.R., Rice, A., Skehin, N., Sohan, R.: Mockdroid: Trading privacy for application functionality on smartphones. In: HotMobile, pp. 49–54 (2011)
3. Bouajjani, A., Esparza, J., Maler, O.: Reachability Analysis of Pushdown Automata: Application to Model Checking. In: Mazurkiewicz, A., Winkowski, J. (eds.) CONCUR 1997. LNCS, vol. 1243, pp. 135–150. Springer, Heidelberg (1997)
4. Bugiel, S., Davi, L., Dmitrienko, A., Fischer, T., Sadeghi, A.-R., Shastry, B.: Towards taming privilege-escalation attacks on android. In: NDSS (2012)
5. Christodorescu, M., Jha, S.: Static analysis of executables to detect malicious patterns. In: 12th USENIX Security Symposium, pp. 169–186 (2003)
6. Christodorescu, M., Jha, S., Seshia, S.A., Song, D.X., Bryant, R.E.: Semantics-aware malware detection. In: IEEE Symposium on Security and Privacy, pp. 32–46 (2005)
7. Dietz, M., Shekhar, S., Pisetsky, Y., Shu, A., Wallach, D.S.: Quire: Lightweight provenance for smart phone operating systems. In: USENIX Security Symposium (2011)
8. Enck, W., Gilbert, P., Gon Chun, B., Cox, L.P., Jung, J., McDaniel, P., Sheth, A.: Taintdroid: An information-flow tracking system for realtime privacy monitoring on smartphones. In: OSDI (2010)
9. Enck, W., Octeau, D., McDaniel, P., Chaudhuri, S.: A study of android application security. In: USENIX Security Symposium (2011)
10. Enck, W., Ongtang, M., McDaniel, P.D.: On lightweight mobile phone application certification. In: ACM Conference on Computer and Communications Security (2009)
11. Esparza, J., Hansel, D., Rossmanith, P., Schwoon, S.: Efficient algorithm for model checking pushdown systems. In: Emerson, E.A., Sistla, A.P. (eds.) SPIN 2000. LNCS, vol. 1885, pp. 232–247. Springer, Heidelberg (2000)
12. Felt, A.P., Wang, H.J., Moshchuk, A., Hanna, S., Chin, E.: Permission re-delegation: Attacks and defenses. In: USENIX Security Symposium (2011)
13. Gibler, C., Crussell, J., Erickson, J., Chen, H.: AndroidLeaks: Automatically detecting potential privacy leaks in android applications on a large scale. In: Katzenbeisser, S., Weippl, E., Camp, L.J., Volkamer, M., Reiter, M., Zhang, X. (eds.) TRUST 2012. LNCS, vol. 7344, pp. 291–307. Springer, Heidelberg (2012)
14. Grace, M.C., Zhou, Y., Zhang, Q., Zou, S., Jiang, X.: Riskranker: Scalable and accurate zero-day android malware detection. In: MobiSys (2012)
15. Hornyack, P., Han, S., Jung, J., Schechter, S.E., Wetherall, D.: These aren't the droids you're looking for: retrofitting android to protect data from imperious applications. In: ACM CCS, pp. 639–652 (2011)
16. Kim, J., Yoon, Y., Yi, K., Shin, J.: Scandal: Static analyzer for detecting privacy leaks in android application. In: Mobile Security Technologies 2012 (2012)
17. Kinder, J., Katzenbeisser, S., Schallhart, C., Veith, H.: Detecting malicious code by model checking. In: Julisch, K., Kruegel, C. (eds.) DIMVA 2005. LNCS, vol. 3548, pp. 174–187. Springer, Heidelberg (2005)
18. Lal, A., Reps, T., Balakrishnan, G.: Extended weighted pushdown systems. In: Etessami, K., Rajamani, S.K. (eds.) CAV 2005. LNCS, vol. 3576, pp. 434–448. Springer, Heidelberg (2005)

19. Mann, C., Starostin, A.: A framework for static detection of privacy leaks in android applications. In: SAC, pp. 1457–1462 (2012)

20. Nauman, M., Khan, S., Zhang, X.: Apex: Extending android permission model and enforcement with user-defined runtime constraints. In: ASIACCS, pp. 328–332 (2010)

21. Octeau, D., Jha, S., McDaniel, P.: Retargeting Android applications to Java bytecode. In: SIGSOFT FSE (2012)

22. Ongtang, M., McLaughlin, S.E., Enck, W., McDaniel, P.D.: Semantically rich application-centric security in android. In: ACSAC (2009)

23. Reps, T.W., Schwoon, S., Jha, S.: Weighted pushdown systems and their application to interprocedural dataflow analysis. In: Cousot, R. (ed.) SAS 2003. LNCS, vol. 2694, pp. 189–213. Springer, Heidelberg (2003)

24. Singh, P.K., Lakhotia, A.: Static verification of worm and virus behavior in binary executables using model checking. In: IAW, pp. 298–300 (2003)

25. Song, F., Touili, T.: Efficient malware detection using model-checking. In: Giannakopoulou, D., Méry, D. (eds.) FM 2012. LNCS, vol. 7436, pp. 418–433. Springer, Heidelberg (2012)

26. Song, F., Touili, T.: Pushdown model checking for malware detection. In: Flanagan, C., König, B. (eds.) TACAS 2012. LNCS, vol. 7214, pp. 110–125. Springer, Heidelberg (2012)

27. Song, F., Touili, T.: LTL model-checking for malware detection. In: Piterman, N., Smolka, S.A. (eds.) TACAS 2013. LNCS, vol. 7795, pp. 416–431. Springer, Heidelberg (2013)

28. Song, F., Touili, T.: Model-checking for Android Malware Detection. Technical report, Shanghai Key Laboratory of Trustworthy Computing (2014),
http://research.sei.ecnu.edu.cn/~song/publications/APLAS14.pdf

29. Zhou, Y., Jiang, X.: Dissecting android malware: Characterization and evolution. In: IEEE Symposium on Security and Privacy, pp. 95–109 (2012)

30. Zhou, Y., Wang, Z., Zhou, W., Jiang, X.: Hey, you, get off of my market: Detecting malicious apps in official and alternative android markets. In: NDSS (2012)

Necessary and Sufficient Preconditions
via Eager Abstraction*

Mohamed Nassim Seghir[1] and Peter Schrammel[2]

[1] University of Edinburgh, UK
[2] University of Oxford, UK

Abstract. The precondition for safe execution of a procedure is useful for understanding, verifying and debugging programs. We have previously presented a CEGAR-based approach for inferring necessary and sufficient preconditions based on the iterative abstraction-refinement of the set of safe and unsafe states until they become disjoint. A drawback of that approach is that safe and unsafe traces are explored separately and each time they are built entirely before being checked for consistency. In this paper, we present an *eager* approach that explores shared prefixes between safe and unsafe traces conjointly. As a result, individual state sets, by construction, fulfil the property of separation between safe and unsafe states without requiring any refinement. Experiments using our implementation of this technique in the precondition generator P-Gen show a significant improvement compared to our previous CEGAR-based method. In some cases the running time drops from several minutes to several seconds.

1 Introduction

Procedure preconditions must hold when invoking a procedure in order to guarantee its intended, safe behaviour during its execution. They are an important concept in design-by-contract, and commonly found in code documentation, e.g. for libraries, in order to help the developer understand how to use a procedure in the current calling context.

However, it is notoriously difficult to come up with preconditions that guarantee that all assertions in the procedure hold under all possible inputs that satisfy them (*sufficient preconditions*), but, at the same time, do not rule out safe behaviour (*necessary preconditions*).

Computing the weakest sufficient or strongest necessary preconditions syntactically is not always possible as programs (due to loops) often contain an infinite number of paths. On the one hand, over-approximating these infinite sets may include unsafe paths which lead to the violation of the assertion and thus giving an unsound result. On the other hand, under-approximating them

---

* The first author was supported by EPSRC under grant number EP/K032666/1 "App Guarden". The second author was supported by the ARTEMIS Joint Undertaking under grant number 295311 "VeTeSS".

may exclude safe paths which might rule out desirable safe behaviour and hence render the precondition unusable. *True*, the precondition that allows all traces of the program, is always a valid (over-approximating) necessary precondition, and *false*, the precondition that forbids program execution, is always a valid (under-approximating) sufficient precondition. Obviously, the former is not sound and the latter is not useful, in general.

In our previous work [1], we proposed a solution to this problem based on iteratively abstracting both the set of safe and unsafe states and refining them until they become disjoint. Thus, the resulting precondition is sufficient and also necessary for the validity of the assertions. This guarantees the absence of false alarms. Of course, this is only possible if the precondition is expressible in the chosen abstract domain (or predicate language); otherwise the algorithm fails to find a suitable precondition. A disadvantage of that approach is the exploration of safe and unsafe states separately. Hence, we do not know the frontier between safe and unsafe states to guide the abstraction at early stages and the refinement is only applied after entire traces are built. Moreover, this laziness in the abstraction process introduces redundant computation steps which can be avoided if safe and unsafe states are explored conjointly.

In this paper, we present an eager approach for inferring necessary and sufficient preconditions in a monotonic fashion[1]. Based on the observation that safe and unsafe traces share most of their prefixes and only differ by small portions in the traces, our approach explores safe and unsafe states conjointly as pairs. Hence the criterion for guiding the abstraction is that each two elements forming pairs of safe and unsafe states at a given location must be disjoint. This new procedure has many advantages:

- Inferring relevant and general predicates at early stages, hence boosting the convergence of the fix-point computation.
- By construction, states fulfil the global constraint of separating the set of safe states from unsafe ones. Hence, the refinement process is totally skipped and a series of iteration steps are avoided.
- Computational redundancies are eliminated as shared prefixes between safe and unsafe traces are explored conjointly.

The inferred preconditions have the same expressiveness as those obtained by our previous method [1], however, the new approach exhibits an enormous improvement in algorithmic efficiency.

We have implemented our approach in the precondition generator P-Gen and performed a comparative study with our CEGAR-based technique. The results clearly demonstrate that our new method is not just a side optimisation but rather represents the right way to proceed for inferring necessary and sufficient preconditions. For all the programs we have tested, the eager approach performs better than the lazy (CEGAR) one. For some cases where the lazy approach takes several minutes, the eager one just requires several seconds.

The remainder of the paper is organised as follows: Section 2 illustrates the intuition behind our approach through an example. Section 3 introduces some

---

[1] By monotonic, we mean that the set of states will only increase.

preliminary material. Section 4 formally exposes our precondition inference approach. Section 5 presents an experimental comparative study and Section 6 surveys related work.

2 Example

To highlight the advantages of our new approach for precondition inference, we briefly recall our previous work [1] and illustrate both techniques on the procedure copy in Figure 1. The procedure takes as parameters two arrays a and b, and copies a range of elements of b to the corresponding range in array a. The access to array a is safe if the index expression is in the range $[0..a\_l - 1]$, where a_l is the length of array a. It is trivial to see that the lower bound is not violated. The safety condition for the upper bound is expressed by the assertion at location ℓ_2. Our goal is to find a necessary and sufficient precondition for procedure copy which guarantees that this assertion is never violated. It means that it should neither be too strong nor too weak. To ease the presentation, we solely focus on the specified assertion, assuming that there are no other run-time exceptions caused by null dereferences, i.e., $a \neq null$ and $b \neq null$.

```
void copy(int a[], int b[])
{
        int i;
ℓ₀ : i = 0;
ℓ₁ : while(b[i] != 0)
        {
ℓ₂ :        assert(i < a_l);
            a[i] = b[i];
            i++;
        }
}
```

Fig. 1. A simple program that copies a range of elements from array b to array a. The limit of the range to be copied is implicitly delimited via the sentinel value 0, and a_l is the length of array a.

For illustration, we formally represent programs in terms of transition constraints over primed and unprimed program variables. The set of transition constraints corresponding to program copy (Figure 1) is given in Figure 2(a) and the associated control flow graph is given in Figure 2(b). The program counter is modelled explicitly using the variable pc, which ranges over the set of control locations. The assertion in the original program is replaced with a conditional branch whose condition is the negation of the assertion and whose target is the *error* location ℓ_E. The special location ℓ_F is the *final* location, and has no successor. Observe that the error location is only reachable if $i \geq a\_l$ evaluates to true at location ℓ_2. The final location ℓ_F is reached in paths without error. Arrays a and b are represented by uninterpreted function symbols, and $a[x := e]$ denotes function update (the expression is equal to a where the xth element has been replaced by e).

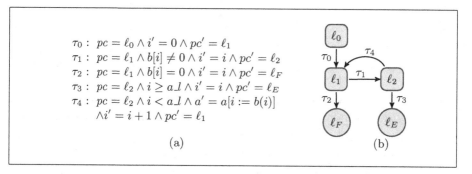

$$\tau_0 : \; pc = \ell_0 \wedge i' = 0 \wedge pc' = \ell_1$$
$$\tau_1 : \; pc = \ell_1 \wedge b[i] \neq 0 \wedge i' = i \wedge pc' = \ell_2$$
$$\tau_2 : \; pc = \ell_1 \wedge b[i] = 0 \wedge i' = i \wedge pc' = \ell_F$$
$$\tau_3 : \; pc = \ell_2 \wedge i \geq a\_l \wedge i' = i \wedge pc' = \ell_E$$
$$\tau_4 : \; pc = \ell_2 \wedge i < a\_l \wedge a' = a[i := b(i)]$$
$$\qquad \wedge i' = i+1 \wedge pc' = \ell_1$$

(a)   (b)

Fig. 2. Transition constraints for program copy (a) and the corresponding control flow graph (b)

CEGAR-Based Precondition Inference. The CEGAR-based approach for precondition generation consists of building abstractions of safe and unsafe states and refining them until they become disjoint. It mainly comprises the following steps:

1. Build abstraction: abstract both the set of safe and unsafe states.
2. Find a counterexample: two abstract traces, a safe one and an unsafe one, beginning with a common initial state.
3. Check counterexample: checks if the two traces can be concretised in the original program. The check is carried out by computing the weakest precondition for each trace.
4. Refine: the spurious counterexample is ruled out by adding predicates that refine the abstraction making the two traces no longer sharing their initial state.

In the refinement phase (steps 3 and 4), safe and unsafe traces are separately explored backwards, and the consistency check is only applied when the initial location is reached. Considering the example of Figure 1, let us assume that the safe trace $\langle \tau_0, \tau_1, \tau_4, \tau_2 \rangle$ and the unsafe one $\langle \tau_0, \tau_1, \tau_4, \tau_1, \tau_3 \rangle$ are generated by entering the loop once. The backward analysis of these two traces is illustrated in Figure 3. On the left (a) is the safe trace and on the right (b) is the unsafe one. With each state of the trace, is associated a set of predicates (in rectangular frames). Predicates without the $\bullet$ superscript, that we call *base* predicates, are obtained by computing the weakest precondition as shown by the solid arrows. Hence their conjunction represents the weakest precondition to reach the final location ℓ_F (respectively error location ℓ_E) in the safe trace (respectively

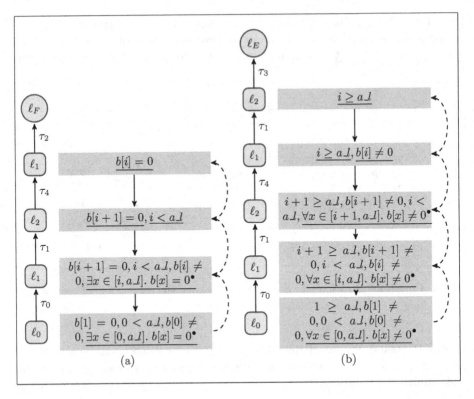

Fig. 3. Illustration of the refinement approach used in [1] on program copy. The underlined predicates are selected by the refinement process and predicates associate with the superscript • are computed using a system of inference rules.

error trace). The predicates associated with the superscript •, called *general* predicates, are inferred using a generalisation procedure based on a system of inference rules as described in [1] (see Appendix A).

The details about the inference rules are not important to the contribution of this paper. The relevant point to retain is that we have a generalisation procedure able to infer new (general) predicates which logically represent consequences of the conjunctions of base predicates. For example, in the state belonging to the error trace (b) and associated with location ℓ_0, we have the general predicate $\forall x \in [0, a\_l].\ b[x] \neq 0$ which is a logical consequence of the base predicates at that state. We have $a\_l = 1$ due the predicates $1 \geq a\_l$ and $0 < a\_l$, and we have $b[0] \neq 0$ and $b[1] \neq 0$, thus all elements of array b in the range $[1..a\_l]$ are not null.

The same procedure is applied to the safe trace (a). Once we reach the initial location, a minimisation procedure is called to keep only relevant predicates which are underlined. This procedure gives priority to general predicates. In our case, we keep $\exists x \in [0, a\_l].\ b[x] = 0$ and $\forall x \in [0, a\_l].\ b[x] \neq 0$ for the safe trace and unsafe one respectively at location ℓ_0 as they are the ones showing that the two traces are inconsistent.

The next step is to perform a dependency analysis starting from the two new states (retained predicates) and going forward in the direction of dashed arrows. Here also, we give priority to general predicates over base predicates. For example, in the state associated with location ℓ_1 of the safe trace, just before the initial state (location ℓ_0), we keep predicate $\exists x \in [i, a\_l].\ b[x] = 0$ as it is the one on which the predicate $\exists x \in [0, a\_l].\ b[x] = 0$ at location ℓ_0 depends.

A drawback of this approach is that it induces redundant computations. There are inter-trace redundancies due to shared parts between traces. For example, the two traces in Figure 3 are sharing a large part of their prefixes, namely $\langle \ell_0, \ell_1, \ell_2, \ell_1 \rangle$. There are also intra-trace redundancies due to backtracking, i.e, going backward for the predicate generation and forward for the dependency analysis. Our new approach remedies these weaknesses.

Eager-Abstraction-Based Precondition Inference. In our new approach the refinement process is completely skipped, states are explored backwards and predicates are added on the fly until a fix-point is reached. To be able to proceed so, we need first to find a node such that all the traces reaching it are common prefixes (going forward) for error traces and safe traces. Hence, such a node simply represents a common dominator for the error location and the final one. We choose the closest common dominator[2] as it maximises the length of common prefixes of traces. Up to that node, traces are explored separately, and from it and going further traces are explored conjointly.

This new scheme is illustrated in Figure 4. First, the two traces (safe and unsafe) are explored separately backwards up to the location ℓ_1 which represents a common dominator for the final location ℓ_F and the error location ℓ_E. At that point, we have $\varphi_F \equiv (b[i] = 0)$ as safe state, and $\varphi_E \equiv (i \geq a\_l \wedge b[i] \neq 0)$ as error state. We can see that φ_F and φ_E are inconsistent. Then, using the system of rules (from [1], see Appendix A), we try to infer a general predicate φ' from φ_F such that its negation $\neg\varphi'$ can be inferred from φ_E using the same system of rules. Hence we have $\varphi_F \Rightarrow \varphi'$ and $\varphi_E \Rightarrow \neg\varphi'$. If we find such a predicate φ', we keep it together with its negation $\neg\varphi'$ and throw all other predicates. It means that φ' becomes the new safe state and $\neg\varphi'$ the error one. Otherwise, we just keep all base predicates forming φ_F and φ_E.

Using the system of inference rules (Appendix A), we see that such a predicate (φ') cannot be inferred at the first encounter of location ℓ_1, so we keep all base predicates. Going one step further using the weakest precondition, at location ℓ_2 we obtain $\varphi_F \equiv (b[i+1] = 0 \wedge i < a\_l)$ and $\varphi_E \equiv (i+1 \geq a\_l \wedge b[i+1] \neq 0 \wedge i < a\_l)$. From φ_E we infer $\forall x \in [i+1, a\_l].\ b[x] \neq 0$, but its negation $\exists x \in [i+1, a\_l].\ b[x] = 0$ cannot be inferred from φ_F via our system of inference rules. Again, we keep all base predicates and continue with the next step backwards. At the second encounter of location ℓ_1, this time we have $\varphi_F \equiv (b[i+1] = 0 \wedge i < a\_l \wedge b[i] \neq 0)$ and $\varphi_E \equiv (i+1 \geq a\_l \wedge b[i+1] \neq 0 \wedge i < a\_l \wedge b[i] \neq 0)$. From φ_E we can infer $\forall x \in [i, a\_l].\ b[x] \neq 0$ which represents φ' as its negation

---

[2] The closest common (or immediate) dominator for a set of nodes S is a node d which dominates S such that any other dominator d' for S is also a dominator for d.

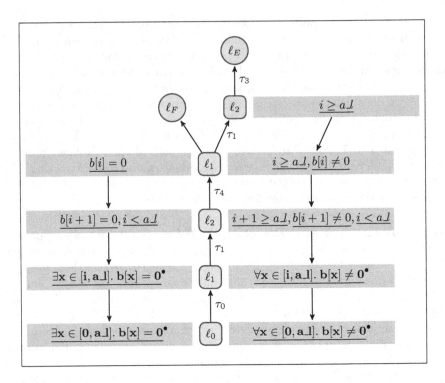

Fig. 4. Illustration of the new refinement approach based on analysing safe and unsafe traces conjointly. The underlined predicates are selected by the refinement process and predicates associate with the superscript • are computed using a system of inference rules.

$\exists x \in [i, a\_l].\ b[x] = 0$ can be inferred from φ_F as well. Thus, we retain φ' and $\neg\varphi'$, and proceed further backwards with the same procedure as shown in Figure 4. We keep applying this procedure to generate states until reaching a fix-point (no new state found). At the end, we obtain the precondition $\exists x \in [0, a\_l].\ b[x] = 0$. Observe that this precondition is sufficient as having an element of array b in the interval $[0, a\_l]$ which is null guarantees the loop termination before violating the assertion condition. It is also necessary as its negation, $\forall x \in [0, a\_l].\ b[x] \neq 0$, allows the loop to iterate at least until the variable i becomes equal to a_l which causes the violation of the assertion.

We call this process *eager abstraction* as opposed to the lazy abstraction governing the CEGAR process. This procedure reduces intra-trace redundancies induced by the refinement which traverses traces back and forth to generate predicates and perform a dependency analysis. Here we can also decide at early stages about relevant predicates to keep, and states are monotonically generated. By construction, safe traces and error traces always contain enough information to show their inconsistency. The new procedure also reduces inter-trace redundancies as common prefixes are explored in parallel. All these points lead to a faster convergence of the fix-point computation.

In our experiments with the program in Fig. 1 including the side assertions to avoid null-pointer dereferencing of a and b (**assert**(a!=NULL); **assert**(b!=NULL)) and access out of bounds for b (**assert**(i<b_l); in ℓ_1 and ℓ_2), we
obtain the precondition $b \neq null \wedge (a \neq null \vee b[0] = 0) \wedge \exists x.\ 0 \leq x \leq a_l \wedge x <
b_l \wedge b[x] = 0$ which is both necessary and sufficient for safe execution.

3   Preliminaries

In this section, we provide background on some ingredients used in our algorithm.

Program. A program is given as a set $\mathcal{TC}$ of transition constraints τ. A transition
constraint τ is a formula of the form

$$g(X) \wedge \left(x'_1 = e_1(X)\right) \wedge \ldots \wedge \left(x'_n = e_n(X)\right) \tag{1}$$

where $X = \langle x_1, \ldots, x_n \rangle$ is a vector of program variables, which include the
program counter pc. In (1), unprimed variables refer to the program state before
performing the transition and primed ones represent the program state after
performing the transition. Formula $g(X)$ is called the *guard* and the remaining
conjuncts of τ are the *update* or *assignment*.

Representing states symbolically. Let us write $V = \{x_1, \ldots, x_n\}$ for the set of
variables of the program (including the program counter pc). For a variable $x \in
V$, $Type(x)$ is the type (range) of x and $\sigma(x)$ is a valuation of x such that $\sigma(x) \in
Type(x)$. The variable pc ranges over the set of all program locations. For a vector
X of variables, a program state is the valuation $\sigma(X) = \langle \sigma(x_1), \ldots, \sigma(x_n) \rangle$.
   A set of program states S is represented symbolically by means of the *char-
acteristic function* of S. The formula φ represents the set of all those states that
correspond to a satisfying assignment of φ, i.e., $\{\sigma(X) \mid \varphi[\sigma(X)/X]\}^3$. We will
use sets and their characteristic functions interchangeably. Symbolic states (for-
mulas) are partially ordered via the implication operator $\Rightarrow$, i.e., $\varphi' \subseteq \varphi$ means
$\varphi' \Rightarrow \varphi$.

State transformer. For a formula φ, the application of the operator **pre** with
respect to the transition constraint τ returns a formula representing the set of
all predecessor states of φ under the transition constraint τ, formally

$$\mathsf{pre}(\tau, \varphi(X)) =_{\mathsf{def}} g(X) \wedge \varphi[\langle e_1(X), \ldots, e_n(X) \rangle / X] \,.$$

For the whole program $\mathcal{TC}$, **pre** is given by

$$\mathsf{pre}(\varphi(X)) =_{\mathsf{def}} \bigvee_{\tau \in \mathcal{TC}} \mathsf{pre}(\tau, \varphi(X)) \,.$$

---

[3] The notation $f[Y/X]$ represents the expression obtained by replacing all occurrences
of every variable from the vector X in f with the corresponding variable (value) from
Y. It naturally extends to a collection (set or list) of expressions.

For a trace $\pi = \tau_1; \ldots; \tau_n$, we have

$$\mathsf{pre}(\tau_1; \ldots; \tau_n, \varphi) =_{\mathsf{def}} \mathsf{pre}(\tau_1, \ldots \mathsf{pre}(\tau_{n-1}, \mathsf{pre}(\tau_n, \varphi)))\ .$$

If $\mathsf{pre}(\pi, \varphi)$ is not equivalent to false, then the trace π is *feasible*.

(Un)Safe states. To ease the presentation, let us assume that the program contains a single error location ℓ_E and a single final location ℓ_F ($\ell_E \neq \ell_F$).[4] We denote by bad the set of *error states*, which is simply given by $pc = \ell_E$. Similarly, we call final the set of *final states*, which is represented by $pc = \ell_F$.

The set of safe states safe contains all states from which a final state is reachable. Formally,

$$\mathsf{safe} =_{\mathsf{def}} \mathsf{lfp}(\mathsf{pre}, \mathsf{final}) \tag{2}$$

where $\mathsf{lfp}(\mathsf{pre}, \varphi)$ denotes the least fix-point of the operator pre above φ. Similarly, unsafe is the set of all states from which an error (bad) state is reachable:

$$\mathsf{unsafe} =_{\mathsf{def}} \mathsf{lfp}(\mathsf{pre}, \mathsf{bad})\ . \tag{3}$$

The least fix-points represent inductive backwards invariants, which we denote by ψ_{bad} and ψ_{final}, respectively. The invariants are inductive under pre, i.e.,

- bad $\subseteq \psi_{\mathsf{bad}}$ and final $\subseteq \psi_{\mathsf{final}}$
- $\mathsf{pre}(\psi_{\mathsf{bad}}) \subseteq \psi_{\mathsf{bad}}$ and $\mathsf{pre}(\psi_{\mathsf{final}}) \subseteq \psi_{\mathsf{final}}$

In the absence of non-determinism in the program, the sets of unsafe and safe states are disjoint, and we have

$$\mathsf{unsafe} \wedge \mathsf{safe} = \mathsf{false}\ .$$

Predicate abstraction. Predicate abstraction consists in approximating a state φ with a formula φ' constructed as a Boolean combination of predicates taken from a set P. Here, the term approximation means that any model that satisfies φ must satisfy φ'. Thus, a suitable approximation is obtained via the logical implication "$\Rightarrow$", i.e., φ' is the strongest Boolean combination built up from predicates taken from the finite set P such that $\varphi \Rightarrow \varphi'$.

Defining the abstraction function α as being the strongest Boolean combination of predicates in P is not practical because of the exponential complexity of the problem. Therefore, we use a lightweight version of α that builds the strongest conjunction of predicates in P:

$$\alpha(\varphi) =_{\mathsf{def}} \bigwedge p\ \ s.t.\ \ p \in P \wedge \varphi \Rightarrow p\ .$$

Let us have $\mathcal{D}^{\sharp}$ the domain of formulas built up from the finite set of predicates P. The domain $\mathcal{D}^{\sharp}$ is not closed under pre, therefore, we define $\mathsf{pre}^{\sharp}$ under which

---

[4] In case of multiple assertions, we add an edge from each assertion (guarded with the negation of the assertion) to ℓ_E. Similar treatment can be applied in the case of multiple return locations.

$\mathcal{D}^\sharp$ is closed. Let us associate the concretization function $\gamma : \mathcal{D}^\sharp \to \mathcal{D}$ to α, we simply choose γ to be the identity function. Functions α and γ form a *Galois connection* with respect to $\subseteq$ ($\Rightarrow$) being the partial order relation for both $\mathcal{D}$ and $\mathcal{D}^\sharp$. Formally speaking

$$\forall x \in \mathcal{D} \; \forall y \in \mathcal{D}^\sharp. \; \alpha(x) \subseteq y \Leftrightarrow x \subseteq \gamma(y) \;.$$

Hence, we define $\mathsf{pre}^\sharp : \mathcal{D}^\sharp \to \mathcal{D}^\sharp$, the abstract version of pre, as follows:

$$\mathsf{pre}^\sharp(\varphi) =_{\mathsf{def}} \alpha(\mathsf{pre}(\gamma(\varphi))) \;,$$

and thus

$$\mathsf{pre}^\sharp(\tau, \varphi) = \alpha(\mathsf{pre}(\tau, \varphi)) = \bigwedge p \;\; s.t. \;\; p \in P \wedge \mathsf{pre}(\tau, \varphi) \Rightarrow p \;.$$

Moreover, for a disjunction we have

$$\mathsf{pre}^\sharp(\tau, \bigvee_{j \in J} \varphi_j) =_{\mathsf{def}} \bigvee_{j \in J} \mathsf{pre}^\sharp(\tau, \varphi_j) \;.$$

As seen for pre, the operator $\mathsf{pre}^\sharp$ also extends to traces. Henceforth, whenever we write $\mathsf{pre}^\sharp_P$ we mean that the abstraction (image) is computed by considering predicates from the set P.

The lattice of abstract states $(\mathcal{L}, \Rightarrow)$ is finite as the set of predicates is finite. Therefore, $\mathsf{lfp}(\mathsf{pre}^\sharp, \mathsf{bad})$ (resp. $\mathsf{lfp}(\mathsf{pre}^\sharp, \mathsf{final})$), the least fixpoint for $\mathsf{pre}^\sharp$ above bad (resp. final) in $\mathcal{L}$, is computable.

4   Eager Abstraction

In this section, we present our approach for the inference of necessary and sufficient preconditions. We recall that a necessary and sufficient precondition φ is a precondition under which no error trace is feasible, and no safe trace is excluded. In other words, it is neither too strong nor too weak. As mentioned previously (Section 3), it is not always possible to compute the set of safe (or unsafe) states using the weakest precondition transformer pre. Therefore, we use its abstract version $\mathsf{pre}^\sharp$. Formally speaking, our goal is to find a set of predicates P which allows us to compute φ such that the two constraints below are fulfilled:

$$\mathsf{lfp}(\mathsf{pre}^\sharp_P, \mathsf{final}) \subseteq \varphi \text{ (no exclusion of safe states)} \tag{4}$$

$$\mathsf{lfp}(\mathsf{pre}^\sharp_P, \mathsf{bad}) \wedge \varphi \equiv \mathsf{false} \text{ (no inclusion of unsafe states)} \tag{5}$$

As opposed to our previous work [1], our goal here is to compute φ monotonically in a single pass. To this end, our algorithm needs to have some features such as:

- A guidance criterion so that at each state exploration step, the two constraints (4) and (5) hold as an invariant of our algorithm.

Algorithm 1. EagerPrecond

Input: set of transition constraints (program) $\mathcal{TC}$
Output: formula (precondition)

1 **Var** P: set of predicates;
2 **Var** ψ_F, ψ_E: formulas;
3 Find a common dominator node ℓ_d for locations ℓ_F and ℓ_E;
4 Let φ_{dF} be the necessary and sufficient precondition for final at ℓ_d;
5 Let φ_{dE} be the necessary and sufficient precondition for bad at ℓ_d;
6 **if** $\varphi_{dF} \wedge \varphi_{dE} \not\equiv$ false **then abort** "failure";
7 $\psi_F := \varphi_{dF}$;
8 $\psi_E := \varphi_{dE}$;
9 **while** true **do**
10 | $\psi_F^0 := \psi_F$;
11 | $\psi_E^0 := \psi_E$;
12 | **foreach** $\tau \in \mathcal{TC}$ **do**
13 | | $P := \mathsf{SplitPreds}(\tau, \psi_F, \psi_E)$;
14 | | **if** $P = \emptyset$ **then abort** "failure";
15 | | $\psi_F := \psi_F \vee \mathsf{pre}_P^\sharp(\tau, \psi_F)$;
16 | | $\psi_E := \psi_E \vee \mathsf{pre}_P^\sharp(\tau, \psi_E)$;
17 | **if** $\psi_F \subseteq \psi_F^0 \wedge \psi_E \subseteq \psi_E^0$ **then return** ψ_F;

- The previous point implies inferring predicates on the fly, as fixing predicates in advance reduces the ability of building abstractions satisfying (4) and (5) at each step.

Hence, we explore safe and unsafe states in parallel taking into account their disjointness as condition that must hold at each step. This idea is translated to the Algorithm EagerPrecond (Algorithm 1).

In the algorithm, the set of safe and unsafe states are symbolically represented via the formulae ψ_F and ψ_E. As the final location ℓ_F and error location ℓ_E are separate, the first question to be answered is: from which location do we start exploring safe and unsafe states conjointly? We choose this location to be the dominator location ℓ_d which is common to ℓ_F and ℓ_E, as any program trace must go through it to reach any of them.

Remark 1. Computing the necessary and sufficient precondition for reaching ℓ_F and ℓ_E (lines 4 and 5 of Algorithm 1) from the dominator node ℓ_d is in practice straightforward, as in most of the programs we have tested, all the paths leading from the dominator location to ℓ_F and ℓ_E are loop-free. However, in the presence of loops, we can use our CEGAR-based technique [1] to compute the precondition up to ℓ_d and then apply the eager approach.

We then compute the weakest precondition to reach ℓ_F and ℓ_E (lines 4 and 5 of Algorithm 1) which respectively gives φ_{dF} and φ_{dE} and they should be disjoint (see line 6). From location ℓ_d onward, states are explored conjointly by taking each time the same transition τ (lines 15 and 16). This step depends on

---

Algorithm 2. SplitPred

Input: formula ψ_F, ψ_E, transition constraint τ
Output: set of predicates

1 **Var** P, P': set of predicates;
2 **Var** ψ_F, ψ_E: formula;
3 $\psi_F := \psi_F \vee \mathsf{pre}(\tau, \psi_F)$;
4 $\psi_E := \psi_E \vee \mathsf{pre}(\tau, \psi_E)$;
5 **if** $\psi_F \wedge \psi_E \not\equiv \mathsf{false}$ **then** **return** $\emptyset$;
6 Let $\tau.pc = \ell$;
7 Let $\psi_{F\ell} \equiv (\psi_F \wedge pc = \ell)$ be of the form $\bigvee_{(i \in I)} \varphi_i$;
8 Let $\psi_{E\ell} \equiv (\psi_E \wedge pc = \ell)$ be of the form $\bigvee_{(j \in J)} \varphi'_j$;
9 $P := \emptyset$;
10 **foreach** $(i, j) \in I \times J$ **do**
11 $\quad$ **if** $\exists\, p \ s.t \ (p \in \mathsf{InferGen}(\varphi_i) \wedge \neg p \in \mathsf{InferGen}(\varphi'_j))$ **then** $P := P \cup \{p, \neg p\}$;
12 $\quad$ **else** $P := P \cup \mathsf{atoms}(\varphi_i) \cup \mathsf{atoms}(\varphi'_j)$;
13 **return** P;

---

the set of predicates computed by calling the procedure SplitPred at line 13. The set of predicates P is computed in a way that the new abstractions obtained via $\mathsf{pre}_P^\#$ are disjoint. This process is iterated until no new safe or unsafe states are discovered (line 17).

Remark 2. The formula ψ_F computed by Algorithm 1 represents all the states which potentially reach the final location from different program locations. To get the precondition at the initial location ℓ_0, it suffices to project ψ_F on ℓ_0, which is simply expressed by the formula $\psi_F \wedge pc = \ell_0$.

SplitPred. Let us now have a look inside the procedure SplitPred (Algorithm 2). The role of this procedure is to deliver the set of predicates under which the next computed abstractions fulfil the separation criterion between safe and unsafe states. It takes as parameters two formulae ψ_F and ψ_E and a transition constraint τ, and returns a set of predicates P such that

$$(\psi_F \vee \mathsf{pre}_P^\#(\tau, \psi_F)) \wedge (\psi_E \vee \mathsf{pre}_P^\#(\tau, \psi_E)) \equiv \mathsf{false} \tag{6}$$

In other words, the over-approximations of the predecessor sets with respect to the transition constraint τ and the set of predicates P are disjoint. First, the exact predecessor sets are computed using the pre operator (lines 3 and 4 in Algorithm 2), if the resulting formulae are not disjoint, there is no need to go further (line 5) as the abstraction will make them even weaker.

We are then interested in the states associated with the program location given by $\ell = \tau.pc^5$ as they are the potentially newly generated ones obtained via

---

[5] The notation $\tau.pc$ simply refers to the program counter value in the pre-state of the transition τ.

transition τ. We obtain this subset by projecting each global set of states on the location ℓ as shown at lines 7 and 8. These sets $\psi_{F\ell}$ and $\psi_{E\ell}$ are disjunctions of formulae, such that every disjunct (φ_i's and φ'_j's) represents a symbolic state and is a conjunction of predicates according to our definition of the predicate transformer (see Section 3).

For each pair of states (φ_i, φ'_j) respectively belonging to the set of safe states and unsafe ones at location ℓ, we try to extract general predicates which they induce using the procedure InferGen (line 11). The extraction of new predicates is based on the system of inference rules [1] (see Appendix A).

If there exists a general predicate p which can be inferred from φ_i and its negation $\neg p$ can be inferred from φ'_j, then it is selected together with its negation (line 11). In fact, p is implied by φ_i and is inconsistent with φ'_j (i.e., $\varphi'_j \wedge p \equiv false$) as $\neg\varphi$ is implied by φ'_j. Hence both p and $\neg p$ are good potential candidates for building new separate states. If we cannot infer such a predicate p, then we return the set of atoms forming the two states (line 12), which keeps the resulting states separated. The function atoms is simply defined as atoms$(\varphi_1 \wedge \ldots \wedge \varphi_n) = \{\varphi_1, \ldots, \varphi_n\}$. It takes a conjunction as argument and returns the set of conjuncts forming it.

Remark 3. Note that SplitPred returns an interpolant [2] for the predecessors of the two formulae taken as parameters. Hence, we could also use an interpolation procedure as a replacement of SplitPred. The investigation of this possibility is left for future work.

Proposition 1. *The formula computed by Algorithm 1 is a necessary and sufficient precondition, i.e. it satisfies (4) and (5).*

Proof. Let us denote by φ the formula returned by Algorithm 1. For (4), φ (which represents ψ_F) is a fix-point according to the termination criterion at line 17 of Algorithm 1. For (5), we have lfp$(\mathsf{pre}_P^\sharp, \mathsf{bad}) \subseteq \psi_E$. Also ψ_E is inconsistent with ψ_F as they are initially inconsistent (line 6 of Algorithm 1) and all updates at lines 15 and 16 based on the set of predicates returned by SplitPred satisfies (6), hence ψ_E and ψ_F remain inconsistent. Thus lfp$(\mathsf{pre}_P^\sharp, \mathsf{bad}) \wedge \varphi \equiv \mathsf{false}$.

Discussion. Our algorithm aborts if it fails to infer a necessary and sufficient precondition (see lines 6 and 14 in Algorithm 1). This can happen due to several reasons: (1) If the program is non-deterministic then $\psi_F \wedge \psi_E$ might be satisfiable; (2) if the predicates inferred by the inference rules do not give rise to sufficiently precise loop invariants to guarantee separation of ψ_F and ψ_E; or (3) if the SMT solver that we are using is unable to conclude unsatisfiability of $\psi_F \wedge \psi_E$. We chose the SMT solver Z3 for our experiments because it did not exhibit any problems regarding (3). However, we encountered some issues regarding the handling of quantifiers in preliminary experiments with other SMT solvers.

Our algorithm cannot distinguish between terminating and non-terminating traces. The problem to perform such a distinction is known as *conditional termination*, i.e. computing preconditions that ensure termination. The extension of our algorithm in this respect is a direction of future work that we pursue.

Table 1. Experimental comparison between eager abstraction and the counterexample-guided approach (from [1])

Program	Precondition	Predicates		Time (s)	
		Eager	CEGAR	Eager	CEGAR
strncmp	Q + S	12	20	**17.54**	**536.70**
strcat	Q + S	3	4	0.18	0.55
memchr	Q + S	7	4	**4.28**	**64.42**
strlen	Q + S	3	4	0.18	0.54
memcpy	S	4	3	0.063	0.15
strchr	Q + S	6	8	0.65	1.76
r_strcat	Q	5	2	1.08	8.04
r_strncpy	Q + S	7	4	**2.90**	**253.55**
strcspn	Q + S	4	3	0.30	0.57
strspn	Q + S	4	3	0.31	0.56
my_strcmp	Q + S	6	7	0.66	2.35
my_memcmp	Q + S	7	5	3.46	20.9
AllNotNull	Q + S	4	3	0.30	2.07
mvswap	S	3	2	0.056	0.061

A well-known problem in predicate abstraction-based methods is non-termination of the analysis if the predicate generalisation method fails to generate the required loop invariants. Common approaches to force termination are the introduction of aggressive generalisation rules (like widening in abstract interpretation) that guarantee that our algorithm eventually answers "failure", or the restriction to a finite predicate language [3] (corresponding to a finite height domain in abstract interpretation). However, the latter method spoils the advantage of our approach that the predicate language adapts itself to the program being analysed, and due the reduced expressiveness our algorithm would answer "failure" more often.

5   Experimental Results

We have implemented our precondition inference technique in the P-Gen[6] tool which takes as input a C program containing a procedure annotated with an assertion to be verified and returns a necessary and sufficient precondition for the validity of the specified assertion.

We performed experiments using a desktop computer with 3.7 GB of RAM and a Core 2 processor with 3 GHz, running Linux. P-Gen uses several theorem provers, such as Yices [4], Simplify [5] and Z3 [6], to compute the abstraction and analyse counterexamples. We used Z3 in our experiments as we noticed that it is the one which handles quantifiers best compared to the other theorem provers.

The results of our experiments are illustrated in Table 1. The column "Precondition" shows the type of precondition inferred, "Q" stands for quantified

---

[6] http://www.cs.ox.ac.uk/people/nassim.seghir/pgen-web-page

and "S" stands for simple (quantifier-free). The column "Predicates" represents the number of predicates inferred to abstract the set of unsafe (safe) states. As we are associating different sets of predicates with different locations, similar to [7], we provide the average number of predicates per location instead of the total number of predicates. Both columns "Time" and "Predicates" are divided into two columns "CEGAR" which represents the counterexample-guided precondition inference approach [1], and "Eager" which refers to the current approach. These examples are implementations of routines from the C string library[7]. The assertions ensure freedom of runtime errors like null pointer dereferencing and array-out-of-bounds accesses. All the benchmarks used as well as the (runs) results of the comparative study are available online[8]. The generated preconditions for the different examples are included as well.

The preconditions generated by the two approaches are semantically equivalent for all these benchmarks, but syntactically different in some cases (due to redundancies).

We can see that the eager approach clearly outperforms the CEGAR-based one in all the cases. This difference is even clearer for programs strncmp, memchr and r_strncpy as the running time takes minutes for the CEGAR approach while it does not go beyond 18 seconds for the eager one. This is encouraging and demonstrates the relevance and practicality of our new approach.

6   Related Work

The combination of predicate abstraction [8] with counterexample-guided abstraction refinement [9] has been implemented in many tools [7,10,11,12,13,14]. Most of them use CEGAR to check the validity of a given assertion. We go beyond that by finding the precondition under which the assertion is valid.

Some other tools are inspired by Hoare's reasoning style [15,16,17]. They are based on the reasoning-by-contract principle: pre- and postconditions and loop invariants have to be specified by the user, which is a tedious task in general. Our technique can support the user by generating preconditions for less interesting side verification obligations (internal assertions), allowing him to focus on the functional aspect (postcondition) of the verification task.

Moy [18] proposed a technique to infer preconditions. While his technique is stronger than many existing ones, it is unable to infer quantified preconditions. Our technique infers universally as well as existentially quantified preconditions for array programs.

Blanc and Kroening [19] proposed an approach for precondition generation to optimise the simulation of SystemC code. However, they have no guarantee that the inferred precondition is necessary and sufficient. Taghdiri [20] proposed an approach for generating approximations of relations (over pre- and

---

[7] An implementation of the different functions is available here:
   http://en.wikibooks.org/wiki/C_Programming/Strings

[8] http://homepages.inf.ed.ac.uk/mseghir/benchmarks_and_results_aplas14.
   tar.gz

post-states) induced by functions by bounding the number of loop unrolling, making the approach unsuitable for proving the absence of bugs. Our technique over-approximates the set of all (even infinite) behaviours. Thus, a computed precondition in our case guarantees safety.

Sankaranarayanan et al. [21] presented a technique that combines test and machine learning to infer likely data preconditions. The results obtained by their approach are promising. However, their technique can only suggest preconditions but does not guarantee their validity.

In the context of abstract interpretation, Cousot et al. [22] formulated precisely the contract inference problem for intermittent assertions. The preconditions extracted by their method are necessary preconditions, i.e. they do not exclude unsafe runs. In a later work [23], they took into account the calling context to identify under which circumstances a generated necessary precondition is also sufficient. We compute necessary and sufficient preconditions independently from the calling context of the procedure. Similar techniques for computing necessary preconditions are proposed by Miné [24] using a *lower widening* technique to perform a polyhedral backward analysis, and Bakhirkin et al [25] who combine over-approximative backward analysis with a *subtraction* operation to obtain under-approximations.

The method described in [22, 24, 26, 27] rely on predefined abstract domains. Thus, if the domain is not precise enough, either it is redesigned or another domain is used. In our approach, predicates are inferred syntactically on the fly and the only a priori restriction are the inference rules that are applied to generalise predicates to potential loop invariants. The inference mechanism can be enhanced by introducing new inference rules without having to implement new abstract program transformers. The advantage of this approach is that the domain adapts itself to the program analysed. However, as discussed above, there is no guarantee for termination if the inference rules fail to generate the required loop invariants.

Calcagno et al. [28] presented a technique based on *bi-abduction* to infer pre- and post-specifications of heap structures. Although we can deal with pointers, the properties handled by their technique are out of the scope for our tool as we do not have a theory to reason about heap properties. On the other hand, the preconditions they compute are only necessary, hence false alarms are not ruled out.

Our current approach deals with the precondition generation problem in the context of safety. Extending it to the liveness context such as termination [29,30] is an area we are interested in for future work.

7 Conclusion

In this paper, we have presented an eager abstraction technique for generating necessary and sufficient preconditions. The idea underlying eager abstraction is that the invariant of separating safe and unsafe states is satisfied throughout the algorithm. Hence the abstraction process is monotone and no refinement is required.

The comparative study with our CEGAR-based approach for precondition generation demonstrates that our new method is a significant improvement and represents the right way to proceed for practicability. For all the programs we have tested, the eager approach performs better than the lazy (CEGAR) one. For cases where the lazy approach takes several minutes, the eager one just requires several seconds (< 18s). This is essential since precondition generation is mostly used in interactive development and verification environments, where response time is crucial for the practicability, productivity and the adoption of the environment by verification engineers.

References

1. Seghir, M.N., Kroening, D.: Counterexample-guided precondition inference. In: Felleisen, M., Gardner, P. (eds.) ESO 2013. LNCS, vol. 7792, pp. 451–471. Springer, Heidelberg (2013)
2. Henzinger, T.A., Jhala, R., Majumdar, R., McMillan, K.L.: Abstractions from proofs. In: POPL, pp. 232–244 (2004)
3. Jhala, R., McMillan, K.L.: A practical and complete approach to predicate refinement. In: Hermanns, H., Palsberg, J. (eds.) TACAS 2006. LNCS, vol. 3920, pp. 459–473. Springer, Heidelberg (2006)
4. Dutertre, B., de Moura, L.: A fast linear-arithmetic solver for DPLL(T). In: Ball, T., Jones, R.B. (eds.) CAV 2006. LNCS, vol. 4144, pp. 81–94. Springer, Heidelberg (2006)
5. Detlefs, D., Nelson, G., Saxe, J.B.: Simplify: A theorem prover for program checking. Technical Report HPL-2003-148, HP Lab (2003)
6. de Moura, L., Bjørner, N.: Z3: An efficient smt solver. In: Ramakrishnan, C.R., Rehof, J. (eds.) TACAS 2008. LNCS, vol. 4963, pp. 337–340. Springer, Heidelberg (2008)
7. Henzinger, T.A., Jhala, R., Majumdar, R., Sutre, G.: Lazy abstraction. In: POPL, pp. 58–70 (2002)
8. Graf, S., Saïdi, H.: Construction of abstract state graphs with PVS. In: Grumberg, O. (ed.) CAV 1997. LNCS, vol. 1254, pp. 72–83. Springer, Heidelberg (1997)
9. Clarke, E.M., Grumberg, O., Jha, S., Lu, Y., Veith, H.: Counterexample-guided abstraction refinement. In: Emerson, E.A., Sistla, A.P. (eds.) CAV 2000. LNCS, vol. 1855, pp. 154–169. Springer, Heidelberg (2000)
10. Ball, T., Rajamani, S.K.: The SLAM project: Debugging system software via static analysis. In: POPL, pp. 1–3 (2002)
11. Chaki, S., Clarke, E.M., Groce, A., Jha, S., Veith, H.: Modular verification of software components in C. In: ICSE, pp. 385–395 (2003)
12. Podelski, A., Rybalchenko, A.: ARMC: The logical choice for software model checking with abstraction refinement. In: Hanus, M. (ed.) PADL 2007. LNCS, vol. 4354, pp. 245–259. Springer, Heidelberg (2007)
13. Ivancic, F., Shlyakhter, I., Gupta, A., Ganai, M.K.: Model checking C programs using F-soft. In: ICCD, pp. 297–308 (2005)
14. Clarke, E., Kroning, D., Sharygina, N., Yorav, K.: SATABS: SAT-based predicate abstraction for ANSI-C. In: Halbwachs, N., Zuck, L.D. (eds.) TACAS 2005. LNCS, vol. 3440, pp. 570–574. Springer, Heidelberg (2005)
15. Flanagan, C., Leino, K.R.M., Lillibridge, M., Nelson, G., Saxe, J.B., Stata, R.: Extended static checking for java. In: PLDI, pp. 234–245 (2002)

16. Barnett, M., Chang, B.-Y.E., DeLine, R., Jacobs, B., Leino, K.R.M.: Boogie: A modular reusable verifier for object-oriented programs. In: de Boer, F.S., Bonsangue, M.M., Graf, S., de Roever, W.-P. (eds.) FMCO 2005. LNCS, vol. 4111, pp. 364–387. Springer, Heidelberg (2006)
17. Dahlweid, M., Moskal, M., Santen, T., Tobies, S., Schulte, W.: Vcc: Contract-based modular verification of concurrent c. In: ICSE Companion, pp. 429–430 (2009)
18. Moy, Y.: Sufficient preconditions for modular assertion checking. In: Logozzo, F., Peled, D.A., Zuck, L.D. (eds.) VMCAI 2008. LNCS, vol. 4905, pp. 188–202. Springer, Heidelberg (2008)
19. Blanc, N., Kroening, D.: Race analysis for systemc using model checking. ACM Trans. Design Autom. Electr. Syst. 15 (2010)
20. Taghdiri, M.: Inferring specifications to detect errors in code. In: ASE, pp. 144–153 (2004)
21. Sankaranarayanan, S., Chaudhuri, S., Ivancic, F., Gupta, A.: Dynamic inference of likely data preconditions over predicates by tree learning. In: ISSTA, pp. 295–306 (2008)
22. Cousot, P., Cousot, R., Logozzo, F.: Precondition inference from intermittent assertions and application to contracts on collections. In: Jhala, R., Schmidt, D. (eds.) VMCAI 2011. LNCS, vol. 6538, pp. 150–168. Springer, Heidelberg (2011)
23. Cousot, P., Cousot, R., Fähndrich, M., Logozzo, F.: Automatic inference of necessary preconditions. In: Giacobazzi, R., Berdine, J., Mastroeni, I. (eds.) VMCAI 2013. LNCS, vol. 7737, pp. 128–148. Springer, Heidelberg (2013)
24. Miné, A.: Inferring sufficient conditions with backward polyhedral underapproximations. ENTCS 287, 89–100 (2012)
25. Bakhirkin, A., Berdine, J., Piterman, N.: Backward analysis via over-approximate abstraction and under-approximate subtraction. In: Müller-Olm, M., Seidl, H. (eds.) SAS 2014. LNCS, vol. 8723, pp. 34–50. Springer, Heidelberg (2014)
26. Bourdoncle, F.: Abstract debugging of higher-order imperative languages. In: PLDI, pp. 46–55 (1993)
27. Rival, X.: Understanding the origin of alarms in ASTRÉE. In: Hankin, C., Siveroni, I. (eds.) SAS 2005. LNCS, vol. 3672, pp. 303–319. Springer, Heidelberg (2005)
28. Calcagno, C., Distefano, D., O'Hearn, P.W., Yang, H.: Compositional shape analysis by means of bi-abduction. In: POPL, pp. 289–300 (2009)
29. Bozga, M., Iosif, R., Konečný, F.: Deciding conditional termination. In: Flanagan, C., König, B. (eds.) TACAS 2012. LNCS, vol. 7214, pp. 252–266. Springer, Heidelberg (2012)
30. Cook, B., Gulwani, S., Lev-Ami, T., Rybalchenko, A., Sagiv, M.: Proving conditional termination. In: Gupta, A., Malik, S. (eds.) CAV 2008. LNCS, vol. 5123, pp. 328–340. Springer, Heidelberg (2008)

A   Inference Rules

The system of rules in Figure 5 was proposed in [1] to generalise predicates. Among the symbols used in the system, e refers to linear terms, x is a variable and φ is a formula.

The rule ELIM linearly combines two constraints to eliminate common variables. Rule EQ infers equality constraints, which might be used by rule SUB to substitute occurrences of variables with equal terms. The rule UNIV builds a quantified formula and LINK bridges the intervals of two quantified formulas. Finally, the rule EXIST produces two existentially quantified formulas and the rules EXT_R and EXT_L extend the interval of an existentially quantified formula from the right and the left, respectively.

$$\frac{c_1.e + e_1 \geq 0 \ , \ -c_2.e + e_2 \geq 0}{c_2.e_1 + c_1.e_2 \geq 0} \ (\text{ELIM})$$
$$(c_1, c_2 > 0)$$

$$\frac{x - e \geq 0 \ , \ -x + e \geq 0}{x = e} \ (\text{EQ})$$

$$\frac{\varphi(x) \ , \ x = e}{\varphi(e)} \ (\text{SUB})$$

$$\frac{\varphi(i), \ \neg\varphi(j) \ (i < j)}{\exists x \in \{i, \ldots, j\}. \ \varphi(x), \ \exists x \in \{i, \ldots, j\}. \ \neg\varphi(x)} \ (\text{EXIST})$$

$$\frac{\exists x \in \{i, \ldots, j\}. \ \varphi(x), \ j \leq k}{\exists x \in \{i, \ldots, k\}. \ \varphi(x)} \ (\text{EXT\_R})$$

$$\frac{\exists x \in \{i, \ldots, j\}. \ \varphi(x), \ k \leq i}{\exists x \in \{k, \ldots, j\}. \ \varphi(x)} \ (\text{EXT\_L})$$

$$\frac{\varphi(i)}{\forall x \in \{i\}. \ \varphi(x)} \ (\text{UNIV})$$

$$\frac{\forall x \in \{j, \ldots, i\}. \ \varphi(x) \ , \ \forall x \in \{i+1, \ldots, k\}. \ \varphi(x)}{\forall x \in \{j, \ldots, k\}. \ \varphi(x)} \ (\text{LINK})$$

i and j are integer variables appearing in a linear index expression in φ ($\neg\varphi$).

Fig. 5. Rules for general predicate inference

Resource Protection Using Atomics
Patterns and Verification

Afshin Amighi, Stefan Blom, and Marieke Huisman

Formal Methods and Tools, University of Twente, Enschede, The Netherlands
{a.amighi,s.blom,m.huisman}@utwente.nl

Abstract. For the verification of concurrent programs, it is essential to be able to show that synchronisation mechanisms are implemented correctly. A common way to implement such sychronisers is by using atomic operations. This paper identifies what different synchronisation patterns can be implemented by using atomic read, write and compare-and-set operation. Additionally, this paper proposes also a specification of these operations in Java's `AtomicInteger` class, and shows how different synchronisation mechanisms can be built and verified using atomic integer as the synchronisation primitive.

The specifications for the methods in the `AtomicInteger` class are derived from the classical concurrent separation logic rule for atomic operations. A main characteristic of our specification is its ease of use. To verify an implementation of a synchronisation mechanism, the user only has to specify (1) what are the different roles of the threads participating in the synchronisation, (2) what are the legal state transitions in the synchroniser, and (3) what share of the resource invariant can be obtained in a certain state, given the role of the current thread. The approach is illustrated on several synchronisation mechanisms. For all implementations, we provide a machine-checked proof that the implementations correctly implement the synchroniser.

1 Introduction

Motivation To increase performance, multi-threaded applications should make optimal use of multi-core architectures. Typically, these applications exploit synchronisation to ensure that there are no conflicting accesses to shared resources. In shared-memory concurrency, atomic variables, *i.e.* variables that may only be accessed using atomic operations, are used to implement these synchronisation mechanisms. Such variables are called *atomic synchronisers*. In programming languages like Java, atomic variables along with three basic atomic operations (atomic read, write and compare-and-set) are encapsulated in *atomic classes*. To guarantee the correctness of concurrent programs it is essential to be able to reason about these atomic classes. This paper proposes an approach to specify the behavior of an *atomic class* as a synchroniser.

Approach. We provide specifications for the basic atomic operations, read, write and conditional update, which can be used to verify the implementation of different synchronisation classes. These specifications are derived from the general

J. Garrigue (Ed.): APLAS 2014, LNCS 8858, pp. 255–274, 2014.

rule for atomic operations from a well-established program logic, Concurrent Separation Logic (CSL) [23]. The specifications have been designed to be easy to use: when using them to show the correctness of a concrete synchroniser implementation, only a few intuitive parameters have to be provided. This paper, presents a specification for atomic integers, as it is the base for most of the synchronisation classes in Java. However, our approach also works for the other atomic classes.

In our approach, any thread has a local view of the atomic variable. The global state is then defined in terms of the atomic variable and all the local views. In addition, the atomic variable is instrumented with a protocol that describes what the legal state transitions are. The protocol is used by the thread to derive the guarantees that the environment provides. Additionally, a resource invariant is declared, which specifies which resources are protected by the synchroniser. The derived specifications for the `AtomicInteger` operations are thus parametrised by this protocol and the resource invariant. This specification expresses how `AtomicInteger`, as an atomic synchroniser, grants and retains permissions to access the shared resource specified by the resource invariant *exclusively*. To describe the specifications and the predicates encoding the views and the protocol, we use permission-based separation logic for Java [3,9].

Before presenting the specification of `AtomicInteger`, we introduce several synchronisation patterns, each supported by an example. For each of these synchronisation patterns, we discuss how the specification parameters have to be defined. Moreover, for each example, we present a machine-checked correctness proof, showing that it indeed protects a shared resource, and avoids data races.

Contributions. The main contributions of this paper are the following: (1) an overview of typical synchronisation patterns using the basic atomic operations; (2) a general specification for the basic atomic operations that together can synchronise a group of threads; (3) a simple, practical and thread-modular contract for `AtomicInteger` as a synchroniser; and (4) verification of several examples implementing the synchronisation patterns using our VerCors tool set [25].

Outline. This paper is structured as follows: in Section 2 we present the different synchronisation patterns using `AtomicInteger` as a synchronisation primitive. Section 3 derives contracts for atomic read, write, and compare-and-set. Section 4 explains the generalised specification of the `AtomicInteger` class and discusses correctness proofs of the clients using `AtomicInteger`. Finally, Section 5 presents related work and Section 6 draws conclusions, and discusses future work.

2   Synchronisation in Java

To support thread-safe access to single variables, Java provides the package `java.util.concurrent.atomic`, as part of Java's general concurrency API. This package provides wrappers for `volatile` variables with appropriate atomic operations for read, write, and compare-and-swap. In Java, changes to a volatile variable are immediately visible to other threads, *i.e.* their value will never be cached thread-locally. This makes volatile variables suitable to implement synchronisation mechanisms, where it is essential that all threads have a consistent view of the synchroniser.

This paper particularly studies the `AtomicInteger` class, which encapsulates a volatile field of type integer. Essentially, it provides the following methods: `get()`, returning the value that was last written to the field; `set(int v)`, atomically assigning the value `v` to the field; and `compareAndSet(int x,int n)`, atomically checking the current value and updating it to `n`, if it is equal to the expected value `x`, otherwise leaving the state unchanged, and returning a boolean to indicate whether the update succeeded.

Synchronisation Patterns. In a shared-memory concurrency setting, two kinds of thread interactions via a synchronizer can be distinguished: *cooperation* and *competition* [18]. In a cooperative interaction, threads employ a *cooperative synchroniser* as a communication channel to cooperatively share a resource. In a competitive interaction, a *competitive synchroniser* runs a competition and provides (temporary) access to the shared resource to the winner. A synchroniser can behave cooperatively or competitively in different states, this is called a *hybrid* interaction. Various patterns of synchronisation can be described in terms of atomic integer operations:

GS (get and set). Threads can cooperatively interact using atomic read and write. Every thread has a designated state in which it obtains the resource, and all threads attempt to reach their designated state. When a thread writes to the atomic integer, it implicitly signals who *should* own the resource next (cooperation). Based on the value written into the synchroniser, ownership of the resource is transferred to the appropriate thread waiting for that particular value. Producer-Consumer and Dekker's critical section algorithm are examples of this pattern. Lst. 1 shows `ProducerConsumer` with two methods `produce` and `consume`, sharing a field `data`, that implements this algorithm. Typically, these methods will be executed as part of a surrounding loop. The `AtomicInteger` denotes the state of the buffer: full (`F`) or empty (`E`). Both the producer and the consumer wait until the buffer gets into their desired state. As soon as the state changes to the expected value, the waiting thread obtains the shared resource. When it is done, it changes the state, so that the other thread can access the resource.

SC (set and compareAndSet). Atomic write and conditional update can be used to implement a competitive synchroniser. Threads are competing to obtain the protected resource by calling `compareAndSet`. A thread that succeeds in changing the state, obtains the resource. When it no longer needs the resource, it sets the state to the initial value, to signal its availability. Failing threads continue to try to acquire the resource by checking whether the state is reverted back to the initial state. A spin-lock implementation using `AtomicInteger` (see Lst. 2) is a known example of this pattern where the atomic integer value encapsulates the state of the lock: locked (`L`) or unlocked (`U`). If a thread successfully updates the state from `U` to `L`, it acquires

```
public class ProducerConsumer{
  private final int E = 0, F=1;
  private AtomicInteger sync;
  private int data; // shared buffer
  ProducerConsumer(){
    sync = new AtomicInteger(E);
  }
  void produce(){
    write();
    sync.set(F); // signal
    while(sync.get() == F); // wait
  }
  void consume(){
    while(sync.get()==E); // wait
    read();
    sync.set(E); // signal
  }
  // methods write() and read()
}
```

```
public class SpinLock{
  private final int U = 0, L=1;
  private AtomicInteger sync;
  SpinLock(){
    sync = new AtomicInteger(U);
  }

  void lock(){
    while(!sync.compareAndSet(U,L));
  }

  void unlock(){
    sync.set(U);
  }
}
```

Lst. 1. ProducerConsumer: cooperation   **Lst. 2.** SpinLock: competition

the lock (method `lock`). Consequently, failing threads enter a try-wait loop, until the lock is released. To release the lock, the thread holding the lock executes `set(U)` (method `unlock`).

GC (get and `compareAndSet`). Atomic read and conditional update are suited to implement a synchronisation mechanism that *partially* transfers the resources between the participating threads. Shared reading synchronisation mechanisms using `AtomicInteger` like `Semaphore` and `CountDownLatch` are typical instances of this pattern. Also lock-free pointer-based data structures using `AtomicReference` are examples of this pattern. Since, here, we are only looking at exclusive synchronisation mechanisms, we do not discuss this pattern further. However, a generalisation of our approach to reason about partial resource ownership using atomics is ongoing work.

GSC (get, set and `compareAndSet`). All basic operations of `AtomicInteger` can be used together to implement a hybrid synchroniser. Threads compete with each other to obtain the resource by calling `compareAndSet`. A thread that succeeds in changing the state, wins the resource. Failing threads may not compete any more to change the state. But, they have to wait for the resource availability. When the winner thread no longer needs the resource, it updates the state to signal how the resource should be used afterwards. Lst. 3 shows the implementation of a `SingleCell` algorithm, which illustrates a hybrid pattern[1]. It provides a single method to find or put a value in a shared storage cell. The storage cell is always in one of these states: empty (E), writing (W) or done (D). The cell containing the value (the state D) must be immutable. Initially, all threads are competing to assign their value. If a thread succeeds in obtaining writing access to the resource, the state becomes W. After completing the assignment, it will report its success (returns PUT). All other threads have to wait until the value is assigned, and then they

---

[1] This is a simplified version of a lock-less hash table, especially designed for state space exploration in the multi-core model checker LTSmin [12].

```
public class SingleCell{
  final private int E = 0, W=1, D=2;
  final private int PUT = 0, SEEN = 1, COLN = 2;
  private AtomicInteger sync;
  private int data;
  SingleCell(){ sync = new AtomicInteger(E); }

  int findOrPut(int v){
    if(sync.compareAndSet(E,W)){ data = v;   sync.set(D);   return PUT; }
    if(sync.get()!=E){
      while(sync.get()==W); // wait
      if(sync.get() == D)
        if(data == v)  return SEEN;
        else  return COLN;
    }
  }
}
```

Lst. 3. `SingleCell`: hybrid

check the stored value. If the value in the cell is equal to the value the thread holds, it will return the value SEEN, otherwise it will signal a collision (returns COLN).

3   Ownership Exchange via Atomics

This section derives permission-based Separation Logic contracts for atomic read, write, and compare-and-set operations. Separation Logic (SL) is an extension of Hoare Logic, originally developed to reason about programs with pointers [19]. A key characteristic of SL is that it allows to reason about disjointness of heaps. This ability also makes SL suitable to reason in a thread-modular way about multi-threaded programs, as demonstrated by O'Hearn [15], who introduced Concurrent Separation Logic (CSL) to verify correct access of synchronised threads to dynamically allocated memory. CSL also introduced the notion of *ownership*, to specify how a synchronisation construct *exclusively* exchanges ownership of a memory location. To be able to verify programs where multiple threads concurrently read a shared address, permission-based separation logic [3] extends CSL with fractional permissions [4]. In a fractional permission model, a thread holds a permission $\pi \in (0, 1]$ to access a heap location. Full ownership, providing write permission, is indicated by the full permission 1, while any permission $\pi \in (0, 1)$ indicates a read-only access.

Let E denote arithmetic expressions, B boolean expressions and R pure resource formulas. In our fragment of CSL, the syntax for assertions P is defined as follows:

$$
\begin{aligned}
B & ::= \neg B \mid B_1 \wedge B_2 \mid B_1 \vee B_2 \\
R & ::= \mathsf{emp} \mid E_1 \overset{\pi}{\hookrightarrow} E_2 \mid R_1 * R_2 \mid R_1 \mathbin{-\!\!*} R_2 \\
P & ::= B \mid R \mid B * R \mid B \implies R \mid \forall x.\, P \mid \exists x.\, P \mid \underset{i \in \mathsf{I}}{\circledast} P_i
\end{aligned}
$$

In addition to the classical connectives and first order quantifiers, the main assertions are: (1) the empty heap assertion, written emp, (2) the *points-to* predicate $E_1 \overset{\pi}{\mapsto} E_2$, meaning that expresssion E_1 points to a location on the heap, has permission π to access this location, and this location contains the value E_2, (3) the *separating conjunction* operator $*$, expressing that two formulas are valid for disjoint parts of the heap, (4) a magic wand (also known as resource implication) formula $R_1 \twoheadrightarrow R_2$ which holds for any heap that has the following property: if the heap is extended with a *disjoint* heap that satisfies R_1, then the combined heap satisfies R_2, and finally (5) an iterative separating conjunction over a set I, written $\underset{i\in I}{\circledast} P_i$. Below, we use $[E]$ to denote the contents of the heap at location E and we use $E \mapsto -$ to indicate that the content stored at location $[E]$ is not important.

Permissions can be transferred between threads at synchronisation points (including thread creation and joining). Moreover, permissions can be split and combined to change between read and write permissions:

$$E_1 \overset{\pi}{\mapsto} E_2 * E_1 \overset{\pi'}{\mapsto} E_2 \Leftrightarrow E_1 \overset{\pi+\pi'}{\mapsto} E_2$$

The addition of two permissions is undefined if the result is greater than the full permission. Soundness of the logic ensures that the total number of permissions on a location never exceeds 1. Thus, at most one thread at a time can be writing to a location, and whenever a thread has a read permission, all other threads holding a permission on this location simultaneously must have a read permission. This in turn ensures that there are no data races in verified programs.

3.1   Basic Rules

Next we show how the contracts in permission-based SL for the basic atomic operations can be derived. We base ourselves on the work by Vafeiadis [23], which enables us to define a language where atomic commands, denoted $\langle C \rangle$, are the only constructs for synchronisation.

We divide the domain of the heap into a set of *atomic* locations ALoc (*e.g.*, the volatile field of AtomicInteger) and a set of *non-atomic* locations NLoc (*e.g.*, data in Lst. 1). An atomic location $s \in$ ALoc may only be accessed using: (1) get(s) for atomic read of the atomic location s, (2) set(s, n) for atomic update of s with n, and (3) cas(s, x, n) for atomic conditional update of s. We use the term *atomic value* to refer to the value that an atomic variable contains and the term *resources* to refer to *non-atomic* locations of the heap.

As proposed by O'Hearn, in a concurrent setting a resource invariant is attached with a synchroniser. This associates ownership of a part of the state space with possible states of the synchroniser [15]. For example, the resource invariant for a lock lock $\in$ ALoc that protects the resource x $\in$ NLoc is defined as:

$$I_{\mathsf{lock}} = \exists\, v \in \{0,1\}.\ \mathsf{lock} \overset{1}{\mapsto} v * ((v = 1 \implies \mathsf{emp}) * (v = 0 \implies \mathsf{x} \overset{1}{\mapsto} -))$$

This expresses that full ownership of the location x is available to win when $[\mathsf{lock}] = 0$, while if $[\mathsf{lock}] = 1$ then emp (interpreted as nothing) can be obtained.

In general, using a function res that maps an atomic value to a set of disjoint resources, given Val as the set of values and $s \in$ ALoc, the resource invariant I_s is defined as:

$$I_s = \exists\, v \in \text{Val.}\ s \overset{1}{\mapsto} v * S(s,v) \quad \text{where} \quad S(s,v) = \underset{r \in \text{res}(s,v)}{\circledast}\ r \overset{1}{\mapsto} -$$

In CSL, a judgment $I \vdash \{P\}\ C\ \{Q\}$ expresses the following: given a globally accessible resource invariant I and a local precondition P, if a statement C starts its execution in a state satisfying $P * I$, and if C terminates, then its final state satisfies $Q * I$. The proof rule for atomic commands [23] expresses that to prove correctness of $\langle C \rangle$, the resource invariant I can be used for the verification of the atomic body C. Thus, I is not accessible to the environment. Moreover, within the body C, the resource invariant I may be invalidated, because it is not visible to the environment, but it must be re-established before C is finished:

$$\frac{\text{emp} \vdash \{P * I\}\ C\ \{I * Q\}}{I \vdash \{P\}\ \langle C \rangle\ \{Q\}} \quad [\textsc{Atomic}]$$

We use the rule [$\textsc{Atomic}$] to derive specifications for the basic atomic operations get, set and cas when they are coordinating a set of threads to (exclusively) access a shared resource. The specifications should capture all exclusive synchronisation patterns mentioned above: cooperative, competitive and hybrid. Therefore, we need to enrich the resource invariant definition with an abstraction of local state and feasible states, which allows one to deduce what the environment guarantees. Next,we instantiate the [$\textsc{Atomic}$] rule to derive the resources that set, get and cas exchange to perform exclusive access synchronisation.

3.2   Synchronisation Protocol

Assuming a set of threads Thr, for each atomic location s that is synchronising the threads, we define the *view* of a thread $t \in$ Thr as an *atomic ghost variable*, denoted s_t. Each thread stores the last visited atomic value in its view. We define the view to be atomic in order to restrict the thread t, using ghost code, to update *its* view *only* inside an atomic block. To do so, the ownership of a view is split in half between the owner thread and the resource invariant, *i.e.* the shared state. Therefore, a thread can always read its own view, but it can only update its view when it captures the other half permission inside an atomic block by accessing the resource invariant. Views of threads indexed by thread identifiers are written as a vector of views $\vec{s_t}$. Similarly, $\vec{v_t}$ denotes a vector of values pointed to by the views, indexed by the corresponding thread identifiers, while $\vec{v_t}_{\{v_\tau = x\}}$ denotes a vector such that the item indexed with τ is equal to x. For the sake of simplicity we assume that there is only one single atomic location s functioning as the synchroniser. However, the approach is generalisable for multiple atomic location.

We define the *(global) atomic state* as a tuple of the atomic value and all thread local views of it, denoted $(s, \vec{s_t})$. An atomic state is *admissible* if at least one thread has a correct view of the synchroniser. An admissible atomic state is *feasible* if either (1) it is an initialisation state where all the threads have an identical view of the initialised atomic location, or (2) it is reachable from the initialisation state by a finite set of atomic operations.

As the views must be updated only inside the atomic operations, they can reflect the actions that the environment can perform w.r.t. the atomic location. The current definition of the resource invariant is too restrictive to reflect this. So, first, we define the protocol of the synchroniser in terms of the atomic state:

$$P_s^{\mathsf{Thr}} = \bigvee_{v, \vec{w_t} \in \mathsf{Val} \cdot \mathsf{fsbl}(v, \vec{w_t})} ([s] = v \wedge [\vec{s_t}] = \vec{w_t})$$

where fsbl determines whether the *atomic state* is feasible.

Example 1 (Protocol for ProducerConsumer*).* To illustrate our definition of feasible states, consider the ProducerConsumer example, where we have two threads p (producer) and c (consumer) with corresponding views, *i.e.* s_p and s_c, respectively, given an atomic variable s:

$$P_s^{\{p,c\}} = (\ ([s] = E \wedge [s_p] = E \wedge [s_c] = E) \vee ([s] = F \wedge [s_p] = F \wedge [s_c] = E) \vee$$
$$([s] = F \wedge [s_p] = F \wedge [s_c] = F) \vee ([s] = E \wedge [s_p] = F \wedge [s_c] = E)\ )$$

Note that $([s] = F, [s_p] = E, [s_c] = F)$ is not a feasible state. Therefore, when p believes that the buffer is empty (E), it can safely *rely* on the fact that no other thread is allowed to modify s to full (F). Thus, p deduces that it exclusively owns s, so $[s]$ *must be* E when $[s_p] = E$.

Example 2 (Protocol for SpinLock*).* Consider the SpinLock example, which is a competititve pattern. Its protocol is defined as follows:

$$P_s^{\mathsf{Thr}} = ([s] = U \ \wedge (\forall\, t \in \mathsf{Thr}.\ [s_t] = U)) \vee$$
$$([s] = L \ \wedge (\exists\, \tau \in \mathsf{Thr}.\ [s_\tau] = L \ \wedge \forall\, t \in \mathsf{Thr} \setminus \{\tau\}.\ [s_t] = U))$$

This expresses that either the lock is available and all threads have a correct view of the state, or there is only one thread that has acquired the lock and updated its view while all others have failed to change their beliefs. This makes it possible for the unlocking thread to rely on its view, knowing that it will be the only one that has the correct view.

The protocol suffices to derive the contracts for the basic atomic operations when they are involved in a *competitive* pattern. To cover cooperative patterns, where *threads obtain the shared resources based on their views*, in addition, the resource invariant has to express what resources are protected in terms of the atomic state. In fact, instead of one single atomic variable s, $(s, \vec{s_t})$ plays the role of a global synchroniser. Similar to res, we define ares to map the atomic state to a set of disjoint resources. Therefore, we replace $S(s, v)$ with $R(s, v, \vec{s_t}, \vec{w_t})$ to denote all the resources associated with $[s] = v$ and $[\vec{s_t}] = \vec{w_t}$.

Now we are ready to define precisely what we mean by a synchronisation primitive, based on our extended definition of resource invariant.

Definition 1 (State-based Synchroniser). *An atomic location s together with the basic atomic operations* ACmd = {get, set, cas} *define a* state-based *primitive synchronisation mechanism for a set of threads* Thr *if it is instrumented with a resource invariant defined as follows:*

$$I_s = \exists v, \overrightarrow{w_t} \in \mathsf{Val} \cdot s \overset{1}{\mapsto} v * (\underset{t \in \mathsf{Thr}}{\circledast}\ s_t \overset{\frac{1}{2}}{\mapsto} w_t) * R(s, v, \overrightarrow{s_t}, \overrightarrow{w_t}) * P_s^{\mathsf{Thr}}$$

where $R(s, v, \overrightarrow{s_t}, \overrightarrow{w_t}) = \underset{r \in ares(s,v,\overrightarrow{s_t},\overrightarrow{w_t})}{\circledast}\ r \overset{1}{\mapsto} -.$

Example 3 (Synchroniser for ProducerConsumer*).* Based on the protocol defined in Example 1, we define the resource invariant of the atomic synchroniser s to synchronise p and c:

$$I_s = \exists v, w_p, w_c \in \{E, F\} \cdot s \overset{1}{\mapsto} v * s_p \overset{\frac{1}{2}}{\mapsto} w_p * s_c \overset{\frac{1}{2}}{\mapsto} w_c * R(s, v, \overrightarrow{s_t}, \overrightarrow{w_t}) * P_s^{\{p,c\}}$$

where $R(s, v, \overrightarrow{s_t}, \overrightarrow{w_t})$ is data $\overset{1}{\mapsto} -$ if $v = E$, $w_p = F$, $w_c = E$ and $v = F$, $w_p = F$, $w_c = E$, and $R(s, v, \overrightarrow{s_t}, \overrightarrow{w_t})$ is emp if threads agree on the value of s. This expresses that s holds the full ownership of data when threads do not agree on the value of the synchroniser (*i.e.*, during the transition phase).

Example 4 (Synchroniser for SpinLock*).* Considering the SpinLock protocol in Example 2, we define the resource invariant for s. Here, regardless of the views of the threads, the resource invariant holds the full resource when the state is U, otherwise the winning thread holds it.

$$I_s = \exists v, \overrightarrow{w_t} \in \{U, L\} \cdot s \overset{1}{\mapsto} v * (\underset{t \in \mathsf{Thr}}{\circledast}\ s_t \overset{\frac{1}{2}}{\mapsto} w_t) * R(s, v, \overrightarrow{s_t}, \overrightarrow{w_t}) * P_s^{\mathsf{Thr}}$$

where $R(s, v, \overrightarrow{s_t}, \overrightarrow{w_t})$ will be data $\overset{1}{\mapsto} -$ when $v = U$ and emp when $v = L$.

Next we investigate how the three basic atomic operations can exchange the shared resources.

3.3 Specifications of Atomics

This section derives contracts for the three basic atomic operations for state-based synchronisation. The contracts, shown in Figure 1, essentially express that in an exclusive state-based synchronisation, the thread τ executing an atomic operation to update the state of the synchroniser, should *provide* the resources associated with the state after the operation, and in return will *receive* the resources associated with the previous state of the synchroniser. In Figure 1, we used $R_s^{\mathsf{Thr}}(\tau, x, y)$ to denote all the resources when $s = x$ and $s_\tau = y$.

Our technical report [1] presents the complete derivations. Basically, for each basic atomic operation we propose an implementation using basic instructions. We instantiate [ATOMIC] for each operation with a precondition about the

$$\text{Let } R_s^{\text{Thr}}(\tau, x, y) = \underset{\overrightarrow{v_t}\{v_\tau = y\} \in \text{Val.fsbl}(x, \overrightarrow{v_t}\{v_\tau = y\})}{\circledast} R(s, x, \overrightarrow{s_t}, \overrightarrow{v_t}\{v_\tau = y\})$$

$$\frac{\forall\, v, \overrightarrow{v_t} \in \text{Val. } v_\tau = d \wedge \text{fsbl}(v, \overrightarrow{v_t}\{v_\tau = d\}) \implies \text{fsbl}(n, \overrightarrow{v_t}\{v_\tau = n\})}{I_s \vdash \{s_\tau \overset{\frac{1}{2}}{\mapsto} d * R_s^{\text{Thr}}(\tau, n, n)\} \; \text{set}_\tau(s, n) \; \{s_\tau \overset{\frac{1}{2}}{\mapsto} n * R_s^{\text{Thr}}(\tau, d, d)\}} \quad [\text{WATM}]$$

$$\frac{}{I_s \vdash \{s_\tau \overset{\frac{1}{2}}{\mapsto} d\} \; \text{get}_\tau(s) \; \{s_\tau \overset{\frac{1}{2}}{\mapsto} ret * (R_s^{\text{Thr}}(\tau, ret, ret) \twoheadrightarrow R_s^{\text{Thr}}(\tau, ret, d))\}} \quad [\text{RATM}]$$

$$\frac{\forall\, v, \overrightarrow{v_t} \in \text{Val. } v_\tau = x \wedge \text{fsbl}(v, \overrightarrow{v_t}\{v_\tau = x\}) \implies \text{fsbl}(n, \overrightarrow{v_t}\{v_\tau = n\})}{\begin{array}{c} I_s \vdash \{s_\tau \overset{\frac{1}{2}}{\mapsto} x * R_s^{\text{Thr}}(\tau, n, n)\} \\ \text{cas}_\tau(s, x, n) \\ \{(ret = \text{true} \wedge s_\tau \overset{\frac{1}{2}}{\mapsto} n * R_s^{\text{Thr}}(\tau, x, x)) \vee (ret = \text{false} \wedge s_\tau \overset{\frac{1}{2}}{\mapsto} x * R_s^{\text{Thr}}(\tau, n, n))\} \end{array}} \quad [\text{CATM}]$$

Fig. 1. Contracts derived for **set**, **get** and **cas**

thread's view and thread's local state, containing the required resources. Then we derive the postcondition from the precondition and the body, taking into account that I_s is available inside the body, providing the resources associated to the current state of the synchroniser. Inside the body, either the atomic location or the view of the thread is updated. The derivations show that the thread consumes the resources it currently holds to re-establish I_s and exits the atomic body with an updated atomic state and the resources it obtains as the result of the update.

Atomic Write. Operation $\text{set}_\tau(s, n)$ denotes the atomic update of s with n by a particular thread τ. We derive rule [WATM], expressing that the executing thread with the view d delivers all the resources associated with the feasible atomic state after the update. We should stress here that this contract is specific to using atomic write for synchronisation, it is not the most general contract possible.

For an atomic synchroniser for *exclusive* resource access, it is crucial that the value inferred by the protocol coincides with the thread's view. In other word, the protocol embedded in the resource invariant must prove that the thread executing an atomic write has the *full permission* to do the **set** action, otherwise, it is not guaranteed that the thread intended to execute **set**, can indeed accomplish this safely.

Atomic read. The read action for a particular thread $\tau \in \text{Thr}$ with a view s_τ that has the last visited value d from the atomic value s is indicated by $\text{get}_\tau(s)$. In the rule [RATM], the contract of the atomic read specifies that the atomic variable does not change its value, while the atomic state is modified because the reading thread updates its view. So the thread has to establish the resource invariant with the resources associated with the updated view inside the atomic body. As a result, it obtains the remainder as its postcondition, which is formalised using a magic wand operator. According to [19] this rule is correct if our resource assertions are *strictly exact*. In a fragment of CSL that we use as our specification language, all resource formulas are indeed strictly exact.

$$\dfrac{\forall\, v, \vec{v_t} \in \mathsf{Val}.\; v_\tau = \mathsf{d} \wedge \mathsf{fsbl}(v, \vec{v_t}_{\{v_\tau = d\}}) \implies \mathsf{fsbl}(n, \vec{v_t}_{\{v_\tau = n\}})}{I_s \vdash \{s_\tau \overset{\frac{1}{2}}{\mapsto} \mathsf{d} * S(s, n) * T(s_\tau, d)\}\; \mathsf{set}_\tau(s, n)\; \{s_\tau \overset{\frac{1}{2}}{\mapsto} n * S(s, d) * T(s_\tau, n)\}} \quad [\text{WATM}]$$

$$\dfrac{}{I_s \vdash \{s_\tau \overset{\frac{1}{2}}{\mapsto} \mathsf{d} * T(s_\tau, d)\}\; \mathsf{get}_\tau(s)\; \{s_\tau \overset{\frac{1}{2}}{\mapsto} ret * T(s_\tau, ret)\}} \quad [\text{RATM}]$$

$$\dfrac{\forall\, v, \vec{v_t} \in \mathsf{Val}.\; v_\tau = x \wedge \mathsf{fsbl}(v, \vec{v_t}_{\{v_\tau = x\}}) \implies \mathsf{fsbl}(n, \vec{v_t}_{\{v_\tau = n\}})}{I_s \vdash \{s_\tau \overset{\frac{1}{2}}{\mapsto} x * S(s, n) * T(s_\tau, x)\}\; \mathsf{cas}_\tau(s, x, n)} \quad [\text{CATM}]$$

$$\{(ret = \mathsf{true} \wedge s_\tau \overset{\frac{1}{2}}{\mapsto} n * S(s, x) * T(s_\tau, n)) \vee (ret = \mathsf{false} \wedge s_\tau \overset{\frac{1}{2}}{\mapsto} x * S(s, n) * T(s_\tau, x))\}$$

Fig. 2. Thread-modular specifications of atomic operations

Conditional update. Finally, rule [CATM] specifies $\mathsf{cas}_\tau(s, x, n)$ with the expected value x and the value to be updated n. The calling thread assumes that the synchroniser contains a value equal to an expected value and then calls the operation to try to modify the atomic synchroniser to n. Therefore, the thread has to provide the resources associated with the updated atomic state and it will gain the resources associated with the expected value, if the operation succeeds. Otherwise, the operation returns all the provided resources.

3.4 Thread-Modular Contracts

The last step is to adapt the derived contracts for the atomic operations to a thread-modular specification. In particular, this means that the specifications should express the pre- and postconditions using local information only, *i.e.*, using (1) the atomic value as a globally known state, and (2) local information that contains the view of the executing thread.

Note that the resource invariant expresses when the *synchroniser* holds the resources. For example, the resource invariant of `ProducerConsumer` does *not* specify when a particular thread can obtain the buffer. Generally, in cooperative patterns, the synchroniser holds the resource *temporarily*, until one of the waiting threads updates its view. We take advantage of this to simplify the contracts by defining the resources using two components: (1) the resources that the *synchroniser* holds for the competition, which is used to associate resources to the atomic values in classical definition of the resource invariant, *i.e.* S, and (2) the resources that *threads* obtain when they are updating their views, denoted with T. Basically, $T(s_\tau, v)$ indicates resources to be held by thread τ when $s_\tau = v$. We exploit these two components to decompose $R_s^{\mathsf{Thr}}(\tau, x, y)$ (defined in Figure 1) into a global and a thread local components.

These resources are either associated to the atomic value x, which will be obtained competitively using a `cas` operation, or associated to a particular view of a thread, which will be obtained by updating the view. We can formally express this decomposition for $\tau \in \mathsf{Thr}$, $x, y \in \mathsf{Val}$ as:

$$R_s^{\mathsf{Thr}}(\tau, x, y) \Leftrightarrow \mathsf{S}(s, x) * \underset{t \in \mathsf{Thr}, v_t \in \mathsf{Val}}{\circledast} (\mathsf{T}(s_t, v_t) \mathbin{-\!\!*} \mathsf{T}(s_t, x))$$

where $\mathsf{T}(s_t, v_t) \mathbin{-\!\!*} \mathsf{T}(s_t, x)$ specifies the resources that thread t exchanges when it updates its view from v_t to x.

In summary, for a competitive pattern, resources are merely associated with the state of the synchroniser using $\mathsf{S}(s, x)$. A *cooperative pattern* exploits the definition of $\mathsf{T}(s_t, v_t)$, which associates the resources to the view of a thread expressing when the *thread* holds a resource. A *hybrid pattern* uses both $\mathsf{T}(s_t, v_t)$ and $\mathsf{S}(s, x)$ to reason about the resource exchanges.

We use this decomposition and update the contracts based on the fact that the executing thread may have resources obtained based on its *current* view. This results in thread-modular specifications for the basic atomic operations, as shown in Figure 2. which generally express that the executing thread must *provide* (1) the resources associated with its current view, and (2) the resources associated with the new state of the synchroniser. In return the thread *obtains* (1) the resources associated with its updated view, and (2) the resources associated with the previous state of the synchroniser. Note that in the patterns that we studied, the `cas` and `set` operations do not exchange resources using the thread views, and we are not aware of algorithms where these operations can transfer ownership based on their views.

4   Contracts of `AtomicInteger`

Based on the specifications derived above, we specify the behaviour of the `AtomicInteger` class as an *exclusive-access atomic synchronisation primitive*. First, we introduce our concrete specification language, which is a combination of permission-based SL and JML [5]. Then, we explain all predicates and functions that we use to specify `AtomicInteger`, and finally we present the complete specification.

4.1   Specification Language

As we reason about Java programs, we use Parkinson's variant of SL for Java, where the expression pointing into the heap is a *field access of an object* [16], extended with permissions for concurrency.

In our assertion language we distinguish between *resource expressions* (R, typical elements r_i) and *functional expressions* (E, typical elements e_i), with the subset of logical expressions of type boolean (B, typical elements b_i). Formulas in our logic are defined by the following grammar:

$$R ::= b \mid \mathsf{Perm}(e.\mathsf{f}, \mathsf{frac}) \mid r_1 \mathbin{*\!*} r_2 \mid r_1 \mathbin{-\!*} r_2$$
$$\mid (\backslash\mathsf{forall} * \; \mathsf{T} \; v; b; r) \mid b_1 \mathbin{==\!\!>} r_2 \mid e.\mathsf{P}(e_1, \cdots, e_n)$$
$$E ::= \text{any } pure \text{ expression} \quad B ::= \text{any } pure \text{ expression of type boolean}$$

where T is an arbitrary type, v is a variable name, P is an abstract predicate [17] of a special type resource, f is a field name, and frac denotes a fractional permission.

The assertion Perm($e.f, \pi_i$) expresses the access permission π_i of the field $e.f$. The notation for implication ==> is borrowed from JML. We also divert from the classical SL notation of * for the separating conjunction to ** in order to avoid name clashes with the multiplication operator. Given b as a constraint on the range of the quantifier we use \forall* to define the universal separating conjunction.

Assertions can also contain abstract predicates (P) that encapsulate the state space [17]. In our specification language $e.P(e_1, \cdots, e_n)$ expresses an invocation of the predicate P on the object e with arguments $e_1, \cdots, e_n$. Verifying a program, the abstract predicates should be explicitly opened when they are in scope, otherwise their body cannot be used. In the specification below, we sometimes require the predicate to be a group. Any predicate that is linear in its fractional arguments can be defined as a group. This means that the predicate can be split over permissions, see [8] for more details. When the value of a field is important we write PointsTo(x.f,p,v), which is equivalent to Perm(x.f,p) && x.f==v. Finally, we use the *minimum non-zero permission* [13], denoted as +0, to read an immutable location with the following axiom:

$$\text{Perm}(x.f, +0) ** \text{Perm}(x.f, +0) = \text{Perm}(x.f, +0)$$

In addition, method and class specifications can be preceded by a given clause, declaring the method and class specification-only parameters. Method specification parameters are passed (implicitly) at method calls, class parameters are passed at type declaration and instance creation, resembling the parametric types mechanism of Java.

4.2 Predicates and Parameters

Any client program instantiating the AtomicInteger class as an exclusive atomic synchronisation primitive has to provide the *protocol* of the synchroniser object. In fact, a protocol of a synchronisation construct is an abstract state machine instrumented with an interpretation function that maps each state of the state machine to a fraction of the resources that the synchroniser object or a particular thread must hold in that state. Especially, in our settings, a protocol of a synchronisation construct must specify: (1) identification of the participants, (2) the shared resource that has to be protected by the synchronisation construct, (3) the fraction of the shared resource to be held by the synchroniser or a thread in each atomic state, and (4) the transitions that are valid for the synchroniser object.

To make a single specification of AtomicInteger that can capture all exclusive access patterns, the specification is parametrised by (1) a set of roles, which basically is an abstraction of the participating threads' identification, (2) an abstract predicate as a resource invariant, specifying the shared resources to be protected by `AtomicInteger`, (3) a function to associate the states of the atomic integer as the synchroniser with the fraction of the shared resource, (4) a boolean predicate, encoding all the valid transitions that a particular instance of `AtomicInteger` can take, and (5) a handle token.

A *role* abstraction abstracts the identity of threads to a set of roles. This makes our specification unbounded in the number of threads. The synchroniser is defined as a globally known, special role, written S, that coordinates the threads. This role is declared as a publicly visible constant in class `AtomicInteger`, to hold the resource when the class runs the competition.

The validity of the transitions is encoded in the `trans` predicate. More importantly this encoding enables us to extract the set of the feasible states. The `trans` predicate expects as arguments the role of the invoking thread, the current and the intended update state of the synchroniser.

The shared resources are described by `inv(frac p)`, a resource formula parametrised with permissions (of type `frac`), and defined as a `group`, *i.e.* it should be splittable over permissions. To associate the *fraction of the shared resources* with the state of the atomic integer, we define the function `share`, which is parametrised by a role, and the value of the atomic integer. Our role abstraction allows us to express S and T in the specification presented in Figure 2 using only `inv` parametrised with `share`.

For example, instantiating `AtomicInteger` for `ProducerConsumer` we define:

```
group inv(frac p) = Perm(data,p);
pred trans(role r,int c,int n)=
    (r == P && c == E && n == F) || (r == C && c == F && n == E);
frac  share(role r,int s){
    return (r == P && s == E) ? 1: ((r == C && s == F) ? 1: 0); }
```

where the definition of `share` shows that the full ownership of the shared resource, *i.e.* `data`, is only associated with the views of the threads. In the specification presented in Figure 2 this would mean that the S component would be `emp` and the T component associates the full ownership of `data` to the views of the threads. Similarly, instantiating `AtomicInteger` for `SpinLock` we use these definitions:

```
group inv = resinv;
pred trans(role r,int c,int n) = (c==U && n==L) || (c==L && n==U);
frac share(role r,int s){ return (r == S && s == U) ? 1 : 0;  };
```

where `resinv` would be the shared resource to be protected by the lock which is passed as a class parameter to `SpinLock`. As it is specified in the definition of `share` the synchroniser, defined with the globally known role S, will hold the full resource when its state is U (unlocked). This can be expressed in the specification presented in Figure 2 with T defined as `emp` while the component S associates the full ownership of `resinv` to the unlocked state of the atomic location.

To invoke an operation from `AtomicInteger`, the calling thread must provide the correct required arguments which are demanded by the contracts. For this purpose, the `AtomicInteger` specification defines a special token, called `handle`, which can be used to prove that a thread has the right to invoke an action.

```
   //@ given group (frac−>group) inv;
2  //@ given (role,int−>frac) share;
   //@ given (role,int,int−> boolean) trans;
4  //@ given Set<role> rs;
   class AtomicInteger {
6    private volatile int value;
     //@ group handle(role r,int d,frac p);

     /*@
10   requires inv(share(S,v));
     ensures (\forall* role r; rs.contains(r) ; handle(r,v,1)); @*/
12   AtomicInteger(int v);

14   /*@ given role r, int d, frac p;
     requires handle(r,d,p) ** inv(share(r,d));
16   ensures handle(r,\result,p) ** inv(share(r,\result)); @*/
     public int get();

     /*@ given role r, int d, frac p;
20   requires handle(r,d,p) ** trans(r,d,v);
     requires inv(share(S,v)) ** inv(share(r,d));
22   ensures handle(r,v,p) ** inv(share(S,d)) ** inv(share(r,v)); @*/
     public void set(int v);

     /*@ given role r, frac p;
26   requires handle(r,x,p)** trans(r,x,n);
     requires inv(share(S,n)) ** inv(share(r,x));
28   ensures \result==> (handle(r,n,p) ** inv(share(S,x)) ** inv(share(r,n)));
     ensures !\result==> (handle(r,x,p) ** inv(share(S,n)) ** inv(share(r,x))); @*/
30   boolean compareAndSet(int x, int n);
   }
```

Lst. 4. Contracts for `AtomicInteger`

The postcondition ensures that appropriate new handles for new actions are handed out to the invoking thread. The handle is carrying the role of the calling thread which witnesses its role and its view from the state (last observed value) of `AtomicInteger`. Any instance of a synchronisation mechanism is associated with a particular set of threads. Therefore any thread (1) without a handle (*i.e.* outside of the coordinated threads), (2) with an incorrect role, or (3) with a visited value that is outside of the synchroniser's reachable states, will therefore not be able to interfere with the threads that participate in this synchronisation.

Handles are specified as **group** without a definition. At the initialisation of the `AtomicInteger`, the constructor issues a full handle for all roles that are passed to the synchroniser. These full handles are all given back to the thread that created the `AtomicInteger`. These full handles may then be split and passed on to any other thread participating in the synchronisation.

4.3 Specification

Finally, Lst. 4 shows the complete specification of class `AtomicInteger`. We briefly discuss the method specifications.

The constructor requires the fraction associated to the initial value of the atomic integer. These are the resources that are initially stored inside the synchroniser (S), and that can be won by the winning thread in a competition.

Notice that in a cooperative synchronisation mechanism, the resources initially are supposed to be with one of the threads, and the synchroniser is only used as a medium to pass the resources on to the next thread. The postcondition of the constructor provides handles for all roles (except the S role) that are involved in the synchronisation, which can be split and passed to all threads that want to access the shared resource.

The contracts of the methods in `AtomicInteger` are all specified based on the specifications we derived in Figure 2 of Section 3. Given the role of the invoking thread, its last visited value from the state (view) and the fraction of `handle`, they all require handles carrying this information. New handles are returned as part of the postconditions. State changing methods, *i.e.* `set` and `compareAndSet`, require that the intended transition is valid, as specified by the `trans` predicate. Finally, the fraction of the resource invariant to be exchanged is specified using `inv` and `share` based on the specifications derived for the basic atomic operations.

4.4   Verification

In verifying client programs using `AtomicInteger`, it is vital to check the definition of `share`, as it should not allow the synchroniser to invent permissions. The distribution defined by `share` should satisfy the following property: *in all states, the total sum of the permissions held by the threads for a resource must not exceed the full permission.* To ensure that the definition of `share` fulfils the condition, we generate proof obligations stating that in any snapshot of the execution, the sum of the fractions assigned to all the threads and the synchroniser must not exceed 1. To show that this proof obligation is respected, we use the definitions of `trans` to extract the set of the valid states, and `share` to determine the resource distribution. The former draws the *maximal state machine* for each role, which shows *all possible transitions* that a role can take. The latter assigns the fraction that each role must hold in each state. Finally, the product of the maximal state machines is exploited to reason about the sum of the shares for each *feasible snapshot*.

Due to space limit, the complete correctness proof of the case studies, including the sanity check of the `share` functions and the proof outline of the programs, are provided in the technical report [1]. Here we only present the correctness of the `findOrPut` method from our `SingleCell` example to illustrate how the specification of `AtomicInteger` works. In Lst. 5 the proof outline of this method demonstrates how the contracts of `AtomicInteger` exchange resources. To show available resources in each step, the outline is annotated with the intermediate states. To instantiate the `SingleCell` class we use these definitions:

```
group inv(frac p) = Perm(data,p);
pred trans(role r,int c,int n) = (c==E && n==W) || (c==W && n==D);
frac  share(role r,int v) { return (r==S && v==E) ? 1 :
          ((r==S && v==D) ? +0: ((r==T && v==D) ? +0:0)); }
```

All the case studies discussed above are verified with our VerCors tool set available at [25]. This tool set is currently being developed to reason about

```
   //@ given frac f;
 2 //@ requires handle(T,E,f);
   //@ ensures \result == PUT ==> handle(T,D,f) ** PointsTo(data,+0,v);
 4 //@ ensures \result == SEEN ==> handle(T,D,f) ** PointsTo(data,+0,v);
   int findOrPut(int v){
 6 {handle(T,E,f) ** inv(share(T,E)) ** inv(share(S,W)) }
     if(sync.compareAndSet(E,W)){
 8 {handle(T,W,f) ** inv(share(T,W)) ** inv(share(S,E)) }
       data = v;  //unfold inv(share(S,E)) for Perm(data,1)
10 {handle(T,W,f) ** PointsTo(data,1,v)}
   {handle(T,W,f) ** inv(share(S,D)) ** inv(share(T,W))}
12     sync.set(D);
   {handle(T,D,f) ** inv(share(S,W)) ** inv(share(T,D)) ** (data==v)}
14 {handle(T,D,f) ** PointsTo(data,+0,v)}
       return PUT;
16   }
   {handle(T,E,f) ** inv(share(T,E)) ** inv(share(S,W)) }
18   if(sync.get()!=E){
   {handle(T,val,f) ** inv(share(T,val)) ** (val!=E) }
20     while(sync.get()==W);
   {handle(T,val,f) ** inv(share(T,val)) ** (val!=E) ** (val!=W)}
22   if(sync.get() == D)
   {handle(T,D,f) ** inv(share(T,D))}  // unfold inv(share(T,D))
24     if(data == v)
         {handle(T,D,f) ** PointsTo(data,+0,v)}
26       return SEEN;
       else
28       {handle(T,D,f) ** PointsTo(data,+0,val) ** (val!=v)}
         return COLN;
30   }
   }
```

Lst. 5. Verification of the `findOrPut` method from `SingleCell`

multithreaded Java programs annotated with permission-based SL. The tool leverages existing verification solutions to multi-threaded Java programs, by encoding verification problems into the Chalice language [13]. The Chalice verifier is then used to prove the translated program correct w.r.t. its specification. All case studies are verified automatically, after providing a few proof hints in terms of intermediate state annotations that we left out here for clarity of presentation. The complete correctness proof of the case studies are presented in the technical report [1] using VerCors syntax which are also available online at [24]. In the presented proof outlines, for clarity, we only annotated the intermediate states of the proof with the predicates that transform resources between the synchroniser and the participating threads.

5   Related Work

Different program logics based on Separation Logic for concurrent programs can be found in the literature. Vafeiadis and Parkinson combined Rely-Guarantee reasoning and SL in RGSep to reason about fine-grained concurrent programs [22]. Assertions in RGSep distinguish between local and shared state, and actions are used to describe the interferences on the shared state between parallel processes. Later, Young et al. embedded permission-annotated actions in their assertion language and extended abstract predicates [17] to Concurrent Abstract Predicates

(CAP) [6]. Abstract predicates in CAP encapsulate both resources and interferences, which allows one to reason about the client program without having to deal with all the underlying interferences and resources. The rule for atomics in CAP uses a so called *repartitioning operator*, to extract the resources that the atomic operation requires or ensures.

In CAP it is not possible to reason about synchroniser objects that protect *external* shared resources. Inspired by Jacobs and Piessens [11], and Dodds *et al.* [7], CAP was extended by Svendsen and Birkedal resulting in Higher-Order CAP (HOCAP) [21] and later Impredicative CAP (iCAP) [20] to specify client usage protocols, suitable for synchronisers. iCAP is an important step towards reasoning about synchronisation mechanisms that protect client defined external states.

Ley-Wild and Nanevski [14] proposed Subjective CSL where the thread's *self* view and an *other* view (as a collective effect of the environment) are used to reason about coarse-grained concurrency. Finally, Hobor *et al.* [10] proposed a rule in CSL to reason about programs using barriers as their main synchronisation construct. But they didn't verify the implementation of the barrier.

All techniques mentioned above develop new program logics to reason about concurrent programs. Instead, here, we treat synchronisers at the specification level and we reuse existing verification technology to derive our practical and easy to use specifications from O'Hearn's classical CSL.

6   Conclusion

This paper proposes an approach to specify and reason about atomics as synchronisation constructs. Our approach separates the verification of (1) the correctness of the communication protocol, and (2) the code obeying the protocol, which carries out a rely-guarantee style proof in SL.

Moreover, the paper discusses different patterns to synchronise a set of threads to access a shared resource using atomic read, write and compare-and-set. Based on these patterns, we provide a simple, thread-modular and practical specification of the class AtomicInteger from the java.util.concurrent.atomic API, using permission-based SL. The specification is easy and intuitive to be used, it only has to be instantiated by: the threads' roles; the shared resources that are protected by the synchroniser; a relation defining allowed state changes; a function that describes for each state change which share of the shared resource is transferred from the thread to the synchroniser, or vice versa; and the handle, as a witness for the provided information.

Using CSL, as a well-established logic, we derived the specification from the standard proof rule for atomic statements. To ensure overall soundness of the approach, it has to be ensured that the sharing function does not implicitly allow the creation of resources. We also briefly discussed how this can be verified.

We are in the process of extending our approach to shared reading synchronisers, which allows us to verify reference implementations of shared usage synchronisation classes such as Semaphore, ReadWriteReentrantLock and

CountDownLatch, see [2] for preliminary results. As future work, we will also develop a specification of the AtomicReference. This will allow us to verify lock-free pointer-based data structures from java.util.concurrent.

Acknowledgments. The work presented in this paper is supported by ERC grant 258405 for the VerCors project.

References

1. Amighi, A., Blom, S.C.C., Huisman, M.: Resource protection using atomics: patterns and verifications. Technical Report TR-CTIT-13-10, Centre for Telematics and Information Technology, University of Twente, Enschede (May 2013)
2. Amighi, A., Blom, S., Huisman, M., Mostowski, W., Zaharieva-Stojanovski, M.: Formal specifications for Java's synchronisation classes. In: Lafuente, A.L., Tuosto, E. (eds.) 22nd Euromicro International Conference on Parallel, Distributed, and Network-Based Processing, pp. 725–733. IEEE Computer Society (2014)
3. Bornat, R., Calcagno, C., O'Hearn, P., Parkinson, M.: Permission accounting in separation logic. In: Palsberg, J., Abadi, M. (eds.) POPL, pp. 259–270. ACM (2005)
4. Boyland, J.: Checking interference with fractional permissions. In: Cousot, R. (ed.) SAS 2003. LNCS, vol. 2694, pp. 55–72. Springer, Heidelberg (2003)
5. Burdy, L., Cheon, Y., Cok, D., Ernst, M., Kiniry, J., Leavens, G., Leino, K., Poll, E.: An overview of JML tools and applications. STTT 7(3), 212–232 (2005)
6. Dinsdale-Young, T., Dodds, M., Gardner, P., Parkinson, M.J., Vafeiadis, V.: Concurrent abstract predicates. In: D'Hondt, T. (ed.) ECOOP 2010. LNCS, vol. 6183, pp. 504–528. Springer, Heidelberg (2010)
7. Dodds, M., Jagannathan, S., Parkinson, M.J.: Modular reasoning for deterministic parallelism. In: Proceedings of the 38th Annual ACM SIGPLAN-SIGACT Symposium on Principles of Programming Languages, POPL 2011, pp. 259–270. ACM, New York (2011)
8. Haack, C., Huisman, M., Hurlin, C.: Reasoning about Java's reentrant locks. In: Ramalingam, G. (ed.) APLAS 2008. LNCS, vol. 5356, pp. 171–187. Springer, Heidelberg (2008)
9. Haack, C., Huisman, M., Hurlin, C., Amighi, A.: Permission-based separation logic for multithreaded Java programs (submitted, 2014)
10. Hobor, A., Gherghina, C.: Barriers in concurrent separation logic. In: Barthe, G. (ed.) ESOP 2011. LNCS, vol. 6602, pp. 276–296. Springer, Heidelberg (2011)
11. Jacobs, B., Piessens, F.: Expressive modular fine-grained concurrency specification. In: Proceedings of the 38th Annual ACM SIGPLAN-SIGACT, POPL 2011, pp. 271–282. ACM, New York (2011)
12. Laarman, A., van de Pol, J., Weber, M.: Boosting multi-core reachability performance with shared hash tables. In: Bloem, R., Sharygina, N. (eds.) FMCAD, pp. 247–255. IEEE (2010)
13. Leino, K., Müller, P., Smans, J.: Verification of concurrent programs with Chalice. In: Aldini, A., Barthe, G., Gorrieri, R. (eds.) FOSAD 2007/2008/2009. LNCS, vol. 5705, pp. 195–222. Springer, Heidelberg (2009)
14. Ley-Wild, R., Nanevski, A.: Subjective auxiliary state for coarse-grained concurrency. In: Giacobazzi, R., Cousot, R. (eds.) POPL, pp. 561–574. ACM (2013)
15. O'Hearn, P.W.: Resources, concurrency and local reasoning. Theoretical Computer Science 375(1-3), 271–307 (2007)

16. Parkinson, M.J.: Local reasoning for Java. Tech. Rep. UCAM-CL-TR-654, University of Cambridge, Computer Laboratory (November 2005)
17. Parkinson, M., Bierman, G.: Separation logic, abstraction and inheritance. In: Principles of Programming Languages (POPL 2008), pp. 75–86. ACM Press (2008)
18. Raynal, M.: Concurrent Programming - Algorithms, Principles, and Foundations. Springer (2013)
19. Reynolds, J.: Separation logic: A logic for shared mutable data structures. In: Logic in Computer Science, pp. 55–74. IEEE Computer Society (2002)
20. Svendsen, K., Birkedal, L.: Impredicative concurrent abstract predicates. In: Shao, Z. (ed.) ESOP 2014. LNCS, vol. 8410, pp. 149–168. Springer, Heidelberg (2014)
21. Svendsen, K., Birkedal, L., Parkinson, M.: Modular reasoning about separation of concurrent data structures. In: Felleisen, M., Gardner, P. (eds.) ESOP 2013. LNCS, vol. 7792, pp. 169–188. Springer, Heidelberg (2013)
22. Vafeiadis, V., Parkinson, M.: A marriage of rely/guarantee and separation logic. In: Caires, L., Vasconcelos, V.T. (eds.) CONCUR 2007. LNCS, vol. 4703, pp. 256–271. Springer, Heidelberg (2007)
23. Vafeiadis, V.: Concurrent separation logic and operational semantics. Electr. Notes Theor. Comput. Sci. 276, 335–351 (2011)
24. Synchronisers in vercors, https://fmt.ewi.utwente.nl/redmine/projects/vercors-verifier/wiki/Synchronizers
25. Vercors tool set, http://www.utwente.nl/vercors/

Resource Analysis of Complex Programs with Cost Equations

Antonio Flores-Montoya and Reiner Hähnle

TU Darmstadt, Dept. of Computer Science, Germany
{aflores,haehnle}@cs.tu-darmstadt.de

Abstract. We present a novel static analysis for inferring precise complexity bounds of imperative and recursive programs. The analysis operates on cost equations. Therefore, it permits uniform treatment of loops and recursive procedures. The analysis is able to provide precise upper bounds for programs with complex execution flow and multi-dimensional ranking functions. In a first phase, a combination of control-flow refinement and invariant generation creates a representation of the possible behaviors of a (possibly inter-procedural) program in the form of a set of execution patterns. In a second phase, a cost upper bound of each pattern is obtained by combining individual costs of code fragments. Our technique is able to detect dependencies between different pieces of code and hence to compute a precise upper bounds for a given program. A prototype has been implemented and evaluated to demonstrate the effectiveness of the approach.

1 Introduction

Automatic resource analysis of programs has been subject to intensive research in recent years. This interest has been fuelled by important advances in termination proving, including not only ranking function inference [6, 16], but complete frameworks that can efficiently prove termination of complex programs [3, 7, 10]. Termination proving is, however, only one aspect of resource bound inference.

There are several approaches to obtain upper bounds for imperative programs [3, 8, 9, 12–15, 17, 18]. Most pay little attention to interprocedural, in particular, to recursive programs. Only SPEED [14] and the recent paper [8] address recursive procedures. The extent to which SPEED can deal with complex recursive procedures is hard to evaluate (they provide only one example). The approach of [8] ignores the output of recursive calls which, however, can be essential to obtain precise bounds (see Fig.1).

A different line of work is based on *Cost Equations*, a particular kind of *non-deterministic recurrence relations*, annotated with constraints. This is the approach followed by the COSTA group [1, 2, 4, 5]. One advantage of Cost Equations is that they can deal with both loops and recursion in a *uniform* manner. However, the approach does not cope well with loops that exhibit multiple phases or with programs whose termination proof requires multiple linear ranking functions for a single loop/recursive procedure.

J. Garrigue (Ed.): APLAS 2014, LNCS 8858, pp. 275–295, 2014.
© Springer International Publishing Switzerland 2014

We use the program in Fig.1 to illustrate some of the problems we address in this paper. The program is annotated with structured comments containing cost labels of the form [*Cost x*]. These indicate that at the given program point x resource units are consumed. The program consists of two methods. Method `move` behaves differently depending on the value of boolean variable `fwd`. If `fwd` is true, it may call itself recursively with $n' = n + 1$ and consume two resource units. If `fwd` is false, it may call itself with $n' = n - 1$ and consume one resource unit. Method `main` has a loop that calls `move` and updates the value of n with the result of the call. Additionally, at any iteration, it can change the value of `fwd` to true.

This example is challenging for several reasons: (i) `move` behaves differently depending on the value of `fwd`, so we ought to analyse its different behaviors separately; (ii) the return value of `move` influences the subsequent behavior of the `main` method and has to be taken into account;

Program 1

```
 1 main(int m, int n){
 2  //assume(m>n>0)
 3  bool fwd=false;
 4  while(n > 0){
 5     n=move(n,m,fwd);
 6     if(?) fwd=true;
 7  }
 8 }
 9 int move(int n,m, bool fwd){
10  if(fwd){
11    if(m > n && ?){
12      ...; //[Cost 2]
13      return move(n+1,m,fwd);
14    }
15  }else{
16    if(n > 0 && ?){
17      ...; //[Cost 1]
18      return move(n-1,m,fwd);
19    }
20  }
21  return n;
22 }
```

Fig. 1. Program example

(iii) the `main` method might not terminate and yet its cost is finite. Moreover, the upper bound of terminating and non-terminating executions is different. Below we present a table that summarizes the possible upper bounds of this program.

Pattern (1) occurs when `move` decrements `n` for a while but without reaching 0 (the initial `n` is an upper bound of the cost); then the guard in

Execution pattern	(1)	(2)	(3)
Upper bound	$n + 2m$	$2(m - n)$	n
Terminating	×	×	✓

line 6 is true and `move` increases `n` up to `m`, incurring a cost of $2m$. The loop in `main` never terminates because n does not reach 0. In pattern (2) the guard in line 6 is true at the beginning and `move` increases `n` to `m` consuming $2 * (m - n)$. Finally, in pattern (3), the guard in line 6 is never true (or only when $n = 0$). Then `move` decrements `n` to 0 and the main loop may terminate, consuming n resource units.

The techniques presented in our paper can deal fully automatically with complex examples such as the program above. Our main contributions are: first, a static analysis for both imperative and (linearly) recursive programs that can infer precise upper bounds for programs with complex execution patterns as above. The analysis combines a control-flow refinement technique in the abstract context of cost equations and a novel upper bound inference algorithm. The latter exploits dependencies between different parts of a program during the computation of upper bounds and it takes into account multiple upper bound candidates at the same time. Second, we provide an implementation of our approach. It is publicly available (see Sec. 6) and it has been evaluated in comparison with KoAT [8], PUBS [1] and Loopus[17]. The experimental evaluation shows how the analysis deals with most examples presented as challenging in the literature.

2   Cost Equations

In this section, we introduce the necessary concepts for the reasoning with cost equations. The symbol $\bar{x}$ represents a sequence of variables $x_1, x_2, \cdots , x_n$ of any length. The expression $vars(t)$ denotes the set of variables in a generic term t. A variable assignment $\alpha : V \mapsto D$ maps variables from the set of variables V to elements of a domain D and $\alpha(t)$ denotes the replacement of each $x \in vars(t)$ by $\alpha(x)$. A *linear expression* has the form $q_0 + q_1 * x_1 + \cdots + q_n * x_n$ where $q_i \in \mathbb{Q}$ and $x_1, x_2, \cdots , x_n$ are variables. A *linear constraint* is $l_1 \leq l_2, l_1 = l_2$ or $l_1 < l_2$, where l_1 and l_2 are linear expressions. A *cost constraint* φ is a conjunction of linear constraints $l_1 \wedge l_2 \wedge \cdots \wedge l_n$. The expression $\varphi(\bar{x})$ represents a cost constraint φ instantiated with the variables $\bar{x}$. A cost constraint φ is *satisfiable* if there exists an assignment $\alpha : V \mapsto \mathbb{Z}$ such that $\alpha(\varphi)$ is valid (α satisfies φ).

Definition 1 (Cost expression). *A cost expression e is defined as:*

$$e ::= q \mid nat(l) \mid e + e \mid e * e \mid nat(e - e) \mid \max(S) \mid \min(S)$$

where $q \in \mathbb{Q}^+$, l is a linear expression, S is a non-empty set of cost expressions and $nat(e) = \max(e, 0)$. We often omit $nat()$ wrappings in the examples.

Definition 2 (Cost equation). *A cost equation c has the form $\langle C(\bar{x}) = e + \sum_{i=1}^{n} D_i(\bar{y_i}), \varphi \rangle$ ($n \geq 0$), where C and D_i are cost relation symbols; all variables $\bar{x}, \bar{y_i}$, and $vars(e)$ are distinct; e is a cost expression; and φ is a conjunction of linear constraints that relate the variables of c.*

A cost equation $\langle C(\bar{x}) = e + \sum_{i=1}^{n} D_i(\bar{y_i}), \varphi \rangle$ states that the cost of $C(\bar{x})$ is e plus the sum of the costs of each $D_i(\bar{y_i})$. The relation φ serves two purposes: it restricts the applicability of the equation with respect to the input variables and it relates the variables $\bar{x}, vars(e)$, and $\bar{y_i}$. One can view C as a non-deterministic procedure that calls $D_1, D_2, \ldots, D_n$.

Fig. 2 displays the cost equations corresponding to the program in Fig. 1. To simplify presentation in the examples we reuse some variables in different relation symbols. In the implementation they are in fact different variables with suitable equality constraints in φ.

We restrict ourselves to linear recursion, i.e., we do not allow recursive equations with more than one recursive call. Our approach could be combined with existing analyses for multiple recursion such as the one in [4]. Input and output variables are both included in the cost equations and treated without distinction. By convention, output variable names end with "o" so they can be easily recognized. In a procedure, the output variable corresponds to the return variable

SCC	Nr	Cost Equation
S_1	1	$main(n,m) = while(n,m,0)$ $n \geq 1 \wedge m \geq n+1$
S_2	2	$while(n,m,fwd) = 0$ $n \leq 0$
	3	$while(n,m,fwd) = move(n,m,fwd,no) + while(no,m,fwd)$ $n > 0$
	4	$while(n,m,fwd) = move(n,m,fwd,no) + while(no,m,1)$ $n > 0$
S_3	5	$move(n,m,fwd,no) = 2 + move(n+1,m,fwd,no)$ $fwd = 1 \wedge n < m$
	6	$move(n,m,fwd,no) = 0$ $fwd = 1 \wedge n = no$
	7	$move(n,m,fwd,no) = 1 + move(n-1,m,fwd,no)$ $fwd = 0 \wedge n > 1$
	8	$move(n,m,fwd,no) = 0$ $fwd = 0 \wedge n = no$

Fig. 2. Cost equations of the example program from Fig. 1

(*no* in the method move). In a loop, the output variables are the local variables that might be modified inside the loop. In the while loop from Fig.2, we would have $while(n,m,fwd,no,fwdo)$ where no and $fwdo$ are the final values of n and fwd, but the cost equations have been simplified for better readability.

Generating Cost Equations. Cost equations can be generated from source code or low level representations. Loop extraction and partial evaluation are combined to produce a set of cost equations with only direct recursion [1]. The details are in the cited papers and omitted for lack of space. The resulting system is a sequence of strongly connected components (SCCs) $S_1, \ldots, S_n$ such that each S_i is a set of cost equations of the form $\langle C(\overline{x}) = e + \sum_{j=1}^{k} D_j(\overline{y_j}) + \sum_{j=1}^{n} C(\overline{y_j}), \varphi \rangle$ with $k \geq 0$ and $n \in \{0,1\}$ and each $D_j \in S_{i'}$ where $i' > i$. Each SCC is a set of directly recursive equations with at most one recursive call and k calls to SCCs that appear later in the sequence. Hence, S_1 is the outermost SCC and entry point of execution while S_n is the innermost SCC and has no calls to other SCCs. Each resulting cost equation is a complete iteration of a loop or recursive procedure.

Example 1. In Fig. 2, the cost equations of Program 1 are grouped by SCC. Each SCC defines only one cost relation symbol: *main*, *while*, and *move* occur in S_1, S_2, and S_3, respectively. However, the cost equations in any SCC may contain references to equations that appear later. For instance, equations 3 and 4 in S_2 have references to *move* in S_3.

A concrete execution of a relation symbol C in a set of cost equations is generally defined as a (possibly infinite) evaluation tree $T = node(r, \{T_1, \ldots T_n\})$, where $r \in \mathbb{R}^+$ is the cost of the root (an instance of the cost expression in C) and $T_1, \ldots T_n$ are sub-trees corresponding to the calls in C. In the following we will not need this general definition. A formal definition of evaluation trees and their semantics is in [1].

3   Control-Flow Refinement of Cost Equations

As noted in Sec. 1, we have to generate all possible execution patterns and discard unfeasible patterns that might reduce precision or even prevent us from obtaining an upper bound. Our cost equation representation allows us to look at one SCC at a time. If we consider only the cost equations within one SCC, we have sequences of calls instead of trees (we are only considering SCCs with linear recursion). That does not prevent each cost equation in the sequence from having calls to other SCCs.

Example 2. Given S_3 from Fig. 2, the sequence $5 \cdot 5 \cdot 6$ represents a feasible execution where equation 5 is executed twice followed by one execution of 6. On the other hand, the execution $5 \cdot 8$ is infeasible, because the cost constraints of its elements are incompatible ($fwd = 1$ and $fwd = 0$).

Given an SCC C consisting of cost equations S_C, we can represent its execution patterns as regular expressions over the alphabet of cost equations in S_C. We use a specific form of execution patterns that we call *chain*:

Definition 3 (Phase, Chain). *Let $S_C = c_1, \ldots, c_r$ be the cost equations of an SCC C. A phase is a regular expression $(c_{i_1} \vee \ldots \vee c_{i_m})^+$ over S_C (executed a positive number of times). A special case is a phase where exactly one equation is executed: $(c_{i_1} \vee \ldots \vee c_{i_m})$.*
A chain is a regular expression over S_C composed of a sequence of phases $ch = ph_1 \cdot ph_2 \cdots ph_n$ such that its phases do not share any common equation. That is, if $c \in ph_i$, then $c \notin ph_j$ for all $j \neq i$.

We say that a cost equation that has a recursive call is *iterative* and a cost equation with no recursive calls is *final*. Given an SCC C consisting of cost equations S_C, we use the name convention $i_1, i_2 \ldots i_n$ for the iterative equations and $f_1, f_2 \ldots f_m$ for the final equations in S_C. All possible executions of an SCC can be summarized in three basic chains: (1) $ch_n = (i_1 \vee i_2 \vee \cdots \vee i_n)^+ \cdot (f_1 \vee f_2 \vee \cdots \vee f_m)$ an arbitrary sequence of iterations that terminates with one of the base cases; (2) $ch_b = (f_1 \vee f_2 \vee \cdots \vee f_m)$ a base case without previous iterations; (3) an arbitrary sequence of iterations that never terminates $ch_i = (i_1 \vee i_2 \vee \cdots \vee i_n)^+$.

Example 3. The basic chains of method *move* (SCC S_3 of Fig.2) are: $ch_n = (5 \vee 7)^+ (6 \vee 8)$, $ch_b = (6 \vee 8)$ and $ch_i = (5 \vee 7)^+$. Obviously, these chains include a lot of unfeasible call sequences which we want to exclude.

3.1   Chain Refinement of an SCC

Our objective is to specialize a chain into more refined ones according to the constraints φ of its cost equations. To this end, we need to analyse the possible sequences of phases in a chain. We use the notation $c \in ch$ to denote that the cost equation c appears in the chain ch.

Definition 4 (Dependency). *Let $c, d \in ch$, $c = \langle C(\bar{x}_c) = \ldots + C(\bar{z}), \varphi_c \rangle$, $d = \langle C(\bar{x}_d) = \ldots, \varphi_d \rangle$; then $c \preceq d$ iff the constraint $\varphi_c \wedge \varphi_d \wedge (\bar{z} = \bar{x}_d)$ is satisfiable. Intuitively, $c \preceq d$ iff d can be executed immediately after c. The relation $\preceq^*$ is the transitive closure of $\preceq$.*

We generate new phases and chains according to these dependencies. Define $c \equiv d$ iff $c = d$ (syntactic equality) or $c \preceq^* d$ and $d \preceq^* c$. Each equivalence class in $[c]_\equiv$ gives rise to a new phase. If $[c]_\equiv = \{c\}$ and $c \npreceq c$, the new phase is (c). If $[c]_\equiv = \{c_1, \ldots, c_n\}$, the new phase is $(c_1 \vee \cdots \vee c_n)^+$. To simplify notation we identify an equivalence class with the phase it generates. Then $ph \prec ph'$ iff $ph \neq ph'$, $c \in ph$, $d \in ph'$ and $c \preceq d$. $ch' = ph_1 \cdots ph_n$ is a *valid chain* iff for all $1 \leq i < n$: $ph_i \prec ph_{i+1}$.

Example 4. The dependency relation of *move* (SCC S_3 from Fig. 2) is the following: $5 \preceq 5$, $5 \preceq 6$, $7 \preceq 7$ and $7 \preceq 8$. This produces the following phases: $(5)^+$, $(7)^+$, (6) and (8), which in turn give rise to chains: non-terminating chains $(5)^+$, $(7)^+$; terminating chains $(5)^+(6)$, $(7)^+(8)$ and the base cases (6), (8). This refinement captures the important fact that the method cannot alternate the behavior that increases n (cost equation 5) with the one that decreases it (cost equation 7).

Theorem 1 (Refinement completeness). *Let $ch_1, \ldots, ch_n$ be the generated chains for a SCC S from the basic chains of S. Any possible sequence of cost equation applications of S is covered by at least one chain ch_i, $i \in 1..n$ (a proof can be found in [11]).*

3.2 Forward and Backward Invariants

We can use invariants to improve the precision of the inferred dependencies and to discard unfeasible execution patterns. Given a chain $ch = ph_1 \cdots ph_n$ in S_i with C as cost relation symbol, we can infer forward invariants (*fwdInv*) that propagate the context in which the chain is called from ph_1 to the subsequent phases. Additionally, we can propagate the relation between the variables from the final phase ph_n to the previous phases until calling point ph_1, obtaining backward invariants (*backInv*). These invariants provide us with extra information at each phase ph_i coming from the phases that appear before (*fwdInv*) or after (*backInv*) ph_i.

$fwdInv_{ch}(ph_i)$ and $backInv_{ch}(ph_i)$ denote forward and backward invariants valid at any application of the equations in the phase ph_i of chain ch. If it is obvious which chain is referred to, we leave out the subscript ch. The forward invariant at the beginning of a chain ch in an SCC S_i is given by the conditions under which ch is called in other SCCs. The backward invariant at the end of a chain ch is defined by the constraints φ of the base case ph_n for terminating chains. For non-terminating chains, the backward invariant at the end of a chain is the empty set of constraints (*true*). The backward invariant of the first phase of a chain ch represents the input-output relations between the variables. It can be seen as a summary of the behavior of ch. The procedure for computing these invariants can be found in [11].

Additionally, we define φ_{ph} and φ_{ph^*} for iterative phases. The symbol φ_{ph} represents the relation between the variables before and after any positive number of iterations of ph, while φ_{ph^*} represents the relation between the variables before and after zero or more iterations.

Example 5. Some of the inferred invariants for the chains of S_3 of our example:
$$backInv_{(5)+(6)}((5)^+) = fwd = 1 \wedge m > n \wedge m \geq no \wedge no > n$$
$$backInv_{(7)+(8)}((7)^+) = fwd = 0 \wedge n > 0 \wedge no \geq 0 \wedge n > no$$

These invariants reflect applicability conditions (Such as $fwd = 0$) and the relation between the input and the output variables. For example, $no > n$ holds when n is increased and $n > no$ when it is decreased. The condition $m \geq no$ is derived from the fact that at the end of phase $(5)^+$ we have $m > n$, in phase (6) $n' = no'$ and the transition is $n' = n + 1 \wedge no' = no$.

We can use forward and backward invariants to improve the precision of the inferred dependencies. At the same time, a more refined set of chains will allow us to infer more precise invariants. Hence, we can iterate this process (chain refinement and invariant generation) until no more precision is achieved or until we reach a compromise between precision and performance. We can also use the inferred invariants to discard additional cost equations or chains. Let $c = \langle C(\bar{x}) = \ldots + C(\bar{z}), \varphi \rangle \in phi$, if $\varphi \wedge backInv_{ch}(\overline{phi}) \wedge fwdInv_{ch}(phi)$ is unsatisfiable, c cannot occur and can be eliminated from phi in the chain ch. If any invariant belonging to a chain is unsatisfiable its pattern of execution cannot possibly occur and the chain can be discarded.

3.3   Terminating Non-termination

In our refinement procedure, we distinguish terminating and non-terminating chains explicitly. Given a chain $ph_1 \cdots ph_n$, it is assumed that every phase ph_i with $i \in 1..n-1$ is terminating. This is safe, because for each ph_i that is iterative we generated another chain of the form $ph_1 \cdots ph_i$, where ph_i is assumed not to terminate. That is, we consider both the case when ph_i terminates and when it does not terminate. Given a non-terminating chain, if we prove termination of its final phase, we can safely discard that chain.

Consider a phase $(c_1 \vee c_2 \vee \ldots \vee c_m)^+$, we obtain a (possibly empty) set of linear ranking functions for each c_i, denoted RF_i, using the techniques of [6, 16]. A linear ranking function of a cost equation $\langle C(\bar{x}) = \cdots + C(\bar{x}'), \varphi \rangle$ with a recursive call $C(\bar{x}')$ is a linear expression f such that (1) $\varphi \Rightarrow f(\bar{x}) \geq 0$ and (2) $\varphi \Rightarrow f(\bar{x}) - f(\bar{x}') \geq 1$.

For each ranking function f of c_i, we check whether its value can be incremented in any other $c_j = \langle C(\bar{x}) = \cdots + C(\bar{x}'), \varphi_j \rangle$, $j \neq i$ (whether $\varphi_j \wedge f(\bar{x}) - f(\bar{x}') < 0$ is satisfiable). If f can be increased in c_j we say that f depends on c_j. As in [3], the procedure for proving termination consists in eliminating the cost equations that have a ranking function without dependencies first. Then, incrementally eliminate the cost equations that have ranking functions whose dependencies have been already removed until there are no cost equations remaining. The set of ranking functions and their dependencies will be used again later to introduce specific bounds for the number of calls to each c_i.

Nr	$Cost\ Equation$
3.1	$while(n, m, fwd) = move_{(5)+(6)}(n, m, fwd, no) + while(no, m, fwd)$
	$\quad n > 0 \wedge \mathbf{fwd = 1} \wedge \mathbf{m > n} \wedge \mathbf{m \geq no} \wedge \mathbf{no > n}$
3.2	$while(n, m, fwd) = move_{(6)}(n, m, fwd, no) + while(no, m, fwd)$
	$\quad n > 0 \wedge \mathbf{fwd = 1} \wedge \mathbf{no = n}$
3.3	$while(n, m, fwd) = move_{(7)+(8)}(n, m, fwd, no) + while(no, m, fwd)$
	$\quad n > 0 \wedge \mathbf{fwd = 0} \wedge \mathbf{no \geq 0} \wedge \mathbf{n > no}$
3.4	$while(n, m, fwd) = move_{(8)}(n, m, fwd, no) + while(no, m, fwd)$
	$\quad n > 0 \wedge \mathbf{fwd = 0} \wedge \mathbf{n = no}$

Fig. 3. Refinement of Cost equation 3 from Fig. 2

Example 6. The ranking functions for the phases $(5)^+$ and $(7)^+$ are $m - n$ and n respectively. With such ranking functions, we can discard the non-terminating chains $(5)^+$ and $(7)^+$. The remaining chains are $(5)^+(6)$, $(7)^+(8)$, (7) and (8).

3.4 Propagating Refinements

The refinement of an SCC S_i in a sequence $S_1, \ldots, S_n$ can affect both predecessors and successors of S_i. The initial forward invariants from SCCs that are called in S_i, the forward invariants of the SCCs $S_{i+1}, \ldots, S_n$ might be strengthened by the refinement of S_i. The preceding SCCs that have calls to S_i can be specialized so they call the refined chains. The backward invariants can be included in the calling cost equations thus introducing a "loop summary" of S_i's behavior.

Each cost equation containing a call to S_i, say $\langle D(\bar{x}) = \ldots + C_{ch}(\bar{z}), \varphi \rangle \in S_j$ with $j < i$, can be replaced with a set of cost equations $\langle D(\bar{x}) = \ldots + C_{ch'}(\bar{z}), \varphi' \rangle$, where $ch' = ph_1 ph_2 \cdots ph_m$ is one of the refined chains of ch, and $\varphi' := \varphi \wedge backInv_{ch'}(\overline{ph_1})$. If φ' is unsatisfiable, the cost equation can be discarded.

Example 7. We propagate the refinement of method *move* (SCC S_3) to *while* (SCC S_2). Fig. 3 shows how cost equation 3 is refined by substituting the calls to *move* by calls to specific chains of *move* and by adding the backward invariants of the callees to its cost constraint φ. Analogously, cost equation 4 is refined into 4.1, 4.2, 4.3, and 4.4. The only difference is that the latter have a recursive call to *while* with $fwd = 1$. The cost equations of *move* are not changed because the do not have calls to other SCCs.

The new phases are $(3.1 \vee 3.2 \vee 4.1 \vee 4.2)^+$, $(3.3 \vee 3.4)^+$, (4.3), (4.4) and (2). Phase $(3.1 \vee 3.2 \vee 4.1 \vee 4.2)^+$ represents iterations of the loop when $fwd = 1$. The fact that fwd is explicitly set to 1 in 4.1 and 4.2 does not have any effect. Phase $(3.3 \vee 3.4)^+$ represents the iterations when $fwd = 0$ and is kept that way in the recursive call. Finally, (4.3) and (4.4) are the cases where fwd is changed from 0 to 1. If we use the initial forward invariant $n \geq 1 \wedge m > n$ of *main* (in SCC S_1), we obtain the following chains:

Pattern (1)	Pattern (2)	Pattern (3)
$(3.3 \vee 3.4)^+(4.3)(3.1 \vee 3.2 \vee 4.1 \vee 4.2)^+$	$(4.3)(3.1 \vee 3.2 \vee 4.1 \vee 4.2)^+$	$(3.3 \vee 3.4)^+(2)$
$(3.3 \vee 3.4)^+(4.4)(3.1 \vee 3.2 \vee 4.1 \vee 4.2)^+$	$(4.4)(3.1 \vee 3.2 \vee 4.1 \vee 4.2)^+$	$(3.3 \vee 3.4)^+$

They are grouped according to the execution patterns that were intuitively presented in Sec. 1. Note that neither $(3.1 \vee 3.2 \vee 4.1 \vee 4.2)^+$ or $(3.3 \vee 3.4)^+$ are always terminating as we can iterate indefinitely on 3.2, 4.2 and 3.4. These cases correspond to a call to *move* that immediately returns without modifying n. Therefore, we cannot discard any of the non-terminating chains.

4 Upper Bound Computation

4.1 Cost Structures

At this point, a refined program consists of a sequence of SCCs $S_1, \ldots, S_n$ where each SCC S_i contains a set of chains. We want to infer safe upper bounds for each chain individually but, at the same time, take their dependencies into account. The standard approach on cost equations [1] consists in obtaining a cost expression that represents the cost of each SCC S_i and substituting any call to that S_i by the inferred cost expression. That way, we can infer closed-form upper bounds for all SCCs in a bottom up approach (From S_n to S_1). This approach turns out not to be adequate to exploit the dependencies between different parts of the code as we illustrate in the next example.

Example 8. Let us obtain an upper bound for method *main* when it behaves as in chain $(3.3 \vee 3.4)^+(2)$. This is a simple pattern, where *move* only increases or leaves n unchanged. Following the standard approach, we first obtain the upper bound for *move* when called in 3.3 and 3.4, that is, when *move* behaves as in $(7)^+(8)$ and (8). By multiplying the maximum number of recursive calls with the maximum cost of each call the upper bound we obtain is n and 0, respectively. The cost of $(3.3 \vee 3.4)^+(2)$ is then the maximum cost of each iteration n multiplied by the maximum number of iterations. However, 3.4 can iterate indefinitely, so we fail to obtain an upper bound.

If we apply the improved method of [4] after the refinement, we consider 3.3 and 3.4 independently. Phase 3.3 has zero cost and 3.4 has a ranking function n, yielding a bound of n^2 for this chain (while a more precise bound is n).

To overcome this problem, we define a new upper bound computation method based on an intermediate structure that summarizes all the cost components while maintaining part of the internal structure of what generated the cost.

Definition 5 (Cost Structure). *A cost structure CT is a pair $SE : CS$. Here SE is a cost expression of the form $SE = \sum_{i=1}^{n} SE_i * iv_i + e \ (n \geq 0)$, where e is a cost expression and iv_i is a symbolic variable representing a natural number. We refer to the iv_i as iteration variables, to a product $SE_i * iv_i$ as iteration component and to SE as structured cost expression. CS is a (possibly empty) set of constraints of the form $\sum_{j=1}^{m} iv_j \leq e \ (m \geq 1)$, such that all its* *iteration variables appear in SE. The constraints relate iteration variables with cost expressions. We use the notation $\sum iv \leq e$ when the number of iteration variables is irrelevant.*

Intuitively, a structured cost expression represents a fixed cost e plus a set of iterative components $SE_i * iv_i$, where each iterative component is executed iv_i times and each iteration has cost SE_i. The set of constraints CS binds the values of the iteration variables iv and can express dependencies among iteration components. For instance, a constraint $iv_1 + iv_2 \leq e$ expresses that the iteration components iv_1 and iv_2 are bound by e and that the bigger iv_1 is, the smaller iv_2 must be.

We denote with IV the set of iteration variables in a cost structure. Let $val : IV \rightarrow E$ be an assignment of the iteration variables to cost expressions, a valid cost of a cost structure $CT = \sum_{i=1}^{n} SE_i * iv_i + e : CS$ is defined as $val(SE) = \sum_{i=1}^{n} val(SE_i) * val(iv_i) + e$ such that $val(CS)$ is valid.[1] A cost structure can represent multiple upper bound candidates.

Example 9. Consider a cost structure $a * iv_1 + b * iv_2 + c : \{iv_1 \leq d, iv_1 + iv_2 \leq e\}$ where a, b, c, d, and e are cost expressions. If $a > b$ and $d < e$, an upper bound is $a * d + b * nat(e - d) + c$ (The $nat()$ wrapping can be omitted). In case of $a < b$, an upper bound is $b * e + c$.

We follow a bottom up approach from S_n to S_1 and infer cost structures for cost equations, phases and chains, detailed in Secs. 4.3, 4.4, and 4.5 below. Sec. 4.2 contains a complete example. In Sec. 5, we present a technique to obtain maximal cost expressions from cost structures. They key of the procedure is to safely combine individual cost structures while detecting dependencies among them. The intermediate cost structures are correct, that is, at the end of our analysis of our example (Fig. 1) we will not only have upper bounds of *main* but also a correct upper bound of *move*.

We define the operations that form the basis or our analysis.

Definition 6 (Cost Expression Maximization). *Given a cost expression e, a cost constraint φ, and a set of variables $\bar{v}$, the operation $bd(e, \varphi, \bar{v})$ returns a set E of cost expressions that only contain variables in $\bar{v}$ and that are safe upper bounds. That is, for each $e' \in E$, we have that for all variable assignments to integers $\alpha : vars(e') \cup vars(e) \rightarrow \mathbb{Z}$ that satisfy $\varphi: \alpha(e') \geq \alpha(e)$. It is possible that $bd(e, \varphi, \bar{v})$ returns the empty set. In this case, no finite upper bound is known.*

For $bd(e, \varphi, \bar{v}) = \{e_1, \ldots, e_n\}$ define $\min(bd(e, \varphi, \bar{v})) = \min(e_1, \ldots, e_n)$. Note that if $bd(e, \varphi, \bar{v}) = \emptyset$, $\min(bd(e, \varphi, \bar{v})) = \infty$. Cost expression maximization can be implemented using geometrical projection over the dimensions of $\bar{v}$ in the context of the polyhedra abstract domain or as existential quantification of the variables of e and φ that do not appear in $\bar{v}$. This operation is done independently

---

[1] Cost structures have some similarities to the multiple counter instrumentation described in [14]. Iteration variables can be seen as counters for individual loops or recursive components and constraints represent dependencies among these counters.

SCC	$Chain$	$Execution$

$$2 \quad (3.3 \vee 3.4)^+(2) \quad c_{3.?}(\overline{x}_1) \to \cdots c_{3.3}(\overline{x}_i) \to \cdots \to c_{3.?}(\overline{x}_f) \to c_2(\overline{x}_{f+1})$$
$$\downarrow \cdots \qquad\qquad \downarrow \qquad\qquad \cdots \downarrow \qquad\qquad |$$
$$3 \quad (7)^+(8) \qquad\qquad c_7(\overline{y}_1) \; \overline{\to \cdots \to c_7(\overline{y}_f)} \to c_8(\overline{y}_{f+1})$$

Fig. 4. Schema of executing chain $(3.3 \vee 3.4)^+(2)$

for each l in the cost expression. The results can be safely combined as linear expressions appear always inside a $nat()$ in cost expressions.

Definition 7 (Structured Cost Expression Maximization). *We define recursively the bound of a structured cost expression as* $Bd(\sum_{i=1}^{n} SE_i * iv_i + e, \varphi, \bar{v}) = \sum_{i=1}^{n} Bd(SE_i, \varphi, \bar{v}) * iv_i + \min(bd(e, \varphi, \bar{v})).$

4.2 Example of Upper Bound Computation

Fig. 4 represents the execution of chain $(3.3 \vee 3.4)^+(2)$. The execution of the phase $(3.3 \vee 3.4)^+$ consists on a series of applications of either 3.3 or 3.4. Each equation application has a call to *move*. In particular, 3.3 calls $move_{(7)+(8)}$ and 3.4 calls $move_{(8)}$. In Fig. 4, only one call to $move_{(7)+(8)}$ is represented. $c_n(\overline{x})$ represents an instance of cost equation n with variables $\overline{x}$.

Cost of move. In order to compute the cost of the complete chain, we start by computing the cost of the innermost SCCs. In this case, the cost of *move*. The cost of one application of 8 ($c_8(\overline{y}_{f+1})$) and 7 ($c_7(\overline{y}_i)$) are 0 and 1 respectively (taken directly from the cost equations in Fig. 2). The cost of phase $(7)^+$ is the sum of the costs of all applications of c_7: $c_7(\overline{y}_1), c_7(\overline{y}_2), \cdots, c_7(\overline{y}_f)$. If c_7 is applied iv_7 times, the total cost will be $1 * iv_7$. Instead of giving a concrete value to iv_7, we collect constraints that bind its value and build a cost structure. In Sec. 3.3 we obtained the ranking function n for 7 so we have $iv_7 \leq nat(n_1)$. Moreover, the number of iterations is also bounded by $nat(n_1 - n_f)$, the difference between the initial and the final value of n in phase $(7)^+$ (see Lemma 1). Consequently, the cost structure for $(7)^+$ is $1 * iv_7 : \{iv_7 \leq n_1, iv_7 \leq n_1 - n_f\}$ (we omit the $nat()$ wrappings). If we had more ranking functions for 7, we could add extra constraints. This is important because we do not know yet which ranking function will yield the best upper bound. Additionally, we keep the cost per iteration and the number of iterations separated so we can later reason about them independently (detect dependencies). The cost of $(7)^+(8)$ is the cost of $(7)^+$ plus the cost of (8) but expressed according to the initial variables $\overline{y}_1$. We add the cost structures and maximize them (Bd) using the corresponding invariants. We obtain $1 * iv_7 : \{iv_7 \leq n_1, iv_7 \leq n_1 - no_1\}$ (because $n_f > n_{f+1} = no_{f+1} = no_1$).

Cost of one application of 3.3, 3.4 *and* 2. The cost of (2) is 0. The cost of one application of 3.4 is the cost of a call to $move_{(8)}$, that is, 0. Conversely, the cost of one application of 3.3 is the cost of one call to $move_{(7)+(8)}$. We want the cost of $c_{3.3}(\overline{x}_i)$ expressed in terms of the entry variables $\overline{x}_i$ and the variables of the corresponding recursive call $\overline{x}_{i+1}$. We maximize the cost structure of $move_{(7)+(8)}$ using the cost constraints of 3.3 ($\varphi_{3.3}$). This results in the cost structure $1 * iv_7 : \{iv_7 \leq n_i, iv_7 \leq n_i - n_{i+1}\}$ (the output no is n_{i+1} in the recursive call).

Cost of phase $(3.3 \vee 3.4)^+$. The cost of phase $(3.3 \vee 3.4)^+$ is the sum of the cost of all applications of $c_{3.3}$ and $c_{3.4}$: $c_{3.?}(\overline{x}_1), c_{3.?}(\overline{x}_2), \cdots, c_{3.?}(\overline{x}_f)$. We group the summands originating from 3.3 and from 3.4 and assume that $c_{3.3}$ and $c_{3.4}$ are applied $iv_{3.3}$ and $iv_{3.4}$ times respectively. The sum of all applications of $c_{3.4}$ is $0 * iv_{3.4} = 0$. However, the cost of each $c_{3.3}(\overline{x}_i)$ might be different (depends on $\overline{x}_i$) so we cannot simply multiply. Using the invariant $\varphi_{(3.3 \vee 3.4)^*}$ and $\varphi_{3.3}$ we know that $n_1 \geq n_i \wedge n_i > n_{i+1} \wedge n_{i+1} \geq 0$. Maximizing each of these constraints yields $iv_7 \leq n_1$ and we obtain a cost structure $1 * iv_7 : \{iv_7 \leq n_1\}$ that is greater or equal than all $1 * iv_7 : \{iv_7 \leq n_i, iv_7 \leq n_i - n_{i+1}\}$ (because $n_1 \geq n_i$). Therefore, a valid (but imprecise) cost of $(3.3 \vee 3.4)^+$ is $(1 * iv_7) * iv_{3.3} : \{iv_7 \leq n_1, iv_{3.3} \leq n_1, iv_{3.3} \leq n_1 - n_f\}$ (n is a ranking function of 3.3). If we solve the cost structure, we will obtain the upper bound n^2.

Inductive constraint compression. Because we kept the different components of the cost separated, we can easily obtain a more precise cost structure Each call to $move$ starts where the last one left it and all of them together can iterate at most n times. This is reflected by the constraint $iv_7 \leq n_i - n_{i+1}$. We can compress all the iterations $(n_1 - n_2) + (n_2 - n_3) + \cdots + (n_{f-1} - n_f) \leq n_1 - n_f$, pull out the iteration component $1 * iv_7$ and obtain a more precise cost structure $(1 * iv_7) + (0 * iv_{3.3}) : \{iv_7 \leq n_1 - n_f, iv_{3.3} \leq n_1, iv_{3.3} \leq n_1 - n_f\}$. Then, we can eliminate $(0 * iv_{3.3})$ arriving at $(1 * iv_7) : \{iv_7 \leq n_1 - n_f\}$ which will result in an upper bound n.

4.3 Cost Structure of an Equation Application

Consider a cost equation $c = \langle C(\overline{x}) = \sum_{i=1}^{n} D_i(\overline{y}_i) + e + C(\overline{x}'), \varphi \rangle$, where $C(\overline{x}')$ is a recursive call. We want to obtain a cost structure $SE_c : CS_c$ that approximates the cost of $\sum_{i=1}^{n} D_i(\overline{y}_i) + e$ and we want such a cost structure to be expressed in terms of $\overline{x}$ and $\overline{x}'$.

Example 10. Consider cost equation 3.3 from Fig. 3 which is part of SCC S_2:
$$while(n, m, fwd) = move_{(7)+(8)}(n'', m'', fwd'', no) + while(n', m', fwd')$$
Assume φ contains $n'' = n \wedge n' = no$. The cost of one application of 3.3 is the cost of $move_{(7)+(8)}(n, m, fwd, no)$ expressed in terms of n, m, fwd and n', m', fwd'. Let the cost of $move_{(7)+(8)}$ be $1 * iv_7 : \{iv_7 \leq n'', iv_7 \leq n'' - no\}$, then we obtain an upper bound by maximizing the structured cost expression and the constraints in terms of the variables n, m, fwd and n', m', fwd'. The obtained cost structure is $1 * iv_7 : \{iv_7 \leq n, iv_7 \leq n - n'\}$.

Let $SE_i : CS_i$ be the cost structure of the chain D_i, then the structured cost expression can be computed as $SE_c = \sum_{i=1}^{n} Bd(SE_i, \varphi, \overline{x}) + min(bd(e, \varphi, \overline{x}))$. By substituting each call $D_i(\bar{y}_i)$ by its structured cost expression and maximizing with respect to $\bar{x}$, we obtain a valid structured cost expression in terms of the entry variables.

A set of valid constraints CS_c is obtained simply as the union of all sets CS_i expressed in terms of the entry and recursive call variables ($\bar{x}$ and $\bar{x}'$): $CS_c \supseteq \{\sum iv \leq e' | \sum iv \leq e \in CS_i, e' \in bd(e, \varphi, \bar{x}\bar{x}')\}$. Should the cost equation not have a recursive call, all the maximizations will be performed only with respect to the entry variables $\bar{x}$.

Constraint Compression. In order to obtain tighter bounds, one can try to detect dependencies among the constraints when they have a linear cost expression. Let $\sum iv_i \leq nat(l_i) \in CS_i$ and $\sum iv_j \leq nat(l_j) \in CS_j$, $j \neq i$. Now assume there exist $l_{new} \in bd(l_i + l_j, \varphi, \bar{x}\bar{x}')$, $l'_i \in bd(l_i, \varphi, \bar{x}\bar{x}')$, and $l'_j \in bd(l_j, \varphi, \bar{x}\bar{x}')$ such that $\varphi \Rightarrow (l_{new} \leq (l'_i + l'_j) \wedge l_{new} \geq l_i \wedge l_{new} \geq l_j)$. $nat(l_{new})$ might bind $nat(l_i)$ and $nat(l_j)$ tighter than $nat(l'_i)$ and $nat(l'_j)$. Then we can add $\sum iv_i + \sum iv_j \leq nat(l_{new})$ to the new set of constraints $C\bar{S}_c$.

Example 11. Suppose the cost equation from the previous example had two consecutive calls to *move*: $while(n, m, fwd) = move_{(7)+(8)}(n_1, m_1, fwd_1, no_1) + move_{(7)+(8)}(n_2, m_2, fwd_2, no_2) + while(n', m', fwd')$ with $\{n_1 = n \wedge no_1 = n_2 \wedge no_2 = n'\} \subseteq \varphi$. The resulting cost structure would be $1 * iv_{7.1} + 1 * iv_{7.2} * 2 :$ $\{iv_{7.1} \leq n, iv_{7.1} \leq n - n', iv_{7.2} \leq n, iv_{7.2} \leq n - n'\}$ ($iv_{7.1}$ and $iv_{7.2}$ correspond to the iterations of the two instances of phase $(7)^+$). However, we could compress $iv_{7.1} \leq n_1 - no_1$ and $iv_{7.2} \leq n_2 - no_2$ (from Ex. 10) into $iv_{7.1} + iv_{7.2} \leq n - n'$ and add it to the final set of constraints. This set represents a tighter bound and captures the dependency between the first and the second call.

4.4   Cost Structure of a Phase

Refined phases have the form of a single equation (c) or an iterative phase $(c_1 \vee c_2 \vee \ldots \vee c_n)^+$. The cost of (c) is simply the cost of c. The cost of an iterative phase is the sum of the costs of all applications of each c_i (see Sec. 4.2). Let $CT_i = SE_i : CS_i$ be the cost of one application of c_i, we group the summands according to each c_i and assign a new iteration variable iv_i that represents the number of times such a cost equation is applied. The total cost of the phase is $\sum_{i=1}^{n}(\sum_{j=1}^{iv_i} SE_i(x_j))$ where $SE_i(x_j)$ is an instance of SE_i with the variables corresponding to the j-th application of c_i.

For each c_i in the phase $(c_1 \vee c_2 \vee \ldots \vee c_n)^+$ we obtain a structured cost expression $Bd(SE_i, \varphi_{ph^*}, \bar{x}_1)$ where φ_{ph^*} is an auxiliary invariant that relates $\bar{x}_1$ (the variables at the beginning of the phase) to any $\bar{x}_j$ as defined in Sec. 3.2. That structured cost expression is valid for any application of c_i during the phase. This allows us to transform each sum $\sum_{j=1}^{iv_i} SE_i(\bar{x}_j)$ into a product $iv_i * Bd(SE_i, \varphi_{ph^*}, \bar{x}_1)$. Similarly, we maximize the cost expressions in the constraints. A set of valid constraints is $CS_{ph} = \bigcup_{i=1}^{n}(\{\sum iv_i \leq e'_i | \sum iv_i \leq e_i \in CS_i, e'_i \in bd(e_i, \varphi_{ph^*} \wedge \varphi_{c_i}, \bar{x}_1)\}) \cup CS_{new}$, where CS_{new} is a new set of constraints that bounds the new iteration variables ($iv_1, iv_2, \cdots, iv_n$). The maximization of the constraints is equivalent to the maximization of the iteration variables inside SE_i (a proof can be found in [11]).

Bounding the iterations of a phase. To generate the constraints in CS_{new}, we use the ranking functions and their dependencies obtained when proving termination (see Sec. 3.3).

Example 12. Consider a phase formed by the following cost equations expressed in compact form (we assume that all have the condition $a, b, c \geq 0$):
$1 : p(a, b, c) = p(a - 1, b, c) \mid 2 : p(a, b, c) = p(a + 2, b - 1, c) \mid 3 : p(a, b, c) = p(a, c, c - 1)$
(3) has a ranking function c with no dependencies. We can add $iv_3 \leq c$ to the constraints. (2) has b as a ranking function but it depends on (3). Every time (3) is executed, b is "restarted". Fortunately, the value assigned to b has a maximum (the initial c). Therefore, we can add the constraint $iv_2 \leq b + c * c$. Finally, (1) has a as a ranking function that depends on (2). a is incremented by 2 in every execution of (2) whose number of iterations is at most $b + c * c$. We add the constraint $iv_1 \leq a + 2 * (b + c * c)$.

More formally, we have a set RF_i for each c_i in a phase. Each $f \in RF_i$ has a (possibly empty) dependency set to other c_j. Given a ranking function f that occurs in all sets $RF_{i_1}, \ldots, RF_{i_m}$ for a maximal m, $i_k \in 1..n$. If f has no dependencies, then $nat(f)$ expressed in terms of $\bar{x}_1$ is an upper bound on the number of iterations of $c_{i_1}, \ldots, c_{i_m}$ and we add $\sum_{k=1}^{m} iv_{i_k} \leq nat(f)$ to CS_{new}.

If f depends on $c_{j_1}, \ldots, c_{j_l}$ ($j_i \in 1..n$) and $ub_{j_1}, \ldots, ub_{j_l}$ are upper bounds on the number of iterations of $c_{j_1}, \ldots, c_{j_l}$, then we distinguish two types of dependencies: (1) if c_{j_i} increases f by a constant t_{j_i} then each execution of c_{j_i} can imply t_{j_i} extra iterations. We add $ub_{j_i} * t_{j_i}$ to f; (2) otherwise, if f can be "restarted" in every execution of c_{j_i}, then $R_{j_i}^f \in bd(f(\bar{x}_3), \varphi_{ph^*}(\bar{x}_1\bar{x}_2) \wedge \varphi_{c_{j_i}}(\bar{x}_2\bar{x}_3), \bar{x}_1)$ represents the maximum value that f can take in c_{j_i} (if it exists) and we add $ub_{j_i} * nat(R_{j_i}^f)$. Taken together, we can add $\sum_{k=1}^{m} iv_{i_k} \leq nat(f) + \sum_{i=1}^{p} ub_{j_i} * t_{j_i} + \sum_{i=p}^{l} ub_{j_i} * nat(R_{j_i}^f)$ to CS_{new} where $c_{j_1}, c_{j_2} \cdots c_{i_p}$ are the dependencies of type (1) and $c_{i_p}, c_{i_{p+1}} \cdots c_{i_l}$ the ones of type (2).

On top of this, we add constraints that depend on the value of the variables after the phase (see the cost of $(7)^+$ Sec.4.2). This will allow us to perform constraint compression afterwards.

Lemma 1. *Given a sequence of r calls $c_{i_1}(\bar{x}_1) \cdot c_{i_2}(\bar{x}_2) \cdots c_{i_r}(\bar{x}_r) \cdot c'(\bar{x}_{r+1})$, during which c_i occurred p times and $f \in RF_i$, and for all $\langle c_{i_j}(\bar{x}_j) = \cdots + c_{i_{j+1}}(\bar{x}_{j+1}), \varphi \rangle$, $\varphi \Rightarrow (f(\bar{x}_j) - f(\bar{x}_{j+1}) \geq 0)$. We have that $f(\bar{x}_1) - f(\bar{x}_{r+1}) \geq p$.*

If f is a ranking function in $RF_{i_1}, \ldots, RF_{i_m}$ as above, if f has no dependencies, we can use Lemma 1 (a proof can be found in [11]) to add $\sum_{k=1}^{m} iv_{i_k} \leq nat(f(\bar{x}_1) - f(\bar{x}_f))$ to CS_{new} where $\bar{x}_f$ are the variables at the end of the phase.

Inductive constraint compression. We generalize the *constraint compression* presented in Sec. 4.3. Instead of compressing two constraints, we compress an arbitrary number of them inductively. This is the mechanism used to obtain a linear bound for the chain $(3.3 \vee 3.4)^+$ at the end of Sec. 4.2.

When a constraint is compressed, its iteration variables should be removed from constraints that cannot be compressed. Removing an iteration variable from a constraint is always safe but can introduce imprecision.

Given a cost expression e_i that we want to compress to $\sum iv \leq e_i$, we start with a copy e_i' of e_1 as our candidate. First, prove the base case $\varphi_i \Rightarrow e_i' \geq e_i$ (which is trivial given that e_i and e_i' are equal). Then prove the induction step $\varphi_{ph}(\bar{x}_1\bar{x}_2) \wedge \varphi_{ph^*}(\bar{x}_2\bar{x}_3) \wedge \varphi_i(\bar{x}_3\bar{x}_4) \Rightarrow e_i'(\bar{x}_1\bar{x}_4) \geq e_i'(\bar{x}_1\bar{x}_2) + e_i(\bar{x}_3\bar{x}_4)$. Assuming e_i' is valid for a number of iterations (represented as $\varphi_{ph}(\bar{x}_1\bar{x}_2)$), this shows that it is valid for one more iteration ($\varphi_i(\bar{x}_3\bar{x}_4)$) even if there are interleavings with other c_j ($\varphi_{ph^*}(\bar{x}_2\bar{x}_3)$). Once we proved that, we can add the constraint $\sum iv' \leq e_i'$ and pull the corresponding iteration components out of the corresponding product (a proof can be found in [11]).

If we can prove the stronger inequality $e_i'(\bar{x}_1\bar{x}_4) \geq e_i'(\bar{x}_1\bar{x}_2) + e_i(\bar{x}_3\bar{x}_4) + 1$, then we know that e_i' also decreases with the iterations of c_i. In this case we derive a new constraint $\sum iv' + iv_i \leq e_i'$. We can generalize this procedure to compress constraints that originate from different equations. This is demonstrated by the following example.

Example 13. Consider the phase $(3.1 \vee 3.2 \vee 4.1 \vee 4.2)^+$. Both 3.1 and 4.1 have a call to $move_{(5)+(6)}$ and their cost structures are $iv_{5.1} * 2 : \{iv_{5.1} \leq n' - n, iv_{5.1} \leq m - n\}$ and $iv_{5.2} * 2 : \{iv_{5.2} \leq n' - n, iv_{5.2} \leq m - n\}$. We can compress both iteration variables obtaining $iv_{5.1} * 2 + iv_{5.2} * 2 : \{iv_{5.1} + iv_{5.2} \leq n' - n\}$ (3.2 and 4.2 have zero cost) that when maximized will give us $iv_{5.1} * 2 + iv_{5.2} * 2 : \{iv_{5.1} + iv_{5.2} \leq m - n\}$ which represents the upper bound $2(m - n)$.

4.5 Cost Structure of a Chain

Given a chain $ch = ph_1 \cdots ph_n$ whose phases have cost structures $CT_1, \ldots CT_n$, we want to obtain a cost structure $CT_{ch} = SE_{ch} : CS_{ch}$ for the total cost of the chain. This is analogous to computing the cost structure of an equation in Sec. 4.3. One constructs a cost constraint φ_{ch} relating all variables of the calls to the entry variables and to each other: $\varphi_{ch} = \varphi_{ph_1}(x_1x_2) \wedge \varphi_{ph_2}(x_2x_3) \wedge \cdots \wedge \varphi_{ph_n}(x_n)$. This cost constraint can be enriched with the invariants of the chain.

The structured cost expression is $SE_{ch} = \sum_{i=1}^n Bd(SE_i, \varphi_{ch}, \bar{x})$ and the constraints are $CS_c \supseteq \{\sum iv \leq e' | \sum iv_i \leq e \in CS_i, e' \in bd(e, \varphi_{ch}, \bar{x})\}$. Again, we can apply *constraint compression* to combine constraints from different phases.

Example 14. The cost of patterns (2) and (3) in Ex. 7 derive directly from the cost of their phases (see Sec. 4.2 and Ex. 13). We examine the cost of pattern (1), that is, $(3.3 \vee 3.4)^+(4.3)(3.1 \vee 3.2 \vee 4.1 \vee 4.2)^+$. Considering that variables are subscripted with 1, 2 and 3 for their value before the first, second and third phase, the cost structures of the phases are: $1 * iv_{7.1} : \{iv_{7.1} \leq n_1 - n_2\}$, $1 * iv_{7.2} : \{iv_{7.2} \leq n_2 - n_3\}$ and $iv_{5.1} * 2 + iv_{5.2} * 2 : \{iv_{5.1} + iv_{5.2} \leq n_4 - n_3\}$. The joint invariants guarantee that $n_3 \geq 0 \wedge n_4 \leq m$. We can compress the constraints $iv_{7.1} \leq n_1 - n_2$ and $iv_{7.2} \leq n_2 - n_3$ and maximize with respect to the initial variables obtaining $1 * iv_{7.1} + 1 * iv_{7.2} + 2 * iv_{5.1} + 2 * iv_{5.2} : \{iv_{7.1} + iv_{7.2} \leq n_1, iv_{5.1} + iv_{5.2} \leq m_1\}$. Such a cost structure represents the bound $n + 2m$ as expected.

5 Solving Cost Structures

Solving a cost structure $SE : CS$ means to look for a maximizing assignment val_{max} from iteration variables to cost expressions (without iteration variables) such that $CS \Rightarrow val_{max}(SE) \geq SE$ is valid. Even though iteration variables range over natural numbers, we consider a relaxation of the problem where iteration variables can take any non-negative real number. The maximization of $val_{max}(SE)$ represents the cost structure SE where each iv has been substituted by $val_{max}(iv)$ and $val_{max}(SE)$ is an upper bound of the cost structure $SE : CS$.

Let $SE = \sum_{i=1}^{n} SE_i * iv_i + e$, The maximization of each SE_i can be performed independently, because its iteration variables depend neither on other iteration variables of SE_j for $j \neq i$ nor on any iv_i. Let e_i be the maximization of SE_i, then we obtain $\sum_{i=1}^{n} e_i * iv_i + e$ as well as a set of constraints over the iv_i. As the e_i's can be symbolic expressions, not necessarily comparable to each other, we need a procedure to find an upper bound independently of the e_i.

We group iteration components (Def. 5) based on dependencies. Two iteration components depend on each other if their iteration variables appear together in a constraint. An iteration group IG is a partial cost structure $\sum_{i=1}^{m} e_{j_i} * iv_{j_i} : CS$ ($1 \leq j_i \leq n$ for $i \in 1..m$) where its iteration components depend on each other.

A constraint $\sum_{i=1}^{m} iv_{j_i} \leq e$ is *active* for assignment val iff $\sum_{i=1}^{m} val(iv_{j_i}) = e$. Let $C = \sum_{i=1}^{m} iv_{j_i} \leq e$, $C' = \sum_{i=1}^{m+k} iv_{j_i} \leq e'$ be constraints such that $C \subseteq C'$ and val any assignment: (i) If C is active for val, then $C = e$ and we substitute $\sum_{i=m+1}^{m+k} iv_{j_i} \leq nat(e' - e)$ for C' making the two constraints independent; (ii) If C is not active, we ignore C and consider the rest of the constraints.

Consider an IG $SE : CS$ that we want to maximize. For each $C, C' \in CS$ with $C \subseteq C'$, we use the observation in the previous paragraph to derive simplified constraints CS_1, CS_2. We solve both constraints and obtain val_1, val_2. The maximum cost of IG is $\min(val_1(SE), val_2(SE))$. Constraints with only one iv can always be reduced. We repeat the procedure until the constraints cannot be further simplified. The constraints can now be grouped into irreducible IGs. A trivial IG is one with a single iv constraint $iv \leq e$ whose maximal assignment is $val(iv) = e$. All constraints in an irreducible, non-trivial IG have at least two iteration variables.

Example 15. Consider the following cost structure $iv_1 * 1 + iv_2 * (b) + iv_3 * (iv_4 * 2) :$ $\{iv_1 + iv_2 + iv_3 \leq a + b, iv_1 + iv_2 \leq c, iv_4 \leq d\}$. First, we maximize the internal iteration component $iv_4 * 2$ which contains a trivial IG $iv_4 \leq d$. The result is $iv_1 *$ $1 + iv_2 * (b) + iv_3 * (2d) : \{iv_1 + iv_2 + iv_3 \leq a + b, iv_1 + iv_2 \leq c\}$. This cost structure forms a single IG with two constraints one contained in the other. (1) We assume $iv_1 + iv_2 \leq c$ is active. Then we have $\{iv_3 \leq nat(a + b - c), iv_1 + iv_2 \leq c\}$ which contains two irreducible IG. The first one is $iv_3 = nat(a + b - c)$ and the second one has two possibilities $iv_1 = c, iv_2 = 0$ or $iv_1 = 0, iv_2 = c$ (Thm. 2 below). The result is then $nat(a + b - c) + max(b * c, 2d * c)$. (2) If $iv_1 + iv_2 \leq c$ is not active, we have only $iv_1 + iv_2 + iv_3 \leq a + b$ which yields $max(a + b, b * (a + b), 2d * (a + b))$. The cost is $min(nat(a + b - c) + max(b * c, 2d * c), max(a + b, b * (a + b), 2d * (a + b)))$.

We could have dropped the second constraint from the beginning and obtain a less precise bound $max(a + b, b * (a + b), 2d * (a + b))$. We can even split the constraint $iv_1 + iv_2 + iv_3 \leq a + b$ into $iv_1 \leq a + b, iv_2 \leq a + b$ and $iv_3 \leq a + b$ and obtain $(1 + b + 2d) * (a + b)$. That way we can balance precision and performance.

Definition 8 (*IG* **dependency graph**). *Let $IG = SE : CS$. Its dependency graph $G(IG)$ is defined as follows: for each $C \in CS$ G has a node C. For each $C \cap C'$ such that $C, C' \in CS$ and $C \cap C' \neq \emptyset$ G has a node $d(C \cap C')$, and edges from C to $d(C \cap C')$ and from $d(C \cap C')$ to C'.*

Example 16. Given the *IG* $\{iv_1 + iv_2 \leq a, iv_2 + iv_3 \leq b, iv_2 + iv_4 \leq c\}$, its dependency graph contains the nodes $n_1 = "iv_1 + iv_2 \leq a"$, $n_2 = "iv_2 + iv_3 \leq b"$, $n_3 = "iv_2 + iv_4 \leq c"$ and $n_4 = "d(iv_2)"$. The edges are $(n_1, n_4), (n_2, n_4), (n_3, n_4)$.

Theorem 2. *Given an irreducible, non-trivial IG. If $G(IG)$ is acyclic there exists a maximizing assignment val_{max} such that there is an active constraint with only one non-zero iteration variable.*

If $G(IG)$ is acyclic, we apply Thm. 2 to solve IG incrementally. Let $C_i = \sum_{j=1}^{r} iv_{i_j} \leq e \in CS$: we obtain a partial assignment val_{ik} such that $val_{ik}(iv_k) = e$ for some $iv_k \in C_i$ and all other iteration variables in C_i being assigned 0. We update CS with val_{ik} and obtain a constraint system with less iteration variables and constraints whose graph is still acyclic, and so on. Once no iteration variable is left, we end up with a set of assignments $MaxVal$. The maximum cost of $IG = SE : CS$ is $max_{val \in MaxVal} val(SE)$.

Example 17. We obtain one of the assignments in $MaxVal$ for the IG of Ex. 16. We take the constraint $iv_1 + iv_2 \leq a$ and assign $iv_1 = a$ and $iv_2 = 0$. The resulting constraints are $iv_3 \leq b$ and $iv_4 \leq c$ that are trivially solved. The resulting assignment is $iv_1 = a, iv_2 = 0, iv_3 = b$ and $iv_4 = c$.

The requirement of $G(IG)$ being acyclic can be relaxed. A discussion and the proof of Thm. 2 is in [11]. One can always obtain an acyclic IG by dropping constraints or by removing iteration variables from a given constraint. Such transformations are safe since they only relax the conditions imposed on the iteration variables. In practice, we perform a pre-selection of the constraints to be considered based on heuristics to improve performance.

6   Related Work and Experiments

This work builds upon the formalism developed in the COSTA group [1, 2, 4, 5], however, the are important differences in how upper bounds are inferred. In [1], upper bounds are computed independently for each SCC and then combined without taking dependencies into account. The precision of that approach is improved in [2] for certain kinds of loops. The paper [5] presents a general approach for obtaining amortized upper bounds that, although powerful, does not scale well. In [4] SCCs are decomposed into sparse cost equations systems. Then it is possible to use the ideas of [5] to solve the sparse cost equations precisely.

In our work, we also decompose programs, but driven by possible sequences of cost applications. This technique, known as control-flow-refinement, has been applied to the resource analysis of imperative programs in [9, 13]. In addition, our refinement technique can deal with programs with linear recursion (non necessarily tail recursive) and multiple procedures. In our analysis we do not refine the whole program at once. Instead, we refine each SCC and then propagate the changes. Our technique allows to leave parts of the program unrefined to increase performance. Paper [15] uses disjunctive invariants to summarize inner loops instead of control-flow-refinement. This technique can also deal with some kinds of non-terminating programs. However, it can only bound the number of visits to a single location in a single procedure. In contrast, our tool can count the number of visits to several locations in multiple procedures derived from cost annotations. The tool Loopus [18] uses disjunctive invariants, collects the inner paths of each loop and also uses contextualization which is a form of control-flow refinement. Both [15, 18] obtain ranking functions based on given patterns and combine them using proof rules. Instead, we infer linear ranking functions using linear programming [6, 16] and combine them to form lexicographic ranking functions (see Sec. 4.4).

SPEED [14] makes use of multiple counters to bound and detect dependencies of different loops. SPEED computes cost summaries for the (non-recursive) procedure calls. Therefore, it cannot detect dependencies among different procedure calls. KoAT [8] adopts an iterative approach, where size analysis and complexity analysis are interleaved and improve each other. That paper also extends transitions systems to deal with inter-procedural and recursive programs. Very recently, a new version of Loopus has been released [17]. They use a simple abstraction and achieve very high performance and great effectiveness. They can also obtain amortized cost for complex nested loops. However, their analysis is limited to imperative programs and cannot deal with recursion.

For our experimental evaluation we took the problem set used by KoAT's evaluation[2] [8], except those with multiple recursion (671 problems). We executed each problem with PUBS [1], KoAT, and our tool CoFloCo (SPEED

	1	$log\,n$	n	$n\,log\,n$	n^2	n^3	$> n^3$	No res.
CoFloCo	120	0	158	0	51	2	3	298
KoAT	117	0	120	0	51	0	4	340
PUBS	112	2	90	5	42	5	3	373
Loopus³	128	0	141	0	73	11	4	275
CoFloCo	1	0	16	0	14	7	0	1
PUBS	1	2	13	3	12	6	0	2
Loopus³	2	0	11	0	7	4	0	15

and the first version of Loopus [18] are not publicly available). The problems are taken from the literature on resource analysis [3, 13–15, 18] and include most of the problems used in the evaluation of [7] (632 problems in the first part of the table) and the ones of the evaluation of PUBS [1] (39 problems in the second part).

The problems of the first part were automatically translated from KoAT's input format to cost equations. That includes performing loop extraction (and

---

[2] http://aprove.informatik.rwth-aachen.de/eval/IntegerComplexity/

generating invariants for PUBS). No slicing took place so the input cost equations might have many more variables than needed. For the second set we used the original cost equations for PUBS and CoFloCo. We decided not to include these problems for KoAT as the translation generated in [8] is not sound (we found several problems where KoAT yields an incorrect upper bound). We summarize the number of problems solved by each tool in different complexity categories. Each problem was run with a time-out of 60 secs. The same set of problems[3] has been used to evaluate the new version of Loopus [17]. We include the results of their evaluation[4] in a shaded row to emphasize that we did not run the experiments ourselves.

CoFloCo obtains a bound asymptotically better than KoAt in 79 problems and better than PUBS in 96 problems. Conversely, KoAt obtains a better bound than CoFloCo in 21 problems and PUBS is better than CoFloCo in 4 problems. CoFloCo obtains better results than Loopus in 67 of the problems analyzed by both. Loopus obtains better results than CoFloCo in 78 problems. However, in 37 of these problems, Loopus reports an upper bound as a function of `call_to_nondet_line_X` where X is a line number. It seems that Loopus assumes a specific symbolic value whenever a non-deterministic assignment is executed whereas CoFloCo does not make such an assumption and fails to provide a bound. The complete experimental data and the implementation are available.[5]

At this time, CoFloCo is just prototype and can be greatly improved. It fails on 23 problems because of irreducible loops. Irreducible loops can be transformed and the approach could be extended to handle other domains including non-linear constraints, logarithmic bounds, etc. The invariants could also be improved with the termination information of Sec.3.3 following the ideas of [8]. CoFloCo had 70 time-outs. Most occurred with problems with many variables where slicing could be applied. In some occasions, the control-flow-refinement of cost equations can generate exponentially many chains. However, these chains have many fragments in common and part of the invariant and upper bound computation can be reused. Moreover, some SCCs can be left unrefined to achieve a compromise between performance and precision.

We presented a control-flow-refinement algorithm that can be applied to linear recursive programs (other approaches do not support recursion). The algorithm distinguishes terminating and non-terminating executions explicitly which allows obtaining better invariants for the terminating executions. This also allows to have intermediate cost expressions depending on the output variables (see the cost of $(7)^+(8)$) and thus obtain amortized cost bounds. We obtain an upper bound for each execution pattern (chain), which often provides more precise information than a generic upper bound for any possible execution. The upper bounds are also precise because cost structures allow us to maintain several upper bound candidates, detect dependencies among different parts of the code (using *constraint compression*) and obtain complex upper bound expressions.

---

[3] 18 problems included here were left out of the evaluation of Loopus.

[4] http://forsyte.at/static/people/sinn/loopus/CAV14/

[5] www.se.tu-darmstadt.de/se/group-members/antonio-flores-montoya/cofloco

Acknowledgements. Research partly funded by the EU project FP7-610582 ENVISAGE: Engineering Virtualized Services. We thank the anonymous reviewers for their careful reading which resulted in numerous improvements. We thank S. Genaim for valuable discussions and help with the experiments.

References

1. Albert, E., Arenas, P., Genaim, S., Puebla, G.: Closed-Form Upper Bounds in Static Cost Analysis. J. of Automated Reasoning 46(2), 161–203 (2011)
2. Albert, E., Genaim, S., Masud, A.N.: More precise yet widely applicable cost analysis. In: Jhala, R., Schmidt, D. (eds.) VMCAI 2011. LNCS, vol. 6538, pp. 38–53. Springer, Heidelberg (2011)
3. Alias, C., Darte, A., Feautrier, P., Gonnord, L.: Multi-dimensional rankings, program termination, and complexity bounds of flowchart programs. In: Cousot, R., Martel, M. (eds.) SAS 2010. LNCS, vol. 6337, pp. 117–133. Springer, Heidelberg (2010)
4. Alonso-Blas, D.E., Arenas, P., Genaim, S.: Precise cost analysis via local reasoning. In: Van Hung, D., Ogawa, M. (eds.) ATVA 2013. LNCS, vol. 8172, pp. 319–333. Springer, Heidelberg (2013)
5. Alonso-Blas, D.E., Genaim, S.: On the limits of the classical approach to cost analysis. In: Miné, A., Schmidt, D. (eds.) SAS 2012. LNCS, vol. 7460, pp. 405–421. Springer, Heidelberg (2012)
6. Bagnara, R., Mesnard, F., Pescetti, A., Zaffanella, E.: A new look at the automatic synthesis of linear ranking functions. Information and Computation 215, 47–67 (2012)
7. Brockschmidt, M., Cook, B., Fuhs, C.: Better termination proving through cooperation. In: Sharygina, N., Veith, H. (eds.) CAV 2013. LNCS, vol. 8044, pp. 413–429. Springer, Heidelberg (2013)
8. Brockschmidt, M., Emmes, F., Falke, S., Fuhs, C., Giesl, J.: Alternating runtime and size complexity analysis of integer programs. In: Ábrahám, E., Havelund, K. (eds.) TACAS 2014. LNCS, vol. 8413, pp. 140–155. Springer, Heidelberg (2014)
9. Chen, H.Y., Mukhopadhyay, S., Lu, Z.: Control flow refinement and symbolic computation of average case bound. In: Van Hung, D., Ogawa, M. (eds.) ATVA 2013. LNCS, vol. 8172, pp. 334–348. Springer, Heidelberg (2013)
10. Cook, B., See, A., Zuleger, F.: Ramsey vs. Lexicographic termination proving. In: Piterman, N., Smolka, S.A. (eds.) TACAS 2013. LNCS, vol. 7795, pp. 47–61. Springer, Heidelberg (2013)
11. Flores-Montoya, A., Hähnle, R.: Resource analysis of complex programs with cost equations. Technical report, TU Darmstadt (2014), https://www.se.tu-darmstadt.de/fileadmin/user_upload/Group_SE/Page_Content/Group_Members/Antonio_Flores-Montoya/APLAS14techReport.pdf
12. Gulavani, B.S., Gulwani, S.: A numerical abstract domain based on expression abstraction and max operator with application in timing analysis. In: Gupta, A., Malik, S. (eds.) CAV 2008. LNCS, vol. 5123, pp. 370–384. Springer, Heidelberg (2008)
13. Gulwani, S., Jain, S., Koskinen, E.: Control-flow refinement and progress invariants for bound analysis. In: PLDI (2009)
14. Gulwani, S., Mehra, K.K., Chilimbi, T.: Speed: Precise and efficient static estimation of program computational complexity. In: POPL, pp. 127–139. ACM, New York (2009)

15. Gulwani, S., Zuleger, F.: The reachability-bound problem. In: PLDI 2010, pp. 292–304. ACM, New York (2010)

16. Podelski, A., Rybalchenko, A.: A Complete Method for the Synthesis of Linear Ranking Functions. In: Steffen, B., Levi, G. (eds.) VMCAI 2004. LNCS, vol. 2937, pp. 239–251. Springer, Heidelberg (2004)

17. Sinn, M., Zuleger, F., Veith, H.: A simple and scalable static analysis for bound analysis and amortized complexity analysis. In: Biere, A., Bloem, R. (eds.) CAV 2014. LNCS, vol. 8559, pp. 745–761. Springer, Heidelberg (2014)

18. Zuleger, F., Gulwani, S., Sinn, M., Veith, H.: Bound analysis of imperative programs with the size-change abstraction. In: Yahav, E. (ed.) SAS 2011. LNCS, vol. 6887, pp. 280–297. Springer, Heidelberg (2011)

Simple and Efficient Algorithms for Octagons

Aziem Chawdhary, Ed Robbins, and Andy King

University of Kent, CT2 7NF, UK

Abstract. The numerical domain of Octagons can be viewed as an exercise in simplicity: it trades expressiveness for efficiency and ease of implementation. The domain can represent unary and binary constraints where the coefficients are $+1$ or -1, so called octagonal constraints, and comes with operations that have cubic complexity. The central operation is closure which computes a canonical form by deriving all implied octagonal constraints from a given octagonal system. This paper investigates the role of incrementality, namely closing a system where only one constraint has been changed, which is a dominating use-case. We present two new incremental algorithms for closure both of which are conceptually simple and computationally efficient, and argue their correctness.

1 Introduction

The octagon domain [16] has become the de facto standard domain for large-scale program analysis. Each invariant in the domain is a system (conjunction) of inequalities over the variables in the program; each inequality takes the restricted form of $\pm x_i \pm x_j \leqslant c$, where x_i and x_j are variables and c is a numerical constant. When $x_i = x_j$ the inequality is unary otherwise it is binary. A unary inequality can express a lower or an upper bound on a variable; whereas a binary inequality places a lower or an upper bound on either the difference between two variables or their sum. A solid planar octagon is expressed as the system

$$x_2 \leqslant 1 \;\wedge\; x_1 + x_2 \leqslant 1 \;\wedge\; x_1 \leqslant 1 \;\wedge\; x_1 - x_2 \leqslant 1 \;\wedge$$
$$-x_2 \leqslant 1 \;\wedge\; -x_1 - x_2 \leqslant 1 \;\wedge\; -x_1 \leqslant 1 \;\wedge\; -x_1 + x_2 \leqslant 1$$

hence the name of the domain. The domain of octagons is more expressive than the domain of intervals [9] because intervals cannot express differences [14]. Moreover, octagons are more expressive than differences [14] since differences cannot bound sums. Yet the domain of octagons is not as rich as the two-variable-per-inequality (TVPI) abstract domain [19] which relaxes the requirement that coefficients are ± 1 and the TVPI domain is, in turn, less expressive than general polyhedra [6] that permit arbitrary n-ary inequalities to be represented.

Domain construction is a balancing act since increasing expressiveness normally degrades performance. The octagon domain has proved to be popular because it is rich enough to support many clients applications, yet all its operations can be reduced to shortest path problems [7,20]. Octagons have been applied in model checking [12], shape analysis [13], interpolation [8], proving program termination [4] and deployed in commercial static analysis tools [5]. Any computational improvement for this domain thus promises to have wide impact.

J. Garrigue (Ed.): APLAS 2014, LNCS 8858, pp. 296–313, 2014.
© Springer International Publishing Switzerland 2014

Miné, who first proposed this domain [16], used difference bound matrices (DBMs) to represent a system of octagonal inequalities. His insight was to introduce auxiliary variables $x'_{2i+1} = -x_i$ and put $x'_{2i} = x_i$ so that inequalities such as $x_i + x_j \leqslant c$ and $-x_i - x_j \leqslant c$ can be translated into differences, namely $x'_{2i} - x'_{2j+1} \leqslant c$ and $x'_{2i+1} - x'_{2j} \leqslant c$, and thereby represented with DBMs. Moreover the unary inequalities $x_i \leqslant c$ and $-x_i \leqslant c$ can also be represented as differences by $x'_{2i} - x'_{2i+1} \leqslant 2c$ and $x'_{2i+1} - x'_{2i} \leqslant 2c$ respectively. Miné derived a canonical form for octagons by applying a Floyd-Warshall style algorithm [7,20] on the DBMs; he also showed how all the domain operations can be reduced to computing this canonical form, which is derived by an operation called closure. The intuition behind closure is that it makes explicit all entailed unary and binary constraints and thereby provides a canonical representation. As well as combining two differences such as $x'_i - x'_j \leqslant c_1$ and $x'_j - x'_k \leqslant c_2$ to derive the entailed inequality $x'_i - x'_k \leqslant c_1 + c_2$, closure amalgamates unary constraints into a binary constraint. This requires special logic since $x_i \leqslant c_1$ and $x_j \leqslant c_2$ are encoded as $x'_{2i} - x'_{2i+1} \leqslant 2c_1$ and $x'_{2j} - x'_{2j+1} \leqslant 2c_2$ which need to be combined to give $x'_{2i} - x'_{2j+1} \leqslant c_1 + c_2$ that encodes $x_i + x_j \leqslant c_1 + c_2$. Likewise $-x_i \leqslant c_1$ and $-x_j \leqslant c_2$ need to be combined to give $-x_i - x_j \leqslant c_1 + c_2$, etc.

Miné adapted the Floyd-Warshall algorithm, which repeatedly combines differences, to handle unary constraints. Later it was independently shown, through an ingenious correctness argument [1], that unary constraints can be handled outside the main loop of the Floyd-Warshall algorithm, in a post-processing step called strengthening. This result led to a performance improvement of approximately 20% [1] which is truly worthwhile. Another worthwhile refinement, which was advocated by Miné himself [15], is to exploit the frequent use-case in which a single inequality is added to a closed system. Miné reordered the columns and rows of the DBM (at least conceptually) so that only entries in the last two columns and rows were recomputed, which led to a quadratic algorithm. Our observation is that an incremental algorithm can be derived by considering paths formed from three inequalities, two of which are expressed in the DBM and the third being the new constraint which is added. As with the strengthening refinement, which is essentially a very clever form of code motion, our observation likewise leads to simpler and more efficient code.

Our contribution is to propose two new incremental algorithms for closing an octagon represented as a DBM. These algorithms represent different points in the design space: the first is simple and efficient; the second is marginally more complex but marginally faster. The correctness of these algorithms is proven and experimental results are presented which quantify their relative speed [1]. Along the way, the paper also proposes a simplification to Miné's incremental algorithm [15] and gives simpler correctness proofs for non-incremental versions of the algorithm. This paper has been designed to be a self-contained guide to implementing closure, which is the key step in realising this abstract domain, hence the paper includes a primer on this domain and its DBM representation.

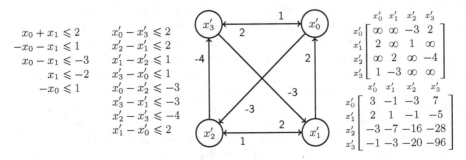

The constraints and figure contents:

$$x_0 + x_1 \leqslant 2$$
$$-x_0 - x_1 \leqslant 1$$
$$x_0 - x_1 \leqslant -3$$
$$x_1 \leqslant -2$$
$$-x_0 \leqslant 1$$

$$x_0' - x_3' \leqslant 2$$
$$x_2' - x_1' \leqslant 2$$
$$x_1' - x_2' \leqslant 1$$
$$x_3' - x_0' \leqslant 1$$
$$x_0' - x_2' \leqslant -3$$
$$x_3' - x_1' \leqslant -3$$
$$x_2' - x_3' \leqslant -4$$
$$x_1' - x_0' \leqslant 2$$

Fig. 1: Example of an octagonal system and its DBM representation

2   Primer on the Octagon Domain

The seminal [15,16] and definitive [1] works on octagons are all long, so this primer is intended to serve as a self-contained short introduction to octagons, in particular the closure operation, on which this paper focuses.

2.1   The Domain and Its Representation

An octagonal constraint is a two variable inequality of the form $\pm x_i \pm x_j \leqslant c$ where x_i and x_j are variables and c is a constant. An octagon is a set of points satisfying a system of octagonal constraints. The octagon domain is the set of all octagons that can be defined over a finite system of variables $x_0 \ldots x_{n-1}$.

An attractive way to implement the octagon domain is to reuse machinery developed for solving difference constraints of the form $x_i - x_j \leqslant c$. Miné [16] showed that octagonal constraints could be translated into differences by working with an extended set of variables $x_0' \ldots x_{2n-1}'$ and letting $x_i = x_{2i}'$ and, most significantly, putting $-x_i = x_{2i+1}'$. Then single octagonal constraints can be translated into a conjunction of one or more difference constraints as follows:

$$x_i - x_j \leqslant c \rightsquigarrow \quad x_{2i}' - x_{2j}' \leqslant c \ \wedge \ x_{2j+1}' - x_{2i+1}' \leqslant c$$
$$x_i + x_j \leqslant c \rightsquigarrow x_{2i}' - x_{2j+1}' \leqslant c \ \wedge \quad x_{2j}' - x_{2i+1}' \leqslant c$$
$$-x_i - x_j \leqslant c \rightsquigarrow x_{2i+1}' - x_{2j}' \leqslant c \ \wedge \quad x_{2j+1}' - x_{2i}' \leqslant c$$
$$x_i \leqslant c \rightsquigarrow x_{2i}' - x_{2i+1}' \leqslant 2c$$
$$-x_i \leqslant c \rightsquigarrow x_{2i+1}' - x_{2i}' \leqslant 2c$$

A system of difference constraints is represented using a difference-bound matrix (DBM). A DBM **m** is a square matrix of dimension $n \times n$, where n is the number of variables in the difference constraint system. The value of the entry $c = \mathbf{m}_{i,j}$ represents the constant c of the inequality $x_i - x_j \leqslant c$ where the indices i, j of **m** range over $\{0 \ldots n - 1\}$. An octagon over n variables $\{x_0 \ldots x_{n-1}\}$ is represented different constraints over $2n$ variables $\{x_0' \ldots x_{2n-1}'\}$ and therefore requires a DBM of dimension $2n \times 2n$.

Example 1. Figure 1 serves as an example of how an octagon can be represented by a system of differences. The entries of the upper DBM correspond to the constants in the difference constraints. Note how differences which are (syntactically) absent from the system lead to entries which take a symbolic value of ∞. Observe too how that DBM can be interpreted as an adjacency matrix for the illustrated graph where the weight of a directed edge abuts its arrow.

Since octagons are more expressive than differences, a DBM representing an octagonal system needs to be interpreted differently to a DBM representing differences. Thus there are two concretisations for DBMs: one for interpreting differences and the other for interpreting octagons, though the latter can be defined in terms of the former:

Definition 1. *Concretisation for rational* $(\mathbb{Q}^n)$ *solutions:*

$$\gamma_{diff}(\mathbf{m}) = \{\langle v_0 \ldots v_{n-1}\rangle \in \mathbb{Q}^n \mid \forall i, j.v_i - v_j \leqslant \mathbf{m}_{i,j}\}$$
$$\gamma_{oct}(\mathbf{m}) = \{\langle v_0 \ldots v_{n-1}\rangle \in \mathbb{Q}^n \mid \langle v_0, -v_0 \ldots v_{n-1}, -v_{n-1}\rangle \in \gamma_{diff}(\mathbf{m})\}$$

where concretisation for integer $(\mathbb{Z}^n)$ *solutions can be defined analogously.*

Example 2. Because binary octagonal inequalities are modelled as two differences, the upper DBM contains duplicated entries, for instance, $\mathbf{m}_{0,2} = \mathbf{m}_{3,1}$.

If a DBM represents an octagon, then any operation on that DBM must maintain equality between the two entries that share the same constant of a binary octagonal inequality. Formally this is stated in a requirement for coherent:

Definition 2. *A DBM* $\mathbf{m}$ *is coherent iff* $\forall i.j.\mathbf{m}_{i,j} = \mathbf{m}_{\bar{j},\bar{i}}$ *where* $\bar{i} = i + 1$ *if* i *is even and* $i - 1$ *otherwise (likewise for* j *and* $\bar{j}$).

Example 3. For the upper DBM observe $\mathbf{m}_{0,3} = -3 = \mathbf{m}_{2,1} = \mathbf{m}_{\bar{3},\bar{0}}$. Coherence holds in degenerate way for unary inequalities, note $\mathbf{m}_{2,3} = -4 = \mathbf{m}_{2,3} = \mathbf{m}_{\bar{3},\bar{2}}$.

When manipulating DBMs care must be taken to preserve coherence either by carefully designed algorithms or by using a data structure which maintains coherence automatically [15, Section 4.5]. One final DBM property is a prerequisite for satisfiability:

Definition 3. *A DBM* $\mathbf{m}$ *is consistent iff* $\forall i.\mathbf{m}_{i,i} \geqslant 0$.

2.2   Closure Algorithms on DBMs

The closure algorithm is key to both differences and octagons: it generates a canonical representation which is required to compute other domain operations such as meet and join [15]. As well as computing a canonical form, closure can decide satisfiability. Bellman [3] showed that the satisfiability of a difference system can be decided using shortest path algorithms on a graph representing the differences. If the graph contains a negative cycle, the difference system is unsatisfiable. The same applies for DBMs representing octagons, where a negative

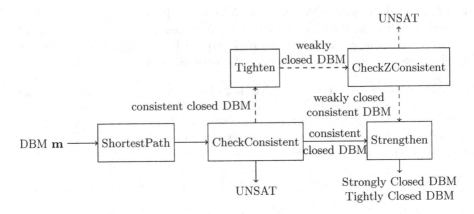

Fig. 2: Architecture of Closure Algorithms for Octagons

cycle results in the diagonal that contains a negative value. Running a shortest path algorithm over a DBM results in its shortest path closure or simply closure. Closure propagates all the implicit (entailed) constraints in a system, leaving each entry in the DBM with the sharpest possible constraint that is entailed between the variables. Closure is formally defined below:

Definition 4. *A consistent DBM* $\mathbf{m}$ *is closed iff*

- $\forall i. \mathbf{m}_{i,i} = 0$
- $\forall i, j, k. \mathbf{m}_{i,j} \leqslant \mathbf{m}_{i,k} + \mathbf{m}_{k,j}$

Example 4. Applying a shortest path algorithm to the upper DBM of Figure 1 yields the lower DBM. The diagonal values preclude the DBM from being consistent and indicate that the difference system, hence the corresponding octagonal system, is unsatisfiable. Indeed observe the graph contains the negative cycle through x_1', x_2' and x_3' stemming from $x_1' - x_2' \leqslant 1$, $x_2' - x_3' \leqslant -4$ and $x_3' - x_1' \leqslant -3$.

Note that closure alone does not provide a canonical representation for an octagonal constraint system: there may be more than one closed DBM which represents the same octagonal system. A stronger property is required, namely strong closure, which additionally propagates the property that if $x_j' - x_{\bar{j}}' \leqslant c_1$ and $x_{\bar{i}}' - x_i' \leqslant c_2$ both hold then $x_j' - x_i' \leqslant (c_1 + c_2)/2$ also holds.

Definition 5. *A DBM* $\mathbf{m}$ *is strongly closed iff*

- $\mathbf{m}$ *is closed*
- $\forall i, j. \mathbf{m}_{i,j} \leqslant \mathbf{m}_{i,\bar{i}}/2 + \mathbf{m}_{\bar{j},j}/2$

Strong closure is necessary to ensure a canonical representation: there is a unique strongly closed DBM for any (non-empty) octagon. Figure 2 gives an

```
1: function STRENGTHEN(m)                    1: function CHECKCONSISTENT(m)
2:    for i ∈ {0 ... 2n − 1} do              2:    for i ∈ {0 ... 2n − 1} do
3:       for j ∈ {0 ... 2n − 1} do           3:       if m_{i,i} < 0 then
4:          m_{i,j} ← min(m_{i,j}, (m_{i,ī}+m_{j̄,j})/2)   4:          return false
5:       end for                             5:       end if
6:    end for                                6:       m_{i,i} ← 0
7: end function                              7:    end for
                                             8:    return true
                                             9: end function
```

```
1: function SHORTESTPATH(m)                  1: function STRONGCLOSURE(m)
2:    for k ∈ {0, 2 ... 2n − 2} do           2:    SHORTESTPATH(m)
3:       for i ∈ {0 ... 2n − 1} do           3:    if ¬CHECKCONSISTENT(m) then
4:          for j ∈ {0 ... 2n − 1} do        4:       return false
5:             t ← m_{i,k} + m_{k,j}         5:    else
6:             m_{i,j} ← min(m_{i,j}, t)     6:       STRENGTHEN(m);
7:          end for                          7:       return true
8:       end for                             8:    end if
9:    end for                                9: end function
10: end function
```

Fig. 3: Strong Closure Algorithm for Octagons

overview of the complete closure algorithm. The algorithm takes in a DBM **m** and performs shortest path closure. Next, the algorithm checks for consistency by checking the diagonal for negative entries, which indicates that the octagonal system represented by **m** is unsatisfiable. If the system is satisfiable then strengthening is applied, resulting in a strongly closed DBM. The dashed lines in Figure 2 represent an alternative path that is taken for integer problems. This is discussed further later in Section 2.3.

Figure 3 reproduces the strong closure algorithm of Miné, refined by applying strengthening outside the main loop of the Floyd-Warshall algorithm, rather than inside it. Bagnara et al. [1] proposed this refinement and showed that it gave a 20% speedup. For presentational reasons the algorithm assumes a matrix representation that enforces coherence (which amounts to updating $\mathbf{m}_{\bar{j},\bar{i}}$ when $\mathbf{m}_{i,j}$ is changed and vice versa). The following theorem [1] justifies this tactic:

Theorem 1. *If* **m** *is a closed DBM and* $\mathbf{m'}_{i,j} = \min(\mathbf{m}_{i,j}, \mathbf{m}_{i,\bar{i}}/2 + \mathbf{m}_{\bar{j},j}/2)$ *then* **m'** *is a strongly closed DBM.*

2.3   Integer Closure

The closure algorithms previously presented have to be modified for integer octagonal constraints, in which the variables are constrained to take integral values. If x_i is integral then $x_i \leqslant c$ can be tightened to $x_i \leqslant \lfloor c \rfloor$. Since $x_i \leqslant c$ is recorded as the difference $x'_{2i} - x'_{2i+1} \leqslant 2c$ tightening the unary constraint is achieved by tightening the difference to $x'_{2i} - x'_{2i+1} \leqslant 2\lfloor c/2 \rfloor$, so that the tightened constant $2\lfloor c/2 \rfloor$ is even.

Definition 6. *A DBM* **m** *is tightly closed iff*

- **m** *is strongly closed*
- $\forall i.\mathbf{m}_{i,\bar{\imath}}$ *is even*

The algorithm for strong closure needs to be modified in the integer case by running a so-called tightening step. This is shown in Figure 4. Tightening makes use of an alternative consistency check, namely CHECKZCONSISTENT. This check exploits the observation that the shortest path algorithm does not need to be rerun after tightening to check consistency; it is sufficient to check that $\mathbf{m}_{i,\bar{\imath}} + \mathbf{m}_{\bar{\imath},i} < 0$ [1]. One subtlety that is worthy of note is that after running the TIGHTEN function on a closed DBM, the resulting DBM will not necessarily be closed but will instead satisfy a weaker property, namely weak closure:

Definition 7. *A DBM* **m** *is weakly closed iff*

- $\forall i.\mathbf{m}_{i,i} = 0$
- $\forall i, j, k.\mathbf{m}_{i,k} + \mathbf{m}_{k,j} \geqslant \min(\mathbf{m}_{i,j}, \mathbf{m}_{i,\bar{\imath}}/2 + \mathbf{m}_{\bar{\jmath},j}/2)$

Strong closure can be recovered from its weak counterpart by strengthening [1]:

Theorem 2. *Let* **m** *be a weakly closed DBM and define* **m**' *as follows:*

$$\mathbf{m}'_{i,j} = \min(\mathbf{m}_{i,j}, \frac{\mathbf{m}_{i,\bar{\imath}}}{2} + \frac{\mathbf{m}_{\bar{\jmath},j}}{2}) \tag{2.2}$$

Then **m**' *is strongly closed.*

2.4   Incremental Closure

A common use-case for the octagon domain is adding a single constraint to an already strongly closed system. Miné [15] designed an incremental algorithm for such a situation based on the observation that one constraint will effect few variables of a strongly closed DBM **m**. The left pane of Figure 5 illustrates this tactic for when the new constraint involves x'_{2n-2} and x'_{2n-1}. The constraint will effect the last two rows and columns of **m**, the shaded region, for which there are $8n - 4$ entries in total; the remaining $4n^2 - 4n + 4$ entries of **m** will remain unchanged. This observation leads to a specialised fast algorithm for strong closure which is presented in the right pane of Figure 5. The intuition is that the body of the loop is only executed for the shaded region of **m**. When the constraint involves variables x'_a and x'_b other than x'_{2n-2} and x'_{2n-1} the rows and columns for x'_a and x'_b can be swapped with those for x'_{2n-2} and x'_{2n-1}. This can achieved either physically or virtually. The rows or columns are literally exchanged in the case of the former. An extra layer of indirection is introduced in the case of the latter between the indices and the rows and columns of **m**

```
1: function TIGHTEN(m)
2:     for i ∈ {0...2n − 1} do
3:         m_{i,ī} ← 2⌊m_{i,ī}/2⌋
4:     end for
5: end function
```

```
1: function CHECKZCONSISTENT(m)
2:     for i ∈ {0...2n − 1} do
3:         if m_{i,ī} + m_{ī,i} < 0 then
4:             return false
5:         end if
6:     end for
7:     return true
8: end function
```

```
1: function TIGHTCLOSURE(m)
2:     SHORTESTPATHCLOSURE(m)
3:     if ¬CHECKCONSISTENT(m) then
4:         return false
5:     end if
6:     m ← TIGHTEN(m)
7:     if ¬CHECKZCONSISTENT(m) then
8:         return false
9:     end if
10:    STRENGTHEN(m)
11:    return true
12: end function
```

Fig. 4: Tightening for integer DBMs

[15] so as to simulate swaps by exchanging pointers. However, this layer can be avoided altogether by reformulating the algorithm to work directly over rows a and b and columns a and b, as shown in listing of Figure 6. Both versions of the algorithm require the entry of $\mathbf{m}$ to be updated prior to applying incremental closure; the second version requires the indices a and b to be passed as well.

3   Improved Incremental Strong Closure Algorithms

Figure 7 presents a new incremental shortest path algorithm inspired by an incremental Floyd-Warshall variant for differences [2]. The new algorithm updates the constraint system represented by the DBM $\mathbf{m}$ with the constraint $x'_a - x'_b \leq d$, and is best understood using the graph interpretation of $\mathbf{m}$. The algorithm examines routes in $\mathbf{m}$ which may be shortened by travelling via the path from x'_a to x'_b and updates $\mathbf{m}$ accordingly, as illustrated below:

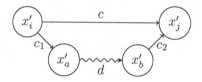

Paths passing via x'_a to x'_b are updated in one of the four following ways:

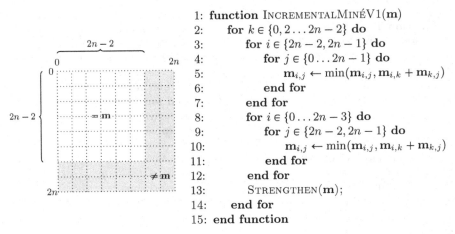

```
1: function INCREMENTALMINéV1(m)
2:     for k ∈ {0, 2 ... 2n − 2} do
3:         for i ∈ {2n − 2, 2n − 1} do
4:             for j ∈ {0 ... 2n − 1} do
5:                 m_{i,j} ← min(m_{i,j}, m_{i,k} + m_{k,j})
6:             end for
7:         end for
8:         for i ∈ {0 ... 2n − 3} do
9:             for j ∈ {2n − 2, 2n − 1} do
10:                m_{i,j} ← min(m_{i,j}, m_{i,k} + m_{k,j})
11:            end for
12:        end for
13:        STRENGTHEN(m);
14:    end for
15: end function
```

Fig. 5: Incremental closure [15] with strengthening [1]

- If $i \neq a$ and $j \neq b$ the path from x'_i to x'_j of length c is shortened if there exist paths x'_i to x'_a and x'_b to x'_j of lengths c_1 and c_2, such that $c_1 + d + c_2 < c$.
- If $i = a$ the path from x'_a to x'_j of length c is shortened if there exists a path x'_b to x'_j of length c_2 such that $d + c_2 < c$.
- If $j = b$ the path from x'_i to x'_b of length c is shortened if there exists a path x'_i to x'_b of length c_1 such that $c_1 + d < c$.
- If $i = a$ and $j = b$ the path from x'_a to x'_b of length c is shortened if $d < c$.

The second algorithm in Figure 7 is a refinement of the first: it only compares paths for those entries in the DBM which *could* change. The shortest path from x'_i to x'_j can only only be changed if either the distance from x'_i to x'_b or the distance x'_a to x'_j are decreased by travelling via the new constraint. Values of i and j for which this is not true do not need to be considered.

The correctness of INCREMENTALDIFFERENCEV1 follows from:

Theorem 3. *Given a closed DBM* **m**, INCREMENTALDIFFERENCEV1 *will return a closed DBM.*

The correctness of INCREMENTALDIFFERENCEV2 is a special case of Theorem 3.

Figures 8 and 9 present two new shortest path algorithms, INCREMENTALOC-TAGONV1 and INCREMENTALOCTAGONV2, for octagons. These, in turn, induce new incremental algorithms for strong closure obtained by replacing line 2 of STRONGCLOSURE with INCREMENTALOCTAGONV1 or INCREMENTALOC-TAGONV2. The novelty of INCREMENTALOCTAGONV1 and INCREMENTALOC-TAGONV2 is that they update the DBM by simultaneously considering the effect of two differences $x'_a − x'_b \leqslant d$ and $x'_{a'} − x'_{b'} \leqslant d$. These differences are derived by the function *split* which applies the translation rules detailed in Sec. 2.1 to the octagonal constraint O. The correctness of INCREMENTALOCTAGONV1 and IN-CREMENTALOCTAGONV2 is founded on the following lemma, which states that there is no harm in computing the effect of the two inequalities in parallel; one difference cannot interfere with the other.

```
1: function INCREMENTALMINÉV2(m, a, b)
2:     for k ∈ {0, 2 . . . 2n − 2} do
3:         for i ∈ {a, b} do
4:             for j ∈ {0 . . . 2n − 1} do
5:                 m_{i,j} ← min(m_{i,j}, m_{i,k} + m_{k,j})
6:             end for
7:         end for
8:         for i ∈ {0 . . . 2n − 1} do
9:             for j ∈ {a, b} do
10:                 m_{i,j} ← min(m_{i,j}, m_{i,k} + m_{k,j})
11:            end for
12:        end for
13:        STRENGTHEN(m);
14:    end for
15: end function
```

Fig. 6: Incremental closure [15] with strengthening [1] and static rows and columns

Lemma 1. *Given a strongly closed DBM* $\mathbf{m}$ *and an octagonal constraint* O, *let* $\mathbf{m}' = \textsc{IncrementalOctagonV1}(\mathbf{m}, O)$ *then* $\mathbf{m}'$ *satisfies:*

$$\forall i, j.\ \mathbf{m}'_{i,j} \leqslant (\mathbf{m}_{i,a} + d + \mathbf{m}_{b,j} \wedge \mathbf{m}_{i,a'} + d + \mathbf{m}_{b',j})$$

The following theorem justifies the new incremental closure algorithm:

Theorem 4. *Given a strongly closed DBM* $\mathbf{m}$ *and an octagonal constraint* O, *let* $\mathbf{m}' = \textsc{StrongClosure}(\mathbf{m})$ *where line 2 has been replaced by* $\textsc{IncrementalOctagonV1}(\mathbf{m}, O)$. *Then* $\mathbf{m}'$ *is strongly closed.*

Proof Sketch   First it must be shown that INCREMENTALOCTAGONV1 preserves closedness. A direct proof strategy is employed based on a case-by-case analysis of:

$$\forall i, j, k. \mathbf{m}'_{i,j} \leqslant \mathbf{m}'_{i,k} + \mathbf{m}'_{k,j}$$

Cases covers whether or not the values of $\mathbf{m}'_{i,j}$, $\mathbf{m}'_{k,j}$ and $\mathbf{m}'_{k,j}$ have changed. For space reasons we include an illustrating case:

– **Case** $\mathbf{m}'_{i,j} = \mathbf{m}_{i,j}$**:** By the properties of *min* the following facts are known which will prove useful later

$$\mathbf{m}_{i,j} \leqslant \mathbf{m}_{i,a} + d + \mathbf{m}_{b,j} \text{ and } \mathbf{m}_{i,j} \leqslant \mathbf{m}_{i,a'} + d + \mathbf{m}_{b',j} \qquad (3.1)$$

• **Case:** $\mathbf{m}'_{i,k} \neq \mathbf{m}_{i,k}$ and $\mathbf{m}'_{k,j} \neq \mathbf{m}_{k,j}$
Here there are four cases to consider. Only the following case is shown in which both entries have changed via different constraints:

$$\mathbf{m}'_{i,k} = \mathbf{m}_{i,a} + d + \mathbf{m}_{b,k} \wedge \mathbf{m}'_{k,j} = \mathbf{m}_{k,a'} + d + \mathbf{m}_{b',j}$$

```
1: function INCREMENTALDIFFERENCEV1(m, x_a − x_b ⩽ d)
2:     for i ∈ {0 … 2n − 1} do
3:         for j ∈ {0 … 2n − 1} do
4:             m_{i,j} ← min(m_{i,j}, m_{i,a} + d + m_{b,j});
5:         end for
6:     end for
7: end function
```

```
1: function INCREMENTALDIFFERENCEV2(m, x_a − x_b ⩽ d)
2:     Q_1 ← Q_2 ← ∅
3:     for i ∈ {0 … 2n − 1} do
4:         if m_{i,a} + d < m_{i,b} then Q_1 ← Q_1 ∪ {i}
5:         end if
6:     end for
7:     for i ∈ {0 … 2n − 1} do
8:         if m_{b,j} + d < m_{a,j} then Q_2 ← Q_2 ∪ {j}
9:         end if
10:    end for
11:    for i ∈ Q_1 do
12:        for j ∈ Q_2 do
13:            m_{i,j} ← min(m_{i,j}, m_{i,a} + d + m_{b,j});
14:        end for
15:    end for
16: end function
```

Fig. 7: Incremental closure algorithms for adding single constraints

From the above it follows that:

$$
\begin{aligned}
\mathbf{m}'_{i,k} + \mathbf{m}'_{k,j} &= \mathbf{m}_{i,a} + d + \mathbf{m}_{b,k} + \mathbf{m}_{k,a'} + d + \mathbf{m}_{b',j} \\
&\geqslant \mathbf{m}_{i,a} + d + \mathbf{m}_{b,k} + \mathbf{m}_{k,j} \qquad \text{by Lemma 1} \\
&\geqslant \mathbf{m}_{i,a} + d + \mathbf{m}_{b,j} \qquad \text{by closure of } \mathbf{m} \\
&\geqslant \mathbf{m}_{i,j} = \mathbf{m}'_{i,j} \qquad \text{by Eq 3.1} \\
& \qquad\qquad\qquad\qquad\qquad \text{and assumption}
\end{aligned}
$$

Theorem 1 guarantees that executing STRENGTHEN after INCREMENTALOC-TAGONV1 will result in a strongly closed DBM.   □

The soundness of INCREMENTALOCTAGONV2 is a special case of Theorem 4.

A key point to note here is the simplicity of our proof: it is direct and uses fundamental properties of DBMs. This approach simplifies existing proofs concerning *non-incremental* closure algorithms defined previously [1,16], which are outlined in the next section.

4   Simpler Proofs of Strong and Integer Closure

The proof of Theorem 4 is simple and compelling since it follows from basic definitions of DBMs and closure. A similar approach can be applied to obtain

```
1: function INCREMENTALOCTAGONV1(m, O: octagonal constraint)
2:     (x_a - x_b ≤ d, x_a' - x_b' ≤ d) = split(O);
3:     for i ∈ {0...2n - 1} do
4:         for j ∈ {0...2n - 1} do
5:             m_{i,j} ← min(m_{i,j}, m_{i,a} + d + m_{b,j}, m_{i,a'} + d + m_{b',j})
6:         end for
7:     end for
8: end function
```

Fig. 8: New Incremental Closure Algorithms (without queueing)

```
 1: function INCREMENTALOCTAGONV2(m, O: octagonal constraint)
 2:     (x_a - x_b ≤ d, x_a' - x_b' ≤ d) = split(O);
 3:     Q_1 ← Q_2 ← ∅
 4:     for i ∈ {0...2n - 1} do
 5:         if m_{i,a} + d < m_{i,b} ∨ m_{i,a'} + d < m_{i,b'} then
 6:             Q_1 ← Q_1 ∪ {i}
 7:         end if
 8:     end for
 9:     for j ∈ {0...2n - 1} do
10:         if m_{b,j} + d < m_{a,j} ∨ m_{b',j} + d < m_{a',j} then
11:             Q_2 ← Q_2 ∪ {j}
12:         end if
13:     end for
14:     for i ∈ Q_1 do
15:         for j ∈ Q_2 do
16:             m_{i,j} ← min(m_{i,j}, m_{i,a} + d + m_{b,j}, m_{i,a'} + d + m_{b',j})
17:         end for
18:     end for
19: end function
```

Fig. 9: New Incremental Closure Algorithms (with queueing)

a more direct proof for the *non-incremental* strong closure and integer closure algorithms defined in [1].

Theorem 1. *If* m *is a closed DBM and* $m'_{i,j} = \min(m_{i,j}, m_{i,\bar{i}}/2 + m_{\bar{j},j}/2)$ *then* m' *is a strongly closed DBM.*

Proof Sketch   Two properties need to be shown: strong closure (Def. 5) and closure (Def. 4). The first amounts to showing that m' satisfies the following:

$$\forall i, j.\ 2m'_{i,j} \leq m'_{i,\bar{i}} + m'_{\bar{j},j}$$

Pick some arbitrary i and j. There are several cases to consider. The following is illustrative:

− **Case:** $m'_{i,j} = m_{i,j}$

- **Case** $m'_{i,\bar{\imath}} \neq m_{i,\bar{\imath}}$ and $m'_{\bar{\jmath},j} \neq m_{\bar{\jmath},j}$

$$
\begin{aligned}
2m'_{i,\bar{\imath}} + 2m'_{\bar{\jmath},j} &= m_{i,\bar{\imath}} + m_{i,\bar{\imath}} + m_{\bar{\jmath},j} + m_{\bar{\jmath},j} \\
&= 2(m_{i,\bar{\imath}} + m_{\bar{\jmath},j}) \\
&\geqslant 2(2m_{i,j}) \qquad\qquad\qquad \text{Since } m'_{i,j} = m_{i,j}
\end{aligned}
$$

The operation must be shown to preserve closure: $\forall i, j, k. m'_{i,j} \leqslant m'_{i,k} + m'_{k,j}$. Again a single illustrative case is presented:

- **Case:** $m'_{i,j} = m_{i,j}$:
  - **Case:** $m'_{i,k} \neq m_{i,k}$ and $m'_{k,j} \neq m_{k,j}$:

$$
\begin{aligned}
2m'_{i,k} + 2m'_{k,j} &= m_{i,\bar{\imath}} + m_{\bar{k},k} + m_{k,\bar{k}} + m_{\bar{\jmath},j} \\
&\geqslant m_{i,\bar{\imath}} + m_{\bar{k},\bar{k}} + m_{\bar{\jmath},j} \qquad && \text{by closure of } m \\
&= m_{i,\bar{\imath}} + 0 + m_{\bar{\jmath},j} \qquad && \text{by closure of } m \\
&\geqslant 2m_{i,j} = 2m'_{i,j} \qquad && \text{by } m'_{i,j} = m_{i,j}
\end{aligned}
$$

$\square$

4.1 Integer Closure

The following is a sketch of a simple proof strategy for theorem 2, which is crucial to the soundness proof for integer tightening: theorem 2 is used to show that running strengthen on a weakly closed DBM is sufficient to regain strong closure. This theorem is part of the following proof strategy by Bagnara et al. which amounts to showing that the tighten procedure on a closed DBM produces a weakly closed DBM, and that strengthen then returns a strongly closed DBM. Bagnara then shows that the floor function in the integer strengthen routine also returns tightly closed DBM.

We have produced a simpler proof of correctness for part of the integer tightening algorithm. The proof of theorem 2 is more direct in comparison to [1] since it avoids induction. This theorem corresponds to the strengthen box in figure 2 with input via CHECKZCONSISTENCY.

Theorem 2. *Let* m *be a weakly closed DBM and define* m' *as follows:*

$$
m'_{i,j} = \min(m_{i,j}, \frac{m_{i,\bar{\imath}}}{2} + \frac{m_{\bar{\jmath},j}}{2}) \tag{2.2}
$$

Then m' *is strongly closed.*

Proof Sketch   First it must be shown that m' is closed: $\forall i, j, k. m'_{i,j} \leqslant m'_{i,k} + m'_{k,j}$. Again, an exemplar case is used:

- **Case** $m'_{i,j} = m_{i,j}$
  By the properties of *min* it is known:

$$
\frac{m_{i,\bar{\imath}}}{2} + \frac{m_{\bar{\jmath},j}}{2} \geqslant m_{i,j} \tag{4.1}
$$

• **Case** $\mathbf{m}'_{i,k} \neq \mathbf{m}_{i,k}$ **and** $\mathbf{m}'_{k,j} \neq \mathbf{m}_{k,j}$

$$\begin{aligned}
\mathbf{m}'_{i,k} + \mathbf{m}'_{k,j} &= \frac{\mathbf{m}_{i,\bar{\imath}}}{2} + \frac{\mathbf{m}_{\bar{k},k}}{2} + \frac{\mathbf{m}_{k,\bar{k}}}{2} + \frac{\mathbf{m}_{\bar{\jmath},j}}{2} \\
&\geqslant \mathbf{m}_{i,j} + \frac{\mathbf{m}_{\bar{k},k}}{2} + \frac{\mathbf{m}_{k,\bar{k}}}{2} \qquad \text{By assumption 4.1} \\
&\geqslant \mathbf{m}_{i,j} = \mathbf{m}'_{i,j} \qquad\qquad \text{by consistency of } \mathbf{m}
\end{aligned}$$

Having sketched how to prove closure it must now be shown that $\mathbf{m}'$ is strongly closed. By definition of $\mathbf{m}'$, one of the two following equations is true:

$$\mathbf{m}'_{i,j} = \mathbf{m}_{i,j} \leqslant \frac{\mathbf{m}_{i,\bar{\imath}}}{2} + \frac{\mathbf{m}_{\bar{\jmath},j}}{2} \tag{4.2}$$

$$\mathbf{m}'_{i,j} = \frac{\mathbf{m}_{i,\bar{\imath}}}{2} + \frac{\mathbf{m}_{\bar{\jmath},j}}{2} \tag{4.3}$$

Both cases satisfy Def. 5 as required. □

5 Experiments

To evaluate the performance of the incremental closure algorithms, three different versions of the algorithm have been separately implemented and tuned for performance. The first is Miné's incremental algorithm [15] refined by moving strengthen outside of the main loop [1]. This represents state-of-the-art. In addition, this implementation applies the refinement introduced in Section 2 which avoids swapping updated rows and columns (or equivalently any layer of indirection that seeks to make the swaps virtual [15]). The implementation follows Figure 6 and constitutes a robust baseline to assess any new algorithm against. The second implementation realises the incremental closure algorithm listed in Figure 8 while the third follows the listing of Figure 9, the latter using queues to focus recalculation only on those entries of the DBM that may have changed.

To stress these algorithms, all three implementations have been integrated into a SMT solver over the theory of (quantifier-free) integer octagons. Apart from the incremental theory solver (which uses incremental closure), the solver is a straightforward extension of a solver originally devised for quantifier-free integer difference logic (QF_IDL) [17]. Both solvers apply constraint reification to orchestrate information flow between the propositional and theory components. The idea is to reify each inequality in the SMT formula with a propositional variable. Such a variable is bound to true if the inequality is entailed by the theory store and bound to false if it is disentailed. Entailment and disentailment can be detected by comparing the constant of the octagonal inequality against the corresponding entry in the closed DBM. Conversely, if the propositional variable is bound to true, the corresponding inequality is added to the DBM,

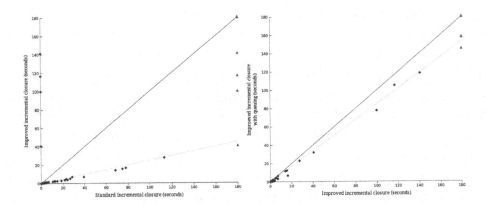

Fig. 10: Execution time

which is then closed. In response to binding the variable to false, the negation of the inequality is added to the DBM which, in the integer case, amounts to adding a non-strict inequality to the DBM and then reapplying closure.

Logic programming languages provide synchronisation primitives for efficiently realising constraint propagation and reification, and these can be used to implement such an SMT architecture [17]. Rather surprisingly, though implemented in Prolog, the resulting QF_IDL solver is capable of solving benchmarks in a time that is comparable to CVC3 and CVC4 [17]. The crucial point is that the closure algorithm is a plug-in into the architecture and the SMT solver provides a way of exercising an incremental solver on large problems, where some SMT instances have even been deliberately engineered to be computationally difficult. In particular, the solver was benchmarked against the first two hundred QF_IDL problems drawn from the latest (2013) SMTLIB suite of benchmarks. Quite apart from comparing the results obtained with different versions of incremental closure, all problems in SMTLIB are labelled according to whether they are satisfiable or not, which provides another check for correctness. Unfortunately SMTLIB does not currently provide integer octagonal problems.

The experiments were run on a single core of a Xeon workstation with a 2.6GHz processor and 128GB of memory, using SICStus Prolog 4.2.1 to run the solvers as interpreted bytecode. Timeouts were set to 180 seconds. The left pane of Figure 10 shows the walltime of the first solver (using the first incremental closure algorithm) against that of the second. The right pane compares the walltime of the second solver against the third. In either graph, results in red triangles indicate a benchmark for which at least one of the two solvers timed out. Note that the runtime of these solvers is dominated by closure, so the experiments constitute an accurate measure of the relative performance of the closure operations themselves (the solvers do not randomly restart and are entirely deterministic).

In order to maintain independence from implementation specifics, from both the machine and the language, the experiments were repeated comparing: the total number of comparisons made in all invocations of incremental closure; and

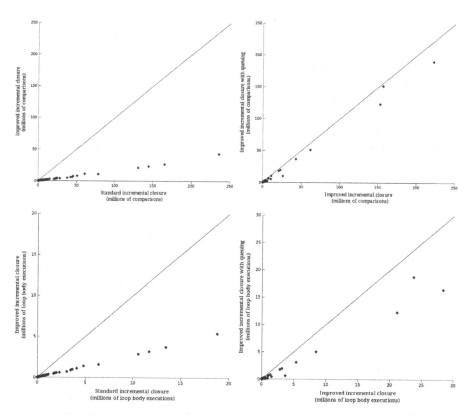

Fig. 11: Total number of comparisons and total number of iterations of inner loop

then the total number of iterations of the inner loop of the closure algorithms. Figure 11 presents these results. Note that these graphs have been pruned to remove data points for which there was a timeout. In such a case, the faster solver receives a higher count because it precedes further and so, without this data cleaning, the graph would suggest that the faster solver was actually slower.

6   Discussion

Figure 10 shows that the second incremental algorithm consistently outperforms the first, appearing to be approximately four times as fast as indicated by the thin blue line with gradient 25%. This result is supported by Figure 11 which shows that the second incremental algorithm performs significantly fewer comparisons and loop iterations.

Figure 10 also shows that the second closure algorithm is able to determine satisfiability of four more benchmarks within the 180 second time frame. The third algorithm that employs queueing improves this by two more. The line in the right pane of Figure 10 has a gradient of 85% showing that the third (queueing) version of the algorithm is uniformly faster. Interestingly, the bottom right pane of Figure 11 indicates that the third algorithm performs significantly fewer loop iterations than second, but the top right pane shows that the number of comparisons is not similarly reduced. This is no doubt because of the extra comparisons incurred while building the queues.

Overall, the distribution of the points in the graphs is similar whether for elapsed time, loop body executions, or comparisons. This suggests that the number of loop body executions and comparisons can be used as a proxy for wall-time and therefore the results are not specific to our Prolog implementation.

7   Related Work

There is arguably no better example of a weakly relational abstract domain than octagons. Miné defined the octagon domain is his thesis [15] and subsequent journal paper [16] and developed an open source implementation [11]. By using DBMs, Miné was able to exploit existing algorithms on solving difference constraints. However the encoding of octagonal constraints into differences requires some conditions, encapsulated in the notion of strong closure, to define a canonical representation of octagons using DBMs. Miné [15,16] showed that strong closure was cubic and that, by swapping rows and columns in the DBM, an incremental version of the algorithm could be derived. Independently a faster algorithm for strong closure was discovered [1], based on the observation that strong closure could be decomposed into two separate algorithmic phases. Our incremental algorithm was inspired by a refinement to the Floyd-Warshall algorithm that was suggested for disjunctive spatial reasoning for solving constraint satisfaction problems [2], and the research question of whether, when adapted to DBMs and octagons, the refinement could improve on Miné's incremental algorithm. The solver proposed in [2] resembles another independently proposed [10] for incrementally solving integer unit two-variable constraints. Though incremental, the integer solver [10] does not decompose constraint solving into the layers of closure, strengthening and tightening, which appears to be important for overall efficiency [1]. The work presented in this paper can be viewed as bringing incrementality to a decomposed solver architecture for DBMs.

8   Conclusions

The widespread use of the octagon domain means that any computational improvement could impact on many areas of analysis and verification. Two new incremental closure algorithms have been presented geared towards the popular DBM representation of octagons [16]. The simplicity of the algorithms paired with their computational efficiency make them an attractive choice for any implementor. [18].

Acknowledgements. We thank Nadia Alshahwan, Earl Barr, David Clark, Jacob Howe and Axel Simon for discussions on TVPI constraints, binary analysis and wrapping that provided impetus for this work.

References

1. Bagnara, R., Hill, P.M., Zaffanella, E.: Weakly-relational Shapes for Numeric Abstractions: Improved Algorithms and Proofs of Correctness. Formal Methods in System Design 35(3), 279–323 (2009)
2. Baykan, C.A., Fox, M.S.: Spatial Synthesis by Disjunctive Constraint Satisfaction. Artificial Intelligence for Engineering, Design, Analysis and Manufacturing 11(4), 245–262 (1997)
3. Bellman, R.: On a Routing Problem. Quarterly of Applied Mathematics 16, 87–90 (1958)
4. Berdine, J., Chawdhary, A., Cook, B., Distefano, D., O'Hearn, P.: Variance Analyses from Invariance Analyses. In: POPL, pp. 211–224. ACM (2007)
5. Cousot, P., Cousot, R., Feret, J., Mauborgne, L., Miné, A., Monniaux, D., Rival, X.: The ASTREÉ Analyzer. In: Sagiv, M. (ed.) ESOP 2005. LNCS, vol. 3444, pp. 21–30. Springer, Heidelberg (2005)
6. Cousot, P., Halbwachs, N.: Automatic Discovery of Linear Restraints among Variables of a Program. In: POPL, pp. 84–97. ACM Press (1978)
7. Floyd, R.W.: Algorithm 97: Shortest Path. CACM 5(6), 345 (1962)
8. Gulavani, B.S., Chakraborty, S., Nori, A.V., Rajamani, S.K.: Automatically Refining Abstract Interpretations. In: Ramakrishnan, C.R., Rehof, J. (eds.) TACAS 2008. LNCS, vol. 4963, pp. 443–458. Springer, Heidelberg (2008)
9. Harrison, W.H.: Compiler Analysis for the Value Ranges of Variables. IEEE Transactions on Software Engineering SE-3(3), 243–250 (1977)
10. Harvey, W., Stuckey, P.J.: A Unit Two Variable Per Inequality Integer Constraint Solver for Constraint Logic Programming. In: Patel, M., Kotagiri, R. (eds.) Twentieth Australasian Computer Science Conference, pp. 102–111. Macquarie University (1997), Also available as TR 95/30 from University of Melbourne
11. Jeannet, B., Miné, A.: APRON: A Library of Numerical Abstract Domains for Static Analysis. In: Bouajjani, A., Maler, O. (eds.) CAV 2009. LNCS, vol. 5643, pp. 661–667. Springer, Heidelberg (2009)
12. Jhala, R., Majumdar, R.: Software Model Checking. ACM Computing Surveys 41(4), 21:1–21:54 (2009)
13. Magill, S., Berdine, J., Clarke, E., Cook, B.: Arithmetic Strengthening for Shape Analysis. In: Riis Nielson, H., Filé, G. (eds.) SAS 2007. LNCS, vol. 4634, pp. 419–436. Springer, Heidelberg (2007)
14. Miné, A.: A New Numerical Abstract Domain Based on Difference-Bound Matrices. In: Danvy, O., Filinski, A. (eds.) PADO 2001. LNCS, vol. 2053, pp. 155–172. Springer, Heidelberg (2001)
15. Miné, A.: Weakly Relational Numerical Abstract Domains. PhD thesis, École Polytechnique (2004), http://www.di.ens.fr/~mine/these/these-color.pdf
16. Miné, A.: The Octagon Abstract Domain. HOSC 19(1), 31–100 (2006)
17. Robbins, E., Howe, J.M., King, A.: Theory Propagation and Reification. Science of Computer Programming (to appear), http://kar.kent.ac.uk/37600
18. Simon, A., King, A.: Taming the Wrapping of Integer Arithmetic. In: Riis Nielson, H., Filé, G. (eds.) SAS 2007. LNCS, vol. 4634, pp. 121–136. Springer, Heidelberg (2007)
19. Simon, A., King, A., Howe, J.M.: The Two Variable Per Inequality Abstract Domain. HOSC 31(1), 182–196 (2010), http://kar.kent.ac.uk/30678
20. Warshall, S.: A Theorem on Boolean Matrices. JACM 9(1), 11–12 (1962)

Compositional Entailment Checking
for a Fragment of Separation Logic

Constantin Enea[1], Ondřej Lengál[2], Mihaela Sighireanu[1], and Tomáš Vojnar[2]

[1] Univ. Paris Diderot, LIAFA CNRS UMR 7089, France
[2] FIT, Brno University of Technology, IT4Innovations Centre of Excellence, Czech Republic

Abstract. We present a (semi-)decision procedure for checking entailment between separation logic formulas with inductive predicates specifying complex data structures corresponding to finite nesting of various kinds of linked lists: acyclic or cyclic, singly or doubly linked, skip lists, etc. The decision procedure is compositional in the sense that it reduces the problem of checking entailment between two arbitrary formulas to the problem of checking entailment between a formula and an atom. Subsequently, in case the atom is a predicate, we reduce the entailment to testing membership of a tree derived from the formula in the language of a tree automaton derived from the predicate. We implemented this decision procedure and tested it successfully on verification conditions obtained from programs using singly and doubly linked nested lists as well as skip lists.

1 Introduction

Automatic verification of programs manipulating dynamic linked data structures is highly challenging since it requires one to reason about complex program configurations having the form of graphs of an unbounded size. For that, a highly expressive formalism is needed. Moreover, in order to scale to large programs, the use of such a formalism within program analysis should be highly efficient. In this context, *separation logic* (SL) [14,21] has emerged as one of the most promising formalisms, offering both high expressiveness and scalability. The latter is due to its support of *compositional reasoning* based on the separating conjunction $*$ and the frame rule, which states that if a Hoare triple $\{\phi\}P\{\psi\}$ holds and P does not alter free variables in σ, then $\{\phi * \sigma\}P\{\psi * \sigma\}$ holds too. Therefore, when reasoning about P, one has to manipulate only specifications for the heap region altered by P.

Usually, SL is used together with higher-order *inductive definitions* that describe the data structures manipulated by the program. If we consider general inductive definitions, then SL is undecidable [5]. Various decidable fragments of SL have been introduced in the literature [1,13,18,3] by restricting the syntax of the inductive definitions and the boolean structure of the formulas.

In this work, we focus on a fragment of SL with inductive definitions that allows one to specify program configurations (heaps) containing finite nestings of various kinds of linked lists (acyclic or cyclic, singly or doubly linked, skip lists, etc.), which are common in practice. This fragment contains formulas of the form $\exists \overrightarrow{X} . \Pi \wedge \Sigma$ where X is a set of variables, Π is a conjunction of (dis)equalities, and Σ is a set of *spatial atoms* connected by the separating conjunction. Spatial atoms can be *points-to atoms*,

J. Garrigue (Ed.): APLAS 2014, LNCS 8858, pp. 314–333, 2014.

which describe values of pointer fields of a given heap location, or *inductively defined predicates*, which describe data structures of an unbounded size. We propose a novel (semi-)decision procedure for checking the validity of entailments of the form $\varphi \Rightarrow \psi$ where φ may contain existential quantifiers and ψ is a quantifier-free formula. Such a decision procedure can be used in Hoare-style reasoning to check inductive invariants but also in program analysis frameworks to decide termination of fixpoint computations. As usual, checking entailments of the form $\bigvee_i \varphi_i \Rightarrow \bigvee_j \psi_j$ can be soundly reduced to checking that for each i there exists j such that $\varphi_i \Rightarrow \psi_j$.

The key insight of our decision procedure is an idea to use the semantics of the separating conjunction in order to reduce the problem of checking $\varphi \Rightarrow \psi$ to the problem of checking a set of simpler entailments where the right-hand side is an inductively-defined predicate $P(\ldots)$. This reduction shows that the compositionality principle holds not only for deciding the validity of Hoare triples but also for deciding the validity of entailments between two formulas. To infer (dis)equalities implied by spatial atoms, our reduction to checking simpler entailments is based on boolean unsatisfiability checking, which is in co-NP but can usually be checked efficiently by current SAT solvers.

Further, to check entailments $\varphi \Rightarrow P(\ldots)$ resulting from the above reduction, we define a decision procedure based on the membership problem for tree automata (TA). In particular, we reduce the entailment to testing membership of a tree derived from φ in the language of a TA $\mathcal{A}[P]$ derived from $P(\ldots)$. The tree encoding of φ preserves some edges of the graph, called *backbone edges*, while others are re-directed to new nodes, related to the original destination by special symbols. Roughly, such a symbol may be a variable represented by the original destination, or it may show how to reach the original destination using backbone edges only.

Our procedure is complete for formulas speaking about non-nested singly as well as doubly linked lists. Moreover, it runs in polynomial time modulo an oracle for deciding validity of a boolean formula. The procedure is incomplete for nested list structures because it does not consider all possible ways in which targets of inner pointer fields of nested list predicates can be aliased. The construction can be easily extended to become complete even in such cases, but then it becomes exponential. However, even in this case, it is exponential in the size of the definition of the inductive predicates, and not in the size of the formulas, which remains acceptable in practice.

We implemented our decision procedure and tested it successfully on verification conditions obtained from programs using singly and doubly linked nested lists as well as skip lists. The results show that our procedure does not only have a theoretically favorable complexity (for the given context), but it also behaves nicely in practice, at the same time offering the additional benefit of compositionality that can be exploited within larger verification frameworks caching the simpler entailment queries.

Contribution. Overall, the contribution of this paper is a novel (semi-)decision procedure for a rich class of verification conditions with singly as well as doubly linked lists, nested lists, and skip lists. As discussed in more detail in Section 9, existing works that can efficiently deal with fragments of SL capable of expressing verification conditions for programs handling complex dynamic data structures are still rare. Indeed, we are not aware of any technique that could decide the class of verification conditions considered in this paper at the same level of efficiency as our procedure. In particular, compared with other approaches using TAs [13,12], our procedure is compositional as it uses TAs recognizing models of predicates, not models of entire formulas (further differences are discussed in the related work section). Moreover, our TAs recognize in fact formulas that entail a given predicate, reducing SL entailment to the membership problem for TAs, not the more expensive inclusion problem as in other works.

2   Separation Logic Fragment

Let *Vars* be a set of *program variables*, ranged over using x, y, z, and *LVars* a set of *logical variables*, disjoint from *Vars*, ranged over using X, Y, Z. We assume that *Vars* contains a distinguished variable nil. Also, let $\mathbb{F}$ be a set of *fields*.

We consider the fragment of separation logic whose syntax is given below:

$x, y \in$ *Vars* program variables $X, Y \in$ *LVars* logical variables $E, F ::= x \mid X$

$f \in \mathbb{F}$ fields $\rho \subseteq \mathbb{F} \times ($ *Vars* $\cup$ *LVars* $)$ $P \in \mathbb{P}$ predicates

$\overrightarrow{B} \in ($ *Vars* $\cup$ *LVars* $)^*$ vectors of variables

$$\Pi ::= E = F \mid E \neq F \mid \Pi \wedge \Pi \qquad \text{pure formulas}$$
$$\Sigma ::= emp \mid E \mapsto \rho \mid P(E, F, \overrightarrow{B}) \mid \Sigma * \Sigma \qquad \text{spatial formulas}$$
$$\varphi \triangleq \exists \overrightarrow{X}. \Pi \wedge \Sigma \qquad \text{formulas}$$

W.l.o.g., we assume that existentially quantified logical variables have unique names. The set of program variables used in a formula φ is denoted by $pv(\varphi)$. By $\varphi(\overrightarrow{E})$ (resp. $\rho(\overrightarrow{E})$), we denote a formula (resp. a set of field-variable couples) whose set of free variables is $\overrightarrow{E}$. Given a formula φ, $pure(\varphi)$ denotes its pure part Π. We allow set operations to be applied on vectors. Moreover, $E \neq \overrightarrow{B}$ is a shorthand for $\bigwedge_{B_i \in \overrightarrow{B}} E \neq B_i$.

The *points-to atom* $E \mapsto \{(f_i, F_i)\}_{i \in \mathcal{I}}$ specifies that the heap contains a location E whose f_i field points to F_i, for all i. W.l.o.g., we assume that each field f_i appears at most once in a set of pairs ρ. The fragment is parameterized by a set $\mathbb{P}$ of *inductively defined predicates*; intuitively, $P(E, F, \overrightarrow{B})$ describes a possibly empty *nested list segment* delimited by its arguments, i.e., all the locations it represents are reachable from E and allocated on the heap except the locations in $\{F\} \cup \overrightarrow{B}$.

Inductively defined predicates. We consider predicates defined as

$$P(E, F, \overrightarrow{B}) \triangleq (E = F \wedge emp) \vee$$
$$\left(E \neq \{F\} \cup \overrightarrow{B} \wedge \exists X_{t1}. \Sigma(E, X_{t1}, \overrightarrow{B}) * P(X_{t1}, F, \overrightarrow{B}) \right) \tag{1}$$

where Σ is an existentially-quantified formula, called *the matrix of* P, of the form:

$$\Sigma(E, X_{t1}, \overrightarrow{B}) \triangleq \exists \overrightarrow{Z}. E \mapsto \rho(\{X_{t1}\} \cup \overrightarrow{V}) * \Sigma' \qquad \text{where } \overrightarrow{V} \subseteq \overrightarrow{Z} \cup \overrightarrow{B} \text{ and}$$
$$\Sigma' ::= Q(Z, U, \overrightarrow{Y}) \mid \circlearrowright^{1+} Q[Z, \overrightarrow{Y}] \mid \Sigma' * \Sigma' \tag{2}$$
$$\text{for } Z \in \overrightarrow{Z}, U \in \overrightarrow{Z} \cup \overrightarrow{B} \cup \{E, X_{t1}\}, \overrightarrow{Y} \subseteq \overrightarrow{B} \cup \{E, X_{t1}\}, \text{ and}$$
$$\circlearrowright^{1+} Q[Z, \overrightarrow{Y}] \triangleq \exists Z'. \Sigma_Q(Z, Z', \overrightarrow{Y}) * Q(Z', Z, \overrightarrow{Y}) \text{ where } \Sigma_Q \text{ is the matrix of } Q.$$

The formula Σ specifies the values of the fields defined in E (using the atom $E \mapsto \rho(\{X_{t1}\} \cup \overrightarrow{V})$, where the fields in ρ are constants in $\mathbb{F}$) and the (possibly cyclic) nested

singly linked lists:
$$\mathtt{ls}(E,F) \triangleq lemp(E,F) \vee (E \neq F \wedge \exists X_{t1}.\, E \mapsto \{(f, X_{t1})\} * \mathtt{ls}(X_{t1},F))$$
lists of acyclic lists:
$$\mathtt{nll}(E,F,B) \triangleq lemp(E,F) \vee (E \neq \{F, B\} \wedge \exists X_{t1}, Z.\, E \mapsto \{(s, X_{t1}), (h, Z)\} *$$
$$\mathtt{ls}(Z,B) * \mathtt{nll}(X_{t1},F,B))$$
lists of cyclic lists:
$$\mathtt{nlcl}(E,F) \triangleq lemp(E,F) \vee (E \neq F \wedge \exists X_{t1}, Z.\, E \mapsto \{(s, X_{t1}), (h, Z)\} *$$
$$\circlearrowleft^{1+} \mathtt{ls}[Z] * \mathtt{nlcl}(X_{t1},F))$$
skip lists with three levels:
$$\mathtt{skl3}(E,F) \triangleq lemp(E,F) \vee (E \neq F \wedge \exists X_{t1}, Z_1, Z_2.\, E \mapsto \{(f_3, X_{t1}), (f_2, Z_2),$$
$$(f_1, Z_1)\} * \mathtt{skl1}(Z_1, Z_2) * \mathtt{skl2}(Z_2, X_{t1}) * \mathtt{skl3}(X_{t1}, F))$$
$$\mathtt{skl2}(E,F) \triangleq lemp(E,F) \vee (E \neq F \wedge \exists X_{t1}, Z_1.\, E \mapsto \{(f_3, \mathtt{nil}), (f_2, X_{t1}),$$
$$(f_1, Z_1)\} * \mathtt{skl1}(Z_1, X_{t1}) * \mathtt{skl2}(X_{t1}, F))$$
$$\mathtt{skl1}(E,F) \triangleq lemp(E,F) \vee (E \neq F \wedge \exists X_{t1}.\, E \mapsto \{(f_3, \mathtt{nil}), (f_2, \mathtt{nil}),$$
$$(f_1, X_{t1})\} * \mathtt{skl1}(X_{t1}, F))$$

Fig. 1. Examples of inductive definitions ($lemp(E,F) \triangleq E = F \wedge emp$)

list segments starting at the locations $\overrightarrow{Z}$ referenced by fields of E. We assume that Σ contains a single points-to atom in order to simplify the presentation. Notice that the matrix of a predicate P does not contain applications of P.

The macro $\circlearrowleft^{1+} Q[Z, \overrightarrow{Y}]$ is used to represent a *non-empty* cyclic (nested) list segment on Z whose shape is described by the predicate Q.

We consider several restrictions on Σ which are defined using its *Gaifman graph* $Gf[\Sigma]$. The set of vertices of $Gf[\Sigma]$ is given by the set of free and existentially quantified variables in Σ, i.e., $\{E, X_{t1}\} \cup \overrightarrow{B} \cup \overrightarrow{Z}$. The edges in $Gf[\Sigma]$ represent spatial atoms: for every (f, X) in ρ, $Gf[\Sigma]$ contains an edge from E to X labeled by f; for every predicate $Q(Z, U, \overrightarrow{Y})$, $Gf[\Sigma]$ contains an edge from Z to U labeled by Q; and for every macro $\circlearrowleft^{1+} Q[Z, \overrightarrow{Y}]$, $Gf[\Sigma]$ contains a self-loop on Z labeled by Q.

The first restriction is that $Gf[\Sigma]$ contains no cycles other than self-loops built solely of edges labeled by predicates. This ensures that the predicate is *precise*, i.e., for any heap, there exists at most one sub-heap on which the predicate holds. Precise assertions are very important for concurrent separation logic [11].

The second restriction requires that all the maximal paths of $Gf[\Sigma]$ start in E and end either in a self-loop or in a node from $\overrightarrow{B} \cup \{E, X_{t1}\}$. This restriction ensures that (a) all the heap locations in the interpretation of a predicate are reachable from the head of the list and that (b) only the locations represented by variables in $F \cup \overrightarrow{B}$ are dangling. Moreover, for simplicity, we require that every vertex of $Gf[\Sigma]$ has at most one outgoing edge labeled by a predicate.

For example, the predicates defined in Fig. 1 describe singly linked lists, lists of acyclic lists, lists of cyclic lists, and skip lists with three levels.

We define the relation $\prec_{\mathbb{P}}$ on the set of predicates $\mathbb{P}$ by $P_1 \prec_{\mathbb{P}} P_2$ iff P_2 occurs in the matrix of P_1. The reflexive and transitive closure of $\prec_{\mathbb{P}}$ is denoted by $\prec_{\mathbb{P}}^*$. For example, if $\mathbb{P} = \{\mathtt{skl1}, \mathtt{skl2}, \mathtt{skl3}\}$, then $\mathtt{skl3} \prec_{\mathbb{P}} \mathtt{skl2}$ and $\mathtt{skl3} \prec_{\mathbb{P}}^* \mathtt{skl1}$.

Given a predicate P of the matrix Σ as in (2), let $\mathbb{F}_{\mapsto}(P)$ denote the set of fields f occurring in a pair (f, X) of ρ. For example, $\mathbb{F}_{\mapsto}(\mathtt{nll}) = \{s, h\}$ and $\mathbb{F}_{\mapsto}(\mathtt{skl3}) =$

$$(S, H) \models P(E, F, \vec{B}) \qquad \text{iff there exists } k \in \mathbb{N} \text{ s.t. } (S, H) \models P^k(E, F, \vec{B}) \text{ and}$$
$$ldom(H) \cap (\{S(F)\} \cup \{S(B) \mid B \in \vec{B}\}) = \emptyset$$
$$(S, H) \models P^0(E, F, \vec{B}) \quad \text{iff } (S, H) \models E = F \wedge emp$$
$$(S, H) \models P^{k+1}(E, F, \vec{B}) \text{ iff } (S, H) \models E \neq \{F\} \cup \vec{B} \wedge$$
$$\exists X_{\mathrm{tl}}. \Sigma(E, X_{\mathrm{tl}}, \vec{B}) * P^k(X_{\mathrm{tl}}, F, \vec{B})$$

Fig. 2. The semantics of predicate atoms

$\mathbb{F}_\mapsto(\mathtt{skl}_1) = \{f_3, f_2, f_1\}$. Also, let $\mathbb{F}_\mapsto^*(P)$ denote the union of $\mathbb{F}_\mapsto(P')$ for all $P \prec_\mathbb{P}^* P'$. For example, $\mathbb{F}_\mapsto^*(\mathtt{nll}) = \{s, h, f\}$.

We assume that $\prec_\mathbb{P}^*$ is a partial order, i.e., there are no mutually recursive definitions in $\mathbb{P}$. Moreover, for simplicity, we assume that for any two predicates P_1 and P_2 which are incomparable w.r.t. $\prec_\mathbb{P}^*$, it holds that $\mathbb{F}_\mapsto(P_1) \cap \mathbb{F}_\mapsto(P_2) = \emptyset$. This assumption avoids predicates named differently but having exactly the same set of models.

Semantics. Let *Locs* be a set of *locations*. A *heap* is a pair (S, H) where $S : Vars \cup LVars \rightarrow Locs$ maps variables to locations and $H : Locs \times \mathbb{F} \rightharpoonup Locs$ is a partial function that defines values of fields for some of the locations in *Locs*. The domain of H is denoted by $dom(H)$ and the set of locations in the domain of H is denoted by $ldom(H)$. As usual, we assume that $\mathtt{nil}$ is interpreted to a location $S(\mathtt{nil}) \notin ldom(H)$. We say that a location ℓ (resp., a variable E) is *allocated* in the heap (S, H) or that (S, H) allocates ℓ (resp., E) iff ℓ (resp., $S(E)$) belongs to $ldom(H)$.

The set of heaps satisfying a formula φ is defined by the relation $(S, H) \models \varphi$. For brevity, we define in Fig. 2 the relation $\models$ for predicate atoms only. The complete definition of $\models$ can be found in [8]. Note that a heap satisfying a predicate atom $P(E, F, \vec{B})$ doesn't allocate any variable in $F \cup \vec{B}$; the locations represented by these variables don't belong to its domain. A heap satisfying this property is called *well-formed w.r.t. the atom* $P(E, F, \vec{B})$. The set of models of a formula φ is denoted by $[\![\varphi]\!]$. Given two formulas φ_1 and φ_2, we say that φ_1 entails φ_2, denoted by $\varphi_1 \Rightarrow \varphi_2$, iff $[\![\varphi_1]\!] \subseteq [\![\varphi_2]\!]$. By an abuse of notation, $\varphi_1 \Rightarrow E = F$ (resp., $\varphi_1 \Rightarrow E \neq F$) denotes the fact that E and F are interpreted to the same location (resp., different locations) in all models of φ_1.

3   Compositional Entailment Checking

We define a procedure for reducing the problem of checking the validity of an entailment between two formulas to the problem of checking the validity of an entailment between a formula and an atom. We assume that the right-hand side of the entailment is a quantifier-free formula (which usually suffices for checking verification conditions in practice). The reduction can be extended to the general case, but it becomes incomplete.

3.1   Overview of the Reduction Procedure

We consider the problem of deciding validity of entailments $\varphi_1 \Rightarrow \varphi_2$ with φ_2 quantifier-free. We assume $pv(\varphi_2) \subseteq pv(\varphi_1)$; otherwise, the entailment is not valid.

$\varphi_1 \leftarrow \text{norm}(\varphi_1); \varphi_2 \leftarrow \text{norm}(\varphi_2);$ // normalization
if $\varphi_1 = \textit{false}$ **then return** true **if** $\varphi_2 = \textit{false}$ **then return** false **if** $\textit{pure}(\varphi_1) \not\Rightarrow \textit{pure}(\varphi_2)$
then return false;   // entailment of pure parts
foreach a_2 : *points-to atom in* φ_2 **do**   // entailment of shape parts
    $\varphi_1[a_2] \leftarrow \text{select}(\varphi_1, a_2);$
    if $\varphi_1[a_2] \not\Rightarrow a_2$ **then return** false
for $P_2 \leftarrow \max_\prec(\mathbb{P})$ *down to* $\min_\prec(\mathbb{P})$ **do**
    forall the $a_2 = P_2(E, F, \vec{B})$: *predicate atom in* φ_2 *s.t.* $\textit{pure}(\varphi_1) \not\Rightarrow E = F$ **do**
      $\varphi_1[a_2] \leftarrow \text{select}(\varphi_1, a_2);$
      if $\varphi_1[a_2] \not\Rightarrow_{sh} a_2$ **then return** false
return $\text{isMarked}(\varphi_1);$

Fig. 3. Compositional entailment checking ($\prec$ is any total order compatible with $\prec_{\mathbb{P}}^*$)

The main steps of the reduction are given in Fig. 3. The reduction starts by a normalization step (described in Sec. 3.2), which adds to each of the two formulas all (dis-)equalities implied by spatial sub-formulas and removes all atoms $P(E, F, \vec{B})$ representing *empty* list segments, i.e., those where $E = F$ occurs in the pure part. The normalization of a formula outputs *false* iff the input formula is unsatisfiable.

In the second step, the procedure tests the entailment between the pure parts of the normalized formulas. This can be done using any decision procedure for quantifier-free formulas in the first-order theory with equality.

For the spatial parts, the procedure builds a mapping from spatial atoms of φ_2 to sub-formulas of φ_1. Intuitively, the sub-formula $\varphi_1[a_2]$ associated to an atom a_2 of φ_2, computed by select, describes the region of a heap modeled by φ_1 that should satisfy a_2. For predicate atoms $a_2 = P_2(E, F, \vec{B})$, select is called (in the second loop) only if there exists a model of φ_1 where the heap region that should satisfy a_2 is non-empty, i.e., $E = F$ does not occur in φ_1. In this case, select does also check that for any model of φ_1, the sub-heap corresponding to the atoms in $\varphi_1[a_2]$ is well-formed w.r.t. a_2 (see Sec. 3.3). This is needed since all heaps described by a_2 are well-formed.

Note that in the well-formedness check above, one cannot speak about $\varphi_1[a_2]$ alone. This is because without the rest of φ_1, $\varphi_1[a_2]$ may have models which are not well-formed w.r.t. a_2 even if the sub-heap corresponding to $\varphi_1[a_2]$ is well-formed for any model of φ_1. For example, let $\varphi_1 = \text{ls}(x, y) * \text{ls}(y, z) * z \mapsto \{(f, t)\}$, $a_2 = \text{ls}(x, z)$, and $\varphi_1[a_2] = \text{ls}(x, y) * \text{ls}(y, z)$. If we consider only models of φ_1, the sub-heaps corresponding to $\varphi_1[a_2]$ are all well-formed w.r.t. a_2, i.e., the location bound to z is not allocated in these sub-heaps. However, $\varphi_1[a_2]$ alone has lasso-shaped models where the location bound to z is allocated on the path between x and y.

Once $\varphi_1[a_2]$ is obtained, one needs to check that all sub-heaps modeled by $\varphi_1[a_2]$ are also models of a_2. For points-to atoms a_2, this boils down to a syntactic identity (modulo some renaming given by the equalities in the pure part of φ_1). For predicate atoms a_2, a special entailment operator $\Rightarrow_{sh}$ (defined in Sec. 3.5) is used. We cannot use the usual entailment $\Rightarrow$ since, as we have seen in the example above, $\varphi_1[a_2]$ may have models which are not sub-heaps of models of φ_1. Thus, $\varphi_1[a_2] \Rightarrow_{sh} a_2$ holds iff all models of $\varphi_1[a_2]$, which are well-formed w.r.t. a_2, are also models of a_2.

If there exists an atom a_2 of φ_2, which is not entailed by the associated sub-formula, then $\varphi_1 \Rightarrow \varphi_2$ is not valid. By the semantics of the separating conjunction, the sub-formulas of φ_1 associated with two different atoms of φ_2 must not share spatial atoms. Due to this, the spatial atoms obtained from each application of select are marked and cannot be reused in the future. Note that the mapping is built by enumerating the atoms of φ_2 in a particular order: first, the points-to atoms and then the inductive predicates, in a decreasing order wrt $\prec_{\mathbb{P}}$. This is important for completeness (see Sec. 3.3).

The procedure select is detailed in Sec. 3.3. It returns emp if the construction of the sub-formula of φ_1 associated with the input atom fails (this implies that also the entailment $\varphi_1 \Rightarrow \varphi_2$ is not valid). If all entailments between formulas and atoms are valid, then $\varphi_1 \Rightarrow \varphi_2$ holds provided that all spatial atoms of φ_1 are marked (tested by isMarked). In Sec. 3.5, we introduce a procedure for checking entailments between a formula and a spatial atom.

Graph Representations. Some of the sub-procedures mentioned above work on a graph representation of the input formulas, called *SL graphs* (which are different from the Gaifman graphs of Sec. 2). Thus, a formula φ is represented by a directed graph $G[\varphi]$ where each node represents a maximal set of variables equal w.r.t. the pure part of φ, and each edge represents a disequality $E \neq F$ or a spatial atom. Every node n is labeled by the set of variables $\mathrm{Var}(n)$ it represents; for every variable E, $\mathrm{Node}(E)$ denotes the node n s.t. $E \in \mathrm{Var}(n)$. Next, (1) a disequality $E \neq F$ is represented by an undirected edge from $\mathrm{Node}(E)$ to $\mathrm{Node}(F)$, (2) a spatial atom $E \mapsto \{(f_1, E_1), \ldots, (f_n, E_n)\}$ is represented by n directed edges from $\mathrm{Node}(E)$ to $\mathrm{Node}(E_i)$ labeled by f_i for each $1 \leq i \leq n$, and (3) a spatial atom $P(E, F, \vec{B})$ is represented by a directed edge from $\mathrm{Node}(E)$ to $\mathrm{Node}(F)$ labeled by $P(\vec{B})$. Edges are referred to as disequality, points-to, or predicate edges, depending on the atom they represent. For simplicity, we may say that the graph representation of a formula is simply a formula.

Running Example. In the following, we use as a running example the entailment $\psi_1 \Rightarrow \psi_2$ between the following formulas:

$$\psi_1 \equiv \exists Y_1, Y_2, Y_3, Y_4, Z_1, Z_2, Z_3.\, x \neq z \wedge Z_2 \neq z \wedge \tag{3}$$
$$x \mapsto \{(s, Z_2), (h, Z_1)\} * Z_2 \mapsto \{(s, y), (h, Z_3)\} * \mathrm{ls}(Z_1, z) * \mathrm{ls}(Z_3, z) *$$
$$\mathrm{ls}(y, Y_1) * \mathrm{skl}_2(y, Y_3) * \mathrm{ls}(Y_1, Y_2) *$$
$$Y_3 \mapsto \{(f_2, t), (f_1, Y_4)\} * Y_4 \mapsto \{(f_2, \mathrm{nil}), (f_1, t)\} * t \mapsto \{(s, Y_2)\}$$
$$\psi_2 \equiv y \neq t \wedge \mathrm{nll}(x, y, z) * \mathrm{skl}_2(y, t) * t \mapsto \{(s, y)\} \tag{4}$$

The graph representations of these formulas are drawn in the top part of Fig. 4.

3.2   Normalization

To infer the implicit (dis-)equalities in a formula, we adapt the boolean abstraction proposed in [10] for our logic. Therefore, given a formula φ, we define an equisatisfiable boolean formula $\mathrm{BoolAbs}[\varphi]$ in CNF over a set of boolean variables containing the boolean variable $[E = F]$ for every two variables E and F occuring in φ and the boolean variable $[E, a]$ for every variable E and spatial atom a of the form $E \mapsto \rho$ or $P(E, F, \vec{B})$ in φ. The variable $[E = F]$ denotes the equality between E and F while $[E, a]$ denotes the fact that the atom a describes a heap where E is allocated.

Initially: $\psi_1 \Rightarrow \psi_2$

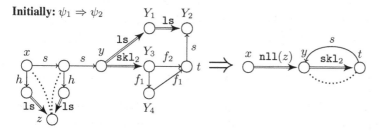

After normalization: $\text{norm}(\psi_1) \Rightarrow \text{norm}(\psi_2)$

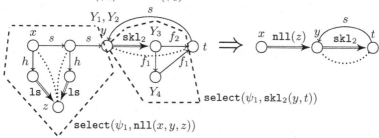

Fig. 4. An example of applying compositional entailment checking. Points-to edges are represented by simple lines, predicate edges by double lines, and disequality edges by dashed lines. For readability, we omit the points-to edge from Y_4 to $\texttt{nil}$, some of the labeling with existentially-quantified variables, and some of the disequality edges in the normalized graphs.

Given $\varphi \triangleq \exists \vec{X}. \Pi \wedge \Sigma$, $\mathsf{BoolAbs}[\varphi] \triangleq F(\Pi) \wedge F(\Sigma) \wedge F_= \wedge F_*$ where $F(\Pi)$ and $F(\Sigma)$ encode the atoms of φ (using $\oplus$ to denote xor), $F_=$ encodes reflexivity, symmetry, and transitivity of equality, and F_* encodes the semantics of the separating conjunction:

$$F(\Pi) \triangleq \bigwedge_{E=F \in \Pi} [E = F] \wedge \bigwedge_{E \neq F \in \Pi} \neg[E = F] \qquad F(\Sigma) \triangleq \bigwedge_{a=E \mapsto \rho \in \Sigma} [E, a] \wedge \bigwedge_{a=P(E,F,\vec{B}) \in \Sigma} [E, a] \oplus [E = F]$$

$$F_= \triangleq \bigwedge_{E_1 \text{ variable in } \varphi} [E_1 = E_1] \wedge \bigwedge_{E_1, E_2 \text{ variables in } \varphi} ([E_1 = E_2] \Leftrightarrow [E_2 = E_1]) \wedge$$
$$\bigwedge_{E_1, E_2, E_3 \text{ variables in } \varphi} ([E_1 = E_2] \wedge [E_2 = E_3] \Rightarrow [E_1 = E_3]) \tag{5}$$

$$F_* \triangleq \bigwedge_{\substack{E, F \text{ variables in } \varphi \\ a, a' \text{ different atoms in } \Sigma}} ([E = F] \wedge [E, a]) \Rightarrow \neg[F, a']$$

For the formula ψ_1 in our running example (Eq. 3), $\mathsf{BoolAbs}[\psi_1]$ is a conjunction of several formulas including:

1. $[y, \texttt{skl}_2(y, Y_3)] \oplus [y = Y_3]$, which encodes the atom $\texttt{skl}_2(y, Y_3)$,
2. $[Y_3, Y_3 \mapsto \{(f_1, Y_4), (f_2, t)\}]$ and $[t, t \mapsto \{(s, Y_2)\}]$, encoding points-to atoms,
3. $([y = t] \wedge [t, t \mapsto \{(s, Y_2)\}]) \Rightarrow \neg[y, \texttt{skl}_2(y, Y_3)]$, which encodes the separating conjunction between $t \mapsto \{(s, Y_2)\}$ and $\texttt{skl}_2(y, Y_3)$,
4. $([Y_3 = t] \wedge [t, t \mapsto \{(s, Y_2)\}]) \Rightarrow \neg[Y_3, Y_3 \mapsto \{(f_1, Y_4), (f_2, t)\}]$, which encodes the separating conjunction between $t \mapsto \{(s, Y_2)\}$ and $Y_3 \mapsto \{(f_1, Y_4), (f_2, t)\}$.

Proposition 1. *Let φ be a formula. Then,* BoolAbs$[\varphi]$ *is equisatisfiable with φ, and for any variables E and F of φ,* BoolAbs$[\varphi] \Rightarrow [E = F]$ *(resp.,* BoolAbs$[\varphi] \Rightarrow \neg[E = F]$*) iff $\varphi \Rightarrow E = F$ (resp. $\varphi \Rightarrow E \neq F$).*

For example, BoolAbs$[\psi_1] \Rightarrow \neg[y = t]$, which is a consequence of the sub-formulas we have given above together with $F_=$.

If BoolAbs$[\varphi]$ is unsatisfiable, then the output of $\mathrm{norm}(\varphi)$ is *false*. Otherwise, the output of $\mathrm{norm}(\varphi)$ is the formula φ' obtained from φ by (1) adding all (dis-)equalities implied by BoolAbs$[\varphi]$ and (2) removing all predicates $P(E, F, \overrightarrow{B})$ s.t. $E = F$ occurs in the pure part. For example, the normalizations of ψ_1 and ψ_2 are given in the bottom part of Fig. 4. Note that the ls atoms reachable from y are removed because BoolAbs$[\psi_1] \Rightarrow [y = Y_1]$ and BoolAbs$[\psi_1] \Rightarrow [Y_1 = Y_2]$.

The following result is important for the completeness of the select procedure.

Proposition 2. *Let $\mathrm{norm}(\varphi)$ be the normal form of a formula φ. For any two distinct nodes n and n' in the SL graph of $\mathrm{norm}(\varphi)$, there cannot exist two disjoint sets of atoms A and A' in $\mathrm{norm}(\varphi)$ s.t. both A and A' represent paths between n and n'.*

If we assume for contradiction that $\mathrm{norm}(\varphi)$ contains two such sets of atoms, then, by the semantics of the separating conjunction, $\varphi \Rightarrow E = F$ where E and F label n and n', respectively. Therefore, $\mathrm{norm}(\varphi)$ does not include all equalities implied by φ, which contradicts its definition.

3.3   Selection of Spatial Atoms

Points-to Atoms. Let $\varphi_1 \triangleq \exists \overrightarrow{X}.\, \Pi_1 \wedge \Sigma_1$ be a normalized formula. The procedure $\mathrm{select}(\varphi_1, E_2 \mapsto \rho_2)$ outputs the sub-formula $\exists \overrightarrow{X}.\, \Pi_1 \wedge E_1 \mapsto \rho_1$ s.t. $E_1 = E_2$ occurs in Π_1 if it exists, or *emp* otherwise. The procedure select is called only if φ_1 is satisfiable and consequently, φ_1 cannot contain two different atoms $E_1 \mapsto \rho_1$ and $E_1' \mapsto \rho_1'$ such that $E_1 = E_1' = E_2$. Also, if there exists no such points-to atom, then $\varphi_1 \Rightarrow \varphi_2$ is not valid. Indeed, since φ_2 does not contain existentially quantified variables, a points-to atom in φ_2 could be entailed only by a points-to atom in φ_1.

In the running example, $\mathrm{select}(\psi_1, t \mapsto \{(s, y)\}) = \exists Y_2.\, y = Y_2 \wedge \ldots \wedge t \mapsto \{(s, Y_2)\}$ (we have omitted some existential variables and pure atoms).

Predicate Atoms. Given an atom $a_2 = P_2(E_2, F_2, \overrightarrow{B_2})$, $\mathrm{select}(\varphi_1, a_2)$ builds a sub-graph G' of $G[\varphi_1]$, and then it checks whether the sub-heaps described by G' are well-formed w.r.t. a_2. If this is not true or if G' is empty, then it outputs *emp*. Otherwise, it outputs the formula $\exists \overrightarrow{X}.\, \Pi_1 \wedge \Sigma'$ where Σ' consists of all atoms represented by edges of the sub-graph G'. Let $\mathrm{Dangling}[a_2] = \mathrm{Node}(F_2) \cup \{\mathrm{Node}(B) \mid B \in \overrightarrow{B_2}\}$.

The sub-graph G' is defined as the union of all paths of $G[\varphi_1]$ that (1) consist of edges labeled by fields in $\mathbb{F}_{\mapsto}^*(P_2)$ or predicates Q with $P_2 \preceq_{\mathbb{P}}^* Q$, (2) start in the node labeled by E_2, and (3) end either in a node from $\mathrm{Dangling}[a_2]$ or in a cycle, in which case they must not traverse nodes in $\mathrm{Dangling}[a_2]$. The paths in G' that end in a node from $\mathrm{Dangling}[a_2]$ must not traverse other nodes from $\mathrm{Dangling}[a_2]$. Therefore, G' does not contain edges that start in a node from $\mathrm{Dangling}[a_2]$. The instances of G' for $\mathrm{select}(\psi_1, \mathrm{nll}(x, y, z))$ and $\mathrm{select}(\psi_1, \mathrm{skl}_2(y, t))$ are emphasized in Fig. 4.

Next, the procedure `select` checks that in every model of φ_1, the sub-heap described by G' is well-formed w.r.t. a_2. Intuitively, this means that all the cycles in the sub-heap are explicitly described in the inductive definition of P_2. For example, if $\varphi_1 = \text{ls}(x, y) * \text{ls}(y, z)$ and $\varphi_2 = a_2 = \text{ls}(x, z)$, then the graph G' corresponds to the entire formula φ_1 and it may have lasso-shaped models (z may belong to the path between x and y) that are not well-formed w.r.t. $\text{ls}(x, z)$ (whose inductive definition describes only acyclic heaps). Therefore, the procedure `select` returns emp, which proves that the entailment $\varphi_1 \Rightarrow \varphi_2$ does not hold. For our running example, for any model of ψ_1, in the sub-heap modeled by the graph $\text{select}(\psi_1, \text{skl}_2(y, t))$ in Fig. 4, t should not be (1) interpreted as an allocated location in the list segment $\text{skl}_2(y, Y_3)$ or (2) aliased to one of nodes labeled by Y_3 and Y_4.

The well-formedness test is equivalent to the fact that for every variable $V \in \{F_2\} \cup \overrightarrow{B_2}$ and every model of φ_1, the interpretation of V is different from all allocated locations in the sub-heap described by G'. This is in turn equivalent to the fact that for every variable $V \in \{F_2\} \cup \overrightarrow{B_2}$, the two following conditions hold:

1. For every predicate edge e included in G' that does not end in $\text{Node}(V)$, V is allocated in all models of $E \neq F \wedge (\varphi_1 \setminus G')$ where E and F are variables labeling the source and the destination of e, respectively, and $\varphi_1 \setminus G'$ is obtained from φ_1 by deleting all *spatial* atoms represented by edges of G'.

2. For every variable V' labeling the source of a points-to edge of G', $\varphi_1 \Rightarrow V \neq V'$.

The first condition guarantees that V is not interpreted as an allocated location in a list segment described by a predicate edge of G' (this trivially holds for predicate edges ending in $\text{Node}(V)$). If V was not allocated in some model (S, H_1) of $E \neq F \wedge (\varphi_1 \setminus G')$, then one could construct a model (S, H_2) of G' where e would be interpreted to a non-empty list and $S(V)$ would equal an allocated location inside this list. Therefore, there would exist a model of φ_1, defined as the union of (S, H_1) and (S, H_2), in which the heap region described by G' would not be well-formed w.r.t. a_2.

For example, in the graph $\text{select}(\psi_1, \text{skl}_2(y, t))$ in Fig. 4, t is not interpreted as an allocated location in the list segment $\text{skl}_2(y, Y_3)$ since t is allocated (due to the atom $t \mapsto \{(s, Y_2)\}$) in all models of $y \neq Y_3 \wedge (\psi_1 \setminus \text{select}(\psi_1, \text{skl}_2(y, t)))$.

To check that variables are allocated, we use the following property: given a formula $\varphi \triangleq \exists \overrightarrow{X}. \Pi \wedge \Sigma$, a variable V is allocated in every model of φ iff $\exists \overrightarrow{X}. \Pi \wedge \Sigma * V \mapsto \{(f, V_1)\}$ is unsatisfiable. Here, we assume that f and V_1 are not used in φ. Note that, by Prop. 1, unsatisfiability can be decided using the boolean abstraction BoolAbs.

The second condition guarantees that V is different from all allocated locations represented by sources of points-to edges in G'. For the graph $\text{select}(\psi_1, \text{nll}(x, y, z))$ in Fig. 4, the variable z must be different from all existential variables labeling a node which is the source of a points-to edge. These disequalities appear explicitly in the formula. In general, by Prop. 1, $\varphi_1 \Rightarrow V \neq V'$ can be decided using the boolean abstraction.

3.4 Soundness and Completeness

The following theorem states that the procedure given in Fig. 3 is sound and complete. The soundness is a direct consequence of the semantics. The completeness is a

consequence of Prop. 1 and 2. In particular, Prop. 2 implies that the sub-formula returned by $\texttt{select}(\varphi_1, a_2)$ is the only one that can describe a heap region satisfying
a_2.

Theorem 1. *Let φ_1 and φ_2 be two formulas s.t. φ_2 is quantifier-free. Then, $\varphi_1 \Rightarrow \varphi_2$
iff the procedure in Fig. 3 returns* $\texttt{true}$.

3.5   Checking Entailments between a Formula and an Atom

Given a formula φ and an atom $P(E, F, \vec{B})$, we define a procedure for checking that
$\varphi \Rightarrow_{sh} P(E, F, \vec{B})$, which works as follows: (1) $G[\varphi]$ is transformed into a tree $T[\varphi]$
by splitting nodes that have multiple incoming edges, (2) the inductive definition of
$P(E, F, \vec{B})$ is used to define a TA $\mathcal{A}[P]$ s.t. $T[\varphi]$ belongs to the language of $\mathcal{A}[P]$ only
if $\varphi \Rightarrow_{sh} P(E, F, \vec{B})$. Notice that we do not require the reverse implication in order to
keep the size of $\mathcal{A}[P]$ polynomial in the size of the inductive definition of P. Thus, $\mathcal{A}[P]$
does not recognize the tree representations of all formulas φ s.t. $\varphi \Rightarrow_{sh} P(E, F, \vec{B})$.
The transformation of graphs into trees is presented in Sec. 4 while the definition of the
TA is introduced in Sec. 5. In Sec. 6, we also discuss how to obtain a complete method
by generating a TA $\mathcal{A}[P]$ of an exponential size.

4   Representing SL Graphs as Trees

We define a canonical representation of SL graphs in the form of trees, which we use
for checking $\Rightarrow_{sh}$. In this representation, the disequality edges are ignored because they
have been dealt with previously when checking entailment of pure parts.

We start by explaining the main concepts of the tree
encoding using the generic labeled graph in Fig. 5(a).
We consider a graph G where all nodes are reachable
from a distinguished node called *Root* (this property is
satisfied by all SL graphs returned by the $\texttt{select}$ procedure). To construct a tree representation of G, we start
with its spanning tree (emphasized using bold edges)
and proceed with splitting any node with at least two
incoming edges, called a *join node*, into several copies,
one for each incoming edge not contained in the spanning tree. The obtained tree is given in Fig. 5(b).

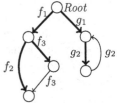

(a) A labeled graph G

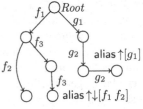

(b) A tree representation of G

Not to loose any information, the copies of nodes
should be labeled with the identity of the original node,
which is kept in the spanning tree. However, since the
representation does not use node identities, we label every original node with a representation of the path from
Root to this node in the spanning tree, and we assign every copied node a label describing how it can reach the

Fig. 5. The tree representation
of a generic graph

original node in the spanning tree. For example, if a node n has the label $\text{alias}\!\uparrow[g_1]$,
this denotes the fact that n is a copy of some join node, which is the first ancestor of

n in the spanning tree that is reachable from *Root* by a path formed of a (non-empty) sequence of g_1 edges. Further, n labelled by alias $\uparrow\downarrow[f_1\ f_2]$ denotes roughly that (1) the original node is reachable from *Root* by a path formed by a (non-empty) sequence of f_1 edges followed by a (non-empty) sequence of f_2 edges, and (2) the original node can be reached from n by going up in the tree until the first node that is labelled by a prefix of $f_1\ f_2$ and then down until the first node labelled with $f_1\ f_2$. The exact definition of these labels can be found later in this section. In general, a label of the form alias $\uparrow[\ldots]$ will be used when breaking loops while a label of the form alias $\uparrow\downarrow[\ldots]$ will be used when breaking parallel paths between nodes. Moreover, if the original node is labeled by a variable, e.g., x, then we will use a label of the form alias $[x]$. This set of labels is enough to obtain a tree representation from SL graphs that can entail a spatial atom from the considered fragment; for arbitrary graphs, this is not the case.

When applying this construction to an SL graph, the most technical part consists in defining the spanning tree. Based on the inductive definition of predicates, we consider a total order on fields $\prec_{\mathbb{F}}$ that is extended to sequences of fields, $\prec_{\mathbb{F}^*}$, in a lexicographic way. Then, the spanning tree is defined by the set of paths labeled by sequences of fields which are minimum according to the order $\prec_{\mathbb{F}^*}$.

Intuitively, the order $\prec_{\mathbb{F}}$ reflects the order in which the unfolding of the inductive definition of P is done: (1) Fields used in the atom $E \mapsto \rho$ of the matrix of P are ordered before fields of any other predicate called by P. (2) Fields appearing in ρ and going "one-step forward" (i.e., occurring in a pair (f, X_{t1})) are ordered before fields going "down" (i.e., occurring in a pair (f, Z) with $Z \in \vec{Z}$), which are ordered before fields going to the "border" (i.e., occurring in a pair (f, X) with $X \in \vec{B} \setminus \{\text{nil}\}$).

Formally, given a predicate P with the matrix Σ as in (2), we identify in the set $\mathbb{F}_{\mapsto}(P)$ three disjoint sets: (a) $\mathbb{F}_{\mapsto X_{t1}}(P)$ is the set of fields f occurring in a pair (f, X_{t1}) of ρ, (b) $\mathbb{F}_{\mapsto \vec{Z}}(P)$ the set of fields f occurring in a pair (f, Z) of ρ with $Z \in \vec{Z}$, and (c) $\mathbb{F}_{\mapsto \vec{B}}(P)$ the set of fields f occurring in a pair (f, X) of ρ with $X \in \vec{B} \setminus \{\text{nil}\}$. Then, we assume that there exists a total order $\prec_{\mathbb{F}}$ on fields s.t., for all P, P_1, P_2 in $\mathbb{P}$:

$$\forall f_1 \in \mathbb{F}_{\mapsto X_{t1}}(P)\ \forall f_2 \in \mathbb{F}_{\mapsto \vec{Z}}(P)\ \forall f_3 \in \mathbb{F}_{\mapsto \vec{B}}(P).\ f_1 \prec_{\mathbb{F}} f_2 \prec_{\mathbb{F}} f_3 \text{ and}$$

$$(f_1 \in \mathbb{F}_{\mapsto}(P_1) \land f_2 \in \mathbb{F}_{\mapsto}(P_2) \land f_1 \neq f_2 \land P_1 \prec_{\mathbb{P}} P_2) \Rightarrow f_1 \prec_{\mathbb{F}} f_2.$$

For example, if $\mathbb{P} = \{\text{nll}, \text{ls}\}$ or $\mathbb{P} = \{\text{nlcl}, \text{ls}\}$, then $s \prec_{\mathbb{F}} h \prec_{\mathbb{F}} f$; and if $\mathbb{P} = \{\text{skl}_2, \text{skl}_1\}$, then $f_2 \prec_{\mathbb{F}} f_1$. The order $\prec_{\mathbb{F}}$ is extended to a lexicographic order $\prec_{\mathbb{F}^*}$ over sequences in $\mathbb{F}^*$. Note that the pointer fields going to nil are not involved in the constraints above (they are not included in neither one of the sets $\mathbb{F}_{\mapsto X_{t1}}(P)$, $\mathbb{F}_{\mapsto \vec{Z}}(P)$, or $\mathbb{F}_{\mapsto \vec{B}}(P)$). They are treated differently because, by definition, there is no pointer field defined in nil. For example, if $\mathbb{P} = \{\text{skl}_1\}$, then $f_2 \prec_{\mathbb{F}} f_1$ and $f_1 \prec_{\mathbb{F}} f_2$ are both valid total orderings on fields.

An *f-edge* of an SL graph is a points-to edge labeled by f or a predicate edge labeled by $P(\vec{N})$ s.t. the minimum field in $\mathbb{F}_{\mapsto}(P)$ w.r.t. $\prec_{\mathbb{F}}$ is f.

Let G be an SL graph and $P(E, F, \vec{B})$ an atom for which we want to prove that $G \Rightarrow_{sh} P(E, F, \vec{B})$. We assume that all nodes of G are reachable from the node *Root* labeled by E, which is ensured when G is constructed by select. The tree encoding of G

is computed by the procedure $\mathtt{toTree}(G, P(E, F, \vec{B}))$ that consists of four consecutive steps that are presented below (see also [8]).

Node Marking. First, $\mathtt{toTree}$ computes a mapping $\mathbb{M}$, called *node marking*, which defines the spanning tree of G. Intuitively, for each node n, $\mathbb{M}(n)$ is the sequence of fields labeling a path reaching n from *Root* that is minimal w.r.t. $\prec_{\mathbb{F}^*}$. Formally, let π be a path in G starting in *Root* and consisting of the sequence of edges $e_1 e_2 \ldots e_n$. The *labeling of* π, denoted by $\mathbb{L}(\pi)$, is the sequence of fields $f_1 f_2 \ldots f_n$ s.t. for all i, e_i is an f_i-edge. The node marking is defined by

$$\forall n \in G \qquad \mathbb{M}(n) \triangleq Reduce(min_{\prec_{\mathbb{F}}}(\mathbb{F}_{\mapsto}(P)) \cdot \mathbb{L}_{\min}(n)), \qquad (6)$$

$$\mathbb{L}_{\min}(n) \triangleq min_{\prec_{\mathbb{F}^*}}\{\mathbb{L}(\pi) \mid Root \xrightarrow{\pi} n\} \qquad (7)$$

where *Reduce* rewrites the sub-words of the form f^+ to f, for any field f. For technical reasons, we add the minimum field (w.r.t. $\prec_{\mathbb{F}}$) in $\mathbb{F}_{\mapsto}(P)$ at the beginning of all $\mathbb{M}(n)$.

Fig. 6(b)–(c) depicts two graphs and the markings of their nodes. (For readability, we omit the markings of the nodes labeled by y and t.)

Splitting Join Nodes. The join nodes are split in two consecutive steps, denoted as $\mathtt{splitLabeledJoin}$ and $\mathtt{splitJoin}$, depending on whether they are labeled by variables in $\{E, F\} \cup \vec{B}$ or not. In both cases, only the edges of the spanning tree are kept in the tree, the other edges are redirected to fresh copies labeled by some alias $[..]$.

For any join node n, the spanning tree edge is the f-edge (m, n) such that $Reduce(\mathbb{M}(m) f) = \mathbb{M}(n)$, i.e., (m, n) is at the end of the minimum path leading to n. (For *Root*, all incoming edges are not in the spanning tree.)

In $\mathtt{splitLabeledJoin}$, a graph G' is obtained by replacing in G any edge (m, n) such that n is labeled by some $V \in \{E, F\} \cup \vec{B}$ and (m, n) is not in the spanning tree by an edge (m, n') with the same label, where n' is a fresh copy of n labeled by alias $[V]$. Moreover, for uniformity, all (even non-join) nodes labeled by a variable $V \in F \cup \vec{B}$ are labeled by alias $[V]$ in G'. Fig. 6(a) gives the output graph of $\mathtt{splitLabeledJoin}$ on the SL graphs returned in our running example by $\mathtt{select}(\psi_1, \mathtt{nll}(x, y, z))$ and $\mathtt{select}(\psi_1, \mathtt{skl_2}(y, t))$.

Subsequently, $\mathtt{splitJoin}$ builds from G' a tree by splitting unlabeled join nodes as follows. Let n be a join node and (m, n) an edge not in the spanning tree of G' (and G). The edge (m, n) is replaced in the tree by an edge (m, n') with the same edge label, where n' is a fresh copy of n labeled by:

- alias $\uparrow[\mathbb{M}(n)]$ if m is reachable from n and all predecessors of m (by a simple path) marked by $\mathbb{M}(n)$ are also predecessors of n. Intuitively, this label is used to break loops, and it refers to the closest predecessor of n' having the given marking. The use of this labeling is illustrated in Fig. 6(b).
- alias $\uparrow\downarrow[\mathbb{M}(n)]$ if there is a node p which is a predecessor of m s.t. all predecessors of m that have a unique successor marked by $\mathbb{M}(n)$ are also predecessors of p, and n is the unique successor of p marked by $\mathbb{M}(n)$. Intuitively, this transformation is used to break multiple paths between p and n as illustrated in Fig. 6(c).[1]

---

[1] The combination of up and down arrows in the label corresponds to the need of going up and then down in the resulting tree—whereas in the previous case, it suffices to go up only.

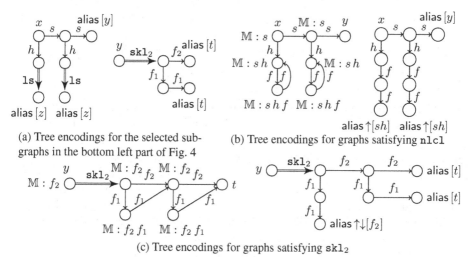

(a) Tree encodings for the selected sub-graphs in the bottom left part of Fig. 4

(b) Tree encodings for graphs satisfying $\mathtt{nlcl}$

(c) Tree encodings for graphs satisfying $\mathtt{skl_2}$

Fig. 6. Tree encodings

If the relation between n and n' does not satisfy the constraints mentioned above, the result of $\mathtt{splitJoin}$ is an error, i.e., the $\bot$ tree.

At the end of these steps, we obtain a tree with labels on edges (using fields $f \in \mathbb{F}$ or predicates $Q(\vec{B})$) and labels on nodes of the form alias $[..]$.

Updating the Labels. In the last step, two transformations are done on the tree. First, the labels of predicate edges are changed in order to replace each argument X different from $\{F\} \cup \vec{B}$ by a label alias $\uparrow[\mathrm{M}(n)]$ or alias $\uparrow\downarrow[\mathrm{M}(n)]$, which describes the position of the node n labeled by X w.r.t. *the source node of the predicate edge.*

Finally, as the generated trees will be tested for membership in the language of a TA which accepts node-labelled trees only, the labels of edges are moved to the labels of their source nodes and concatenated in the order given by $\prec_\mathbb{F}$ (predicates in the labels are ordered according to the minimum field in their matrix).

The following property ensures the soundness of the entailment procedure:

Proposition 3. *Let $P(E, F, \vec{B})$ be an atom and G an SL graph. If $\mathtt{toTree}(G, P(E, F, \vec{B})) = \bot$, then $G \not\Rightarrow P(E, F, \vec{B})$.*

5   Tree Automata Recognizing Tree Encodings of SL Graphs

Next, we proceed to the construction of tree automata $\mathcal{A}[P(E, F, \vec{B})]$ that recognize tree encodings of SL graphs that imply atoms of the form $P(E, F, \vec{B})$. Due to space constraints, we cannot provide a full description of the TA construction (which we give in [8]). Instead, we give an intuitive description only and illustrate it on two typical examples (for now, we leave our running examples, TAs for which are given in [8]).

Tree Automata. A (non-deterministic) *tree automaton* recognizing tree encodings of SL graphs is a tuple $\mathcal{A} = (Q, q_0, \Delta)$ where Q is a set of states, $q_0 \in Q$ is the initial state, and Δ is a set of transition rules of the form $q \hookrightarrow a_1(q_1), \ldots, a_n(q_n)$ or $q \hookrightarrow a$, where

$n > 0, q, q_1, \ldots, q_n \in Q$, a_i is an SL graph edge label (we assume them to be ordered w.r.t. the ordering of fields as for tree encodings), and a is alias$\uparrow[m]$, alias$\uparrow\downarrow[m]$, or alias$[V]$. The set of trees $L(\mathcal{A})$ recognized by $\mathcal{A}$ is defined as usual.

Definition of $\mathcal{A}[P(E, F, \vec{B})]$**.** The tree automaton $\mathcal{A}[P(E, F, \vec{B})]$ is defined starting from the inductive definition of P. If P does not call other predicates, the TA simply recognizes the tree encodings of the SL graphs that are obtained by "concatenating" a sequence of Gaifman graphs representing the matrix $\Sigma(E, X_{\mathtt{t1}}, \vec{B})$ and predicate edges $P(E, X_{\mathtt{t1}}, \vec{B})$. In these sequences, occurrences of the Gaifman graphs representing the matrix and the predicate edges can be mixed in an arbitrary order and in an arbitrary number. Intuitively, this corresponds to a partial unfolding of the predicate P in which there appear concrete segments described by points-to edges as well as (possibly multiple) segments described by predicate edges. Concatenating two Gaifman graphs means that the node labeled by $X_{\mathtt{t1}}$ in the first graph is merged with the node labeled by E in the other graph. This is illustrated on the following example.

Consider a predicate $P_1(E, F, B)$ that does not call other predicates and that has the matrix

$$\Sigma_1 \triangleq E \mapsto \{(f_1, X_{\mathtt{t1}}), (f_2, X_{\mathtt{t1}}), (f_3, B)\}.$$

The tree automaton $\mathcal{A}_1$ for $P_1(E, F, B)$ has transition rules given in Fig. 7. Rules (1)–(3) recognize the tree encoding of the Gaifman graph of Σ_1, assuming the following total order on the fields: $f_1 \prec_{\mathbb{F}} f_2 \prec_{\mathbb{F}} f_3$. Rule (4) is used to distinguish the "last" instance of this tree encoding, which ends in the node labeled by alias$[F]$ accepted by Rule (5). Finally, Rules (6) and (7) recognize predicate edges labeled by $P_1(B)$. As in the previous case, we distinguish the predicate edge that ends in the node labeled by alias$[F]$.

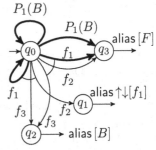

(1) $q_0 \hookrightarrow f_1(q_0), f_2(q_1), f_3(q_2)$
(2) $q_1 \hookrightarrow$ alias$\uparrow\downarrow[f_1]$
(3) $q_2 \hookrightarrow$ alias$[B]$
(4) $q_0 \hookrightarrow f_1(q_3), f_2(q_3), f_3(q_2)$
(5) $q_3 \hookrightarrow$ alias$[F]$
(6) $q_0 \hookrightarrow P_1(B)(q_0)$
(7) $q_0 \hookrightarrow P_1(B)(q_3)$

Fig. 7. $\mathcal{A}[P_1(E, F, B)]$

Note that the TA given above exhibits the simple and generic skeleton of TAs accepting tree encodings of list segments defined in our SL fragment: The initial state q_0 is used in a loop to traverse over an arbitrary number of folded (Rule 6) and unfolded (Rule 1) occurrences of the list segments, and the state q_3 is used to recognize the end of the backbone (Rule 5). The other states (here, q_2) are used to accept alias labels only. The same skeleton can be observed in the TA recognizing tree encodings of singly linked lists, which is given in Fig. 8.

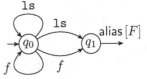

Fig. 8. $\mathcal{A}[\mathtt{ls}(E, F)]$

When P calls other predicates, the automaton recognizes tree encodings of concatenations of more general SL graphs, obtained from $Gf[\Sigma]$ by replacing predicate edges with unfoldings of these predicates. On the level of TAs, this operation corresponds to a substitution of transitions labelled by predicates with TAs for the nested predicates. During this substitution, alias$[..]$ labels occurring in the TA for the nested predicate need to be modified. Labels of the form alias$\uparrow[m]$ and alias$\uparrow\downarrow[m]$ are adjusted by prefixing m with the marking of the source state of the transition. Moreover, labels of the form alias$[V]$ are substituted by the marking of Node(V) w.r.t. the higher-level matrix.

Let us consider a predicate $P_2(E, F)$ that calls P_1 and that has the matrix

$$\Sigma_2 \triangleq \exists Z.\, E \mapsto \{(g_1, X_{t1}), (g_2, Z)\} \wedge \circlearrowleft^{1+} P_1[Z, E].$$

The TA $\mathcal{A}_2$ for $P_2(E, F)$ includes the transition rules given in Fig. 9. These rules are complemented by the rules of $\mathcal{A}_1$ where alias $[F]$ is substituted by alias $\uparrow[g_1\, g_2]$, alias $[B]$ by alias $\uparrow[g_1]$, and alias $\uparrow\downarrow[f_1]$ is substituted by alias $\uparrow\downarrow[g_1\, g_2\, f_1]$. Rule (1') and the ones imported (after renaming of the labels) from $\mathcal{A}_1$ describe

$(1')\ qq_0 \hookrightarrow g_1(qq_0), g_2(q_0)$
$(2')\ qq_0 \hookrightarrow g_1(qq_1), g_2(q_0)$
$(3')\ qq_1 \hookrightarrow \text{alias}\,[F]$
$(4')\ qq_0 \hookrightarrow P_2(qq_0)$
$(5')\ qq_0 \hookrightarrow P_2(qq_1)$

Fig. 9. $\mathcal{A}[P_2(E, F)]$

trees obtained from the tree encoding of $Gf[\Sigma_2]$ by replacing the edge looping in Z with a tree recognized by $\mathcal{A}_1$. According to $Gf[\Sigma_2]$, the node marking of Z is $g_1\, g_2$, and so the label alias $[F]$ shall be substituted by alias $\uparrow[g_1\, g_2]$, and the marking alias $\uparrow\downarrow[f_1]$ shall be substituted by alias $\uparrow\downarrow[g_1\, g_2\, f_1]$.

The following result states the correctness of the tree automata construction.

Theorem 2. *For any atom* $P(E, F, \overrightarrow{B})$ *and any SL graph* G*, if the tree generated by* $\texttt{toTree}(G, P(E, F, \overrightarrow{B}))$ *is recognized by* $\mathcal{A}[P(E, F, \overrightarrow{B})]$*, then* $G \Rightarrow P(E, F, \overrightarrow{B})$*.*

6   Completeness and Complexity

In general, there exist SL graphs that entail $P(E, F, \overrightarrow{B})$ whose tree encodings are *not* recognized by $\mathcal{A}[P(E, F, \overrightarrow{B})]$. The models of these SL graphs are nested list segments where inner pointer fields specified by the matrix of P are aliased. For example, the TA for $\texttt{skl}_2$ does not recognize tree encodings of SL graphs modeling heaps where X_{t1} and Z_1 are interpreted to the same location.

The construction of TAs explained above can be easily extended to cover such SL graphs (cf. [8]), but the size of the obtained automata may become exponential in the size of P (defined as the number of symbols in the matrices of all Q with $P \prec_{\mathbb{P}}^* Q$) as the construction considers all possible aliasing scenarios of targets of inner pointer fields permitted by the predicate definition.

For the verification conditions that we have encountered in our experiments, the TAs defined above are precise enough in the vast majority of the cases. In particular, note that the TAs generated for the predicates for $\texttt{ls}$ and $\texttt{dll}$ (defined below) are precise. We have, however, implemented even the above mentioned extension and realized that it also provides acceptable performance.

In conclusion, the overall complexity of the semi-decision procedure (where aliases between variables in the definition of a predicate are ignored) runs in polynomial time modulo an oracle for deciding validity of a boolean formula (needed in normalization procedure). The complete decision procedure is exponential in the size of the predicates, and not of the formulas, which remains acceptable in practice.

7   Extensions

The procedures presented above can be extended to a larger fragment of SL that uses more general inductively defined predicates. In particular, they can be extended to cover finite nestings of singly or doubly linked lists (DLL). To describe DLL segments between two locations E and F where P is the predecessor of E and S is the successor of F, one can use the predicate

$$
\begin{aligned}
\mathtt{dll}(E,F,P,S) \triangleq {}& (E = S \wedge F = P \wedge emp) \vee \Big(E \neq S \wedge F \neq P \wedge \\
& \exists X_{\mathtt{t1}}.\, E \mapsto \{(next, X_{\mathtt{t1}}), (prev, P)\} * \mathtt{dll}(X_{\mathtt{t1}}, F, E, S) \Big).
\end{aligned}
\tag{8}
$$

Finite nestings of such list segments can be defined by replacing the matrix $E \mapsto \{(next, X_{\mathtt{t1}}), (prev, P)\}$ with more general formulas that include other predicates.

The key point in this extension is the definition of the tree encoding. Basically, one needs to consider two more types of labels for the tree nodes: alias $\uparrow^2[\alpha]$ with $\alpha \in \mathbb{F}^*$, which denotes the fact that the node is a copy of its second predecessor of marking α, and alias $\uparrow\downarrow_{\mathsf{last}}[\alpha]$ with $\alpha \in \mathbb{F}^*$, which denotes the fact that the node is a copy of the last successor of marking α of its first predecessor that has a successor of marking α. The first label is needed to handle inner nodes of doubly linked lists, which have two incoming edges, one from their successor and one from their predecessor, while the second label is needed to "break" cyclic doubly linked lists. In the latter case, the label is used for the copy of the predecessor of the head of the list (cf. [8] for more details).

8 Implementation and Experimental Results

We implemented our decision procedure in a solver called SPEN (SeParation logic ENtailment). The tool takes as input an entailment problem $\varphi_1 \Rightarrow \varphi_2$ (including the definition of the used predicates) encoded in the SMTLIB2 format. For non-valid entailments, SPEN prints the atom of φ_2 which is not entailed by a sub-formula of φ_1. The tool is based on the MINISAT solver for deciding unsatisfiability of boolean formulas and the VATA library [15] as the tree automata backend.

We applied SPEN to entailment problems that use various recursive predicates. First, we considered the benchmark provided in [16], which uses only the ls predicate. This benchmark has been used in the ls division of the first competition of Separation Logic solvers, SL-COMP 2014[2]. It consists of 292 problems split into three classes: the first two classes contain problems generated randomly according to the rules specified in [16], whereas the last class contains problems obtained from the verification conditions generated by the tool SMALLFOOT [2]. SPEN solved the full benchmark in less than 8 seconds (CPU time), which is the second time of the division; the winner of the division was a specialized solver for the ls predicate, Asterix [17], which spent less than 4 seconds for the ls benchmark. An explanation for this result is that in the current version of SPEN, a new TA has to be built for each ls edge, which is time-consuming for problems with several ls edges (this issue will be remedied in future versions).

Moreover, the TA for ls is quite small, and so the above experiments did not evaluate thoroughly the performance of our procedure for checking entailments between formulas and atoms. For that, we further considered the experiments listed in Table 1,

---

[2] The participants in this competition are available at
http://smtcomp.sourceforge.net/2014/participants.shtml, and the
benchmarks for all divisions of the competition are available at
https://github.com/mihasighi/smtcomp14-sl.

Table 1. Running SPEN on entailments between formulas and atoms.

φ_2	nll			nlcl			skl$_3$			dll		
φ_1	tc1	tc2	tc3	tc1	tc2	tc3	tc1	tc2	tc3	tc1	tc2	tc3
Time [ms]	344	335	319	318	316	317	334	349	326	358	324	322
Status	vld	vld	inv	vld	vld	inv	vld	vld	inv	vld	vld	inv
States/Trans. of $\mathcal{A}[\varphi_2]$	6/17			6/15			80/193			9/16		
Nodes/Edges of $T(Gf[\varphi_1])$	7/7	7/7	6/7	10/9	7/7	6/6	7/7	8/8	6/6	7/7	7/7	5/5

among which skl$_3$ required the extension of our approach to a full decision procedure as discussed in Sec. 6. The full benchmark is available with our tool [9] and it includes the 43 problems of the division "fixed definitions" of SL-COMP 2014. The entailment problems are extracted from verification conditions of operations like adding or deleting an element at the start, in the middle, or at the end of various kinds of list segments. Table 1 gives for each example the running time, the valid/invalid status, and the size of the tree encoding and TA for φ_1 and φ_2, respectively. SPEN was the winner in this division of SL-COMP 2014 (in front of [4,6]) and it was the only tool that solved all problems of this division.

9 Related Work

Several decision procedures for fragments of SL have been introduced in the literature [1,5,7,10,13,12,16,18,19,4].

Some of these works [1,5,7,16] consider a fragment of SL that uses only one predicate describing singly linked lists, which is a much more restricted setting than what is considered in this paper. In particular, Cook et al [7] prove that the satisfiability/entailment problem can be solved in polynomial time. Piskac et al [18] show that the boolean closure of this fragment can be translated to a decidable fragment of first-order logic, and this way, they prove that the satisfiability/entailment problem can be decided in NP/co-NP. Furthermore, they consider the problem of combining SL formulas with constraints on data using the Nelson-Oppen theory combination framework. Adding constraints on data to SL formulas is considered also in Qiu et al [20].

A fragment of SL covering overlaid nested lists was considered in our previous work [10]. Compared with it, we currently do not consider overlaid lists, but we have enlarged the set of inductively-defined predicates to allow for nesting of cyclic lists and doubly linked lists (DLLs). We also provide a novel and more efficient TA-based procedure for checking simple entailments.

Brotherston et al [4] define a generic automated theorem prover relying on the notion of cyclic proofs and instantiate it to prove entailments in a fragment of SL with inductive definitions and disjunctions more general than what we consider here. However, they do not provide a fragment for which completeness is guaranteed. Iosif et al [13] also introduce a decidable fragment of SL that can describe more complex data structures than those considered here, including, e.g., trees with parent pointers or trees with linked leaves. However, [13] reduces the entailment problem to MSO on graphs with a bounded tree width, resulting in a multiply-exponential complexity.

The recent work [12] considers a more restricted fragment than [13], incomparable with ours. The work proposes a more practical, purely TA-based decision procedure, which reduces the entailment problem to *language inclusion* on TAs, establishing EXPTIME-completeness of the considered fragment. Our decision procedure deals with the boolean structure of SL formulas using SAT solvers, thus reducing the entailment problem to the problem of entailment between a formula and an atom. Such simpler entailments are then checked using a polynomial semi-decision procedure based on the *membership problem* for TAs. The approach of [12] can deal with various forms of trees and with entailment of structures with skeletons based on different selectors (e.g., DLLs viewed from the beginning and DLLs viewed from the end). On the other hand, it currently cannot deal with structures of zero length and with some forms of structure concatenation (such as concatenation of two DLL segments), which we can handle.

10   Conclusion

We proposed a novel (semi-)decision procedure for a fragment of SL with inductive predicates describing various forms of lists (singly or doubly linked, nested, circular, with skip links, etc.). The procedure is compositional in that it reduces the given entailment query to a set of simpler queries between a formula and an atom. For solving them, we proposed a novel reduction to testing membership of a tree derived from the formula in the language of a TA derived from a predicate. We implemented the procedure, and our experiments show that it not only has a favourable theoretical complexity, but that it also efficiently handles practical verification conditions.

In the future, we plan to investigate extensions of our approach to formulas with a more general boolean structure or using more general inductive definitions. Concerning the latter, we plan to investigate whether some ideas from [12] could be used to extend our decision procedure for entailments between formulas and atoms. From a practical point of view, apart from improving the implementation of our procedure, we plan to integrate it into a complete program analysis framework.

Acknowledgement. This work was supported by the Czech Science Foundation (project 14-11384S), the BUT FIT projects FIT-S-12-1 and FIT-S-14-2486, and the EU/Czech IT4Innovations Centre of Excellence project CZ.1.05/1.1.00/02.0070.

References

1. Berdine, J., Calcagno, C., O'Hearn, P.W.: A decidable fragment of separation logic. In: Lodaya, K., Mahajan, M. (eds.) FSTTCS 2004. LNCS, vol. 3328, pp. 97–109. Springer, Heidelberg (2004)
2. Berdine, J., Calcagno, C., O'Hearn, P.W.: Smallfoot: Modular automatic assertion checking with separation logic. In: de Boer, F.S., Bonsangue, M.M., Graf, S., de Roever, W.-P. (eds.) FMCO 2005. LNCS, vol. 4111, pp. 115–137. Springer, Heidelberg (2006)
3. Brotherston, J., Fuhs, C., Gorogiannis, N., Pérez, J.N.: A decision procedure for satisfiability in separation logic with inductive predicates. In: Proceedings of CSL-LICS. ACM (to appear, 2014)

4. Brotherston, J., Gorogiannis, N., Petersen, R.L.: A generic cyclic theorem prover. In: Jhala, R., Igarashi, A. (eds.) APLAS 2012. LNCS, vol. 7705, pp. 350–367. Springer, Heidelberg (2012)

5. Calcagno, C., Yang, H., O'Hearn, P.W.: Computability and complexity results for a spatial assertion language for data structures. In: Hariharan, R., Mukund, M., Vinay, V. (eds.) FSTTCS 2001. LNCS, vol. 2245, pp. 108–119. Springer, Heidelberg (2001)

6. Chin, W.-N., David, C., Nguyen, H.H., Qin, S.: Automated verification of shape, size and bag properties via user-defined predicates in separation logic. Sci. Comput. Program. 77(9), 1006–1036 (2012)

7. Cook, B., Haase, C., Ouaknine, J., Parkinson, M., Worrell, J.: Tractable reasoning in a fragment of separation logic. In: Katoen, J.-P., König, B. (eds.) CONCUR 2011. LNCS, vol. 6901, pp. 235–249. Springer, Heidelberg (2011)

8. Enea, C., Lengál, O., Sighireanu, M., Vojnar, T.: Compositional entailment checking for a fragment of separation logic. Technical Report FIT-TR-2014-01, FIT BUT (2014), http://www.fit.vutbr.cz/~ilengal/pub/FIT-TR-2014-01.pdf

9. Enea, C., Lengál, O., Sighireanu, M., Vojnar, T.: Spen (2014), http://www.liafa.univ-paris-diderot.fr/spen

10. Enea, C., Saveluc, V., Sighireanu, M.: Compositional invariant checking for overlaid and nested linked lists. In: Felleisen, M., Gardner, P. (eds.) ESOP 2013. LNCS, vol. 7792, pp. 129–148. Springer, Heidelberg (2013)

11. Gotsman, A., Berdine, J., Cook, B.: Precision and the conjunction rule in concurrent separation logic. Electronic Notes in Theoretical Computer Science 276, 171–190 (2011)

12. Iosif, R., Rogalewicz, A., Vojnar, T.: Deciding entailments in inductive separation logic with tree automata. In: Cassez, F., Raskin, J.-F. (eds.) ATVA 2014. LNCS, vol. 8837, pp. 201–218. Springer, Heidelberg (2014)

13. Iosif, R., Rogalewicz, A., Simacek, J.: The tree width of separation logic with recursive definitions. In: Bonacina, M.P. (ed.) CADE 2013. LNCS (LNAI), vol. 7898, pp. 21–38. Springer, Heidelberg (2013)

14. Ishtiaq, S., O'Hearn, P.W.: BI as an assertion language for mutable data structures. In: POPL, pp. 14–26. ACM (2001)

15. Lengál, O., Šimáček, J., Vojnar, T.: VATA: A library for efficient manipulation of non-deterministic tree automata. In: Flanagan, C., König, B. (eds.) TACAS 2012. LNCS, vol. 7214, pp. 79–94. Springer, Heidelberg (2012)

16. Navarro Pérez, J.A., Rybalchenko, A.: Separation logic + superposition calculus = heap theorem prover. In: Proc. of PLDI 2011, pp. 556–566. ACM (2011)

17. Navarro Pérez, J.A., Rybalchenko, A.: Separation logic modulo theories. In: Shan, C.-C. (ed.) APLAS 2013. LNCS, vol. 8301, pp. 90–106. Springer, Heidelberg (2013)

18. Piskac, R., Wies, T., Zufferey, D.: Automating separation logic using SMT. In: Sharygina, N., Veith, H. (eds.) CAV 2013. LNCS, vol. 8044, pp. 773–789. Springer, Heidelberg (2013)

19. Piskac, R., Wies, T., Zufferey, D.: Automating separation logic with trees and data. In: Biere, A., Bloem, R. (eds.) CAV 2014. LNCS, vol. 8559, pp. 711–728. Springer, Heidelberg (2014)

20. Qiu, X., Garg, P., Stefanescu, A., Madhusudan, P.: Natural proofs for structure, data, and separation. In: PLDI, pp. 231–242. ACM (2013)

21. Reynolds, J.C.: Separation logic: A logic for shared mutable data structures. In: Proc. of LICS 2002, pp. 55–74. IEEE (2002)

Automatic Constrained Rewriting Induction towards Verifying Procedural Programs*

Cynthia Kop[1] and Naoki Nishida[2]

[1] Institute of Computer Science, University of Innsbruck, Austria
Cynthia.Kop@uibk.ac.at
[2] Graduate School of Information Science, Nagoya University, Japan
nishida@is.nagoya-u.ac.jp

Abstract. This paper aims at developing a verification method for procedural programs via a transformation into logically constrained term rewriting systems (LCTRSs). To this end, we adapt existing rewriting induction methods to LCTRSs and propose a simple yet effective method to generalize equations. We show that we can handle realistic functions, involving, e.g., integers and arrays. An implementation is provided.

1 Introduction

A problem familiar to many computer science lecturers, is the marking of student programming assignments. This can be large time drain, as it typically involves checking dozens (or hundreds!) of unnecessarily complicated programs at once.

An obvious solution is automatic testing. For example, one might run assignments on a fixed set of input files; this quickly weeds out incorrect solutions, but has a high risk of false positives. Alternatively (or in addition), we can try to automatically prove correctness. Several methods for this have been investigated (see e.g. [9]). However, most of them require expert knowledge to use, like *assertions* in the code to trace relevant properties; this is not useful in our setting.

An interesting alternative is *inductive theorem proving*, which is well investigated in the field of functional programming (see, e.g., [2]). For a functional program f to be checked against a specification f_{spec}, it suffices if $f(\overrightarrow{x}) \approx f_{spec}(\overrightarrow{x})$ is an *inductive theorem* of the combined system of f and f_{spec}. For this initial setting, no expert knowledge is needed, only the definitions of f and f_{spec}.

Recently, analyses of procedural programs (in C, Java Bytecode, etc.) via transformations into term rewriting systems have been investigated [4,6,8,17]. In particular, *constrained rewriting systems* are popular for these transformations, since logical constraints used for modeling the control flow can be separated from terms expressing intermediate states [4,6,8,16,20]. To capture the existing approaches for constrained rewriting in one setting, the framework of *logically constrained term rewriting systems* (LCTRS) has been proposed [13].

---

* This research is supported by the Austrian Science Fund (FWF) international project I963, the Japan Society for the Promotion of Science (JSPS) and *Nagoya University's Graduate Program for Real-World Data Circulation Leaders* from *MEXT*, Japan.

J. Garrigue (Ed.): APLAS 2014, LNCS 8858, pp. 334–353, 2014.

In this paper, we develop a verification method for LCTRSs, designed in particular for LCTRSs obtained from procedural programs. We use rewriting induction [18], one of the well-investigated methods for inductive theorem proving, together with a generalization technique that works particularly well for transformed iterative functions. Although our examples focus on integers and static integer arrays, the results can be used with various theories.

Of course, verification also has applications outside the academic world. Although we initially focus on typical homework assignments (small programs, which require only limited language features), we hope to additionally lay a basis for more extensive program analysis using constrained term rewriting systems.

In this paper, we first recall the LCTRS formalism from [13] (Section 2), and sketch a way to translate procedural programs to LCTRSs (Section 3). Then we adapt existing rewriting induction methods for earlier notions of constrained rewriting [5,20] to LCTRSs (Section 4), which is strengthened with a dedicated generalization technique (Section 5). Finally, we briefly discuss implementation ideas (Section 6), give a comparison with related work (Section 7) and conclude. *An extended version of this paper, including all proofs, is available in [14].*

2   Preliminaries

In this section, we briefly recall *Logically Constrained Term Rewriting Systems (LCTRSs)*, following the definitions in [13].

Many-Sorted Terms. We assume given a set $\mathcal{S}$ of *sorts* and an infinite set $\mathcal{V}$ of *variables*, each variable equipped with a sort. A *signature* Σ is a set of *function symbols* f, disjoint from $\mathcal{V}$, each symbol equipped with a *sort declaration* $[\iota_1 \times \cdots \times \iota_n] \Rightarrow \kappa$, with all ι_i and κ sorts. The set $\mathit{Terms}(\Sigma, \mathcal{V})$ of *terms* over Σ and $\mathcal{V}$, contains any expression s such that $\vdash s : \iota$ can be derived for some sort ι, using:

$$\frac{}{\vdash x : \iota}\ (x : \iota \in \mathcal{V}) \qquad \frac{\vdash s_1 : \iota_1 \ \ \cdots \ \ \vdash s_n : \iota_n}{\vdash f(s_1, \ldots, s_n) : \kappa}\ (f : [\iota_1 \times \cdots \times \iota_n] \Rightarrow \kappa \in \Sigma)$$

Fixing Σ and $\mathcal{V}$, every term has a unique sort ι such that $\vdash s : \iota$; we say that ι is the sort of s. Let $Var(s)$ be the set of variables occurring in s. A term s is *ground* if $Var(s) = \emptyset$. A *substitution* is a sort-preserving mapping $[x_1 := s_1, \ldots, x_k := s_k]$ from variables to terms; $s\gamma$ denotes s with occurrences of any x_i replaced by s_i.

Given a term s, a *position* in s is a sequence p of integers such that $s_{|p}$ is defined, where $s_{|\epsilon} = s$ and $f(s_1, \ldots, s_n)_{|i \cdot p} = (s_i)_{|p}$. We say that $s_{|p}$ is a *subterm* of s. If $\vdash s_{|p} : \iota$ and $\vdash t : \iota$, then $s[t]_p$ denotes s with the subterm at position p replaced by t. A *context* C is a term containing one or more typed *holes* $\square_i : \iota_i$. If $s_1 : \iota_1, \ldots, s_n : \iota_n$, we define $C[s_1, \ldots, s_n]$ as C with each $\square_i$ replaced by s_i.

Logical Terms. We fix a signature $\Sigma = \Sigma_{terms} \cup \Sigma_{theory}$ (with possible overlap, as discussed below). The sorts occurring in Σ_{theory} are called *theory sorts*, and the symbols *theory symbols*. We assume given a mapping $\mathcal{I}$ which assigns to each theory sort ι a set $\mathcal{I}_\iota$, and a mapping $\mathcal{J}$ which maps each $f : [\iota_1 \times \cdots \times \iota_n] \Rightarrow \kappa \in \Sigma_{theory}$ to a function $\mathcal{J}_f$ in $\mathcal{I}_{\iota_1} \times \cdots \times \mathcal{I}_{\iota_n} \Longrightarrow \mathcal{I}_\kappa$. For all theory sorts ι we also fix a set $Val_\iota \subseteq \Sigma_{theory}$ of *values*: function symbols $a : [] \Rightarrow \iota$, where $\mathcal{J}$ gives a bijective mapping from Val_ι to $\mathcal{I}_\iota$. We require that $\Sigma_{terms} \cap \Sigma_{theory} \subseteq Val = \bigcup_\iota Val_\iota$.

A term in $Terms(\Sigma_{theory}, V)$ is called a *logical term*. For ground logical terms, let $[\![f(s_1, \ldots, s_n)]\!] := \mathcal{J}_f([\![s_1]\!], \ldots, [\![s_n]\!])$. Every ground logical term s corresponds to a unique value c such that $[\![s]\!] = [\![c]\!]$; we say that c is the value of s. A *constraint* is a logical term φ of some sort bool with $\mathcal{I}_{bool} = \mathbb{B} = \{\top, \bot\}$, the set of *booleans*. We say φ is *valid* if $[\![\varphi\gamma]\!] = \top$ for *all* substitutions γ which map $Var(\varphi)$ to values, and *satisfiable* if $[\![\varphi\gamma]\!] = \top$ for *some* substitution γ which maps $Var(\varphi)$ to values. A substitution γ *respects* φ if $\gamma(x)$ is a value for all $x \in Var(\varphi)$ and $[\![\varphi\gamma]\!] = \top$.

Formally, terms in $Terms(\Sigma_{terms}, V)$ have no special function, but we see them as the primary objects of the term rewriting system: a reduction would typically begin and end with such terms, with elements of $\Sigma_{theory} \setminus Val$ (also called *calculation symbols*) only used in intermediate terms.

We typically choose a theory signature with $\Sigma_{theory} \supseteq \Sigma_{theory}^{core}$, where Σ_{theory}^{core} contains the core theory symbols: true, false : bool, $\wedge, \vee, \Rightarrow$: [bool × bool] $\Rightarrow$ bool, $\neg$: [bool] $\Rightarrow$ bool, and, for all sorts ι, symbols $=_\iota, \neq_\iota$: [$\iota \times \iota$] $\Rightarrow$ bool, and an evaluation function $\mathcal{J}$ that interprets these symbols as expected. We omit the sort subscripts from = and $\neq$ when they can be derived from context.

The standard integer signature Σ_{theory}^{int} is $\Sigma_{theory}^{core} \cup \{+, -, *, \exp, \text{div}, \text{mod} :$ [int × int] $\Rightarrow$ int; $\leq, <$: [int × int] $\Rightarrow$ bool$\} \cup \{n : \text{int} \mid n \in \mathbb{Z}\}$. Here, values are true, false and n for all $n \in \mathbb{Z}$. We let $\mathcal{J}$ be defined in the natural way, but (since all $\mathcal{J}_f$ must be total) $\mathcal{J}_{\text{div}}(n, 0) = \mathcal{J}_{\text{mod}}(n, 0) = \mathcal{J}_{\exp}(n, k) = 0$ for all n and all $k < 0$. However, when constructing LCTRSs, we normally avoid such calls.

Rules and Rewriting. A *rule* is a triple $\ell \to r\ [\varphi]$ where ℓ and r are terms of the same sort and φ is a constraint. Here, ℓ is not a logical term (so also not a variable, as $V \subseteq Terms(\Sigma_{theory}, V)$). If $\varphi =$ true with $\mathcal{J}(\text{true}) = \top$, the rule is usually just denoted $\ell \to r$. We define $LVar(\ell \to r\ [\varphi])$ as $Var(\varphi) \cup (Var(r) \setminus Var(\ell))$. A substitution γ *respects* $\ell \to r\ [\varphi]$ if $\gamma(x)$ is a value for all $x \in LVar(\ell \to r\ [\varphi])$, and $\varphi\gamma$ is valid. Note that it is allowed that $Var(r) \not\subseteq Var(\ell)$, but fresh variables in the right-hand side may only be instantiated with *values*. This is done to model user input or random choice, both of which would typically produce a value. Variables on the left do not need to be instantiated with values (unless they also occur in the constraint); this is needed for instance for lazy evaluation.

We assume given a set of rules $\mathcal{R}$, and let $\mathcal{R}_{\text{calc}}$ be the set $\{f(x_1, \ldots, x_n) \to y\ [y = f(\overrightarrow{x})] \mid f : [\iota_1 \times \cdots \times \iota_n] \Rightarrow \kappa \in \Sigma_{theory} \setminus Val\}$ (writing $\overrightarrow{x}$ for $x_1, \ldots, x_n$). The *rewrite relation* $\to_\mathcal{R}$ is a binary relation on terms, defined by:

$$C[\ell\gamma] \to_\mathcal{R} C[r\gamma] \text{ if } \ell \to r\ [\varphi] \in \mathcal{R} \cup \mathcal{R}_{\text{calc}} \text{ and } \gamma \text{ respects } \ell \to r\ [\varphi]$$

We say the reduction occurs at position p if $C = C[\Box]_p$. Let $s \leftrightarrow_\mathcal{R} t$ if $s \to_\mathcal{R} t$ or $t \to_\mathcal{R} s$. A reduction step with $\mathcal{R}_{\text{calc}}$ is called a *calculation*. A term is in *normal form* if it cannot be reduced with $\to_\mathcal{R}$. If $f(\ell_1, \ldots, \ell_n) \to r\ [\varphi] \in \mathcal{R}$ we call f a *defined symbol*; non-defined elements of Σ_{terms} and all values are *constructors*. Let $\mathcal{C}ons$ be the set of all constructors. A *logically constrained term rewriting system* (LCTRS) is the abstract rewriting system $(Terms(\Sigma, V), \to_\mathcal{R})$, usually given by supplying Σ, $\mathcal{R}$, and maybe $\mathcal{I}$ and $\mathcal{J}$ if these are not clear from context.

Example 1. To implement an LCTRS calculating the *factorial* function, we let $\mathcal{I}_{\mathsf{int}} = \mathbb{Z}$, $\mathcal{I}_{\mathsf{bool}} = \mathbb{B}$, $\Sigma_{theory} = \Sigma_{theory}^{int}$, $\mathcal{J}$ defined as discussed above, and:

$$\Sigma_{terms} = \{\ \mathsf{fact} : [\mathsf{int}] \Rightarrow \mathsf{int}\} \cup \{\mathsf{n} : \mathsf{int} \mid n \in \mathbb{Z}\ \}$$
$$\mathcal{R}_{fact} = \{\ \mathsf{fact}(x) \rightarrow 1\ [x \leq 0]\ ,\quad \mathsf{fact}(x) \rightarrow x * \mathsf{fact}(x-1)\ [\neg(x \leq 0)]\ \}$$

Using infix notation, examples of logical terms are $5 + 9$ and $0 = 0 + -1$ and $x + 3 \geq y + -42$; the latter two are constraints. We can reduce $5 + 9$ to 14 with a calculation (using $x + y \rightarrow z\ [z = x+y]$), and $\mathsf{fact}(3)$ reduces in ten steps to 6.

Example 2. To implement an LCTRS calculating the sum of elements in an array, let $\mathcal{I}_{\mathsf{bool}} = \mathbb{B}$, $\mathcal{I}_{\mathsf{int}} = \mathbb{Z}$ and $\mathcal{I}_{\mathsf{array(int)}} = \mathbb{Z}^*$, so $\mathsf{array(int)}$ is mapped to finite-length integer sequences. Let $\Sigma_{theory} = \Sigma_{theory}^{int} \cup \{\mathsf{size} : [\mathsf{array(int)}] \Rightarrow \mathsf{int}, \mathsf{select} : [\mathsf{array(int)} \times \mathsf{int}] \Rightarrow \mathsf{int}\} \cup \{\mathsf{a} \mid a \in \mathbb{Z}^*\}$. (So we do not encode arrays as lists: every array a corresponds to a unique symbol a.) The interpretation function $\mathcal{J}$ behaves on Σ_{theory}^{int} as usual and has $\mathcal{J}_{\mathsf{size}}(a) = k$ when $a = \langle n_0, \ldots, n_{k-1}\rangle$, and $\mathcal{J}_{\mathsf{select}}(a, i) = n_i$ if $a = \langle n_0, \ldots, n_{k-1}\rangle$ with $0 \leq i < k$, otherwise 0. In addition:

$$\Sigma_{terms} = \{\ \mathsf{sum} : [\mathsf{array(int)}] \Rightarrow \mathsf{int}, \mathsf{sum1} : [\mathsf{array(int)} \times \mathsf{int}] \Rightarrow \mathsf{int}\ \} \cup$$
$$\{\ \mathsf{n} : \mathsf{int} \mid n \in \mathbb{Z}\ \} \cup \{\ \mathsf{a} \mid a \in \mathbb{Z}^*\ \}$$
$$\mathcal{R}_{\mathsf{sum}} = \left\{ \begin{array}{ll} \mathsf{sum}(x) \rightarrow \mathsf{sum1}(x, \mathsf{size}(x) - 1) & \\ \mathsf{sum1}(x, k) \rightarrow \mathsf{select}(x, k) + \mathsf{sum1}(x, k-1)\ [k \geq 0] \\ \mathsf{sum1}(x, k) \rightarrow 0 & [k < 0] \end{array} \right\}$$

Note the special role of *values*, which are new in LCTRSs compared to older styles of constrained rewriting. They are the representatives of the underlying theory. All values are constants (constructor symbols $v()$ which do not take arguments), even if they represent complex structures, as seen in Example 2. However, not all constants are values. Because, unlike traditional TRSs and e.g. [6,8], values are not term-generated. we can easily have uncountably many of them (for example an LCTRS over the real number field $\mathbb{R}$), and do not have to match modulo theories (for example equating $0 + (x + y)$ with $y + x$).

Quantification. The definition of LCTRSs does *not* permit quantifiers. In for instance an LCTRS over integers and arrays, we cannot specify a rule $\mathsf{extend}(arr, x) \rightarrow \mathsf{addtoend}(x, arr)\ [\forall y \in \{0, \ldots, \mathsf{size}(arr) - 1\} : x \neq \mathsf{select}(arr, y)]$ (where $\mathsf{addtoend} : [\mathsf{int} \times \mathsf{array(int)}] \Rightarrow \mathsf{array(int)} \in \Sigma_{theory}$ and extend is a defined symbol).

However, one of the key features of LCTRSs is that theory symbols, including predicates, are not confined to a fixed list. Therefore, what we *can* do when defining an LCTRS, is to add a new symbol to Σ_{theory} (and $\mathcal{J}$). For the extend rule, we could for instance introduce a symbol $\mathsf{notin} : [\mathsf{int} \times \mathsf{array(int)}] \Rightarrow \mathsf{bool}$ with $\mathcal{J}_{\mathsf{notin}}(u, \langle a_0, \ldots, a_{n-1}\rangle) = \top$ if for all i: $u \neq a_i$, and replace the constraint by $\mathsf{notin}(x, arr)$. This generates the same reduction relation as the original rule.

Thus, we can permit quantifiers in the constraints of rules, as intuitive notation for fresh predicates. However, as the reduction relation $\rightarrow_{\mathcal{R}}$ is only decidable if all $\mathcal{J}_f$ are, an *unbounded* quantification would likely not be useful in practice.

Differences to [13]. In [13], where LCTRSs are first defined, we assume that $\mathcal{V}$ contains unsorted variables, and use a separate *variable environment* for typing terms. Also, $\rightarrow_{\mathcal{R}}$ is there defined as the union of $\rightarrow_{\texttt{rule}}$ (using rules in $\mathcal{R}$) and $\rightarrow_{\texttt{calc}}$ (using calculations). These changes give equivalent results, but the current definitions cause a bit less bookkeeping.

A non-equivalent change is the requirement on rules: in [13] left-hand sides must have a root symbol in $\Sigma_{terms} \setminus \Sigma_{theory}$. We follow [12] in weakening this.

2.1 Rewriting Constrained Terms

In LCTRSs, the objects of study are *terms*, with $\rightarrow_{\mathcal{R}}$ defining the relation between them. However, for analysis it is often useful to consider *constrained terms*: pairs $s\,[\varphi]$ of a term s and a constraint φ. A constrained term $s\,[\varphi]$ represents all terms $s\gamma$ where γ respects φ, and can be used to reason about such terms.

Different constrained terms might represent the same terms; for example $f(0)\,[\texttt{true}]$ and $f(x)\,[x = 0]$, or $g(x,y)\,[x > y]$ and $g(z,u)\,[u \leq z-1]$. We consider these terms *equivalent*. Formally, $s\,[\varphi] \sim t\,[\psi]$ if for all substitutions γ which respect φ there is a substitution δ which respects ψ such that $s\gamma = t\delta$, and vice versa. Note that $s\,[\varphi] \sim s\,[\psi]$ if and only if $\forall \overrightarrow{x}[\exists \overrightarrow{y}[\varphi] \leftrightarrow \exists \overrightarrow{z}[\psi]]$ holds, where $Var(s) = \{\overrightarrow{x}\}$, $Var(\varphi) \setminus Var(s) = \{\overrightarrow{y}\}$ and $Var(\psi) \setminus Var(s) = \{\overrightarrow{z}\}$.

For a rule $\rho := \ell \rightarrow r\,[\psi] \in \mathcal{R} \cup \mathcal{R}_{\texttt{calc}}$ and position q, we let $s\,[\varphi] \rightarrow_{\rho,q} t\,[\varphi]$ if $s_{|q} = \ell\gamma$ and $t = s[r\gamma]_q$ for some substitution γ with $\gamma(x)$ a variable in $Var(\varphi)$ or value for all $x \in LVar(\rho)$ and $\varphi \Rightarrow (\psi\gamma)$ valid. Let $s\,[\varphi] \rightarrow_{\texttt{base}} t\,[\varphi]$ if $s\,[\varphi] \rightarrow_{\rho,q} t\,[\varphi]$ for some ρ, q. The relation $\rightarrow_{\mathcal{R}}$ on constrained terms is: $\sim \cdot \rightarrow_{\texttt{base}} \cdot \sim$. We say $s\,[\varphi] \rightarrow_{\mathcal{R}} t\,[\psi]$ at position q by rule ρ if $s\,[\varphi] \sim \cdot \rightarrow_{\rho,q} \cdot \sim t\,[\psi]$.

Example 3. In the factorial LCTRS from Example 1, we have that $\mathsf{fact}(x)\,[x > 3] \rightarrow_{\mathcal{R}} x * \mathsf{fact}(x-1)\,[x > 3]$. This constrained term can be further reduced using the calculation rule $x - y \rightarrow z\,[z = x - y]$, but here we must use the $\sim$ relation, as follows: $x * \mathsf{fact}(x-1)\,[x > 3] \sim x * \mathsf{fact}(x-1)\,[x > 3 \wedge z = x - 1] \rightarrow_{\texttt{base}} x * \mathsf{fact}(z)\,[x > 3 \wedge z = x - 1]$, as $\forall x[x > 3 \leftrightarrow \exists z[x > 3 \wedge z = x - 1]]$.

Example 4. The relation $\sim$ allows us to reformulate the constraint both before and after a reduction, which is particularly useful for *irregular* rules, where the constraint contains variables not occurring in the left-hand side. The calculation rules are a particular example of such rules, as we saw in Example 3. For a different example, with the rule $f(x) \rightarrow g(y)\,[y > x]$, we have: $f(x)\,[x > 3] \sim f(x)\,[x > 3 \wedge y > x] \rightarrow_{\texttt{base}} g(y)\,[x > 3 \wedge y > x] \sim g(y)\,[y > 4]$. Similarly, $f(x-1)\,[x > 0]$ reduces with a calculation to $f(y)\,[y \geq 0]$. We do *not* have that $f(x)\,[\texttt{true}] \rightarrow_{\mathcal{R}} g(x+1)\,[\texttt{true}]$, as $x + 1$ cannot be instantiated to a value.

Example 5. A constrained term does not always need to be reduced in the most general way. With the rule $f(x) \rightarrow g(y)\,[y > x]$, we have $f(0)\,[\texttt{true}] \sim f(0)\,[y > 0] \rightarrow_{\texttt{base}} g(y)\,[y > 0]$, but we also have $f(0)\,[\texttt{true}] \sim f(0)\,[1 > 0] \rightarrow_{\texttt{base}} g(1)$.

As intended, constrained reductions give information about usual reductions:

Theorem 6 ([13]). *If $s\,[\varphi] \rightarrow_{\mathcal{R}} t\,[\psi]$, then for all substitutions γ which respect φ there is a substitution δ which respects ψ such that $s\gamma \rightarrow_{\mathcal{R}}^{+} t\delta$.*

3   Transforming Imperative Programs into LCTRSs

Transformations of imperative programs into integer rewriting systems are investigated in e.g. [4,6,8]. These papers use different variations of constrained rewriting, but the proposed transformations are easily adapted to produce LCTRSs that operate on integers, i.e., use Σ_{theory}^{int}. What is more, we can extend the ideas to also handle advanced programming structures, like function calls and arrays.

Following the ideas of [4,6,8], we transform each function f separately. Let $\vec{v}$ be the vector of all parameters and local variables in f (we disallow global variables for now). For all basic blocks in the function (i.e., straight-line code segments), we introduce a new function symbol u_i. A transition from block i to block j is encoded as a rule $u_i(\vec{v}) \rightarrow u_j(\vec{r})\ [\varphi]$, with assignments reflected by argument updates in the right-hand side, and conditions by the constraint. Return statements return e are encoded by reducing to $return_f(e)$, where $return_f$ is a new constructor.

Finally, the generated LCTRS is optimized to make it more amenable to analysis: we combine rules whose root symbols occur only once in left-hand sides [6], remove unused parameters (in particular, variables not in scope at a given location), and, if appropriate, simplify the constraint (e.g. by removing duplicate clauses or replacing a term like $\neg(x > y)$ by $y \geq x$.

Example 7. Consider the following small C-function fact, calculating the factorial function from Example 1. Here, $\vec{v}$ is $\langle x, i, z \rangle$. There are three basic blocks: u_1 (the initialization of the local variables, which includes both int z = 1 and int i = 1), u_2 (the loop body), and u_3 (the block containing the return-statement).

```
int fact(int x) {
    int z = 1;
    for(int i = 1; i <= x; i++)
        z *= i;
    return z;
}
```

We obtain the following initial LCTRS (left) and simplification (right):

$$fact(x) \rightarrow u_1(x, i, z)$$
$$u_1(x, i, z) \rightarrow u_2(x, 1, 1)$$
$$u_2(x, i, z) \rightarrow u_2(x, i+1, z*i)\ [i \leq x]$$
$$u_2(x, i, z) \rightarrow u_3(x, i, z)\qquad [\neg(i \leq x)]$$
$$u_3(x, i, z) \rightarrow return_{fact}(z)$$

$$fact(x) \rightarrow u_2(x, 1, 1)$$
$$u_2(x, i, z) \rightarrow u_2(x, i+1, z*i)\ [i \leq x]$$
$$u_2(x, i, z) \rightarrow return_{fact}(z)\qquad [i > x]$$

Note that there is nothing special about the integers; the definition of LCTRSs allows values from all kinds of underlying domains. So, with a suitable theory signature, we could also handle e.g. doubles, encoding them as real numbers. *Pointers* are more difficult to handle, but *static arrays* are not so problematic. Consider for instance the following two implementations of the same assignment: *given an integer array and its length, return the sum of the array's elements.*

```
int sum1(int arr[],int n){
    int ret=0;
    for(int i=0;i<n;i++)
        ret+=arr[i];
    return ret;
}
```

```
int sum2(int *arr, int k) {
    if (k <= 0) return 0;
    return arr[k-1] +
        sum2(arr, k-1);
}
```

To encode these functions, we use Σ_{theory} as in Example 2. To handle illegal program behavior, we reduce to an additional error$_f$ constructor in cases when we index an array out of bounds. To handle function calls (as in sum2), we execute the call in a separate parameter, and then examine the result. These ideas result in the following simplified translations (using the same return and error symbols in both cases, because we want to be able to compare the resulting functions):

(1) $\text{sum1}(arr, n) \rightarrow \text{u}(arr, n, 0, 0)$

(2) $\text{u}(arr, n, ret, i) \rightarrow \text{error}$ $[i < n \wedge (i < 0 \vee i \geq \text{size}(arr))]$

(3) $\text{u}(arr, n, ret, i) \rightarrow \text{u}(arr, n, ret + \text{select}(arr, i), i + 1)$

                           $[i < n \wedge 0 \leq i < \text{size}(arr)]$

(4) $\text{u}(arr, n, ret, i) \rightarrow \text{return}(ret)$ $[i \geq n]$

(5) $\text{sum2}(arr, k) \rightarrow \text{return}(0)$ $[k \leq 0]$

(6) $\text{sum2}(arr, k) \rightarrow \text{error}$ $[k - 1 \geq \text{size}(arr)]$

(7) $\text{sum2}(arr, k) \rightarrow \text{w}(\text{select}(arr, k - 1), \text{sum2}(arr, k - 1))$

                           $[0 \leq k - 1 < \text{size}(arr)]$

(8) $\text{w}(n, \text{error}) \rightarrow \text{error}$

(9) $\text{w}(n, \text{return}(r)) \rightarrow \text{return}(n + r)$

Here, a constraint $x \leq y < b$ should be read as: $x \leq y \wedge y < b$. Note that sum2 differs from the system in Example 2 only by adding error-handling.

In general, we can encode arrays of any data type, including arrays of arrays, by defining $\mathcal{I}_{\text{array}(\iota)} = \mathcal{I}_\iota^*$ for any ι with $\mathcal{J}_\iota \neq \emptyset$ (we need some default value $0_\iota \in \mathcal{Val}_\iota$ for out-of-bound selects). We can also handle array updates: let store : $[\text{array}(\iota) \times \text{int} \times \iota] \Rightarrow \text{array}(\iota)$, and $\mathcal{J}_{\text{store}}(\langle a_0, \ldots, a_{n-1} \rangle, k, v) = \langle a_0, \ldots, a_{k-1}, v, a_{k+1}, \ldots, a_{n-1} \rangle$ if $0 \leq k < n$ and $\langle \overrightarrow{a} \rangle$ otherwise. To reflect side effects, we include updated array parameters in the return value.

Example 8. The function void empty(char arr[]) { arr[0] = '\0'; } is translated to the following LCTRS:

$$\text{empty}(arr) \rightarrow \text{error}_{\text{empty}} \qquad [0 \geq \text{size}(arr)]$$
$$\text{empty}(arr) \rightarrow \text{return}(\text{store}(arr, 0, 0)) \ [0 < \text{size}(arr)]$$

A more extensive discussion of this translation, including global variables, integer overflow and dynamic pointers, is available online in [14, Section 3].

4   Rewriting Induction for LCTRSs

In this section, we adapt the inference rules from [18,5,20] to inductive theorem proving with LCTRSs. This provides the core theory to use rewriting induction, which will be strengthened with a lemma generalization technique in Section 5.

We start by listing some restrictions we need to impose on LCTRSs for the method to work (Section 4.1). Then, we provide the theory for the technique (Section 4.2), making several changes compared to [18,5,20] to handle the new formalism. We complete with two illustrative examples (Section 4.3).

4.1   Restrictions

In order for rewriting induction to be successful, we need to impose certain restrictions. We limit interest to LCTRSs which satisfy the following properties:

1. all core theory symbols $(\wedge, \vee, \Rightarrow, \neg$ and each $=_{\iota}, \neq_{\iota})$ are present in Σ_{theory};
2. the LCTRS is terminating, so there is no infinite reduction $s_1 \rightarrow_{\mathcal{R}} s_2 \rightarrow_{\mathcal{R}} \ldots$;
3. the system is *quasi-reductive*, i.e., for every term s either $s \in \mathcal{T}erms(\mathcal{C}ons, \emptyset)$
   (we say s is a *ground constructor term*), or there is some t such that $s \rightarrow_{\mathcal{R}} t$;[1]
4. there are ground terms of every sort occurring in Σ.

Property 1 is just the standard assumption we saw in Section 2. We will need these symbols, for instance, to add new information to a constraint. Termination (property 2) is crucial in the inductive derivation, as the method uses induction on terms, oriented with an extension of $\rightarrow_{\mathcal{R}}$. Property 3 which, together with termination, provides *sufficient completeness*, makes it possible to do an exhaustive case analysis on the rules applicable to an equation. It also allows us to assume that variables are always instantiated by ground constructor terms. The last property is natural, since the method considers *ground* terms; function symbols which cannot be assigned ground arguments can simply be omitted.

Methods to prove quasi-reductivity and termination have been published for different styles of constrained rewriting; see e.g. [5] for quasi-reductivity and [7,19] for termination. These methods are easily adapted to LCTRSs: see [14, Appendix A] for quasi-reductivity and [12] for termination. The LCTRSs obtained from procedural programs following Section 3 are always quasi-reductive.

4.2   Rewriting Induction

We now introduce the notions of *constrained equations* and *inductive theorems*.

Definition 9. *A* (constrained) equation *is a triple* $s \approx t$ $[\varphi]$ *with s and t terms and φ a constraint. Let $s \simeq t$ $[\varphi]$ denote either $s \approx t$ $[\varphi]$ or $t \approx s$ $[\varphi]$. A substitution γ respects $s \approx t$ $[\varphi]$ if γ respects φ and $Var(s) \cup Var(t) \subseteq Dom(\gamma)$. We say γ is a* ground constructor substitution *if all $\gamma(x)$ are ground constructor terms.*

An equation $s \approx t$ $[\varphi]$ is an inductive theorem *of an LCTRS $\mathcal{R}$ if $s\gamma \leftrightarrow^{*}_{\mathcal{R}} t\gamma$ for any ground constructor substitution γ that respects this equation.*

Intuitively, if an equation $f(\overrightarrow{x}) \approx g(\overrightarrow{x})$ $[\varphi]$ is an inductive theorem, then f and g define the same function (conditional on φ, and assuming confluence).

To prove that an equation is an inductive theorem, we will consider five inference rules, originating in [18,5,20]. These rules modify a *proof state*: a pair $(\mathcal{E}, \mathcal{H})$ where $\mathcal{E}$ is a set of equations and $\mathcal{H}$ a set of constrained rewrite rules with $\rightarrow_{\mathcal{R}\cup\mathcal{H}}$ terminating. A rule in $\mathcal{H}$ plays the role of an *induction hypothesis* for proving that the equations in $\mathcal{E}$ are inductive theorems, and is called an *induction rule*.

---

[1] A more standard definition of this property would be that for every defined or calculation symbol f and suitable ground constructor terms $s_1, \ldots, s_n$, the term $f(s_1, \ldots, s_n)$ reduces. As observed in [14, Appendix A], this definition is equivalent.

SIMPLIFICATION If $s \approx t\,[\varphi] \to_{\mathcal{R} \cup \mathcal{H}} u \approx t\,[\psi]$, where $\approx$ is seen as a fresh constructor for the purpose of constrained term reduction,[2] then we may derive:

$$(\mathcal{E} \uplus \{(s \simeq t\,[\varphi])\}, \mathcal{H}) \vdash_{\texttt{ri}} (\mathcal{E} \cup \{(u \approx t\,[\psi])\}, \mathcal{H})$$

DELETION If $s = t$ or φ is not satisfiable, we can delete $s \approx t\,[\varphi]$ from $\mathcal{E}$:

$$(\mathcal{E} \uplus \{s \approx t\,[\varphi]\}, \mathcal{H}) \vdash_{\texttt{ri}} (\mathcal{E}, \mathcal{H})$$

EXPANSION Let $Expd(s, t, \varphi, p)$ be a set containing, for all rules $\ell \to r[\psi] \in \mathcal{R}$[3] such that ℓ is unifiable with $s_{|p}$ with most general unifier γ and $\varphi\gamma \wedge \psi\gamma$ is (or may be)[4] satisfiable, an equation $s' \approx t'\,[\varphi']$ where $s[\ell]_p\gamma \approx t\gamma\,[(\varphi\gamma) \wedge (\psi\gamma)] \to_{\mathcal{R}} s' \approx t'\,[\varphi']$ with rule $\ell \to r\,[\psi]$ at position $1 \cdot p$. Here, as in SIMPLIFICATION, $\approx$ is seen as a fresh constructor for the purpose of constrained term reduction. Intuitively, $Expd$ generates all resulting equations if a ground constructor instance of $s \approx t\,[\varphi]$ is reduced at position p of s. Now, if p is a position of s such that $s_{|p}$ is *basic* (i.e., $s_{|p} = f(s_1, \ldots, s_n)$ with f a defined symbol and all s_i constructor terms) we may derive:

$$(\mathcal{E} \uplus \{s \simeq t\,[\varphi]\}, \mathcal{H}) \vdash_{\texttt{ri}} (\mathcal{E} \cup Expd(s, t, \varphi, p), \mathcal{H})$$

If, moreover, $\mathcal{R} \cup \mathcal{H} \cup \{s \to t\,[\varphi]\}$ is terminating, we may even derive:

$$(\mathcal{E} \uplus \{s \simeq t\,[\varphi]\}, \mathcal{H}) \vdash_{\texttt{ri}} (\mathcal{E} \cup Expd(s, t, \varphi, p), \mathcal{H} \cup \{s \to t\,[\varphi]\})$$

Note that, if $\to_{\mathcal{R}}$ is non-deterministic (which may for instance happen when considering irregular rules), we can choose how to build $Expd$.

EQ-DELETION If all $s_i, t_i \in \mathit{Terms}(\Sigma_{theory}, \mathit{Var}(\varphi))$, then we can derive:

$$(\mathcal{E} \uplus \{C[s_1, \ldots, s_n] \simeq C[t_1, \ldots, t_n]\,[\varphi]\}, \mathcal{H}) \vdash_{\texttt{ri}}$$
$$(\mathcal{E} \cup \{C[s_1, \ldots, s_n] \approx C[t_1, \ldots, t_n]\,[\varphi \wedge \neg(\bigwedge_{i=1}^{n} s_i = t_i)]\}, \mathcal{H})$$

$C[\ ]$ is allowed to contain symbols in Σ_{theory}. Intuitively, if $\bigwedge_{i=1}^{n} s_i = t_i$ holds, then $C[s_1, \ldots, s_n]\gamma \leftrightarrow^{*}_{\mathcal{R}_{calc}} C[t_1, \ldots, t_n]\gamma$ and thus, we are done. We exclude this case from the equation by adding $\neg(\bigwedge_{i=1}^{n} s_i = t_i)$ to the constraint.

GENERALIZATION If for all substitutions γ which respect φ there is a substitution δ which respects ψ with $s\gamma = s'\delta$ and $t\gamma = t'\delta$, then we can derive:

$$(\mathcal{E} \uplus \{s \approx t\,[\varphi]\}, \mathcal{H}) \vdash_{\texttt{ri}} (\mathcal{E} \cup \{s' \approx t'\,[\psi]\}, \mathcal{H})$$

---

[2] It is not enough if $s\,[\varphi] \to_{\mathcal{R}} u\,[\psi]$: when reducing constrained terms, we may manipulate unused variables at will, which causes problems if they are used in t. For example, $f(x + 0)\,[x > y] \sim f(x + 0)\,[z = x + 0] \to_{\texttt{base}} f(z)\,[z = x + 0] \sim f(x)\,[y < x]$, but we would not want to replace an equation $f(x+0) \approx g(y)\,[x > y]$ by $f(x) \approx g(y)\,[x < y]$!

[3] Here, we assume that the variables in the rules are distinct from the ones in s, t, φ.

[4] Although we do not *have* to include equations in $Expd(s, t, \varphi, p)$ which correspond to rules that give an unsatisfiable constraint, it is sometimes convenient to postpone the satisfiability check; the resulting equations can be removed with DELETION.

The first three of these rules originate in [18], but they are adapted in several ways. Partially, this is because we consider LCTRSs rather than plain TRSs, and have to handle the constraints: hence we use constrained reduction rather than normal reduction in SIMPLIFICATION, and include an unsatisfiability case in DELETION. In EXPANSION, we have made more structural changes; our definition also differs from the corresponding rules in [5,20], where the method is defined for different styles of constrained rewriting.

To start, we use constrained reduction, whereas the authors of [18,5,20] use direct instantiation (e.g. $Expd(s,t,p)$ contains elements $s[r\gamma]_p \approx t$ when $\ell \to r \in \mathcal{R}$ and $s_{|p}$ unifies with ℓ with most general unifier γ). This was changed to better handle irregular rules, especially those where the right-hand side introduces fresh variables, i.e. $\ell \to r\ [\varphi]$ where $Var(r) \cap Var(\varphi) \not\subseteq Var(\ell)$. Such rules occur for example in transformed iterative functions where variables are declared but not immediately initialized. The alternative formulation of $\mathcal{R}$ in Section 5, which is essential for our lemma generalization technique, also uses such irregular rules.

Second, the case where no rule is added is new. This is needed to allow progress in cases when adding the rule might cause loss of termination. It somewhat corresponds to, but is strictly stronger than, CASE-SIMPLIFY in [5].

EQ-DELETION originates in [20] and can, in combination with DELETION, be seen as a generalized variant of THEORY$_\top$ in [5]. Most importantly, this inference rule provides a link between the equation part $s \approx t$ and the constraint. The last rule, GENERALIZATION, can be seen as a special case of POSTULATE in [18]. By generalizing an equation, the EXPANSION rule gives more powerful induction rules, which (as discussed in Section 5) is often essential to prove a theorem.

The inference rules are used for *rewriting induction* by the following theorem:

Theorem 10. *Let an LCTRS with rules $\mathcal{R}$ and signature Σ, satisfying the restrictions from Section 4.1, be given; let $\mathcal{E}$ be a finite set of equations. If $(\mathcal{E}, \emptyset) \vdash_{ri} \cdots \vdash_{ri} (\emptyset, \mathcal{H})$, then every $e \in \mathcal{E}$ is an inductive theorem of $\mathcal{R}$.*

Proof Sketch: We follow the proof method of [20] (with a few adaptations), which builds on the original proof idea in [18]. That is, we define $\leftrightarrow_\mathcal{E}$ in the expected way (treating an equation as a rule) and prove the equivalent statement that $\leftrightarrow^*_\mathcal{E} \subseteq \leftrightarrow^*_\mathcal{R}$ on ground terms by making the following observations:

1. If $(\mathcal{E}_1, \mathcal{H}_1) \vdash_{ri} (\mathcal{E}_2, \mathcal{H}_2)$, then $\leftrightarrow_{\mathcal{E}_1} \subseteq \to^*_{\mathcal{R}\cup\mathcal{H}_2} \cdot (\leftrightarrow_{\mathcal{E}_2} \cup =) \cdot \leftarrow^*_{\mathcal{R}\cup\mathcal{H}_2}$ on ground terms (which we see by a careful analysis of all inference rules); using induction we obtain that $\leftrightarrow_\mathcal{E} \subseteq \to^*_{\mathcal{R}\cup\mathcal{H}} \cdot = \cdot \leftarrow^*_{\mathcal{R}\cup\mathcal{H}} \subseteq \leftrightarrow^*_{\mathcal{R}\cup\mathcal{H}}$.
2. If $(\mathcal{E}_1, \mathcal{H}_1) \vdash_{ri} (\mathcal{E}_2, \mathcal{H}_2)$ and $\to_{\mathcal{R}\cup\mathcal{H}_1} \subseteq \to_\mathcal{R} \cdot \to^*_{\mathcal{R}\cup\mathcal{H}_1} \cdot (\leftrightarrow_{\mathcal{E}_1} \cup =) \cdot \leftarrow^*_{\mathcal{R}\cup\mathcal{H}_1}$, then also $\to_{\mathcal{R}\cup\mathcal{H}_2} \subseteq \to_\mathcal{R} \cdot \to^*_{\mathcal{R}\cup\mathcal{H}_2} \cdot (\leftrightarrow_{\mathcal{E}_2} \cup =) \cdot \leftarrow^*_{\mathcal{R}\cup\mathcal{H}_2}$ (which follows by a case analysis, paying particular attention to the EXPANSION rule); using induction we obtain that $\to_{\mathcal{R}\cup\mathcal{H}} \subseteq \to_\mathcal{R} \cdot \to^*_{\mathcal{R}\cup\mathcal{H}} \cdot \leftarrow^*_{\mathcal{R}\cup\mathcal{H}}$.
3. By point 2 and induction on $\to_{\mathcal{R}\cup\mathcal{H}}$, we find that $\leftrightarrow^*_\mathcal{R} = \leftrightarrow^*_{\mathcal{R}\cup\mathcal{H}}$.

Details are provided in our technical report [14]. $\square$

Following e.g. [1], there are many other potential inference rules we could consider. For space reasons, we limit interest to the rules needed for our examples.

4.3   Some Illustrative Examples

To show how the method works, recall the sum1 and sum2 rules from Section 3 (page 340). We want to see that these two implementations are equivalent, at least when the input makes sense, so the given length is at least 0 and does not exceed the array size. This is the case if the following equation is an inductive theorem:

$$\text{(A)}\ \ \text{sum1}(a, k) \approx \text{sum2}(a, k)\ [0 \le k \le \text{size}(a)]$$

Thus, we start the procedure with $(\{(A)\}, \emptyset)$. From SIMPLIFICATION, we obtain:

$$(\{(B)\ \ u(a, k, 0, 0) \approx \text{sum2}(a, k)\ [0 \le k \le \text{size}(a)]\}, \emptyset)$$

None of SIMPLIFICATION, EQ-DELETION, DELETION and CONSTRUCTOR is applicable, so we apply EXPANSION to the right-hand side of (B) at the root. Since $k \le \text{size}(a)$ and $k - 1 \ge \text{size}(a)$ cannot both hold, the error rule leads to an unsatisfiable constraint. Therefore, this step only gives two new equations:

$$\left(\left\{ \begin{array}{l} \text{(C)} : \text{return}(0) \approx u(a, k, 0, 0)\ [0 \le k \le \text{size}(a) \wedge k \le 0] \\ \text{(D)} : w(\text{select}(a, k - 1), \text{sum2}(a, k - 1)) \approx u(a, k, 0, 0) \\ \qquad\quad [0 \le k \le \text{size}(a) \wedge 0 \le k - 1 < \text{size}(a)] \end{array} \right\}, \{(B^{-1})\} \right)$$

Here, (B^{-1}) should be read as the rule generated from (B) right-to-left, so $\text{sum2}(a, k) \to u(a, k, 0, 0)\ [0 \le k \le \text{size}(a)]$. We use SIMPLIFICATION with rule (4) to reduce (C) to $\text{return}(0) \approx \text{return}(0)\ [\ldots]$, which we quickly delete. Simplifying the right-hand side of (D) with rule (3), we obtain $(\{(E)\}, \{(B^{-1})\})$, with:

$$\text{(E)} : w(\text{select}(a, k - 1), \text{sum2}(a, k - 1)) \approx u(a, k, 0 + \text{select}(a, 0), 0 + 1)$$
$$[0 \le k \le \text{size}(a) \wedge 0 \le k - 1 < \text{size}(a)]$$

Next we use SIMPLIFICATION with the calculation rules. As these rules are irregular, this requires some care. There are three standard ways to do this:

- if $s \to_{\text{calc}} t$ then $s\,[\varphi] \to_{\mathcal{R}} t\,[\varphi]$, e.g. $f(0 + 1) \approx r\ [\varphi]$ reduces to $f(1) \approx r\ [\varphi]$;
- a calculation can be replaced by a fresh variable, which is defined in the constraint, e.g. $f(x + 1) \approx r\ [\varphi]$ reduces to $f(y) \approx r\ [\varphi \wedge y = x + 1]$;
- a calculation *already* defined in the constraint can be replaced by the relevant variable, e.g. $f(x + 1) \approx r\ [\varphi \wedge y = x + 1]$ reduces to $f(y) \approx r\ [\varphi \wedge y = x + 1]$.

These ways are not functionally different; if an equation e reduces both to e_1 and e_2 with a calculation at the same position, then it is easy to see that $e_1 \sim e_2$.

We can do more: recall that, by definition of constrained term reduction, we can rewrite a constraint φ with variables $\overrightarrow{x}, \overrightarrow{y}$ in a constrained term $s\,[\varphi]$, to any constraint ψ over $\overrightarrow{x}, \overrightarrow{z}$ such that $\exists \overrightarrow{y}\,[\varphi]$ is equivalent to $\exists \overrightarrow{z}\,[\psi]$ (if $Var(s) = \{\overrightarrow{x}\}$). We use this observation to write constraints in a simpler form after SIMPLIFICATION or EXPANSION, for instance by removing redundant clauses.

Using six more SIMPLIFICATION steps with the calculation rules on (E), and writing the constraint in a simpler form, we obtain:

$$\left(\left\{ \begin{array}{l} \text{(F)} : \qquad w(n, \text{sum2}(a, k')) \approx u(a, k, r, 1)\ [k' = k - 1 \wedge \\ \quad 0 \le k' < \text{size}(a) \wedge n = \text{select}(a, k') \wedge r = 0 + \text{select}(a, 0)] \end{array} \right\}, \{(B^{-1})\} \right)$$

Then, using SIMPLIFICATION with the induction rule (B^{-1}):

$$\left(\left\{ \begin{array}{l} (G): \quad \mathsf{w}(n, \mathsf{u}(a, k', 0, 0)) \approx \mathsf{u}(a, k, r, 1) \ [k' = k - 1 \ \wedge \\ \qquad 0 \le k' < \mathsf{size}(a) \wedge n = \mathsf{select}(a, k') \wedge r = 0 + \mathsf{select}(a, 0)] \end{array} \right\}, \left\{ (B^{-1}) \right\} \right)$$

As the simpler inference rules do not apply, we expand in the right-hand side:

$$\left(\left\{ \begin{array}{l} (H): \quad \mathsf{u}(a, k, r + \mathsf{select}(a, 1), 1 + 1) \approx \mathsf{w}(n, \mathsf{u}(a, k', 0, 0)) \\ \qquad [k' = k - 1 \wedge 0 \le k' < \mathsf{size}(a) \wedge n = \mathsf{select}(a, k') \wedge \\ \qquad\quad r = 0 + \mathsf{select}(a, 0) \wedge 1 < k \wedge 0 \le 1 < \mathsf{size}(a)] \\ (I): \quad \mathsf{return}(r) \approx \mathsf{w}(n, \mathsf{u}(a, k', 0, 0)) \ [k' = k - 1 \wedge 0 \le k' < \\ \qquad \mathsf{size}(a) \wedge n = \mathsf{select}(a, k') \wedge r = 0 + \mathsf{select}(a, 0) \wedge 1 \ge k] \end{array} \right\}, \left\{ \begin{array}{l} (B^{-1}) \\ (G^{-1}) \end{array} \right\} \right)$$

We have again omitted the error rule, as the corresponding constraint is not satisfiable. For (I), the constraint implies that $k = 1$, so SIMPLIFICATION with rule (4) followed by (9) and prettifying the constraint gives $\mathsf{return}(r) \approx \mathsf{return}(n + 0) \ [k' = 0 < \mathsf{size}(a) \wedge n = \mathsf{select}(a, k') \wedge r = \mathsf{select}(a, 0)]$. EQ-DELETION gives an unsatisfiable constraint $\ldots \wedge \neg(r = n + 0)$; we complete with DELETION.

We continue with $(\{(H)\}, \{(B^{-1}), (G^{-1})\})$. After applying SIMPLIFICATION with (3) and calculation rules a few times, we have $(\{(J)\}, \{(B^{-1}), (G^{-1})\})$:

$$(J): \mathsf{u}(a, k, r_1, 2) \approx \mathsf{w}(n, \mathsf{u}(a, k', r, 1)) \ [k' = k - 1 \wedge 0 \le k' \wedge 1 < k \le \mathsf{size}(a) \wedge \\ n = \mathsf{select}(a, k') \wedge r = 0 + \mathsf{select}(a, 0) \wedge r_1 = r + \mathsf{select}(a, 1)]$$

Here, we have used the third style of calculation simplification to reuse r.

We can use EXPANSION again, this time on the left-hand side. But now a pattern starts to arise. If we continue like this, simplifying as long as we can, and then using whichever of the other core rules is applicable, we get:

$(K): \mathsf{u}(a, k, r_2, 3) \approx \mathsf{w}(n, \mathsf{u}(a, k', r_1, 2)) \ [k' = k - 1 \wedge 2 < k \le \mathsf{size}(a) \wedge \ldots]$
$(L): \mathsf{u}(a, k, r_3, 4) \approx \mathsf{w}(n, \mathsf{u}(a, k', r_2, 3)) \ [k' = k - 1 \wedge 3 < k \le \mathsf{size}(a) \wedge \ldots]$

That is, we have a *divergence*: a sequence of increasingly complex equations, each generated from the same leg in an EXPANSION (see also the *divergence critic* in [22]). Yet the previous induction rules never apply to the new equation. So, consider the following equation (we will say more about it in Section 5):

$(M): \mathsf{u}(a, k, r, i) \approx \mathsf{w}(n, \mathsf{u}(a, k', r', i')) \ [k' = k - 1 \wedge 0 \le i' < k \le \mathsf{size}(a) \wedge \\ i' = i - 1 \wedge r = r' + \mathsf{select}(a, i') \wedge n = \mathsf{select}(a, k')]$

It is easy to see that (J) is an instance of (M); we apply GENERALIZATION and continue with $(\{(M)\}, \{(B^{-1}), (G^{-1})\})$. Using EXPANSION, we obtain:

$$\left(\left\{ \begin{array}{l} (N): \quad \mathsf{u}(a, k, r + \mathsf{select}(a, i), i + 1) \approx \mathsf{w}(n, \mathsf{u}(a, k', r', i')) \\ \qquad [k' = k - 1 \wedge 0 \le i' < k \le \mathsf{size}(a) \wedge i' = i - 1 \wedge r = r' + \\ \qquad \mathsf{select}(a, i') \wedge n = \mathsf{select}(a, k') \ \wedge i < k \ \wedge 0 \le i < \mathsf{size}(a)] \\ (O): \quad \mathsf{return}(r) \approx \mathsf{w}(n, \mathsf{u}(a, k', r', i')) \\ \qquad [k' = k - 1 \wedge 0 \le i' < k \le \mathsf{size}(a) \wedge i' = i - 1 \wedge \\ \qquad r = r' + \mathsf{select}(a, i') \wedge n = \mathsf{select}(a, k') \wedge i \ge k] \end{array} \right\}, \left\{ \begin{array}{l} (B^{-1}) \\ (G^{-1}) \\ (M) \end{array} \right\} \right)$$

Again, the result of the error rule is omitted, because $i < 0$ cannot hold if both $0 \leq i'$ and $i' = i - 1$, and $i \geq \text{size}(a)$ cannot hold if both $i < k$ and $k \leq \text{size}(a)$.

Consider (O). Investigating the constraint, we can simplify it with rules (4) and (9), and then complete with EQ-DELETION and DELETION.

Only (N) remains. We simplify this equation with the normal rules, giving:

$$u(a, k, r'', i'') \approx w(n, u(a, k', r, i))$$
$$[k' = k - 1 \wedge 0 \leq i' < k \leq \text{size}(a) \wedge i' = i - 1 \wedge r = r' + \text{select}(a, i') \wedge$$
$$n = \text{select}(a, k') \wedge i < k \wedge 0 \leq i < \text{size}(a) \wedge i'' = i + 1 \wedge r'' = r + \text{select}(a, i)]$$

But now note that the induction rule (M) applies! This rule is irregular, so for the constrained reduction step we use a substitution that also affects variables not occurring in its left-hand side: $\gamma = [a := a, k := k, r := r'', i := i'', n := n, k' := k', r' := r, i' := i]$. Using SIMPLIFICATION, the equation is reduced to $w(n, u(a, k', r, i)) \approx w(n, u(a, k', r, i))$ [...], which is removed using DELETION.

As $(\{(A)\}, \emptyset) \vdash_{\mathtt{ri}}^* (\emptyset, \mathcal{H})$ for some $\mathcal{H}$, we see that (A) is an inductive theorem.

For another example, let us look at an assignment to implement `strlen`, a string function which operates on 0-terminated `char` arrays. As `char` is a numeric data type, the LCTRS translation can implement this as integer arrays again (although using another underlying sort $\mathcal{I}_{\text{char}}$ would make little difference). The example function and its LCTRS translation are as follows:

```
int strlen(char *str) {
  for (int i = 0; ; i++)
    if (str[i] == 0) return i;
}
```

$$(10) \quad \text{strlen}(x) \rightarrow u(x, 0)$$
$$(11) \quad u(x, i) \rightarrow \text{error} \qquad [i < 0 \vee i \geq \text{size}(x)]$$
$$(12) \quad u(x, i) \rightarrow \text{return}(i) \quad [0 \leq i < \text{size}(x) \wedge \text{select}(x, i) = 0]$$
$$(13) \quad u(x, i) \rightarrow u(x, i + 1) \ [0 \leq i < \text{size}(x) \wedge \text{select}(x, i) \neq 0]$$

Note that the overflow checks guarantee termination.

To see that `strlen` does what we would expect it to do, we want to know that for *valid C-strings*, $\text{strlen}(a)$ returns the first integer i such that $a[i] = 0$:

$$(P) \qquad\qquad \text{strlen}(x) \approx \text{return}(n)$$
$$[0 \leq n < \text{size}(x) \wedge \forall i \in \{0, n - 1\}[\text{select}(x, i) \neq 0] \wedge \text{select}(x, n) = 0]$$

Here, we use bounded quantification, which, as described in Section 2, can be seen as syntactic sugar for an additional predicate, e.g. `nonzero_until`.

Starting with $(\{(P)\}, \emptyset)$, we first use SIMPLIFICATION with rule (10), creating:

$$(Q) \qquad\qquad u(x, 0) \approx \text{return}(n)$$
$$[0 \leq n < \text{size}(x) \wedge \forall i \in \{0, n - 1\}[\text{select}(x, i) \neq 0] \wedge \text{select}(x, n) = 0]$$

We continue with EXPANSION; since the constraint implies that $0 < \mathsf{size}(x)$, the error case (11) gives an unsatisfiable constraint; we only get two new equations:

(R) $\mathsf{return}(0) \approx \mathsf{return}(n)$ $[0 \leq n < \mathsf{size}(x) \wedge \forall i \in \{0, n-1\}[\mathsf{select}(x, i) \neq 0] \wedge$
$\mathsf{select}(x, n) = 0 \wedge 0 \leq 0 < \mathsf{size}(x) \wedge \mathsf{select}(x, 0) = 0]$

(S) $\mathsf{u}(x, 0 + 1) \approx \mathsf{return}(n)$ $[0 \leq n < \mathsf{size}(x) \wedge \forall i \in \{0, n-1\}[\mathsf{select}(x, i) \neq 0] \wedge$
$\mathsf{select}(x, n) = 0 \wedge 0 \leq 0 < \mathsf{size}(x) \wedge \mathsf{select}(x, 0) \neq 0]$

As the constraint of (R) implies that $n = 0$ (because of the quantification and $\mathsf{select}(x, 0) = 0$), we can remove (R) using EQ-DELETION and DELETION.

As for (S), we simplify with a calculation, and expand again. This gives an equation $\mathsf{return}(1) \approx \mathsf{return}(n)$ [...] that we can quickly remove again, and an equation (T) which is simplified, expanded and eq-deleted/deleted into:

(U) $\mathsf{u}(x, 2 + 1) \approx \mathsf{return}(n)$ $[0 \leq n < \mathsf{size}(x) \wedge \forall i \in \{0, n-1\}[\mathsf{select}(x, i) \neq 0] \wedge$
$\mathsf{select}(x, n) = 0 \wedge 0 < \mathsf{size}(x) \wedge \mathsf{select}(x, 0) \neq 0 \wedge$
$1 < \mathsf{size}(x) \wedge \mathsf{select}(x, 1) \neq 0 \wedge 2 < \mathsf{size}(x) \wedge \mathsf{select}(x, 2) \neq 0]$

Simplifying and reformulating the constraint, we obtain:

(V) $\mathsf{u}(x, 3) \approx \mathsf{return}(n)$ $[0 \leq n < \mathsf{size}(x) \wedge \forall i \in \{0, n-1\}[\mathsf{select}(x, i) \neq 0] \wedge$
$\mathsf{select}(x, n) = 0 \wedge 0 \leq 2 < \mathsf{size}(x) \wedge \forall j \in \{0, 2\}[\mathsf{select}(x, j) \neq 0]]$

Note that we grouped together the $\neq 0$ statements into a quantification, which looks a lot like the other quantification in the constraint. We apply GENERALIZATION to obtain $(\{(W)\}, \{\ldots\})$, where (W) is $\mathsf{u}(x, k) \approx \mathsf{return}(n)$ $[\varphi]$ with:

$$\varphi : [k = m + 1 \wedge 0 \leq n < \mathsf{size}(x) \wedge \forall i \in \{0, n-1\}[\mathsf{select}(x, i) \neq 0] \wedge$$
$$\mathsf{select}(x, n) = 0 \wedge 0 \leq m < \mathsf{size}(x) \wedge \forall j \in \{0, m\}[\mathsf{select}(x, j) \neq 0]$$

Obviously, (V) is an instance of (W); we proceed with EXPANSION on (W) to obtain the proof status $(\{(X), (Y), (Z)\}, \{\ldots, (W)\})$, where:

(X) $\mathsf{error} \approx \mathsf{return}(n)$ $[\varphi \wedge (k < 0 \vee k \geq \mathsf{size}(x))]$
(Y) $\mathsf{return}(k) \approx \mathsf{return}(n)$ $[\varphi \wedge 0 \leq k < \mathsf{size}(x) \wedge \mathsf{select}(x, k) = 0]$
(Z) $\mathsf{u}(x, k + 1) \approx \mathsf{return}(n)$ $[\varphi \wedge 0 \leq k < \mathsf{size}(x) \wedge \mathsf{select}(x, k) \neq 0]$

For all cases, note that the two $\forall$ statements, together with $\mathsf{select}(x, n) = 0$, imply that $m < n$, so $k \leq n$. Hence the constraint of (X) is unsatisfiable: $k = m + 1$ and $0 \leq m$ imply that $k \not< 0$, and $k \leq n$, $k \geq \mathsf{size}(x)$ imply that $n \not< \mathsf{size}(x)$. By DELETION, we remove (X). For (Y), we use EQ-DELETION. Note that the two $\forall$ statements, together with $\mathsf{select}(x, k) = 0$, imply that $n - 1 < k$, so $n \leq k$. Since also $k \leq n$, the resulting constraint is unsatisfiable; we use DELETION again.

Finally, simplifying (Z) with a calculation, and reformulating the constraint:

$$\mathsf{u}(x, p) \approx \mathsf{return}(n)$$
$[p = k + 1 \wedge \mathsf{select}(x, n) = 0 \wedge 0 \leq n < \mathsf{size}(x) \wedge \forall i \in \{0, n-1\}[\mathsf{select}(x, i) \neq 0]$
$\wedge\ 0 \leq k < \mathsf{size}(x) \wedge \forall j \in \{0, k\}[\mathsf{select}(x, j) \neq 0]\ \wedge \text{some constraints on } m]$

The induction rule (W) lets us simplify this to $\mathsf{return}(n) \approx \mathsf{return}(n)$ [...], which is easily removed using DELETION.

5   Lemma Generalization by Dropping Initializations

Divergence, like we encountered in both examples of Section 4, is very common in inductive theorem proving. This is only natural: in mathematical proofs, when basic induction fails to prove a theorem, we often need a more general claim to obtain a stronger induction hypothesis. Viewed in this light, the generalization of equations, or the generation of suitable auxiliary lemmas is not only part, but even at the heart, of inductive theorem proving. Consequently, this subject has been extensively investigated [3,10,11,16,21,22]. Candidates for such equations are typically generated during solving, when the proof state is in divergence.

In this section, we propose a new method, specialized for constrained systems. The generalizations from Section 4 were found using this technique. Although the method is very simple (at its core, we just drop a part of the constraint), it is particularly effective for LCTRSs obtained from procedural programs.

First, let us state the rules of our sum example differently. When the right-hand side of a rule has a subterm $f(\ldots, n, \ldots)$ with f defined and n a value, we replace n by a fresh variable v_i, and add $v_i = n$ to the constraint. In the LCTRS $\mathcal{R}_{sum}$ from page 340, rules (2)–(9) are not changed, but (1) is replaced by:

$$(1')\quad \mathsf{sum1}(arr, n) \to \mathsf{u}(arr, n, v_1, v_2)\ [v_1 = 0 \wedge v_2 = 0]$$

Evidently, these altered rules generate the same rewrite relation as the original.

Consider what happens now if we use the same steps as in Section 4.3. We do not rename the variables v_i in EXPANSION, and ignore the $v_i = n$ clauses when simplifying the presentation of a constrained term. The resulting induction has the same shape, but with more complex equations. Some instances:

$$(B'):\quad \mathsf{u}(a, k, v_1, v_2) \approx \mathsf{sum2}(a, k)\ [0 \le k \le \mathsf{size}(a) \wedge v_1 = 0 \wedge v_2 = 0]$$

$$(F'):\quad \mathsf{w}(n, \mathsf{sum2}(a, k')) \approx \mathsf{u}(a, k, r_0, i_0)$$
$$[k' = k - 1 \wedge 0 \le k' < \mathsf{size}(a) \wedge v_1 = 0 \wedge v_2 = 0 \wedge n = \mathsf{select}(a, k') \wedge$$
$$r_0 = v_1 + \mathsf{select}(a, v_2) \wedge i_0 = v_2 + 1]$$

$$(J'):\quad \mathsf{u}(a, k, r_1, i_1) \approx \mathsf{w}(n, \mathsf{u}(a, k', r_0, i_0))$$
$$[k' = k - 1 \wedge 0 \le k' < \mathsf{size}(a) \wedge v_1 = 0 \wedge v_2 = 0 \wedge n = \mathsf{select}(a, k') \wedge$$
$$r_0 = v_1 + \mathsf{select}(a, v_2) \wedge i_0 = v_2 + 1 \wedge i_0 < k \wedge 0 \le i_0 < \mathsf{size}(a) \wedge$$
$$i_1 = i_0 + 1 \wedge r_1 = r_0 + \mathsf{select}(a, i_0)]$$

Continuing from (J'), we get equations $\mathsf{u}(a, k, r_2, i_2) \approx \mathsf{w}(n, \mathsf{u}(a, k', r_1, i_1))\ [\varphi]$ and $\mathsf{u}(a, k, r_3, i_3) \approx \mathsf{w}(n, \mathsf{u}(a, k', r_2, i_2))\ [\psi]$ whose main part is the same as that of (J'), modulo renaming of variables, while the constraint grows. Essentially, we keep track of parts of the history of an equation in its constraint.

We generalize (J') by dropping all clauses $v_i = q_i$, where v_i is an initialization variable. Remaining occurrences of v_i are renamed to avoid confusion. This gives:

$$(M')\ \mathsf{u}(a, k, r_1, i_1) \approx \mathsf{w}(n, \mathsf{u}(a, k', r_0, i_0))\quad [k' = k - 1 \wedge 0 \le k' < \mathsf{size}(a) \wedge$$
$$n = \mathsf{select}(a, k') \wedge r_0 = x_1 + \mathsf{select}(a, x_2) \wedge i_0 = x_2 + 1 \wedge i_0 < k \wedge$$
$$0 \le i_0 < \mathsf{size}(a) \wedge i_1 = i_0 + 1 \wedge r_1 = r_0 + \mathsf{select}(a, i_0)]$$

Note that $(M') \sim (M)$: the clauses with x_1 and x_2 can be removed, as suitable x_1, x_2 always exist. Continuing with (M') completes the proof as before.

Discussion. Thus, our equation generalization technique is very straightforward to use: we merely replace initializations by variables in the original rules, then remove the definitions of those initializations when a divergence is detected.

The only downside is that, in order to use this technique, we have to use the altered rules from the beginning, so we keep track of the v_i variables throughout the recursive procedure. For an automatic analysis this is no problem, however.

Note that we can only use this method if the equation part of the divergence has the same shape every time. This holds for sum, because the rule that causes the divergence has the form $u(x_1, \ldots, x_n) \rightarrow u(r_1, \ldots, r_n)\ [\varphi]$, preserving its outer shape. In general, the generalization method is most likely to be successful when analyzing tail-recursive functions (with accumulators), such as those obtained from procedural programs. This includes mutually recursive functions, like $u(x_1, \ldots, x_n) \rightarrow w(r_1, \ldots, r_m)\ [\varphi]$ and $w(y_1, \ldots, y_m) \rightarrow u(q_1, \ldots, q_n)\ [\psi]$. To analyze systems with general recursion, however, we will need different techniques.

The given generalization method also works for strlen from Section 4.3, and for strcpy. In these cases, we additionally have to collect multiple clauses into a quantified clause before generalizing, as was done for equation (W) in Section 4.3.

6   Implementation

We have implemented the rewriting induction and generalization methods in this paper in Ctrl, our tool for analyzing constrained term rewriting. As prerequisites, we have also implemented basic techniques to prove termination and quasi-reductivity. To deal with constraints, the tool is coupled both with a small internal reasoner and the (quantifier-capable) external SMT-solver Z3 [15].

The internal reasoner has two functions. First, it uses standard tricks to detect satisfiability or validity of simple statements, without a call to the external solver; this is both faster, and lets us optimize for often recurring questions (e.g. "find $n_1, \ldots, n_k \in \{-2, \ldots, 2\}$ such that φ is valid", as used for termination). Second, it simplifies the constraints of equations, for instance combining statements into quantifications. In addition, our notion of arrays is not supported by mainstream SMT-solvers, so we translate our array formulas into the SMT-LIB array-format; an array is encoded as a function from $\mathbb{Z}$ to $\mathbb{Z}$, with an additional variable encoding its size.

To obtain Ctrl, see: http://cl-informatik.uibk.ac.at/software/ctrl/.

Strategy. The rewriting induction method of Ctrl uses a simple strategy: we try, in the following order: EQ-DELETION and DELETION together, SIMPLIFICATION, EXPANSION, and GENERALIZATION (simply removing all $v_i = t$ definitions). When a rule succeeds, we continue from the start of the list. When we encounter an obviously unsolvable problem, or have gone too deep without removing any of the main equations, we backtrack and try something else. At the moment, divergence is not automatically detected, although this is an obvious extension.

To rewrite an equation in SIMPLIFICATION (and EXPANSION) with an irregular rule, we instantiate as many variables in the rule by existing variables as possible (as done for (N) in Section 4.3). Other variables are instantiated with fresh variables. When simplifying constraints, clauses which are clearly implied by other clauses (ignoring the $v_i = n$ definitions) or do not play a role are removed. Most importantly, Ctrl introduces *ranged quantifications* $\forall x \in \{k_1, \ldots, k_n\}[\varphi(x)]$ whenever possible (as we also saw in Section 4.3), provided $n \geq 3$. If a boundary of the range is a special variable v_i, we replace it by the value it is defined as, since it is typically better not to generalize the starting point of a quantification.

Experiments. To test performance of Ctrl, we used assignments from a group of students in the first-year programming course in Nagoya. Unfortunately, although we know how to translate C-programs to LCTRSs, we do not yet have an implementation. Therefore, we translated five groups by hand: sum (given n, implement $\sum_{i=1}^{n} i$), fib (calculate the first n Fibonacci numbers), sumfrom (given n and m, implement $\sum_{i=n}^{m} i$), strlen and strcpy. Due to the large effort of manually translating, we only use this small sample space. We considered two further assignments, with our own implementations: arrsum (the array summation from Section 4.3) and fact (the factorial function from Examples 1 and 7).

We quickly found that many implementations were incorrect: students had often forgotten to account for, e.g., negative input. Correcting for this (by altering the constraint, or excluding the benchmark), Ctrl automatically verified most queries, as summarized to the right. Here, for instance "3 / 5" means that 3 out of the 5 different correct functions could automatically be verified. The runtime includes only queries where Ctrl succeeded.

Investigating the failures, the main problem is termination. As Ctrl's termination module is not very strong yet, several times the initial LCTRS could not be handled; also, sometimes a natural induction rule was not

function	verified	time
sum	9 / 13	4.8
fib	10 / 12	11.4
strlen	3 / 5	16.2
strcpy	3 / 6	30.0
sumfrom	2 / 5	5.6
arrsum	1 / 1	14.2
fact	1 / 1	4.3

introduced because it would cause non-termination (although in most of these cases, expanding at a different position still led to a proof). Another weakness is that sometimes, generalizing removes the relation between two variables (e.g. both x and y are initialized to 0, and are both increased by 1 in every loop iteration). This suggests a natural direction for improvements to the technique.

An evaluation page, including exact problem statements, is given at:

> http://cl-informatik.uibk.ac.at/software/ctrl/aplas14/.

7   Related Work

The related work can be split into two categories. First, the literature on rewriting induction; and second, the work on program verification.

Rewriting Induction. Building on a long literature about rewriting induction (see e.g. [1,5,18,20]), the method for inductive theorem proving in this paper is primarily an adaptation of existing techniques to the new LCTRS formalism.

The most relevant related works are [5,20], where rewriting induction is defined for different styles of constrained rewriting. In both cases, the formalisms used are restricted to *integer* functions and predicates; it is not clear how they can be generalized to handle more advanced theories. LCTRSs offer a more general setting, which allows us to use rewriting induction also for systems with for instance arrays, bitvectors or real numbers. Additionally, by not restricting the predicates in Σ_{theory}, we can handle (a limited form of) quantifiers in constraints.

To enable these advantages, we had to make subtle changes to the inference rules, in particular SIMPLIFICATION and EXPANSION. Our changes make it possible to modify constraints of an equation, and to handle *irregular* rules, where the constraint introduces fresh variables. This has the additional advantage that it enables EXPANSION steps when this would create otherwise infeasible rules.

Furthermore, the method requires a very different implementation from previous definitions: we need separate strategies to simplify constraints (e.g. deriving quantified statements), and, in order to permit the desired generality, must rely primarily on external solvers to manipulate constraints.

In addition to the adaptation of rewriting induction, we introduced a completely new lemma generalization technique, which offers a powerful tool for analyzing loops in particular. A similar idea (abstract the initialization values) is used in [16], but the execution is very different. In [16], an equation $s \approx t\ [\varphi]$ is generalized by first adapting $s \approx t$ using templates obtained from the rules, then generalizing φ using a set of relations between positions, which the proof process tracks. In our method, the constraint carries all information. Our method succeeds on all examples in [16], and on some where [16] fails (cf. [14, Appendix B]).

For *unconstrained* systems, there are several generalization methods in the literature, e.g., [10,11,21]. Mostly, these approaches are very different from ours. Most similar, perhaps, is [10], which also proposes a method to generalize initial values. As observed in [16], this is not sufficient even for our simplest benchmarks sum and fact since the argument for the loop variable cannot be generalized. In contrast, our method has no problem with such variables.

As far as we are aware, there is no other work for lemma generation of rewrite systems (or functional programs) obtained from procedural programs.

Automatic Program Verification. Although this paper is a primarily theoretical contribution to the field of constraint rewriting induction, our intended goal is to (automatically) verify correctness properties of procedural programs.

As mentioned in the introduction, however, most existing verifiers require human interaction. Exceptions are the fully automated tools in the *Competition on Software Verification* (SV-COMP, http://sv-comp.sosy-lab.org/), which verify program properties like reachability, termination and memory-safety.

However, comparing our approach to these tools does not seem useful. While we can, to some extent, tackle termination and memory-safety, the main topic of this paper is *equivalence*, which is not studied in SV-COMP. And while technically equivalence problems can be formulated as reachability queries (e.g., $f(x) \approx g(x)\ [c]$ is handled by the main function to the right), neither of the top two tools in the "recursive" category of SV-COMP halts succesfully (in two hours) for our simplest (integer) example sum.

```c
int main() {
  int x =
  __VERIFIER_nondet_int();
  if (c && f(x) != g(x)) {
    ERROR: goto ERROR;
  }
  return 0;
}
```

8 Conclusions

In this paper, we have extended rewriting induction to the setting of LCTRSs. Furthermore, we have shown how this method can be used to prove correctness of procedural programs. LCTRSs seem to be a good analysis backend for this since the techniques from standard rewriting can typically be extended, and native support for logical conditions and data types like integers and arrays is present.

We have also introduced a new technique to generalize equations. The idea of this method is to identify constants used as *variable initializations*, keep track of them during the proof process, and abstract from these constants when a proof attempt diverges. The LCTRS setting is instrumental in the simplicity of this method, as it boils down to dropping a (cleverly chosen) part of a constraint.

In addition to the theory of these techniques, we provide an implementation that automatically verifies inductive theorems. Initial results on a small database of student programs are very promising. In future work, we will aim to increase the strength of this implementation and couple it with an automatic transformation tool which converts procedural programs into LCTRSs.

Acknowledgements. We are grateful to Stephan Falke, who contributed to an older version of this paper, and to both the IJCAR'14 and APLAS'14 referees for their helpful remarks.

References

1. Bouhoula, A.: Automated theorem proving by test set induction. Journal of Symbolic Computation 23(1), 47–77 (1997)
2. Bundy, A.: The automation of proof by mathematical induction. In: Voronkov, A., Robinson, A. (eds.) Handbook of Automated Reasoning, pp. 845–911. Elsevier (2001)
3. Bundy, A., Basin, D., Hutter, D., Ireland, A.: Rippling: Meta-Level Guidance for Mathematical Reasoning. Cambridge University Press (2005)
4. Falke, S., Kapur, D.: A term rewriting approach to the automated termination analysis of imperative programs. In: Schmidt, R.A. (ed.) CADE 2009. LNCS (LNAI), vol. 5663, pp. 277–293. Springer, Heidelberg (2009)
5. Falke, S., Kapur, D.: Rewriting induction + linear arithmetic = decision procedure. In: Gramlich, B., Miller, D., Sattler, U. (eds.) IJCAR 2012. LNCS (LNAI), vol. 7364, pp. 241–255. Springer, Heidelberg (2012)
6. Falke, S., Kapur, D., Sinz, C.: Termination analysis of C programs using compiler intermediate languages. In: Schmidt-Schauß, M. (ed.) 22nd International Conference on Rewriting Techniques and Applications (RTA), Dagstuhl, Leibniz. LIPIcs, vol. 10, pp. 41–50 (2011)
7. Falke, S.: Term Rewriting with Built-In Numbers and Collection Data Structures. Ph.D. thesis, University of New Mexico, Albuquerque, NM, USA (2009)
8. Furuichi, Y., Nishida, N., Sakai, M., Kusakari, K., Sakabe, T.: Approach to procedural-program verification based on implicit induction of constrained term rewriting systems. IPSJ Transactions on Programming 1(2), 100–121 (2008) (in Japanese)(**)

9. Huth, M., Ryan, M.: Logic in Computer Science: Modelling and Reasoning about Systems. Cambridge University Press (2000)

10. Kapur, D., Sakhanenko, N.A.: Automatic generation of generalization lemmas for proving properties of tail-recursive definitions. In: Basin, D., Wolff, B. (eds.) TPHOLs 2003. LNCS, vol. 2758, pp. 136–154. Springer, Heidelberg (2003)

11. Kapur, D., Subramaniam, M.: Lemma discovery in automated induction. In: McRobbie, M.A., Slaney, J.K. (eds.) CADE 1996. LNCS, vol. 1104, pp. 538–552. Springer, Heidelberg (1996)

12. Kop, C.: Termination of LCTRSs. In: 13th International Workshop on Termination (WST), pp. 59–63 (2013)

13. Kop, C., Nishida, N.: Term rewriting with logical constraints. In: Fontaine, P., Ringeissen, C., Schmidt, R.A. (eds.) FroCoS 2013. LNCS (LNAI), vol. 8152, pp. 343–358. Springer, Heidelberg (2013)

14. Kop, C., Nishida, N.: Towards verifying procedural programs using constrained rewriting induction. Technical report, University of Innsbruck (2014), http://arxiv.org/abs/1409.0166

15. de Moura, L., Bjørner, N.: Z3: An efficient SMT solver. In: Ramakrishnan, C.R., Rehof, J. (eds.) TACAS 2008. LNCS, vol. 4963, pp. 337–340. Springer, Heidelberg (2008)

16. Nakabayashi, N., Nishida, N., Kusakari, K., Sakabe, T., Sakai, M.: Lemma generation method in rewriting induction for constrained term rewriting systems. Computer Software 28(1), 173–189 (2010) (in Japanese)(**)

17. Otto, C., Brockschmidt, M., von Essen, C., Giesl, J.: Automated termination analysis of Java bytecode by term rewriting. In: Lynch, C. (ed.) 21st International Conference on Rewriting Techniques and Applications (RTA), Dagstuhl, Leibniz. LIPIcs, vol. 6, pp. 259–276 (2010)

18. Reddy, U.S.: Term rewriting induction. In: Stickel, M.E. (ed.) CADE 1990. LNCS, vol. 449, pp. 162–177. Springer, Heidelberg (1990)

19. Sakata, T., Nishida, N., Sakabe, T.: On proving termination of constrained term rewrite systems by eliminating edges from dependency graphs. In: Kuchen, H. (ed.) WFLP 2011. LNCS, vol. 6816, pp. 138–155. Springer, Heidelberg (2011)

20. Sakata, T., Nishida, N., Sakabe, T., Sakai, M., Kusakari, K.: Rewriting induction for constrained term rewriting systems. IPSJ Transactions on Programming 2(2), 80–96 (2009) (in Japanese)(**)

21. Urso, P., Kounalis, E.: Sound generalizations in mathematical induction. Theoretical Computer Science 323(1-3), 443–471 (2004)

22. Walsh, T.: A divergence critic for inductive proof. Journal of Artificial Intelligence Research 4, 209–235 (1996)

(**) Translations or summaries of marked Japanese papers are available at:
http://www.trs.cm.is.nagoya-u.ac.jp/crisys/

A ZDD-Based Efficient Higher-Order Model Checking Algorithm

Taku Terao and Naoki Kobayashi

The University of Tokyo, Japan

Abstract. The model checking of higher-order recursion schemes, aka. higher-order model checking, has recently been applied to automated verification of higher-order programs. Despite its extremely high worst-case complexity, practical algorithms have been developed that work well for typical inputs that arise in program verification. Even the state-of-the-art algorithms are, however, not scalable enough for verification of thousands or millions of lines of programs. We, therefore, propose a new higher-order model checking algorithm. It is based on Broadbent and Kobayashi's type and saturation-based algorithm HORSAT, but we make two significant modifications. First, unlike HORSAT, we collect flow information (which is necessary for optimization) in linear time by using a sub-transitive flow graph. Thanks to this, the resulting algorithm runs in almost linear time under a fixed-parameter assumption. Secondly, we employ zero-suppressed binary decision diagrams to efficiently represent and propagate type information. We have confirmed through experiments that the new algorithm is more scalable for several families of inputs than the state-of-the-art higher-order model checkers HORSAT and Preface.

1 Introduction

Higher-order model checking is the problem of deciding whether the (possibly infinite) tree generated by a given higher-order recursion scheme (HORS) satisfies a given property [19]. Higher-order model checking has recently been applied to automatic verification of higher-order functional program [9,13,20,12,14].

A major challenge in applying higher-order model checking to practice is to develop an *efficient* higher-order model checker. Actually, the higher-order model checking problem is k-EXPTIME complete for order-k HORS [19,11], so there is no hope to obtain an algorithm that works well for all the inputs. Nevertheless, several practical algorithms have been developed and implemented, which run reasonably fast for many typical inputs [9,8,18,3,21]. The state-of-the-art higher-order model checkers HORSAT [3] and Preface [21] can handle HORS consisting of hundreds of lines of rewriting rules (and it has been reported [21] that Preface works even for thousands of lines of HORS for a specific problem instance). Despite the recent advance, they are still not scalable enough to be applied to verification of thousands or millions of lines of programs.

In the present paper, we improve the HORSAT algorithm [3] in two significant ways. HORSAT computes (a finite representation of) the backward closure of

J. Garrigue (Ed.): APLAS 2014, LNCS 8858, pp. 354–371, 2014.

error configurations (i.e., the set of terms that generate error trees) by using intersection types, and checks whether the initial configuration belongs to the set. It has two main bottlenecks: one is the flow analysis (based on 0CFA [23]) employed to compute only a relevant part of the backward closure. In theory, (the known upper-bound of) the worst-case complexity of the flow analysis is almost cubic time [16], whereas the other part of the HorSat algorithm is actually fixed-parameter linear time.[1] The other bottleneck is that the number of intersection types used for representing a set of terms may blow up quickly. This blow up immediately slows down the whole algorithm, since each saturation step (for computing the backward closure by iteratively computing the backward image of a set of terms) picks and processes each type one by one. To overcome the first problem, we employ a linear-time *sub-transitive* control flow analysis (which constructs a graph whose transitive closure is a flow graph) [5] and use it for the optimization. This guarantees that the whole algorithm runs in time linear in the size of HORS, under the same fixed-parameter assumption as before. To address the second problem, we represent a set of intersection types using a zero-suppressed binary decision diagram (ZDD) [17], and develop a new saturation algorithm that can process a set of intersection types (represented in the form of ZDD) simultaneously.

We have implemented the new algorithm mentioned above and confirmed that it scales better (with respect to the size of HORS) than HorSat and Preface for several classes of inputs parametrized by the size of HORS.

The rest of the paper is structured as follows. Section 2 reviews the higher-order model checking problem, the model checking algorithm HorSat, and ZDD. Section 3 describes our new algorithm. Section 4 reports experiments. Section 5 discusses related work and Section 6 concludes the paper.

2   Preliminaries

We review higher-order recursion schemes (HORS) and higher-order model checking [19]. To save the definitions, we consider here a specialized version of higher-order model checking called co-trivial ATA model checking of HORS [3].

2.1   Higher-Order Recursion Schemes and Co-trivial ATA Model Checking

The set of **sorts**, written **Sorts**, is defined by: $\kappa ::= o \mid \kappa_1 \to \kappa_2$. Intuitively, o describes trees, and $\kappa_1 \to \kappa_2$ describes functions from κ_1 to κ_2. A **sorted alphabet** is a map from a finite set of symbols to **Sorts**. The *arity* and *order* of **Sorts** are defined by:

$$\mathsf{arity}(o) = 0 \qquad \mathsf{arity}(\kappa_1 \to \kappa_2) = 1 + \mathsf{arity}(\kappa_2)$$
$$\mathsf{order}(o) = 0 \qquad \mathsf{order}(\kappa_1 \to \kappa_2) = \max(1 + \mathsf{order}(\kappa_1), \mathsf{order}(\kappa_2))$$

---

[1] Actually, in the previously reported implementation of HorSat [3], the other part also took more than linear time due to the naive implementation. In the present work, we have also improved on that point.

Let X be a sorted alphabet. The (family of) sets $\mathbf{Terms}_{X,\kappa}$ of *applicative terms* of sort κ over X is inductively defined by: (i) If $X(a) = \kappa$, then $a \in \mathbf{Terms}_{X,\kappa}$; and (ii) If $t_1 \in \mathbf{Terms}_{X,\kappa_2 \to \kappa}$ and $t_2 \in \mathbf{Terms}_{X,\kappa_2}$, then $t_1 t_2 \in \mathbf{Terms}_{X,\kappa}$. We write $\mathbf{Terms}_X$ for the union of $\mathbf{Terms}_{X,\kappa}$ for all sorts.

Definition 1 (Higher-order recursion schemes (HORS)). *A **higher-order recursion scheme** is a tuple $\mathcal{G} = (\Sigma, \mathcal{N}, \mathcal{R}, S)$ where: (i) Σ and $\mathcal{N}$ are sorted alphabets, where $\mathcal{N}(S) = o$, $\mathrm{dom}(\Sigma) \cap \mathrm{dom}(\mathcal{N}) = \emptyset$, and $\mathrm{order}(\Sigma(a)) \leq 1$ for every $a \in \mathrm{dom}(\Sigma)$; (ii) $\mathcal{R}$ is a set of rewriting rules of the form $F\, x_1 \cdots x_n \to t$ where $\mathcal{N}(F) = \kappa_1 \to \cdots \to \kappa_n \to o$ and $t \in \mathbf{Terms}_{\Sigma \cup \mathcal{N} \cup \{ x_1:\kappa_1, \ldots, x_n:\kappa_n \}, o}$. We require that $\mathcal{R}$ has exactly one rule for each $F \in \mathrm{dom}(\mathcal{N})$. The **reduction relation** $t_1 \longrightarrow_{\mathcal{G}} t_2$ is the least binary relation on $\mathbf{Terms}_{\Sigma \cup \mathcal{N}, o}$ that satisfies: (i) $F\, t_1 \cdots t_n \longrightarrow_{\mathcal{G}} [t_1/x_1, \ldots, t_n/x_n]t$ if $F\, x_1 \cdots x_n \to t \in \mathcal{R}$, and (ii) $a\, t_1 \cdots t_i \cdots t_n \longrightarrow_{\mathcal{G}} a\, t_1 \cdots t_i' \cdots t_n$ if $t_i \longrightarrow_{\mathcal{G}} t_i'$ and $a \in \mathrm{dom}(\Sigma)$. The **value tree** of $\mathcal{G}$, written $\mathbf{Tree}(\mathcal{G})$, is the least upper bound of $\{ t^{\perp} \mid S \longrightarrow_{\mathcal{G}}^* t \}$ (with respect to the least precongruence $\sqsubseteq$ that satisfies $\perp \sqsubseteq t$ for every tree t), where $t^{\perp}$ is defined by $(F\, t_1 \cdots t_n)^{\perp} = \perp$ for each $F \in \mathrm{dom}(\mathcal{N})$ and $(a\, t_1 \cdots t_n)^{\perp} = a\, t_1^{\perp} \cdots t_n^{\perp}$ for each $a \in \mathrm{dom}(\Sigma)$. We call each x_i in $F\, x_1 \cdots x_n \to t$ a **variable**. We assume that all variables are distinct from each other. $\mathcal{X}$ denotes the sorted alphabet of all variables.*

Intuitively, each symbol $a \in \mathrm{dom}(\Sigma)$ (called a terminal symbol) is a tree constructor of arity $\mathrm{arity}(\Sigma(a))$, and $F \in \mathrm{dom}(\mathcal{R})$ (called a non-terminal symbol) is a (higher-order) function on trees defined by the rewriting rules.

Example 1. Consider the HORS $\mathcal{G}_0 = (\Sigma, \mathcal{N}, \mathcal{R}, S)$ where $\Sigma = \{ \mathsf{a} : o \to o \to o, \mathsf{b} : o \to o, \mathsf{c} : o \}$, $\mathcal{N} = \{ S : o, F : (o \to o) \to o, T : (o \to o) \to o \to o \}$, and $\mathcal{R}$ consists of the rules:

$$S \to F\,(T\,\mathsf{b}) \qquad F\,f \to \mathsf{a}\,(f\,\mathsf{c})\,(F\,(T\,f)) \qquad T\,g\,x \to g(g(x))$$

S is reduced as follows.

$$S \longrightarrow F\,(T\,\mathsf{b}) \longrightarrow \mathsf{a}\,(T\,\mathsf{b}\,\mathsf{c})\,(F\,(T\,(T\,\mathsf{b}))) \longrightarrow \mathsf{a}\,(\mathsf{b}(\mathsf{b}\,\mathsf{c}))\,(F\,(T\,(T\,\mathsf{b}))) \longrightarrow \cdots$$

It generates an infinite tree having a path $\mathsf{a}^k \mathsf{b}^{2^k} \mathsf{c}$ for every $k \geq 1$.

Higher-order model checking is the problem of deciding whether $\mathbf{Tree}(\mathcal{G})$ satisfies a given tree property. We use alternating tree automata (for finite trees) to describe the tree property. We consider below an element of $\mathbf{Terms}_{\Sigma, o}$ as a tree.

Definition 2 (Alternating Tree Automata (ATA)). *An **alternating tree automaton** is a tuple (Σ, Q, δ, q_I) where: (i) Σ is a sorted alphabet; (ii) Q is a finite set; (iii) $\delta \subseteq Q \times \mathrm{dom}(\Sigma) \times 2^{\mathbb{N} \times Q}$ such that whenever $(q, a, U) \in \delta$ and $(i, q') \in U$, $1 \leq i \leq \mathrm{arity}(\Sigma(a))$; and (iv) $q_I \in Q$. A **configuration** is a set of pairs of the form $(t, q) \in \mathbf{Terms}_{\Sigma, o} \times Q$, and the **transition relation** over configurations is defined by:*

$$C \cup \{ (a\, t_1 \cdots t_k, q) \} \longrightarrow C \cup \{ (t_i, q') \mid (i, q') \in U \} \quad (\textit{if } (q, a, U) \in \delta).$$

A tree $t \in \mathbf{Terms}_{\Sigma,o}$ *is* **accepted** *if* $\{(q_I, t)\} \longrightarrow^* \emptyset$. *We write* $\mathcal{L}(\mathcal{A})$ *for the set of trees accepted by* $\mathcal{A}$. *For an ATA* $\mathcal{A} = (\Sigma, Q, \delta, q_I)$ *(with* $\perp \notin \mathrm{dom}(\Sigma)$*), we write* $\mathcal{A}^{\perp}$ *for* $(\Sigma \cup \{\perp \mapsto o\}, Q, \delta, q_I)$.

Example 2. Consider the automaton $\mathcal{A}_0 = (\Sigma, \{q_0, q_1\}, \delta, q_0)$ where Σ is the same as that of Example 1, and δ is:

$$\{(q_i, \mathsf{a}, \{(j, q_i)\}) \mid j \in \{1, 2\}, i \in \{0, 1\}\}$$
$$\cup \{(q_0, \mathsf{b}, \{(1, q_1)\}), (q_1, \mathsf{b}, \{(1, q_0)\}), (q_1, \mathsf{c}, \emptyset)\}$$

It accepts all the trees that have a finite path containing an odd number of b's.

We can now define a special case of higher-order model checking called the co-trivial model checking of HORS [3].

Definition 3 (Co-trivial Model Checking for HORS). *We write* $\mathcal{G} \models \mathcal{A}$ *if there exists a term* t *such that* $S \longrightarrow^* t$ *and* $t^{\perp} \in \mathcal{L}(\mathcal{A}^{\perp})$. *The co-trivial ATA model checking of HORS is the problem of deciding whether* $\mathcal{G} \models \mathcal{A}$ *holds, given an ATA* $\mathcal{A} = (\Sigma, Q, \delta, q_I)$ *and a HORS* $\mathcal{G}$ *as input.*

Intuitively, the ATA describes the property of *invalid* trees, and the condition "$S \longrightarrow^* t$ and $t^{\perp} \in \mathcal{L}(\mathcal{A}^{\perp})$" means that a prefix of $\mathbf{Tree}(\mathcal{G})$ is invalid (hence so is $\mathbf{Tree}(\mathcal{G})$). Note that the co-trivial model checking of $\mathcal{G}$ with respect to $\mathcal{A}$ is equivalent to the trivial model checking of $\mathcal{G}$ with respect to $\overline{\mathcal{A}}$ (where $\overline{\mathcal{A}}$ is the complement of $\mathcal{A}$) considered in [1,9,3].

Example 3. Recall $\mathcal{G}_0$ in Example 1 and $\mathcal{A}_0$ in Example 2. Then, $\mathcal{G}_0 \not\models \mathcal{A}_0$ holds. In other words, every finite path (that ends in c) $\mathbf{Tree}(\mathcal{G})$ contains an even number of b's.

2.2 Broadbent and Kobayashi's Algorithm

We quickly review Broadbent and Kobayashi's saturation-based algorithm HOR-SAT for co-trivial automata model checking of HORS [3]. We fix an ATA $\mathcal{A} = (\Sigma, Q, \delta, q_I)$ and a HORS $\mathcal{G} = (\Sigma, \mathcal{N}, \mathcal{R}, S)$ in the following discussion.

Definition 4 (Intersection types). *The sets* **ITypes** *and* **STypes** *of intersection types and strict types, ranged over by* σ *and* θ *respectively, are defined by:*

$$\sigma ::= \{\theta_1, \ldots, \theta_n\} \qquad \theta ::= q \mid \bigwedge \sigma \to \theta$$

Here $q \in Q$ *and* n *is a non-negative integer.*

Intuitively, the type q describes trees accepted by the automaton from state q, and $\bigwedge \sigma \to \theta$ describes functions that take an argument that has all (strict) types in σ and returns a value of type θ.

We say θ is a **refinement** of κ, written $\theta :: \kappa$, when it is derivable by the following rules.

$$\frac{}{q :: o} \qquad \frac{\sigma :: \kappa_1 \quad \theta :: \kappa_2}{(\bigwedge \sigma \to \theta) :: (\kappa_1 \to \kappa_2)} \qquad \frac{\theta :: \kappa \text{ for each } \theta \in \sigma}{\sigma :: \kappa}$$

An **(intersection) type environment** is a map $\Gamma : \mathrm{dom}(\mathcal{N}) \to \mathbf{ITypes}$ such that $\forall f \in \mathrm{dom}(\mathcal{N}).\ \Gamma(f) :: \mathcal{N}(f)$. The union of type environments $\Gamma_1 \cup \Gamma_2$ is defined by $(\Gamma_1 \cup \Gamma_2)(x) = \Gamma_1(x) \cup \Gamma_2(x)$.

The type judgment relation $\Gamma \vdash_I t : \theta$ is defined by the following typing rules:

$$\frac{\theta \in \Gamma(f)}{\Gamma \vdash_I f : \theta} \qquad \frac{(q, a, U) \in \delta}{\Gamma \vdash_I a : \bigwedge U|_1 \to \cdots \to \bigwedge U|_{\mathsf{arity}(\Sigma(a))} \to q}$$

$$\frac{\Gamma \vdash_I t_1 : \bigwedge \sigma \to \theta \qquad \Gamma \vdash_I t_2 : \theta' \text{ for each } \theta' \in \sigma}{\Gamma \vdash_I t_1 t_2 : \theta}$$

Here, $U|_i = \{ q \mid (j, q) \in U, j = i \}$.

A type environment Γ can be considered a finite representation of the set of terms: $\mathbf{ITerms}_{\Gamma,q_I} = \{ t \mid \Gamma \vdash_I t : q_I \}$. The set $\mathbf{ITerms}_{\emptyset,q_I}$ described by the empty type environment is exactly the set of terms t such that $t^\perp \in \mathcal{L}(\mathcal{A}^\perp)$. HOR-SAT starts from the empty type environment, and iteratively expand it to a type environment Γ such that $\mathbf{ITerms}_{\Gamma,q_I} = \{ t \mid \exists s.t \longrightarrow^* s \wedge s^\perp \in \mathcal{L}(\mathcal{A}^\perp) \} \cap$ **RTerms**, where **RTerms** is an over-approximation of the set of terms reachable from S, i.e., $\{ t \mid S \longrightarrow^* t \}$. Once such Γ is obtained, the co-trivial model checking amounts to checking whether $\Gamma \vdash_I S : q_I$, i.e., whether $q_I \in \Gamma(S)$ holds.

HORSAT makes use of flow information to efficiently compute Γ above.

Definition 5. $\mathbf{Flow}_{ap} : \mathrm{dom}(\mathcal{X}) \to \mathcal{P}(\mathbf{Terms}_{\Sigma \cup \mathcal{N}})$ *(recall that $\mathcal{X}$ is a sorted alphabet of variables in $\mathcal{G}$) is (approximate) flow information, if* $\mathbf{Flow}_{ap}(x_i) \subseteq \mathbf{Terms}_{\Sigma \cup \mathcal{N}, \mathcal{X}(x_i)}$ *and if* $t_i \in \mathbf{Flow}_{ap}(x_i)$ *holds for each* $i \in \{ 1, \ldots, k \}$ *whenever* $S \longrightarrow^* t$ *and* $F t_1 \cdots t_k$ *occurs as a subterm of t with* $F x_1 \cdots x_k \to t \in \mathcal{R}$.

Using $\mathbf{Flow}_{ap}$, the function to iteratively expand a type environment is defined as follows.

Definition 6. *The function $\mathcal{F}_{\mathcal{G}}$ over type environments is given by:*

$$\mathcal{F}_{\mathcal{G}}(\Gamma)(F) = \Gamma(F) \cup \left\{ \bigwedge \Delta(x_1) \to \cdots \to \bigwedge \Delta(x_n) \to q \;\middle|\; \begin{array}{l} F x_1 \cdots x_n \to t \in \mathcal{R}, \\ \Gamma \vdash_I t : q \Longrightarrow \Delta, \\ \mathbf{Inhabited}(\Gamma, \Delta) \end{array} \right\}. \tag{1}$$

Here, $\mathbf{Inhabited}(\Gamma, \Delta) \iff \forall x \in \mathrm{dom}(\Delta). \exists t \in \mathbf{Flow}_{ap}(x). \forall \theta \in \Delta(x). \Gamma \vdash_I t : \theta$. *The relation $\Gamma \vdash_I t : \theta \Longrightarrow \Delta$ is defined by:*

$$\frac{\Gamma \vdash_I t : \theta}{\Gamma \vdash_I t : \theta \Longrightarrow \emptyset} \qquad \frac{\exists t \in \mathbf{Flow}_{ap}(x). \Gamma \vdash_I t : \theta}{\Gamma \vdash_I x : \theta \Longrightarrow \{ x : \theta \}}$$

$$\frac{\Gamma \vdash_I t_1 : \theta_1 \wedge \cdots \wedge \theta_n \to \theta \Longrightarrow \Delta_0 \qquad \forall i \in \{ 1, \ldots, n \}. \Gamma \vdash_I t_2 : \theta_i \Longrightarrow \Delta_i}{\Gamma \vdash_I t_1 t_2 : \theta \Longrightarrow \bigcup_{i=0}^{n} \Delta_i}$$

The rules for $\Gamma \vdash_I t : \theta \Longrightarrow \Delta$ can be read as an algorithm to compute Δ such that $\Gamma \cup \Delta \vdash_I t : \theta$. For example, the rule for $t_1 t_2$ says that given Γ

and θ, we should first enumerate all the pairs $(\theta_1 \wedge \cdots \wedge \theta_n, \Delta_0)$ such that $\Gamma \vdash_I t_1 : \theta_1 \wedge \cdots \wedge \theta_n \to \theta \Longrightarrow \Delta_0$, and then for each such pair, enumerate all $(\Delta_1, \ldots, \Delta_n)$ such that $\Gamma \vdash_I t_2 : \theta_i \Longrightarrow \Delta_i$, and return $\bigcup_{i=0}^{n} \Delta_i$ for all the combinations of $\Delta_0, \Delta_1, \ldots, \Delta_n$.

HORSAT is based on the following theorem, and computes $\Gamma = \bigcup_{i \in \omega} \mathcal{F}_{\mathcal{G}}^i(\emptyset)$ and checks whether $q_I \in \Gamma(S)$ holds.

Theorem 1 ([3]). *Let* $\mathcal{G} = (\Sigma, \mathcal{N}, \mathcal{R}, S)$ *be a HORS.* $q_I \in (\bigcup_{i \in \omega} \mathcal{F}_{\mathcal{G}}^i(\emptyset))(S)$ *if and only if* $\mathcal{G} \models \mathcal{A}$.

Example 4. Recall $\mathcal{G}_0$ in Example 1 and $\mathcal{A}_0$ in Example 2. The map

$$\{ f \mapsto \{ T^k \mathsf{b} \mid k \geq 1 \}, g \mapsto \{ T^k \mathsf{b} \mid k \geq 0 \}, x \mapsto \{ \mathsf{b}^k \mathsf{c} \mid k \geq 0 \} \}$$

is a valid flow map **Flow**$_{ap}$. Since $\emptyset \vdash_I f(f\,x) : q_1 \Longrightarrow \Delta$ and **Inhabited**$(\emptyset, \Delta)$ hold for $\Delta = \{ f : \{ q_0 \to q_1, q_1 \to q_0 \}, x : q_1 \}$, we have $\mathcal{F}_{\mathcal{G}_0}(\emptyset) = \{ S : \emptyset, F : \emptyset, T : \{ (q_0 \to q_1) \wedge (q_1 \to q_0) \to q_1 \to q_1 \} \}$ and $(\bigcup_{i \in \omega} \mathcal{F}_{\mathcal{G}}^i(\emptyset))(S) = \{ q_1 \}$. Thus, we have $\mathcal{G}_0 \not\models \mathcal{A}_0$.

3   A ZDD-Based Algorithm

We now discuss our new algorithm. The main limitations of HORSAT and our approach to address them are summarized as follows.

1. First, although $\bigcup_{i \in \omega} \mathcal{F}_{\mathcal{G}}^i(\emptyset)$ is guaranteed to be finite, it sometimes becomes quite large, containing "similar" types $q_1 \to q_3 \to q$, $q_2 \to q_3 \to q$, $q_1 \to q_4 \to q$, and $q_2 \to q_4 \to q$, which could be represented by a single type $q_1 \vee q_2 \to q_3 \vee q_4 \to q$ if we had union types as well. The blow-up of the size of a type environment also significantly affects the cost of intermediate computation of $\mathcal{F}_{\mathcal{G}}(\Gamma)(F)$, as we have to enumerate Δ such that $\Gamma \vdash_I t : q \Longrightarrow \Delta$ and **Inhabited**(Γ, Δ) one by one, and construct new types. This suggests that the intersection types (in the syntactic representation) may not be an optimal representation for computing $\bigcup_{i \in \omega} \mathcal{F}_{\mathcal{G}}^i(\emptyset)$. We use *ZDD* to represent intersection types and type environments, and re-define $\mathcal{F}_{\mathcal{G}}$ accordingly.

2. Secondly, HORSAT uses 0CFA to compute approximate flow information **Flow**$_{ap}$, whose worst-case complexity is almost cubic time [16]. As the definition of $\mathcal{F}_{\mathcal{G}}$ suggests, however, what we actually need is not **Flow**$_{ap}$ itself but the set $\{ \{ \theta \mid \Gamma \vdash_I t : \theta \} \mid t \in \textbf{Flow}_{ap}(x) \}$ (for each x). The latter can be more efficiently computed (in fact, in *linear time* under a fixed-parameter assumption) by first computing *sub-transitive* flow information [5] and then directly computing the set $\{ \{ \theta \mid \Gamma \vdash_I t : \theta \} \mid t \in \textbf{Flow}_{ap}(x) \}$ using the sub-transitive flow information.

We discuss the first issue in Sections 3.1 and 3.2, and the second issue in Section 3.3.

3.1   ZDD Types

We use ZDD [17] to represent a set of intersection types compactly. ZDD is an efficient data structure for representing a set of (finite) sets. The following description is actually based on set operations, and not tied to the specific data structure of ZDD; thus one may use other representations such as ordered boolean decision diagrams (OBDD) and boolean formulas to implement the algorithm below. Using ZDD, however, we expect that the representation is more compact and the set operations can be efficiently performed: see Remark 1 below.

We first modify the representation of a strict type.

Definition 7 (ZDD types). *Let θ be a strict type. The* **ZDD strict type** *corresponding to θ, written $[\theta]$, is defined as:*

$$[q] = \{q\} \qquad [\bigwedge \sigma \to \theta] = \{(\text{arity}(\bigwedge \sigma \to \theta), \theta') \mid \theta' \in \sigma\} \cup [\theta]$$

A **ZDD intersection type** *is a collection of ZDD strict types. The set of ZDD intersection types is written* **ITypes**$_{ZDD}$. *Let Γ be an intersection type environment, The* **ZDD type environment** *corresponding to Γ, written $[\Gamma]$, is the map from $\text{dom}(\Gamma)$ to ZDD intersection types such that for each $F \in \text{dom}(\Gamma)$, $[\Gamma](F) = \{[\theta] \mid \theta \in \Gamma(F)\}$.*

For example, the strict type $q_1 \wedge q_2 \to q_3 \to q$ is now expressed by the set $\{(2, q_1), (2, q_2), (1, q_3), q\}$.[2] The intersection type (or, the set of strict types):

$$\{q_1 \to q_3 \to q, q_1 \to q_4 \to q, q_2 \to q_3 \to q, q_2 \to q_4 \to q\}$$

is expressed by a set of sets:

$$\{\{(2, q_1), (1, q_3), q\}, \{(2, q_1), (1, q_4), q\}, \{(2, q_2), (1, q_3), q\}, \{(2, q_2), (1, q_4), q\}\}.$$

A careful reader will notice that we can then use a compact representation like $((2, q_1) \vee (2, q_2)) \wedge ((1, q_3) \vee (1, q_4)) \wedge q$ to represent the intersection type. Note that the set representation is *not* nested. For example, $(q_1 \wedge q_2 \to q) \wedge (q_3 \to q) \to q$ is expressed by: $\{(1, q_1 \wedge q_2 \to q), (1, q_3 \to q), q\}$. The strict types $q_1 \wedge q_2 \to q$ and $q_3 \to q$ are lazily converted to ZDD strict types as necessary inside the algorithm described below. We use meta-variables $\bar{\theta}$, $\bar{\sigma}$, and $\bar{\Gamma}$ for ZDD strict types, ZDD intersection types and ZDD type environments respectively. (In general, we shall use $\bar{x}$ as the meta-variable for the ZDD version of x below.)

In the saturation-based algorithm (recall Definition 6), we need to compute the set of pairs (θ, Δ) such that $\Gamma \vdash_I t : \theta \Longrightarrow \Delta$ for given Γ and t. We therefore prepare a representation for such a set.

Definition 8. *Let θ be a strict type, and Δ be an intersection type environment. The* **ZDD constraint type** *corresponding to $\theta \Longrightarrow \Delta$, written $[\theta \Longrightarrow \Delta]$, is defined by:*

$$[\theta \Longrightarrow \Delta] = [\theta] \cup [\Delta]_s \tag{2}$$

$$[\Delta]_s = \{(x, \theta) \mid x \in \text{dom}(\Delta), \theta \in \Delta(x)\} \tag{3}$$

---

[2] This is actually similar to the representation of Ong's *variable profiles* [19]: $(\{(x_2, q_1), (x_2, q_2), (x_1, q_3)\}, q)$.

We use the meta-variable $\overline{\Delta}$ for a subset of $\mathcal{X} \times \mathbf{STypes}$, and τ for a ZDD constraint type. Please notice the difference between $[\Gamma]$ and $[\Delta]_s$. In the former, types are converted to ZDD ones, while in the latter, types are kept as they are. For example, a constraint strict type $q_1 \to q \Longrightarrow \{f : \{q_1 \to q_2\}, x : \{q_1, q_2\}\}$ is represented as a ZDD constraint type $\{q, (1, q_1), (f, q_1 \to q_2), (x, q_1), (x, q_2)\}$. Since ZDD strict type is a subset of $Q \cup (\mathbb{N} \times \mathbf{STypes})$, and a ZDD constraint type is a subset of $Q \cup (\mathbb{N} \times \mathbf{STypes}) \cup (\mathcal{X} \times \mathbf{STypes})$, a collection of them can be represented using ZDD, by treating elements of $Q, \mathbb{N} \times \mathbf{STypes}, \mathcal{X} \times \mathbf{STypes}$ as atomic elements.

Let τ be a collection of ZDD constraint types, $q \in Q$, Θ be a subset of $\mathbb{N} \times \mathbf{STypes}$ and $\overline{\Delta}$ be a subset of $\mathcal{X} \times \mathbf{STypes}$. We write $(q, \Theta, \overline{\Delta}) \in \tau$ when $\{q\} \cup \Theta \cup \overline{\Delta} \in \tau$. We write $(q, \Theta) \in \overline{\sigma}$ when $\overline{\sigma}$ is a ZDD intersection type and $\{q\} \cup \Theta \in \overline{\sigma}$. The notation $\Theta(i)$ and $\overline{\Delta}(x)$ respectively denote the sets $\{\theta \mid (i, \theta) \in \Theta\}$ and $\{\theta \mid (x, \theta) \in \Delta\}$ (which is based on the standard set representation of a map).

We define a conversion from ZDD intersection types to intersection types.

Definition 9. *Let $\overline{\sigma}$ be a ZDD intersection type, and n be a non-negative integer. The intersection type corresponding to $\overline{\sigma}$ with the arity n, written $\mathsf{enum}(\tau, n)$ is defined by:*

$$\mathsf{enum}(\overline{\sigma}, n) = \left\{ \bigwedge \Theta(n) \to \cdots \to \bigwedge \Theta(1) \to q \,\middle|\, (q, \Theta) \in \overline{\sigma} \right\} \qquad (4)$$

3.2 Saturation Algorithm Using ZDD Types

We now present the new saturation-based algorithm using ZDD types.

Definition 10. *Let $\mathcal{G} = (\Sigma, \mathcal{N}, \mathcal{R}, S)$ be a HORS. The function $\overline{\mathcal{F}}_{\mathcal{G}}$ over ZDD type environments is defined by:*

$$\overline{\mathcal{F}}(\overline{\Gamma})(F) = \overline{\Gamma}(F) \cup \left\{ \mathsf{rename}(\mathsf{inhabited}(\tau, \overline{\Gamma})) \,\middle|\, \begin{array}{c} F \, x_n \cdots x_1 \to t \in \mathcal{R}, \\ \overline{\Gamma} \vdash_{ZDD} t : \tau \end{array} \right\} \qquad (5)$$

Here, $\mathsf{rename}(\tau)$, $\mathsf{inhabited}(\tau, \overline{\Gamma})$, and $\overline{\Gamma} \vdash_{ZDD} t : \tau$ are defined by:

$$\mathsf{rename}(\tau) = \{ \{q\} \cup \{ (i, \theta) \mid (x_i, \theta) \in \overline{\Delta} \} \mid (q, \emptyset, \overline{\Delta}) \in \tau \}$$
$$\mathsf{inhabited}(\tau, \overline{\Gamma}) = \{\{q\} \cup \overline{\Delta} \mid (q, \emptyset, \overline{\Delta}) \in \tau, \quad \exists \overline{\sigma}. \overline{\Delta}(x) \subseteq \overline{\sigma} \wedge \overline{\sigma} \in \mathsf{typesof}(x, \overline{\Gamma})\}$$

$$\frac{F \in \mathrm{dom}(\mathcal{N})}{\overline{\Gamma} \vdash_{ZDD} F : \overline{\Gamma}(F)}$$

$$\frac{a \in \mathrm{dom}(\Sigma)}{\overline{\Gamma} \vdash_{ZDD} a : \left\{ \{q\} \cup \left\{ (k, q') \,\middle|\, \begin{array}{c} (j, q') \in U \\ k = \mathsf{arity}(\Sigma(a)) - j + 1 \end{array} \right\} \,\middle|\, \begin{array}{c} q \in Q, \\ (q, a, U) \in \delta \end{array} \right\}}$$

$$\frac{x \in \mathrm{dom}(\mathcal{X})}{\overline{\Gamma} \vdash_{ZDD} x : \left\{ [\theta] \cup \{(x, \theta)\} \mid \theta \in \bigcup \mathsf{typesof}(x, \overline{\Gamma}) \right\}}$$

$$\frac{\overline{\Gamma} \vdash_{ZDD} t_1 : \tau_1 \qquad \overline{\Gamma} \vdash_{ZDD} t_2 : \tau_2 \qquad n = \mathsf{arity}(t_1)}{\overline{\Gamma} \vdash_{ZDD} t_1 \, t_2 : \left\{ \{q\} \cup \Theta' \cup \overline{\Delta} \cup \overline{\Delta}' \; \middle| \; \begin{array}{l} (q, \Theta, \overline{\Delta}) \in \tau_1 \\ \overline{\Delta}' \in \bigotimes_{\theta \in \Theta(n)} g(\tau_2, \theta) \\ \Theta' = \Theta \setminus \{ (n, \theta) \mid \theta \in \Theta(n) \} \end{array} \right\}}$$

where $S_1 \otimes S_2 = \{ s_1 \cup s_2 \mid s_1 \in S_1, s_2 \in S_2 \}$, $\Theta(n) = \{ (j, \theta) \mid (j, \theta) \in \Theta, n = j \}$, and $g(\tau, \theta) = \{ \overline{\Delta} \mid (q, \Theta, \overline{\Delta}) \in \tau, [\theta] = \{q\} \cup \Theta \}$.

$\mathsf{typesof}(x, \overline{\Gamma}) = \{ \mathsf{enum}(\overline{\sigma}_{\overline{\Gamma}, t}, \mathsf{arity}(\mathcal{X}(x))) \mid t \in \mathbf{Flow}_{ap}(x) \}$ where $\overline{\sigma}_{\overline{\Gamma}, t}$ is the (unique) intersection type such that $\overline{\Gamma} \vdash_{ZDD} t : \overline{\sigma}_{\overline{\Gamma}, t}$. (Since t is closed, τ such that $\overline{\Gamma} \vdash_{ZDD} t : \tau$ contains no free variables, hence it is actually a ZDD intersection type.)

Note that the relation $\Gamma \vdash_I t : \theta \Longrightarrow \Delta$ has now been replaced by $\overline{\Gamma} \vdash_{ZDD} t : \tau$. Since τ represents a set of pairs $(\theta_1, \Delta_1), \ldots, (\theta_n, \Delta_n)$, $\overline{\Gamma} \vdash_I t : \tau$ means that $\overline{\Gamma} \vdash_I t : \theta_i \Longrightarrow \Delta_i$ holds for all such pairs. Thanks to this modification, the algorithm to compute τ such that $\overline{\Gamma} \vdash_I t : \tau$ is deterministic, and implemented by using ZDD. The set $\mathsf{typesof}(x, \overline{\Gamma})$ used above is based on flow information $\mathbf{Flow}_{ap}$. How to represent $\mathbf{Flow}_{ap}$ and compute $\mathsf{typesof}(x, \overline{\Gamma})$ using it is explained later in Section 3.3.

The following lemma formally states the correspondence between $\Gamma \vdash_I t : \theta \Longrightarrow \Delta$ and $\overline{\Gamma} \vdash_{ZDD} t : \tau$ mentioned above.

Lemma 1. *Let Γ be an intersection type environment over $\mathcal{N}$, t be an applicative term. For any θ and Δ, if $\Gamma \vdash_I t : \theta \Longrightarrow \Delta$ then there exists τ such that $[\Gamma] \vdash_{ZDD} t : \tau$ and $[\theta \Longrightarrow \Delta] \in \tau$. Conversely, for any φ and τ, if $[\Gamma] \vdash_{ZDD} t : \tau$ and $\varphi \in \tau$, there exist θ and Δ such that $\Gamma \vdash_I t : \theta \Longrightarrow \Delta$ and $\varphi = [\theta \Longrightarrow \Delta]$.*

Based on the above lemma, we can obtain the following correspondence between the step functions used for saturation.

Lemma 2. *Let $\mathcal{G} = (\Sigma, \mathcal{N}, \mathcal{R}, S)$ be a HORS and Γ be an intersection type environment over $\mathcal{N}$. Then the following equation holds.*

$$\mathcal{F}_{\mathcal{G}}([\Gamma]) = [\mathcal{F}_{\mathcal{G}}(\Gamma)] \tag{6}$$

The following theorem is an immediate corollary of Theorem 1 and Lemma 2.

Theorem 2. *Let $\mathcal{G} = (\Sigma, \mathcal{N}, \mathcal{R}, S)$ be a HORS. $q_I \in \bigcup_{i \in \omega} (\overline{\mathcal{F}}_{\mathcal{G}}^i(\emptyset))(S)$ if and only if $\mathcal{G} \models \mathcal{A}$.*

Remark 1. The formalization above does not rely on the specific data structure of ZDD [17]. We could, therefore, use OBDD instead. In fact, our initial implementation used OBDD rather than ZDD. According to our earlier experiments, however, ZDD tends to be more efficient. Our rationale for this is that in many of the benchmarks, while the "width" of each intersection type (i.e., the size σ) tends to be small, the number of strict types θ that occur in a set of intersection types can be large. Due to this property, suppressing zero's in ZDD brings a benefit. This argument is however yet to be confirmed through more experiments.

3.3   Approximation of Control-Flow information

Next, we discuss how to compute $\mathbf{Flow}_{ap}$ and $\mathtt{typesof}(x, \overline{\Gamma})$ efficiently. To obtain (a finite representation of) $\mathbf{Flow}_{ap}$, we use Heintze and Mcallester's subtransitive flow analysis [5].

Definition 11 (Sub-transitive flow graph). *Let* $\mathcal{G} = (\Sigma, \mathcal{N}, \mathcal{R}, S)$ *be a HORS. A **sub-transitive** flow graph of $\mathcal{G}$ is a quadruple (V, E, ξ, ρ) such that: (i) (V, E) is a directed acyclic graph, (ii) each leaf v in V is labeled by $\xi(v) \in$ **Terms**$_{\Sigma \cup \mathcal{N} \cup \mathcal{X}}$, and (iii) $\rho : \mathrm{dom}(\mathcal{X}) \to V$. The **flow map** represented by a sub-transitive flow graph (V, E, ξ, ρ) is the least (with respect to the pointwise ordering) map $h : \mathrm{dom}(\mathcal{X}) \to$ **Terms**$_{\Sigma, \mathcal{N}}$ such that*

$$h(x) = \{\, t \in subst(\xi(v)) \mid v \text{ is reachable from } \rho(x) \,\}.$$

Here, $subst(t)$ is defined inductively by:

$$subst(a) = \{\, a \,\} \qquad subst(F) = \{\, F \,\} \qquad subst(x) = h(x)$$
$$subst(t_1 \; t_2) = \{\, t_1' \; t_2' \mid t_1' \in subst(t_1), t_2' \in subst(t_2) \,\}$$

A sub-transitive flow graph is sound if its flow map h is approximate flow information.

Example 5. Recall $\mathcal{G}_0$ in Example 1. A sub-transitive flow graph for $\mathcal{G}_0$ is depicted as below:

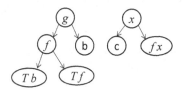

Here, the label for each non-leaf node shows the map f (e.g., x means that $\rho(x)$ is the node labeled by x in the graph), and the label for each leaf node shows the map ξ.

We can compute a sub-transitive flow graph whose flow map is equivalent to the result of 0CFA in time *linear* in the size of HORS by using Heintze and Mcallester's algorithm[5], under the assumption that the size of the largest type used in HORS is fixed. Therefore, the size of the sub-transitive flow graph is also linear in the size of HORS. We use it as a finite representation of $\mathbf{Flow}_{ap}$ below.

Let $G = (V, E, \xi, \rho)$ be a sound sub-transitive flow graph. Let $\overline{\Gamma}$ be a ZDD type environment over $\mathcal{N}$. We present an algorithm to compute $\mathtt{typesof}(x, \overline{\Gamma})$. We define the function $\mathcal{H}_{\overline{\Gamma}} : (\mathrm{dom}(\mathcal{X}) \to \mathcal{P}(\mathbf{ITypes}_{ZDD})) \to (\mathrm{dom}(\mathcal{X}) \to \mathcal{P}(\mathbf{ITypes}_{ZDD}))$ by:

$$\mathcal{H}_{\overline{\Gamma}}(\Xi)(x) = \Xi(x) \cup \{\, \overline{\sigma} \mid v \text{ is reachable from } \rho(x), \overline{\Gamma}; \Xi \vdash_{ZDD} \xi(v) : \overline{\sigma} \,\} \quad (7)$$

where $\overline{\Gamma}; \Xi \vdash_{ZDD} t : \overline{\sigma}$ is given by:

$$\frac{f \in \mathrm{dom}(\mathcal{N}) \cup \mathrm{dom}(\Sigma) \qquad \overline{\Gamma} \vdash_{ZDD} f : \overline{\sigma}}{\overline{\Gamma}, \Xi \vdash_{ZDD} f : \overline{\sigma}}$$

$$\frac{\overline{\sigma} \in \Xi(x)}{\overline{\Gamma}, \Xi \vdash_{ZDD} x : \overline{\sigma}}$$

$$\frac{\overline{\Gamma}, \Xi \vdash_{ZDD} t_1 : \overline{\sigma}_1 \qquad \overline{\Gamma}, \Xi \vdash_{ZDD} t_2 : \overline{\sigma}_2 \qquad n = \mathsf{arity}(t_1)}{\overline{\Gamma}, \Xi \vdash_{ZDD} t_1\, t_2 : \left\{ \{q\} \cup \Theta' \; \middle| \; \begin{array}{l} (q, \Theta) \in \overline{\sigma}_1 \\ \Theta(n) \subseteq \mathsf{enum}(\overline{\sigma}_2, \mathsf{arity}(t_2)) \\ \Theta' = \Theta \setminus \{ (n, \theta) \mid \theta \in \Theta(n) \} \end{array} \right\}}$$

Lemma 3. *Let* $\Xi_0 = \{ x : \emptyset \mid x \in \mathrm{dom}(\mathcal{X}) \}$, *and* $\Xi^{(\omega)} = \bigcup_{n \in \omega} (\mathcal{H}_{\overline{\Gamma}})^n(\Xi_0)$, *and* $x \in \mathrm{dom}(\mathcal{X})$. $\forall t \in \mathbf{Flow}_{ap}(x).\exists \overline{\sigma} \in \Xi^{(\omega)}.\ \overline{\Gamma} \vdash_{ZDD} t : \overline{\sigma}$, *and* $\forall \overline{\sigma} \in \Xi^{(\omega)}(x).\ \exists t \in \mathbf{Flow}_{ap}(x).\ \overline{\Gamma} \vdash_{ZDD} t : \overline{\sigma}$.

Because the number of all intersection types are finite, we can compute $\Xi^{(\omega)}$ and use it to compute $\mathcal{F}_{\mathcal{G}}(\overline{\Gamma})$.

3.4 Fixed-Parameter Linear Time Algorithm

We now discuss how to compute $\bigcup_{i \in \omega}(\overline{\mathcal{F}}_{\mathcal{G}}^i(\emptyset))$ (recall Theorem 2) in time linear in the size of HORS, under the assumption that (i) the largest order and size of types in HORS and (ii) the property automaton $\mathcal{A}$ are fixed. This fixed-parameter assumption is the same as the assumption made in the literature [9,10,8,3,21]. The naive fixed computation of $\bigcup_{i \in \omega}(\overline{\mathcal{F}}_{\mathcal{G}}^i(\emptyset))$ and $\bigcup_{n \in \omega}(\mathcal{H}_{\overline{\Gamma}})^n(\Xi_0)$ is polynomial time, but not linear: both the number of iterations to compute $\overline{\mathcal{F}}_{\mathcal{G}}(\overline{\Gamma})$ and the cost for each iteration are linear in the size of HORS even if we assume $\bigcup_{n \in \omega}(\mathcal{H}_{\overline{\Gamma}})^n(\Xi_0)$ can be computed in linear time. We can, however, use the standard technique for optimizing a fixed-point computation over a finite semi-lattice [22], as follows.

We compute the following information incrementally.

- For each non-terminal F, $\overline{\Gamma}(F)$.
- For each sub-term t of the right-hand side of a rule, τ_t such that $\overline{\Gamma} \vdash_{ZDD} t : \tau_t$ (for the current value of $\overline{\Gamma}$ and typesof).
- For each node v of the sub-transitive flow graph (V, E, ξ, ρ), the set U_v of (ZDD) intersection types that may be taken by the term $\xi(v)$. (Without loss of generality, we assume here that for each subterm t of the right-hand side of a rule, there is a node v such that $\xi(v) = t$.)

The values $\overline{\Gamma}(F)$, τ_t and U_v are updated in an on-demand manner when other values have been updated.

- $\overline{\Gamma}(F)$ is recomputed and updated as necessary, when τ_t for the body t of F's rule or U_v such that $\rho(x_i) = v$ (where x_i is a formal parameter of F) has been updated,

- τ_x is recomputed and updated as necessary, when U_v such that $\rho(x) = v$ has been updated.
- τ_a is updated only initially.
- τ_F is recomputed and updated as necessary, when $\overline{\Gamma}(F)$ has been updated.
- $\tau_{t_1 t_2}$ is recomputed and updated as necessary, when τ_{t_1} or τ_{t_2} has been updated.
- U_v is recomputed and updated as necessary, when (i) $U_{v'}$ such that $(v, v') \in E$ has been updated, (ii) $\xi(v) = F$ and τ_F has been updated, or (iii) $\xi(v) = t_1 t_2$ and $U_{v'}$ such that $\xi(v') \in \{ t_1, t_2 \}$ has been updated.

Since each update monotonically increases the values of $\overline{\Gamma}(F)$, τ_t, and U_v (which range over finite sets), the termination is guaranteed. Under the fixed-parameter assumption, the size of the sets ranged over by $\overline{\Gamma}(F)$, τ_t, and U_v is bounded above by a constant. Thus, each recomputation and update can be performed in a constant time. The number of recomputations is linearly bounded by the size of HORS and the size of the subtransitive flow graph, where the latter is linear in the size of HORS. Thus, the whole algorithm runs in time linear in the size of HORS under the fixed-parameter assumption.

Example 6. Recall $\mathcal{G}_0$ in Example 1 and $\mathcal{A}_0$ in Example 2. After saturation, U_v and $\overline{\Gamma}$ are

$$U_{\rho(x)} = \{ \{ q_0 \}, \{ q_1 \} \}$$
$$U_{\rho(g)} = \{ \{ q_0 \to q_1, q_1 \to q_0 \}, \{ q_0 \to q_0, q_1 \to q_1 \} \}$$
$$\overline{\Gamma}(T) = \{ (q_0 \to q_1) \wedge (q_1 \to q_0) \to q_0 \to q_0, (q_0 \to q_1) \wedge (q_1 \to q_0) \to q_1 \to q_1,$$
$$(q_0 \to q_0) \to q_0 \to q_0, (q_1 \to q_1) \to q_1 \to q_1 \}$$
$$\overline{\Gamma}(F) = \{ (q_1 \to q_1) \to q_1 \} \qquad \overline{\Gamma}(S) = \{ q_1 \}$$

For readability, we wrote types in the non-ZDD notation.

4 Experiments

4.1 Data Sets and Evaluation Environment

We have implemented our ZDD-based algorithm in the tool named HORSATZDD, evaluated its performance by existing problem instances, and compared the results with the two state-of-the-art previous higher-order model checkers: HORSAT [3] and Preface [21].

The problem instances used in the benchmark are classified into three categories. The first one consists of two families of HORS, $\mathcal{G}_{m,n}$ [8] and t_n [21]. They are parametrized by m, n and have been used to evaluate the scalability of Preface [21]. The second one consists of instances automatically generated by program verification tools such as the HMTT verification tool [13], MoCHi [12], PMRS model checker [20], and exact control flow analysis [24]. They have also been used in the benchmarks for HORSAT [3] and Preface [21]. The third one consists of new instances added to clarify the advantages of the new algorithm. They are also parametrized by a size parameter.

We conducted the experiments on a computer with 2.3GHz Intel Core i7 CPU, 16GB RAM and OSX 10.9.3 operating system. HORSATZDD is written in Haskell, and compiled with GHC 7.8.2. HORSAT was compiled with ocamlopt version 4.01.0, and Preface was run on Mono JIT compiler version 3.2.4.

4.2   Experimental Results

Figure 1 and Table 1 show the results of our experiments. In each table, columns D, S, O, and Q represent the expected decision (Y means Yes, N means No), the size of HORS (the number of occurrences of symbols in the righthand side of the rewriting rules), the order of HORS, and the number of states of automaton respectively, and the other columns represent the running time of each model checker measured in seconds.

For the instances $\mathcal{G}_{m,n}$ HORSATZDD scaled almost linearly with respect to the grammar size n. HORSATZDD scaled better than the other model checkers with respect to the grammar order m, although the running time was exponential in the grammar order due to the explosion of the sub-transitive flow graph. For the t_n instances Preface did not scale well (as reported in [21]), while both HORSATZDD and HORSAT scaled well.

HORSATZDD processed all instances in the category 2 within the time limit. HORSATZDD ran in ten seconds for most test cases in the category 2, but HOR-SATZDD is significantly slower than the other model checkers for the instances xhtmlf-div-2, xhtmlf-m-church, jwig-cal_main, and cfa-life2. Except for cfa-life2, this is attributed to the size of the property automaton, which blows up the size of each ZDD. This suggests that further optimization of ZDD implementation is required. As for cfa-life2, the majority of the running time of HORSATZDD was for the computation of the sub-transitive flow graph. This suggests that a further optimization may be necessary on the construction of sub-transitive flow graphs.

Category 3 consists of two families of problem instances: ae3-n and abc-len$n$. The family ae3-n has been manually constructed to clarify the advantage of using ZDD to represent (a set of) intersection types. It consists of the following grammar:

$$S \rightarrow \mathsf{br}\,(F \underbrace{\mathsf{a_1}\ \mathsf{e_1}\quad \cdots \quad \mathsf{a_1}\ \mathsf{e_1}}_{n \text{ repetitions of } \mathsf{a_1}\ \mathsf{e_1}})\,(F\ \mathsf{a_2}\ \mathsf{e_2}\ \cdots\ \mathsf{a_2}\ \mathsf{e_2}\,)\,(F\ \mathsf{a_3}\ \mathsf{e_3}\ \cdots\ \mathsf{a_3}\ \mathsf{e_3}\,)$$

$$F\ f_1\ x_1\ \cdots\ f_n\ x_n \rightarrow f_1(x_1(\cdots(f_n(x_n\mathsf{end}))\cdots))$$

Here, the types of constants are:

$$\mathsf{a}_i : q_i \rightarrow q_0,$$
$$\mathsf{e}_i : q_0 \rightarrow q_i \wedge \bigwedge\{\top \rightarrow q_j \mid j \in \{1,2,3\}\setminus\{i\}\}$$
$$\mathsf{br} : (q_0 \rightarrow \top \rightarrow \top q_0)\wedge(\top \rightarrow q_0 \rightarrow \top \rightarrow q_0)\wedge(\top \rightarrow \top \rightarrow q_0 \rightarrow q_0), \mathsf{end} : q_1 \wedge q_2$$

(The point is that the composition of a_i and e_i has type $q_0 \rightarrow q_0$ for every i.) HORSAT uses the naive representation of intersection types and enumerates

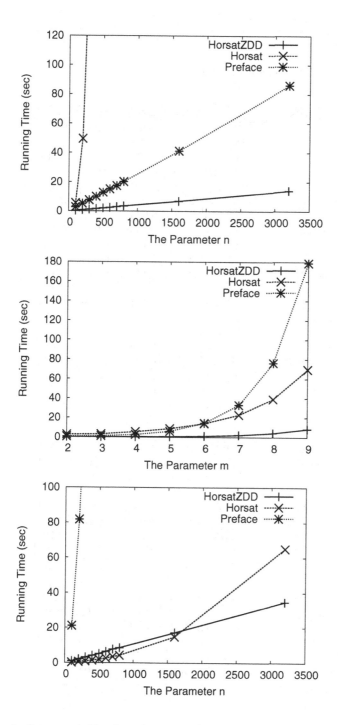

Fig. 1. Category 1: Benchmarks of $\mathcal{G}_{4,n}$ (top), $\mathcal{G}_{m.100}$ (middle), and t_n (bottom)

Table 1. Benchmarks of categories 2 (top) and 3 (bottom)

inputs	D	S	O	Q	ZDD	HorSat	Preface
checknz	Y	93	2	1	0.020	0.003	0.318
merge4-2	N	141	2	27	0.998	0.028	0.369
merge4	Y	141	2	27	0.906	0.031	0.519
gapid-2	Y	182	3	9	0.431	0.027	0.545
last	Y	193	2	1	0.053	0.014	0.326
checkpairs	N	251	2	1	0.055	0.018	0.379
tails	Y	259	3	1	0.063	0.021	0.331
map-plusone	Y	302	5	2	0.165	0.035	0.457
safe-head	Y	354	3	1	0.108	0.030	0.409
mc91-2	Y	358	4	1	0.222	0.060	1.934
map-head-filter	N	370	3	1	0.112	0.076	0.410
mkgroundterm	Y	379	2	1	0.103	0.042	0.347
safe-tail	Y	468	3	1	0.171	0.039	0.445
filter-nonzero	N	484	5	1	0.288	0.064	0.655
risers	Y	563	2	1	0.154	0.047	0.457
safe-init	Y	680	3	1	0.284	0.064	0.481
search-e-church	N	837	6	2	6.065	0.297	4.601
map-head-filter-1	Y	880	3	1	0.475	0.133	0.467
filter-nonzero-1	N	890	5	2	0.887	0.159	2.357
fold_right	Y	1310	5	2	3.647	21.646	0.370
fold_fun_list	Y	1346	7	2	1.421	0.161	0.364
cfa-psdes	Y	1819	7	2	2.796	0.128	0.417
specialize_cps_coerce1-c	Y	2731	3	4	1.606	1.176	0.505
cfa-matrix-1	Y	2944	8	2	4.030	0.307	0.484
zip	Y	2952	4	2	10.425	2.276	0.916
xhtmlf-div-2	N	3003	2	50	105.414	7.846	2.024
xhtmlf-m-church	Y	3027	2	50	56.187	5.808	1.134
filepath	Y	5956	2	1	0.693	0.396	0.665
jwig-cal_main	Y	7627	2	51	73.940	7.852	0.702
cfa-life2	Y	7648	14	2	35.978	1.849	1.15
ae3-6	Y	53	2	4	0.123	0.077	0..380
ae3-8	Y	69	2	4	0.201	4.748	0.320
ae3-10	Y	85	2	4	0.312	DNF	0.309
abc-len6	Y	70	3	1	0.012	0.002	0.372
abc-len8	Y	92	3	1	0.016	0.003	1.056
abc-len10	Y	114	3	1	0.023	0.003	9.597
abc-len12	Y	136	3	1	0.029	0.004	107.766
abc-len14	Y	158	3	1	0.037	0.004	DNF

all the types of the form: $(q_{i_1} \to q_0) \to (q_0 \to q_{i_1}) \to \cdots (q_{i_{n-1}} \to q_0) \to (q_0 \to q_{i_{n-1}}) \to (q_{i_n} \to q_0) \to (\top \to q_{i_n}) \to q_0$ (among others) for F. Since the number of those intersection types is exponential in n, HORSAT shows an exponential behavior. HORSATZDD does not suffer from the problem, since the above set of intersection types can be represented compactly. Preface works well for a different reason: it keeps binding information for all the parameters of each non-terminal together, so that it can utilize information that $f_1, \ldots, f_n$ and $x_1, \ldots, x_n$ are respectively bound to the same value for each application of F. Thus, it enumerates only types of the form: $(q_i \to q_0) \to (q_0 \to q_i) \to \cdots (q_i \to q_0) \to (q_0 \to q_i) \to q_0$. While Preface is effective for ae3-n, the use of the precise flow information causes a problem for the other instance abc-len$n$. It consists of the following rules:

$$S \to F_0 \, G.$$
$$G \, f_1 \, \cdots \, f_n \to f_1(\cdots (f_n \mathsf{e}) \cdots).$$
$$F_i \, f \to \mathsf{br} \, (F_{i+1}(f \, \mathsf{a})) \, (F_{i+1}(f \, \mathsf{b})) \, (F_{i+1}(f \, \mathsf{c})). \text{ (for } i = 0, \ldots, n-1)$$
$$F_n \, f \to f.$$

Preface generates the bindings $\{ f_1 \mapsto x_1, \ldots, f_n \mapsto x_n \}$ for all $x_1, \ldots, x_n \in \{ \mathsf{a}, \mathsf{b}, \mathsf{c} \}$. Thus, Preface suffers from the exponential blow up of the size of the abstract configuration graph with respect to n. The results in Table 1 confirms the observation above. Although these examples have been artificially created, we expect that the same problems can occur in HORS generated mechanically from program verification problems.

5   Related Work

The complexity of higher-order model checking is known to be k-EXPTIME complete for order-k HORS, even when the properties are restricted to safety properties (as in the present paper) [19,11]. Until recently, the main issue has been how to cope with this hyper-exponential worst-case complexity and construct a practical algorithm that works well for typical inputs. Kobayashi [7,9] first developed such an algorithm. Since then, a number of other practical algorithms have been developed [8,18,2]. The recent development of HORSAT and Preface significantly improved the scalability of higher-order model checking, and shifted the focus from how to cope with hyper-exponential complexity to how to achieve (almost) linear-time complexity to deal with thousands of lines of HORS. As already mentioned in Section 1, neither HORSAT nor Preface has fully achieved it; both HORSAT and Preface are fixed-parameter polynomial time algorithms (with the same fixed-parameter assumption), but HORSAT suffers from cubic bottleneck of 0CFA, and Preface runs in time exponential in the largest arity of non-terminals (in other words, the order of polynomials is the largest arity): recall abc-len$n$ in Section 4. The first practical linear-time algorithm is actually due to Kobayashi [8], but because of a large constant factor, it is often slower than other algorithms such as HORSAT, and Preface.

All the algorithms mentioned above are for trivial automata model checking. For more general, modal μ-calculus (or parity tree automata) model checking of HORS (as originally considered in [6] and [19]) some practical algorithms have also been developed [15,4]. The state-of-the-art for the modal μ-calculus mode checking for HORS is, however, much behind that for trivial automata model checking. In theory, the problem still remains fixed-parameter polynomial time [10], but not linear.

Higher-order model checkers have been used as backends of various automated verification tools for higher-order programs [9,12,13,20,24,14]. The HORS obtained in those verification tools are typically several times larger than the source programs. Being able to handle thousands of lines of HORS is, therefore, important for enabling those tools to verify large programs.

6   Conclusion

We have proposed a new saturation-based, fixed-parameter linear time algorithm for higher-order model checking and shown its effectiveness through experiments. Although it is built on Broadbent and Kobayashi's previous algorithm, we have made two important modifications that use sub-transitive flow analysis and ZDD-based representation of (a set of) intersection types. As for future work, the implementation should be improved further, as the current implementation does not exhibit the exact (fixed-parameter) linear time complexity. The use of more accurate flow information (like the one used in Preface) would improve the efficiency further, and achieving it without losing the fixed-parameter linear time complexity is also left for future work.

Acknowledgments. We would like to thank Steven Ramsay for providing the source code of Preface, and anonymous reviewers for useful comments. This work was supported by JSPS KAKENHI 23220001.

References

1. Aehlig, K.: A finite semantics of simply-typed lambda terms for infinite runs of automata. Logical Methods in Computer Science 3(3) (2007)
2. Broadbent, C.H., Carayol, A., Hague, M., Serre, O.: C-SHORe: A collapsible approach to higher-order verification. In: Proceedings of ICFP 2013, pp. 13–24 (2013)
3. Broadbent, C.H., Kobayashi, N.: Saturation-based model checking of higher-order recursion schemes. In: Proceedings of CSL 2013. LIPIcs, vol. 23, pp. 129–148 (2013)
4. Fujima, K., Ito, S., Kobayashi, N.: Practical alternating parity tree automata model checking of higher-order recursion schemes. In: Shan, C.-C. (ed.) APLAS 2013. LNCS, vol. 8301, pp. 17–32. Springer, Heidelberg (2013)
5. Heintze, N., McAllester, D.A.: Linear-time subtransitive control flow analysis. In: Proceedings of PLDI 1997, pp. 261–272 (1997)
6. Knapik, T., Niwiński, D., Urzyczyn, P.: Higher-order pushdown trees are easy. In: Nielsen, M., Engberg, U. (eds.) Fossacs 2002. LNCS, vol. 2303, pp. 205–222. Springer, Heidelberg (2002)

7. Kobayashi, N.: Model-checking higher-order functions. In: Proceedings of PPDP 2009, pp. 25–36. ACM Press (2009)

8. Kobayashi, N.: A practical linear time algorithm for trivial automata model checking of higher-order recursion schemes. In: Hofmann, M. (ed.) FOSSACS 2011. LNCS, vol. 6604, pp. 260–274. Springer, Heidelberg (2011)

9. Kobayashi, N.: Model checking higher-order programs. Journal of the ACM 60(3) (2013)

10. Kobayashi, N., Ong, C.-H.L.: A type system equivalent to the modal mu-calculus model checking of higher-order recursion schemes. In: Proceedings of LICS 2009, pp. 179–188. IEEE Computer Society Press (2009)

11. Kobayashi, N., Ong, C.-H.L.: Complexity of model checking recursion schemes for fragments of the modal mu-calculus. Logical Methods in Computer Science 7(4) (2011)

12. Kobayashi, N., Sato, R., Unno, H.: Predicate abstraction and CEGAR for higher-order model checking. In: Proceedings of PLDI 2011, pp. 222–233. ACM Press (2011)

13. Kobayashi, N., Tabuchi, N., Unno, H.: Higher-order multi-parameter tree transducers and recursion schemes for program verification. In: Proceedings of POPL 2010, pp. 495–508. ACM Press (2010)

14. Kuwahara, T., Terauchi, T., Unno, H., Kobayashi, N.: Automatic termination verification for higher-order functional programs. In: Shao, Z. (ed.) ESOP 2014. LNCS, vol. 8410, pp. 392–411. Springer, Heidelberg (2014)

15. Lester, M.M., Neatherway, R.P., Ong, C.-H.L., Ramsay, S.J.: Model checking liveness properties of higher-order functional programs. In: Proceedings of ML Workshop 2011 (2011)

16. Midtgaard, J., Horn, D.V.: Subcubic control flow analysis algorithms. Higher-Order and Symbolic Computation

17. Minato, S.: Zero-suppressed bdds for set manipulation in combinatorial problems. In: Proceedings of DAC 1993, pp. 272–277 (1993)

18. Neatherway, R.P., Ramsay, S.J., Ong, C.-H.L.: A traversal-based algorithm for higher-order model checking. In: ACM SIGPLAN International Conference on Functional Programming (ICFP 2012), pp. 353–364 (2012)

19. Ong, C.-H.L.: On model-checking trees generated by higher-order recursion schemes. In: Proceedings of LICS 2006, pp. 81–90. IEEE Computer Society Press (2006)

20. Ong, C.-H.L., Ramsay, S.: Verifying higher-order programs with pattern-matching algebraic data types. In: Proceedings of POPL 2011, pp. 587–598. ACM Press (2011)

21. Ramsay, S., Neatherway, R., Ong, C.-H.L.: An abstraction refinement approach to higher-order model checking. In: Proceedings of POPL 2014 (2014)

22. Rehof, J., Mogensen, T.: Tractable constraints in finite semilattices. Science of Computer Programming 35(2), 191–221 (1999)

23. Shivers, O.: Control-Flow Analysis of Higher-Order Languages. Ph.D. thesis, Carnegie-Mellon University (May 1991)

24. Tobita, Y., Tsukada, T., Kobayashi, N.: Exact flow analysis by higher-order model checking. In: Schrijvers, T., Thiemann, P. (eds.) FLOPS 2012. LNCS, vol. 7294, pp. 275–289. Springer, Heidelberg (2012)

Inferring Grammatical Summaries
of String Values

Se-Won Kim, Wooyoung Chin,
Jimin Park, Jeongmin Kim, and Sukyoung Ryu

Department of Computer Science, KAIST, Daejeon, South Korea

Abstract. We present a new kind of static analysis that infers grammatical summaries of string values. We are given a context-free grammar and a program which contains string expressions whose values should be partial sentences of the grammar. A grammatical summary of an expression is a vocabulary string of the grammar that derives all the possible string values of the expression. Our analysis automatically finds out such grammatical summaries. We design the analysis using abstract interpretation framework making it pluggable into conventional data-flow analysis frameworks.

In addition to the theoretical foundation of the analysis, we present how we make the analysis *computable* and *tractable*. While inferring grammatical summaries of a string expression often results in an infinite number of summaries, we make the inference computable by using a CFL-reachability algorithm and finite state automata representation. Additionally, we make the analysis more tractable by several optimization techniques such as keeping only relevant summaries and using two-level grammars. These techniques achieve huge speedup in our experiments.

1 Introduction

Many programs manipulate string values to produce semi-structured data, documents, or programs according to their *reference grammars*, usually context-free grammars (CFGs). Web applications often use strings to generate *HTML documents* or *SQL queries* specified by their corresponding grammars. Scripting languages including JavaScript often produce *program expressions* or *fragments of HTML documents* as string values, and evaluate or render them on the fly. This programming style is widespread especially in web applications on various platforms such as web browsers, smart TVs, and mobile devices.

Figure 1 shows a typical code fragment of such programs. It generates an HTML table using string values. The loop condition '?' denotes an unknown condition. The outer loop constructs a sequence of `tr` elements and the inner loop constructs children `td` elements for each `tr` element using string values. At the end of the code, they complete a `table` element by concatenating the string value with `<table>` and `</table>`. Server-side programs that show tables from databases or client-side programs that construct game boards may have similar pattern.

J. Garrigue (Ed.): APLAS 2014, LNCS 8858, pp. 372–391, 2014.

```
1   x = "";
2   while (?) {
3       x = x . "<tr>";
4       while (?)
5           x = x . "<td>a</td>";
6       x = x . "</tr>";
7   }
8   y = "<table>" . x . "</table>";
```

⟨TABLE⟩ ::= <table>⟨TRS⟩</table>
⟨TRS⟩   ::= ε | ⟨TRS⟩⟨TR⟩
⟨TR⟩   ::= <tr>⟨TDS⟩</tr>
⟨TDS⟩   ::= ε | ⟨TDS⟩⟨TD⟩
⟨TD⟩   ::= <td>a</td>

Fig. 1. An example code generating an HTML table

Fig. 2. An example context-free grammar of an HTML table

While developing such code fragments, programmers often conceptually have grammatical invariant conditions on string values. Figure 2 describes a part of the CFG specification of HTML documents, which we have simplified for exposition. Let us present some invariant conditions and their help in reasoning.

- Before evaluating line 3 in Figure 1, the value of x can be derived from ⟨TRS⟩. Observe that ⟨TR⟩ can appear after ⟨TRS⟩ in the second rule of Figure 2. This allows a programmer to append <tr>, which is a prefix string of ⟨TR⟩.
- Before evaluating line 5, the value of x can be derived from ⟨TRS⟩<tr>⟨TDS⟩. So, one can append <td>a</td> which corresponds to ⟨TD⟩. After the concatenation, we know from the fourth rule of Figure 2 that the value can be derived again from ⟨TRS⟩<tr>⟨TDS⟩.
- Finally, the value of x before evaluating line 8 can also be derived from ⟨TRS⟩. Thus, we can prepend <table> and append </table> based on the first rule of Figure 2, and obtain a string value derivable from ⟨TABLE⟩.

Based on such reasoning, programmers can write codes that generate grammatically correct partial documents.

Let us call such invariant conditions *grammatical summaries* or *summaries* in short. They are *grammatical* because we denote such invariant conditions with sequences of terminal and non-terminal symbols of the reference CFG. We call them *summaries* because the non-terminals in summaries effectively abridges corresponding substrings. In the grammatical summary ⟨TRS⟩<tr>⟨TDS⟩ before line 5, ⟨TRS⟩ and ⟨TDS⟩ correspond to the substrings constructed via the outer loop and inner loop, respectively.

In this paper, we present a useful unprecedented static analysis that infers such grammatical summaries. Existing string analyses [11,14,6,10,15] mainly *check* whether *string expressions of their interest* always produce valid *complete sentences* of the reference grammar. On the other hand, our analysis *infers* grammatical summaries of *any string expressions* that produce valid *partial sentences*. For example, to the best of our knowledge, no existing string analysis can automatically find out the summary ⟨TRS⟩<tr>⟨TDS⟩ for x before line 5, which corresponds to strictly partial sentences. The benefits of the analysis are,

(1) inferred summaries can help understand the logics of non-trivial string constructions, and (2) the analysis can verify and sum up the behavior of functions or code blocks that construct correct partial sentences.

The design of our analysis is generic in two aspects. First, the analysis is an abstract interpretation of string values and string operations. Therefore, other people can integrate our analysis seamlessly into their data-flow analysis frameworks. Second, our analysis can deal with any CFGs unlike existing string analyses that can handle only specific families of CFGs or push-down automata.

In the rest of this paper, we show how we design, implement, and engineer a static analysis for inferring grammatical summaries.

- We rigorously design the analysis within the abstract interpretation framework [3,4,5] (Section 3).
- Since our mathematical design often results in an infinite number of summaries, we present how to make the analysis computable by using finite state automata representation and CFL-reachability algorithms (Section 4).
- To enhance usability of the analysis and reduce grammatical biases, we allow the analysis to use extended CFGs, the right-hand sides of whose production rules are regular expressions (Section 5).
- Then, we develop several optimization techniques to make the analysis provide tractable performance (Section 6).

Finally, we show experimental results of our analysis (Section 7), discuss related work (Section 8), and conclude (Section 9).

2   Preliminaries

We present notations for CFGs and finite state automata in this section.

2.1   Context-Free Grammar

Definition 1 (context-free grammar). *A CFG is a quadruple $G = (N, T, P, S)$. N denotes a finite set of non-terminals, T a non-empty finite set of terminals, $P \subseteq N \times (N \cup T)^*$ a finite set of production rules, and $S \in N$ the initial non-terminal.*

Let V denote the set of vocabulary symbols $N \cup T$ where $N \cap T = \varnothing$. We use A, B, C for non-terminals and u, v, w for vocabulary strings. We write a production rule $(A, u) \in P$ as $A \to u \in P$.

Definition 2 (one-step derivation). *For $uAw \in V^*$, if $A \to v \in P$, we have:*

$$uAw \Rightarrow uvw.$$

Definition 3 (derivation relation). *The derivation relation on vocabulary strings, which is the reflexive and transitive closure of $\Rightarrow$, is denoted by $\Rightarrow^*$. If $u \Rightarrow^* v$, we say u derives to v.*

Definition 4 (language of $\mathcal{G}$). *Given a CFG $\mathcal{G} = (\mathcal{N}, \mathcal{T}, \mathcal{P}, \mathcal{S})$, the language of the grammar $\mathcal{L}(\mathcal{G})$ is:*

$$\mathcal{L}(\mathcal{G}) = \{w \in \mathcal{T}^* \mid \mathcal{S} \Rightarrow^* w\}.$$

We generalize the definition for the language of a vocabulary string $u \in \mathcal{V}^*$:

$$\mathcal{L}(u) = \{w \in \mathcal{T}^* \mid u \Rightarrow^* w\}.$$

So, we have $\mathcal{L}(\mathcal{G}) = \mathcal{L}(\mathcal{S})$.

2.2 Finite State Automaton

Definition 5 (finite state automaton). *A finite state automaton (henceforth, FSA) is a quintuple $\mathcal{A} = (\Sigma, \mathcal{I}, \delta, \sigma, \mathcal{F})$. Σ denotes a finite set of states, $\mathcal{I}$ a finite set of input symbols, $\delta \subseteq \Sigma \times (\{\varepsilon\} \cup \mathcal{I}) \times \Sigma$ a transition relation, σ the initial state, and $\mathcal{F} \subseteq \Sigma$ a set of accepting states.*

We write a transition $(\sigma_1, i, \sigma_2) \in \delta$ as $\sigma_1 \overset{i}{\mapsto} \sigma_2 \in \delta$.

3 Grammatical Summary Inference

For our grammatical summary analysis, we are given a reference CFG $\mathcal{G} = (\mathcal{N}, \mathcal{T}, \mathcal{P}, \mathcal{S})$ and use vocabulary strings of $\mathcal{G}$ as abstractions of string values.

3.1 Galois Connection

First, we describe the relation between string values and grammatical summaries. The target of abstraction is a subset of $\mathcal{T}^*$ since a string expression can have multiple string values during program executions. A vocabulary string $u \in \mathcal{V}^*$ is a summary of $S \subseteq \mathcal{T}^*$ if u derives to each $v \in S$. Note the following two characteristics of grammatical summaries:

- A set $S \subseteq \mathcal{T}^*$ may have multiple grammatical summaries.
- If $S_1 \subseteq S_2 \subseteq \mathcal{T}^*$, the set of summaries of S_2 is a subset of that of S_1.

Therefore, we choose the abstract domain as $(\wp(\mathcal{V}^*), \supseteq)$, and obtain the following Galois connection:

Theorem 1. $(\wp(\mathcal{T}^*), \subseteq) \xleftrightarrow[\alpha]{\gamma} (\wp(\mathcal{V}^*), \supseteq)$ *holds where:*

$$\alpha(S) = \{u \in \mathcal{V}^* \mid \forall v \in S. \ u \Rightarrow^* v\} = \{u \in \mathcal{V}^* \mid S \subseteq \mathcal{L}(u)\}, \ and$$
$$\gamma(U) = \{v \in \mathcal{T}^* \mid \forall u \in U. \ u \Rightarrow^* v\} = \bigcap_{u \in U} \mathcal{L}(u).$$

Notice that the order of the abstract domain is opposite to that of the concrete domain. We denote $\supseteq$, $\cap$, $\cup$, $\mathcal{V}^*$ and $\varnothing$ in the abstract domain by $\sqsubseteq$, $\sqcup$, $\sqcap$, $\bot$ and $\top$, respectively. This notation reduces the confusion with the operations and elements in the concrete and abstract domains and makes the adjoint functions monotone.

We introduce the *upperset* operator "↑" to partially reduce abstract values.

Definition 6 (upperset). *For $U \subseteq \mathcal{V}^*$, the upperset of U according to the grammar derivation relation, denoted by $U\uparrow$, is $\{v \in \mathcal{V}^* \mid \exists u \in U.\ v \Rightarrow^* u\}$.*

We use the notation "↑" since it adds all the *upwardly reachable elements* from U regarding the derivation relation as a pre-order. This operator is monotone, idempotent and reductive. Particularly, although $U\uparrow \subseteq U$, $\gamma(U\uparrow) = \gamma(U)$ holds. The additional vocabulary strings in $U\uparrow$ do not increase the precision of the concretization because their languages are always supersets of those of some vocabulary strings in U. Also note that the upperset operator is not equivalent to the lower closure operator, and it only partially reduces an abstract value towards its lower closure. This operator is crucial for the design and precision of our analysis. It also has an interesting algorithmic counterpart as you will see in Section 4.

3.2   Abstract Operations

Abstraction of String Literals. We abstract string literal expressions in programs using the upperset operator. The set of possible string values of a string literal expression $v \in \mathcal{T}^*$ is $\{v\}$. Thus, we abstract $\{v\}$ for the string literal:

$$\alpha(\{v\}) = \{u \in \mathcal{V}^* \mid \forall v' \in \{v\}.\ u \Rightarrow^* v'\}$$
$$= \{u \in \mathcal{V}^* \mid \exists v' \in \{v\}.\ u \Rightarrow^* v'\} = \{v\}\uparrow,$$

which means the set of all vocabulary strings that can derive v.

Join and Order. The join operation and order checking correspond to the set intersection operation and inclusion checking, respectively, since the order is simply the superset relation on sets. The following properties can be used to avoid some upperset operations.

Fact 1. *For $U_1, U_2 \subseteq \mathcal{V}^*$,*

- $U_1\uparrow \sqcup U_2\uparrow$ *is also an upperset.*
- $U_1\uparrow \subseteq U_2\uparrow$ *if and only if $U_1\uparrow \subseteq U_2$.*

Concatenation. String concatenation is one of the most frequent operations in programs of our interest. For $U_1, U_2 \in \wp(\mathcal{V}^*)$, our abstract concatenation operation '$\odot$' is:

$$U_1 \odot U_2 = \begin{cases} (U_1 \cdot U_2)\uparrow & \text{if } U_1 \neq \bot \wedge U_2 \neq \bot \\ \bot & \text{otherwise} \end{cases} \tag{1}$$

where '$\cdot$' denotes the collection of pairwise concatenations of two vocabulary strings from each set.

Lemma 1. *The operation '$\odot$' is monotone and a sound abstraction of the concrete concatenation '$\cdot$' on $(\wp(\mathcal{T}^*), \subseteq)$. The soundness is,*

$$\forall U_1, U_2 \in \wp(\mathcal{V}^*), \gamma(U_1) \cdot \gamma(U_2) \subseteq \gamma(U_1 \odot U_2).$$

3.3   Remarks on Inferring Grammatical Summaries

Our analysis is general in two aspects:

- Our analysis can also verify string expressions whose string values should be complete sentences using the special summary S. Assume that, for $S \subseteq \mathcal{T}^*$, $\alpha(S) \sqsubseteq U$ which means that U is a set of summaries of S. Then, for $u \in U$, we have $S \subseteq \mathcal{L}(u)$ from $S \subseteq \gamma(U) \subseteq \mathcal{L}(u)$. When $S \in U$, we can guarantee that all the strings in S are valid sentences of $\mathcal{G}$.
- Our analysis can accept any CFGs regardless of whether they are ambiguous or non-deterministic. It is often delicate to rewrite a grammar to make it unambiguous, deterministic or $LR(k)$. It is particularly difficult when the grammar specification is at character level instead of lexical token level. On the other hand, in our analysis we can specify reference grammars at character level without such concerns. Character-level grammars are particularly useful when we have to deal with strings with partial tokens.

Our analysis does not have precision changes with minor changes in programs:

- Splitting a long string literal into several concatenated string literals and vice versa do not affect the analysis precision. Because, for any $u_1, u_2 \in \mathcal{T}^*$, $\alpha(\{u_1\}) \odot \alpha(\{u_2\}) = \alpha(\{u_1\} \cdot \{u_2\})$.
- Since our concatenation operation is associative, changing the order of concatenations does not affect the analysis precision.

4   Finite Representation and Algorithm

In this section, we describe how we achieve a *computable* analysis from the mathematical design of our summary inference analysis described in Section 3. We first point out the problem of an infinite number of summaries, and we remedy the problem by using FSAs whose alphabets are $\mathcal{V}$, and a CFL-reachability closure algorithm for computing uppersets.

4.1   Problem of an Infinite Number of Summaries

The analysis described in Section 3 often leads to an infinite number of summaries when the reference grammar has epsilon production rules. Assume the reference grammar has a production rule, $A \rightarrow \varepsilon$. Then, for any non-empty $U \subseteq \mathcal{V}^*$, $U\uparrow$ is infinite because for $u \in U$, $U\uparrow$ also should contain uA, uAA, $uAAA$, and so on.

While transforming the grammar with the epsilon elimination algorithm may be a possible solution to the problem, it may result in undesirable precision loss for frequent patterns of string constructions. Consider the program in Figure 1 again. Using the grammar in Figure 2 our analysis infers $\langle \text{TRS} \rangle$ as a summary of x before line 3. This is possible since $\langle \text{TRS} \rangle$ is a summary of the empty string. However, if we apply epsilon elimination to the grammar, $\langle \text{TRS} \rangle$ cannot derive the empty string and is no loner a summary of x before line 3. Since such string constructions are frequent, we should find a way to use the grammar with epsilon production rules as it is.

Algorithm 1. CFL-reachability closure of an FSA using $\mathcal{G} = (\mathcal{N}, \mathcal{T}, \mathcal{P}, \mathcal{S})$

---

input : $\mathcal{A} = (\Sigma, \mathcal{V}, \delta, \sigma, \mathcal{F})$
output: $Clos_\mathcal{G}(\mathcal{A})$
$\delta' := \delta$
repeat
   foreach $(\sigma_0, \sigma_n \in \Sigma, A \to u_1 \cdots u_n \in \mathcal{P})$ **do**
      if $\exists \sigma_1, \ldots, \sigma_{n-1}. \ \forall i \in \{0, \ldots, n-1\}. \ \sigma_i \overset{u_{i+1}}{\mapsto} \sigma_{i+1} \in \delta'$ **then**
         $\delta' := \delta' \cup \{\sigma_0 \overset{A}{\mapsto} \sigma_n\}$
      end
   end
until δ' *has not changed*
return $(\Sigma, \mathcal{V}, \delta', \sigma, \mathcal{F})$

4.2 FSA Representation and CFL Reachability

To remedy the problem, we choose to focus on regular sets in the abstract domain and use FSAs to represent abstract values. FSAs are convenient finite representation for regular sets which include some infinite sets. The downside of this decision is that we cannot make use of the entire abstract domain $(\mathcal{P}(\mathcal{V}^*), \subseteq)$. However, this compromise is essential to any finite representation for the abstract domain since the domain is uncountable. From now on, we allow FSAs or regular expressions to denote abstract values.

As a side note, more powerful representations do not help our analysis much. In fact, the abstractions of string literals, the results of join and abstract concatenation of regular sets are all regular. The regularity of an abstract value itself does not mean that it cannot express context-free properties. For example, an FSA representing $\{\mathcal{S}\}$ asserts that its corresponding set of string values are sentences of the CFG. Our usage of $\mathcal{V}$ for input symbols of FSAs is crucial for the expressive power and distinguishes our work from other string analyses using FSAs [22,25,24]. On the other hand, if we use more powerful representations like push-down automata, the operations including order decision will become expensive or even undecidable.

We can compute the upperset of a regular set by a CFL-reachability algorithm [16,19,13,20] on the FSA. Algorithm 1 shows how to compute the CFL-reachability closure of an FSA $\mathcal{A}$ using $\mathcal{G}$, which we denote by $Clos_\mathcal{G}(\mathcal{A})$. Essentially, the algorithm repeatedly finds out paths in the FSA corresponding to right-hand sides of production rules, and adds shortcut non-terminal edges. More specifically, for some $A \to v \in \mathcal{P}$ and a path from σ_0 to σ_n labeled with v, we add an edge from σ_0 to σ_n labeled with A. Note that the length of a path can be 0, in which case the path label is ε. The following Theorem 2 shows the equivalence of our CFL-reachability algorithm on FSAs and the upperset operation on regular sets.

Theorem 2. *For FSA* $\mathcal{A} = (\Sigma, \mathcal{V}, \delta, \sigma, \mathcal{F})$ *and* $U \subseteq \mathcal{V}^*$,

$$\text{if } \mathcal{L}(\mathcal{A}) = U \text{ then } \mathcal{L}(Clos_\mathcal{G}(\mathcal{A})) = U\uparrow.$$

Proof. We prove the following bidirectional inclusion relations:

- Case $\mathcal{L}(Clos_G(\mathcal{A})) \subseteq U\uparrow$:

  Let $\mathcal{A}_i$ be the automaton after adding i shortcut edges to $\mathcal{A}$. We prove $\forall i \in \mathbb{N}. \mathcal{L}(\mathcal{A}_i) \subseteq U\uparrow$ by induction. For $i = 0$, from $\mathcal{A}_0 = \mathcal{A}$ and the assumption, we have $\mathcal{L}(\mathcal{A}_0) = U \subseteq U\uparrow$. For $i = j + 1$, assume $\mathcal{L}(\mathcal{A}_j) \subseteq U\uparrow$. $\mathcal{A}_i$ may have one additional transition $\sigma_0 \overset{A}{\mapsto} \sigma_n$ for some production rule $A \to u \in \mathcal{P}$ and some path from σ_0 to σ_n labeled by u in $\mathcal{A}_j$. For $v \in \mathcal{A}_i$, $\mathcal{A}_i$ may use the new transition to accept it. So, we have $v = v_1 A v_2 A \cdots v_n$ and $v' = v_1 u v_2 u \cdots v_n \in \mathcal{L}(\mathcal{A}_j)$. From $v' \in U\uparrow$ and the property of the upperset, we have $v \in U\uparrow$. Therefore, $\mathcal{L}(\mathcal{A}_i) \subseteq U\uparrow$ holds. Finally, since $Clos_G(\mathcal{A})$ is $\mathcal{A}_n$ for some n, we have $\mathcal{L}(Clos_G(\mathcal{A})) \subseteq U\uparrow$.

- Case $\mathcal{L}(Clos_G(\mathcal{A})) \supseteq U\uparrow$:

  Let $u \in U\uparrow$. There exists some $v \in U$ such that $u \Rightarrow^* v$. From $\mathcal{L}(\mathcal{A}) = U$, we can find a path in $\mathcal{A}$ that accepts v. If we draw all the additional transitions of $Clos_G(\mathcal{A})$ on the path, we find a path that represents u. Thus, $u \in \mathcal{L}(Clos_G(\mathcal{A}))$. Therefore, $\mathcal{L}(Clos_G(\mathcal{A})) \supseteq U\uparrow$.   □

4.3   Abstract Operations with FSA Representation

Now, we can perform the required operations in Section 3.2 using basic FSA operations and $Clos_G$.

Abstraction of String Literals For a string literal v, we construct a linear automaton $\mathcal{A}$ that accepts only v and apply $Clos_G$ on $\mathcal{A}$.

Join and Order We use the intersection of FSAs for join and the FSA language inclusion checking for order decision.

Concatenation To compute Equation (1), we first concatenate two operand FSAs, and apply $Clos_G$ on the concatenated FSA.

Widening In addition to the usual operations, we require a widening operator to guarantee termination. Because the height of the domain $(\wp(\mathcal{V}^*), \sqsubseteq)$ restricted to regular sets is infinite, analyzing a loop may not converge in a finite number of iterations. Consider the following program with production rules $A \to \mathtt{a}$ and $B \to \mathtt{b} \mid \varepsilon$:

```
x = "a";
while (?) x = x . "b";
output x;
```

At the start of the loop body, the abstract value of x is $B^*(\mathtt{a}|A)B^*(\mathtt{b}|B)^n B^*$ after $n \geq 0$ iterations, which makes the analysis diverge.

We present a simple widening operator as an example.

Definition 7. *For $\mathcal{A}_1$ and $\mathcal{A}_2$, we let $\mathcal{A}_1 \triangledown \mathcal{A}_2 \triangleq \mathcal{A}_1' \sqcup \mathcal{A}_2$ where $\mathcal{A}_1'$ is obtained by eliminating all edges of $\mathcal{A}_1$ that are in any cyclic paths.*

Lemma 2. ∇ *is a widening operator for regular sets in* $(\wp(\mathcal{V}^*), \sqsubseteq)$.

Proof. Since $\mathcal{A}_1 \sqsubseteq \mathcal{A}_1'$, $\mathcal{A}_1 \sqcup \mathcal{A}_2 \sqsubseteq \mathcal{A}_1 \nabla \mathcal{A}_2$ holds. As $\mathcal{A}_1'$ does not have any cyclic paths, $\mathcal{L}(\mathcal{A}_1')$ is finite. Therefore, by accumulating values to $\mathcal{A}_1'$ using ∇, the value cannot increase infinitely many times in the abstract domain.   □

One can define more advanced widening operators as well.

5   Extended CFG

To make it easy to specify grammars and to reduce grammatical biases, we extend the analysis to use extended CFGs (ECFGs). An ECFG $\mathcal{G}$ is composed of $(\mathcal{N}, \mathcal{T}, \mathcal{P}, \mathcal{S})$ where $\mathcal{P}$ is a function from $\mathcal{N}$ to regular expressions over $\mathcal{V}$. Using ECFGs has the following benefits:

- Regular expressions on the right-hand sides of production rules help specify reference grammars succinctly. For example, the HTML DTD uses regular expressions to specify possible children nodes, and scannerless grammars use regular expressions to describe lexical tokens. If we use an ordinary CFG for such cases, the grammar becomes verbose and error prone.
- The Kleene closure in ECFGs removes some biases that could have existed in ordinary CFG specifications. To describe a sequence of non-terminals, CFGs may have production rules that generate sequences in either a right- or left-recursive way. This bias makes the analysis fail on programs that construct sequences in the opposite way. On the contrary, by using the Kleene closure, we can describe sequences concisely without biases and obtain better precision for either way of construction.

5.1   CFL-Reachability Algorithm Using ECFGs

We compute the CFL reachability closure of an FSA using an ECFG $\mathcal{G} = (\mathcal{N}, \mathcal{T}, \mathcal{P}, \mathcal{S})$ by $EClos_{\mathcal{G}}$, whose naïve implementation is shown in Algorithm 2. The algorithm first constructs FSA $\mathcal{A}_A = (\Sigma_A, \mathcal{V}, \delta_A, \sigma_A, \mathcal{F}_A)$ for each $A \in \mathcal{N}$ from the regular expression $\mathcal{P}(A)$. We call those automata *ECFG automata*. The algorithm uses ECFG automata instead of the regular expressions. Applying $EClos_{\mathcal{G}}$ amounts to using $Clos_{\mathcal{G}'}$ where $\mathcal{G}' = (\mathcal{N}', \mathcal{T}, \mathcal{P}', \mathcal{S})$ is defined as follows.

- $\mathcal{N}' = \mathcal{N} \cup \{[\sigma_1, \sigma_2] \mid \exists A \in \mathcal{N}.\ \sigma_1, \sigma_2 \in \Sigma_A\}$. We call $[\sigma_1, \sigma_2] \in \mathcal{N}' \setminus \mathcal{N}$ a *state pair* and a transition labeled with it a *state pair edge*.
- $\mathcal{P}'$ contains the following production rules:
  - $[\sigma_1, \sigma_1] \rightarrow \varepsilon$ for $A \in \mathcal{N}$ and $\sigma_1 \in \Sigma_A$
  - $[\sigma_1, \sigma_2] \rightarrow u$ for $A \in \mathcal{N}$ and $\sigma_1 \overset{u}{\mapsto} \sigma_2 \in \delta_A$
  - $[\sigma_1, \sigma_3] \rightarrow [\sigma_1, \sigma_2][\sigma_2, \sigma_3]$ for $A \in \mathcal{N}$ and $\sigma_1, \sigma_2, \sigma_3 \in \Sigma_A$
  - $A \rightarrow [\sigma_A, \sigma_1]$ for $A \in \mathcal{N}$ and $\sigma_1 \in \mathcal{F}_A$

Algorithm 2. CFL-reachability closure of an FSA using ECFG $\mathcal{G} = (\mathcal{N}, \mathcal{T}, \mathcal{P}, \mathcal{S})$

---

input : $\mathcal{A} = (\Sigma, \mathcal{V}, \delta, \sigma, \mathcal{F})$
output: $EClos_\mathcal{G}(\mathcal{A})$

$\delta' := \delta$
foreach $A \in \mathcal{N}$ **do**
   | construct $\mathcal{A}_A = (\Sigma_A, \mathcal{V}, \delta_A, \sigma_A, \mathcal{F}_A)$ s.t. $\mathcal{L}(\mathcal{A}_A) = \mathcal{L}(\mathcal{P}(A))$
end
foreach $(\sigma' \in \Sigma,\ A \in \mathcal{N},\ \sigma_1 \in \Sigma_A)$ **do**
   | $\delta' := \delta' \cup \{\sigma' \overset{[\sigma_1, \sigma_1]}{\mapsto} \sigma'\}$
end
repeat
   | **foreach** $(A \in \mathcal{N}, \sigma_1, \sigma_2 \in \Sigma_A, X \in \mathcal{V} \cup \{\varepsilon\}, \sigma'_1, \sigma'_2 \in \Sigma)$ **do**
      | **if** $\sigma_1 \overset{X}{\mapsto} \sigma_2 \in \delta_A$ *and* $\sigma'_1 \overset{X}{\mapsto} \sigma'_2 \in \delta'$ **then**
         | $\delta' := \delta' \cup \{\sigma'_1 \overset{[\sigma_1, \sigma_2]}{\mapsto} \sigma'_2\}$
      | **end**
   | **end**
   | **foreach** $(A \in \mathcal{N}, \sigma_1, \sigma_2, \sigma_3, \in \Sigma_A, \sigma'_1, \sigma'_2, \sigma'_3 \in \Sigma)$ **do**
      | **if** $\sigma'_1 \overset{[\sigma_1, \sigma_2]}{\mapsto} \sigma'_2$ *and* $\sigma'_2 \overset{[\sigma_2, \sigma_3]}{\mapsto} \sigma'_3 \in \delta'$ **then**
         | $\delta' := \delta' \cup \{\sigma'_1 \overset{[\sigma_1, \sigma_3]}{\mapsto} \sigma'_3\}$
      | **end**
   | **end**
   | **foreach** $(A \in \mathcal{N}, \sigma_F \in \mathcal{F}_A, \sigma'_1, \sigma'_2 \in \Sigma)$ **do**
      | **if** $\sigma'_1 \overset{[\sigma_A, \sigma_F]}{\mapsto} \sigma'_2 \in \delta'$ **then**
         | $\delta' := \delta' \cup \{\sigma'_1 \overset{A}{\mapsto} \sigma'_2\}$
      | **end**
   | **end**
until δ' *has not changed*

   foreach $A \in \mathcal{N}, \sigma_1, \sigma_2 \in \Sigma_A, \sigma'_1, \sigma'_2 \in \Sigma$ **do**
      | $\delta' := \delta' \setminus \{\sigma'_1 \overset{[\sigma_1, \sigma_2]}{\mapsto} \sigma'_2\}$
   end

return $(\Sigma, \mathcal{V}, \delta', \sigma, \mathcal{F})$

Although there is nothing theoretically interesting regarding ECFGs and $EClos_\mathcal{G}$, ECFG automata representation is more succinct than the derived CFG $\mathcal{G}'$ and $EClos_\mathcal{G}$ can work more efficiently than $Clos_{\mathcal{G}'}$.

The complexity of $EClos_\mathcal{G}$ is not larger than $O(n^3)$ where $n = |\Sigma|$. In $EClos_\mathcal{G}$, we have to examine paths composed of up to 3 states and this guarantees $O(n^3)$. In fact, in most cases we can sort the states of $\mathcal{A}$ in a topological order, and could have used a sub-cubic algorithm based on Valiant's technique [18]. However, we use a worklist-based algorithm which guarantees $O(n^3)$ for simplicity.

5.2   Preserving State Pair Edges

In the algorithm $EClos_G$, we keep *state pair* edges to avoid redundant work. Since state pair edges are just intermediate edges and originally not essential, one may eliminate them as in the boxed region of Algorithm 2. However, eagerly removing them leads to redundant computations. For example, to concatenate two string literals, we first abstract each string literal adding state pair edges. If we remove the state pair edges from the resulting abstract values right away, we should reconstruct the same edges during the abstract concatenation. Thus, we keep those edges to avoid redundant work.

More interestingly, preserving state pair edges often improves analysis precision because they enrich the abstract domain. Consider the following example with a production rule $A \rightarrow ac \mid bc$:

```
if (?) x = "a"; else x = "b";
x = x . "c";
```

Since the final value of x is either ac or bc, we can summarize it as A. Now let us apply our analysis. Assume we obtained the following ECFG automaton $\mathcal{A}_A$.

$$\text{start} \longrightarrow (\sigma_0) \xrightarrow{a,b} (\sigma_1) \xrightarrow{c} ((\sigma_2))$$

1. If we eliminate the state pair edges, we cannot verify the program. In this case, the vocabulary symbols that we can utilize are $\{a, b, c, A\}$. Then, the abstract value of x after the conditional is ⊤ because there is no vocabulary string that can derive both a and b.
2. On the other hand, we can verify the program if we keep state pair edges. In this case, we can also regard the state pairs such as $[\sigma_0, \sigma_1]$, $[\sigma_1, \sigma_2]$ and $[\sigma_0, \sigma_2]$ as non-terminals. Then, the abstract value of x after the conditional contains $[\sigma_0, \sigma_1]$ since it is a common summary of both $\{a\}$ and $\{b\}$. After we append the abstraction of $\{c\}$ which contains $[\sigma_1, \sigma_2]$, we can successfully infer $[\sigma_0, \sigma_2]$ and A as summaries of the final x.

In addition, for better efficiency and precision, we use minimized FSAs for ECFG automata. Smaller ECFG automata may reduce the computation of the $EClos_G$ algorithm. Also, the less states ECFG automata have, the more likely we find common summaries during the join operation. For the previous example, we could have used the following automaton for $\mathcal{A}_A$:

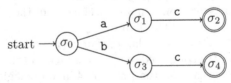

If we use this automaton, we cannot analyze the program even when we keep the state pair edges. We observed that minimized ECFG automata often provide better analysis results than larger ones, although they do not guarantee the best precision.

6   Implementation of Grammatical Summary Inference

In this section, we describe our analysis implementation and several optimization techniques that make our analysis tractable.

6.1   Integration into SAFE

We have implemented our analysis in the SAFE framework [9,12]. The SAFE framework is a general analysis framework for JavaScript, which is designed to be pluggable in the sense that SAFE provides a default type analysis based on abstract interpretation, and one can replace the analysis at his or her disposal. The default type analysis uses a variant of the constant string domain from [8]. In theory, our analysis may subsume the precision of the original domain if we add appropriate production rules. However, because several components of the framework such as object property accesses depend on the original string domain, we have plugged our grammatical summary domain in conjunction with the original domain without replacing the original one.

Our analysis also infers summaries of abstract numbers in string contexts. JavaScript code often use numbers in string contexts as shown by width below:

$$\text{'width="' + width + '" height="'} \tag{2}$$

The number abstract domain is also a constant domain with some special abstract values [8]. When our analysis requires summaries of an abstract number representing a constant, we compute its summaries on the fly. For abstract numbers representing non-constants, we pre-compute and use their summaries obtained by abstracting their possible string representations.

6.2   Optimization Techniques

Deferring Abstraction. We defer abstraction of singleton string values until join or widening operations. This optimization is effective for the following two cases:

- While JavaScript property accesses often use string literals for property names, those string literals evaporate after the accesses. Thus, we avoid inferring summaries of them.
- For a series of concatenations of n string literals, if we defer the abstraction and apply CFL reachability only for the final result, the number of applying CFL reachability reduces from $2n - 1$ to 1.

After the analysis, if the abstract value of a string expression whose abstraction is deferred is queried, we should apply CFL reachability to get its summaries.

Using Two-level Grammars. To infer summaries even for string values that have partial lexical tokens, we specify ECFGs at the character level rather than at the token level. As the expression in (2) shows, JavaScript programs often use partial string tokens. By specifying ECFGs at the character level, we can infer summaries for `'width="'` and `'" height="'`. However, such a precision improvement comes with a performance burden.

To alleviate the performance problem, we first prepare a two-level grammar from a given reference grammar. We first rewrite the grammar so that the right-hand side of each production rule uses either only terminals or only non-terminals. This task is almost mechanical: we replace terminal parts of right-hand sides with new non-terminals and add new production rules deriving the terminal parts. Let the rewritten grammar be $\mathcal{G} = (\mathcal{N}, \mathcal{T}, \mathcal{P}, \mathcal{S})$. The two-level grammar consists of two sub-grammars $\mathcal{G}_1$ and $\mathcal{G}_2$. $\mathcal{G}_1$ is $(\mathcal{N}_1, \mathcal{T}, \mathcal{P}_1, -)$ [1] where $\mathcal{N}_1$ is non-terminals of $\mathcal{G}$ whose right-hand sides use only terminals and $\mathcal{P}_1 = \mathcal{P}|_{\mathcal{N}_1}$. $\mathcal{G}_2$ is $(\mathcal{N}_2, \mathcal{N}_1, \mathcal{P}_2, \mathcal{S})$ where $\mathcal{N}_2 = \mathcal{N} \setminus \mathcal{N}_1$ and $\mathcal{P}_2 = \mathcal{P}|_{\mathcal{N}_2}$. Then, $\mathcal{G}_1$ serves as a lexical token specification of $\mathcal{G}$ and $\mathcal{G}_2$ is a token-level grammar.

Using the two-level grammar, we use two-staged algorithms for string literal abstraction and concatenation. The first stage of each algorithm that uses $\mathcal{G}_1$ is as follows.

- Abstraction of string literals: We use $\mathcal{G}_1$ to selectively add (possibly partial) token edges by mimicking a *longest match strategy* of conventional lexers. A detailed description of the algorithm is shown in Algorithm 3. The complexity of Algorithm 3 is largely due to token suffixes at the starts of literals, token prefixes at the ends of literals, and partial tokens that encompass entire literals. Except that, we use the longest match strategy: if edges $\sigma_k \overset{T_1}{\mapsto} \sigma_l$ and $\sigma_k \overset{T_2}{\mapsto} \sigma_m$ are possible where $k > 0$, $T_1, T_2 \in \mathcal{N}_1$, and $l < m$, we add only $\sigma_k \overset{T_2}{\mapsto} \sigma_m$. Also, to add an edge labeled by $T_2 \in \mathcal{N}_1$ starting at σ_k ($k > 0$), there must be a previously added edge incoming to σ_k representing (suffix of) T_1 where T_1 *can be followed by* T_2, in the sense that there exists $A \in \mathcal{N}_2$ such that $A \Rightarrow^* uT_1T_2v$ for some $u, v \in \mathcal{V}^*$. After applying Algorithm 3, we remove all the terminal edges from the automaton.
- Concatenation: We concatenate two automata representing operands, and apply CFL reachability using $\mathcal{G}_1$ to find tokens that became complete. We remove state pair edges of $\mathcal{G}_1$ that are not at the beginning or end of the concatenated automaton because we allow partial tokens only at boundaries.

The second stage is CFL reachability using $\mathcal{G}_2$ as usual.

Keeping Only Relevant Summaries. During the analysis, we choose to keep only state pair edges in the abstract values. The impact of removing non-terminal edges is not critical because of two reasons. First, we have state pairs that are more specific than usual non-terminals. For example, for a non-terminal A, we have several state pairs refining A: the language of $[\sigma_A, \sigma_1]$ where $\sigma_1 \in \mathcal{F}_A$ is a

---

[1] Since we do not use the initial non-terminal of $\mathcal{G}_1$, we leave it unspecified.

Algorithm 3. Addition of (possibly partial) token edges using a longest match strategy.

---

input : $\mathcal{A} = (\Sigma, \mathcal{V}, \delta, \sigma_0, \{\sigma_n\})$ where
$\quad \Sigma = \{\sigma_0, \cdots, \sigma_n\}$ and
$\quad \delta = \{\sigma_0 \overset{a_1}{\mapsto} \sigma_1, \cdots, \sigma_{n-1} \overset{a_n}{\mapsto} \sigma_n\}$ for $a_1 \cdots a_n \in \mathcal{T}^*$
output: An automaton accepting (partial) token strings.

$\delta' := \delta$
$W := \varnothing$
$P := [\overbrace{\varnothing, \varnothing, \cdots, \varnothing}^{n}]$
foreach $T \in \mathcal{N}_1, s \in \Sigma_T$ **do**
$\quad N := \varnothing$
$\quad \ell := 0$
$\quad t := s$
$\quad$ **while** $\ell < n \wedge \exists t'. t \overset{a_{\ell+1}}{\mapsto} t' \in \delta_T$ **do**
$\quad\quad \ell := \ell + 1$
$\quad\quad t := t'$
$\quad\quad$ **if** $t \in \mathcal{F}_T$ **then**
$\quad\quad\quad N := \varnothing$
$\quad\quad\quad$ **if** $s = \sigma_T$ **then**
$\quad\quad\quad\quad N := N \cup \{\sigma_0 \overset{T}{\mapsto} \sigma_\ell\}$
$\quad\quad\quad$ **end**
$\quad\quad\quad$ **if** s has an incoming edge **then**
$\quad\quad\quad\quad N := N \cup \{\sigma_0 \overset{[s,t]}{\mapsto} \sigma_\ell\}$
$\quad\quad\quad$ **end**
$\quad\quad$ **end**
$\quad$ **end**
$\quad$ **if** $\ell = n \wedge t$ has an outgoing edge **then**
$\quad\quad N := N \cup \{\sigma_0 \overset{[s,t]}{\mapsto} \sigma_\ell\}$
$\quad$ **end**
$\quad$ **foreach** $\sigma_0 \overset{v}{\mapsto} \sigma_\ell \in N$ **do**
$\quad\quad \delta' := \delta' \cup \{\sigma_0 \overset{v}{\mapsto} \sigma_\ell\}$
$\quad\quad$ **if** $\ell < n$ **then**
$\quad\quad\quad P[\ell] := P[\ell] \cup \{T' \in \mathcal{N}_1 \mid$
$\quad\quad\quad\quad \exists A \in \mathcal{N}_2, u, v \in \mathcal{V}^*. A \Rightarrow^* uTT'v\}$
$\quad\quad\quad W := W \cup \{\ell\}$
$\quad\quad$ **end**
$\quad$ **end**
end

while $W \neq \varnothing$ **do**
$\quad k := \min\{i \mid \sigma_i \in W\}$
$\quad W := W \setminus \{\sigma_k\}$
$\quad \ell := k$
$\quad S := \{(T, \sigma_T) \mid T \in P[k]\}$
$\quad N := \varnothing$
$\quad$ **while** $\ell < n \wedge S \neq \varnothing$ **do**
$\quad\quad S' := \varnothing$
$\quad\quad$ **foreach** $(T, t) \in S$ **do**
$\quad\quad\quad$ **if** $\exists t'. t \overset{a_{\ell+1}}{\mapsto} t' \in \delta_T$ **then**
$\quad\quad\quad\quad S' := S' \cup \{(T, t')\}$
$\quad\quad\quad$ **end**
$\quad\quad$ **end**
$\quad\quad S := S'$
$\quad\quad \ell := \ell + 1$
$\quad\quad$ **if** $\exists (T, t) \in S. t \in \mathcal{F}_T$ **then**
$\quad\quad\quad N := \varnothing$
$\quad\quad\quad$ **foreach** $(T, t) \in S$ **do**
$\quad\quad\quad\quad$ **if** $t \in \mathcal{F}_T$ **then**
$\quad\quad\quad\quad\quad N := N \cup \{\sigma_k \overset{T}{\mapsto} \sigma_\ell\}$
$\quad\quad\quad\quad$ **end**
$\quad\quad\quad$ **end**
$\quad\quad$ **end**
$\quad$ **end**
$\quad$ **if** $\ell = n$ **then**
$\quad\quad$ **foreach** $(T, t) \in S$ **do**
$\quad\quad\quad$ **if** t has an outgoing edge **then**
$\quad\quad\quad\quad N := N \cup \{\sigma_k \overset{[\sigma_T, t]}{\mapsto} \sigma_\ell\}$
$\quad\quad\quad$ **end**
$\quad\quad$ **end**
$\quad$ **end**
$\quad \delta' := \delta' \cup N$
$\quad$ **foreach** $\sigma_k \overset{T}{\mapsto} \sigma_\ell \in N$ where $T \in \mathcal{N}_1$ **do**
$\quad\quad$ **if** $\ell < n$ **then**
$\quad\quad\quad P[\ell] := P[\ell] \cup \{T' \in \mathcal{N}_1 \mid$
$\quad\quad\quad\quad \exists A \in \mathcal{N}_2, u, v \in \mathcal{V}^*. A \Rightarrow^* uTT'v\}$
$\quad\quad\quad W := W \cup \{\ell\}$
$\quad\quad$ **end**
$\quad$ **end**
end
return $(\Sigma, \mathcal{V}, \delta', \sigma_0, \{\sigma_n\})$

subset of that of A, and the union of the languages is $\mathcal{L}(A)$. Second, if there is only A transition from σ_1 to σ_2 in some ECFG automaton, we can reconstruct A from $[\sigma_1, \sigma_2]$.

Among the sequences of state pairs, some are verbose or invalid. If an abstract value contains $\phi_1[\sigma_1, \sigma_2][\sigma_2, \sigma_3]\phi_2$, its closure also contains $\phi_1[\sigma_1, \sigma_3]\phi_2$, where the latter is more succinct. Some sequence of state pair edges may be invalid under a given reference grammar. For example, when a reference grammar is an HTML grammar, if $[\sigma_1, \sigma_2]$ is a state pair from **body** and $[\sigma_3, \sigma_4]$ is from **head**, $\phi_1[\sigma_1, \sigma_2][\sigma_3, \sigma_4]\phi_2$ is invalid because **head** should not follow **body** in HTML documents.

Thus, we define relevant state pair sequences and keep only such sequences:

Definition 8 (Relevant state pair sequence). *A state pair sequence $\phi \neq \varepsilon$ is relevant, if for any decomposition of ϕ into $\phi_1[\sigma_1, \sigma_2][\sigma_3, \sigma_4]\phi_2$, one of the followings holds for some $A \in \mathcal{N}$:*

- *$\sigma_2 \in \mathcal{F}_A$, and σ_3 has an in-edge labeled by A; or*
- *σ_2 has an out-edge labeled by A, and $\sigma_3 = \sigma_A$.*

We construct the *filtering* automaton that accepts the relevant state pair sequences by analyzing the ECFG automata. Then, our analysis intersects abstract values with the filtering automaton to keep only the relevant state pair sequences. The filtering automaton consists of one initial state, one accepting state, and two states $\sigma_{A\nearrow}, \sigma_{A\searrow}$ per each non-terminal $A \in \mathcal{N}$. An edge between the states should have the label $[s_1, s_2]$ satisfying the following restrictions:

- If the edge goes to $\sigma_{A\nearrow}$, then $s_2 \in \mathcal{F}_A$.
- If the edge comes from $\sigma_{A\nearrow}$, then s_1 has an incoming edge labeled by A.
- If the edge goes to $\sigma_{A\searrow}$, then s_2 has an outgoing edge labeled by A.
- If the edge comes from $\sigma_{A\searrow}$, then $s_1 = \sigma_A$
- There is no incoming edge to the initial state.
- There is no outgoing edge from the accepting state.

For instance, an edge from $\sigma_{A\nearrow}$ to $\sigma_{B\searrow}$ must be labeled by $[s_1, s_2]$ where s_1 has an incoming edge labeled by A and s_2 has an outgoing edge labeled by B.

7   Evaluation

We evaluate our analysis in two perspectives: 1) how much optimization techniques improve the analysis performance and 2) how precisely our analysis infers summaries of string expressions in a real-world application. Our experiments ran on a Linux machine with an Intel ® Core™ i7-4770 CPU and 32GB of memory. We used OpenJDK-1.6.0_31 and 2GB of maximum heap space.

Table 1 summarizes the programs and functions used for the evaluation. Note that the numbers of operations include the numbers of string literals, string concatenations and control-flow joins. `table2.js` and `table4.js` are two tiny codes generating HTML tables. `iframe.js` is a program generating an **iframe** element. Finally, `displayCaptPieces`, `displayMovesColumns`,

Table 1. Sizes of the test programs and functions

Program/function	# of lines	# of operations	# of literals	Total length of literals
table2.js	8	8	4	19
table4.js	18	13	6	43
iframe.js	52	67	31	188
displayCaptPieces	16	33	14	84
displayMovesColumns	22	42	17	633
displayMovesParagraph	16	40	15	218
htmlBoard	101	163	64	726

Table 2. Performance improvements with optimization techniques

Program	Baseline	Two-level	Relevant	Both	Speedup
table2.js	59.90s	0.56s	2.44s	0.56s	108x
table4.js	>2h	12.90s	10.67s	0.53s	>13500x
iframe.js	>2h	>2h	24.48s	12.22s	>589x
htmlBoard	>2h	>2h	397.68s	42.58s	>169x

displayMovesParagraph, and htmlBoard are 4 functions that generate HTML fragments in WebChess[2], an open-source web-based chess playing application.

Table 2 shows performance improvements of our analysis by the two major optimization techniques, which are using two-level grammars and keeping only relevant summaries. Using small sample programs, we evaluated the impacts of the optimization techniques by measuring analysis time with timeout of 2 hours. The baseline uses deferring singleton abstraction and other minor optimization techniques such as recording both incoming and outgoing transitions for each state in automata. We used a slightly simplified HTML grammar as a reference grammar; it does not express all tag inclusion and exclusion constraints, and ignores specific attributes allowed for each HTML element. However, it specifies the valid sequences of children elements and their repetition constraints, and the syntax of attributes. With the two optimization techniques, we achieve at least 108 times speedup and get the analysis result in reasonable time.

Keeping only the relevant summaries is crucial for the performance. During the analysis, we occasionally minimize the FSAs, to make them smaller. However, in the experiment, we cannot finish some minimization operations without this technique. Our minimization operation involves determinization of FSAs, which could result in exponentially big FSAs. It turns out that the relevant summaries are shorter than irrelevant summaries, and removing irrelevant ones makes the FSAs smaller before the application of determinization.

Table 3 shows our analysis results for 4 relatively complex JavaScript functions that generate HTML fragments in WebChess. This web application uses the

---

[2] http://webchess.sourceforge.net

Table 3. Analysis of JavaScript functions in WebChess

Function	Time	Notable summaries	Additional techniques
displayCaptPieces	5.92s	(flow entity)$^+$	None
displayMovesColumns	4.93s	(flow entity)$^+$	Unroll the first iteration, assume moves.length > 0.
displayMovesParagraph	7.52s	(flow entity)$^+$	None
htmlBoard	42.58s	table element	Unroll the last iteration.

innerHTML property to draw and update game boards. Our analysis found a bug in htmlBoard that contains the following code fragment:

$$\ldots + \text{'" width='} + \text{borderWidth} + \text{'">\ <\/td><\/tr>'}$$

Note that a double quote is missing after width=. After fixing the bug, our analysis can infer summaries like one or more flow entities and the table element precisely. They show that the functions construct valid fragments of HTML documents. While we show only notable summaries for the final string values due to the space limitation, recall that our analysis can provide summaries for all string expressions in a program.

For some functions, additional analysis techniques such as unrolling some iterations, and providing assumptions on non-string values are required to verify those functions. For example, displayMovesColumns internally builds a table element which contains moves.length number of tr elements. The HTML specification states that the content of a table must contain at least one tr element, and moves.length is guaranteed to be positive in the program. However, since our number domain only keeps track of whether a value is non-negative or not, it cannot capture the fact that moves.length is positive. Thus, we apply additional techniques such as loop unrolling to overcome the limitation of the imprecise number domain. However, if we use a more precise number domain our analysis can verify those functions without such additional techniques.

8 Related Work

String Analyses with References. Several string analyses efficiently check string values according to reference CFGs [11,14,6,15]. They essentially use the same technique developed by Christensen et al. [1] to over-approximate possible string values of a string expression into a CFG. However, they cannot use arbitrary reference CFGs unlike our analysis, and they are less composable with other static analyses because they focus on only string values.

Kim and Choe [10] use a special family of push-down automata as references and provide abstraction of string values that are substrings of reference languages. While their analysis is composable with other string analyses, their abstract values consisting of pairs of stack fragments are more difficult to understand than our grammatical summaries. Also, the complexity of their string literal abstraction is $O(2^n)$ in the worst case while that of our analysis is $O(n^3)$ where n is the length of the string literal.

Minamide [13] presented a PHP analyzer to check dynamically generated web pages by resolving various string validation and sanitization operations as finite transducer applications on CFGs. We are developing a general technique to integrate such operations into string analyses designed in the abstract interpretation framework.

Type Analyses of Dynamically Generated SQL Queries. Cook and Rai [2] represent queries as statically typed objects instead of strings so that they can check ill-formed or ill-typed queries at compile time. However, this approach does not work for scripting languages like PHP, JavaScript and legacy web applications, and manipulating such objects rather than strings to build queries is not intuitive nor convenient for developers familiar with query languages. Gould *et al.* [7] check whether a given program generates SQL queries that belong to a given regular grammar, which is an under-approximated SQL, and then check whether the queries are well-typed. Their analysis requires carefully designed regular languages as references.

String Analyses with FSAs. Researchers have proposed various analyses using FSAs to model string values [22,25,21,24,23]. Their FSAs do not consider reference grammars and do not use non-terminal symbols, while our FSAs use non-terminal symbols to precisely infer grammatical summaries. However, they support string operations like substring, regular replacement, and regular matching using various operations on FSAs. Thus, their analyses are complementary to our analysis in the sense that we can use them to analyze such string operations and abstract the languages of their resulting FSAs to our grammatical summaries.

Non-terminals as Summaries. While Thiemann's type system [17] and the derivability condition of Wassermann and Su [20, Definition 3.2] also use grammatical summaries of string values, they have two notable differences from ours:

– We provide a much richer space for string abstraction. Our abstraction of string values is an element in $\wp(\mathcal{V}^*)$ while theirs is an element in $\mathcal{N}$. Because string values in real-world web applications often represent only partial sentences, non-terminals alone cannot summarize them. Recall the summary "⟨TRS⟩ <tr> ⟨TDS⟩" in Section 1, which is a vocabulary string and not a non-terminal.
– Our analysis is reusable in any analyses based on forward data-flow analyses. However, Thiemann provides a type system for a specific functional language, and Wassermann and Su provide a CFG verification algorithm that is not directly applicable to conventional data-flow analysis frameworks.

9   Conclusion

We design, implement, and optimize an analysis that infers grammatical summaries of string values according to a given reference grammar. Our domain provides a simple but intuitive interpretation and a rich set of abstract values. To make the analysis computable, we use FSAs to represent infinite sets of summaries finitely, and CFL reachability on FSAs to infer a possibly infinite number of summaries. We present several optimization techniques to make the analysis tractable and show their impacts with the experimental results.

We are planning to apply our analysis to more applications. Since our analysis can deal with partial sentences, we can analyze PHP or JSP programs that are not complete or that generate only fragments of HTML documents. By using our analysis in development environments for such PHP or JSP programs, we can either report bugs earlier or provide developers with expected grammatical summaries. Also, while persistence libraries like Hibernate[3] internally build and use database query strings, no existing analysis can verify their well-formedness as far as we know. We expect that our analysis can verify them by analyzing query string construction split in many functions.

References

1. Christensen, A.S., Møller, A., Schwartzbach, M.I.: Precise analysis of string expressions. In: Cousot, R. (ed.) SAS 2003. LNCS, vol. 2694, pp. 1–18. Springer, Heidelberg (2003), http://www.brics.dk/JSA/
2. Cook., W.R., Rai, S.: Safe query objects: Statically typed objects as remotely executable queries. In: Proceedings of the 27th International Conference on Software Engineering (2005)
3. Cousot, P., Cousot, R.: Abstract interpretation: A unified lattice model for static analysis of programs by construction or approximation of fixpoints. In: Proceedings of the 4th ACM Symposium on Principles of Programming Languages (1977)
4. Cousot, P., Cousot, R.: Systematic design of program analysis frameworks. In: Proceedings of the 6th ACM Symposium on Principles of Programming Languages (1979)
5. Cousot, P., Cousot, R.: Abstract interpretation frameworks. Journal of Logic and Computation 2(4), 511–547 (1992)
6. Doh, K.-G., Kim, H., Schmidt, D.A.: Abstract parsing: Static analysis of dynamically generated string output using LR-parsing technology. In: Palsberg, J., Su, Z. (eds.) SAS 2009. LNCS, vol. 5673, pp. 256–272. Springer, Heidelberg (2009)
7. Gould, C., Su, Z., Devanbu, P.T.: Static checking of dynamically generated queries in database applications. In: Proceedings of the 26th International Conference on Software Engineering (2004)
8. Jensen, S.H., Møller, A., Thiemann, P.: Type analysis for JavaScript. In: Palsberg, J., Su, Z. (eds.) SAS 2009. LNCS, vol. 5673, pp. 238–255. Springer, Heidelberg (2009)
9. PLRG @ KAIST. SAFE: Scalable Analysis Framework for ECMAScript, http://safe.kaist.ac.kr
10. Kim, S.-W., Choe, K.-M.: String analysis as an abstract interpretation. In: Jhala, R., Schmidt, D. (eds.) VMCAI 2011. LNCS, vol. 6538, pp. 294–308. Springer, Heidelberg (2011)

---

[3] http://hibernate.org

11. Kirkegaard, C., Møller, A.: Static Analysis for Java Servlets and JSP. In: Yi, K. (ed.) SAS 2006. LNCS, vol. 4134, pp. 336–352. Springer, Heidelberg (2006)
12. Lee, H., Won, S., Jin, J., Cho, J., Ryu, S.: SAFE: Formal specification and implementation of a scalable analysis framework for ECMAScript. In: Proceedings of the 2012 International Workshop on Foundations of Object-Oriented Languages (2012)
13. Minamide, Y.: Static approximation of dynamically generated web pages. In: Proceedings of the 14th International Conference on World Wide Web (2005)
14. Minamide, Y., Tozawa, A.: XML validation for context-free grammars. In: Kobayashi, N. (ed.) APLAS 2006. LNCS, vol. 4279, pp. 357–373. Springer, Heidelberg (2006)
15. Møller, A., Schwarz, M.: HTML validation of context-free languages. In: Hofmann, M. (ed.) FOSSACS 2011. LNCS, vol. 6604, pp. 426–440. Springer, Heidelberg (2011)
16. Reps, T.W., Horwitz, S., Sagiv, M.: Precise interprocedural dataflow analysis via graph reachability. In: Proceedings of the 22nd ACM Symposium on Principles of Programming Languages (1995)
17. Thiemann, P.: Grammar-based analysis of string expressions. In: Proceedings of the 2005 ACM SIGPLAN International Workshop on Types in Languages Design and Implementation (2005)
18. Valiant, L.G.: General context-free recognition in less than cubic time. J. Comput. Syst. Sci. 10(2), 308–315 (1975)
19. Wassermann, G., Gould, C., Su, Z., Devanbu, P.T.: Static checking of dynamically generated queries in database applications. ACM Trans. Softw. Eng. Methodol. 16(4) (2007)
20. Wassermann, G., Su, Z.: Sound and precise analysis of web applications for injection vulnerabilities. In: Proceedings of the 28th ACM SIGPLAN Conference on Programming Language Design and Implementation (2007)
21. Yu, F., Alkhalaf, M., Bultan, T.: STRANGER: An automata-based string analysis tool for PHP. In: Esparza, J., Majumdar, R. (eds.) TACAS 2010. LNCS, vol. 6015, pp. 154–157. Springer, Heidelberg (2010)
22. Yu, F., Bultan, T., Cova, M., Ibarra, O.H.: Symbolic string verification: An automata-based approach. In: Havelund, K., Majumdar, R. (eds.) SPIN 2008. LNCS, vol. 5156, pp. 306–324. Springer, Heidelberg (2008)
23. Yu, F., Bultan, T., Hardekopf, B.: String abstractions for string verification. In: Groce, A., Musuvathi, M. (eds.) SPIN 2011. LNCS, vol. 6823, pp. 20–37. Springer, Heidelberg (2011)
24. Yu, F., Bultan, T., Ibarra, O.H.: Symbolic string verification: Combining string analysis and size analysis. In: Kowalewski, S., Philippou, A. (eds.) TACAS 2009. LNCS, vol. 5505, pp. 322–336. Springer, Heidelberg (2009)
25. Yu, F., Bultan, T., Ibarra, O.H.: Relational string verification using multi-track automata. In: Domaratzki, M., Salomaa, K. (eds.) CIAA 2010. LNCS, vol. 6482, pp. 290–299. Springer, Heidelberg (2011)

Syntax-Directed Divide-and-Conquer Data-Flow Analysis

Shigeyuki Sato[1] and Akimasa Morihata[2]

[1] The University of Electro-Communications, Japan
sato@ipl.cs.uec.ac.jp
[2] Graduate School of Arts and Sciences, University of Tokyo, Japan
morihata@graco.c.u-tokyo.ac.jp

Abstract. Link-time optimization, with which GCC and LLVM are equipped, generally deals with large-scale procedures because of aggressive procedure inlining. Data-flow analysis (DFA), which is an essential computation for compiler optimization, is therefore desired to deal with large-scale procedures. One promising approach to the DFA of large-scale procedures is divide-and-conquer parallelization. However, DFA on control-flow graphs is difficult to divide and conquer. If we perform DFA on abstract syntax trees (ASTs) in a syntax-directed manner, the divide and conquer of DFA becomes straightforward, owing to the recursive structure of ASTs, but then nonstructural control flow such as goto/label becomes a problem. In order to resolve it, we have developed a novel syntax-directed method of DFA on ASTs that can deal with goto/label and is ready to divide-and-conquer parallelization. We tested the feasibility of our method experimentally through prototype implementations and observed that our prototype achieved a significant speedup.

Keywords: syntax-directed, divide and conquer, closed semiring.

1 Introduction

Data-flow analysis (DFA) is a classic and fundamental formalization in programming languages and particularly forms the foundation of compiler optimization. Many optimizations consist of a pair of analysis and transformation, and DFA often formulates the analysis part of an optimization and occupies the computational kernel of its optimization pass.

Nowadays, an input to DFA can be very large. For example, state-of-the-art optimizing compilers such as GCC and LLVM are equipped with link-time optimization (LTO), which is to reserve intermediate representations beside executables at compile time and then optimize the whole program at link time by using all reserved intermediate representations of linked executables. An input program of LTO is larger than the one of usual separate compilations. Furthermore, LTO promotes aggressive procedure inlining, which can incur an exponential blow up of input programs. In DFA for LTO, it is therefore desired that large-scale input programs can be dealt with effectively.

J. Garrigue (Ed.): APLAS 2014, LNCS 8858, pp. 392–407, 2014.
© Springer International Publishing Switzerland 2014

One promising approach to dealing with large-scale inputs is parallelization. Since parallel machines are widespread, well-parallelized DFA will benefit many users of LTO. A primary concern is the generation and assignment of parallel tasks. Concretely, load balancing with little overhead is important. Although load balancing is necessary to reduce parallel time, the load balancing itself could incur considerable overhead in processing large-scale inputs. For parallel DFA of large-scale input programs, the divide and conquer directly on input data structures without preprocessing is very much desired because this will result in the immediate generation of parallel finer-grained tasks in recursion.

A naive approach to the divide and conquer of DFA is procedure-level decomposition. In interprocedural as well as intraprocedural analysis, the analysis of each procedure is computationally almost independent of that of the others and therefore can be performed in parallel. This procedure-wise parallelization, however, can incur a poor load balancing in LTO with aggressive inlining. Aggressive inlining expands the main procedures sharply by substituting and eliminating many other procedures; consequently, it reduces the number of procedures and causes a size imbalance among procedures. To obtain better load balancing, the divide and conquer over a procedure is necessary.

DFA usually deals with a procedure in the form of a control-flow graph (CFG). Although there were some earlier studies on parallel DFA that developed divide-and-conquer methods on CFGs, these methods required an auxiliary tree structure [6] or duplication of CFGs [5] and therefore incur significant overhead. These drawbacks stem from the nature of CFGs. The loops and sharing of paths in CFGs make the divide and conquer of DFA difficult because they impose unstructured dependence on parts of the DFA. To resolve this dependence, some preprocessing is generally required. Therefore, DFA on CFGs is essentially difficult to divide and conquer.

In contrast to CFGs, abstract syntax trees (ASTs) are easy to divide and conquer owing to their recursive structures. If we can perform DFA on ASTs, the divide and conquer of DFA will be straightforward in a recursion on ASTs (i.e., a syntax-directed manner) and enable us to perform each DFA of independent AST subtrees in parallel. Rosen developed high-level data-flow analysis [13], a well-formed method of DFA on ASTs, but his method cannot deal with goto/label. Since goto/label causes control flow unrestricted to the structures of ASTs, it introduces into ASTs unstructured dependence similar to that of CFGs. Taming goto/label is therefore essential for general DFA.

To resolve this problem, we have developed a novel parallel syntax-directed method of general DFA that tames goto/label. The proposed method is built upon Tarjan's algebraic formalization [17] of DFA. First, our method summarizes the syntax-directed data flow in a bottom-up parallel sweep of a given AST, while detaching the goto-derived data flow and constructing a compact system of linear equations that represent it. Next, we obtain the summary of the goto-derived data flow by solving the system. Lastly, we merge the syntax-directed data flow with the goto-derived flow. Our method is particularly useful for programs containing few goto/label statements because the divide and conquer over a given AST is applied to the most part of DFA. We can assume such an input thanks to the popularity of structured programming. Furthermore, our method guarantees asymptotically linear speedup.

The following are our two major contributions:

- We have developed a novel syntax-directed divide-and-conquer parallel method of DFA based on Tarjan's formalization [17] (Section 3). The essence of our method is to detach the goto-derived data flow and calculate it afterward. Our method guarantees asymptotically linear speedup.
- We have demonstrated the feasibility of our method experimentally through prototype implementations on a C compiler (Section 4). Our parallel prototype achieved a significant speedup and our sequential prototype achieved reasonable performance compared to the standard implementation.

2   Formalization of Data-Flow Analysis

DFA is to aggregate data-flow values over a given program [4]. The domain of data-flow values is a join-semilattice L whose join operator is $\sqcup$. Each program point has a transfer function over L. The result of DFA is defined as a join-over-all-paths (JOP) solution, namely, a sum of the data-flow values of all executable paths from the entry to the exit (or a target point) in a given program.

The proposed method is based upon Tarjan's formalization over a closed semiring [17]. This first formalizes an input program as the set of all executable paths represented by a *regular path*, which is a regular expression whose alphabet is the set of all program points Π. Then, DFA is defined as a homomorphism h_R from a closed semiring $(R, |, \cdot, \varnothing, \epsilon)$ to another closed semiring $(F, \oplus, \otimes, \overline{0}, \overline{1})$. The former is for regular paths: R is a set of regular paths, addition is the alternation $|$, and multiplication is the concatenation $\cdot$. The latter is for transfer functions: F is the set of transfer functions, the addition $f_1 \oplus f_2 = \lambda x. f_1(x) \sqcup f_2(x)$, the multiplication[1] $f_1 \otimes f_2 = f_2 \circ f_1$, $\overline{0}$ is the zero element, $f \oplus \overline{0} = \overline{0} \oplus f = f$ and $f \otimes \overline{0} = \overline{0} \otimes f = \overline{0}$, and $\overline{1}$ is the multiplicative identity, $f \otimes \overline{1} = \overline{1} \otimes f = f$. Note that from the definition of a closed semiring, Kleene star $f*$ is defined as $f* = \bigoplus_{i=0}^{\infty} f^i$, where $f^0 = \overline{1}$ and $f^i = f^{i-1} \otimes f$. Giving $(F, \oplus, \otimes, \overline{0}, \overline{1})$ and a lift function $\tau : \Pi \to F$, we can characterize the homomorphism of DFA as

$$h_R(\epsilon) = \overline{1},$$
$$h_R(\pi) = \tau(\pi), \quad \text{if } \pi \in \Pi,$$
$$h_R(r_1 \cdot r_2) = h_R(r_1) \otimes h_R(r_2),$$
$$h_R(r_1 \mid r_2) = h_R(r_1) \oplus h_R(r_2),$$
$$h_R(r*) = h_R(r) * .$$

In this paper, we assume that $\varnothing$ is not an input of any DFA. Therefore, $\overline{0}$ can be left undefined and regarded as a special value that behaves as the zero element.

---

[1] Here, we consider forward DFA. For backward DFA, $f_1 \otimes f_2 = f_1 \circ f_2$.

Example of DFA To give readers to a clearer understanding of Tarjan's formalization, here we describe the DFA of reaching definitions. A definition is a pair consisting of an LHS variable and an RHS expression. In this DFA, the domain of data-flow values is a set of definitions, i.e., a binary relation from variables to expressions. The join operation is the set union. The transfer function of an assignment statement $v \leftarrow e$ generates a definition $v \mapsto e$ and kills all other definitions of v that can reach the assignment. Meanwhile, a simple expression e without assignment has no effect on data flow. That is, τ is defined as

$$\tau(v \leftarrow e) = \lambda X. \{v' \mapsto e \in X \mid v \neq v'\} \cup \{v \mapsto e\},$$
$$\tau(e) = \lambda X. X.$$

To define a closed semiring, a general form of transfer functions is necessary. Letting V be a set of variables and D be a set of definitions, we can define it as

$$f(V, D) = \lambda X. \{v \mapsto e \in X \mid v \notin V\} \cup D.$$

By using this f, we can define τ and a closed semiring $(F, \oplus, \otimes, \overline{0}, \overline{1})$ as

$$\tau(v \leftarrow e) = f(\{v\}, \{v \mapsto e\}),$$
$$\tau(e) = f(\varnothing, \varnothing),$$
$$\overline{1} = f(\varnothing, \varnothing),$$
$$f(V_1, D_1) \oplus f(V_2, D_2) = f(V_1 \cap V_2, D_1 \cup D_2),$$
$$f(V_1, D_1) \otimes f(V_2, D_2) = f(V_1 \cup V_2, \{v \mapsto e \in D_1 \mid v \notin V_2\} \cup D_2),$$
$$f(V, D)* = 1 \oplus f(V, D).$$

As seen in the h_R above, Tarjan's approach calculates a *summary*[2], namely a transfer function for a program fragment, rather than data-flow values. By applying the summary from an entry to an exit to a given initial data-flow value, we obtain its JOP solution. This formalization can deal with monotone DFA. Refer to [17,7] for a detailed discussion.

For optimizations, compilers often use JOP solutions from an entry to every point, i.e., all-points JOP solutions. Although the homomorphism above does not calculate the summaries for all-points JOP solutions, it is easy to calculate them. We can obtain a set of summaries from an entry to all points by accumulating summaries over a regular path, similarly to calculating a prefix sum. We call this an all-points summary. By applying each element of an all-points summary to an initial value, we obtain all-points JOP solutions.

In Tarjan's formalization, the primary concern on algorithms is how to construct the regular path of an input program. Tarjan [18] developed a sophisticated algorithm for extracting a regular path from a CFG. However, if an input program is goto-free, namely, in the while language (Fig. 1), we can immediately obtain its regular path representation. This is trivial but notable. Thus, DFA for the while language is performed in a syntax-directed manner as follows:

---

[2] A procedure summary, which is the transfer function of the whole of a procedure, is used extensively for interprocedural analysis [16].

$$P \quad ::= \quad s \qquad\qquad\qquad\qquad\qquad\qquad\qquad \text{(Program)}$$
$$s \quad ::= \quad \textbf{pass} \mid v \leftarrow e \mid s_1\ s_2 \mid \textbf{if}\ (e)\ \{s_1\}\ \textbf{else}\ \{s_2\} \mid \textbf{while}\ (e)\ \{s\} \quad \text{(Statement)}$$

Fig. 1. Syntax of the while language. v and e are respectively the metavariables over variables and expressions; **pass** denotes an empty statement.

$$h(\textbf{pass}) = \overline{1},$$
$$h(v \leftarrow e) = \tau(v \leftarrow e),$$
$$h(s_1\ s_2) = h(s_1) \otimes h(s_2),$$
$$h(\textbf{if}\ (e)\ \{s_1\}\ \textbf{else}\ \{s_2\}) = \tau(e) \otimes (h(s_1) \oplus h(s_2)),$$
$$h(\textbf{while}\ (e)\ \{s\}) = \tau(e) \otimes (h(s) \otimes \tau(e)) * .$$

Here, h calculates the summary of a given program fragment. Throughout this paper, we identify a program fragment given to τ with its program point; thus, τ takes a program fragment and yields a transfer function.

Example We explain the syntax-directed DFA based on Tarjan's formalization by using the following example program:

$$x \leftarrow a\ \textbf{if}\ (x < 0)\ \{x \leftarrow 0\}$$
$$\textbf{else}\ \{\textbf{while}\ (x < 10)\ \{x \leftarrow x + a\}\}.$$

By applying h, we calculate the summary of the above program as

$$\tau(x \leftarrow a) \otimes \tau(x < 0) \otimes (\tau(x \leftarrow 0)$$
$$\oplus (\tau(x < 10) \otimes (\tau(x \leftarrow x + a) \otimes \tau(x < 10))*)).$$

By using the closed semiring of reaching definitions, we can reduce it to

$$f(\{x\}, \{x \mapsto 0,\ x \mapsto x + a\}).$$

Because the initial data-flow value of reaching definitions is $\varnothing$, the JOP solution at the exit is

$$\{x \mapsto 0,\ x \mapsto x + a\}.$$

We can also construct all-points summaries in a syntax-directed manner. An example of such construction is described in Section 3.3.

3   Syntax-Directed Parallel DFA Algorithm

For goto-free programs, the divide and conquer of DFA is immediate from a syntax-directed computation, and its parallelization is therefore straightforward. Syntax-directed jumps (i.e., jumps to ancestors on ASTs) such as break/continue can be dealt with by using Rosen's method [13] in a syntax-directed manner.

Non-syntax-directed (i.e., nonstructural) jumps caused by goto/label, however, require a special attention. In the following, our target language is the while language with goto/label. Letting l be a metavariable over labels, we introduce a goto statement **goto** l and a label statement l:.

The main idea of the proposed method is to discriminate between syntax-directed (i.e., structural) data flow and goto-derived (i.e., nonstructural) data flow. Our method consists of two phases: first, it constructs a summary of structural data flow while detaching nonstructural data flow from an input AST in a syntax-directed manner, and second, it calculates only nonstructural data flow from the obtained summary. After that, we obtain JOP solutions.

In terms of parallelization, the first phase is straightforward from a syntax-directed computation. This is the main benefit of our method. We do not have to parallelize the second phase. The size of a summary obtained in the first phase is quadratic to the number of labels. Because of the popularity of structured programming, we can suppose that labels are few; that is, we assume nonstructural flow to be an exceptional irregularity in an input. The second phase would be cheap and not worth parallelizing. In the rest of this section, we describe the algorithms of both phases and the extension to interprocedural analysis.

3.1 Syntax-Directed Construction of Summaries

It is nontrivial to represent a program that contains goto/label by a single regular path. For example, consider the following program:

while $(\underline{x < 10}_1)$ $\{l: \underline{x \leftarrow x + 1}_2\}$ **if** $(\underline{x > 20}_3)$ $\{$**goto** $l\}$ **else** $\{\underline{\text{pass}}_4\}$,

where a suffix to an underlined part denotes its program point. We cannot construct a Kleene closure only from the while statement above unlike the goto-free case because regular paths containing jumps to l: are unknown. We, however, can decompose by interpreting l: as another entry and **goto** l as another exit, the above program into four goto-free regular paths: $1 \cdot (2 \cdot 1) * \cdot 3 \cdot 4$ (from the entry to the exit), $1 \cdot (2 \cdot 1) * \cdot 3$ (from the entry to **goto** l), $2 \cdot 1 \cdot (2 \cdot 1) * \cdot 3 \cdot 4$ (from l: to the exit), and $2 \cdot 1 \cdot (2 \cdot 1) * \cdot 3$ (from l: to **goto** l). These are immediately obtained from the AST. In the case of two labels l_1 and l_2, we can generally consider nine regular paths as illustrated in Fig. 2, where all goto-derived jumps to l_i are encapsulated in the box labeled by l_i. This decomposition enables us to postpone interpreting goto-derived flow. This is the key idea of our method.

On the basis of this idea, we define a structured summary by a set of transfer functions. Let $\{l_1, \ldots, l_k\}$ be the set of labels and $a_{ij} = h_R(r_{ij})$, where r_{ij} is the goto-free regular path from l_j: (or the entry, if $j = 0$) to **goto** l_i (or the exit, if $i = 0$); then, a structured summary is the following system of linear equations:

$$\left\{ \begin{array}{l} out = a_{00} \oplus (l_1 \otimes a_{01}) \oplus \cdots \oplus (l_k \otimes a_{0k}), \\ l_1 = a_{10} \oplus (l_1 \otimes a_{11}) \oplus \cdots \oplus (l_k \otimes a_{1k}), \\ \vdots \\ l_k = a_{k0} \oplus (l_1 \otimes a_{k1}) \oplus \cdots \oplus (l_k \otimes a_{kk}), \end{array} \right\}$$

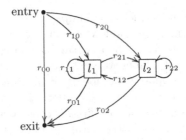

Fig. 2. Regular paths in a program containing labels l_1 and l_2. r_{00} is the regular path from the entry to the exit, r_{0i} is the regular path from l_i: to the exit, r_{i0} is the regular path from the entry to **goto** l_i, and r_{ij} is the regular path from l_j: to **goto** l_i.

where *out* denotes the data flow that goes out from the exit and l_i denotes nonstructural data flow via the label l_i; specifically, l_i denotes an outflow in the LHS and an inflow in the RHS. In the rest of this paper, we omit any equation whose RHS is $\overline{0}$. We can represent the system above by a coefficient matrix,

$$\begin{pmatrix} out \\ x \end{pmatrix} = \begin{pmatrix} \overline{1} \\ x \end{pmatrix}^T A^T, \quad \text{where } x = \begin{pmatrix} l_1 \\ \vdots \\ l_k \end{pmatrix}, \quad A = \begin{pmatrix} a_{00} & \cdots & a_{0k} \\ \vdots & \ddots & \vdots \\ a_{k0} & \cdots & a_{kk} \end{pmatrix}.$$

The matrix multiplication here is defined by using $\oplus$ and $\otimes$ respectively as the scalar addition and the scalar multiplication. Unless otherwise noted, matrix operations are generalized over a semiring. For a structured summary, we intentionally confuse the system of linear equations with its coefficient matrix A.

We define each of the addition, multiplication, and Kleene star over structured summaries as a matrix operation.

The addition is used to merge two independent summaries, such as those of two branches of a conditional statement. It is easy to see that the conventional matrix addition suffices for this purpose; consider the edge-wise union on Fig. 2. In the rest of this paper, we overload $\oplus$ for the matrix addition.

The multiplication is used to connect the summaries of two consecutive statements. This necessitates a little consideration. For example, consider the concatenation of two copies of the regular paths in Fig. 2, as illustrated in the left side of Fig. 3. Although two boxes labeled by l_i exist there, both encapsulate the same kind of control flow. We can therefore contract regular paths by merging both boxes, as illustrated in the right side of Fig. 3. This contraction of regular paths leads to the following definition of the multiplication $\odot$:

$$(c_{ij})_{0 \leq i,j \leq k} = (a_{ij})_{0 \leq i,j \leq k} \odot (b_{ij})_{0 \leq i,j \leq k}$$

$$\text{s.t. } c_{ij} = \begin{cases} a_{00} \otimes b_{00} & (i = j = 0), \\ (a_{0j} \otimes b_{00}) \oplus b_{0j} & (i = 0 \wedge j \neq 0), \\ (a_{00} \otimes b_{i0}) \oplus a_{i0} & (i \neq 0 \wedge j = 0), \\ (a_{0j} \otimes b_{i0}) \oplus a_{ij} \oplus b_{ij} & (i \neq 0 \wedge j \neq 0). \end{cases}$$

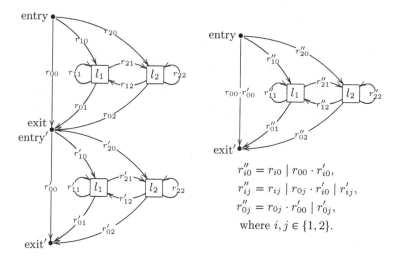

$$r''_{i0} = r_{i0} \mid r_{00} \cdot r'_{i0},$$
$$r''_{ij} = r_{ij} \mid r_{0j} \cdot r'_{i0} \mid r'_{ij},$$
$$r''_{0j} = r_{0j} \cdot r'_{00} \mid r'_{0j},$$
$$\text{where } i, j \in \{1, 2\}.$$

Fig. 3. Concatenation of two copies of the regular paths in Fig. 2, where the left side is the connected view and the right side is the contracted view

Note that $\odot$ is associative and its identity is $\{out = \overline{1}\}$.

By using the addition $\oplus$ and the multiplication $\odot$, we can define the Kleene star in the standard way. However, owing to the idempotence of $\oplus$, we can provide the following equivalent but simpler definition:

$$(a_{ij})_{0 \leq i,j \leq k} * = (a'_{ij})_{0 \leq i,j \leq k}$$

$$s.t.\ a'_{ij} = \begin{cases} a_{00}* & (i = j = 0), \\ a_{0j} \otimes a_{00}* & (i = 0 \wedge j \neq 0), \\ a_{00}* \otimes a_{i0} & (i \neq 0 \wedge j = 0), \\ (a_{0j} \otimes a_{00}* \otimes a_{i0}) \oplus a_{ij} & (i \neq 0 \wedge j \neq 0). \end{cases}$$

Now we are ready to define h_C, which calculates a structured summary from a given AST.

$$h_C(e) = \{out = h(e)\},$$
$$h_C(s) = \{out = h(s)\},$$
$$h_C(l_i:) = \{out = \overline{1} \oplus l_i\},$$
$$h_C(\mathbf{goto}\ l_i) = \{l_i = \overline{1}\},$$
$$h_C(s'_1\ s'_2) = h_C(s'_1) \odot h_C(s'_2),$$
$$h_C(\mathbf{if}\ (e)\ \{s'_1\}\ \mathbf{else}\ \{s'_2\}) = h_C(e) \odot (h_C(s'_1) \oplus h_C(s'_2)),$$
$$h_C(\mathbf{while}\ (e)\ \{s'\}) = h_C(e) \odot (h_C(s') \odot h_C(e))*,$$

where s denotes a metavariable over statements containing no goto/label statement and s' denotes one over statements containing any goto/label statement.

Example We here consider, as an example input, the following program:

> **if** $(i > n)$ $\{l_1\colon x \leftarrow 1\}$ **else** $\{$**while** $(i < n)$ $\{i \leftarrow 2\}$ $l_2\colon x \leftarrow i\}$
> **if** $(x = n)$ $\{i \leftarrow x\}$ **else** $\{$**goto** $l_1\}$.

By applying $h_{\mathcal{C}}$, we calculate a structured summary of the above program as

$$A_1 \odot ((\{out = \bar{1} \oplus l_1\} \odot A_2) \oplus (A_3 \odot \{out = \bar{1} \oplus l_2\} \odot A_4))$$
$$\odot A_5 \odot (A_6 \oplus \{l_1 = \bar{1}\}),$$
$$\text{where } A_1 = \{out = \tau(i > n)\}, \quad A_2 = \{out = \tau(x \leftarrow 1)\},$$
$$A_3 = \{out = \tau(i < n) \otimes (\tau(i \leftarrow 2) \otimes \tau(i < n))*\},$$
$$A_4 = \{out = \tau(x \leftarrow i)\}, \quad A_5 = \{out = \tau(x = n)\},$$
$$A_6 = \{out = \tau(i \leftarrow x)\}.$$

By reducing matrix operations, we obtain

$$\{out = a_1' \oplus (l_1 \otimes a_2') \oplus (l_2 \otimes a_3'), \ l_1 = a_4' \oplus (l_1 \otimes a_5'),\}$$
$$\text{where } a_1' = a_1 \otimes (a_2 \oplus (a_3 \otimes a_4)) \otimes a_5 \otimes a_6,$$
$$a_2' = a_2 \otimes a_5 \otimes a_6, \ a_3' = a_4 \otimes a_5,$$
$$a_4' = a_1 \otimes (a_2 \oplus (a_3 \otimes a_4)) \otimes a_5, \ a_5' = a_2 \otimes a_5$$
$$a_1 = \tau(i > n), \ a_2 = \tau(x \leftarrow 1),$$
$$a_3 = \tau(i < n) \otimes (\tau(i \leftarrow 2) \otimes \tau(i < n))*,$$
$$a_4 = \tau(x \leftarrow i), \ a_5 = \tau(x = n), \ a_6 = \tau(i \leftarrow x).$$

This result exemplifies the notion of a structured summary: a_1' denotes the data flow from the entry to the exit, a_2' denotes that from the l_1: to the exit, a_3' denotes that from l_2: to the exit, a_4' denotes that from the entry to the **goto** l_1, and a_5' denotes that from l_1: to the **goto** l_1. None of these take any nonstructural data flow into account, but the whole system contains the nonstructural data flow of the program. For example, $l_1 = a_4' \oplus (l_1 \otimes a_5')$ denotes that the nonstructural data flow via l_1 is $a_4' \otimes a_5'*$. We can therefore calculate the nonstructural data flow from this structured summary. Finally, we obtain the value of *out*.

Parallel Complexity. We can parallelize $h_{\mathcal{C}}$ immediately in a divide-and-conquer manner because $h_{\mathcal{C}}$ can fork for each child at any internal node of an input AST. For the parallel time complexity of $h_{\mathcal{C}}$, the associativity of $\odot$ is important. We can flatten the nesting of statement sequencing, i.e., convert a nesting $((s_1 \ s_2) \ s_3)$ into a sequence $(s_1 \ s_2 \ s_3)$, because it guarantees both results to be equivalent. Moreover, it enables us to perform parallel reduction for a sequence of statements. The number of parallel recursive steps of $h_{\mathcal{C}}$ therefore is bounded by the maximum if/while nesting d in an input AST. Let k be the number of labels, N be the number of the nodes in an input AST, P be the number of processors, and b be the maximum length of a sequence of statements. The parallel time complexity of $h_{\mathcal{C}}$ is the following:

$$O(k^2(N/P + d \lg \min(b, P))),$$

where we assume closed-semiring operations to be constant-time. This $\lg \min(b, P)$ factor is derived from the parallel reduction of a sequence of statements and is practically negligible. The k^2 factor represents the cost of matrix operations. Note that for an AST containing no label statement, this factor will be k, and for one containing no goto/label statement, it will be a constant. If $N/P > d \lg \min(b, P)$, h_C guarantees asymptotically linear speedup.

3.2   Calculating Join-Over-All-Paths Solutions

To obtain a JOP solution, we have to solve the nonstructural data flow whose calculation has been postponed, i.e., to determine the value of x in a structured summary. As seen in Fig. 2, a structured summary can be regarded as a collapsed CFG. We can therefore apply existing methods on CFGs to solve that. The simplest one is Gaussian elimination [15]. Although it is cubic-time, it is sufficient to solve the nonstructural data flow. Assuming closed-semiring operations to be constant-time, it costs only $O(k^3)$ because of the size of a structured summary as a CFG. This cost is asymptotically negligible compared to the parallel cost of h_C if $N/P + d \lg \min(b, P) > k$. Therefore, the part to solve nonstructural data flow is not worth sophisticating and/or parallelizing.

Once the value of x in a structured summary is obtained, we can determine the value of *out* in $O(k)$ time. By applying a initial value to *out*, we obtain the JOP solution of a given program. It is usually constant-time.

3.3   Construction of All-Points Summaries

We can compute all-points JOP solutions from an all-points summary in embarrassingly parallel because each application of its elements to an initial value is independent. We can construct all-points summaries by using tree accumulation.

The tree accumulation to construct an all-points summary consists of two phases. The first is the same as h_C except for leaving intermediate results at each node in a given AST. The second is a top-down sweep of the AST decorated with intermediate results. In this top-down sweep, we perform the parallel prefix-sum operation with $\odot$ on every sequence of statements and update summaries that decorate each node of the AST. The resultant AST decorated with structured summaries is an all-point summary. Note that $\odot$ used in the second phase has only to calculate the uppermost row vector and the leftmost column vector in a resultant matrix because only the equation of *out* in every element of an all-points summary is used for yielding all-points JOP solutions. The second phase is cheaper than the first one. Therefore, the time complexity of constructing an all-points summary is the same as that of h_C.

Example The above algorithm for constructing all-points summaries is, in fact, applicable to both h and h_C. The difference between them is only on primitive operations: scalar ones (e.g., $\otimes$) used for h and matrix ones (e.g., $\odot$) used for h_C. For simplicity, we describe here the construction of an all-points summary regarding h. We consider the following goto-free program:

$$\textbf{if } (e_1) \ \{s_1 \ s_2 \ s_3\} \ \textbf{else } \{\textbf{while } (e_2) \ \{s_4 \ s_5\} \ s_6\}.$$

We reserve part of the above program as metavariables to concentrate a recursive step. After the first phase of bottom-up tree accumulation, we obtain

$$\textbf{if } (f_1) \ \{f_2 \ f_3 \ f_4\} \ \textbf{else } \{f_6 \ f_7\},$$
$$\text{where } f_1 = h(e_1), \ f_2 = h(s_1), \ f_3 = h(s_2), \ f_4 = h(s_3),$$
$$f_5 = h(e_2), \ f_6 = h(\textbf{while } (e_2) \ \{s_4 \ s_5\}), \ f_7 = h(s_6).$$

Tree accumulation also brings us the summaries of all next-level statements; e.g., we have already had

$$\textbf{while } (f_1') \ \{f_2' \ f_3'\},$$
$$\text{where } f_1' = h(e_2), \ f_2' = h(s_4), \ f_3' = h(s_5).$$

In the second phase, we calculate a top-down prefix sum at each nesting level. The following is the result for the outermost if statement:

$$\textbf{if } (f_1) \ \{(f_1 \otimes f_2) \ (f_1 \otimes f_2 \otimes f_3) \ (f_1 \otimes f_2 \otimes f_3 \otimes f_4)\}$$
$$\textbf{else } \{(f_1 \otimes f_6) \ (f_1 \otimes f_6 \otimes f_7)\}.$$

We then recurse on next-level statements: s_1, s_2, s_3, $\textbf{while } (e_2) \ \{s_4 \ s_5\}$, and s_6. Since we have already had all these summaries in the first phase, we are ready to recurse on them. After recursions on statements at all levels, the resultant AST becomes an all-points summary.

3.4   Interprocedural Analysis

Tarjan's formalization deals essentially with intraprocedural DFA. However, it can be extended to calculate procedure summaries and is therefore useful even for interprocedural DFA. In fact, our method can deal effectively with context-insensitive interprocedural DFA.

We now consider a program P to be a set of top-level procedures. Let p be a metavariable over procedure names. The syntax of a procedure with a body statement s is $p()\{s\}$. The procedure call $p()$ and $\textbf{return}$ are introduced to s. For simplicity, we assume that none of the procedures take arguments or return values. Argument passing and value returning may be implemented by using global variables. For convenience, p_c refers to the current procedure at a point.

Since the information of call sites is neglected in context-insensitive DFA, we can interpret call/return simply as goto/label. We extend h_C as follows:

$$h_C(P) = \bigoplus_{p \in P} h_C(p()\{s\}),$$
$$h_C(p()\{s\}) = \{\} \odot h_C(p_{\text{call}}\colon s \ \textbf{goto } p_{\text{ret}}) \odot \{\},$$
$$h_C(p()) = h_C(\textbf{goto } p_{\text{call}} \ p_{\text{ret}}\colon),$$
$$h_C(\textbf{return}) = h_C(\textbf{goto } p_{\text{ret}}), \quad \text{where } p = p_c.$$

Note that the null system {} denotes no control flow. The same call-site label p_{ret} may be attached to many program points. In such cases, we interpret goto as a nondeterministic jump to one of the corresponding label statements, where we require no change in h_C. The rest of the DFA process, including the constructions of all-points summaries, is the same as the intraprocedural case.

In contrast, our method is less effective for context-sensitive interprocedural DFA because context sensitivity prevents us from factoring out the data flow of calls as a compact linear system. When using our method, the first choice to obtain context sensitivity is procedure inlining. Intraprocedural DFA with inlining is generally more precise than context-sensitive DFA. Furthermore, we usually require code replication similar to inlining for generating context-sensitively optimized code, and in this sense, inlining is essential for utilizing context sensitivity in compiler optimization. Although the drawback of inlining is the expansion of procedure sizes, it is tractable in our method by using divide-and-conquer parallelization. Our method is synergistic with inlining, and aggressive inlining followed by context-insensitive DFA is therefore both appropriate and sufficient.

4 Experiments

We conducted experiments to demonstrate the feasibility and scalability of our algorithm. Note that our aim is not to evaluate our analyzer implementation.

4.1 Prototype Implementations

We implemented our method for the DFA of reaching definitions, which is the most standard and lightweight example of DFA. Because a lightweight computation to a large-scale input is sensitive to the overhead of load balancing, the DFA of reaching definitions is appropriate for demonstrating the scalability of our method. Our implementations built upon COINS[3], a C compiler in Java. We implemented h_C as a simple visitor on an AST. We used a dense matrix for Gaussian elimination to solve nonstructural data flow. We made extensive use of java.util.HashMap for the implementation of the closed semiring of reaching definitions. We call our sequential prototype seq and the parallel one par. This parallelization was very simple; we simply used Java 7 Fork/Join framework for the visitor of h_C. We forked a visitor for each compound statement in a sequence of statements while summarizing segments of atom statements. At the end of a sequence of statements, we waited for all forked visitors one by one and then calculated the summary of the sequence.

As the reference implementation of DFA, we implemented wordwise analysis [3], which is an efficient iterative method for solving the most common DFA, a.k.a. the bit-vector framework. We call this implementation bvf. Since this method uses a wordwise worklist, we implemented a sparse wordwise bit-vector. We used a LIFO queue as the worklist. We constructed a CFG of basic blocks,

---

[3] http://coins-compiler.sourceforge.jp/

and then numbered definitions on the AST through the CFG. After that, we initialized gen/kill sets of each node and performed the iterative method.

Note that bvf by definition calculated all-points JOP solutions, while our prototypes seq and par calculated a procedure summary. The comparison of their absolute performance is therefore unfair. Because this difference on results stems from the difference on style between our method and the iterative method, a truly fair comparison is difficult. However, since the asymptotic time complexity of constructing an all-points summary is the same as h_C (see Section 3.3), in terms of asymptotic performance, seq and par are comparable to bvf.

4.2   Experimental Setup

We generated a large-scale input program normalized in the while language with goto/label statements by using a biased random generation. We set the maximum depth to about 128, the length of block statements to a random number between 1 and 8. An about half of if statements had empty else branches. Each goto statement was guarded by a simple if statement to avoid dead code. An about half of assignments defined new variables. The generated AST had about 1,000,000 statements where the number of goto and label statements were 96 and 20. We used this unrealistically large-scale program for a benchmark to observe asymptotic behaviors of our method. We call it rand.

To obtain a realistic large program, we used procedure inlining of recursive programs. As an example recursive program, we selected the Lua 5.2.3 parser[4], which is known to be written in clean C. After normalization, we applied inlining iteratively to the entry function. We stopped the recursion of inlining at the seventh level. The resultant entry function consisted of about 12,000 statements, where 51 pairs of goto/label statements existed. We call it inl.

We used a server equipped with four Opteron 6380 (16 cores, 2.50 GHz) processors and 128 GB of DDR3-1600 memory running OpenJDK (64-bit Server VM) version 1.7.0_55. We executed each analyzer 20 times for the same AST in memory. To minimize the effect of GC and VM issues, we discarded outliers and considered the median of the remainder as the result.

4.3   Experimental Results

The relative speedup of par given rand, shown in Fig. 4, had a significant scalability up to 15 threads. The relative speedup with 15 threads was 5.82x (while the speedup compared to bvf was 5.00x). A careful control of task granularity was not required. We also tested a granularity-controlled prototype but did not observe any performance gain. Only the divide and conquer of our method was sufficient to obtain a significant speedup. Our method was ready to parallelize and demonstrated that the divide and conquer on input data structures is crucial. The speedup curve in Fig. 4 demonstrates the asymptotically linear speedup of our method and exemplifies Amdahl's law.

---

[4] http://www.lua.org/ftp/lua-5.2.3.tar.gz

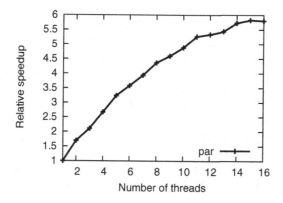

Fig. 4. Relative speedup of **par** given **rand**

Table 1. Breakdown of execution time of **seq**. "Elim" means Gaussian elimination on a structured summary.

Phase		h_C	Elim	Total
Time (ms)	**rand**	810	1	811
	inl	13	1	14

Table 2. Breakdown of execution time of **bvf**. "Cons" means CFG construction, "Ndef" means numbering definitions, "Init" means initializing gen/kill sets, and "Iter" means the iterative method.

Phase		Cons	Ndef	Init	Iter	Total
Time (ms)	**rand**	431	565	971	334	2301
	inl	6	3	6	3	18

Tables 1 and 2 respectively show the breakdowns of the execution time of **seq** and bvf given **rand** and **inl**. For **inl**, both **seq** and bvf were sufficiently fast. For **rand**, **seq** was significantly faster than bvf, but the direct comparison of both is inappropriate as mentioned earlier. What we can justify from these results is that our method is not algorithmically slower than the iterative method. It is notable that the Elim phase in our method incurred no overhead as expected. Therefore, our method is both feasible and useful if label statements in a given program are few, specifically less than about 50.

5   Related Work

Rosen [13,14] proposed the concept and method of high-level DFA. His method performs DFA on a high-level CFG that captures syntactic nesting, by calculating bit-vector equations for each level of statements similarly to interval analysis [2] but in a much finer-grained manner. Although Rosen dealt with break/continue, he did not with goto/label. The equations constructed in his method correspond to structured summaries containing only the leftmost column vector. His method can potentially deal with goto statements (i.e., jump-out) but not with label statements (i.e., jump-in). Mintz et al. [10] implemented Rosen's method integrated with a CFG-based method to deal with goto/label. Their method processes ASTs containing no jump-in similarly to Rosen's. For ASTs containing a jump-in from the outside, it abandons the idea of calculating equations and instead constructs a CFG. For ASTs containing no jump-in from the outside but with a jump(s) between its components, by applying a CFG-based method to the CFG derived from the AST, the CFG is reduced to equations. The primary difference between our method and theirs is how the jump-in is handled. In our method, we detach the data flow of every jump-in completely from an input AST and summarize it into a structured summary. As a result, our method performs syntax-directed computation more thoroughly (e.g., even for context-insensitive interprocedural DFA) than theirs. This trait is quite advantageous in terms of divide-and-conquer parallelization.

In previous studies on parallelizing DFA [6,5], load balancing was the primary concern. Lee et al. [6] improved the parallelization of interval analysis [2], where CFGs are recursively decomposed into substructures called intervals. In interval analysis, exclusive intervals can be processed in parallel, but the size of each interval, i.e., the granularity of parallel tasks is diverse. Lee et al. divided a CFG into controlled-size regions instead of intervals for load balancing and used an auxiliary tree structure to manage the parallelism among regions. Region decomposition itself is a sequential task. Kramer et al. [5] utilized the parallel prefix-sum operation with $\otimes$ for each path of a CFG. Their method unwinds loops to convert a CFG into a directed acyclic graph. This degrades the generality of DFA. To make matters worse, their method expands the sharing of paths in a given CFG. This causes the asymptotic cost of DFA to blow up exponentially[5]. Our method is a simpler and cheaper way of divide-and-conquer parallelization, and furthermore guarantees asymptotically linear speedup.

Many studies on accelerating static analysis [19,8,1,11,12,9] parallelized fixed-point iterations. Multithreading with worklists [19,1,12] worked well for expected inputs in practical usage, but this imposes concurrency issues such as mutual exclusion for worklists, termination detection, deadlock/livelock, and the fairness of underlying schedulers. Parallel implementations specialized for GPUs [8,11] achieved high performance experimentally, but these techniques are very hardware-specific. Speculative parallelization [9] was feasible, but it complicates runtime behaviors. None of these approaches guarantee asymptotic speedup.

6   Conclusion

We have presented a novel syntax-directed parallel method of DFA that tames goto/label, and also experimentally demonstrated its feasibility and scalability.

---

[5] Their worst-case analysis is wrong on the size of a graph that they called a *combining DAG*. It can be exponential to the number of nodes in a given CFG, e.g., a sequence of if-then-else statements, whose regular path is $(r_1 \mid r_2) \cdot (r_3 \mid r_4) \cdots$.

There are two directions for future work. One is to implement our method more seriously by tying it to compiler optimizations and then to evaluate it practically. We expect that our method will simplify the construction of optimizing compilers. The other is to apply our method to other domains, e.g., XML processing. We expect that our approach to taming goto/label will be useful for computation over a mostly hierarchical structure.

Acknowledgments. We thank Hideya Iwasaki for his generous support facilitating this work, and Munehiro Takimoto for his advice encouraging this work.

References

1. Albarghouthi, A., Kumar, R., Nori, A.V., Rajamani, S.K.: Parallelizing Top-Down Interprocedural Analyses. In: Proc. PLDI 2012, pp. 217–228 (2012)
2. Allen, F.E., Cocke, J.: A Program Data Flow Analysis Procedure. Commun. ACM 19(3), 137–147 (1976)
3. Khedker, U.P., Dhamdhere, D.M.: A Generalized Theory of Bit Vector Data Flow Analysis. ACM Trans. Program. Lang. Syst. 16(5), 1472–1511 (1994)
4. Kildall, G.A.: A Unified Approach to Global Program Optimization. In: Proc. POPL 1973, pp. 194–206 (1973)
5. Kramer, R., Gupta, R., Soffa, M.L.: The Combining DAG: A Technique for Parallel Data Flow Analysis. IEEE T. Parall Distr. 5(8), 805–813 (1994)
6. Lee, Y.F., Ryder, B.G., Fiuczynski, M.E.: Region Analysis: A Parallel Elimination Method for Data Flow Analysis. IEEE Software Eng. 21(11), 913–926 (1995)
7. Marlowe, T.J., Ryder, B.G.: Properties of data flow frameworks. Acta Inform. 28(2), 121–163 (1990)
8. Méndez-Lojo, M., Burtscher, M., Pingali, K.: A GPU Implementation of Inclusion-based Points-to Analysis. In: Proc. PPoPP 2012, pp. 107–116 (2012)
9. Méndez-Lojo, M., Mathew, A., Pingali, K.: Parallel Inclusion-based Points-to Analysis. In: Proc. OOPSLA 2010, pp. 428–443 (2010)
10. Mintz, R.J., Fisher, G.A., Sharir, M.: The design of a global optimizer. In: Proc. SIGPLAN Symposium on Compiler Construction 1979, pp. 226–234 (1979)
11. Prabhu, T., Ramalingam, S., Might, M., Hall, M.: EigenCFA: Accelerating Flow Analysis with GPUs. In: Proc. POPL 2011, pp. 511–522 (2011)
12. Rodriguez, J., Lhoták, O.: Actor-Based Parallel Dataflow Analysis. In: Knoop, J. (ed.) CC 2011. LNCS, vol. 6601, pp. 179–197. Springer, Heidelberg (2011)
13. Rosen, B.K.: High-Level Data Flow Analysis. Commun. ACM 20(10), 712–724 (1977)
14. Rosen, B.K.: Monoids for Rapid Data Flow Analysis. SIAM J. Comput. 9(1), 159–196 (1980)
15. Ryder, B.G., Paull, M.C.: Elimination Algorithms for Data Flow Analysis. ACM Comput. Surv. 18(3), 277–316 (1986)
16. Sharir, M., Pnueli, A.: Two Approaches to Inter-Procedural Data-Flow Analysis. Prentice-Hall (1981)
17. Tarjan, R.E.: A Unified Approach to Path Problems. J. ACM 28(3), 577–593 (1981)
18. Tarjan, R.E.: Fast Algorithms for Solving Path Problems. J. ACM 28(3), 594–614 (1981)
19. Vaivaswatha, N., Govindarajan, R.: Parallel Flow-Sensitive Pointer Analysis by Graph-Rewriting. In: Proc. PACT 2013, pp. 19–28 (2013)

Address Chain: Profiling Java Objects without Overhead in Java Heaps

Xiaohua Shi, Junru Xie, and Hengyang Yu

School of Computer Science and Engineering, Beihang University, Beijing, China
xhshi@buaa.edu.cn, xie789852123@163.com, 457713855@qq.com

Abstract. How to efficiently and adequately profile Java objects is one of the key problems for debugging, monitoring, program analysis, and many optimizations. Most current approaches have extra overheads in Java heaps and slow down the runtime performance significantly, or need to modify particular object layouts with limited extendibility and adaptivity. In this paper, we present a novel profiling mechanism, namely *Address Chain*, which has no overhead in Java heaps and does not modify object layouts, class layouts and any other key structures in Java Virtual Machines. So far, the Address Chain mechanism profiles the accurate life cycle, the allocation site in jitted code, as well as the physical memory trace of object movements with time stamps, etc., for every Java object. Furthermore, it provides a profiling framework that can be easily adapted to profile more or less information for future requirements. It is a general mechanism suitable for garbage collectors using mark-and-sweep, copying or generational algorithms. The runtime overheads of our approach are reasonable. We implemented our mechanism on Apache Harmony 6.0 DRLVM, which is a J2SE Virtual Machine with a generational garbage collector. The runtime overheads of the profiler are about 5% on average for SpecJVM2008, less than 8% for SpecJBB2005, and about 8% for Dacapo, respectively. We use a distributed mode to collect and calculate the object information from the profiled data sent via network. For most cases we studied, the object status can be calculated almost simultaneously when Java applications run on another computing device. Our mechanism has the capability of providing online object status in a distributed way. We also demonstrate how to use the profiled data to help optimizations like pretenuring.

Keywords: Profiling, Garbage Collector, Java Virtual Machine.

1   Introduction

Some languages, like Java, have garbage collectors to manage all the objects at runtime. The garbage collectors effectively reduce the memory-related failures, and improve the efficiency of the usage of memory heaps. However, sometime we still need to understand more about what happened to an object at runtime. For instance, memory leaks caused by useless objects still happen in programs written using garbage-collected languages. To determine whether an object could

J. Garrigue (Ed.): APLAS 2014, LNCS 8858, pp. 408–427, 2014.
© Springer International Publishing Switzerland 2014

introduce memory leak, we need to understand every object in terms of its life cycle (when the object was created and how long it lives), allocation site, as well as its last access time, etc. Furthermore, these kinds of information could help compilers to do some useful optimizations, like pretenuring, which could improve the performance of generational garbage collectors by allocating long-term survived objects in mature object areas directly instead of nursery object areas first[3][10]. Therefore, how to efficiently and adequately profile objects at runtime is one of the key problems for debugging, monitoring, program analysis and many optimizations for garbage-collected languages.

When we profile Java objects in heaps, especially for generational or copying garbage collectors, we can not use the address of an object as its unique identity directly, because the object could be moved among different areas at runtime. Some approaches encode the information in object headers or extended the data structures of object layouts, like [13][4][5]. Some approaches add additional fields in object headers to record the profiled information, like [15][16]. These solutions either modify the existing object layouts and core data structures of Java Virtual Machines, or require more space in Java heaps. For the former approaches, if we cannot steal enough bits from the object headers, we have to record approximate values to fit the limited space, or adapt the data structures of object layouts to the profiled data. For the latter ones, we have to pay more memory space for every object in the heap. That could introduce significant overheads to garbage collectors and Java Virtual Machines. Furthermore, many existing approaches are designed to profile some particular information, e.g. object allocation sites or time, etc. It is hard to adapt them to profile more or less information to fulfil further requirements.

In this paper, we introduce a novel mechanism, namely *AddressChain*, for efficiently profiling the accurate life cycle, the allocation site, as well as the physical memory trace of object movements with time stamps, etc., for every Java object. The points of our mechanism include:

- There is NO overhead in Java heaps. It does not modify object layouts, class layouts, etc. It does not modify the jitted code, bytecode, or source code of Java programs as well.
- So far, it profiles the accurate life cycle, the allocation site in jitted code, as well as the physical memory trace of object movements with time stamps, etc., for every Java object. It also provides a profiling framework that can be easily adapted to profile more or less information for further requirements.
- It is a general mechanism suitable for garbage collectors using mark-and-sweep, copying, or generational algorithms.
- The runtime overheads of our approach are reasonable. We implemented our mechanism on Apache Harmony 6.0 DRLVM, which is a J2SE Virtual Machine with a generational garbage collector. The runtime overheads of the profiler are about 5% on average for SpecJVM2008, less than 8% for SpecJBB2005, and about 8% for Dacapo[2], respectively. In practice, the memory requirements of out-of-java-heap profiling buffers are only dozens of kilobytes per Java thread or garbage collector thread.

- We use a distributed mode to calculate the object information from the profiled data sent via network. For most cases we studied, the object status can be calculated almost simultaneously when Java applications run on another computing device. Our mechanism has the capability of providing online object status in a distributed way.
- We present how to use the profiled data to help optimizations like pretenuring as well.

The rest of the paper is structured as follows. Section 2 introduces related works. Section 3 presents the general mechanism of our approach. Section 4 presents our implementations on Harmony DRLVM. Section 5 demonstrates the runtime performance of our implementations. Section 6 concludes this paper.

2   Related Work

Many profiling tools, like JProbe[11] and JProfiler[12], profile Java objects with high runtime overhead, which limits their use.

Hertz et al.[8][9] studied how to profile a garbage collection trace, which is a chronological record of every object allocation, heap pointer update, and object death (object becoming unreachable) over the execution of a program. They used the Merlin object lifetime algorithm to compute object lifetimes. The Merlin algorithm timestamps live objects when they lose an incoming reference and later uses the timestamps to reconstruct the time at which the object became unreachable. The algorithm has better performance comparing with the brute force method that could require over a month for each trace. However, as what the authors declared, even with the improvement Merlin provides to trace generations, the time required to generate a trace is still 70-300 times slower than running the program without tracing.

Bond et al.[5][4] encoded object allocation and last-use sites in object headers. They need some stolen bits in object headers to record the profiled information. Hence, they only profile approximated values for the limited space of stolen bits, and their approach depends on specific JVM implementations. Their previous approach, namely Sleigh, adds 29% execution time overhead, which adaptive profiling reduces to 11%. Their later approach, which only records the approximated last-use time in stolen bits of object headers, has 5% overhead for SpecJVM98 and SpecJBB2000. They use the approximated last-use time of every living object to determine which object should be temporarily removed from heaps. If they want to output the profiled data, the time and space overheads could be much higher for the spending of I/O and profiling dead objects.

Shaham et al.[15] presented a heap-profiling tool for exploring the potential for space savings in Java programs. The heap-profiling tool attached a trailer to every object to keep track of their profiling information, and then wrote the trailer to a log file upon reclamation of the object or upon program termination. An object's trailer fields include its creation time, last use time, length in bytes, nested allocation site and nested last-use site, etc. They did not discuss runtime overheads of their profiler, because they used the profiler and analysed the profiled data in an off-line mode. However, it is easy to imagine, for workloads like SpecJBB2005, the added trailers could require hundreds of Mega bytes in Java heaps, even much higher, for hundreds of millions allocated objects during program execution.

Chilimbiet et al.[6] presented a memory leak detection tool namely SWAT, which could trace the allocations and frees of a program, to detect memory leaks. Their tool has low runtime overhead (less than 5%), and low space overhead (less than 10% in most cases and often less than 5%). Because their approach is a sample-based adaptive profiling scheme, the low overhead mainly thanks to the perfectly designed sampling scheme for a specific purpose, i.e. memory leak detection. Their profiler produces much less object information than our approach.

Ha et al.[7] presented the design, implementation, and evaluation of a concurrent, configurable dynamic analysis framework that efficiently utilizes multi-core cache architectures. Their approach offloads the profiled data to another node as well. However, they did not discuss how to profile Java object at a fine granularity.

Xu et al.[17] introduced a technique, namely copy profiling, that summarizes runtime activity in terms of chains of data copies. The execution time of building their context-insensitive copy graphs is about 10–60 times slower than running programs without profiling. Xu[18] also introduced a tunable profiling technique that explores the middle ground between high precision and high efficiency to find the precision-efficiency sweetspot for various liveness-based optimization techniques. Unlike our approach, they still use a global object ID that may occupy a large amount of Java heap memory to identify different objects.

Odaira et al.[13] proposed two approaches to track the allocation sites of every Java object with only a 1.0% slowdown on average. Their first approach, the Allocation-Site-as-a-Hash-code (ASH) Tracker, encodes the allocation site ID of an object into the hash code field of its header by regarding the ID as part of the hash code. Their second approach, the Allocation-Site-via-a-Class-pointer (ASC) Tracker, makes the class pointer field in an object header refer to the allocation site structure of the object, which in turn points to the actual class structure. However, their approaches need to steal some bits from object headers or modify the object layout. It means that the approaches depend on specific JVM implementations with less extendibility and adaptability. Furthermore, like [5][4], they only record profiled data in live objects, if they want to output the profiled data, the time and space overheads could be much higher for the spending of I/O and profiling dead objects. Odaira et al.[14] also proposed a low-overhead object access profiler using a memory-protection-based approach and adaptive overhead reduction techniques. Their work more focuses on some specified purposes like profiling object access patterns instead of a general profiling approach.

3   Address Chain Mechanism

This section presents the definitions, profiling rules, building methodologies, as well as the adaptivity and extendibility of the Address Chain mechanism.

3.1 Definitions

An Address Chain is a chain with linked vectors. Every vector represents one object, as below:

$$\langle AllocS, T_d, T_0, Addr_0, T_1, Addr_1, ..., T_N, Addr_N \rangle$$

In which, $AllocS$ stands for the allocation site of an object. T_0 stands for its allocation time. We use the number of times garbage collector has been invoked as the allocation time. For instance, if an object was allocated between the second and third garbage collections, T_0 will be 2. The initial physical address of the object will be assigned to $Addr_0$. T_d stands for the dead time of the object. It could be the reclaiming time of the object, or the time the object is explicitly marked as dead by the garbage collector. Like T_0, T_d uses the garbage collection number as its value, too.

A mark-and-sweep garbage collector does not move objects. So, an Address Chain vector only has one pair of T and $Addr$ under this scenario. For compacting, copying and generational garbage collectors, objects could be moved among different areas. When an object has been moved, a new pair of T and $Addr$ will be appended to its vector. For instance, if an object has been moved the third time during the fifth garbage collection, a T_3 with number 5 and an $Addr_3$ with the new target physical address of the object will be appended to its Address Chain vector. With the time sequence, the trace of physical memory movements of an object differentiates itself from others.

3.2 Profiling Rules

The Address Chain does not exist in Java heaps. It is built from the profiled data. The profiling rules at runtime are as follows:

- Allocating a new object. The profiler will output a record as:
  $(NEWOBJ, AllocS, Addr_0)$
    In which, $NEWOBJ$ is a constant number indicating that this data group has 3 elements, including the constant value itself, the allocation site, and the initial physical address of the object.
- Garbage collection starting. Every time a garbage collection starts, the profiler will output a pair of values as:
  $(GCTIME, GC_n)$
    In which, $GCTIME$ is a constant number indicating that the next value, GC_n, is the current garbage collection number.
- Moving an object. The profiler will output a pair of values as:
  $(Addr_{prev}, Addr_{target})$
    When an object has been moved by the garbage collector, the profiler will simply output the previous and target addresses of the object.
- Marking an object as dead. If a garbage collector explicitly marks an object as dead, the profiler will output a pair of values as:
  $(DEADOBJ, Addr_{cur})$
    In which, $DEADOBJ$ is a constant number indicating that the next address belongs to a dead object. The $Addr_{cur}$ is the current physical address of the object.

- Garbage collection finished. Every time a garbage collection finishes, the profiler will output a constant number $GCFINISH$.
- Other scenarios. The profiler does not output any new record.

The profiled data provide enough information for calculating Address Chain vectors, which contain the allocation time, the allocation site, as well as the memory trace for every object. The next section will introduce how to build the Address Chain.

In theory, we could suppose there is a single limitless buffer out of the Java heap to receive the profiled data for all Java threads and garbage collectors, like the left part of Fig. 1. In practice, we use reusable out-of-java-heap buffers with only dozens of kilobytes per Java thread or garbage collector thread to store profiled records, and will send them out immediately to another machine or process via network when buffers are full. So, the memory overheads on the profiling machine are almost negligible. There is no overhead in Java heaps, and out-of-java-heap buffers will be reclaimed automatically when Java threads or garbage collector threads terminate. Section 4 will present more details in terms of implementations.

All the profiled records could be adapted to some specified profiling requirements, except the initial physical address of an object and the $(Addr_{prev}, Addr_{target})$ address pairs, because the trace of physical memory movements of an object differentiates itself from others. The next subsection will explain more.

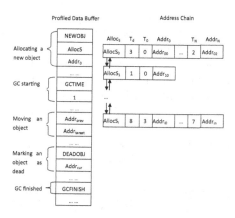

Fig. 1. Profiled data buffer and Address Chain

3.3   Building Address Chain

Address Chain vectors, like the right part of Fig. 1, can be built from the profiled data by the algorithm in Fig. 2. The profiled data buffer will be traversed top down only once. When a record started with $NEWOBJ$ is read, a new Address Chain vector will be created and appended to the end of the chain. $Addr_0$ of the new vector will be set to the value of the next entry of the profiled data buffer. T_0 will be assigned to the value of GC_Time, which equals to the current garbage collection number. The T_d field of the new vector will be set to $NULL$ to indicate the object is live.

When a record started with $DEADOBJ$ is read, the algorithm will search the Address Chain vectors in reverse order, to find out the first vector whose last $Addr$ value equals to the next entry following $DEADOBJ$ in the profiled data buffer. Because garbage collectors could reuse the memory spaces in heaps, different objects may have the same addresses in their vectors, including the last addresses. However, two objects never occupy the same memory space at the same time. The latest object is the one who owns the last address when the $DEADOBJ$ record was profiled. Hence, reversely traversing the Address Chain just finds out the correct object that is dead.

Then, the value of T_d of the found vector will be set to the value of GC_Time to indicate the object is dead.

When a record started with $GCTIME$ is read, the value of GC_Time will be set to the garbage collection number saved in the next entry of the profiled data buffer.

When a record started with $GCFINISH$ is read, the T_d fields of some Address Chain vectors need to be patched for some kinds of garbage collectors. For instance, for a copying or generational garbage collector, the dead objects in some areas will be abandoned and reclaimed automatically, without any explicit marking or reclaiming operation. The vectors belonging to these dead objects should be patched. For instance, most generational garbage collectors simply copy the infant objects to another area with higher generation, without any more operation on the corpses. We also need to patch all the unmoved objects in these copying areas as dead. At this moment, the algorithm will go through the existing Address Chain, find out the live objects whose last T values are smaller than the current GC_Time in the copying areas, and assign their T_d fields to GC_Time to indicate the objects are dead and have been reclaimed.

Beside the scenarios above, the only possible type of records in the profiled data buffer must have a pair of addresses, which consist of the previous and target addresses of a moved object. For the aforementioned reason, the algorithm will search the Address Chain in reverse order to find out the vector whose last address equals to the previous address, and append a new pair of $(T_N, Addr_N)$ with the value of GC_Time and the target address to the end of the vector.

The algorithm in Fig. 2 has $O(N^2)$ time complexity and $O(N)$ space complexity, in which N is the number of objects. However, with the support of a hash table that uses the last addresses of Address Chain vectors as keys, the time complexity could be significantly reduced. Fig. 4 demonstrates the hash table and its relations with the Address Chain. Fig. 3 presents the revised algorithm with hash table support. In Fig. 3, when a new vector has been initialized, a pointer to the vector will be added into the hash table by using its last address

```
currSlot = 0 ; AddressChain = NULL ;
GC_Time = 0 ;
while(!Empty(ProfiledDataBuffer[currSlot])){
 currData = ProfiledDataBuffer[currSlot++];
 switch(currData){
 case NEWOBJ:
  AllocS = ProfiledDataBuffer[currSlot++];
  T0 = GC_Time ;
  Addr0 = ProfiledDataBuffer[currSlot++];
  //Append a new vector to Address Chain
  AddNewVector(AddressChain,AllocS,T0,Addr0);
  break ;
 case DEADOBJ:
  currAddr = ProfiledDataBuffer[currSlot++];
  //Search the AddressChain in reverse order,
  //find the first vector whose last AddrN
  //equals to currAddr.
  pVector=ReverseSearch(AddressChain,currAddr);
  pVector->Td = GC_Time ;   break ;
 case GCTIME:
  GC_Time = ProfiledDataBuffer[currSlot++];
  break ;
 case GCFINISH:
  //For copying and generational GC,
  //we need to patch all the unmoved
  //and live objs in the copying areas
  //as dead & reclaimed.
  while(pVector =
         GetNextLiveVector(AddressChain)){
   if(InCopyArea(pVector)&&pVector->Tn<GC_Time)
    pVector->Td = GC_Time ;
  }
  break ;
 default:
  //A pair of addresses of a moved object
  //previous address == currData
  targetAddr==ProfiledDataBuffer[currSlot++];
  //Search the AddressChain in reverse order,
  //find the first vector whose last AddrN
  //equals to currData.
  pVector=ReverseSearch(AddressChain,currData);
  //Append a new pair of (Tn, AddrN) to pVector,
  //in which Tn = GC_Time, AddrN = targetAddr
  AddNewAddress(pVector, GC_Time, targetAddr);
  //break ;
 }
}
```

Fig. 2. The algorithm of building Address
Chain vectors from the profiled data buffer

```
//... ... means, same as the original
//algorithm in Fig.2.
... ...
 case NEWOBJ:
  ... ...
  AddHashTable(pVector) ;   break ;
 case DEADOBJ:
  ... ...
  pVector=RemoveFromHashTable(currAddr);
  pVector->Td = GC_Time ;   break ;
 case GCTIME:
  ... ...
 case GCFINISH:
  ... ...
  while(pVector=GetNextVectorFromHashTable()) {
   if(InCopyArea(pVector)&& pVector->Tn<GC_Time){
    pVector->Td = GC_Time ;
    RemoveFromHashTable(pVector->AddrN) ;}}
  break ;
 default:
  ... ...
  pVector = RemoveFromHashTable(currData);
  ... ...
  AddNewAddress(pVector, GC_Time, targetAddr);
  AddHashTable(pVector) ;   break ;
```

Fig. 3. Revised algorithm of building Address Chain vectors with hash table support

Fig. 4. Hash table for live objects

($Addr_0$ at this moment) as the key. When a record started with $DEADOBJ$ is read, the revised algorithm will get the dead vector whose last address equals to the profiled address from the hash table by using the profiled address as the key, and remove the vector from the hash table. This process has almost constant time complexity, and is much faster than the original method $ReverseSearch()$ in Fig. 2.

In a similar way, when a pair of addresses of a moved object is read, the revised algorithm will get the corresponding vector from the hash table by using the previous address as the key, and remove the vector from the hash table. Then, it will append the current GC_Time and the target address to the vector, and add the vector to the hash table again by using the target address as the updated key, like Fig. 3.

When a record started with $GCFINISH$ is read, the revised algorithm will patch some live objects as dead, same as the original algorithm. However, it does not traverse the whole Address Chain this time. All the live objects have been added into the hash table, and the hash table only saves live objects. The revised algorithm will traverse the hash table instead of the whole Address Chain to get the live objects and make decisions.

The revised algorithm significantly reduced the time complexity with some more memory overheads from the hash table, which has linear space complexity to the number of live objects.

3.4   Adaptivity and Extendibility

It is easy to adapt the mechanism to profile more or less information for further requirements. All fields in an Address Chain vector, except the orderly sequence of $Addr$s, can be removed or replaced by others to fit the specified profiling requirements. For instance, if we do not want to profile allocation sites of Java objects, we can simply remove $AllocS$ fields from Address Chain vectors, and do not output them at runtime. For instance, if we want to profile the class information for every object, we can simply add one more $CLASS$ field in vectors. When the profiler outputs records headed by $NEWOBJ$, it could output the class handle of the object as well. The algorithm will save class handles in $CLASS$ fields when initializing new vectors, just like allocation sites.

4   Implementations of the Address Chain Mechanism

This section introduces our implementations of the Address Chain mechanism on Apache Harmony 6.0 DRLVM, which is a J2ME Java Virtual Machine with a generational garbage collector namely GCV5.

4.1   GCV5 Garbage Collector of Harmony DRLVM

GCV5 is the default stop-the-world garbage collector of Apache Harmony DRLVM[1]. It partitions the Java heap into three spaces, namely NOS, MOS and

LOS. The nursery object space (NOS) is used for small object allocation, and partitioned into *FromSpace*s and *ToSpace*s. The mature object space (MOS) is used for storing survived objects from NOS. The large object space (LOS) is used for allocating objects with large sizes, e.g. more than 5K bytes. GCV5 collects objects in two kinds of collections, i.e. the major collections and minor collections. During minor collections, GCV5 moves survived objects from *FromSpace*s of NOS to *ToSpace*s, or MOS directly. During major collections, GCV5 collects the NOS and MOS as a whole space by using a move-and-compact mechanism, as well as the LOS by a parallel LISP2-based sliding compactor.

4.2   Implementations of the Profiler

We will introduce two implementations of the profiler with uncompressed and compressed modes in this section. For both implementations, most code of the profiler was instrumented in the garbage collector.

Uncompressed Mode. The implementation of the profiler with uncompressed mode is exactly based on the corresponding profiling rules in Section 3.2, as follows:

- Allocating a new object. In theory, there should be a single limitless buffer out of the Java heap to receive the profiled data for all Java threads , as illustrated in the left part of Fig. 1. In practice, we use a reusable thread-local buffer with 64 kilobytes for every Java thread to save the profiled data, as illustrated in the left part of Fig. 5. Every buffer is headed by the value of GC_Time and an optional record of the current thread ID and a serial number that is identical for every buffer. The optional record helps the profiling data receiver to maintain the completeness of the data.

    Harmony DRLVM allocates new objects through two different interfaces, i.e. $gc\_alloc()$ and $gc\_alloc\_fast()$. They have similar functions, but the later one only handles small objects. We only instrument the two interfaces instead of the jitted code to get object allocation sites by unwinding the call stack to find the nearest Java frame. The allocation sites will be saved in the thread-local buffer with the initial physical addresses of objects. For saving memory, we encode different tags in the last two bits of the profiled records, to indicate their types, like the right part of Fig. 5. Because GCV5 aligns all the objects by 4 bytes on a 32-bit system, the last two bits are always zeros under this scenario. If the new object is allocated in NOS, the lowest two bits of the first word will be set to 01b, otherwise 10b. When the buffer is full, or a garbage collection happens, the profiled data in the buffer will be sent to another process or computing device via sockets. Then the buffer can be reused again, until the Java thread terminates.
- Garbage collection starting. When a garbage collection happens, all the remained profiled data in Java thread buffers will be sent out. Then, the GC_Time value will be increased by 1. It will not be outputted alone, but

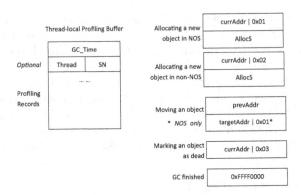

Fig. 5. Thread-local profiling buffer and encoded records

saved in every thread-local buffer as the header. When GCV5 starts multiple concurrent collectors, the profiler will apply a thread-local buffer like Fig. 5 with 64 kilobytes for every collector.

- Moving an object. Objects can only be moved during collections. During minor collections, GCV5 will move the infant objects from *FromSpaces* to *ToSpaces* of NOS, or MOS directly if an object has been moved before during the last collection. The profiler will write the previous address and target address of the moved object to the thread-local buffer at this moment. During major collections, GCV5 will collect the NOS and MOS as a whole space in a move-and-compact mode. Every time an object is moved, its previous address and target address will be recorded in the collector buffer as well. So does the LOS. When a buffer is full, the profiled data in the buffer will be sent out immediately. If the target address of a moved object belongs to NOS, its lowest two bits will be set to 01*b* in the profiled record, like Fig. 5.
- Marking an object as dead. During major collections, MOS collectors will explicitly mark dead objects. The profiler will record their addresses for all dead objects in thread-local buffers with death marks, like Fig. 5. It uses the same buffers as object moving. GCV5 scans LOS during major collections as well. Collectors will go through all objects, including live and dead ones in LOS. The profiler will record the addresses of dead objects in LOS in a similar way. During minor collections, GCV5 copies live objects in NOS to another area with higher generation. The profiler does not output any death information under this scenario. Dead objects in NOS will be picked out by the Address Chain building process later.
- Garbage collection finished. The profiler will output the remaining information in thread-local buffers of collectors, and the *GCFINISH* constant number, like Fig. 5.
- Other scenarios. In theory, the profiler does not output any new record under these scenarios. In practice, by the end of program execution, the profiler will output the remaining information in Java thread buffers.

Compressed Mode. For saving the bandwidth of networks, the profiler could use a compressed mode to buffer the records of allocation sites. Comparing with the amount of millions even hundreds of millions of objects, the amount of allocation sites is limited, about several thousands in most workloads we studied. Therefore, we could compress the profiled data of allocation sites by grouping objects with the same allocation site together. For instance, for every Java thread, the profiler could create an independent buffer for a frequently allocated site that has been executed thousands of times between two garbage collections, besides the unified 64-kilobyte buffer for all sites. An independent buffer is also structured like Fig. 5, but added one more field to record the corresponding allocation site in the header. For all the objects allocated at the same site after the corresponding independent buffer created, they will be profiled together only with their $Addr_0$ values. All the objects in the same independent buffer have the same $AllocS$ value as the added field in the header.

The independent buffers are also reusable, and will be automatically reclaimed when a Java thread finishes or a garbage collection happens. We can use smaller sizes for the independent buffers, e.g. 4 kilobytes per site, for saving memory space. In practice, the additional out-of-java-heap memory overheads required by the independent buffers were only dozens of kilobytes per Java thread on average.

For most workloads we studied, the profiled allocation sites of new objects dominate the whole data sets before compression. Therefore, the compressed mode can obviously reduce the profiled data size and the bandwidth of networks, about 50% on average for SpecJVM2008 and SpecJBB2005. Section 5 will demonstrate more about the runtime performance of the compressed mode.

It is easy to extend the compressed mode for further profiling requirements. For instance, if we want to profile the class information for every object, e.g. its class name or class handle, we could compress the profiled data of objects belonging to the same class as well, in a similar way.

4.3 Implementations of the Address Chain Building Algorithm

This section will introduce the single-threaded and multi-threaded implementations of the Address Chain building algorithm.

Single-Threaded Implementation. The single-threaded implementation of the Address Chain building algorithm basically follows the two algorithms shown in Fig. 2 and Fig. 3. It receives data from the profiler via sockets on another computing device. We use a hash table with 32M buckets mapping to the lowest three bytes of $Addr_N$, for reducing collisions for hundreds of millions of objects initialized by SpecJVM2008 and SpecJBB2005. If the new address of a record belongs to NOS, the lowest two bits marked by $01b$ will be reserved for further usage.

The two algorithms have provided almost all the details of how to handle the object initialization, movements and death records. Beside these scenarios, when a $GCFINISH$ record is read, dead objects in NOS can be picked out by traversing the hash table to find out vectors whose $Addr_N$ fields have been set to $01b$ in the lowest two bits and T_N fields are less than the current GC_Time. These NOS objects have been automatically abandoned by the garbage collector without any explicit reclaiming operation during the last collection. The vectors of dead objects will be removed and freed from both the hash table and the Address Chain, after collecting the statistical information.

Multi-threaded Implementation. Although the revised Address Chain building algorithm in Fig. 3 could significantly reduce the computing complexity, the Address Chain building process could still be time-consuming, especially for workloads with hundreds of millions of objects and hundreds of garbage collections. In fact, one of the most time-consuming parts of the building process is the routine that marks NOS objects as dead and reclaims their memory space. This part will traverse all the buckets of the hash table, find out all abandoned NOS objects and deal with their vectors. However, this traversing routine is bucket-independent. That means, when traversing one bucket, the routine needs not visit any other bucket at all. We can start multiple threads to traverse different buckets concurrently without data exchange between threads. The multi-threaded implementation can obviously improve the runtime performance of the Address Chain building process, e.g. at most 2.5 times faster than the single-threaded approach on an Intel's Core i7-2600 Quad-Core machine for some workloads of SpecJVM2008. Section 5 will demonstrate more about the runtime performance of the multi-threaded implementation.

5   Performance Evaluation

This section presents the performance evaluation of the profiler, as well as the Address Chain building algorithm.

Some analysis results of the profiled data for SpecJVM2008, SpecJBB2005 and Dacapo (DaCapo-9.12-bach) are demonstrated. We also demonstrate how to use the profiled data to help some optimizations like pretenuring.

5.1   Performance of the Profiler

We chose Apache Harmony 6.0 DRLVM with a generational garbage collector as the host platform. The Java Virtual Machine and the Address Chain building algorithm ran on different computing devices. An Intel's Pentium Dual-Core E5200 machine and an AMD's FX-8120 Eight-Core machine were chosen as the host machines of the profiler, and an Intel's Core i7-2600 Quad-Core machine was chosen as the profiled data collector and the Address Chain builder. All these machines were connected via a Gigabit network. The detailed software and hardware configurations of testing machines are shown in Table 1.

All the workloads of SpecJVM2008 and Dacapo ran with a 512M Java heap and default settings. SpecJBB2005 ran with 8 warehouses and a 768M Java

Table 1. Configurations of testing machines

	Profiling PC A	Profiling PC B	Data Collct. PC
CPU Type	Intel Pentium Dual-Core E5200	AMD FX-8120 8-Core	Intel Core i7-2600 Quad-Core
CPU Freq.	2.5G	3.1G	3.4G
Main Mem.	2GB	12GB	4GB
OS	Ubuntu 12.04 LTS	Ubuntu 12.04 LTS	Ubuntu Server 12.04

heap. The original Apache Harmony 6.0 DRLVM only supports *avrora*, *fop*, *h2*, *jython*, *luindex*, *lusearch*, *pmd*, *sunflow*, and *xalan* of Dapaco. Because SpecJVM2008 and Dacapo both have a workload namely *sunflow*, the workload that first appears always belongs to SpecJVM2008 in figures and tables below.

The runtime overheads of the profiler are shown in Fig. 6. We tested the profiler with both uncompressed and compressed modes on the two profiling machines shown in Table 1, respectively. The average overheads of SpecJVM2008 were 5.40% and 6.78% on the two testing machines with the uncompressed mode, respectively. The average overheads of SpecJBB2005 were 7.83% and 10.72% on the two testing machines with the uncompressed mode, respectively. The average overheads of Dacapo were 8.12% on Machine A. For the compressed mode, the average overheads were 6.45% and 8.32% for SpecJVM2008, and 10.07% and 10.32% for SpecJBB2005, respectively. For the compressed mode, the average overheads of Dacapo were 12.31% on Machine A.

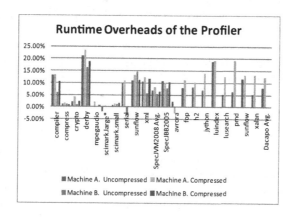

Fig. 6. Runtime overheads of the profiler. *Note: The original Apache Harmony 6.0 DRLVM does not support scimark.large of SpecJVM2008 on Machine B.

In most cases, the compress mode was a little bit slower than the uncompressed mode, as shown in Fig. 6. This is due to the runtime overheads of unifying objects with the same allocation site to the same profiling buffer. Although we used a hash table to speed up the unifying process for every Java thread, it still could slow down the performance about $2 - 4\%$ on average. However, the compressed mode obviously reduced the bandwidth of networks and

Table 2. Bandwidths and profiled data sizes

Benchmark	Network BW. (MB/S) Uncompressed	Network BW. (MB/S) Compressed	Profiled Bytes per obj. Uncompressed	Profiled Bytes per obj. Compressed
compiler	29.45	15.67	8.86	4.73
compress	0.08	0.07	21.71	19.42
crypto	5.57	2.88	8.21	4.28
derby	29.30	14.18	8.03	4.04
mpegaudio	0.06	0.04	9.25	6.07
scimark.large	0.02	0.02	25.51	24.00
scimark.small	0.08	0.05	10.27	7.08
serial	22.77	11.37	8.02	4.10
sunflow	32.12	16.51	8.39	4.28
xml	24.36	12.49	8.06	4.14
SpecJVM2008 Avg.	10.05	5.16	8.30	4.29
SpecJBB2005	22.08	12.13	8.20	4.77
avrora	1.77	1.06	8.33	4.84
fop	9.24	3.49	8.59	5.45
h2	51.88	30.05	8.96	5.60
jython	14.09	7.18	8.38	4.69
luindex	2.70	1.67	10.99	8.92
lusearch	12.80	6.53	8.89	4.62
pmd	12.13	6.23	8.40	4.72
sunflow	31.29	15.45	8.05	4.07
xalan	10.94	6.75	8.64	5.61
Dacapo Avg.	16.31	8.71	8.80	5.39

the size of profiled data, e.g. more than 50% on average for SpecJVM2008 and SpecJBB2005, and about 40% on average for Dacapo, as shown in Table 2. The compressed mode is useful for environments with limited bandwidth or storage capabilities.

Table 2 also shows the network bandwidths and the sizes of profiled data per object for both uncompressed and compressed modes on profiling machine A. For the uncompressed mode, the average bandwidths were 10.05 MB/S, 22.08 MB/S and 16.31 MB/S for SpecJVM2008, SpecJBB2005 and Dacapo, respectively. The highest bandwidth was 51.88 MB/S for $sunflow$ of SpecJVM2008, and the lowest bandwidth was 0.02 MB/S for $scimark.large$ of SpecJVM2008. For the compressed mode, the average bandwidths have been reduced about 50% to 5.16 MS/S and 12.13 MB/S for SpecJVM2008 and SpecJBB2005, respectively. The highest bandwidth was 30.05 MB/S for $h2$ of Dacapo, and the lowest bandwidth was 0.02 MB/S for $scimark.large$ of SpecJVM2008. For a Gigabit network system, all the bandwidths are acceptable for both uncompressed and compressed modes.

For the uncompressed mode, the average sizes of profiled data per object were 8.3, 8.2 and 8.8 bytes for SpecJVM2008, SpecJBB2005 and Dacapo, respectively. For the compressed mode, the average sizes were 4.29, 4.77, and 5.39 bytes, respectively. The workload $scimark.large$ of SpecJVM2008 had the lowest bandwidth, but the largest size of profiled data per object, i.e. 25.41 bytes for uncompressed mode and 24 bytes for compressed mode. The major reason is, a lot of MOS and LOS objects of $scimark.large$ were heavily moved during garbage collections. That caused the profiler to produce many $(Addr_{prev}, Addr_{target})$ pairs that could not be compressed.

5.2   Performance of the Address Chain Building Algorithm

Fig. 7 presents the runtime performance of the single-threaded and multi-threaded implementations of the Address Chain building algorithm shown in Fig. 3, by using the profiling machine A and the data collecting machine shown in Table 1. We compared the calculating time of the building algorithm with the execution time of the corresponding workload. In this figure, 100% means the building algorithm was exactly as fast as the workload, and 80% means the algorithm was 20% faster than the workload.

We can find that the single-threaded implementation of the algorithm was on average about 16%, 77% and 3% slower than the Java Virtual Machine for SpecJVM2008, SpecJBB2005 and Dacapo, respectively. However, the multi-threaded implementation was on average about 4% faster than the Java Virtual Machine for SpecJVM2008, 56% slower for SpecJBB2005, and 6% faster for Dacapo, respectively. The multi-threaded implementation was on average about 33%, 12% and 9% faster than the single-threaded version for SpecJVM2008, SpecJBB2005 and Dacapo on the Intel's Quad-Core machine by using 32 threads to mark dead NOS objects concurrently, respectively. That means, our mechanism has the capability of providing online object status in a distributed way for most workloads we studied.

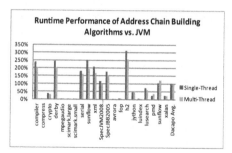

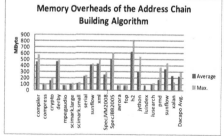

Fig. 7. Runtime performance of Address Chain building algorithm comparing with the Java Virtual Machine

Fig. 8. Memory overheads of the Address Chain building algorithm on the data collecting machine

The memory overheads of the algorithm on the data collecting machine are shown in Fig. 8. The average memory sizes required by the algorithm were about 252M, 494M and 222M bytes for SpecJVM2008, SpecJBB2005 and Dacapo, respectively. The maximum memory sizes were about 572M bytes for the workload *compiler* of SpecJVM2008, 608M bytes for SpecJBB2005, and 798M for *h2* of Dacapo, respectively.

Fig. 9 presents the processed object numbers per second by the multi-threaded algorithm on the data collecting machine. The multi-threaded implementation could process on average more than 1.8, 1.7 and 2.6 million objects per second for their entire life cycles, for SpecJVM2008, SpecJBb2005 and Dacapo, respectively.

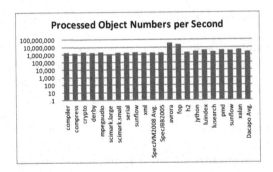

Fig. 9. Objects processed per second by the multi-threaded implementation of the Address Chain building algorithm

5.3   Profiled Data Analysis

Table 3 shows the total object numbers, objects died during major collections, objects died during minor collections, the average life cycles of objects counted in garbage collection times, as well as the total garbage collection times for SpecJVM2008, SpecJBB2005 and Dacapo. The dead objects in MOS and LOS were only marked and reclaimed by GCV5 during major collections. The NOS objects were reclaimed during both minor and major collections. On average, more than 76%, 97% and 69% objects died during minor collections for SpecJVM2008, SpecJBB2005 and Dacapo, respectively. The total object number minus the sum of objects died in major and minor collections equals to the number of objects survived at the end of Java program execution.

Table 3. Object life cycles of SpecJVM2008, SpecJBB2005 and Dacapo

Workload	Obj #	Died in Major GC.	Died in Minor GC.	Avg. Life Cycl.	GC #
compiler	2,687,615,414	9,994,180	2,672,421,727	0.40	347
compress	1,439,278	547,380	533,690	3.05	19
crypto	820,878,761	17,741,796	802,508,705	0.30	421
derby	2,394,376,389	20,040,660	2,372,915,933	0.46	421
mpegaudio	2,810,041	126,477	2,071,807	2.54	31
sci. large	1,531,628	313,733	790,400	5.79	34
sci. small	15,312,110	861,661	14,021,032	2.48	142
serial	1,221,030,456	2,477,287	1,217,080,285	0.08	325
sunflow	1,497,652,655	126,477	1,494,757,222	0.62	177
xml	2,555,748,192	2,509,129,381	40,626,795	0.36	380
JBB2005	214,208,072	7,709,328	701,398,471	0.30	94
avrora	2,977,153	0	177,507	0.04	1
fop	3,134,693	45,970	195,524	0.10	2
h2	135,991,578	10,459,133	115,703,110	0.93	25
jython	46,718,046	38,242,009	2,625,698	0.10	8
luindex	670,397	117,599	175,635	0.40	2
lusearch	11,963,090	390,868	10,126,243	0.24	14
pmd	9,397,088	171,845	7,500,996	0.07	3
sunflow	62,180,768	135,496	56,486,622	0.02	8
xalan	9,781,989	4,350,505	2,286,462	0.07	4

Table 4. Top allocation sites of SpecJVM2008, SpecJBB2005 and Dacapo

Workload	Total Alloc. Sites	Top Sites
compiler	7841	79
compress	5900	101
crypto	6256	4
derby	8362	29
mpegaudio	8989	37
sci. large	5907	103
sci. small	5992	10
serial	6153	12
sunflow	6499	5
xml	10570	30
JBB2005	4951	6
avrora	3535	13
fop	9708	50
h2	3688	36
jython	11329	174
luindex	3237	43
lusearch	3078	51
pmd	4316	84
sunflow	3598	6
xalan	4083	30

Table 4 shows how many allocation sites allocating more than 80% of the total objects. For instance, the workload *compiler* of SpecJVM2008 allocated 80.22% objects at the top 79 allocation sites of the total 7841 sites. With more details of the top allocations sites, these kinds of information could help programmers and compilers to understand the hottest sites regarding memory allocation better.

5.4   Example of Application

Although we demonstrate more about our profiling mechanism itself in this paper, the current profiled data could help some optimizations like pretenuring as well. Table 5 demonstrates some allocation sites that allocated long-term survived objects (died in MOS) much more than short-term survived ones (died in NOS) in SpecJVM2008 and SpecJBB2005. For instance, the allocation site $0xCA14CF$ of SpecJBB2005 method *create_random_a_string()* allocated more than 1.7 million objects, 100% of which died in MOS spaces. If the Java Virtual Machine pretenures these objects in MOS spaces directly, instead of allocating them in NOS first, the performance of the garbage collector could be better.

Table 5. Allocation sites for pretenuring candidates in SpecJVM2008 and SpecJBB2005

Workload	Method	Alloc. Site	% of Obj. Died in MOS	Total Obj.
JBB2005	create_random_ a_string()	0xCA14CF	100%	1,785,160
sci. small	newCharBuffer()	0xAEC501	83.59%	15,784
	newDecoder()	0xAEBDC7	83.58%	15,778
sci. large	RES_GET_ KEY16()	0x7CD8614	88.45%	5,653
mpegaudio	RES_GET_ KEY16()	0x7952614	97.27%	4,801
compress	java.lang.Long. toString()	0x722485E	99.67%	5,491
	java.lang.String. getBytes()	0x844FA73	96.95%	10,049

Of cause, the current profiler could not be used to perform optimizations directly, however, it is possible to enhance the profiler for further requirements.

6   Conclusion

The *AddressChain* mechanism profiles Java objects without overhead in Java heaps. It also provides a profiling framework that can be easily adapted to profile more or less information for further requirements. The runtime performance of the profiler is reasonable. The object status could be calculated almost simultaneously for most workloads we studied in a distributed way. The mechanism is useful for debugging, monitoring, program analysis and many optimizations for garbage-collected languages.

Acknowledgments. This material is based upon works supported by National Natural Science Foundation of China No.61073010 and No.61272166.

References

1. Apache DRLVM GCV5, http://harmony.aparche.org/subcomponents/drlvm/gc-v5.html
2. Blackburn, S.M., Garner, R., Hoffman, C., Khan, A.M., McKinley, K.S., Bentzur, R., Diwan, A., Feinberg, D., Frampton, D., Guyer, S.Z., Hirzel, M., Hosking, A., Jump, M., Lee, H., Moss, J.E.B., Phansalkar, A., Stefanovic, D., Van Drunen, T., von Dincklage, D., Wiedermann, B.: The DaCapo Benchmarks: Java Benchmarking Development and Analysis. In: OOPSLA 2006: Proceedings of the 21st Annual ACM SIGPLAN Conference on Object-Oriented Programing, Systems, Languages, and Applications, Portland, USA, October 22-26 (2006)
3. Blackburn, S.M., Hertz, M., McKinley, K.S., Moss, J.E.B., Yang, T.: Profile-Based Pretenuring. ACM Transactions on Programming Languages and Systems 29(1) (2007)
4. Bond, M.D., McKinley, K.S.: Leak Pruning. In: Proceedings of ASPLOS 2009, Washington, DC, USA (2009)
5. Bond, M.D., McKinley, K.S.: Bell: Bit-Encoding Online Memory Leak Detection. In: Proceedings of ASPLOS 2006, San Jose, California, USA (2006)
6. Chilimbi, T.M., Hauswirth, M.: Low-Overhead Memory Leak Detection Using Adaptive Statistical Profiling. In: Proceedings of ASPLOS 2004, Boston, MA, USA (2004)
7. Ha, J., Arnold, M., Blackburn, S.M.: A Concurrent Dynamic Analysis Framework for Multicore Hardware. In: Proceedings of OOPSLA 2009, Orlando, Florida, USA (2009)
8. Hertz, M., Blackburn, S.M., Moss, J.E.B., McKinley, K.S., Stefanovic, D.: Error-free garbage collection traces: How to cheat and not get caught. In: Proceedings of the International Conference on Measurement and Modeling of Computer Systems, Marina Del Rey, CA, USA (2002)
9. Hertz, M., Blackburn, S.M., Moss, J.E.B., McKinley, K.S., Stefanovic, D.: Generating object lifetime traces with Merlin. ACM Transactions on Programming Languages and Systems (TOPLAS) 28(3), 476–516 (2006)

10. Jump, M., Blackburn, S.M., McKinley, K.S.: Dynamic object sampling for pretenuring. In: Proceedings of the 4th International Symposium on Memory Management, pp. 152–162 (2004)
11. JProbe, http://www.quest.com/jprobe
12. JProfiler, http://www.ej-technologies.com
13. Odaira, R., Ogata, K., Kawachiya, K., Onodera, T., Nakatani, T.: Efficient Runtime Tracking of Allocation Sites in Java. In: Proceedings of VEE 2010, Pittsburgh, Pennsylvania, USA (2010)
14. Odaira, R., Nakatani, T.: Continuous object access profiling and optimizations to overcome the memory wall and bloat. In: Proceedings of ASPLOS XVII, London, England, UK (2012)
15. Shaham, R., Kolodner, E.K., Sagiv, M.: Heap profiling for space-efficient Java. In: Proceedings of PLDI 2001, pp. 104–113 (2001)
16. Sun, Q.Y., Shi, X.H., Xie, J.R.: Profiling Object Life Ranges for Detecting Memory Leaks in Java Virtual Machine. In: Proceedings of PDCAT 2012, Beijing, China (2012)
17. Xu, G., Arnold, M., Mitchell, N., Rountev, A., Sevitsky, G.: Go with the Flow: Profiling Copies To Find Runtime Bloat. In: Proceedings of PLDI 2009, Dublin, Ireland (2009)
18. Xu, G.: Resurrector: A Tunable Object Lifetime Profiling Technique for Optimizing Real-World Programs. In: Proceedings of OOPSLA 2013, Indianapolis, Indiana, USA (2013)

Call-by-Value in a Basic Logic for Interaction

Ulrich Schöpp

Ludwig-Maximilians-Universität München, Germany

Abstract. In game semantics and related approaches to programming language semantics, programs are modelled by interaction dialogues. Such models have recently been used by a number of authors for the design of compilation methods, in particular for applications where resource control is important. The work in this area has focused on call-by-name languages. In this paper we study the compilation of call-by-value into a first-order low-level language by means of an interpretation in a semantic interactive model. We refine the methods developed for call-by-name languages to allow an efficient treatment of call-by-value. We introduce an intermediate language that is based on the structure of an interactive computation model and that can be seen as a fragment of Linear Logic. The main result is that Plotkin's call-by-value CPS-translation and its soundness proof can be refined to target this intermediate language. This refined CPS-translation amounts to a direct compilation of the source language into a first-order language.

1 Introduction

The compilation of programming languages to machine code is usually considered as a series of translation steps between intermediate languages of varying expressiveness. While managing the details of low level intermediate languages is sometimes considered an implementation problem, there are many good reasons for studying the logical principles underlying the low level details of compilation, e.g. for the formal verification of compilers and optimisers, the design of intermediate languages, or the analysis of machine code behaviour and resource usage.

The study of the logical structure of low-level computation has been fruitful in recent work on the compilation of programming languages with strong resource constraints. A number of authors, e.g. [10,11,7,9], have used semantic models related to game semantics to design compilation methods with various resource usage guarantees. Game semantics explains higher-order computation by interaction dialogues and can be used to organise low-level programs into semantic models. The idea is to think of low-level programs as implementations of game semantic strategies, so that interaction dialogues appear as traces of low-level programs. Following this idea, one can construct models that have interesting structure, enough to interpret higher-order languages, but also suitable for fine-grained control of resources. For example, the structure has been shown to allow good control of stack space usage in work on using of higher-order languages for hardware synthesis [10] and for programming in logarithmic space [7].

It is reasonable to ask if such semantically-motivated compilation methods are not useful for analysing and organising compilation even if one does not want to impose resource restrictions. Control of stack space usage, for example, is important in compilation and having logical and semantic principles to account for it should be useful.

J. Garrigue (Ed.): APLAS 2014, LNCS 8858, pp. 428–448, 2014.

One way of assessing this question is to capture the structure of semantically-motivated compilation methods in terms of higher intermediate languages and to study their utility for general compilation. In our case, this entails to study the structure of interactive models built from a low-level language, to define intermediate languages for working with this structure and to assess questions such as: Can existing languages be compiled by translation to such an intermediate language? Would we obtain efficient compilation methods and how would they relate to existing methods? Most importantly, would we gain anything from moving to such a more structured intermediate language? Can we identify logical principles for the intermediate language that allows us to reason about low-level programs, such as for proving compiler correctness or resource bounds?

For the compilation of call-by-name languages, such as PCF, there is growing evidence that these questions have a positive answer. The above-mentioned work on resource-aware compilation considers call-by-name languages that can be seen as fragments of PCF with various resource constraints. By relaxing constraints on resources, it is possible to extend this work to cover all of PCF. It turns out that one obtains efficient compilation methods that are related to standard techniques in the compilation of programming languages, such as CPS-translation and defunctionalization [23]. The translation from PCF to the interactive model can be seen as a thunkifying translation [13] into an intermediate language, such as the one described in [24], and correctness follows immediately from equations in the intermediate language.

In this paper we consider the case of call-by-value source languages, which has received much less attention so far. We present a basic intermediate language close to Tensorial Logic [17] that captures just the structure needed to handle the translation of a call-by-value source language. What we obtain is a translation from source language to low-level language that fully specifies all details of the translation, including closure representation. It is compositional, allows for separate compilation and specifies abstractly the interfaces of compiled modules. We show that standard techniques for equational reasoning in the polymorphic λ-calculus can be transported to the intermediate language, which allows for a simple proof of correctness for the translation from call-by-value source language to low-level language.

The translation is a refined call-by-value CPS-translation. Existing work has shown that interactive models naturally support call-by-name languages, so it seems reasonable to try to reduce the case for call-by-value languages to that for call-by-name languages. Indeed, a standard CPS-translation from call-by-value to call-by-name leads to programs that implement call-by-value programs in a natural way. However, the translation fails to satisfy the well-known requirement that call-by-value translations should be *safe for space* [26], which means that the value of a variable should be discarded after the last use in its scope. It appears that the structure identified so far for call-by-name languages does not give us enough low-level control to satisfy such requirements.

Let us outline the issue concretely, using as an example the language INTML [7], which is a call-by-name language developed for compilation with LOGSPACE guarantees. In INTML stack memory management information is made explicit in the type system. Function types have the form $A \cdot X \multimap Y$, where A is a type of values that the function needs to preserve on the stack when it makes a call to its argument. When the function makes a call to its argument, a value of type A is put on the stack and is kept there until the call returns, whereupon the value of type A is removed from the stack for further use. Thus, values are removed from the stack only when a call returns.

That values are removed from the stack only upon function return is problematic for programming in continuation passing style. Continuations are functions that are invoked, but that typically never return. If one considers CPS-translated call-by-value programs, then this means that no value will ever be discarded in the course of computation. Indeed, if we translate the term let $x=5$ in let $y=x+1$ in let $z=y+4$ in $z+3$ to INTML using Plotkin's CPS-translation (see Section 4.1), then the resulting term can be given type $(\mathsf{nat} \times \mathsf{nat} \times \mathsf{nat}) \cdot (\mathsf{unit} \cdot [\mathsf{nat}] \multimap [0]) \multimap [0]$. The type already shows that the continuation will be called with three natural numbers on the stack, even though only a single number, namely 13, should be needed. Indeed, the stack will contain the triple $\langle 6, 10, 13 \rangle$ of all the intermediate values for x, y and z. The question is therefore how we can give a translation that deallocates values that are not needed anymore.

In this paper we show how to refine the CPS-translation to target an intermediate language derived from an interactive model in a way that addresses this issue of managing values and their deallocation. It turns out that this issue is orthogonal to duplication in the source language. In order to focus on value management, we shall therefore first focus on the linear case. To allow duplication it will be enough to allow duplication in the intermediated language, see Section 5.

In Section 3 we first define a basic linear intermediate language. This intermediate language allows us to formulate the call-by-value translation for a linear source language as a refinement of Plotkin's call-by-value CPS-translation [19] in Section 4. In contrast to standard approaches of compiling with continuations, such as [4], where CPS-translation targets a higher-order intermediate language that still requires closure conversion, the refined CPS-translation fully specifies a translation from source language to the first-order low-level language. The translation appears to be related to defunctionalizing compilation methods [5,6], see also [23]. We believe that it is also related to the call-by-value games of [14,3], in particular [16] seems relevant. Notice, however, that these games do not make explicit which values must be stored for how long. The translation in this paper makes this and other low-level details, such as closure conversion, explicit. In Section 4 we show it nevertheless allows the soundness of the translation to be proved by an argument close to Plotkin's original soundness proof. In Section 5 we then explain how to lift the linearity restriction in order to translate a simply-typed source language.

2   Low-Level Programs

We start by fixing the low-level language, which is essentially a goto language. It is typed and works with values of the following first-order types.

$$\text{Value Types} \quad A, B ::= \alpha \mid \mathsf{nat} \mid \mathsf{unit} \mid A \times B \mid 0 \mid A + B$$
$$\text{Values} \quad v, w ::= x \mid n \mid \langle \rangle \mid \langle v, w \rangle \mid \mathsf{inl}(v) \mid \mathsf{inr}(v)$$

Low-level programs are built from *blocks* of the form $f(x \colon A) \{ b \}$, where f is the block label, x is its formal parameter and b is the body, formed according to the grammar below. Therein, v ranges over values, g over labels and op over primitive operation constants.

$$b ::= \mathsf{let}\, x = op(v)\, \mathsf{in}\, b \mid \mathsf{let}\, \langle x, y \rangle = v\, \mathsf{in}\, b \mid \mathsf{case}\, v\, \mathsf{of}\, \mathsf{inl}(x) \Rightarrow b_1; \mathsf{inr}(y) \Rightarrow b_2 \mid g(v)$$

The set of constants that takes arguments of type A and returns values of type B is defined by a set $Prim(A, B)$. In this paper, we assume $Prim(\mathsf{nat}, \mathsf{unit}) = \{\mathsf{print}\}$, $Prim(\mathsf{nat} \times \mathsf{nat}, \mathsf{int}) = \{\mathsf{add}, \mathsf{times}, \mathsf{div}\}$, $Prim(\mathsf{nat} \times \mathsf{nat}, \mathsf{unit} + \mathsf{unit}) = \{\mathsf{eq}, \mathsf{lt}\}$ and that all other $Prim$-sets are empty.

A *program* p is given by a set of block definitions together with two distinguished labels $entry_p$ and $exit_p$. The program must be such that there are no two block definitions with the same label and that there is no definition of the exit label. We write short $(x \mapsto v)$ for the program with a single block $entry(x\colon A)\,\{\,exit(v)\,\}$ and use informal pattern matching notation, such as writing $(\langle x, y \rangle \mapsto v)$ for $(z \mapsto \mathsf{let}\ \langle x, y \rangle = z\ \mathsf{in}\ v)$. We write Ω_A for the nonterminating program $entry(x\colon A)\,\{\,entry(x)\,\}$.

Programs are assumed to be typed in the canonical way. We write $p\colon A \to B$ if p is a program whose entry and exit labels accept values of type A and B respectively.

Operational Semantics. The operational semantics of a program p is given by a relation $b_1 \xrightarrow{o}_p b_2$, which expresses that body term b_1 reduces to body term b_2 while outputting the sequence of closed values o using the print-operation. We write ε for the empty sequence and $o_1 o_2$ for concatenation of o_1 and o_2.

This relation is defined to be the smallest relation such that $b_1 \xrightarrow{o_1}_p b_2 \xrightarrow{o_2}_p b_3$ implies $b_1 \xrightarrow{o_1 o_2}_p b_3$, such that $f(v) \xrightarrow{\varepsilon}_p b[v/x]$ if p contains a block definition $f(x\colon A)\,\{\,b\,\}$, and such that the following hold.

$$\mathsf{let}\ \langle x, y \rangle = \langle v, w \rangle\ \mathsf{in}\ b \xrightarrow{\varepsilon}_p b[v/x, w/y] \qquad \mathsf{case}\ \mathsf{inl}(v)\ \mathsf{of}\ \mathsf{inl}(y) \Rightarrow b; \ldots \xrightarrow{\varepsilon}_p b[v/y]$$

$$\mathsf{let}\ x = \mathsf{print}(v)\ \mathsf{in}\ b \xrightarrow{v}_p b[\mathsf{unit}/x] \qquad \mathsf{case}\ \mathsf{inr}(v)\ \mathsf{of}\ \ldots; \mathsf{inr}(y) \Rightarrow b \xrightarrow{\varepsilon}_p b[v/y]$$

$$\mathsf{let}\ x = \mathsf{add}(\langle m, n \rangle)\ \mathsf{in}\ b \xrightarrow{\varepsilon}_p b[m + n/x] \qquad \text{(similar cases for mul, div, eq and lt)}$$

Notation. We consider two programs $p, q\colon A \to B$ equal, written $p = q$, if they have the same observable effects and return the same values: Whenever $entry_p(v) \xrightarrow{o}_p b$ then $entry_q(v) \xrightarrow{o}_q b'$ for some b', whenever $entry_p(v) \xrightarrow{o}_p exit_p(w)$ then $entry_q(v) \xrightarrow{o}_q exit_q(w)$, and the same two conditions with the roles of p and q exchanged.

We use standard graphical notation [25] for working with low-level programs. A program $p\colon A_1 + \cdots + A_n \to B_1 + \cdots + B_m$ is depicted like on the left below. Shown next to it are the identity program $id_A\colon A \to A$ and the swapping program $swap_{A,B}\colon B + A \to A + B$. Programs can be composed by vertical and horizontal composition and by taking loops. For two programs $q_1\colon A \to B$ and $q_2\colon C \to D$, their vertical composition is the sum $q_1 + q_2\colon A + C \to B + D$, which is the program obtained by renaming all labels in q_1 and q_2 so that no label appears in both programs and by adding new definitions $entry(x\colon A + C)\,\{\,\mathsf{case}\ x\ \mathsf{of}\ \mathsf{inl}(x_1) \Rightarrow entry_{q_1}(x_1); \mathsf{inr}(x_2) \Rightarrow entry_{q_2}(x_2)\,\}$, $exit_{q_1}(x\colon B)\,\{\,exit(\mathsf{inl}(x))\,\}$ and $exit_{q_2}(x\colon D)\,\{\,exit(\mathsf{inr}(x))\,\}$, where $entry$ and $exit$ are the fresh entry and exit labels of $q_1 + q_2$. The horizontal composition of $r_1\colon A \to B$ and $r_2\colon B \to C$ stands for the sequential composition $r_2 \circ r_1\colon A \to C$ and is defined similarly. Loops are defined by jumping from the exit to entry label.

The values of any closed type A can be encoded into natural numbers, that is one can define programs $\mathrm{encode}_A \colon A \to \mathrm{nat}$ and $\mathrm{decode}_A \colon \mathrm{nat} \to A$ such that $\mathrm{decode}_A \circ \mathrm{encode}_A = id_A$ holds. To simplify the examples, we assume that the encoding and decoding functions for nat are the identity. Given a value-type-with-hole $C[\cdot]$, i.e. a value type with zero or more occurrences of $\cdot$, we write $C[A]$ for the type obtained by replacing each $\cdot$ with A. The encoding and decoding programs can be lifted to $C[\mathrm{encode}_A] \colon C[A] \to C[\mathrm{nat}]$ and $C[\mathrm{decode}_A] \colon C[\mathrm{nat}] \to C[A]$ by induction on C.

3   A Basic Linear Intermediate Language

In this section we introduce a basic linear higher-order intermediate language LIN that can be used to organise low-level programs and to reason about them. It can be seen as a syntactic description of the mathematical structure obtained by applying the Int construction [15] to a term model of the low-level language, see [7]. The intermediate language recombines the ideas developed in [21,7,22] in a way that is suitable to handle also the translation of call-by-value. It was inspired by Melliès' Tensorial Logic [18,17]. We can give here only a concise definition of bare LIN; a richer intermediate language, defined not solely for the study of call-by-value, is described in detail in [24].

The types and terms of LIN are defined by the following grammars, in which A ranges over value types and α ranges over value type variables.

$$\text{Interface Types}\quad X, Y ::= A^{\perp} \mid X \multimap Y \mid \forall \alpha.\, X$$

These types may be thought of as the interfaces of interactive entities that are implemented in the low-level language. The type $A^{\perp}$ is the interface of low-level programs that accept inputs of type A and that never return anything. The type $X \multimap Y$ is the interface of low-level programs that when linked to a program implementing interface X become an implementation of interface Y. Finally, value type polymorphism $\forall \alpha.\, X$ makes it easier to write programs and to reason about them.

The terms of LIN are defined as follows, where p ranges over low-level programs.

$$s, t ::= x \mid p^* t \mid \langle s, t \rangle \mid \mathrm{let}\ \langle x, y \rangle = s\ \mathrm{in}\ t \mid \lambda x{:}X.\, t \mid s\, t \mid \Lambda \alpha.\, t \mid t\, A$$

The typing rules for LIN are given in Fig. 1. We explain the meaning of terms by defining a translation to low-level programs. Each type X represents an interface that consists of two value types X^- and X^+:

$$(A^{\perp})^- = A \qquad (X \multimap Y)^- = X^+ + Y^- \qquad (\forall \alpha.\, X)^- = X^-[\mathrm{nat}/\alpha]$$
$$(A^{\perp})^+ = 0 \qquad (X \multimap Y)^+ = X^- + Y^+ \qquad (\forall \alpha.\, X)^+ = X^+[\mathrm{nat}/\alpha]$$

The idea is that an implementation of interface X is a program of type $X^- \to X^+$. For contexts we let $(-)^- = (-)^+ = 0$ and $(\Gamma, x \colon X)^- = \Gamma^- + X^-$ and $(\Gamma, x \colon X)^+ = \Gamma^+ + X^+$. A program of type $\Gamma^- \to \Gamma^+$ thus consists of an implementation of the interface of each variable in Γ.

A typing sequent $\Gamma \vdash t \colon X$ is translated as a low-level program $[\![\Gamma \vdash t \colon X]\!]$ of type $\overline{\Gamma^+ + X^-} \to \overline{\Gamma^- + X^+}$, where we write $\overline{(-)}$ for the operation of substituting nat for all free type variables. The intention is that if one connects an implementation e of the interface of Γ as follows, then one obtains a program implementing interface X.

$$\text{AX} \frac{}{x: X \vdash x: X} \qquad \text{WEAK} \frac{\Gamma \vdash t: Y}{\Gamma, x: X \vdash t: Y} \qquad \text{EXCH} \frac{\Gamma, y: Y, x: X, \Delta \vdash t: Z}{\Gamma, x: X, y: Y, \Delta \vdash t: Z}$$

$$0 \frac{}{\vdash \star: 0^{\perp}} \qquad \text{ACT} \frac{p: A \to B \qquad \Gamma \vdash t: B^{\perp}}{\Gamma \vdash p^{*}t: A^{\perp}}$$

$$\langle\rangle_{\text{I}} \frac{\Gamma \vdash s: A^{\perp} \qquad \Delta \vdash t: B^{\perp}}{\Gamma, \Delta \vdash \langle s, t \rangle: (A + B)^{\perp}} \qquad \langle\rangle_{\text{E}} \frac{\Gamma \vdash s: (A + B)^{\perp} \qquad \Delta, x: A^{\perp}, y: B^{\perp} \vdash t: X}{\Gamma, \Delta \vdash \text{let } \langle x, y \rangle = s \text{ in } t: X}$$

$$\multimap \text{I} \frac{\Gamma, x: X \vdash t: Y}{\Gamma \vdash \lambda x: X. t: X \multimap Y} \qquad \multimap \text{E} \frac{\Gamma \vdash s: X \multimap Y \qquad \Delta \vdash t: X}{\Gamma, \Delta \vdash s\, t: Y}$$

$$\forall \text{I} \frac{\Gamma \vdash t: X}{\Gamma \vdash \Lambda \alpha. t: \forall \alpha. X} \; \alpha \text{ not in } \Gamma \qquad \forall \text{E} \frac{\Gamma \vdash t: \forall \alpha. X}{\Gamma \vdash t\, A: X[A/\alpha]}$$

Fig. 1. Linear Intermediate Language

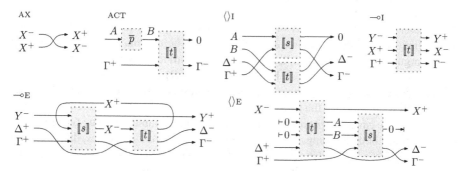

The translation is defined by induction on the derivation and is given in graphical notation below. Strictly speaking, we define an interpretation of derivations rather than sequents. We write only $[\![\Gamma \vdash t: X]\!]$, as different derivations of the same sequent will be equal in the sense defined in the next section. We also write just $[\![t]\!]$ when context and type are clear from the context. For readability, we omit the operation $\overline{(-)}$ on types – it is assumed to be applied to all types in the figure below.

The basic rules AX, WEAK, EXCH, $\multimap$I and $\multimap$E amount to a standard interpretation of the linear λ-calculus in the monodial closed structure that one obtains from applying the categorical Int construction to the low-level language, see [7]. It is the same structure that one finds in the Geometry of Interaction [1] and in Game Semantics [2]. The rules for functions formalise the view that the type $X \multimap Y$ is implemented by programs that, when linked with a program implementing interface X, implement interface Y. Rule $\multimap$E implements the linking of a function program to its argument program.

Rule $-\circ$I amounts to a reinterpretation of the interface of $[\![t]\!]$, so that an application will link the argument program to variable x.

Polymorphism is implemented by using nat in place of any type variable α. Since the values of any type can be encoded into nat, we can recover any type instance by using the encoding and decoding programs defined above. Rule $\forall$I is the identity, just like $-\circ$I, as the type variable α has already been substituted by nat. Rule $\forall$E realises the encoding and decoding of values of type A into ones of type nat. Let $F[\cdot] = \overline{X^-[\cdot/\alpha]}$ and $G[\cdot] = \overline{X^+[\cdot/\alpha]}$. We then have programs $F[\text{encode}_{\overline{A}}]\colon F[\overline{A}] \to F[\text{nat}]$ and $G[\text{decode}_{\overline{A}}]\colon G[\text{nat}] \to G[\overline{A}]$. Note $F[\text{nat}] = \overline{X^-}$ and $\overline{X^+} = G[\text{nat}]$. To obtain $[\![t\,A]\!]$, we pre- and post-compose $[\![t]\!]$ with these programs.

It remains to define the structural rules and 0. Weakening is defined such that any input on the weakened port results in a diverging computation, and exchange permutes the input and output wires. The conclusion in rule 0 is interpreted as $id_0\colon 0 \to 0$.

3.1 Equational Theory

We intend LIN to be used as language for constructing low-level programs and for reasoning about them. For equational reasoning, the notion of equality for LIN should be defined to reflect a reasonable notion of equality of low-level programs. In this section we define a notion of equality for LIN that allows us to reason about program correctness: closed terms of base type are equal if and only if they translate to equal programs.

To define equality, one possible option would be to consider two terms equal when they translate to equal low-level programs. This definition would validate the β-equality $(\lambda x{:}X.\,t)\,s = t[s/x]$ if s is closed, but it would not validate other reasonable instances of it. For example, if t does not contain x, then s is dead code and the β-equality would correspond to reasonable dead code elimination. However, if s has free variables, then it may be possible to distinguish the low-level programs interpreting $(\lambda x{:}X.\,t)\,s$ and $t[s/x]$ by interacting with the dead code that would otherwise never be used.

This motivates the definition of a coarser equality relation for LIN. We define it so that we can use the parametricity of polymorphism for equality reasoning. We therefore use a relational definition of term equality for LIN, where terms are equal if they map related arguments to related results, just like in standard models of polymorphism [27].

A *value type relation* is given by a triple (A, A', R) of two closed value types A and A' and a binary relation R between the closed values of type A and those of type A'. We write $R \subseteq A \times A'$ for the triple (A, A', R).

A *value type environment* ρ is a mapping from type variables to value type relations. If σ and σ' are both mappings from type variables to closed value types, then we write $\rho \subseteq \sigma \times \sigma'$ if $\rho(\alpha)$ is a relation $R_\alpha \subseteq \sigma(\alpha) \times \sigma'(\alpha)$. For such σ we write $X\sigma$ for the type obtained from X by substituting any variable α with $\sigma(\alpha)$.

For each value type A and each $\rho \subseteq \sigma \times \sigma'$, define a relation $[\![A]\!]_\rho \subseteq A\sigma \times A\sigma'$ by:

$$[\![\alpha]\!]_\rho = \rho(\alpha)$$
$$[\![A + B]\!]_\rho = \{(\text{inl}(v), \text{inl}(v')) \mid v\ [\![A]\!]_\rho\ v'\} \cup \{(\text{inr}(w), \text{inr}(w')) \mid w\ [\![B]\!]_\rho\ w'\}$$
$$[\![A \times B]\!]_\rho = \{(\langle v, w\rangle, \langle v', w'\rangle) \mid v\ [\![A]\!]_\rho\ v', w\ [\![B]\!]_\rho\ w'\}$$
$$[\![A]\!]_\rho = \{(v, v) \mid v\ \text{value of type } A\} \text{ if } A \text{ is a base type } (0, \text{unit}, \text{nat}).$$

For any interface type X and any type environment $\rho \subseteq \sigma \times \sigma'$ we define a relation $[\![X]\!]_\rho$ between low-level programs of type $(X\sigma)^- \to (X\sigma)^+$ and $(X\sigma')^- \to (X\sigma')^+$:

$$p \,[\![A^\perp]\!]_\rho\, p' \text{ iff } \forall v, v'. \; v \,[\![A]\!]_\rho\, v' \Rightarrow \forall o. \; ((\exists b. \; \mathsf{entry}_p(v) \xrightarrow{o}_p b) \Leftrightarrow$$
$$(\exists b'. \; \mathsf{entry}_{p'}(v') \xrightarrow{o}_{p'} b')$$
$$p \,[\![X \multimap Y]\!]_\rho\, p' \text{ iff } \forall q, q'. \; q \,[\![X]\!]_\rho\, q' \Rightarrow \mathsf{app}(p, q) \,[\![Y]\!]_\rho\, \mathsf{app}(p', q')$$
$$p \,[\![\forall \alpha.X]\!]_\rho\, p' \text{ iff } \forall R \subseteq A \times A'. \; \mathsf{inst}_{(\forall \alpha.X)\sigma}(p, A) \,[\![X]\!]_{\rho[R/\alpha]} \mathsf{inst}_{(\forall \alpha.X)\sigma'}(p', A')$$

In these cases, we use the following notation. For programs $p: A + B \to C + D$ and $q: C \to A$, we write $\mathsf{app}(p, q)$ for the following program of type $B \to D$.

$$\mathsf{app}(p, q) = \quad \begin{array}{c} B \longrightarrow \boxed{p} \longrightarrow D \\ A \; \overline{} \; {\scriptstyle \leftarrow C \leftarrow} \boxed{q} \; \overline{} \end{array}$$

If p is a program of type $\overline{X^-} \to \overline{X^+}$ then we write $\mathsf{inst}_{\forall \alpha.X}(p, A)$ for the program obtained by pre- and post-composing with $F[\mathsf{encode}_A]$ and $G[\mathsf{decode}_A]$, where $F[\cdot] = X^-[\cdot/\alpha]$ and $G[\cdot] = X^+[\cdot/\alpha]$. We write $\mathsf{inst}_{\forall \vec{\alpha}.X}(p, \sigma)$ for iterated application of inst.

Definition 1 (Equality). *Suppose $\Gamma \vdash s: X$ and $\Gamma \vdash t: X$ are derivable. Suppose $\vec{\alpha}$ is a list of the free type variables in these sequents and suppose Γ is $x_1: X_1, \ldots, x_n: X_n$. Then we write $\Gamma \models s = t: X$ if: For any value type environment $\rho \subseteq \sigma \times \tau$ and all $\vec{p}$ and $\vec{q}$ with $p_i \,[\![X_i]\!]_\rho\, q_i$ for $i = 1, \ldots, n$, $\mathsf{app}(\mathsf{inst}_{(\forall \vec{\alpha}.\Gamma \multimap X)\sigma}([\![\Gamma \vdash s: X]\!], \sigma), \vec{p})$ and $\mathsf{app}(\mathsf{inst}_{(\forall \vec{\alpha}.\Gamma \multimap X)\tau}([\![\Gamma \vdash t: X]\!], \tau), \vec{q})$ are $[\![X]\!]_\rho$-related.*

This definition requires some justification, in particular that it does not depend on the choice of derivation of $\Gamma \vdash s: X$ or $\Gamma \vdash t: X$. It is possible to define equality for derivations and show coherence, i.e. that two derivations of the same derivation have equal interpretations, see [24] for more details. For the results in this paper, it would be just as well to work with derivations and without coherence, so we do not spell this out.

The parametricity lemma takes the form:

Lemma 1 (Parametricity). *If $\Gamma \vdash t: X$ then $\Gamma \models t = t: X$.*

Lemma 2 (Identity Extension). *For any σ, we have $\models s = t: X\sigma$ if and only if $[\![s]\!] \,[\![X]\!]_{\Delta_\sigma}\, [\![t]\!]$, where $\Delta_\sigma(\alpha) = \{(v, v) \mid v \text{ is closed value of type } \sigma(\alpha)\}$.*

Equality is symmetric and transitive and a congruence with respect to the term constructors. We state further properties of equality in the following lemmas. In them, as in rest of this paper, we write just $s = t$ to mean that $\Gamma \models s = t: X$ holds for any Γ and X that make both terms well-typed.

Lemma 3. *The following β-equalities are valid.*

$$(\lambda x{:}X.\, s)\, t = s[t/x] \quad (\Lambda \alpha.t)\, A = t[A/\alpha] \quad (\mathsf{let}\ \langle x, y \rangle = \langle s, t \rangle\ \mathsf{in}\ r) = r[s/x, t/y]$$

Lemma 4. *The equations $\mathsf{id}^* t = t$ and $p^*(q^* t) = (q \circ p)^* t$ are valid. Moreover, if $p = q$ then $p^* t = q^* t$.*

We note that LIN allows duplication of values of type $A^\perp$. If $\Gamma, x_1\colon A^\perp, x_2\colon A^\perp \vdash t\colon Y$ then $\Gamma, x\colon A^\perp \vdash \text{let } \langle x_1, x_2\rangle = \nabla_A^* x \text{ in } t\colon Y$, where $\nabla_A\colon A + A \to A$ is the canonical low-level program of its type, i.e. the one mapping both $\text{inl}(v)$ and $\text{inr}(v)$ to v. If one substitutes a closed term s for x, then one has $(\text{let } \langle x_1, x_2\rangle = \nabla_A^* s \text{ in } t) = t[s/x_1, s/x_2]$, as the following lemma shows.

Lemma 5. *The equations* $(x \mapsto \text{inl}(x))^*\langle s, t\rangle = s$ *and* $(x \mapsto \text{inr}(x))^*\langle s, t\rangle = t$ *are valid. Moreover, if t is closed then we have* $\nabla_A^* t = \langle t, t\rangle$.

Relational parametricity is useful, as it justifies dinaturality properties, e.g. that $\vdash s\colon \forall\alpha.\, \alpha^\perp \multimap \alpha^\perp$ satisfies $(x \mapsto v)^*(s\; A\; t) = s\; B\;((x \mapsto v)^* t)$ for any $\vdash t\colon A^\perp$ and any value v of appropriate type. It would be possible to write this paper without polymorphism in LIN, but at the expense of having to establish such equations explicitly as invariants in all constructions. In Lemma 9 we use the following instance of dinaturality. Its proof is much like the proof that parametricity implies dinaturality in [20].

Lemma 6. *Suppose* $\vdash s\colon \forall\alpha.\,(\forall\beta.\, X \multimap \forall\gamma.\, Y \multimap \alpha^\perp) \multimap \alpha^\perp$, *where α is not free in X or Y. Then* $(y \mapsto v)^*(s\; A\; t) = s\; B\;(\Lambda\beta.\, \lambda x{:}X.\, \Lambda\gamma.\, \lambda y{:}Y.\,(y \mapsto v)^*(t\; x))$ *holds for any value v and any closed t of correct type.*

4   Linear Call-by-Value

The rest of the paper is devoted to showing how a call-by-value λ-calculus can be translated to intermediate languages based on LIN. To handle the full call-by-value λ-calculus, we shall need to extend LIN with a form of duplication in Section 5. In this section we first show that a *linear* fragment of the call-by-value λ-calculus can be translated to LIN. We do so by refining Plotkin's call-by-value CPS-translation to target LIN instead of the λ-calculus. While the linear source language is very simple, it is instructive to consider the translation for it first, as this already requires us to develop the main infrastructure needed for the translation.

By composing the refined CPS-translation to LIN with the translation from LIN to the low-level language, we obtain a fully specified translation from higher-order source language to first-order low-level language. The point is that LIN is low-level enough to give us fine-grained control over low-level programs, for example to make the closure representation and memory management issues explicit, but at the same time it is high-level enough to carry out essentially the standard correctness proof of the CPS-translation.

As the source language we consider a λ-calculus with a base type of natural numbers and a diverging term Ω that allows one to observe the evaluation order.

Source Types	$X, Y ::= \mathbb{N} \mid X \to Y$
Source Values	$V, W ::= x \mid \lambda x{:}X.\, M \mid n$ (natural number constant)
Source Terms	$M, N ::= V \mid M\; N \mid \text{add}(V, W) \mid \text{if0}(V, M, N) \mid \Omega$

The source terms are typed as follows:

$$\frac{}{\Gamma, x\colon X \vdash x\colon X} \qquad \frac{\Gamma, x\colon X \vdash M\colon Y}{\Gamma \vdash \lambda x{:}X.\,M\colon X \to Y} \qquad \frac{\Gamma \vdash M\colon X \to Y \quad \Gamma \vdash N\colon X}{\Gamma \vdash M\,N\colon Y}$$

$$\frac{}{\Gamma \vdash n\colon \mathbb{N}} \qquad \frac{\Gamma \vdash V_i\colon \mathbb{N}}{\Gamma \vdash \mathsf{add}(V_1, V_2)\colon \mathbb{N}} \qquad \frac{\Gamma \vdash V\colon \mathbb{N} \quad \Gamma \vdash N_i\colon \mathbb{N}}{\Gamma \vdash \mathsf{if0}(V, N_1, N_2)\colon \mathbb{N}} \qquad \frac{}{\Gamma \vdash \Omega\colon \mathbb{N}}$$

In this section we moreover impose the linearity restriction that in a source term any variable may be used at most once. (Duplication of variables of type $\mathbb{N}$ could also be allowed in this section, but we do without for simplicity.)

The terms for addition and if-then-else are restricted to values for technical convenience; one can write an addition function as $\lambda x{:}\mathbb{N}.\,\lambda y{:}\mathbb{N}.\,\mathsf{add}(x, y)$, for example. The if-then-else is restricted to the base type $\mathbb{N}$; we discuss this in Section 5.

We use a standard call-by-value reduction semantics: $(\lambda x{:}X.\,M)\,V \longrightarrow M[V/x]$, $\mathsf{add}(m, n) \longrightarrow m + n$, $\mathsf{if0}(0, M, N) \longrightarrow M$, $\mathsf{if0}(n + 1, M, N) \longrightarrow N$, $\Omega \longrightarrow \Omega$, $M_1\,N \longrightarrow M_2\,N$ if $M_1 \longrightarrow M_2$, and $V\,N_1 \longrightarrow V\,N_2$ if $N_1 \longrightarrow N_2$.

4.1 CPS-Translation

The aim is now to move Plotkin's call-by-value CPS-translation to LIN as the target language. We first recall Plotkin's CPS-translation [19] and its typing [12], that is, a variant that always puts the continuation first [8] and that covers our source language.

To any source type X, we assign a continuation type $\mathcal{K}(X)$ defined by:

$$\mathcal{K}(X) = \mathcal{A}(X) \to \bot \qquad \mathcal{A}(\mathbb{N}) = \mathbb{N} \qquad \mathcal{A}(X \to Y) = \mathcal{K}(Y) \to \mathcal{K}(X)$$

A source term of type $x_1\colon X_1, \ldots, x_n\colon X_n \vdash M\colon X$ is translated to a term of type $x_1\colon \mathcal{A}(X_1), \ldots, x_n\colon \mathcal{A}(X_n) \vdash \mathsf{cps}(M)\colon \mathcal{T}(X)$ where $\mathcal{T}(X) = \mathcal{K}(X) \to \bot$:

$$\mathsf{cps}(x) = \lambda k.\,k\,x \qquad \mathsf{cps}(\lambda x.\,M) = \lambda k.\,k\,(\lambda k_1.\,\lambda x.\,\mathsf{cps}(M)\,k_1)$$

$$\mathsf{cps}(n) = \lambda k.\,k\,n \qquad \mathsf{cps}(M\,N) = \lambda k.\,\mathsf{cps}(M)\,(\lambda f.\,\mathsf{cps}(N)\,(\lambda x.\,f\,k\,x))$$

$$\mathsf{cps}(\Omega) = \lambda k.\,\Omega_\bot \quad \mathsf{cps}(\mathsf{add}(V, W)) = \lambda k.\,\mathsf{cps}(V)\,(\lambda x.\,\mathsf{cps}(W)\,(\lambda y.\,k\,(x + y)))$$

$$\mathsf{cps}(\mathsf{if0}(V, M, N)) = \lambda k.\,\mathsf{cps}(V)\,(\lambda x.\,\mathsf{if0}(x, \mathsf{cps}(M)\,k, \mathsf{cps}(N)\,k))$$

4.2 Refining the CPS-Translation

While the CPS-translation above is completely linear, it is not obvious how to adapt it to target LIN. The problem is that in LIN we must make explicit which values to keep for later use. Consider for example the addition term $x\colon \mathbb{N},\, y\colon \mathbb{N} \vdash x + y\colon \mathbb{N}$ used in the above translation. We cannot just represent $\mathbb{N}$ in LIN by an interface from which we can get a single number at a time: in order to compute the sum we must have both summands at the same time. We address this issue by making the environment of variables explicit.

We decompose $\mathcal{A}(X)$ into two parts: First there is a *code type* $\mathcal{C}_\varphi(X)$, which is a value type. This is the type of codes that represent the values of type X. The code for a natural number would be just the number itself, while the code for a function might be the tuple of the values of the free variables in the body of the function, or similar.

Second, there is an *access type* $\mathcal{A}_\varphi(X)$, which is a LIN-type. The terms of type $\mathcal{A}_\varphi(X)$ will represent low-level programs that can interpret codes of type $\mathcal{C}_\varphi(X)$. They allow us to use such codes without knowledge of the encoding details.

The parameter φ in $\mathcal{C}_\varphi(X)$ and $\mathcal{A}_\varphi(X)$ is a value type variable that allows for information hiding. The code for a natural number should always be the number itself, but for a function, any possible encoding should be acceptable. We do not need to inspect the codes for functions; it suffices that they are accepted by access types. The type variable φ represents a type of abstract codes that we do not know anything about other than that it is accepted by the terms of access type.

For the given source language, the type of continuations is thus refined to:

$$\mathcal{K}_\alpha(X) = \forall\varphi.\, \mathcal{A}_\varphi(X) \multimap (\mathcal{C}_\varphi(X) \times \alpha)^\perp$$
$$\mathcal{C}_\varphi(\mathbb{N}) = \mathsf{nat} \quad \mathcal{C}_\varphi(X \to Y) = \varphi$$
$$\mathcal{A}_\varphi(\mathbb{N}) = 0^\perp \quad \mathcal{A}_\varphi(X \to Y) = \forall\beta.\, \mathcal{K}_\beta(Y) \multimap \mathcal{K}_{\varphi\times\beta}(X)$$

The type $\mathcal{K}_\alpha(X)$ of continuations refines $\mathcal{K}(X)$. A continuation accepts inputs that may be encoded using any encoding type φ. For this to work, the continuation must know how to use such an encoded value, which is what the argument of type $\mathcal{A}_\varphi(X)$ provides. Then, any value of type $\mathcal{C}_\varphi(X) \times \alpha$, i.e. the code of an actual value (we ignore α for now and come back to it below), can be thrown into the continuation.

The access types are defined as explained above. For natural numbers we do not need an access type, as the code type does not use φ. Indeed, we have $\mathcal{K}_\alpha(\mathbb{N}) = \forall\varphi.\, 0^\perp \multimap (\mathsf{nat} \times \alpha)^\perp$ and this type is isomorphic to $(\mathsf{nat} \times \alpha)^\perp$. A continuation of type $\mathbb{N}$ therefore just expects to be passed a natural number (again, ignore α for now).

Finally, we define a type $\mathcal{T}_\gamma(X)$ by

$$\mathcal{T}_\gamma(X) = \forall\alpha.\, \mathcal{K}_\alpha(X) \multimap (\gamma \times \alpha)^\perp.$$

The CPS-translation will be such that terms of source type X are translated to LIN-terms of type $\mathcal{T}_G(X)$, where $G = \mathsf{unit} \times \mathcal{C}_{\varphi_1}(X_1) \times \cdots \times \mathcal{C}_{\varphi_n}(X_n)$ is a type containing the codes for the values of the free variables of the term.

Example 1. Let us explain concretely how to understand the type

$$\mathcal{T}_{\mathsf{unit}}(\mathbb{N} \to \mathbb{N}) \cong \forall\alpha.\, \left(\forall\varphi.\, \mathcal{A}_\varphi(\mathbb{N} \to \mathbb{N}) \multimap (\mathcal{C}_\varphi(\mathbb{N} \to \mathbb{N}) \times \alpha)^\perp \right) \multimap (\mathsf{unit} \times \alpha)^\perp$$
$$\cong \forall\alpha.\, \left(\forall\varphi.\, (\forall\beta.\, (\mathsf{nat} \times \beta)^\perp \multimap (\mathsf{nat} \times (\varphi \times \beta))^\perp) \multimap (\varphi \times \alpha)^\perp \right) \multimap \alpha^\perp.$$

Closed terms of this type are translated to programs with the following interface (up to removal of ports of type 0).

A function $f\colon \mathbb{N} \to \mathbb{N}$ is implemented by such a program in the following way. To start the evaluation of the function itself, we pass any value $\langle\langle\rangle, s\rangle\colon \overline{\mathsf{unit} \times \alpha}$ to the first input port. The low-level program then returns a pair $\langle c, s\rangle\colon \overline{\varphi \times \alpha}$, where the first component c is a code for the value of f and the second component is our initial value s (this

If Γ declares the variables $\vec{z}$ and these all appear free in M, then define $\mathsf{cps}(\Gamma \vdash M)$ by:

$$\mathsf{cps}(x : X \vdash x) = \Lambda\alpha.\,\lambda k.\,(\langle\langle\langle\rangle, x\rangle, s\rangle \mapsto \langle x, s\rangle)^*(k\,\varphi_x\,x)$$

$$\mathsf{cps}(\vdash n) = \Lambda\alpha.\,\lambda k.\,(\langle\langle\rangle, s\rangle \mapsto \langle n, s\rangle)^*(k\,\mathsf{unit}\,\star)$$

$$\mathsf{cps}(\Gamma \vdash \lambda x{:}X.\,M) = \Lambda\alpha.\,\lambda k.\,k\,C(\Gamma)\,(\Lambda\beta.\,\lambda k_1.\,\Lambda\varphi_x.\,\lambda x.\,(\langle a, \langle\vec{z}, t\rangle\rangle \mapsto \langle\langle\vec{z}, a\rangle, t\rangle)^*$$
$$(\mathsf{cps}(\Gamma, x : X \vdash M)\,\beta\,k_1))$$

$$\mathsf{cps}(\Gamma \vdash M\,N) = \Lambda\alpha.\,\lambda k.\,(\langle\vec{z}, s\rangle \mapsto \langle\vec{z}, \langle\vec{z}, s\rangle\rangle)^*\mathsf{cps}(\Gamma \vdash M)\,(C(\Gamma) \times \alpha)\,t$$
$$\text{where } t = (\Lambda\varphi.\,\lambda f.\,(\langle\varphi, \langle\vec{z}, s\rangle\rangle \mapsto \langle\vec{z}, \langle\varphi, s\rangle\rangle)^*$$
$$\mathsf{cps}(\Gamma \vdash N)\,(\varphi \times \alpha)\,(\Lambda\beta.\,\lambda x.\,f\,\alpha\,k\,\beta\,x))$$

$$\mathsf{cps}(x : \mathbb{N}, y : \mathbb{N} \vdash \mathsf{add}(x, y)) = \Lambda\alpha.\,\lambda k.\,(\langle\langle\langle\langle\rangle, m\rangle, n\rangle, s\rangle \mapsto \langle m + n, s\rangle)^*(k\,\mathsf{unit}\,\star)$$

$$\mathsf{cps}(x : \mathbb{N}, y : \mathbb{N} \vdash \mathsf{add}(y, x)) = \Lambda\alpha.\,\lambda k.\,(\langle\langle\langle\langle\rangle, n\rangle, m\rangle, s\rangle \mapsto \langle m + n, s\rangle)^*(k\,\mathsf{unit}\,\star)$$

$$\mathsf{cps}(x : \mathbb{N} \vdash \mathsf{add}(x, n)) = \Lambda\alpha.\,\lambda k.\,(\langle\langle\langle\rangle, m\rangle, s\rangle \mapsto \langle m + n, s\rangle)^*(k\,\mathsf{unit}\,\star)$$

$$\mathsf{cps}(x : \mathbb{N} \vdash \mathsf{add}(m, x)) = \Lambda\alpha.\,\lambda k.\,(\langle\langle\langle\rangle, n\rangle, s\rangle \mapsto \langle m + n, s\rangle)^*(k\,\mathsf{unit}\,\star)$$

$$\mathsf{cps}(\vdash \mathsf{add}(m, n)) = \Lambda\alpha.\,\lambda k.\,(\langle\langle\rangle, s\rangle \mapsto \langle m + n, s\rangle)^*(k\,\mathsf{unit}\,\star)$$

$$\mathsf{cps}(\Gamma \vdash \mathsf{if0}(x, M, N)) = \Lambda\alpha.\,\lambda k.\,\mathsf{let}\,\langle k_1, k_2\rangle = \nabla^*_{\mathsf{nat}}(k\,\mathsf{unit}\,\star)\,\mathsf{in}$$
$$(\langle\vec{z}, s\rangle \mapsto \mathsf{if}\,x = 0\,\mathsf{then}\,\mathsf{inl}(\langle\vec{z}, s\rangle)\,\mathsf{else}\,\mathsf{inr}(\langle\vec{z}, s\rangle))^*$$
$$\langle\mathsf{cps}(\Gamma \vdash M)\alpha(\Lambda\varphi.\lambda x.k_1), \mathsf{cps}(\Gamma \vdash N)\alpha(\Lambda\varphi.\lambda x.k_2)\rangle$$

$$\mathsf{cps}(\Gamma \vdash \mathsf{if0}(0, M, N)) = \mathsf{cps}(\Gamma \vdash M)$$

$$\mathsf{cps}(\Gamma \vdash \mathsf{if0}(n + 1, M, N)) = \mathsf{cps}(\Gamma \vdash N)$$

$$\mathsf{cps}(\vdash \Omega_N) = \Lambda\alpha.\,\lambda k.\,\Omega^*_{\mathsf{unit}}(k\,\mathsf{unit}\,\star)$$

If Γ declares more than the free variables of M, let Δ be the subcontext declaring just the free variables of M, let $\vec{z}$ and $\vec{y}$ be the list of variables defined in Γ and Δ respectively and define $\mathsf{cps}(\Gamma \vdash M) = \Lambda\alpha.\,\lambda k.\,(\langle\vec{z}, s\rangle \mapsto \langle\vec{y}, s\rangle)^*(\mathsf{cps}(\Delta \vdash M)\,\alpha\,k)$.

Fig. 2. Call-by-Value CPS translation into LIN

follows from parametricity). We do not know how c encodes f, but we may use this code to apply the function to concrete arguments. We may pass $\langle n, \langle c, t\rangle\rangle : \overline{\mathsf{nat} \times (\varphi \times \beta)}$ to the second input port. What we get is the desired value $\langle f(n), t\rangle : \overline{\mathsf{nat} \times \beta}$.

The values s and t are both returned unchanged. They are useful, as our simple low-level language cannot store values for later use. Instead of storing values, the values may be encoded in s and t and then decoded when these values are returned.

Having defined the types of the CPS-translation, we now come to the terms. In Fig. 2 we define the term $\mathsf{cps}(\Gamma \vdash M)$, where M is a source term and Γ is a finite list of source variable declarations $x_1 : X_1, \ldots, x_n : X_n$ under which M is well-typed. In the figure we use the following notation. We choose a fresh type variable φ_x for each source variable x, write $C(\Gamma)$ for the value type $\mathsf{unit} \times C_{\varphi_{x_1}}(X_1) \times \cdots \times C_{\varphi_{x_n}}(X_n)$, associated to the left, and $A(\Gamma)$ for the LIN-context $x_1 : A_{\varphi_{x_1}}(X_1), \ldots, x_n : A_{\varphi_{x_n}}(X_n)$. For a list of pairwise distinct variables $\vec{z}$, we also write $\vec{z}$ for tuples of variables, i.e. ε denotes $\langle\rangle$ and $\vec{z}, x$ denotes $\langle\vec{z}, x\rangle$. In Fig. 2 we have omitted type annotations in LIN-terms for better readability, as these will be uniquely determined by the types. The types of the terms in that figure are specified by the following proposition, which one should keep in mind when reading the figure. This proposition is proved by induction on M.

Proposition 1. *If $\Gamma \vdash M \colon X$ in the source language with linearity restriction, then $\mathcal{A}(\Gamma) \vdash \mathsf{cps}(\Gamma \vdash M) \colon \mathcal{T}_{\mathcal{C}(\Gamma)}(X)$ in* LIN.

Let us now explain informally the CPS-translation of abstraction and application. Notice first that, by parametricity, values of type α and β cannot be inspected, but only be passed along. This is used in the translation to preserve certain values for later use.

For abstraction, consider a fully applied term of the form $\mathsf{cps}(\Gamma \vdash \lambda x \colon X. M)\, \alpha\, K$. It has type $(\mathcal{C}(\Gamma) \times \alpha)^{\perp}$ and it expects to be sent (the codes of) the values of its free variables and some arbitrary value s of type α. By definition, it sends this data unchanged to $(K\, \mathcal{C}(\Gamma)\, (\ldots))$, which also has type $(\mathcal{C}(\Gamma) \times \alpha)^{\perp}$. But K expects as its first argument the type that encodes the function value and here we use $\mathcal{C}(\Gamma)$. This means that the tuple of the values of the free variables is now considered as the code of the function. The second argument to K is the access term that explains how this tuple can be used to apply the function to arguments. If we fully apply this second argument, then we obtain a term of type $(\mathcal{C}_{\varphi_x}(X) \times (\mathcal{C}(\Gamma) \times \beta))^{\perp}$. If we pass a value $\langle a, \langle \varphi, t \rangle \rangle$ to this term, then this value is transformed to $\langle \langle a, \varphi \rangle, t \rangle \colon \mathcal{C}(\Gamma, x \colon X) \times \beta$ and then passed to the CPS-translation of the function body M, as expected.

For application, consider $\mathsf{cps}(\Gamma \vdash M\, N)\, \alpha\, K$, which has type $(\mathcal{C}(\Gamma) \times \alpha)^{\perp}$. If we pass to this term the pair $\langle \vec{z}, s \rangle$, where $\vec{z}$ are the values of the free variables, then first $\langle \vec{z}, \langle \vec{z}, s \rangle \rangle$ is passed to the CPS-translation of M. When its evaluation is finished, it sends the value $\langle c, \langle \vec{z}, s \rangle \rangle$ to the continuation, where c is the code of the function value and the second component $\langle \vec{z}, s \rangle$ is returned unchanged. The CPS-translation of the application is defined such that then $\langle \vec{z}, \langle c, s \rangle \rangle$ is passed to the argument N. This causes the argument to be evaluated; it passes $\langle a, \langle c, s \rangle \rangle$ to the continuation, where a is the value of the function argument and the pair $\langle c, s \rangle$ is again returned unchanged. But the continuation is defined so that it just invokes the access term provided by the function M with the code c for the function and a for the argument. It thus invokes the program to perform the requested function application.

Example 2. We illustrate the CPS-translation and how it relates to low-level programs by translating the simple example term $\vdash (\lambda x \colon \mathbb{N}. \mathsf{add}(x, 5))\, 3 \colon \mathbb{N}$. In this example we let $\gamma := \mathsf{unit}$. In the following, α, β and φ are type variables and we have $\overline{\alpha} = \overline{\beta} = \overline{\varphi} = \mathsf{nat}$.

First we have

$$\mathsf{cps}(\vdash 3) = \Lambda \alpha.\, \lambda k.\, (\langle \langle \rangle, s \rangle \mapsto \langle 3, s \rangle)^{*}(k\, \mathsf{unit}\, \star) \colon \mathcal{T}_{\gamma}(\mathbb{N})$$
$$\mathsf{cps}(x \colon \mathbb{N} \vdash \mathsf{add}(x, 5)) = \Lambda \alpha.\, \lambda k.\, (\langle \langle \langle \rangle, m \rangle, s \rangle \mapsto \langle m + 5, s \rangle)^{*}(k\, \mathsf{unit}\, \star) \colon \mathcal{T}_{\gamma}(\mathbb{N}) \ .$$

These terms translate to the following programs.

$$[\![\mathsf{cps}(\vdash 3)]\!] = \qquad \gamma \times \overline{\alpha} \longrightarrow \boxed{\langle \langle \rangle, s \rangle \mapsto \langle 3, s \rangle} \longrightarrow \mathsf{nat} \times \overline{\alpha}$$

$$[\![\mathsf{cps}(x \colon \mathbb{N} \vdash \mathsf{add}(x, 5))]\!] = \quad (\gamma \times \mathsf{nat}) \times \overline{\alpha} \longrightarrow \boxed{\langle \langle \langle \rangle, x \rangle, s \rangle \mapsto \langle x + 5, s \rangle} \longrightarrow \mathsf{nat} \times \overline{\alpha}$$

(The encoding and decoding programs arising from the type application with unit are the identity and have been removed.) Each of these programs takes a pair as an input. The first component in this pair is the tuple of the code values for free variables of the term. The second component may be any value, which must be returned unchanged (by parametricity). A caller may use this second component to 'store' values across the call. The translation of the abstraction $\mathsf{cps}(\vdash \lambda x{:}X.\,\mathsf{add}(x,5)){:}\ \mathcal{T}_\gamma(\mathbb{N}\to\mathbb{N})$ is the term

$$\Lambda\alpha.\,\lambda k.\,k\ \gamma\ (\Lambda\beta.\,\lambda k_1.\,\Lambda\varphi_x.\,\lambda x.\ (\langle a,\langle\langle\rangle,t\rangle\rangle \mapsto \langle\langle\langle\rangle,a\rangle,t\rangle)^*$$
$$(\mathsf{cps}(x\colon \mathbb{N}\vdash \mathsf{add}(x,5))\ \beta\ k_1))$$

It translates to the following program, whose interface is as in Example 1.

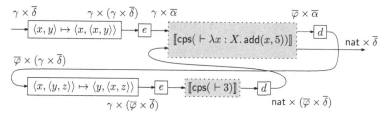

An input to the topmost input port corresponds to a request to compute the value of the function. It takes an argument of type $\gamma \times \overline{\alpha}$, whose first component is the tuple of the free values of the term (in this case none). The return value $\overline{\varphi} \times \overline{\alpha}$ must be the pair of the code for the function together and the value of type $\overline{\alpha}$ that was given as input. As the code for the function, the translation uses the (encoding of) tuple of the codes of the values of its free variables.

The second input port allows function application. It takes as input the function argument (of type nat) and the code for the function (of type $\overline{\varphi}$). Its third argument is again an arbitrary value that must be returned unchanged. To compute the function application, the program first constructs the tuple of (the codes of) the values of free variables of the body of the λ-term. It can do so, since the code for a function is just the tuple of (the codes of) its free variables, and the function argument value is also supplied. The program then just invokes the program for the body of the λ-term.

Notice the similarity to the implementation of functions using defunctionalization, such as [6]. Functions are represented by first order values and there is static program code for application of any function.

Finally, the CPS-translation of the application $\mathsf{cps}(\vdash (\lambda x{:}X.\,\mathsf{add}(x,5))\ 3)$ is given by the term $\Lambda\delta.\,\lambda k.\,(\langle\langle\langle\rangle,s\rangle \mapsto \langle\langle\rangle,\langle\langle\rangle,s\rangle\rangle)^*\mathsf{cps}(\vdash \lambda x{:}X.\,\mathsf{add}(x,5))\ (\gamma \times \delta)\ t$, where t abbreviates $(\Lambda\varphi.\,\lambda f.\,(\langle x,\langle\langle\rangle,s\rangle\rangle \mapsto \langle\langle\rangle,\langle x,s\rangle\rangle)^*\mathsf{cps}(\vdash 3)\ (\varphi \times \delta)\ (\Lambda\beta.\,\lambda x.\,f\ \delta\ k\ \beta\ x))$. This term translates to the following low-level program, in which each e abbreviates $(id \times \mathsf{encode}_A)$, i.e. $(\langle x,y\rangle \mapsto \langle x,\mathsf{encode}_A(y)\rangle)$ for an appropriate type A. Likewise, each d abbreviates $(id \times \mathsf{decode}_A)$ for an appropriate A.

In this program, the value of type γ is duplicated, as it is needed twice, once for the evaluation of the function and once for its argument. The copy is encoded in the callee-save value and the function value is computed. When this it is returned, the value of type γ is restored, as it is needed in general to compute the function argument. While computing the function argument, the code of the function is encoded and put in the callee-save value. When the argument value is returned, the function code is decoded and both argument and function code are passed to the program for application.

This outlines how one can understand the translation on the level of low-level programs. On input $\langle\langle\rangle, s\rangle$, the above program outputs $\langle 8, s\rangle$, as expected.

One may also understand the program directly in LIN using the equations from Section 3.1. By using only the β-equations from Lemma 3, we get

$$\mathsf{cps}(\vdash (\lambda x{:}X.\,\mathsf{add}(x,5))\,3)\,\alpha\,k = (\langle\langle\langle\rangle, s\rangle \mapsto \langle\langle\rangle, \langle\langle\rangle, s\rangle\rangle))^* \mathsf{cps}(\vdash \lambda x{:}X.\,\mathsf{add}(x,5))\,(\gamma \times \alpha)t$$

$$= \cdots = (\langle\langle\rangle, s\rangle \mapsto \langle\langle\rangle, \langle\langle\rangle, s\rangle\rangle))^* (\langle\varphi, \langle\langle\rangle, s_1\rangle\rangle \mapsto \langle\langle\rangle, \langle\varphi, s_1\rangle\rangle)^* (\langle\langle\langle\rangle, s_2\rangle \mapsto \langle 3, s_2\rangle))^*$$

$$(\langle a, \langle\langle\rangle, t\rangle\rangle \mapsto \langle\langle\langle\rangle, a\rangle, t\rangle)^* (\langle\langle\langle\rangle, m\rangle, s_3\rangle \mapsto \langle m + 5, s_3\rangle)^* (k\,\mathsf{unit}\,\star)$$

Using Lemma 4, this term can be simplified to $(\langle\langle\rangle, s\rangle \mapsto \langle 8, s\rangle)^* (k\,\mathsf{unit}\,\star)$, which also shows that the term behaves as expected.

4.3 Soundness

In this section we show that correctness of the refined CPS-translation can be shown much in the same way as for the original CPS-translation. We show:

Theorem 1. *If* $\vdash M : \mathbb{N}$ *and* $M \longrightarrow^* n$*, where* n *is a value, then* $\mathsf{cps}(\vdash M)\,\mathsf{unit}\,K = (\langle\vec{z}, s\rangle \mapsto \langle n, s\rangle)^* (K\,\mathsf{unit}\,\star)$ *for any closed continuation* $K : \mathcal{K}_{\mathsf{unit}}(\mathbb{N})$*.*

Corollary 1. *If* $\vdash M : \mathbb{N}$ *then* $[\![\mathsf{cps}(\vdash M)\,\mathsf{unit}]\!]$ *is, up to isomorphism, a program of type* unit $\to$ nat *with the property that it maps* $\langle\rangle$ *to* n *if* $M \longrightarrow^* n$ *holds.*

Proof. We have $[\![\mathsf{cps}(\vdash M)\,\mathsf{unit}]\!] : (0 + 0) + \mathsf{unit} \times \mathsf{unit} \to (0 + \mathsf{nat} \times \mathsf{unit}) + 0$ by definition and the type is isomorphic to unit $\to$ nat.

If we choose K to be $\Lambda\varphi.\,\lambda a.\,(x{:}\mathsf{nat} \mapsto \mathsf{let}\,\_{=}\mathsf{print}(x)\,\mathsf{in}\,\Omega)$, then Theorem 1 tells us that $[\![\mathsf{cps}(\vdash M)\,\mathsf{unit}\,K]\!]$ is a program of type unit $\times$ unit $\to 0$ that on input $\langle\langle\rangle, \langle\rangle\rangle$ prints n if and only if M reduces to n. By definition of the translation from LIN to low-level programs, this means that $[\![\mathsf{cps}(\vdash M)\,\mathsf{unit}]\!]$ must map $\mathsf{inr}(\langle\langle\rangle, \langle\rangle\rangle)$ to $\mathsf{inl}(\mathsf{inr}(\langle n, \langle\rangle\rangle))$, from which the result follows. $\square$

We now come to the proof of Theorem 1, which follows that of Plotkin [19]. This is an important point of this paper; it shows that with little adaptation, existing proof methods can be applied to a translation going directly into first-order code.

For any source value V with $\Gamma \vdash V : X$, we define a value type $\mathcal{P}(\Gamma \vdash V)$, a low-level value $\eta(V)$ of type $\mathcal{C}_{\mathcal{P}(\Gamma \vdash V)}(X)$ and a LIN-term $\Psi(\Gamma \vdash V)$ by

$$\eta(x) = x \qquad\qquad \mathcal{P}(\Gamma \vdash x) = \varphi_x \qquad\qquad \Psi(\Gamma \vdash x) = x$$
$$\eta(n) = n \qquad\qquad \mathcal{P}(\Gamma \vdash n) = \mathsf{unit} \qquad\qquad \Psi(\Gamma \vdash n) = \star$$
$$\eta(\lambda x{:}X.\,t) = \vec{y} \qquad\quad \mathcal{P}(\Gamma \vdash \lambda x{:}X.\,M) = \mathcal{C}(\Delta)$$
$$\Psi(\Gamma \vdash \lambda x{:}X.\,t) = \Lambda\beta.\,\lambda k_1.\,\Lambda\varphi_x.\,\lambda x.\,\mathsf{cps}(\Delta, x : X \vdash t)\,\beta\,k_1,$$

where in the last two lines Δ is the context obtained from Γ by deleting all declarations of variables that are not free in $\lambda x{:}X.\,M$ and $\vec{y}$ is the tuple of variables declared in Δ. The notation Ψ comes from [19].

We shall often write just $\mathcal{P}(M)$ and $\Psi(M)$, when a typing context Γ for M is clear from the context. The point of these definitions is the following lemma.

Lemma 7. $\mathsf{cps}(\Gamma \vdash V) = \Lambda\alpha.\,\lambda k.\,(\langle \vec{z}, s \rangle \mapsto \langle \eta(V), s \rangle)^*(k\,\mathcal{P}(V)\,\Psi(\Gamma \vdash V))$ *for any value* V.

Lemma 8. *Let* M *be a source term that is well-typed in context* Γ. *Let* Δ *be a reordering of the context* Γ. *Let* $\vec{z}$ *and* $\vec{y}$ *be the lists of variables declared in* Γ *and* Δ *respectively. Then* $\mathsf{cps}(\Gamma \vdash M) = \Lambda\alpha.\,\lambda k.\,(\langle \vec{z}, s \rangle \mapsto \langle \vec{y}, s \rangle)^*(\mathsf{cps}(\Delta \vdash M)\,\alpha\,k)$.

Lemma 9. *For any value* V, *any* α *and any closed* K *of the appropriate type, we have*

$$\mathsf{cps}(\Gamma \vdash M[V/x])\,\alpha\,K =$$
$$(\langle \vec{z}, s \rangle \mapsto \langle \langle \vec{z}, \eta(V) \rangle, s \rangle)^*(\mathsf{cps}(\Gamma, x\colon X \vdash M)[\Psi(V)/x, \mathcal{P}(V)/\varphi_x]\,\alpha\,K)\;.$$

Proof. The proof goes by induction on M. The most difficult case is that when M is a λ-abstraction $\lambda y{:}Y.\,N$. We show the sub-case where $x \neq y$ and where y is free in N.

$$(\langle \vec{z}, s \rangle \mapsto \langle \langle \vec{z}, \eta(V) \rangle, s \rangle)^*(\mathsf{cps}(\Gamma, x\colon X \vdash \lambda y.\,N)[\Psi(V)/x, \mathcal{P}(V)/\varphi_x]\,\alpha\,K)$$
$$= (\langle \vec{z}, s \rangle \mapsto \langle \langle \vec{z}, \eta(V) \rangle, s \rangle)^*$$
$$(K\,\varphi_{\vec{z},x}\,(\Lambda\beta.\,\lambda k_1.\,\Lambda\varphi_y.\,\lambda y.\,\mathsf{cps}(\Gamma, x\colon X, y\colon Y \vdash N)[\Psi(V)/x, \mathcal{P}(V)/\varphi_x]\,\beta\,k_1))$$
$$= (\langle \vec{z}, s \rangle \mapsto \langle \langle \vec{z}, \eta(V) \rangle, s \rangle)^* \qquad\qquad\text{(Lemma 9)}$$
$$(K\,\varphi_{\vec{z},x}\,(\Lambda\beta.\,\lambda k_1.\,\Lambda\varphi_y.\,\lambda y.\,(\langle\langle\langle \vec{z}, x \rangle, y \rangle, s \rangle \mapsto \langle\langle\langle \vec{z}, y \rangle, x \rangle, s \rangle)^*$$
$$(\mathsf{cps}(\Gamma, y\colon Y, x\colon X \vdash N)[\Psi(V)/x, \mathcal{P}(V)/\varphi_x]\,\beta\,k_1)))$$
$$= K\,\varphi_{\vec{z}}\,(\Lambda\beta.\,\lambda k_1.\,\Lambda\varphi_y.\,\lambda y.\,(\langle\langle \vec{z}, a \rangle, s \rangle \mapsto \langle\langle \vec{z}, \eta(V) \rangle, a \rangle, s \rangle)^* \qquad\text{(Lemma 6)}$$
$$(\langle\langle\langle \vec{z}, x \rangle, y \rangle, s \rangle \mapsto \langle\langle\langle \vec{z}, y \rangle, x \rangle, s \rangle)^*$$
$$(\mathsf{cps}(\Gamma, y\colon Y, x\colon X \vdash N)[\Psi(V)/x, \mathcal{P}(V)/\varphi_x]\,\beta\,k_1))$$
$$= K\,\varphi_{\vec{z}}\,(\Lambda\beta.\,\lambda k_1.\,\Lambda\varphi_y.\,\lambda y.\,(\langle\langle \vec{z}, a \rangle, s \rangle \mapsto \langle\langle\langle \vec{z}, a \rangle, \eta(V) \rangle, s \rangle)^*$$
$$(\mathsf{cps}(\Gamma, y\colon Y, x\colon X \vdash N)[\Psi(V)/x, \mathcal{P}(V)/\varphi_x]\,\beta\,k_1))$$
$$= K\,\varphi_{\vec{z}}\,(\Lambda\beta.\,\lambda k_1.\,\Lambda\varphi_y.\,\lambda y.\,\mathsf{cps}(\Gamma, y\colon Y \vdash |N[V/x]|)\,k_1) \qquad\text{(IH)}$$
$$= \mathsf{cps}(\Gamma \vdash \lambda y{:}Y.\,N[V/x])\,\alpha\,K \qquad\qquad\qquad\qquad\qquad\qquad \square$$

To prove correctness of the CPS-translation, Plotkin defines a term $M{:}K$, which is the term that one gets from $\mathsf{cps}(M)\,K$ by reduction of administrative redexes. We adapt this definition to the current situation and define $M :_A^\Gamma K$ as follows.

$$N :_\alpha^\Gamma K = (\langle \vec{z}, s \rangle \mapsto \langle \eta(N), s \rangle)^*(K\,\mathcal{P}(N)\,\Psi(N)) \qquad (N \text{ is closed value})$$
$$M\,N :_\alpha^\Gamma K = (\langle \vec{z}, s \rangle \mapsto \langle \vec{z}, \langle \vec{z}, s \rangle \rangle)^* \qquad\qquad\qquad (M \text{ is not a value})$$
$$(M :_\alpha^\Gamma (\Lambda\varphi.\,\lambda f.\,(\langle \varphi, \langle \vec{z}, s \rangle \rangle \mapsto \langle \vec{z}, \langle \varphi, s \rangle \rangle)^*$$
$$\mathsf{cps}(\Gamma \vdash N)\,(\varphi \times \alpha)\,(\Lambda\beta.\,\lambda x.\,(f\,\alpha\,K\,\beta\,x)))$$
$$M\,N :_\alpha^\Gamma K = (\langle \vec{z}, s \rangle \mapsto \langle \vec{z}, \langle \eta(M), s \rangle \rangle)^* \qquad (M \text{ is a value, } N \text{ is not a value})$$
$$(N :_{\mathcal{P}(M) \times \alpha}^\Gamma (\Lambda\beta.\,\lambda x.\,(\Psi(M)\,\alpha\,K\,\beta\,x)))$$
$$M\,N :_\alpha^\Gamma K = (\langle \vec{z}, s \rangle \mapsto \langle \eta(N), \langle \eta(M), s \rangle \rangle)^* \qquad (M \text{ and } N \text{ are values})$$
$$(\Psi(M)\,\alpha\,K\,\mathcal{P}(N)\,\Psi(N))$$
$$\mathsf{if0}(0, M, N) :_\alpha^\Gamma K = M :_\alpha^\Gamma K \qquad\qquad \mathsf{if0}(n+1, M, N) :_\alpha^\Gamma K = N :_\alpha^\Gamma K$$
$$\mathsf{add}(m, n) :_\alpha^\Gamma K = (m+n) :_\alpha^\Gamma K$$

We show the following lemma by case distinction on M.

Lemma 10. *Let* $\Gamma \vdash M : X$ *in the source language. Then, for all* α *and all closed* K *such that* $\mathsf{cps}(\Gamma \vdash M)\,\alpha\,K$ *is well-typed, we have* $\mathsf{cps}(\Gamma \vdash M)\,\alpha\,K = M :_\alpha^\Gamma K$.

Lemma 11. *If* $M \longrightarrow N$ *then* $M :_\alpha^\Gamma K = N :_\alpha^\Gamma K$ *for any* α *and closed* K *of the appropriate type.*

Proof. We show the representative case where M is $(\lambda x.M_1)\,M_2$, M_2 is a value and x is free in M_1. Let Δ be the subcontext of Γ defining just the free variables of $(\lambda x.M_1)$.

$$((\lambda x{:}X.\,M_1)\,M_2) :_\alpha^\Gamma K$$
$$= (\langle \vec{z}, s\rangle \mapsto \langle\langle \eta(\lambda x.\,M_1), \eta(M_2)\rangle, s\rangle)^* (\Psi(\lambda x{:}X.\,M_1)\,\alpha\,K\,\mathcal{P}(M_2)\,\Psi(M_2))$$
$$= (\langle \vec{z}, s\rangle \mapsto \langle\langle \eta(\lambda x.\,M_1), \eta(M_2)\rangle, s\rangle)^*$$
$$\quad ((\Lambda\beta.\,\lambda k'.\,\Lambda\varphi_x.\,\lambda x.\,\mathsf{cps}(\Delta, x{:}\,X \vdash M_1)\,\beta\,k')\,\alpha\,K\,\mathcal{P}(M_2)\,\Psi(M_2))$$
$$= (\langle \vec{z}, s\rangle \mapsto \langle\langle \eta(\lambda x.\,M_1), \eta(M_2)\rangle, s\rangle)^* (\mathsf{cps}(\Delta, x{:}\,X \vdash M_1)\,\alpha\,K)[\Psi(M_2)/x, \mathcal{P}(M_2)/\varphi_x]$$
$$= (\langle \vec{z}, s\rangle \mapsto \langle\langle \vec{z}, \eta(M_2)\rangle, s\rangle)^* ((\langle\langle \vec{z}, x\rangle, s'\rangle \mapsto \langle\langle \eta(\lambda x.M_1), x\rangle, s'\rangle)^*$$
$$\quad (\mathsf{cps}(\Delta, x{:}\,X \vdash M_1)\,\alpha\,K))[\Psi(M_2)/x, \mathcal{P}(M_2)/\varphi_x]$$
$$= \mathsf{cps}(\Gamma \vdash M_1[M_2/x])\,\alpha\,K = M_1[M_2/x] :_\alpha^\Gamma K \qquad \square$$

Theorem 1 is now a direct consequence of Lemmas 10 and 11. Each reduction step in the source language can be followed by an equality in LIN and, for a value n, the definition of $n :_\alpha K$ is just as required.

The soundness argument shows that we can trace reduction steps in the source language with equalities in LIN. We are not aware of such results for direct translations from source to a first-order target language, e.g. for defunctionalization compilation.

4.4   On Resource Usage

Let us come back to the issue of memory space usage that has motivated this work. Consider a source program of the form let $x_1=M_1$ in let $x_2=M_2$ in ... let $x_k=M_k$ in N, where (let $x=M$ in N) abbreviates $(\lambda x{:}X.\,N)\,M$. The refined call-by-value CPS-translation is defined such that the values of the terms $M_1, \ldots, M_k$ are computed in this order in the low-level language. Moreover, by construction, at the time when the computation of M_i starts, only values of variables are being stored that are free in N or some M_j with $j \geq i$. In particular, the value of each x_i is only kept as long as it is needed. This means that the proposed CPS-translation solves the issue discussed with an INTML-example in the Introduction.

Take the concrete example $M = $ let $x=5$ in let $y=x+1$ in let $z=y+4$ in $z+3$ from the introduction. The program $[\![M]\!]$ maps $\langle\langle\rangle, s\rangle$ to $\langle 13, s\rangle$. The following table traces the computation through this program. In the two steps where values are discarded, the case at the bottom of Figure 2 applies. For example, the definition of the CPS-translation $\mathsf{cps}(x{:}\,\mathbb{N}, y{:}\,\mathbb{N} \vdash $ let $z=y+4$ in $z+3)$ is just

$$(\langle\langle\langle\langle\rangle, y\rangle, z\rangle, s\rangle \mapsto \langle\langle\langle\rangle, z\rangle, s\rangle)^* \mathsf{cps}(y{:}\,\mathbb{N} \vdash \text{let } z=y+4 \text{ in } z+3),$$

which explains that the value 5 is discarded from line three to four.

Value at entry	Subprogram
$\langle\langle\rangle, s\rangle$	$[\![\mathsf{cps}(\ \vdash \mathsf{let}\ x{=}5\ \mathsf{in}\ \mathsf{let}\ y{=}x + 1\ \mathsf{in}\ \mathsf{let}\ z{=}y + 4\ \mathsf{in}\ z + 3)]\!]$
$\langle\langle\langle\rangle, 5\rangle, s\rangle$	$[\![\mathsf{cps}(x : \mathbb{N} \vdash \mathsf{let}\ y{=}x + 1\ \mathsf{in}\ \mathsf{let}\ z{=}y + 4\ \mathsf{in}\ z + 3)]\!]$
$\langle\langle\langle\langle\rangle, 5\rangle, 6\rangle, s\rangle$	$[\![\mathsf{cps}(x : \mathbb{N},\ y : \mathbb{N} \vdash \mathsf{let}\ z{=}y + 4\ \mathsf{in}\ z + 3)]\!]$
$\langle\langle\langle\rangle, 6\rangle, s\rangle$	$[\![\mathsf{cps}(y : \mathbb{N} \vdash \mathsf{let}\ z{=}y + 4\ \mathsf{in}\ z + 3)]\!]$
$\langle\langle\langle\langle\rangle, 6\rangle, 10\rangle, s\rangle$	$[\![\mathsf{cps}(y : \mathbb{N},\ z : \mathbb{N} \vdash z + 3)]\!]$
$\langle\langle\langle\rangle, 10\rangle, s\rangle$	$[\![\mathsf{cps}(z : \mathbb{N} \vdash z + 3)]\!]$

5   Call-by-Value

In this section we observe that the linearity restriction on the source language can be lifted if the intermediate language allows contraction. We describe a simple way of extending LIN with contraction by adding exponentials $!X$. We believe that for applications in compilation it would be better to use the more fine-grained *subexponentials* $A \cdot X$ of INTML [7], see [24, §6] for a discussion. For lack of space and for simplicity, we consider just exponentials here.

A simple way of expressing this is by defining an intermediate language EXP, which extends LIN with a type $!X$ and the following typing rules.

$$\frac{\Gamma, x : X \vdash t : Y}{\Gamma, x : !X \vdash t : Y} \qquad \frac{\Gamma, x : !X, y : !X \vdash t : Y}{\Gamma, x : !X \vdash t[x/y] : Y} \qquad \frac{\Gamma \vdash s : !X \multimap Y \qquad !\Delta \vdash t : X}{\Gamma, !\Delta \vdash s\,t : Y}$$

The translation of LIN to the low-level language can be extended to EXP by choosing $(!X)^- = \mathsf{nat} \times X^-$ and $(!X)^+ = \mathsf{nat} \times X^+$ and by interpreting the exponential rules in a standard way [1].

The definition of equality is extended from LIN to EXP by letting $[\![!X]\!]_\rho$ be the smallest relation such that $q\ [\![X]\!]_\rho\ q'$ implies $(id_{\mathsf{nat}} \times q)\ [\![!X]\!]_\rho\ (id_{\mathsf{nat}} \times q')$. The results from Section 3.1 remain true.

This extension of LIN to EXP suffices to translate the full source language. Define $\mathcal{C}_\varphi(X)$, $\mathcal{A}_\varphi(X)$, $\mathcal{K}_\alpha(X)$ and $\mathcal{T}_\varphi(X)$ just as in Section 4, but with $!(-) \multimap (-)$ instead of $(-) \multimap (-)$. The CPS-translation of terms to EXP is defined exactly as in Fig. 2.

Proposition 2. *If* $\Gamma \vdash M : X$ *in the source language without the linearity restriction, then* $!\mathcal{A}(\Gamma) \vdash \mathsf{cps}(\Gamma \vdash M) : \mathcal{T}_{\mathcal{C}(\Gamma)}(X)$ *in* EXP.

Theorem 2. *If* $\vdash M : \mathbb{N}$ *in the source language without the linearity restriction and* $M \longrightarrow^* n$*, where* n *is a value, then* $\mathsf{cps}(\vdash M)\ \mathsf{unit}\ K = (\langle \vec{z}, s \rangle \mapsto \langle n, s \rangle)^*(K\ \mathsf{unit}\ \star)$ *for any closed continuation* $K : \mathcal{K}_{\mathsf{unit}}(\mathbb{N})$.

We end this section by noting that with contraction in the source language we can define a term $\mathsf{if0}(V, M, N)$ for M and N of any source type X. The definition goes by induction on X. At function type $X_1 \to X_2$ one defines $\lambda x{:}X_1.\,\mathsf{if0}(V, M\ x, N\ x)$, where the body is obtained from the induction hypothesis.

This definition may look undesirable for compilation, as the case distinction is performed every time the function is invoked. But consider what happens to terms of the form $\mathsf{if0}(V, (\lambda x{:}\mathbb{N}.\ M), (\lambda x{:}\mathbb{N}.\ N))$ in defunctionalizing compilers, such as [6].

The two abstractions would be represented by two constructors, $C_1(\dots)$ and $C_2(\dots)$, say. The function value of the whole term could be either $C_1(\dots)$ or $C_2(\dots)$. When this function is applied, a case distinction over the two possible constructors is performed in order to execute the correct function, so a similar case distinction is performed here. It seems that is a certain amount of case distinction is unavoidable in order to find the right code to execute. The precise properties of the above definition of case distinction on higher types remain to be investigated, however.

6   Conclusion

We have given a new interpretation of call-by-value in an intermediate language that represents the structure of an interactive computation model constructed from a first-order low-level language. The interpretation makes low-level details explicit that are interesting for compilation, such as which values are stored at any point in the execution of the resulting low-level programs. The interpretation is motivated by game semantic models [3,14] which however abstract away some important (for us) low-level details.

We have shown that well-known logical tools, such as parametric polymorphism, are useful managing the low level details of the interpretation. We have formulated these principles in terms of a simple intermediate language LIN. Its use has simplified the handling of encoding details, for example in the encoding of function values. The utility of studying intermediate languages like LIN is also demonstrated by the fact that the soundness proof of the refined CPS-translation presented here can be carried out by a refinement of the standard proof. While it would certainly be possible to define the translation to the low-level language in a single step, it is not immediate how to track reduction on source terms on the level of compiled low-level programs. We hope that other logical tools will find use in the context of low level languages.

We should remark that for call-by-name a thunkifying translation [13] into EXP is possible. In essence, this is the translation of INTML [7]. Indeed, INTML integrates a call-by-name CPS-translation, see [23], that can be factored through EXP.

For further work, we are optimistic that it will be possible to extend the approach to more expressive source languages, e.g. with recursion. We should also like to clarify the relation to defunctionalizing compilation methods for call-by-value languages, such as the very successful [6].

In another direction, it should also be interesting to apply the results to the resource usage analysis of call-by-value languages. For instance, one may consider the design of a call-by-value functional language for LOGSPACE computation, using an approach similar to that of INTML [7] for call-by-name. To remain within LOGSPACE one would need to restrict nat in the low-level language. We believe that this can be done if one replaces $\forall \alpha.\, X$ in LIN by bounded quantification $\forall \alpha \lhd A.\, X$ using the ideas from [21]. One may also consider such bounded quantification to reduce the amount of encoding operations into nat arising from the low-level implementation of universal quantification. The situation should be similar that of exponentials and subexponentials [24, §6].

Acknowledgments. I am grateful for support by the Fondation Sciences Mathématiques de Paris as part of the PROOFS program.

References

1. Abramsky, S., Haghverdi, E., Scott, P.: Geometry of interaction and linear combinatory algebras. Mathematical Structures in Computer Science 12(5), 625–665 (2002)
2. Abramsky, S., Jagadeesan, R., Malacaria, P.: Full abstraction for PCF. Inf. Comput. 163(2), 409–470 (2000)
3. Abramsky, S., McCusker, G.: Call-by-value games. In: Nielsen, M., Thomas, W. (eds.) CSL 1997. LNCS, vol. 1414, pp. 1–17. Springer, Heidelberg (1998)
4. Appel, A.W.: Compiling with Continuations. Cambridge University Press (2006)
5. Banerjee, A., Heintze, N., Riecke, J.G.: Design and correctness of program transformations based on control-flow analysis. In: Kobayashi, N., Pierce, B.C. (eds.) TACS 2001. LNCS, vol. 2215, pp. 420–447. Springer, Heidelberg (2001)
6. Cejtin, H., Jagannathan, S., Weeks, S.: Flow-directed closure conversion for typed languages. In: Smolka, G. (ed.) ESOP/ETAPS 2000. LNCS, vol. 1782, pp. 56–71. Springer, Heidelberg (2000)
7. Dal Lago, U., Schöpp, U.: Functional programming in sublinear space. In: Gordon, A.D. (ed.) ESOP 2010. LNCS, vol. 6012, pp. 205–225. Springer, Heidelberg (2010)
8. Fischer, M.J.: Lambda calculus schemata. SIGACT News (14), 104–109 (1972)
9. Fredriksson, O., Ghica, D.R.: Abstract machines for game semantics, revisited. In: LICS, pp. 560–569. IEEE (2013)
10. Ghica, D.R.: Geometry of synthesis: A structured approach to VLSI design. In: Hofmann, M., Felleisen, M. (eds.) POPL, pp. 363–375. ACM (2007)
11. Ghica, D.R., Smith, A., Singh, S.: Geometry of synthesis IV: Compiling affine recursion into static hardware. In: Chakravarty, M.M.T., Hu, Z., Danvy, O. (eds.) ICFP, pp. 221–233 (2011)
12. Harper, R., Lillibridge, M.: Polymorphic type assignment and cps conversion. Lisp and Symbolic Computation 6(3-4), 361–380 (1993)
13. Hatcliff, J., Danvy, O.: Thunks and the lambda-calculus. J. Funct. Program. 7(3), 303–319 (1997)
14. Honda, K., Yoshida, N.: Game-theoretic analysis of call-by-value computation. Theor. Comput. Sci. 221(1-2), 393–456 (1999)
15. Joyal, A., Street, R., Verity, D.: Traced monoidal categories. Math. Proc. Cambridge Philos. Soc. 119(3), 447–468 (1996)
16. Laird, J.: Game semantics and linear cps interpretation. Theor. Comput. Sci. 333(1-2), 199–224 (2005)
17. Melliès, P.A.: Game semantics in string diagrams. In: LICS, pp. 481–490. IEEE (2012)
18. Melliès, P.A., Tabareau, N.: Resource modalities in game semantics. In: LICS, pp. 389–398 (2007)
19. Plotkin, G.D.: Call-by-name, call-by-value and the lambda-calculus. Theor. Comput. Sci. 1(2), 125–159 (1975)
20. Plotkin, G.D., Abadi, M.: A logic for parametric polymorphism. In: Bezem, M., Groote, J.F. (eds.) TLCA 1993. LNCS, vol. 664, pp. 361–375. Springer, Heidelberg (1993)
21. Schöpp, U.: Stratified bounded affine logic for logarithmic space. In: LICS, pp. 411–420 (2007)
22. Schöpp, U.: Computation-by-interaction with effects. In: Yang, H. (ed.) APLAS 2011. LNCS, vol. 7078, pp. 305–321. Springer, Heidelberg (2011)

23. Schöpp, U.: On interaction, continuations and defunctionalization. In: Hasegawa, M. (ed.) TLCA 2013. LNCS, vol. 7941, pp. 205–220. Springer, Heidelberg (2013)

24. Schöpp, U.: Organising low-level programs using higher types. In: PPDP 2014 (to appear, 2014)

25. Selinger, P.: A survey of graphical languages for monoidal categories. In: New Structures for Physics. Lecture Notes in Physics, vol. 813, pp. 289–355. Springer (2011)

26. Shao, Z., Appel, A.W.: Efficient and safe-for-space closure conversion. ACM Trans. Program. Lang. Syst. 22(1), 129–161 (2000)

27. Wadler, P.: Theorems for free! In: FPCA, pp. 347–359 (1989)

A Precise and Abstract Memory Model for C Using Symbolic Values*

Frédéric Besson[1], Sandrine Blazy[2], and Pierre Wilke[2]

[1] Inria, Rennes, France
[2] Irisa - Université Rennes 1, Rennes, France

Abstract. Real life C programs are often written using C dialects which, for the ISO C standard, have undefined behaviours. In particular, according to the ISO C standard, reading an uninitialised variable has an undefined behaviour and low-level pointer operations are implementation defined. We propose a formal semantics which gives a well-defined meaning to those behaviours for the C dialect of the CompCert compiler. Our semantics builds upon a novel memory model leveraging a notion of symbolic values. Symbolic values are used by the semantics to delay the evaluation of operations and are normalised lazily to genuine values when needed. We show that the most precise normalisation is computable and that a slightly relaxed normalisation can be efficiently implemented using an SMT solver. The semantics is executable and our experiments show that the enhancements of our semantics are mandatory to give a meaning to low-levels idioms such as those found in the allocation functions of a C standard library.

1 Introduction

Semantics of programming languages give a formal basis for reasoning about the behaviours of programs. In particular, the correctness guarantee of C compilers [14] and verification frameworks [4] is stated with respect to the program semantics. However, the C programming language is specified in such a way that certain operations are either undefined, unspecified or implementation-defined. Typically, reading uninitialised memory is an undefined behaviour; the order of evaluation of function arguments is unspecified; the size of the int type is implementation-defined. A C program is *strictly conforming* if it does not trigger any undefined, unspecified or implementation-defined behaviour.

This leads to an unsettling question: what is the guarantee provided by a compiler when the program is not strictly conforming, *i.e.* when its semantics is undefined? The short answer is none. The C standard [10] explains that anything can happen with undefined behaviours: the compiler may fail to compile, but it could – and usually does – produce an executable code. The behaviour of the executable depends on compiler flags, especially optimisation levels. The executable code may behave as expected by the programmer, but it can also ignore

---

* This work was supported by Agence Nationale de la Recherche, grant number ANR-12-INSE-002 BinSec.

J. Garrigue (Ed.): APLAS 2014, LNCS 8858, pp. 449–468, 2014.

the statements that lead to undefined behaviours, or even crash at runtime. For instance, for the sake of optimisation, the compiler may choose to remove pieces of code that result in an undefined behaviour [19]. In summary, the advantage of undefined behaviours is that they can be exploited by C compilers to optimise the generated code; the downside is that C programs with undefined behaviours may have unexpected results.

In practice, undefined behaviours have been responsible for serious flaws in major open source software [19] – optimisations triggered by undefined behaviours have introduced vulnerabilities in the target code. Moreover, some low-level idioms cannot be expressed without resorting to unspecified behaviours of the C semantics. A compelling example is the memory allocation primitives of the C standard library which are written using the C syntax but do not have a *strictly conforming* semantics. One reason for this is that the low-level bit manipulation of pointers that is necessary for efficient and robust implementation of memory allocation is implementation defined.

To alleviate the problem, a common approach consists in setting compiler flags to disable optimisations known to exploit undefined behaviours [19, Section 3.1]. In a sense, flag tweaking is a fragile way to get the desired program semantics. Wang, Zeldovich *et al.* [20] propose a more principled compiler approach where they identify and report code whose optimisation depends on undefined behaviours. In this work, we advocate for a semantics-based approach and propose an executable extension of a C semantics ruling out unspecified behaviours originating from low-level pointer arithmetic and undefined behaviours due to access to uninitialised data.

The C standard describes only an informal semantics, but several realistic C formal semantics have been defined [17,3,7,12]. They describe precisely the defined behaviours of C programs, as well as some undefined behaviours. Yet, none of them accommodates for all low-level pointer manipulations; uninitialised data are only dealt with in a very limited fashion by the semantics of Ellison and Roşu [7, 6.2.2].

One formal semantics is the C semantics used by the CompCert formally verified C compiler [14]. CompCert is equipped with a machine-checked correctness proof establishing that the generated assembly code behaves exactly as prescribed by the semantics of the C source, eliminating all possibilities of compiler-introduced bugs and generating unprecedented confidence in this compiler. Yet, as for any compiler, the guarantee offered by CompCert only holds for programs with a defined behaviour. In general, the CompCert compiler provides a stronger guarantee than an ISO C compiler because its source language CompCert C is more defined than the ISO C99 language. Our goal is to extend the semantics expressiveness of CompCert C further by ruling out more undefined or unspecified behaviours.

The contributions of this work can be phrased as follows:

- We present the first formal semantics for CompCert C able to give a meaning to low-level idioms (bit-level pointer arithmetic and access to uninitialised data) without resorting to a concrete representation of the memory.

- The semantics operates over a novel memory model where *symbolic* values represent delayed computations and are normalised lazily to *concrete* values.
- We demonstrate that the most precise normalisation is decidable and explain how to devise an efficient implementation using an SMT solver.
- The semantics is executable and the software development is available at http://www.irisa.fr/celtique/ext/csem/.
- We show in our experiments that our extensions are mandatory to give a defined meaning to low-level idioms found in existing C code.

The remainder of this paper is organised as follows. Section 2 introduces relevant examples of programs having undefined or unspecified behaviours. Section 3 defines our extension of CompCert's semantics with symbolic values. Section 4 specifies our normalisation of symbolic values. Section 5 deals with the implementation of the normalisation using SMT solvers over the theory of bitvectors. Section 6 describes the experimental evaluation of our implementation. Related work is discussed in section 7, followed by concluding remarks.

2 Motivating Examples

An example of unspecified behaviour is the order of evaluation of the arguments of a function call. The relative size of numeric types is defined but the precise number of bits is implementation defined. An undefined behaviour is for instance the access of an array outside its bounds. Unsafe programming languages like C have by nature undefined behaviours and there is no way to give a meaningful semantics to an out-of-bound array access.[1] Yet, certain undefined behaviours of C were introduced on purpose to ease either the portability of the language across platforms or the development of efficient compilers. As illustrated below, our novel memory model gives a formal semantics to low-level idioms such as access to uninitialised memory or low-level pointer arithmetic.

2.1 Access to Uninitialised Variables

The C standard states that any read access to uninitialised memory triggers undefined behaviours [10, section 6.7.8, §10]: "If an object that has automatic storage duration is not initialised explicitly, its value is indeterminate." Here, "indeterminate" means that the behaviour is undefined. To illustrate a benefit of our semantics, consider the code snippet of Fig. 1, representative of an existing C pattern (see Section 6.3).

The program declares a status variable and sets its least significant bit using the set function. It then tests whether the least significant bit is set using the isset function. According to the C standard, this program has undefined behaviour because the set function reads the value of the status variable before it is ever written.

---

[1] Typed languages detect illegal accesses and typically throw an exception.

However, we argue that this program should have a well-defined semantics and should always return the value 1. The argument is that whatever the initial value of the variable status, the least significant bit of status is known to be 1 after the call set(status,0). Moreover, the value of the other bits is irrelevant for the return value of the call isset(status,0) which returns 1 if and only if the least significant bit of the variable status is 1. More formally, the program should return the value of the expression (status|(1≪0))&(1≪0) != 0 which evaluates to 1 whatever the value of status. Our semantics constructs symbolic values and normalises them to a genuine value when the evaluation yields a unique possible value.

2.2 Low-Level Pointer Arithmetic

In ISO C, the bit width and the alignment of pointers are implementation defined. We consider here that pointers are encoded with 4 bytes and that the malloc function returns pointers that are 16-byte aligned (i.e. the 4 least significant bits are zeros). The C standard also states that arithmetic operations on pointers are limited to certain comparisons, the addition (or subtraction) of an integer offset to a pointer and the subtraction of two pointers pointing to the same object. In order to perform arbitrary operations over a pointer, it is possible to cast it to an unsigned integer of type uintptr_t for which the ISO C standard provides the following specification [10, Section 7.18.1.4].

> [The type uintptr_t] designates an unsigned integer type with the property that any valid pointer to void can be converted to this type, then converted back to pointer to void, and the result will compare equal to the original pointer.

Note that this specification is very weak and does not ensure anything if a pointer, cast to uintptr_t, is modified before being cast back. Here, uintptr_t is implemented by a 4 bytes unsigned integer, and a cast between pointers and uintptr_t preserves the binary representation of both pointers and integers (i.e. it is essentially a no-op).

With these assumptions in mind, consider the expected behaviour of the code snippet of Fig. 2. The pointer p is a 16-byte aligned pointer to a heap-allocated integer obtained by malloc. Therefore, it has 4 trailing spare bits. The pointer q is obtained from the pointer p by filling the 4 trailing bits (hence the bitwise and with 0xF) with a hash of the pointer p. Note that this pattern is used in practice as a hardening technique to enforce pointer integrity [13]. Then, the evaluation

```
int set(int p, int flag) { return p | (1 ≪ flag); }
int isset(int p, int flag) { return (p & (1 ≪ flag)) != 0; }
int main() {  int status = set(status,0); return isset(status,0);     }
```

Fig. 1. Undefined behaviour: reading the uninitialised variable status

```
char hash(void* ptr);
int main(){
    int * p = (int *) malloc(sizeof(int));
    *p = 0;
    int * q = (int *) ((uintptr_t) p | (hash(p) & 0xF));
    int * r = (int *) (((uintptr_t) q >> 4) << 4);
    return *r;    }
```

Fig. 2. Unspecified behaviour: low-level pointer arithmetic

of r clears out the 4 trailing bits of q using logical shifts. We argue that r is equal to p and that the program has a well-defined semantics and returns *p (that is 0). Our semantics computes the expected behaviour of this program without resorting to a concrete representation of pointers as machine integers.

2.3   Summary of Differences with the ISO C Standard

The ISO C standard leaves certain behaviours implementation defined. Among these, our semantics is parametrised by the size of the pointers and the alignment constraint of malloc. Our semantics also stipulates that pointer and uintptr_t types have the same size and that casts between these types preserve the binary representation of the objects. The ISO C standard states that reading uninitialised memory is undefined behaviour. Our semantics is more flexible and simulates the read of an arbitrary value. Operationally, our semantics propagates a symbolic undefined value through the execution. These extensions are sufficient to give a well-defined (and intuitive) semantics to the previous examples.

3   A C Semantics with Symbolic Values

Our semantics is able to model low-level idioms, in particular bit-level manipulation of pointers, while retaining abstraction properties of the current block-based memory model of CompCert. Our approach consists in computing symbolic values *lazily* delaying evaluation until values are really needed. A symbolic value sv evaluates to a value v if for every possible concrete memory M, sv evaluates to the same value v.

CompCert defines the semantics of a dozen of intermediate languages ranging from CompCert C to assembly. All the languages share the same memory model. The compiler transforms programs from one language to another and proves the correctness of the transformations with respect to that memory model. The two highest-level languages are CompCert C (source language) and Clight, a simpler version of CompCert C with side-effect free expressions. For the sake of presentation, we introduce our new memory model on the Clight semantics. However, our implementation leverages the existing CompCert C interpreter enhanced with our new memory model.

In this section, we first describe our memory model with symbolic values. Then, we show how to enhance the Clight semantics [3] with symbolic values.

Memory locations: $l ::= (b, i)$ (block, integer offset)

Values: $v ::= \mathtt{int}(i) \mid \mathtt{float}(f)$
                        $\mid \mathtt{ptr}(l) \mid \mathtt{undef}$

Memory chunks: $\kappa ::= \mathtt{Mint8signed}$ 8-bit integers
                        $\mid \mathtt{Mint8unsigned}$
                        $\mid \mathtt{Mint16signed}$ 16-bit integers
                        $\mid \mathtt{Mint16unsigned}$
                        $\mid \mathtt{Mint32}$ 32-bit integers or pointers
                        $\mid \mathtt{Mfloat32}$ 32-bit floats

Operations over memory states:

$\mathtt{alloc}(M, lo, hi) = (M', b)$	Allocate a fresh block with bounds $[lo, hi[$.
$\mathtt{free}(M, b) = M'$	Free (invalidate) the block b
	Read consecutive bytes (as determined by κ) at
$\mathtt{load}(\kappa, M, b, i) = \lfloor v \rfloor$	block b, offset i of memory state M. If successful,
	return the contents of these bytes as value v.
	Store the value v as one or several consecutive
$\mathtt{store}(\kappa, M, b, i, v) = \lfloor M' \rfloor$	bytes (as determined by κ) at offset i of block b.
	If successful, return an updated memory state M'.
$\mathtt{bound}(M, b)$	Return the bounds $[lo, hi[$ of block b.

Fig. 3. CompCert's memory model

3.1   The CompCert Memory Model

The semantics of operations involving pointers relies on a memory model defining how values are represented. The most concrete memory model is an array of bytes, where pointers and integers are indistinguishable. It can give a precise semantics, but reasoning on programs at such a low level is cumbersome (e.g. reasoning on forbidden memory accesses to detect buffer overflows). CompCert is using a more abstract block-based model [15] where memory is divided into disjoint blocks, each block corresponding to an allocated variable. A memory is a collection of blocks, each block being an array of concrete bytes. Intuitively, a block represents a C variable or an invocation of `malloc`.

Values stored in memory are defined in Fig. 3. They are the disjoint union of 32-bit integers (written as `int`(i)), 32-bit floating-point numbers (written as `float`(f)), locations (written as `ptr`(b,i)), and the special value **undef** representing the content of uninitialised memory. Locations `ptr`(b,i) are composed of a block identifier b (i.e. an abstract address) and an integer byte offset i within this block. Pointer arithmetic modifies the offset part of a location, keeping its block identifier part unchanged. Memory chunks appear in memory operations `load` and `store`, to describe concisely the size, type and signedness of the value being stored. These functions return option types: we write $\emptyset$ for failure and $\lfloor x \rfloor$ for a successful return of a value x.

The memory is modelled as a map associating to each location an 8-bit elementary memory value of type `memval`. A `memval` value is a byte-sized quantity that describes the current content of a memory cell. It can be either `Undef` to model uninitialised memory; `Byte(b)` to model a concrete byte b; or `Pointer(b, i, n)` to represent the n-th byte ($n \in \{1, 2, 3, 4\}$) of the location $\mathtt{ptr}(b, i)$.

3.2   A New Memory Model with Symbolic Values

Our memory model is built on top of CompCert's, where we replace the values with symbolic values, defined as follows.

$$
\begin{array}{lll}
sv ::= v & & \\
\quad | \quad op_1^\tau\ sv & & \text{unary arithmetic operation} \\
\quad | \quad sv\ ^\tau op_2^\tau\ sv & & \text{binary arithmetic operation} \\
\quad | \quad sv^\tau\ ?\ sv^\tau : sv^\tau & & \text{conditional expression} \\
\quad | \quad (\tau)sv^\tau & & \text{type cast (to a C type } \tau\text{)}
\end{array}
$$

Symbolic values are annotated by C types that are needed to disambiguate overloaded C operators. Symbolic values are side-effect free and therefore their evaluation is independent of the memory content. To account for alignment properties we associate with each block of the memory a *mask* that the concrete address of the block needs to satisfy. Formally, the concrete address a of a block with mask msk must be such that $a \mathbin{\&} msk = a$. The allocation primitive is modified accordingly, and we add a function that returns the mask of a given block. The primitives `load` and `store` now operate over symbolic values instead of values.

$$
\begin{array}{l}
\mathtt{alloc}(M, lo, hi, msk) = (M', b) \\
\mathtt{mask}(M, b) = msk \\
\mathtt{load}(\kappa, M, b, i) = \lfloor sv \rfloor \\
\mathtt{store}(\kappa, M, b, i, sv) = \lfloor M' \rfloor
\end{array}
$$

We also adapt the `memval` type to accommodate for symbolic values. To that purpose, we replace the `Pointer` constructor by a generalised `Symbolic(sv, n)` constructor which represents the n-th byte of a symbolic value sv.

To perform these memory primitives, we define a key operation `extr(sv,i)`, which extracts the ith byte of a symbolic value. The reverse operation is the concatenation of a symbolic value sv1 with a symbolic value sv2 representing 8 bits. Assuming that the symbolic value represents a 32-bit value, these operations can be defined as

$$
\begin{array}{l}
\mathtt{extr(sv,i)} = (sv \gg (8*i))\ \&\ \mathtt{0xFF} \\
\mathtt{concat(sv1,sv2)} = sv1 \ll 8 + sv2
\end{array}
$$

3.3   Parametrised Semantics of Clight Values

Expressions cannot be kept symbolic forever. Our semantics is equipped with a partial normalisation function $\mathtt{normalise}(M, \tau, sv)$ which converts a symbolic

Expressions in l-value position:

$$\frac{G, E \vdash a, M \Rightarrow sv \quad \texttt{normalise}(M, \texttt{type}(a), sv) = \lfloor \texttt{ptr}(\ell) \rfloor}{G, E \vdash {*}a, M \Leftarrow \ell} \quad (1)$$

Expressions in r-value position:

$$\frac{G, E \vdash a_1, M \Rightarrow sv_1 \quad \texttt{type}(a_1) = \tau}{G, E \vdash op_1\ a_1, M \Rightarrow op_1^\tau\ sv_1} \quad (2)$$

$$\frac{G, E \vdash a_1, M \Rightarrow sv_1 \quad G, E \vdash a_2, M_1 \Rightarrow sv_2 \quad \texttt{type}(a_1) = \tau_1 \quad \texttt{type}(a_2) = \tau_2}{G, E \vdash a_1\ op_2\ a_2, M \Rightarrow sv_1{}^{\tau_1} op_2{}^{\tau_2}\ sv_2} \quad (3)$$

$$\frac{G, E \vdash a_1, M \Rightarrow sv_1 \quad \texttt{type}(a_1) = \tau_1}{G, E \vdash a_2, M \Rightarrow sv_2 \quad \texttt{type}(a_2) = \tau_2 \quad G, E \vdash a_3, M \Rightarrow sv_3 \quad \texttt{type}(a_3) = \tau_3}{G, E \vdash a_1\ ?\ a_2 : a_3, M \Rightarrow sv_1^{\tau_1}\ ?\ sv_2^{\tau_2} : sv_3^{\tau_3}} \quad (4)$$

$$\frac{G, E \vdash a, M \Rightarrow sv_1 \quad \texttt{type}(a) = \tau_1}{G, E \vdash (\tau)a, M \Rightarrow (\tau)sv_1^{\tau_1}} \quad (5)$$

Fig. 4. Semantics of Clight with symbolic values (excerpt)

value sv to a concrete value of type τ, depending on masks and bounds of blocks of memory M. The modified Clight semantics of expressions is given in Fig. 4. It is defined by judgements, parametrised by a global environment G, a local environment E and an initial memory state M. The evaluation of an expression in l-value (resp. r-value) position results in a location (resp. symbolic value). In the judgements, a, a_1, a_2, a_3 range over syntactic expressions and sv, sv_1, sv_2, sv_3 range over symbolic values.

$$G, E \vdash a, M \Leftarrow \ell \quad \text{(evaluation of an expression in l-value position)}$$
$$G, E \vdash a, M \Rightarrow sv \quad \text{(evaluation of an expression in r-value position)}$$

Compared to the existing Clight semantics [3], expressions are not completely evaluated but mapped to symbolic values. Moreover, the rules explicitly introduce calls to a normalisation function (see Section 4). These calls are inserted when a genuine value is required, *i.e.* when reading from or writing to memory, when evaluating the condition of a loop or **if-then-else** statement, or when exiting the program.

For instance, to evaluate ${*}a$, rule (1) recursively evaluates the expression a to get the symbolic value sv. To get a genuine location l, rule (1) explicitly normalises sv to get l. Now, l can be used to perform a **store** memory operation. Rule (2) specifies the evaluation of unary expression $op_1\ a_1$: it recursively evaluates the expression a_1 to get the symbolic value sv_1. Instead of evaluating the operator op_1, the semantics delays the evaluation and constructs the symbolic value $op_1^\tau\ sv_1$ where τ is the type of the expression a_1. Similarly, the evaluation of binary expressions (rule (3)), conditional expressions (rule (4)) and cast expressions (rule (5)) recursively evaluate their arguments and construct a symbolic value. Note that for the original Clight semantics, two rules are needed to give a semantics to conditional expressions [3, Fig.6, rules (12) and (13)] depending on whether the condition holds or not. With symbolic values, we delay the evaluation and therefore have a single rule.

4   A Sound and Complete Normalisation

Our semantics with symbolic values aims at giving a defined meaning to low-level idioms that are out-of-reach of the current Clight. To do so, we need to instantiate the semantics with an aggressive normalisation function. The existing Clight semantics can be obtained by a suitable normalisation function. This semantics is trustworthy because it has been carefully designed, thoroughly reviewed and intensively tested. However, for more aggressive normalisation (which is what we aim at), this validation methodology does not scale and therefore provides a limited trustworthiness.

In this section, we give a formal specification of the `normalise` function. We define the notions of soundness and completeness of a normalisation function with respect to a concrete memory model. We will later show (Section 5) how to get efficient executable implementations from this specification.

4.1   Soundness of the Normalisation of Symbolic Values

Our semantics is parametrised by the normalisation function `normalise`. In this part, we describe the soundness conditions that this normalisation should fulfil. Symbolic values denote low-level values of types either `Tint` or `Tfloat`. The mapping between high-level C types and low-level types is performed by the function `ctyp` defined as follows: $\mathtt{ctyp}(\tau) = \mathtt{Tfloat}$ if $\tau = \mathtt{Tfloat}$, and $\mathtt{ctyp}(\tau) = \mathtt{Tint}$ otherwise. Notice that all the pointer types are mapped to the type `Tint`. Indeed, at low-level, addresses are not distinguishable from genuine integers. To map locations (b, i) to integers, the low-level evaluation is equipped with a mapping A from block identifiers to concrete addresses, which assigns an address to each memory block and therefore fixes a memory layout. In general, the low-level evaluation of a symbolic value is not a single value but a set because the value `undef` represents an arbitrary low-level value. Definition 1 formalises the low-level evaluation of symbolic values.

Definition 1 (Low-level evaluation). *Let A be an allocation function mapping block identifiers to concrete addresses. The low-level evaluation $[\![\cdot]\!]_A^\tau$ of a symbolic value e of type τ is inductively defined by the following rules.*

$$\frac{}{\mathtt{int}(n) \in [\![\mathtt{int}(n)]\!]_A^{\mathtt{Tint}}} \qquad \frac{}{\mathtt{float}(f) \in [\![\mathtt{float}(f)]\!]_A^{\mathtt{Tfloat}}}$$

$$\frac{\mathtt{ctyp}(\tau) = \mathtt{Tint}}{\mathtt{int}(A(b) + i) \in [\![\mathtt{ptr}(b, i)]\!]_A^\tau} \qquad \frac{\mathtt{ctyp}(\tau) = \mathtt{Tfloat}}{\mathtt{float}(n) \in [\![\mathtt{undef}]\!]_A^\tau}$$

$$\frac{\mathtt{ctyp}(\tau) = \mathtt{Tint}}{\mathtt{int}(n) \in [\![\mathtt{undef}]\!]_A^\tau}$$

$$\frac{v_1 \in [\![sv_1]\!]_A^{\tau_1} \quad \texttt{eval\_unop}(op_1, v_1, \texttt{ctyp}(\tau_1)) = \lfloor v \rfloor \quad \texttt{type}(v) = \texttt{ctyp}(\tau)}{v \in [\![op_1^{\tau_1} \, sv_1]\!]_A^{\tau}}$$

$$\frac{v_1 \in [\![sv_1]\!]_A^{\tau_1} \quad v_2 \in [\![sv_2]\!]_A^{\tau_2} \quad \texttt{type}(v) = \texttt{ctyp}(\tau)}{\texttt{eval\_binop}(op_2, v_1, \texttt{ctyp}(\tau_1), v_2, \texttt{ctyp}(\tau_2)) = \lfloor v \rfloor}{v \in [\![sv_1 \,^{\tau_1} op_2^{\tau_2} \, sv_2]\!]_A^{\tau}}$$

$$\frac{v_1 \in [\![sv_1]\!]_A^{\tau_1} \quad v_2 \in [\![sv_2]\!]_A^{\tau} \quad \texttt{is\_true}(v_1, \texttt{ctyp}(\tau_1))}{v_2 \in [\![sv_1^{\tau_1} \, ? \, sv_2^{\tau} \, : \, sv_3^{\tau}]\!]_A^{\tau}}$$

$$\frac{v_1 \in [\![sv_1]\!]_A^{\tau_1} \quad v_3 \in [\![sv_3]\!]_A^{\tau} \quad \texttt{is\_false}(v_1, \texttt{ctyp}(\tau_1))}{v_3 \in [\![sv_1^{\tau_1} \, ? \, sv_2^{\tau} \, : \, sv_3^{\tau}]\!]_A^{\tau}}$$

$$\frac{v_1 \in [\![sv_1]\!]_A^{\tau_1} \quad \texttt{cast}(v_1, \texttt{ctyp}(\tau)) = \lfloor v \rfloor}{v \in [\![(\tau)sv_1^{\tau_1}]\!]_A^{\tau}}$$

By construction, the denotation of a symbolic value of type τ is a set of values of type $\texttt{ctyp}(\tau)$. Symbolic values that are not well-typed have an empty low-level evaluation. As a side-remark, notice that the types of symbolic values cannot be uniquely inferred (undef can have an arbitrary type), and are therefore explicitly given. Moreover, the low-level evaluation of a symbolic value is reusing the existing high-level operators eval_unop and eval_binop with the difference that types are low-level types.

The normalisation of a symbolic value s should return a defined value v ($v \neq$ undef) such that s evaluates to v for all possible concrete valid memory layouts. Definition 2 specifies valid memory layouts.

Definition 2 (Valid memory layout). *An allocation A from blocks to concrete addresses is a valid memory layout for memory M (written $A \vdash M$) iff:*

1. *addresses from distinct blocks do not overlap,*
2. *the address of a block satisfies its mask, i.e. $\forall b, A(b) \,\&\, \texttt{mask}(M, b) = A(b)$*
3. *addresses are not equal to zero.*

With the previous definitions we are ready to state what it means for a normalisation to be sound.

Definition 3 (Sound normalisation). *A normalisation function is sound iff for any symbolic value sv, it returns a value v ($\texttt{normalise}(M, \tau, sv) = \lfloor v \rfloor$) such that v is not undef ; v has type τ and v has the same evaluation as sv for any valid allocation layout i.e. $\forall A \vdash M.[\![sv]\!]_A^{\tau} = [\![v]\!]_A^{\tau}$.*

Note that because v differs from undef, $[\![v]\!]_A^{\tau}$ is necessarily a singleton. Yet, certain symbolic values containing undef can nonetheless be normalised, for instance, $\texttt{normalise}(\texttt{M}, \texttt{Tint}, \texttt{undef} \,\&\, \texttt{0x0}) = \lfloor 0 \rfloor$.

4.2 Reconstructing the Original Clight Semantics

The more precise the normalisation, the more defined the semantics. There is a hierarchy of normalisations of different precision. We therefore aim at identifying a normalisation which is not only precise but also tractable. The least precise normalisation, which always returns $\emptyset$, is sound but useless: it fails to provide a semantics to any expression. The original Clight semantics can be modelled by a normalisation function which recursively evaluates symbolic values.

$$\frac{\text{type}(v) = \tau}{\text{normalise}(M, \tau, v) = \lfloor v \rfloor}$$

$$\frac{\text{normalise}(M, \tau_1, e_1) = \lfloor v_1 \rfloor \quad \text{eval\_unop}(op_1, v_1, \tau_1) = \lfloor v \rfloor \quad \text{type}(v) = \tau}{\text{normalise}(M, \tau, op_1^{\tau_1} e_1) = \lfloor v \rfloor}$$

$$\frac{\text{normalise}(M, \tau_1, e_1) = \lfloor v_1 \rfloor \quad \text{normalise}(M, \tau_2, e_2) = \lfloor v_2 \rfloor}{\text{normalise}(M, \tau, e_1 \;^{\tau_1} op_2^{\tau_2} e_2) = \lfloor v \rfloor}$$

As explained in the introduction, this normalisation is unable to give a semantics to low-level pointer operations (e.g. $\text{ptr}(b,i)$ & $0x0$) or expressions with undefined sub-terms (e.g. undef & $0x0$). The original Clight semantics could be enriched to cope with these simple expressions. However, dealing with arbitrarily complex expressions using *ad hoc* simplifications would not be manageable.

4.3   Completeness of the Normalisation of Symbolic Values

Whenever possible, the most precise normalisation should always return some value. Yet there are rare cases where distinct values are sound normalisations. This is illustrated by Example 1.

Example 1. Consider the normalisation of the symbolic value $\text{ptr}(b, 0) + 2^{31} - 1$ for a pointer type τ in a memory M made of an unaligned block b with bounds $[0, 2^{31} - 1[$ and a 2-byte aligned block b' with bounds $[0, 2^{31}[$. Because the maximum capacity of the memory is $2^{32} - 1$ bytes (0 is not a valid address), the memory is full. Moreover, the alignment constraint of b' prevents it from being allocated at address 1. It follows that the only valid memory layout of M is $A = [b \mapsto 1; b' \mapsto 2^{31}]$.

As we have $[\![\text{ptr}(b, 0) + 2^{31} - 1]\!]_A^\tau = [\![\text{ptr}(b, 2^{31} - 1)]\!]_A^\tau = [\![\text{ptr}(b', 0)]\!]_A^\tau = \{\text{int}(2^{31})\}$, both $\text{ptr}(b, 2^{31} - 1)$ and $\text{ptr}(b', 0)$ are sound normalisations.

In this example, the normalisation $\text{ptr}(b', 0)$ is more valuable because it represents a valid address (i.e. within the bounds of the allocated block). Definition 4 formalises what it means for a normalisation to be complete by stipulating an ordering $\prec_M$ on values such that $\text{ptr}(b', 0) \prec_M \text{ptr}(b, 2^{31} - 1)$.

Definition 4 (Complete normalisation). *A normalisation function* norm *is complete if for all sound normalisations* norm'*, we have:*

$$\text{norm}(M, \tau, e) \preccurlyeq_M \text{norm}'(M, \tau, e)$$

where $\preccurlyeq_M$ *is the reflexive closure of the ordering* $\prec_M$ *inductively defined below and* $<$ *is an arbitrary total order over locations.*

$$\lfloor v \rfloor \prec_M \emptyset \quad (6) \qquad \frac{i \in \text{bound}(M, b) \quad i' \notin \text{bound}(M, b')}{\lfloor \text{ptr}(b, i) \rfloor \prec_M \lfloor \text{ptr}(b', i') \rfloor} \quad (7)$$

$$\frac{i \in \text{bound}(M, b) \quad i' \in \text{bound}(M, b') \quad (b, i) < (b', i')}{\lfloor \text{ptr}(b, i) \rfloor \prec_M \lfloor \text{ptr}(b', i') \rfloor} \quad (8)$$

$$\frac{i \notin \text{bound}(M, b) \quad i' \notin \text{bound}(M, b') \quad (b, i) < (b', i')}{\lfloor \text{ptr}(b, i) \rfloor \prec_M \lfloor \text{ptr}(b', i') \rfloor} \quad (9)$$

Rule (6) ensures that a complete normalisation is maximally defined and as much as possible does not return $\emptyset$. Rules (7), (8) and (9) ensure that a complete normalisation should, as much as possible, return a valid address.

There are memories M for which there is no valid memory layout A. The simple case is when the size of the allocated memory exceeds $2^{32}-1$ bytes. In general, reasoning about the size of the allocated memory is not enough because the memory can be fragmented due to alignment constraints. In such cases, Definition 4 is not sufficient to ensure that there is a unique sound and complete normalisation function. The reason is that when there is no valid memory layout, *any* value v is a correct normalisation. Moreover, as the order $\prec_M$ is not total, Definition 4 does not rule out these spurious cases. The good news is that all sound and complete normalisations compute the same result as soon as there exists a valid memory layout. Our normalisation algorithm (see Section 5) checks the existence of a valid memory layout and fails to normalise when there is none.

5   Evaluating Symbolic Values Using an SMT Solver

We have adapted the CompCert C semantics and its executable interpreter to work with symbolic values. As already demonstrated for the Clight semantics, the addition of symbolic values is not very intrusive and reuses most of the semantics infrastructure of the existing interpreter.

The difficulty lies in the implementation of the normalisation function. Given a memory M, there are finitely many valid memory layouts A. It is thus decidable to compute a sound and complete normalisation and the naive algorithm consists in enumerating over the valid memory layouts and checking that the symbolic values always evaluate to the same values. Yet, this is not tractable. As shown below, the normalisation can be recast as a decision problem over the logic of bitvectors. However, implementing (and proving) in Coq an efficient decision procedure for this logic would require a substantial engineering effort. Therefore, our current implementation leverages an external Satisfiability Modulo Theory (SMT) solver, Z3 [6].

5.1   An Executable Semantics of Symbolic Values

We have adapted the CompCert C interpreter to work with symbolic values. The modification requires to change the type of values to the type of symbolic values and to replace the existing memory model by our implementation accommodating for symbolic values. As it is illustrated for Clight, the evaluation of

C operators now builds symbolic values and calls to the **normalise** function are placed at certain points, as discussed below.

Our memory model stores (resp. reads) symbolic values to (resp. from) memory but the address needs to be a location (b,i). Therefore, we apply the normalisation function before calling the **store** and **load** primitives of the memory model. The normalisation is also called to compute the target of conditional jumps (e.g. **for**, **while** or **if** statements). A last normalisation is applied before ending the program because the program status needs to be a genuine integer. If the normalisation succeeds and returns some value, then the execution continues normally. Otherwise, the semantics gets stuck and the interpreter returns that it encountered an undefined behaviour. We detail in Section 6 some representative programs of our benchmarks.

5.2   Normalisation as a Satisfiability Problem

The normalisation function is axiomatised and implemented by an external (trusted) call to the SMT solver Z3 [6]. As stated earlier, the problem of computing the most precise normalisation is decidable. Yet, a naive approach does not provide a tractable algorithm. A better solution consists in encoding the normalisation problem as an SMT problem over the logic of bitvectors and uninterpreted function symbols. A bitvector of size n is the logic counterpart of a machine integer with n bits. This logic is therefore a perfect match for reasoning about machine integers.

First, we *axiomatise* the memory and define a logical function *size* mapping each block to its size and a logical function *mask* mapping each block to the mask to be verified by the concrete address. Next, we axiomatise the valid memory layout relation by directly translating Definition 2 in first-order logic.

Example 2. Consider a memory M restricted to two blocks b_1 and b_2, with b_1 of bounds $[0,4[$ aligned on word boundaries (i.e. the 4 trailing bits are zeros) and b_2 of bounds $[0,8[$ with no alignment constraint. The axiomatisation of M is given by the following formulae.

$$\text{Block sizes:} \quad size(b) = \begin{cases} 4 \text{ if } b = b_1 \\ 8 \text{ if } b = b_2 \\ 0 \text{ otherwise} \end{cases}$$

$$\text{Block masks:} \quad mask(b) = \begin{cases} \text{0xFFFC if } b = b_1 \\ \text{0xFFFF if } b = b_2 \\ \text{0xFFFF otherwise} \end{cases}$$

$$\text{No overlap:} \quad \forall b, b', o, o'. \bigwedge \begin{cases} b \neq b' \\ o < size(b) \\ o' < size(b') \end{cases} \Rightarrow A(b) + o \neq A(b') + o'$$

$$\text{Addresses are not 0:} \quad \forall b, o. o < size(b) \Rightarrow A(b) + o \neq 0$$

$$\text{Alignment :} \quad \forall b, A(b) \,\&\, mask(b) = A(b)$$

We process the symbolic value e to be normalised into a logical symbolic value e^* and replace occurrences of **undef** by distinct fresh logical variables thus modelling that **undef** may take any value.

Normalising into an integer. To normalise into an integer, we generate the SMT query: $e^* = i$, where i is a fresh logical variable. Suppose the formula is satisfiable for a value v for logical variable i. This means that there exists a valid memory layout such that e is evaluated as the value v. However, this value v is only a sound normalisation if it is the evaluation for *every* possible valid memory layout. To ensure this, we generate the second SMT query: $e^* = i \wedge i \neq v$. If this is unsatisfiable, then we will return v as the normalisation of e.

Normalising into a pointer. Getting the normalisation of a pointer value is more complicated by the fact that there are several ways of decomposing an integer into a location made of a base and an offset. Yet, as we are only interested in valid addresses (i.e. with an offset inside the bounds of the block), there is only a single choice. Therefore, we generate the following SMT query:

$$e^* = A(b) + o \wedge o < size(b).$$

Given a model (b', o') for location (b, o), we have to ensure that the evaluation of the expression is independent from the memory layout. Since blocks do not overlap, there is only one block such that the pointer is valid, so we just need to check that b' is the only possible block that makes a valid pointer, i.e. that the following formula is unsatisfiable:

$$e^* = A(b) + o \wedge o < size(b) \wedge b \neq b'$$

Example 3. Consider again the memory M of Example 2 and the symbolic value $e = \mathtt{ptr}(b_1, 1) - \mathtt{ptr}(b_2, 2) + \mathtt{ptr}(b_2, 4) + \mathtt{undef}\&0\mathtt{x}0$. We process e into a logical expression e^* by replacing $\mathtt{undef}$ by the fresh variable x_1:

$$e^* = A(b_1) + 1 - A(b_2) - 2 + A(b_2) + 4 + x_1\&0\mathtt{x}0$$

Notice that the two occurrences of $A(b_2)$ cancel out each other, and that we have $\forall x, x\&0\mathtt{x}0 = 0$. As a result, we can simplify this expression e^* into $A(b_1) + 3$.

Normalising into an integer. We need to solve the following SMT query, with i the unknown: $A(b_1) + 3 = i$. We then get a first solution (e.g. $v = 19$, with $A(b_1) = 16$). However, this is not the only possibility because we get a second solution with $A(b_1) = 32$ for example, which yields $v = 35$. This expression has therefore no normalisation as an integer.

Normalising into a pointer. Now, the SMT query we need to solve is:

$$A(b_1) + 3 = A(b) + o \wedge o < size(b)$$

A solution is $b' = b_1$ and $o' = 3$, and we can see that this is the only solution to this equation. Therefore the expression e is normalised into the location $\mathtt{ptr}(b_1, 3)$.

5.3   Relaxation and Optimisation of the SMT Encoding

The previous encoding of the memory depends on the number of allocated blocks. Thus, as the memory gets bigger, the normalisation would get slower. In practice, we observe that the size of the memory has a dramatic (negative) impact on SMT solvers. To tackle the problem, we propose a relaxation of the SMT query that is independent of the number of allocated blocks and only depends on the size of the symbolic value to be normalised.

A key observation is that a symbolic value can only be normalised if the corresponding SMT query has a unique solution. As a result, it is always sound to relax the SMT query and generate a weaker one (i.e. with potentially more solutions) provided the initial formula is satisfiable. Indeed, if there are more solutions, the normalisation will fail – this is always sound.

In our relaxation, we do not fully axiomatise the memory but only specify the bounds and masks of the memory blocks B that appear syntactically in the symbolic value to be normalised. When normalising a symbolic pointer, we also state explicitly in the SMT query that the normalisation, if it exists, should be a location (b, i) such that $b \in B$.

This relaxation will only miss a normalisation if the memory is almost full and blocks $b \in B$ cannot be allocated at certain addresses because of bound or alignment constraints of other blocks $b' \notin B$. This is illustrated by Example 4.

Example 4. Consider a memory with 3 unaligned blocks b_1, b_2 and b_3 of size 1 and a last block b_4 of size $2^{32} - 4$ that is 4-byte-aligned, i.e. the last two bits are zeros. Because of alignment and size constraints, the block b_4 can only be allocated at address 4 while other blocks can be allocated at the remaining addresses (i.e. 1, 2 and 3). As a result, the symbolic value $\mathtt{ptr}(b_1,0)\mathtt{+ptr}(b_2,0)\mathtt{+ptr}(b_3,0)$ evaluates to 6 which corresponds to the valid location $(b_4, 2)$.

The normalisation of Example 4 requires a full axiomatisation of the memory and cannot be obtained using our relaxation. In practice, we have never encountered such a pathological case.

6   Experimental Evaluation

As stated earlier, we have adapted the CompCert C interpreter so that we could test our semantics on real programs. This required only minor changes to get it to work with symbolic values. However, we put slightly more effort in designing stubs in the interpreter to model system calls such as `mmap` that are used e.g. in the source code of the `malloc` implementation we used. This system call is mapped to the `alloc` primitive of our memory model. Other system calls such as `open`, `read` or `write` are resolved using the OCaml equivalent functions.

We have tested our C semantics with symbolic values on the CompCert benchmarks. Their size ranges between a few hundreds and a few thousands lines of code. We checked the absence of regression: when the CompCert interpreter returns a defined value, our interpreter enhanced with symbolic values returns the exactly same value.

We have also run our interpreter over Doug Lea's memory allocator [13] and on parts of the NaCl cryptographic library [2], which are challenging programs because they perform low-level pointer arithmetic; their size is about a few thousands lines of code. For this experiment, we model the system call mmap by a call to the alloc primitive of our memory model with a mask specifying the alignment of a page. Our interpreter succeeds in giving a semantics to memory management functions, such as malloc, memalign or free, built on top of mmap. As there is no other formal C semantics able to deal with low-level pointer arithmetic, we checked that the result of our interpreter was matching the output of gcc. Programs reading uninitialised variables have undefined semantics and gcc could exploit this to perform arbitrary computations. Yet, the output of gcc and our interpreter agree on examples similar to Fig. 1. In the following, we detail some interesting patterns found in the benchmarks.

6.1   Pointer Arithmetic Using Alignment and Bitwise Operations

The malloc function sometimes needs to check a pointer's distance to an alignment boundary. This is equivalent to getting the last bits of the pointer. For instance, this is done with the C expression p & 15, which gets the 4 last bits of pointer p. For our experiments, pointers are allocated by mmap and are therefore known to be aligned on more than 16 bytes boundaries. For a pointer p=ptr(b,3), our SMT encoding models that the last 4 bits of b are zeros and the code evaluates to 3&15 (i.e. 3). In general, with the previous alignment constraints, we have that the symbolic value ptr(b,o) & 15 returns the offset o of the pointer.

A similar example is the function memalign(al,nb), where al must be a power of two (i.e. $al = 2^n$). The function dynamically allocates a nb-byte region, and ensures that the address returned has the n last bits to zero. When called with $al = 32$, the function computes checks such as p&31 == 0 to check that the 5 last bits are zeros. The left-hand side of the comparison is evaluated in the same manner as the example above, and the comparison is computed trivially.

6.2   Comparison Between Pointers and -1

Several system calls, such as mmap or sbrk, are expected to return pointers but return -1 on error. When a function calls mmap for example, there is typically a check that the system call succeeded (i.e. the returned value is not -1).

```
void *p = mmap(...); if (p == −1) { ... }
```

Our normalisation gives a semantics to this programming pattern using the following reasoning. We know that pointers returned by mmap are aligned on a page boundary (2^{12} in our implementation, i.e. the 11 last bits of the pointer are zeros). When the allocation succeeds, the pointer can therefore never be -1 (in binary 0xFFFFFFFF) thus allowing to evaluate this comparison.

6.3   Operations on Undefined Values

The example shown is Fig. 1 is a simplified version of a C expression that appears in real-life programs. For example, the `memalign` function described above features this kind of operations on undefined values.

The memory managed by the dynamic allocation functions is organised in memory chunks, which consist of two 32-bit words of meta-data and the memory chunk itself. The second word of meta-data stores the size of the chunk and two bits of other information. Initialising the meta-data is done with the C code `*p = (*p & 0b1)|size|0b10` (the `0b` prefix applies to constants in binary format). When the memory pointed by p is undefined, this ends up with the symbolic value `(undef & 0b1)|size|0b10`. It does not evaluate as a value, because the last bit is still undefined.

However, our semantics enables us to keep a symbolic value holding information about all the other bits instead of getting stuck. For instance, the symbolic value `((undef & 0b1)|size|0b10) & 0b10` has the well-defined normalisation `0b10` and retrieves the second last bit of the meta-data. This reasoning is made possible by the fact that `size` is a multiple of 4 (i.e. the last two trailing bits of `size` are zeros).

6.4   Copying Bytes between Memory Areas with `memmove`

Our semantics requires the target of jump instructions to be unique. This is a consequence of the fact that a symbolic value representing a conditional should normalise to some fixed boolean value. In other words, a program whose control-flow depends on the memory layout has an undefined behaviour. This dependance on the memory layout (e.g. on the memory allocator) is a portability bug that is detected by our semantics.

Indeed, in our experiments, we have encountered this situation for the `memmove` function (see Fig. 5) which implements a memory copy even when the origin and destination memory regions do overlap. To cope with this situation, the `memmove` function performs the pointer comparison `dest <= src`. If the pointers `dest` and `src` point to distinct memory blocks, this comparison depends on the memory layout and is therefore undefined for our memory model.

```
void * memmove( void * s1, const void * s2, size_t n ) {
  char * dest = (char *) s1;
  const char * src = (const char *) s2;
  if ( dest <= src )
     while ( n— ) { *dest++ = *src++; }
  else {
     src += n; dest += n;
     while ( n— ) { *—dest = *—src; }
  }
  return s1;
}
```

Fig. 5. `memmove` with an undefined semantics

We have solved the issue by replacing the original condition dest <= src with the more involved condition src <= dest & dest < src + n. This condition explicitly tests whether the memory regions overlap using the integer n which is the number of bytes to be copied. Notice that we use on purpose the bitwise & operator (and not the lazy boolean && operator). A && would force the evaluation of src <= dest which cannot be normalised. The new condition with a & constructs a symbolic value which is independent from the memory layout and has therfore always a defined normalisation. In particular, if the pointers are from distinct blocks, the condition is always false because locations from distinct blocks cannot overlap.

7   Related Work

Wang *et al.* have shown that undefined behaviours of the ISO C standard have a negative impact on the security of software [19]. To tackle the problem Wang *et al.* propose a compiler-based approach to identify pieces of code whose optimised generated code exploit undefined behaviours [20]. We adopt a semantics-based approach that aims at giving a meaning to programs that do not have a defined behaviour according to the ISO C standard.

Memory models have been proposed to ease the reasoning about low-level code. The VCC system [4] generates verification conditions using an abstract typed memory model [5] where the memory is a mapping from typed pointers ($p \in T \times \mathbb{B}^{|u64|}$) to structured C values. This memory model is not formally verified. Using the Isabelle/HOL proof assistant, the Autocorres tool [8,9] constructs provably correct abstractions of C programs. Following Tuch *et al.* [18], a concrete memory is abstracted by an abstract memory $m \in \, 'a \; ptr \rightarrow \, 'a \; option$ where $'a$ represents the type of the pointer. The memory models of VCC [5] and Autocorres [9] ensure separation properties of pointers for high-level code and are complete with respet to the concrete memory model. For the CompCert memory model [15], separation properties of pointers are for free because pointers are modelled as abstract locations $l \in block \times offset$. For our symbolic extension, the completeness (and correctness) of the normalisation is defined with respect to a concrete memory model and therefore allows to reason about low-level idioms.

Several formal semantics of C are defined over a block based memory model where pointers are modelled by a location $l \in block \times offset$ [7,12,14]. The different models differ upon their precise interpretation of the ISO C standard. The CompCert C semantics [3] provides the specification for the correctness of the CompCert compiler [14]. CompCert is used to compile safety critical embedded systems [1] and the semantics departs from the ISO C standard to capture existing practices. Our semantics extends the existing CompCert semantics and benefits from its infrastructure.

Krebbers also extends the CompCert semantics but aims at being as close as possible to the C standard and proposes a formalisation of sequence points in non-deterministic programs [12] and of strict aliasing restrictions in **union** types of C11 [11]. These aspects are orthogonal to the focus of our semantics which gives a meaning to implementation defined low-level pointer arithmetic. Ellison and Roşu [7] propose an executable C semantics using the K framework [16]. Unlike our semantics with symbolic values, they do not model low-level pointer arithmetic and only have a partial symbolic support for uninitialised values [7, Section 6.2.2].

8 Conclusion

We propose an executable semantics for C programs that augments the block based memory model of CompCert with the ability to reason about low-level pointer arithmetic and uninitialised values. The key insight is the use of symbolic values that represent delayed computations: symbolic values are only normalised when a concrete value is really needed. The normalisation is executable and efficient in practice thanks to the use of SMT solvers.

As future work, we shall investigate how to adapt the correctness proof of the CompCert compiler to our new memory model. A difficulty is that our model makes explicit that the memory is finite as the normalisation exploits the fact that pointers are indistinguishable from C integers. Moreover, our memory model is general enough and should be helpful to add in CompCert new target architectures where integer and float values are not so clearly separated in memory or in registers (e.g. SIMD architecture).

As another line of research, we intend to study how to ground security analyses upon our enhanced memory model. A feature of our memory model is that the normalisation, seen as an SMT query, implicitly enumerates all the possible concrete memory configurations. We shall investigate how to augment the axiomatisation of the memory to assess the consequences of a memory violation (e.g. use-after-free), and perform detailed vulnerability analyses.

References

1. Bedin França, R., Blazy, S., Favre-Felix, D., Leroy, X., Pantel, M., Souyris, J.: Formally verified optimizing compilation in ACG-based flight control software. In: ERTS2 2012: Embedded Real Time Software and Systems (2012)
2. Bernstein, D.J., Lange, T., Schwabe, P.: The Security Impact of a New Cryptographic Library. In: Hevia, A., Neven, G. (eds.) LATINCRYPT 2012. LNCS, vol. 7533, pp. 159–176. Springer, Heidelberg (2012)
3. Blazy, S., Leroy, X.: Mechanized Semantics for the Clight Subset of the C Language. J. Autom. Reasoning 43(3), 263–288 (2009)
4. Cohen, E., Dahlweid, M., Hillebrand, M., Leinenbach, D., Moskal, M., Santen, T., Schulte, W., Tobies, S.: VCC: A practical System for Verifying Concurrent C. In: Berghofer, S., Nipkow, T., Urban, C., Wenzel, M. (eds.) TPHOLs 2009. LNCS, vol. 5674, pp. 23–42. Springer, Heidelberg (2009)
5. Cohen, E., Moskal, M., Tobies, S., Schulte, W.: A Precise Yet Efficient Memory Model for C. ENTCS 254, 85–103 (2009)
6. de Moura, L., Bjørner, N.: Z3: An Efficient SMT solver. In: Ramakrishnan, C.R., Rehof, J. (eds.) TACAS 2008. LNCS, vol. 4963, pp. 337–340. Springer, Heidelberg (2008)

7. Ellison, C., Roşu, G.: An executable formal semantics of C with applications. In: POPL, pp. 533–544. ACM (2012)
8. Greenaway, D., Andronick, J., Klein, G.: Bridging the Gap: Automatic Verified Abstraction of C. In: Beringer, L., Felty, A. (eds.) ITP 2012. LNCS, vol. 7406, pp. 99–115. Springer, Heidelberg (2012)
9. Greenaway, D., Lim, J., Andronick, J., Klein, G.: Don't sweat the small stuff: Formal verification of C code without the pain. In: PLDI. ACM (2014)
10. ISO. ISO C Standard 1999. Technical report (1999)
11. Krebbers, R.: Aliasing restrictions of C11 formalized in Coq. In: Gonthier, G., Norrish, M. (eds.) CPP 2013. LNCS, vol. 8307, pp. 50–65. Springer, Heidelberg (2013)
12. Krebbers, R.: An operational and axiomatic semantics for non-determinism and sequence points in C. In: POPL, pp. 101–112. ACM (2014)
13. Lee, D.: A memory allocator, http://gee.cs.oswego.edu/dl/html/malloc.html
14. Leroy, X.: Formal verification of a realistic compiler. Comm. ACM 52(7), 107–115 (2009)
15. Leroy, X., Appel, A.W., Blazy, S., Stewart, G.: The CompCert memory model. In: Program Logics for Certified Compilers. Cambridge University Press (2014)
16. Lucanu, D., Şerbănuţă, T.F., Roşu, G.: K Framework Distilled. In: Durán, F. (ed.) WRLA 2012. LNCS, vol. 7571, pp. 31–53. Springer, Heidelberg (2012)
17. Norrish, M.: C formalised in HOL. PhD thesis, University of Cambridge (1998)
18. Tuch, H., Klein, G., Norrish, M.: Types, bytes, and separation logic. In: POPL, pp. 97–108. ACM (2007)
19. Wang, X., Chen, H., Cheung, A., Jia, Z., Zeldovich, N., Kaashoek, M.F.: Undefined behavior: What happened to my code? In: APSYS 2012, pp. 1–7 (2012)
20. Wang, X., Zeldovich, N., Kaashoek, M.F., Solar-Lezama, A.: Towards Optimization-safe Systems: Analyzing the Impact of Undefined Behavior. In: SOSP 2013, pp. 260–275. ACM (2013)

Hereditary History-Preserving Bisimilarity: Logics and Automata*

Paolo Baldan and Silvia Crafa

Dipartimento di Matematica, Università di Padova, Italy
`baldan,crafa@math.unipd.it`

Abstract. We study hereditary history-preserving (hhp-) bisimilarity, a canonical behavioural equivalence in the true concurrent spectrum, by means of logics and automata. We first show that hhp-bisimilarity on prime event structures can be characterised in terms of a simple logic whose formulae just observe events in computations and check their executability. The logic suggests a characterisation of hhp-bisimilarity based on history-dependent automata, a formalism for modelling systems with dynamic allocation and deallocation of resources, where the history of resources is traced over time. Prime event structures can be naturally mapped into history-dependent automata in a way that hhp-bisimilarity exactly corresponds to the canonical behavioural equivalence for history-dependent automata.

1 Introduction

Behavioural equivalences play a key role in the formal analysis of system specifications. They can be used to equate specifications that, although syntactically different, denote the same system behaviour, or to formally state that a system enjoys a desired property. A number of behavioural equivalences have been defined which take into account different concurrency features of computations. In particular, true concurrent equivalences (see, e.g., [1]) are a natural choice when one is interested in analysing properties concerning the dependencies between computational steps (e.g. causality). They can be convenient also because they provide some relief to the so-called state-space explosion problem in the analysis of concurrent systems (see, e.g., [2]).

Hereditary history preserving (hhp-)bisimilarity [3], the finest equivalence in the true concurrent spectrum in [1], has been shown to arise as a canonical behavioural equivalence when considering partially ordered computations [4]. True concurrent models, such as Winskel's event structures [5], often describe the behaviour of systems in terms of events in computations and dependency relations between such events, like causal dependency or concurrency. Hhp-bisimilarity then precisely captures the interplay between branching, causality and concurrency. Roughly, hhp-bisimilarity requires that events of one system are simulated by events of the other system with the same causal history and the same

---

* Work partially supported by the MIUR PRIN project CINA.

J. Garrigue (Ed.): APLAS 2014, LNCS 8858, pp. 469–488, 2014.

concurrency. The last constraint is often captured by means of a sort of back-tracking condition: for any two related computations, the computations obtained by reversing a pair of related events must be related too. As a consequence, hhp-bisimilarity, together with other variants of forward-reverse equivalences, are considered appropriate behavioural equivalences for systems with reversible computations [6,7,8].

Recently, the logical characterisation of hhp-bisimilarity has received a renewed interest and corresponding event-based logics have been introduced, where formulae include variables which can be bound to events. The logic $\mathcal{L}$ in [9] explicitly refers to relations between events, namely causality and concurrency. More precisely, $\mathcal{L}$ includes two main operators. The formula $(x, \overline{y} < \mathsf{a}\, z)\varphi$ is satisfied in a state when an a-labelled future event exists, which causally depends on the event bound to x, and is independent from the event bound to y; such an event is bound to variable z and then φ is required to hold. In general, x and y can be replaced by tuples of variables. The formula $\langle z \rangle\, \varphi$ says that the event bound to z is enabled in the current state, and after its execution φ holds. Instead, the logic EIL (Event Identifier Logic) in [10] relies on a backward step modality: the formula $\langle\!\langle x \rangle\, \varphi$ holds when the event bound to x can be undone and then φ holds. This is similar to the past tense or future perfect modality studied in [4,11,3,12].

In this paper we provide a logical characterisation of hhp-bisimilarity in terms of a simple logic $\mathcal{L}_0$, a core fragment of $\mathcal{L}$, which only predicates over existence and executability of events, without explicitly referring to their dependencies. Formally, the operator $(x, \overline{y} < \mathsf{a}\, z)\varphi$ is replaced by $(\mathsf{a}\, z)\varphi$. Syntactically, $\mathcal{L}_0$ is also a subset of EIL, but it is different in spirit (as quantification is performed only on future events and it does not include a backward modality). In particular, although all such logics characterise hhp-bisimilarity, the modalities of EIL and $\mathcal{L}$ are not interdefinable.

The fact that the logic $\mathcal{L}_0$ allows one to observe and track events in computations suggests a connection with *history-dependent automata (HD-automata)* [13], a computational formalism for modelling systems with dynamic allocation and deallocation of resources, tracing the history of such resources over time. Indeed, by considering events in computations as resources manipulated by automata, we identify a class of HD-automata, called HDE-automata, where prime event structures (PESs) can be naturally mapped, in a way that the canonical behavioural equivalence for HD-automata coincides with hhp-bisimilarity over PESs. More precisely, transitions of HDE-automata correspond to planning an activity or event (which could be not immediately executable due to unsatisfied dependencies with other activities), executing a previously planned activity and dismissing a planned activity (without executing it). We provide an encoding of any prime event structure $\mathcal{E}$ into an HDE-automaton $\mathcal{H}(\mathcal{E})$ such that two prime event structures are hhp-bisimilar if and only if the corresponding HDE-automata are bisimilar. The proof relies on a logical characterisation of bisimilarity on HDE-automata in terms of a logic $\mathcal{L}_{hd}$, a slight variant of the logic $\mathcal{L}_0$, which adds an operator for deallocation, i.e., for forgetting an event planned and not yet executed. Mappings of logic $\mathcal{L}_0$ into $\mathcal{L}_{hd}$ and back are provided, in a way that a PES $\mathcal{E}$ satisfies a formula in $\mathcal{L}_0$ if and only if $\mathcal{H}(\mathcal{E})$ satisfies the corresponding formula in $\mathcal{L}_{hd}$ and vice versa. Although developed for a specific class of HD-automata, in our opinion the logical characterisation of HD-bisimilarity has an interest which goes beyond the specific application in this paper and deserves to be further investigated.

Moreover, our characterisation of hhp-bisimilarity in terms of HD-automata, besides shedding light on the nature of this behavioural equivalence, can be helpful in studying the decidability boundary for hhp-bisimilarity, which is undecidable for many basic models of concurrency, even in the finite state case (e.g., it is known that hhp-bisimilarity is undecidable for safe finite Petri nets [14]). Indeed, the characterisation in terms of HD-automata naturally suggests effective approximations of hhp-bisimilarity, which can be obtained by establishing bounds k on the distance in the future of planned events. The detailed study of such approximations is postponed to the extended version of the paper. We focus here on an insightful investigation about the logical and the automata-theoretic characterisations of hhp-bisimilarity.

The rest of the paper is structured as follows. In Section 2 we review the definition of hhp-bisimilarity over prime event structures. In Section 3 we define the logic $\mathcal{L}_0$ and show that hhp-bisimilarity is the logical equivalence induced by $\mathcal{L}_0$ on (image finite) PESs. In Section 4 we study HDE-automata: the class of HD-automata operating over resources which can be seen as activities or events in a computation. In Section 5 we provide a bisimilarity-preserving encoding of prime event structures into HDE-automata. In Section 6 we comment on some related work and outline future research.

2   Event Structures and hhp-Bisimilarity

Prime event structures [5] are a widely known model of concurrency. They describe the behaviour of a system in terms of events and dependency relations between such events. Throughout the paper $\mathbb{E}$ is a fixed countable set of events, Λ a set of labels ranged over by $\mathsf{a}, \mathsf{b}, \mathsf{c} \ldots$ and $\lambda : \mathbb{E} \to \Lambda$ a labelling function.

Definition 1 (prime event structure). *A (Λ-labelled) prime event structure (PES) is a tuple $\mathcal{E} = \langle E, \leq, \# \rangle$, where $E \subseteq \mathbb{E}$ is the set of events and $\leq$, $\#$ are binary relations on E, called* causality *and* conflict *respectively, such that:*

1. *$\leq$ is a partial order and $\lceil e \rceil = \{e' \in E \mid e' \leq e\}$ is finite for all $e \in E$;*
2. *$\#$ is irreflexive, symmetric and hereditary with respect to $\leq$, i.e., for all $e, e', e'' \in E$, if $e \# e' \leq e''$ then $e \# e''$.*

In the following, we will assume that the components of an event structure $\mathcal{E}$ are named as in the definition above, possibly with subscripts.

Definition 2 (consistency, concurrency). *Let $\mathcal{E}$ be a PES. We say that $e, e' \in E$ are* consistent, *written $e \frown e'$, if $\neg(e \# e')$. A subset $X \subseteq E$ is called* consistent *if $e \frown e'$ for all $e, e' \in X$. We say that e and e' are* concurrent, *written $e \parallel e'$, if $e \frown e'$ and $\neg(e \leq e')$, $\neg(e' \leq e)$.*

Causality and concurrency will be sometimes used on set of events. Given $X \subseteq E$ and $e \in E$, by $X < e$ we mean that for all $e' \in X$, $e' < e$. Similarly $X \parallel e$, resp. $X \frown e$, means that for all $e' \in X$, $e' \parallel e$, resp. $e' \frown e$.

The concept of (concurrent) computation for event structures is captured by the notion of configuration.

Definition 3 (configuration). *Let $\mathcal{E}$ be a* PES. *A (finite) configuration in $\mathcal{E}$ is a (finite) consistent subset of events $C \subseteq E$ closed w.r.t. causality (i.e., $\lceil e \rceil \subseteq C$ for all $e \in C$). The set of finite configurations of $\mathcal{E}$ is denoted by $\mathcal{C}(\mathcal{E})$.*

Observe that the empty set of events $\emptyset$ is always a configurations, which can be interpreted as the initial state of the computation. Hereafter, unless explicitly stated otherwise, all configurations will be assumed to be finite.

Definition 4 (residual). *Let $\mathcal{E}$ be a* PES. *For a configuration $C \in \mathcal{C}(\mathcal{E})$, the residual of $\mathcal{E}$ after C, is defined as $\mathcal{E}[C] = \{e \mid e \in E \setminus C \ \wedge \ C \frown e\}$.*

Concurrent behavioural equivalences can then be defined on the transition system where configurations are states.

Definition 5 (transition system). *Let $\mathcal{E}$ be a* PES *and let $C \in \mathcal{C}(\mathcal{E})$. Given $e \in \mathcal{E}[C]$, if $C \cup \{e\} \in \mathcal{C}(\mathcal{E})$ then we write $C \xrightarrow{e} C \cup \{e\}$.*

A PES $\mathcal{E}$ is called *image finite* if for every $C \in \mathcal{C}(\mathcal{E})$ and $\mathsf{a} \in \Lambda$, the set of events $\{e \in E \mid C \xrightarrow{e} C' \ \wedge \ \lambda(e) = \mathsf{a}\}$ is finite. All the PESs considered in this paper will be assumed to be image finite, a standard requirement for getting a logical characterisation of a behavioural equivalence based on a finitary logic.

Several equivalences have been defined in order to capture the concurrency features of a system to different extents (see, e.g., [1]). Hereditary history-preserving (hhp-)bisimilarity arises as a canonical equivalence for PESs [4] which fully takes into account the interplay between causality, concurrency and nondeterminism of events.

We need to fix some further notation. A consistent subset $X \subseteq E$ of events will be often seen as a *pomset* (partially ordered multiset) $(X, \leq_X, \lambda_X)$, where $\leq_X$ and λ_X are the restrictions of $\leq$ and λ to X. Given $X, Y \subseteq E$ we will write $X \sim Y$ if X and Y are isomorphic as pomsets and write $f : X \xrightarrow{\sim} Y$ for a pomset isomorphism.

Definition 6 (posetal product). *Given two* PESs $\mathcal{E}_1$, $\mathcal{E}_2$, *the posetal product of their configurations, denoted $\mathcal{C}(\mathcal{E}_1) \bar{\times} \mathcal{C}(\mathcal{E}_2)$, is defined as*

$$\{(C_1, f, C_2) \mid C_1 \in \mathcal{C}(\mathcal{E}_1), \ C_2 \in \mathcal{C}(\mathcal{E}_2), \ f : C_1 \xrightarrow{\sim} C_2\}$$

A subset $R \subseteq \mathcal{C}(\mathcal{E}_1) \bar{\times} \mathcal{C}(\mathcal{E}_2)$ is called a posetal relation. We say that R is downward closed whenever for any $(C_1, f, C_2), (C'_1, f', C'_2) \in \mathcal{C}(\mathcal{E}_1) \bar{\times} \mathcal{C}(\mathcal{E}_2)$, if $(C_1, f, C_2) \subseteq (C'_1, f', C'_2)$ pointwise and $(C'_1, f', C'_2) \in R$ then $(C_1, f, C_2) \in R$.

Given a function $f : X_1 \to X_2$ we will use the notation $f[x_1 \mapsto x_2] : X_1 \cup \{x_1\} \to X_2 \cup \{x_2\}$ for the function defined by $f[x_1 \mapsto x_2](x_1) = x_2$ and $f[x_1 \mapsto x_2](z) = f(z)$ for $z \in X_1 \setminus \{x_1\}$. Note that this can represent an update of f, when $x_1 \in X_1$, or an extension of its domain, otherwise.

Definition 7 ((hereditary) history-preserving bisimulation). *A history-preserving (hp-)bisimulation is a posetal relation* $R \subseteq \mathcal{C}(\mathcal{E}_1) \bar{\times} \mathcal{C}(\mathcal{E}_2)$ *such that if* $(C_1, f, C_2) \in R$ *and* $C \xrightarrow{e_1} C_1'$ *then* $C_2 \xrightarrow{e_2} C_2'$, *with* $(C_1', f[e_1 \mapsto e_2], C_2') \in R$, *and vice versa. We say that* $\mathcal{E}_1$, $\mathcal{E}_2$ *are* history preserving (hp-)bisimilar *and write* $\mathcal{E}_1 \sim_{hp} \mathcal{E}_2$ *if there exists a hp-bisimulation* R *such that* $(\emptyset, \emptyset, \emptyset) \in R$.

A hereditary history-preserving (hhp-)bisimulation *is a downward closed hp-bisimulation. When* $\mathcal{E}_1, \mathcal{E}_2$ *are* hereditary history-preserving (hhp-)bisimilar *we write* $\mathcal{E}_1 \sim_{hhp} \mathcal{E}_2$.

3   A Logic for hhp-Bisimilarity

In this section we introduce the syntax and the semantics of a logic $\mathcal{L}_0$, used to characterise hhp-bisimilarity. The formulae of $\mathcal{L}_0$ predicate over existence and executability of events in computations. As already mentioned, $\mathcal{L}_0$ is a small core of the logic $\mathcal{L}$ in [9], where the operators do not explicitly refer to the dependencies between events. Still $\mathcal{L}_0$ is sufficiently powerful to capture such dependencies and its logical equivalence is the same as that of the full logic in that they both correspond to hhp-bisimilarity.

Definition 8 (syntax). *Let Var be a countable set of variables ranged over by* x, y, z.... *The logic* $\mathcal{L}_0$ *over the set of labels* Λ *is defined by the following syntax:*

$$\varphi ::= \mathsf{T} \mid \varphi \wedge \varphi \mid \neg \varphi \mid (\mathsf{a}\, z)\varphi \mid \langle z \rangle \varphi$$

Disjunction $\varphi \vee \psi$ is defined, as usual, by duality as the formula $\neg(\neg\varphi \wedge \neg\psi)$. Similarly, we write F for $\neg\mathsf{T}$.

The operator $(\mathsf{a}\, z)$ acts as a binder for the variable z. Accordingly, the free variables of a formula φ are defined as follows:

$$fv((\mathsf{a}\, z)\varphi) = fv(\varphi) \setminus \{z\} \qquad fv(\langle z \rangle\, \varphi) = fv(\varphi) \cup \{z\}$$

$$fv(\mathsf{T}) = \emptyset \quad fv(\neg\varphi) = fv(\varphi) \quad fv(\varphi_1 \wedge \varphi_2) = fv(\varphi_1) \cup fv(\varphi_2)$$

Formulae are considered up to α-conversion of bound variables. The logic $\mathcal{L}_0$ is interpreted over PESs. In particular, the satisfaction of a formula is defined with respect to pairs (C, η), where $C \in \mathcal{C}(\mathcal{E})$ is a configuration representing the state of the computation, and $\eta : Var \to E$ is a function, called *environment*, that maps the free variables of φ to events.

Since, intuitively, a formula φ describes possible future computations, the environment should map variables to events consistent with C and pairwise consistent. The first condition ensures that the formula actually refers to events that belong to the future (residual) of the current state. The second condition prevents the direct observation of conflicts, in accordance with the observational power of hhp-bisimilarity (Some examples are provided below, after defining the semantics.) Formally, this is captured by the notion of legal pair.

Definition 9 (legal pair). *Given a PES* $\mathcal{E}$, *let* $Env_{\mathcal{E}}$ *denote the set of environments, i.e., of functions* $\eta : Var \to E$. *Given a formula* φ *in* $\mathcal{L}_0$, *a pair* $(C, \eta) \in \mathcal{C}(\mathcal{E}) \times Env_{\mathcal{E}}$ *is* legal *for* φ *if* $C \cup \eta(fv(\varphi))$ *is a consistent set of events. We write* $lp_{\mathcal{E}}(\varphi)$ *for the set of legal pairs for* φ.

$$
\begin{array}{ccc}
b \quad d & & b \quad a \\
| \quad | & & | \quad | \\
a \cdots\cdots c \quad\quad a \quad b \quad\quad a \cdots\cdots b \\
\mathcal{E}_1 \quad\quad\quad \mathcal{E}_2 \quad\quad\quad \mathcal{E}_3
\end{array}
$$

Fig. 1. The PES $\mathcal{E}_1$ for $a.b + c.d$, $\mathcal{E}_2$ for $a \mid b$ and $\mathcal{E}_3$ for $a.b + b.a$

We omit the subscripts and write Env and $lp(\varphi)$ when the PES $\mathcal{E}$ is clear from the context.

Definition 10 (semantics). *Let $\mathcal{E}$ be a* PES. *The denotation of a formula φ, written $\{\!|\varphi|\!\}^{\mathcal{E}} \in 2^{\mathcal{C}(\mathcal{E}) \times Env}$ is defined inductively as follows:*

$$\{\!|\mathsf{T}|\!\}^{\mathcal{E}} \;=\; \mathcal{C}(\mathcal{E}) \times Env_{\mathcal{E}}$$

$$\{\!|\varphi_1 \wedge \varphi_2|\!\}^{\mathcal{E}} \;=\; \{\!|\varphi_1|\!\}^{\mathcal{E}} \cap \{\!|\varphi_2|\!\}^{\mathcal{E}} \cap lp(\varphi \wedge \psi)$$

$$\{\!|\neg\varphi|\!\}^{\mathcal{E}} \;=\; lp(\varphi) \setminus \{\!|\varphi|\!\}^{\mathcal{E}}$$

$$
\{\!|(\mathsf{a}\,z)\,\varphi|\!\}^{\mathcal{E}} \;=\; \{(C,\eta) \mid \exists e \in \mathcal{E}[C].e \frown \eta(fv(\varphi) \setminus \{z\})
$$
$$
\lambda(e) = \mathsf{a} \wedge\ (C, \eta[z \mapsto e]) \in \{\!|\varphi|\!\}^{\mathcal{E}}\}
$$

$$\{\!|\langle z\rangle\,\varphi|\!\}^{\mathcal{E}} \;=\; \{(C,\eta) \mid C \xrightarrow{\eta(z)} C' \wedge\ (C',\eta) \in \{\!|\varphi|\!\}^{\mathcal{E}}\ \}$$

When $(C,\eta) \in \{\!|\varphi|\!\}^{\mathcal{E}}$ we say that the PES *$\mathcal{E}$ satisfies the formula φ in the configuration C and environment $\eta : Var \to E$, and write $\mathcal{E}, C \models_\eta \varphi$. For closed formulae φ, we write $\mathcal{E} \models \varphi$, when $\mathcal{E}, \emptyset \models_\eta \varphi$ for some η.*

In words, the formula $(\mathsf{a}\,z)\,\varphi$ holds in (C,η) when in the future of the configuration C there is an a-labelled event e consistent with the events already observed (which are bound to free variables in φ) and binding such event e to the variable z, the formula φ holds. The formula $\langle z\rangle\,\varphi$ states that the event bound to z is currently enabled, hence it can be executed producing a new configuration which satisfies the formula φ. An environment η is a total function, but it can be shown that the semantics of a formula φ depends only on the value of the environment on the free variables $fv(\varphi)$. In particular, for closed formulae the environment is irrelevant. Moreover, it can be easily seen that α-equivalent formulae have the same semantics.

As an example, consider the PES $\mathcal{E}_1$ in Fig. 1 corresponding to the CCS process $a.b + c.d$, where dotted lines represent immediate conflict and the causal order proceeds upwards along the straight lines. The empty configuration satisfies the formula $\varphi = (\mathsf{b}\,x)\mathsf{T}$, i.e., $\mathcal{E}_1 \models \varphi$ since in the future of the empty configuration there is a b-labelled event. However $\mathcal{E}_1 \not\models (\mathsf{b}\,x)\langle x\rangle\,\mathsf{T}$ since such event is not immediately executable.

Observe also that $\mathcal{E}_1 \models (\mathsf{b}\,x)\mathsf{T} \wedge (\mathsf{d}\,y)\mathsf{T}$, since there are two possible (incompatible) future computations starting from the empty configuration that contain, respectively, a b-labelled and a d-labelled event. For a similar reason, we have

Fig. 2. The PES $\mathcal{E}_4$ for $a.b$, $\mathcal{E}_5$ for $a.b + a.b$.

also $\mathcal{E}_1 \models (a\,x)\langle x\rangle\, \mathsf{T} \wedge (c\,y)\langle y\rangle\, \mathsf{T}$. Finally observe that $\mathcal{E}_1 \models (a\,x)(c\,y)\mathsf{T}$ since in this case, after binding the variable x to the a-labelled event, we can bind y to the c-labelled event because x is not free in the remaining subformula T.

As a further example, consider the PESs $\mathcal{E}_2$ and $\mathcal{E}_3$ in Fig. 1, corresponding to the CCS processes $a \mid b$ and $a.b + b.a$, respectively. They are distinguished by the formula $(a\,x)(b\,y)(\langle x\rangle\,\langle y\rangle\,\mathsf{T} \wedge \langle y\rangle\,\langle x\rangle\,\mathsf{T})$ that states that there are two events, labelled a and b, that can be executed in any order. The formula is satisfied by the first but not by the second PES. In a similar way, the processes $a \mid a$ and $a.a$ are distinguished by the formula $(a\,x)(a\,y)(\langle x\rangle\,\langle y\rangle\,\mathsf{T} \wedge \langle y\rangle\,\langle x\rangle\,\mathsf{T})$.

On the other hand, the PESs $\mathcal{E}_4$ and $\mathcal{E}_5$ in Fig. 2, corresponding to the processes $a.b$ and $a.b + a.b$, are hhp-equivalent; accordingly, they both satisfy the formula $\varphi_1 = (a\,x)(a\,y)\mathsf{T}$ and falsify $\varphi_2 = (a\,x)(a\,y)\langle x\rangle\,\langle y\rangle\,\mathsf{T}$. In particular, for $\mathcal{E}_4$ to satisfy φ_1 both x and y must be bound to the unique a-labelled event. These PESs can be also used for clarifying the need of restricting to legal pairs in the semantics. Consider the formula $\varphi = (a\,x)(b\,y)\langle x\rangle\,\neg\langle y\rangle\,\mathsf{T}$. While, clearly, $\mathcal{E}_4 \not\models \varphi$, one could believe that $\mathcal{E}_5 \models \varphi$ since after binding the variable x to the right a-labelled event, we could think of binding y to the left b-labelled event, thus satisfying the remaining subformula $\langle x\rangle\,\neg\langle y\rangle\,\mathsf{T}$. However, this is not correct: since x occurs free in the subformula $\langle x\rangle\,\neg\langle y\rangle\,\mathsf{T}$, the event bound to y must be consistent to that bound to x in order to lead to a legal pair, hence the only possibility is to choose the b-labelled event caused by that bound to x.

Roughly speaking, the logic $\mathcal{L}_0$ observes conflicting futures, as long as conflicting events are kept separate and not combined in a computation. This corresponds to the observational power of hhp-bisimilarity, which captures the interplay between branching and causality/concurrency without explicitly observing conflicts. We observe that the fragment $\mathcal{L}_0$ is less expressive than the full logic $\mathcal{L}$. For instance, it can be shown that the formula $(a\,x)(x < a\,y)\mathsf{T}$ in $\mathcal{L}$, which states the existence of two causally dependent a-labelled events at arbitrary causal distance, is not encodable by a finite formula of $\mathcal{L}_0$. Still, $\mathcal{L}_0$ is sufficiently expressive to capture the same logical equivalence of $\mathcal{L}$, i.e., hhp-bisimilarity.

In the following we will denote lists of variables like $x_1, ..., x_n$ by $\boldsymbol{x}$.

Theorem 1 (hhp-bisimilarity, logically). *Let $\mathcal{E}_1, \mathcal{E}_2$ be two PESs. Then $\mathcal{E}_1 \sim_{hhp} \mathcal{E}_2$ iff $\mathcal{E}_1$ and $\mathcal{E}_2$ satisfy the same closed formulae in $\mathcal{L}_0$.*

Proof (Sketch). The only if part follows from [9, Theorem 1], since the logic $\mathcal{L}_0$ is a fragment of $\mathcal{L}$. For the converse implication, fix a surjective environment $\eta_1 : Var \to E_1$. Then given an event $e \in E_1$, we let x_e denote a chosen variable such that $\eta_1(x_e) = e$. For a configuration $C_1 = \{e_1, \ldots, e_n\}$ we denote by X_{C_1} the set of variables $\{x_{e_1}, \ldots, x_{e_n}\}$.

Then one can prove that the posetal relation $R \subseteq \mathcal{C}(\mathcal{E}_1) \bar{\times} \mathcal{C}(\mathcal{E}_2)$ defined by:

$$R = \{ (C_1, f, C_2) \mid \forall \varphi \in \mathcal{L}_0.\ fv(\varphi) \subseteq X_{C_1} \tag{1}$$
$$(\mathcal{E}_1, \emptyset \models_{\eta_1} \varphi \text{ iff } \mathcal{E}_2, \emptyset \models_{f \circ \eta_1} \varphi) \}$$

is a hhp-bisimulation. Above, given an isomorphism of pomsets $f : C_1 \to C_2$, we denote by $f \circ \eta_1$ an environment such that $f \circ \eta_1(x) = f(\eta_1(x))$ for $x \in X_{C_1}$ and $f \circ \eta_1(x)$ has any value, otherwise (the semantics of φ only depends on the value of the environment on $fv(\varphi)$ and $fv(\varphi) \subseteq X_{C_1}$ by construction). Note that R relates two configurations C_1 and C_2 when the same formulae φ are satisfied by the empty configuration (rather than by the configurations C_1 and C_2 themselves). The formulae φ considered in (1) refer to events in C_1 and in C_2 by means of their free variables. This is according to the intuition that hhp-bisimilarity does not only compare the future of two configurations but also their alternative evolutions, that is evolutions from the past.   □

Similarly to what has been done in [9] for the full logic $\mathcal{L}$, one can identify fragments of $\mathcal{L}_0$ that characterise various other behavioural equivalences in the true concurrent spectrum [1]. First of all notice that the standard Hennessy-Milner logic can be recovered as the following fragment of $\mathcal{L}_0$, where whenever we state the existence of an event we are forced to execute it:

$$\varphi ::= \top \mid \varphi \wedge \varphi \mid \neg\varphi \mid (\mathsf{a}\,x)\langle x \rangle\,\varphi$$

In such a fragment variables are irrelevant: the formula $(\mathsf{a}\,x)\langle x \rangle\,\varphi$ states the existence of an a-labelled event, which is immediately executable from the current configuration and whose execution produces a new configuration in which φ holds. The event is bound to variable x which, however, is no longer referred to in the formula. Hence $(\mathsf{a}\,x)\langle x \rangle$ is completely analogous to the diamond modality of standard Hennessy Milner logic and the induced logical equivalence is (interleaving) bisimilarity [15].

Along the lines of [9, Theorem 4], one can prove that history-preserving bisimilarity (Definition 7) corresponds to the logical equivalence induced by the following fragment of $\mathcal{L}_0$:

$$\varphi ::= \top \mid \varphi \wedge \varphi \mid \neg\varphi \mid \langle\!| \boldsymbol{x}, \overline{\boldsymbol{y}} < \mathsf{a}\,z |\!\rangle \varphi$$

where $\boldsymbol{x}, \boldsymbol{y}$ are lists of variables and $\langle\!| \boldsymbol{x}, \overline{\boldsymbol{y}} < \mathsf{a}\,z |\!\rangle\varphi$ denotes the formula

$$(\mathsf{a}\,z)(\langle \boldsymbol{x} \rangle \langle z \rangle \langle \boldsymbol{y} \rangle \top \wedge \langle \boldsymbol{x} \rangle \langle \boldsymbol{y} \rangle \top \wedge \bigwedge_{\boldsymbol{x}' \subset \boldsymbol{x}} \neg\langle \boldsymbol{x}' \rangle \langle z \rangle \top \wedge \varphi). \tag{2}$$

Above, given a list of variables $\boldsymbol{x} = x_1 \ldots x_n$ the abbreviation $\langle \boldsymbol{x} \rangle$ is used as a shortcut for $\langle x_1 \rangle \ldots \langle x_n \rangle$. Intuitively, the formula (2) states the existence of an a-labelled event, which is bound to z, that causally depends on the events bound to $\boldsymbol{x}$ and that is concurrent with the events bound to $\boldsymbol{y}$. In fact, z can be executed only after x, while y can be executed after or before z. The event is required to be immediately executable, and once executed, formula φ holds. For the above to work, the events bound to x and y must form a $\leq$-closed set, i.e., $\lceil \eta(w) \rceil \subseteq \eta(x \cup y)$ for any $w \in x \cup y$. More formally, it is not difficult to prove that $\{\!| \langle x, \overline{y} < \text{a } z \rangle \varphi |\!\}^{\mathcal{E}}$ is

$$\{\langle C, \eta \rangle \mid \exists e \in \mathcal{E}[C].\ e \frown \eta(fv(\varphi) \setminus \{z\}) \wedge$$
$$C \xrightarrow{e} C \cup \{e\} \wedge \lambda(e) = \text{a } \wedge$$
$$\eta(x) < e \wedge \eta(y) \,\|\, e \wedge \eta(x \cup y) \leq\text{-closed} \wedge$$
$$\langle C \cup \{e\}, \eta[z \mapsto e] \rangle \in \{\!| \varphi |\!\}^{\mathcal{E}}\}$$

Incidentally, this derived operator illustrates how $\mathcal{L}_0$ formulae can be used to express causal (in)dependence between events.

The fact that this fragment has a reduced expressivity, corresponding exactly to hd-bisimilarity can be intuitively explained as follows. As noticed above, a formula in the fragment can "observe" an event only by executing it. Hence the observation of an event automatically discards all future conflictual events. As a consequence it is not possible to observe alternative conflicting futures involving common events, namely the fragment cannot fully describe the interplay between causality/concurrency and branching as required for hhp-bisimilarity. Still, it allows one to capture the dependencies of the observed events with previously executed events, a capability which corresponds to the observational power of hp-bisimilarity.

Analogously, fragments of $\mathcal{L}_0$ inducing pomset and step bisimilarity can be identified.

4   History-Dependent Automata over Events

The logic $\mathcal{L}_0$ for hhp-bisimilarity, singled out in the previous section, allows one to trace events in computations and check their executability. This hints at a connection with HD-automata, a generalised model of automata that has been indeed introduced to describe systems with dynamic allocation and deallocation of resources, tracing the history of such resources over time [13]. In this section we lay the basis of such a connection by identifying a class of HD-automata where PESs can be naturally mapped and providing a logical characterisation of bisimilarity for this class of automata in terms of a mild extension of $\mathcal{L}_0$.

4.1   HDE-Automata and HD-Bisimilarity

HD-automata extend ordinary automata in order to manipulate resources generically identified as names. The allocation of a resource is modelled by the generation of a fresh name and the usage of a resource in a transition is modelled by observing the corresponding name in the transition label. Concretely, with respect to an ordinary automaton, states of an HD-automaton are enriched with a set of local names corresponding to the resources that are active at that states.

Transitions, in turn, modify these sets and explicitly trace the correspondence between the local names of the source and the target states.

We introduce a class of HD-automata, referred to as HDE-automata, where PESs will be naturally encodable. In HDE-automata the names can be thought of as activities or events in a computation. HDE transitions are of three kinds: $\texttt{plan}(e), \texttt{exec}(e), \texttt{drop}(e)$ which can be interpreted, respectively, as planning an activity or event e (which might be not immediately executable due to unsatisfied dependencies with other activities), executing a previously planned activity and dismissing a planned activity (without executing it).

Formally, as before, we fix a countable set $\mathbb{E}$ whose elements are thought of as activities, labelled by $\lambda : \mathbb{E} \to \Lambda$. Given two subsets $A_1, A_2 \subseteq \mathbb{E}$, a *labelled bijection*, denoted $\delta : A_1 \overset{\sim}{\to} A_2$, is a bijection such that for any $e_1 \in A_1$, it holds that $\lambda(e_1) = \lambda(\delta(e_1))$. Let $R(\mathbb{E})$ be the set of *renamings*, i.e., label preserving partial injective functions $\rho : \mathbb{E} \to \mathbb{E}$. Given $\rho \in R(\mathbb{E})$, we write $dom(\rho)$ and $cod(\rho)$ for the domain and codomain of ρ, respectively. The set of labels for the automata transitions is $L(\mathbb{E}) = \{\texttt{plan}(e), \texttt{exec}(e), \texttt{drop}(e) \mid e \in \mathbb{E}\}$.

Definition 11 (HDE-automata). *A HDE-automaton $\mathcal{H}$ is a tuple $\langle Q, n, q_0, \to \rangle$ where Q is a set of states, $n : Q \to 2^{\mathbb{E}}$ associates with each state a set of activities and $\to \subseteq Q \times L(\mathbb{E}) \times R(\mathbb{E}) \times Q$ is a transition relation, written $q \overset{\ell}{\to}_\rho q'$ for $(q, \ell, \rho, q') \in \to$, such that $dom(\rho) \subseteq n(q')$ and $cod(\rho) \subseteq n(q)$ (hence ρ is a partial injection $n(q') \to n(q)$) and*

- *if $q \xrightarrow{\texttt{plan}(e)}_\rho q'$ then $cod(\rho)=n(q)$, $dom(\rho)=n(q') \setminus \{e\}$;*
- *if $q \xrightarrow{\texttt{exec}(e)}_\rho q'$ or $q \xrightarrow{\texttt{drop}(e)}_\rho q'$ then $cod(\rho)=n(q) \setminus \{e\}$ and $dom(\rho)=n(q')$.*

For a $\texttt{plan}(e)$ transition the mapping ρ is a bijection between $n(q)$ and $n(q')\setminus\{e\}$. Intuitively, e is the newly planned activity, while $n(q')\setminus\{e\}$ represents, via the renaming ρ, activities already planned in q. In an $\texttt{exec}(e)$ transition the activity e is executed, while in a $\texttt{drop}(e)$ transition the activity e is dropped without being executed. In both cases the other activities planned in the source state are kept, and the correspondence between source and target is established by ρ which is a bijection between $n(q)\setminus\{e\}$ and $n(q')$.

Note that when dealing with event structures, states of a computation are given by configurations, namely sets of events which have been already executed. Logic $\mathcal{L}_\mathbf{0}$ observes events in the future of a configuration, but these are not part of the state and are implicitly garbage collected when they are no longer referred by the formula. Instead, the states of a HDE-automaton have a richer structure as they explicitly include a set of activities planned but not yet executed (which intuitively correspond to events observed and not yet executed). As a consequence, also dismissing a planned activity is an explicit operation which requires a $\texttt{drop}(\cdot)$ transition.

We write $q \to_\rho q'$ when $q \overset{\ell}{\to}_\rho q'$ for some label $\ell \in L(\mathbb{E})$, and we denote by $\to_\rho^*$ the reflexive and transitive closure of the transition relation, with ρ resulting as the composition of the involved renamings, i.e., $q \to_{id}^* q$ and if $q \to_\rho^* q' \to_{\rho'} q''$ then $q \to_{\rho' \circ \rho}^* q''$.

$$n(q_1) \xleftarrow{\ \rho_1\ } n(q_1')$$

$$\delta \downarrow \qquad\qquad \downarrow \delta'$$

$$n(q_2) \xleftarrow{\ \rho_2\ } n(q_2')$$

Fig. 3. HD-bisimulation

The theory of HD-automata [13] provides a notion of behavioural equivalence, which we specialise in the following to the case of HDE-automata. First, according to the general theory, it is not restrictive to assume that all HDE-automata are *irredundant*, i.e. that all names occurring in a state are eventually used. Actually, we work with a slightly strengthened notion of irredundancy, i.e., we will assume that for any $e \in n(q)$ there exists a state reachable from q where e can be executed. Formally, we assume that for any $q \in Q$ and any $e \in n(q)$ there exists some $q' \in Q$ such that $q \to_\rho^* q'$ and $q' \xrightarrow{\texttt{exec}(e')}_{\rho'} q''$ with $\rho(e') = e$.

Definition 12 (HD-bisimilarity). *Let $\mathcal{H}_1$ and $\mathcal{H}_2$ be two HDE-automata. A HD-bisimulation is a relation*

$$R = \{(q_1, \delta, q_2) \mid q_1 \in Q_1 \ \wedge \ q_2 \in Q_2 \ \wedge \ \delta : n_1(q_1) \overset{\sim}{\to} n_2(q_2)\}$$

such that, whenever $(q_1, \delta, q_2) \in R$,

1. *if $q_1 \xrightarrow{\texttt{plan}(e_1)}_{\rho_1} q_1'$, then there exists a transition $q_2 \xrightarrow{\texttt{plan}(e_2)}_{\rho_2} q_2'$ such that $(q_1', \delta', q_2') \in R$;*

2. *if $q_1 \xrightarrow{\texttt{exec}(e_1)}_{\rho_1} q_1'$, resp. $q_1 \xrightarrow{\texttt{drop}(e_1)}_{\rho_2} q_1'$, then there exists a transition $q_2 \xrightarrow{\texttt{exec}(e_2)}_{\rho_1} q_2'$, resp. $q_2 \xrightarrow{\texttt{drop}(e_2)}_{\rho_2} q_2'$, such that $\delta(e_1) = e_2$ and $(q_1', \delta', q_2') \in R$;*

where both for 1) and 2) it holds $\rho_2 \circ \delta' = \delta \circ \rho_1$ (see Fig. 3). Dually, transitions of $\mathcal{H}_2$ are simulated in $\mathcal{H}_1$.

We say that $\mathcal{H}_1$ and $\mathcal{H}_2$ are HD-bisimilar, written $\mathcal{H}_1 \sim_{hd} \mathcal{H}_2$, when there exists a HD-bisimulation R such that $(q_{01}, \delta, q_{02}) \in R$ for some δ.

Observe that, by commutativity of the diagram in Fig. 3, in case (1) we get that $\delta' = \rho_2^{-1} \circ \delta \circ \rho_1 \cup \{(e_1, e_2)\}$ and in case (2) $\delta = \rho_2 \circ \delta' \circ \rho_1^{-1} \cup \{(e_1, e_2)\}$. Hence, since the δ-component in R is a labelled bijection, whenever we match two transitions, the involved activities are required to have the same label.

The behavioural equivalence is referred to as HD-bisimilarity rather than HDE-bisimilarity since it is just the general notion [13] instantiated to our specific subclass of HD-automata.

4.2 Logical Characterisation of HD-Bisimilarity

We next show that HD-bisimilarity admits a natural logical characterisation in terms of a mild extension of the logic $\mathcal{L}_0$ introduced in Section 3.

Definition 13 ($\mathcal{L}_{hd}$ syntax). *Let Var be a countable set of variables ranged over by x, y, z.... The logic $\mathcal{L}_{hd}$ over the set of labels Λ is defined as:*

$$\varphi ::= \top \mid \varphi \wedge \varphi \mid \neg\varphi \mid (\mathsf{a}\, z)\varphi \mid \langle z \rangle \varphi \mid {\downarrow} z\, \varphi$$

The logic $\mathcal{L}_{hd}$, besides the operators of $\mathcal{L}_0$ for planning and executing activities, includes an additional operator ${\downarrow}\, z$ that represents the dismissal of a planned activity. More precisely, the formula ${\downarrow} z\, \varphi$ holds if $\eta(z) \in n(q)$, i.e., $\eta(z)$ is a planned activity in the current state (namely, an active name), and after dismissing such activity (i.e., forgetting the corresponding name) φ holds.

The free variables of a formula in $\mathcal{L}_{hd}$ are defined as in Section 3, with the additional clause $fv({\downarrow} z\, \varphi) = fv(\varphi) \cup \{z\}$. Concerning the semantics, $\mathcal{L}_{hd}$ formulae are now interpreted over HDE-automata. More precisely, let Env be the set of environments, i.e., functions $\eta : Var \to \mathbb{E}$. Given a HDE-automaton $\mathcal{H}$ and a formula φ in $\mathcal{L}_{hd}$, the denotation of φ will be a set of pairs $(q, \eta) \in Q \times Env$. Note that the semantics of $\mathcal{L}_{hd}$ does not involve a notion of legal pair, which was essential in Section 3 to correctly deal with the conflict relation distinctive of PESs. In fact, as observed before, the states of HDE-automata explicitly include a set of planned activities which intuitively corresponds to events observed and not yet executed in PESs. The activities planned in a state are pairwise consistent by construction: for a state q of a HDE-automaton, the fact that a new activity e is in conflict with some activities which have been already planned in q is represented by the absence of a $\mathtt{plan}(e)$ transition from state q, i.e., by the impossibility of planning activity e in state q.

Below given a renaming $\rho \in R(\mathbb{E})$ and an environment $\eta : Var \to \mathbb{E}$ we write $\eta; \rho^{-1}$ for the environment defined by $\eta; \rho^{-1}(x) = \rho^{-1}(\eta(x))$ when $\eta(x) \in cod(\rho)$ and $\eta; \rho^{-1}(x) = \eta(x)$, otherwise.

Definition 14 (semantics). *Let $\mathcal{H}$ be a HDE-automaton. The denotation of a formula φ, written $\{\!|\varphi|\!\}^{\mathcal{H}} \in 2^{Q \times Env}$, is inductively defined as follow:*

$$\{\!|\top|\!\}^{\mathcal{H}} = Q \times Env$$

$$\{\!|\varphi_1 \wedge \varphi_2|\!\}^{\mathcal{H}} = \{\!|\varphi_1|\!\}^{\mathcal{H}} \cap \{\!|\varphi_2|\!\}^{\mathcal{H}}$$

$$\{\!|\neg\varphi|\!\}^{\mathcal{H}} = (Q \times Env) \setminus \{\!|\varphi|\!\}^{\mathcal{H}}$$

$$\{\!|(\mathsf{a}\, z)\varphi|\!\}^{\mathcal{H}} = \{(q, \eta) \mid \exists q \xrightarrow{\mathtt{plan}(e)}_\rho q' \wedge \lambda(e) = \mathsf{a} \wedge$$
$$(q', \eta; \rho^{-1}[z \mapsto e]) \in \{\!|\varphi|\!\}^{\mathcal{H}} \}$$

$$\{\!|\langle z \rangle\, \varphi|\!\}^{\mathcal{H}} = \{(q, \eta) \mid q \xrightarrow{\mathtt{exec}(\eta(z))}_\rho q' \wedge (q', \eta; \rho^{-1}) \in \{\!|\varphi|\!\}^{\mathcal{H}}\}$$

$$\{\!|{\downarrow} z\, \varphi|\!\}^{\mathcal{H}} = \{(q, \eta) \mid q \xrightarrow{\mathtt{drop}(\eta(z))}_\rho q' \wedge (q', \eta; \rho^{-1}) \in \{\!|\varphi|\!\}^{\mathcal{H}}\}$$

When $(q, \eta) \in \{\!|\varphi|\!\}^{\mathcal{H}}$ we say that the automaton $\mathcal{H}$ satisfies the formula φ in the state q and environment $\eta : Var \to E$, and write $\mathcal{H}, q \models_\eta \varphi$. For closed formulae φ, we write $\mathcal{H} \models \varphi$, when $\mathcal{H}, q_0 \models_\eta \varphi$ for some η.

The logical equivalence induced by $\mathcal{L}_{hd}$ over HDE-automata can be shown to be HD-bisimilarity. Actually, as it commonly happens when dealing with a finitary logic (with finite conjunctions), the result holds under suitable hypotheses which restrict the branching cardinality of HDE-automata. The standard requirement is image-finiteness, which, however, for HDE-automata would be too restrictive as $\mathtt{plan}(\cdot)$ steps allow one to plan activities which are executable unboundedly far in the future. Instead, we assume the following weaker notion of boundedness for HDE-automata.

Definition 15 (bounded HDE-automata). *A HDE-automaton $\mathcal{H}$ is called bounded if for any $q \in Q$, $k \in \mathbb{N}$ and $A \subseteq_{fin} \Lambda$ the set below is finite:*

$$q(k, A) = \{e \in \mathbb{E} \mid q \xrightarrow{\mathtt{plan}(e)}_{\rho} q' \xrightarrow{\ell_1}_{\rho_1} q_1 \ldots \xrightarrow{\ell_k}_{\rho_k} q_k \xrightarrow{\mathtt{exec}(e')} q_{k+1}$$
$$\wedge\ \rho_k \circ \ldots \circ \rho_1(e') = e \ \wedge\ \lambda(e) \in A \ \wedge$$
$$for\ i \in \{1, \ldots, k\},\ if\ \ell_i = \mathtt{plan}(e_i)\ then\ \lambda(e_i) \in A\}.$$

In words, $q(k, A)$ is the set of activities labelled over A which can be planned in the current state and executed in k steps, using only already planned activities or new activities labelled in A. This set is required to be finite when A is finite. We will show later that the automaton corresponding to a PES is bounded if and only if the original PES is image finite. Under the boundedness hypothesis, we can prove that the logical equivalence induced by $\mathcal{L}_{hd}$ on HDE-automata is HD-bisimilarity.

Proposition 1 (HD-bisimilarity, logically). *Let $\mathcal{H}_1$, $\mathcal{H}_2$ be bounded HDE-automata. Then $\mathcal{H}_1 \sim_{hd} \mathcal{H}_2$ iff $\mathcal{H}_1$, $\mathcal{H}_2$ satisfy the same closed formulae in $\mathcal{L}_{hd}$.*

The boundedness hypothesis is essential to ensure the existence of a finite formula distinguishing any two non bisimilar HDE-automata. Roughly, the point is that a $\mathtt{plan}(e_1)$ transition of an automaton could be simulated, in principle, by infinitely many $\mathtt{plan}(e_2)$ transitions of the other. However, by the irredundancy assumption on the class of HDE-automata, we know that e_1 is executable in some reachable state. Let k be the number of transitions of a run leading to a state where e_1 is executable and let A be the set of labels of events planned in such run. Then it is not difficult to see that the event e_2 of the simulating transition $\mathtt{plan}(e_2)$ must be itself executable within k steps, involving only already planned events or events labelled in the set A. By the boundedness hypothesis there are only finitely many such events, a fact which plays a basic role in the proof of Proposition 1.

5 Hhp-Bisimilarity via HD-Automata

In order to obtain a characterisation of hhp-bisimilarity in terms of HD-automata we proceed as follows: first we provide an encoding of PESs into the class of HDE-automata. Then we encode the logic $\mathcal{L}_0$ into $\mathcal{L}_{hd}$ and back, in a way that a PES satisfies a formula in $\mathcal{L}_0$ if and only if the corresponding automaton satisfies the

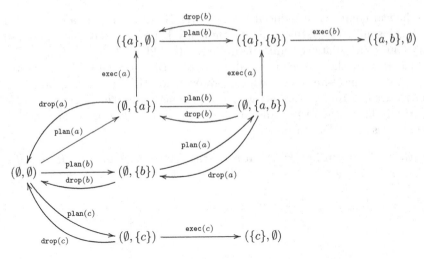

Fig. 4. HDE automaton corresponding to the CCS process $a.b + c$.

formula in $\mathcal{L}_{hd}$. Finally we rely on the logical characterisations of HD-bisimilarity and of hhp-bisimilarity to show that two PESs are hhp-bisimilar if and only if their corresponding HDE-automata are HD-bisimilar.

5.1   From Event Structures to HDE-Automata

We next provide an encoding of PESs into HDE-automata which is later shown to preserve and reflect behavioural equivalence. Throughout this section, the correspondence between activities in the source, label and target of a transition are given by (partial) identities and hence kept implicit.

Definition 16 (from PES to HDE-automata). *Let $\mathcal{E}$ be a PES. The HDE-automaton $\mathcal{H}(\mathcal{E}) = (Q, q_0, n, \rightarrow)$ is defined as*

- $Q = \{\langle C, X \rangle \mid C \in \mathcal{C}(\mathcal{E}) \wedge X \subseteq_{fin} \mathcal{E}[C] \wedge X \times X \subseteq \frown \}$
- $q_0 = (\emptyset, \emptyset)$
- $n(\langle C, X \rangle) = X$
- *the transition relation is given as follows where it is assumed that $e \notin X$*
  - $\langle C, X \rangle \xrightarrow{\text{plan}(e)} \langle C, X \cup \{e\} \rangle$ *when $e \in \mathcal{E}[C]$ and $e \frown X$;*
  - $\langle C, X \cup \{e\} \rangle \xrightarrow{\text{exec}(e)} \langle C \cup \{e\}, X \rangle$ *when $C \cup \{e\} \in \mathcal{C}(\mathcal{E})$;*
  - $\langle C, X \cup \{e\} \rangle \xrightarrow{\text{drop}(e)} \langle C, X \rangle$.

In words, a PES $\mathcal{E}$ corresponds to an automaton $\mathcal{H}(\mathcal{E})$ whose states are pairs $\langle C, X \rangle$ where $C \in \mathcal{C}(\mathcal{E})$ represents the current state of the computation, and X is a set of events belonging to a possible future computation extending C, planned but not yet executed. Note that, in order to represent a set of events which can occur in a computation starting from C, the events in X must be both pairwise consistent and consistent with C. Instead, we do not require X to be causally closed, that is we do not require $C \cup X \in \mathcal{C}(\mathcal{E})$.

According to this intuition, given a state $\langle C, X \rangle$, the transition $\mathtt{plan}(e)$ allows one to plan a new event e whenever e is compatible both with C and its future X. On the other hand, any event planned and not yet executed, i.e., any event $e \in X$ can be dismissed by means of a $\mathtt{drop}(e)$ transition. Finally, an event e can be executed if it belongs to the planned future X and it is enabled by the configuration C. As an example, the automaton corresponding to the (PES associated with the) CCS process $a.b+c$ is given in Fig. 4. Observe that the HDE-automaton obtained from a PES is irredundant. Roughly, $\mathtt{plan}(\cdot)$ and $\mathtt{drop}(\cdot)$ transitions allow one to construct alternative futures of the current configuration. The concurrent structure of such futures can then be analysed by means of $\mathtt{exec}(\cdot)$ moves.

Note that, as mentioned above, the ρ-component of transitions is omitted and it is implicitly assumed to be a partial identity. More precisely when $\langle C, X \rangle \xrightarrow{\ell}$ $\langle C', X' \rangle$, the renaming is $\rho = id_{X \cap X'}$. For instance, when $\langle C, X \rangle \xrightarrow{\mathtt{plan}(e)} \langle C, X \cup \{e\} \rangle$, the renaming $\rho : X \cup \{e\} \to X$ is defined by $\rho(e') = e'$ for $e' \in X$ and $\rho(e)$ undefined.

The image finiteness property for PESs exactly corresponds, through the encoding, to the boundedness property for HDE-automata as introduced in Definition 15.

Proposition 2 (image finiteness). *Let $\mathcal{E}$ a PES. Then $\mathcal{E}$ is image finite iff $\mathcal{H}(\mathcal{E})$ is bounded.*

5.2   From $\mathcal{L}_0$ to $\mathcal{L}_{hd}$ and Back: Hhp-Bisimilarity via hd-Bisimilarity

In order to prove that behavioural equivalence is preserved and reflected by the encoding of PESs into HDE-automata we rely on the logical characterisation of such equivalences, which is given in terms of very similar logics. Specifically, here we prove that a tight link exists between satisfaction of $\mathcal{L}_0$ formulae by PESs and satisfaction of $\mathcal{L}_{hd}$ formulae by the corresponding HDE-automata, in a way that the two logical equivalences can then be shown to coincide. Below, we write $\models^{\mathcal{L}_0}$ and $\models^{\mathcal{L}_{hd}}$ in order to clarify to which notion of satisfaction we are referring to.

First of all, notice that although $\mathcal{L}_0$ is syntactically a subset of $\mathcal{L}_{hd}$, for a PES $\mathcal{E}$ and a formula φ in $\mathcal{L}_0$, it is not the case that if $\mathcal{E} \models^{\mathcal{L}_0} \varphi$ then $\mathcal{H}(\mathcal{E}) \models^{\mathcal{L}_{hd}} \varphi$. As an example, consider the PES $\mathcal{E}_1$ in Fig. 1 associated with the process $a.b + c.d$ and the formula $\varphi = (a\, x)((c\, y)\langle y \rangle \top \wedge (b\, z)\langle x \rangle \langle z \rangle \top)$. Then $\mathcal{E}_1 \models^{\mathcal{L}_0} \varphi$, because $\emptyset \models^{\mathcal{L}_0}_{\eta[x \to a]} (c\, y)\langle y \rangle \top$ and $\emptyset \models^{\mathcal{L}_0}_{\eta[x \to a]} (b\, z)\langle x \rangle \langle z \rangle \top$. In fact, for the first subformula, note that y can be bound to the c-labelled event even though it is in conflict with a, since x is no longer free in the subformula.

Instead, $\mathcal{H}(\mathcal{E}_1) \not\models^{\mathcal{L}_{hd}} \varphi$ since satisfaction reduces to $(\emptyset, \{a\}) \models^{\mathcal{L}_{hd}}_{\eta[x \to a]} (c\, y)\langle y \rangle \top$ and $(\emptyset, \{a\}) \models^{\mathcal{L}_{hd}}_{\eta[x \to a]} (b\, z)\langle x \rangle \langle z \rangle \top$. The first is false since the automaton cannot perform a $\mathtt{plan}(c)$ step as long as the conflicting event a belongs to the planned future. However, $\mathcal{H}(\mathcal{E}_1) \models^{\mathcal{L}_{hd}} (a\, x)(\downarrow x\, (c\, y)\langle y \rangle \top \wedge (b\, z)\langle x \rangle \langle z \rangle \top)$ since, in this case, after planning a, the left branch forgets it in a way that b can be planned and executed.

More generally, a $\mathcal{L}_0$ formula φ can be encoded into a $\mathcal{L}_{hd}$ formula that uses the $\downarrow$ operator to explicitly drop planned events that intuitively no longer pertain to the future that the formula describes, i.e., events planned but no longer referred to by free variables in the remaining part of the formula. Formally, given $\varphi \in \mathcal{L}_0$, we define an encoding of φ into $\mathcal{L}_{hd}$ which is parametric on a set of variables X such that $fv(\varphi) \subseteq X$, representing the events planned in the past. Given a set of variables $Z = \{z_1, \ldots, z_n\}$ we write $\downarrow Z$ for $\downarrow x_1 \ldots \downarrow x_n$.

Definition 17 (from $\mathcal{L}_0$ to $\mathcal{L}_{hd}$). *The encoding function* $[\![\cdot]\!] : \mathcal{L}_0 \times 2^{Var} \to \mathcal{L}_{hd}$ *is inductively defined as follows:*

$$[\![\mathsf{T}]\!]_X = \mathsf{T}$$
$$[\![\neg\varphi]\!]_X = \neg[\![\varphi]\!]_X$$
$$[\![\varphi_1 \wedge \varphi_2]\!]_X = [\![\varphi_1]\!]_X \wedge [\![\varphi_2]\!]_X$$
$$[\![\langle x \rangle \, \varphi]\!]_X = \langle x \rangle \, [\![\varphi]\!]_X$$
$$[\![(\mathsf{a}\,x)\varphi]\!]_X = \downarrow Z \,(\mathsf{a}\,x)[\![\varphi]\!]_{fv(\varphi)\cup\{x\}}$$

where, in the last clause, $Z = X \backslash (fv(\varphi) \backslash \{x\})$.

In words, before binding a new event to x, the $\mathcal{L}_{hd}$ encoding drops any (previously planned) event that is not bound to the free variables of the subformula.

As an example, consider the formula $\varphi = (\mathsf{a}\,x)((\mathsf{c}\,y)\langle y \rangle \, \mathsf{T} \ \wedge \ (\mathsf{b}\,z)\langle x \rangle \, \langle z \rangle \, \mathsf{T})$ in $\mathcal{L}_0$ discussed at the beginning of the section, satisfied by $\mathcal{E}_1$ but not by $\mathcal{H}(\mathcal{E}_1)$. The formula $[\![\varphi]\!]_\emptyset$ is exactly the $\mathcal{L}_{hd}$ formula previously constructed by hand in order to be satisfied by the automaton, i.e., $(\mathsf{a}\,x)(\downarrow x\,(\mathsf{c}\,y)\langle y \rangle \, \mathsf{T} \ \wedge \ (\mathsf{b}\,z)\langle x \rangle \, \langle z \rangle \, \mathsf{T})$. As a further example, consider the $\mathcal{L}_0$ formulae $\varphi_1 = (\mathsf{a}\,x)(\mathsf{b}\,y)(\mathsf{c}\,z)\langle z \rangle \, \mathsf{T}$ and $\varphi_2 = (\mathsf{a}\,x)(\mathsf{b}\,y)(\langle y \rangle \, \mathsf{T} \wedge (\mathsf{c}\,z)\langle z \rangle \, \mathsf{T})$, which are both true for the PES consisting of three pairwise conflicting events. Then we have that $[\![\varphi_1]\!]_\emptyset = (\mathsf{a}\,x) \downarrow x\,(\mathsf{b}\,y) \downarrow y\,(\mathsf{c}\,z)\langle z \rangle \, \mathsf{T}$ and $[\![\varphi_2]\!]_\emptyset = (\mathsf{a}\,x) \downarrow x\,(\mathsf{b}\,y)(\langle y \rangle \, \mathsf{T} \wedge \downarrow y\,(\mathsf{c}\,z)\langle z \rangle \, \mathsf{T})$.

We next prove a technical lemma. It roughly asserts that, given a formula $\varphi \in \mathcal{L}_0$, the satisfaction of its encoding in $\mathcal{L}_{hd}$ by a state of the HD-automaton does not depend on planned events bound to variables which are not free in the formula, as long as the encoding takes care of dropping such events.

Lemma 1. *Let $\mathcal{E}$ be a PES. Let $\varphi \in \mathcal{L}_{hd}$ be a formula, $\eta : Var \to \mathbb{E}$ an environment and $X_1, X_2 \subseteq Var$ sets of variables such that $fv(\varphi) \subseteq X_i$ and $C \cup \eta(X_i)$ is compatible for $i \in \{1, 2\}$. Then in the HDE-automata $\mathcal{H}(\mathcal{E})$ it holds*

$$\langle C, \eta(X_1) \setminus C \rangle \models_\eta [\![\varphi]\!]_{X_1} \quad iff \quad \langle C, \eta(X_2) \setminus C \rangle \models_\eta [\![\varphi]\!]_{X_2}.$$

Then we can prove the following.

Lemma 2 (from $\mathcal{L}_0$ to $\mathcal{L}_{hd}$). *Let $\mathcal{E}$ be a PES. For any closed formula $\varphi \in \mathcal{L}_0$ it holds $\mathcal{E} \models^{\mathcal{L}_0} \varphi$ iff $\mathcal{H}(\mathcal{E}) \models^{\mathcal{L}_{hd}} [\![\varphi]\!]_\emptyset$.*

Conversely, we show how formulae of $\mathcal{L}_{hd}$ can be encoded in $\mathcal{L}_0$. This is somehow more difficult since the notion of satisfaction in $\mathcal{L}_0$ relies on simpler states, those of PESs, consisting only of a configuration (executed events), while states of HDE-automata, where $\mathcal{L}_{hd}$ satisfaction is defined, include explicitly also those events which have been planned and not executed. In order to fill this gap the idea is to "keep" events planned but not yet executed as free variables in the formulae of $\mathcal{L}_0$.

Definition 18 (from $\mathcal{L}_{hd}$ to $\mathcal{L}_0$). *Given a set of variables $X=\{x_1,\ldots,x_n\} \subseteq Var$, let $st(X)$ denote the formula in $\mathcal{L}_0$*

$$st(X) = (\textstyle\bigvee_{i=1}^{n}\langle x_i\rangle \mathsf{T}) \vee \mathsf{T}$$

The encoding function $\|\cdot\| : \mathcal{L}_{hd} \times 2^{Var} \to \mathcal{L}_0$ is inductively defined as follows:

$$\|\mathsf{T}\|_X = \mathsf{T}$$

$$\|\neg\varphi\|_X = \neg\|\varphi\|_X$$

$$\|\varphi_1 \wedge \varphi_2\|_X = \|\varphi_1\|_X \wedge \|\varphi_2\|_X$$

$$\|(\mathsf{a}\,x)\varphi\|_X = (\mathsf{a}\,x)(\|\varphi\|_{X\cup\{x\}} \wedge st(X))$$

$$\|\downarrow\!x\ \varphi\|_X = \begin{cases} \|\varphi\|_{X\setminus\{x\}} & \text{if } x \in X \\ \mathsf{F} & \text{otherwise} \end{cases}$$

$$\|\langle x\rangle\ \varphi\|_X = \begin{cases} \langle x\rangle\ \|\varphi\|_{X\setminus\{x\}} & \text{if } x \in X \\ \mathsf{F} & \text{otherwise} \end{cases}$$

Observe that the encoding of a formula of $\mathcal{L}_{hd}$ into $\mathcal{L}_0$ is parametric w.r.t. a set of variables which represent those events which have been planned but not yet dropped or executed. In order to understand this, note that in the formula $st(X)$ the disjunction with T does not make it trivially equivalent to true. In fact $fv(st(X)) = X$, and thus $st(X)$ is satisfied only by pairs (C,η) which are legal, i.e., such that $\eta(X) \subseteq C[E]$ and pairwise consistent. The role of $st(X)$ is exactly to keep alive the events associated with variable in X and impose that they are consistent. It can be proved inductively that, more generally, $fv(\|\varphi\|_X) \subseteq X$.

Lemma 3 (from $\mathcal{L}_{hd}$ to $\mathcal{L}_0$). *Let $\mathcal{E}$ be a PES, let $\mathcal{H}(\mathcal{E})$ be the corresponding automaton. For any closed formula $\varphi \in \mathcal{L}_{hd}$, $\mathcal{H}(\mathcal{E}) \models^{\mathcal{L}_{hd}} \varphi$ iff $\mathcal{E} \models^{\mathcal{L}_0} \|\varphi\|_\emptyset$.*

Combining the results above we can immediately deduce that hhp-bisimilarity between PESs is faithfully captured by bisimilarity of the corresponding HDE-automata.

Theorem 2 (hhp-bisimilarity vs. hd-bisimilarity). *Let $\mathcal{E}_1$ and $\mathcal{E}_2$ be PESs. Then $\mathcal{E}_1 \sim_{hhp} \mathcal{E}_2$ iff $\mathcal{H}(\mathcal{E}_1) \sim_{hd} \mathcal{H}(\mathcal{E}_2)$.*

6   Conclusions: Related and Future Work

We studied hhp-bisimilarity, a canonical behavioural equivalence in the true concurrent spectrum, by means of logics and automata. We provided a characterisation in terms of an event-based logic $\mathcal{L}_0$ that predicates over the existence and executability of events. This in turn suggests a connection with HD-automata. More precisely, we defined a class of HD-automata whose transitions allow one to plan the execution of an activity, execute a planned activity and to dismiss a planned activity. We then showed that PESs can be mapped into such class of automata in a way that the canonical behavioural equivalence for HD-automata coincides with hhp-bisimilarity over the corresponding PESs.

Both characterisations show that, in order to capture hhp-bisimilarity, the observer must be able to compare states by checking unboundedly large concurrent computations in the future of such states. Intuitively, this can be seen as a source of ineffectiveness of hhp-bisimilarity which indeed is known to be undecidable for many basic models of concurrency, even in the finite state case (e.g., it is known that hhp-bisimilarity is undecidable for safe finite Petri nets [14]).

The results in the paper can be helpful in the study of decidable approximations of hhp-bisimilarity, possibly opening the road to the development of verification techniques. This represents an interesting line of future research. Indeed, some preliminary investigations show that fixing a bound on the distance of the future that an observer is allowed to check, one gets effective approximations of hhp-bisimilarity. More precisely, when fixing such a bound, regular PESs (which typically arise as semantics of finite state systems [16]) can be transformed into finite HD-automata for which bisimilarity checking is decidable. On these bases, algorithms for checking such approximations of $\sim_{hhp}$-bisimilarity can be obtained by simply providing an explicit construction of the finite HD-automata for specific formalisms. E.g., for finite $(n\text{-})$safe Petri nets this could be done along the lines of the work in [17,18] for history preserving bisimilarity. The construction could also take inspiration from that in [19], used for proving decidability of approximations of hhp-bisimilarity on finite safe Petri nets.

The fact that HDE-automata deal with infinite sets of events, but with the possibility of testing only equality and labels, suggests a connection with register automata and, more generally, with the recent line of work on nominal automata (see, e.g., [20] and references therein), which would be interesting to deepen.

In order to capture hhp-bisimilarity in the setting of HD-automata, we provided a characterisation of HD-bisimilarity in terms of a logic $\mathcal{L}_{hd}$ that enriches $\mathcal{L}_0$ with an operator for explicitly dropping activities planned but not yet executed. Interestingly, even if it is defined over HDE-automata, we think that the logic $\mathcal{L}_{hd}$ will be useful to establish a precise connection with the logic EIL in [10], which includes a reverse step-modality which is related to the drop transitions and the $\downarrow \cdot$ modality in $\mathcal{L}_{hd}$. We believe a further investigation of the relation between $\mathcal{L}_0$ and EIL (and the other logics for concurrency in the literature) can bring some interesting insights, at least at conceptual level. This, despite the fact that it is clear that some modalities of $\mathcal{L}_0$ and EIL are not interdefinable. For instance, the formula $(x : a)\varphi$ in EIL which binds x to an a-labelled event in the current configuration is not encodable in $\mathcal{L}_0$. Conversely, the formula $(\mathsf{a}\,x)\varphi$ where x is bound to an a-labelled event in the future of the current configuration is not encodable in EIL. A connection to be further investigated seems to exist also with the work on higher-dimensional automata and ST-configuration structures in [21], where a logic, again with backward step modalities, is proposed for hhp-bisimilarity.

We also believe that the logical characterisation of HD-bisimilarity has an interest which goes beyond the specific class of HD-automata considered in this paper and deserves to be studied further.

Acknowledgments. We are grateful to Alberto Meneghello for several insightful discussions on this work at its early stages of development. We are also indebted with the anonymous reviewers for providing detailed comments and insightful suggestions which helped us to improve our work.

References

1. van Glabbeek, R., Goltz, U.: Refinement of actions and equivalence notions for concurrent systems. Acta Informatica 37(4/5), 229–327 (2001)
2. Esparza, J., Heljanko, K.: Unfoldings - A Partial order Approach to Model Checking. EACTS Monographs. Springer (2008)
3. Bednarczyk, M.A.: Hereditary history preserving bisimulations or what is the power of the future perfect in program logics. Technical report, Polish Academy of Sciences (1991)
4. Joyal, A., Nielsen, M., Winskel, G.: Bisimulation from open maps. Information and Computation 127(2), 164–185 (1996)
5. Winskel, G.: Event Structures. In: Brauer, W., Reisig, W., Rozenberg, G. (eds.) APN 1986. LNCS, vol. 255, pp. 325–392. Springer, Heidelberg (1987)
6. Phillips, I., Ulidowski, I.: A hierarchy of reverse bisimulations on stable configuration structures. Mathematical Structures in Computer Science 22(2), 333–372 (2012)
7. Phillips, I., Ulidowski, I.: Reversing algebraic process calculi. Journal of Logic and Algebraic Programming 73(1-2), 70–96 (2007)
8. Cristescu, I., Krivine, J., Varacca, D.: A compositional semantics for the reversible p-calculus. In: Proc. of LICS 2013, pp. 388–397. IEEE Computer Society (2013)
9. Baldan, P., Crafa, S.: A logic for true concurrency. Journal of the ACM 61(4), 24:1–24:36 (2014)
10. Phillips, I., Ulidowski, I.: Event identifier logic. Mathematical Structures in Computer Science 24(2), 1–51 (2014)
11. Nielsen, M., Clausen, C.: Games and logics for a noninterleaving bisimulation. Nordic Journal of Computing 2(2), 221–249 (1995)
12. Hennessy, M., Stirling, C.: The power of the future perfect in program logics. Information and Control 67(1-3), 23–52 (1985)
13. Montanari, U., Pistore, M.: History-Dependent automata: An introduction. In: Bernardo, M., Bogliolo, A. (eds.) SFM-Moby 2005. LNCS, vol. 3465, pp. 1–28. Springer, Heidelberg (2005)
14. Jurdzinski, M., Nielsen, M., Srba, J.: Undecidability of domino games and hhp-bisimilarity. Information and Computation 184(2), 343–368 (2003)

15. Hennessy, M., Milner, R.: Algebraic laws for nondeterminism and concurrency. Journal of the ACM 32(1), 137–161 (1985)
16. Thiagarajan, P.S.: Regular event structures and finite petri nets: A conjecture. In: Brauer, W., Ehrig, H., Karhumäki, J., Salomaa, A. (eds.) Formal and Natural Computing. LNCS, vol. 2300, pp. 244–256. Springer, Heidelberg (2002)
17. Vogler, W.: Deciding history preserving bisimilarity. In: Leach Albert, J., Monien, B., Rodríguez-Artalejo, M. (eds.) ICALP 1991. LNCS, vol. 510, pp. 495–505. Springer, Heidelberg (1991)
18. Montanari, U., Pistore, M.: Minimal transition systems for history-preserving bisimulation. In: Reischuk, R., Morvan, M. (eds.) STACS 1997. LNCS, vol. 1200, pp. 413–425. Springer, Heidelberg (1997)
19. Fröschle, S., Hildebrandt, T.: On plain and hereditary history-preserving bisimulation. In: Kutyłowski, M., Wierzbicki, T., Pacholski, L. (eds.) MFCS 1999. LNCS, vol. 1672, pp. 354–365. Springer, Heidelberg (1999)
20. Bojanczyk, M., Klin, B., Lasota, S.: Automata with group actions. In: Proc. of LICS 2011, pp. 355–364. IEEE Computer Society (2011)
21. Prisacariu, C.: The glory of the past and geometrical concurrency. CoRR abs/1206.3136 (2012)

Author Index